Societies in Eclipse

Societies in Eclipse

Archaeology of the Eastern

Woodlands Indians, A.D. 1400–1700

Edited by David S. Brose, C. Wesley Cowan,

and Robert C. Mainfort Jr.

SMITHSONIAN INSTITUTION PRESS / Washington and London

Copy editor: Jane Kepp
Production editor: E. Anne Bolen
Designer: Janice Wheeler

Library of Congress Cataloging-in-Publication Data
Societies in eclipse: archaeology of the Eastern Woodlands Indians,
A.D. 1400–1700 / edited by David S. Brose, C. Wesley
Cowan, and Robert C. Mainfort, Jr.
        p. cm.
    Includes bibliographical references and index
    ISBN 1-56098-956-4 (alk. paper)—ISBN 1-56098-981-5 (pbk. : alk.
paper)
    1. Woodland Indians—Antiquities. 2. Woodland Indians—First
contact with Europeans. 3. Woodland Indians—Social life and
customs. 4. Social archaeology—East (U.S.) 5. Land settlement
patterns—East (U.S.)—History. 6. East (U.S.) Antiquities. I.
Brose, David S., 1939– II. Cowan, C. Wesley, 1951– III. Mainfort,
Robert C., 1948–
E78.E2 S63 2001
974′.01—dc21   2001020515

British Library Cataloguing-in-Publication Data is available

Manufactured in the United States of America
08 07 06 05 04 03 02 01   5 4 3 2 1

♾ The paper used in this publication meets the minimum requirements
of the American National Standard for Information Sciences—
Permanence of Paper for Printed Library Materials ANSI Z39.48-1984.

Contents

Figures

Tables

Contributors

David G. Anderson, Southeast Regional Office, National Park Service, Atlanta, GA

James W. Bradley, Robert S. Peabody Museum of Archaeology, Andover, MA

David S. Brose, Schiele Museum of Natural History, Gastonia, NC

James A. Brown, Department of Anthropology, Northwestern University, Evanston, IL

C. Wesley Cowan, Terrace Park, OH

R. P. Stephen Davis Jr., Research Laboratories of Anthropology, University of North Carolina, Chapel Hill, NC

Penelope B. Drooker, New York State Museum, Albany, NY

William R. Fitzgerald, Bruce County Museum and Archives, Ontario, Canada

Jeffrey L. Hantman, Department of Anthropology, University of Virginia, Charlottesville, VA

William C. Johnson, Cultural Resources Section, Michael Baker Jr., Inc., Pittsburgh, PA

Robert C. Mainfort Jr., Arkansas Archeological Survey, Fayetteville, AR

William H. Marquardt, Florida Museum of Natural History, Gainesville, FL

George R. Milner, Department of Anthropology, Pennsylvania State University, University Park, PA

Robert F. Sasso, Department of Sociology and Anthropology, University of Wisconsin–Parksdale, Kenosha, WI

Marvin T. Smith, Department of Sociology, Anthropology, and Criminal Justice, Valdosta State University, Valdosta, GA

Dean R. Snow, Department of Anthropology, Pennsylvania State University, University Park, PA

David Hurst Thomas, American Museum of Natural History, New York

H. Trawick Ward, Research Laboratories of Anthropology, University of North Carolina, Chapel Hill, NC

Stephen Williams, emeritus, Peabody Museum, Harvard University, Cambridge, MA

Preface

In 1992, C. Wesley Cowan, curator of archaeology at the Cincinnati Museum of Natural History, was invited to organize a symposium centered "sort of around Pittsburgh," where the annual meeting of the Society for American Archaeology was being held. The topic—changes undergone by Native American societies in eastern North America immediately before and after Columbus's landfall in the Caribbean—was timely, and the symposium (a two-session affair) was well attended.

The fifteenth and sixteenth centuries marked the end for many eastern Native American societies and the diminishing of a former way of life for most of the others. Defining eclipse as "a reduction or loss of splendor, status, reputation, etc.; any obscuring or overshadowing," Cowan titled the symposium "Societies in Eclipse: Pittsburgh and Environs at the Dawn of Colonization." Its Wednesday evening venue permitted the inclusion of only five papers, so Cowan decided to expand the topic's areal coverage by organizing a second, larger symposium, which was presented the following day during the concurrent sessions. He titled this symposium "Societies in Eclipse: Eastern North America at the Dawn of Colonization."

As so often happens with successful symposia that offer fresh perspectives and important new data, Cowan recognized the value of refining the presentations and capturing them in a more enduring medium. He was encouraged to pursue the project by Daniel Goodwin, then editor at the Smithsonian Institution Press. Aware of the limited representation the symposium offered, Cowan asked several symposium contributors to suggest additional scholars who might be asked to write chapters.

Nearly all of the expanded chapters were in Cowan's hands by the late summer of 1993, and after receiving a publishing contract from the Smithsonian Institution Press, Cowan worked throughout 1994 on the final, edited draft. In 1995, however, following the amalgamation of the Cincinnati Museum of Natural History with several other Cincinnati institutions, Cowan left the museum and launched an independent business. From home, he continued to work with authors and the press on *Societies in Eclipse,* but lacking any academic institutional support, the project inevitably lagged.

At that point, Brose, as senior editor of the *Midcontinental Journal of Archaeology,* asked Cowan if he would entertain an offer of assistance to complete the project. Cowan accepted immediately and by the summer of 1996 had turned the project over to Brose entirely. Brose asked Mainfort, editor of *Southeastern Archaeology,* to assist in resuscitating the volume. In the winter of 1997 we received approval from the press to move forward as co-editors of *Societies in Eclipse.* We felt strongly that the five years since the presentation of such paradigm-changing data at the Pittsburgh conference were not an impossibly long time. We believed the book would not quickly be outdated: it remained the first synthetic and comprehensive book to turn the illumination of a generation of anthropological archaeology toward those few generations of American Indians who lived between prehistory and removal from unfettered control of the eastern continent.

Nevertheless, because it had been more than two years since any of the manuscripts had been revised, we asked every author to review the most recent version of his or her chapter, and if significant new data or publications had appeared, to refer to them in a separate, concluding section. Only if we were persuaded that the new studies were significant enough to require reinterpretation of existing conclusions did we ask authors to rewrite those portions of their manuscripts.

The chapters in this book follow the format originally envisioned by Cowan and Goodwin. Cultural developments in each area are divided into broad precontact and postcontact dimensions. Important characteristics of each are summarized, with major emphases on changing settlement size and structure, social relationships, mortuary patterns, and exchange networks. Each chapter also summarizes what is known about the relationship between archaeology and the historical record.

Cowan wanted the chapters to present substantive new interpretations of cultural changes that were under way before European contact in the Eastern Woodlands, from the northeastern Appalachians to the trans-Mississippi southern prairies. Penelope Drooker graciously agreed to work with Wes Cowan to bring the middle Ohio region up to date, and Mainfort filled a key areal gap by contributing a chapter on the central Mississippi Valley. Finally, David Hurst Thomas prepared some concluding remarks. Though one paper was retracted from publication, all the other chapters in the volume were originally presented at the Society for American Archaeology meeting in Pittsburgh. Though updated and altered, their focus remains the same.

While each contributor acknowledges the contributions that myriad readers and researchers made to his or her chapter, it is appropriate to thank several individuals and institutions that made this publication possible. Daniel Goodwin deserves special thanks for his encouragement of the concept and the initial steps necessary to turn a collection of new data and interpretation into a real book. Robert Lockhart carried the task forward after Dan left the Smithsonian Institution Press, and Scott Mahler offered the final

allotment of patience in what must have seemed to all like an endless stream of "you'll be receiving the manuscript any day now" communications.

Cowan, as symposium organizer, and the three of us, as volume editors, appreciate the patience each contributor has shown throughout the process of soliciting and editing manuscripts and the final production of this book. The authors' uniform enthusiasm and willingness to revise manuscripts, to include or remove "one more figure," to incorporate or limit one more table, or to delete what the editors in their ignorance called "inappropriate" sections are convincing evidence of the collective belief in the value of this volume.

At the Cincinnati Museum of Natural History, Robert Genheimer helped to keep the Archaeology Division functioning while Cowan was writing and doing the initial editing. Genheimer also hunted through uncounted drawers and offices to ensure that all manuscripts and illustrations reached the ultimate editorial hands. Kathryn DiCarlo and Mary Pamboukdjian, in the associate director's office at the Royal Ontario Museum, assisted Brose while he worked to resurrect the volume. Lana Ward helped complete the task from the director's office at the Schiele Museum of Natural History. It is no exaggeration to add that Brose would never have persisted with the task had it not been for Mainfort's encouragement and his immense, well-organized editorial efforts. At the Arkansas Archeological Survey, Lindi Holmes prepared the final manuscript and comprehensive bibliography, and Mary Lynn Kennedy assisted with a number of graphics. We also want to thank Anne Bolen, production editor at the Smithsonian Institution Press, and Jane Kepp, freelance editor and arbiter, for "putting the wheels on" this academic vehicle and keeping it running.

C. Wesley Cowan is clearly the spirit behind this publication. As authors, we (Brose and Mainfort) appreciate his optimism and dedication. He envisioned that many of the chapters in this book would become benchmarks, referred to by future generations at every level of expertise.

Inevitably, data accumulate, and the boundaries of an area are rethought as methods develop and the "important" questions change. Another, richer version of *Societies in Eclipse* eventually will be assembled by another editor. We hope it will run a less circuitous editorial gauntlet.

David S. Brose and Robert C. Mainfort Jr.

Societies in Eclipse

1

Introduction to Eastern North America at the Dawn of European Colonization

Curiosity about the aboriginal people of the New World is as great in the United States today as it was among Europeans five hundred years ago, when Native Americans met the first Europeans since the Norsemen to arrive on the Atlantic shore. The history of American Indian cultural traditions has always been part of North American collective history. Yet the collective image of American Indian societies exists largely in terms of European and Anglo-American ideas of science and history that prevailed in the past. The American public has little appreciation for the real depth of the aboriginal cultural traditions that mediated social interactions between Native Americans and the Europeans and white Americans who largely replaced them on the land. Nor have most Americans any effective understanding of how American Indians' ancient traditions mediated their interactions with one another in the face of nonaboriginal pressures. Indeed, most of the public's common misunderstandings about Native American social and ecological relationships can be attributed to the fact that until recently, United States history as a national tradition expropriated examples of Native American contact and resistance, along with isolated, emotionally affecting stories, ignoring nearly everything else. With an inadequate grasp of the depth and tempo of cultural phenomena, public perception of the American Indian collapses like a half-filled balloon. And this is because few thought it might matter.

Neither the seventeenth-century French and English colonists who penetrated the St. Lawrence and Mississippi waterways and crossed the Appalachians nor the eighteenth-century American settlers envisioned the persistence of the American Indian societies they encountered. Against generations of economic sanctions, psychological and biological warfare, and what we would today call ethnic cleansing, attempts at resistance by eastern American Indians proved heroic failures. Having been declared in the early eighteenth century to be people without a cultural future, American Indians discovered that they had also lost to the Old World the remote past, which might have given them a historic claim to the lands of which they were being swiftly dispossessed.

The colonizers' encounters with the New World coincided with western Europe's era of immense intellectual ferment—a movement from theodicy to the appreciation of newly discovered ancient authorities and on to the creation of critical historiography and the development of experimental science. In the years between the Renaissance and the Reformation, western Europeans explored not only the globe but also the roots of their own society. Poorly known societies encountered far away were compared to poorly known societies of long ago—lost Israelites, Teutons, Phoenicians, Babylonians. American Indian societies appeared so unlike current European ones that all but their languages and their most glaring cultural differences were obscured in learned debates over their theological qualifications and biblical lineage. Those who first encountered native tribes and

DAVID S. BROSE

bands along the coasts of eastern North America came fresh from the violent subjugation of the early states of Mexico and Peru. Narragansett and Powhatan, Creek and Cherokee became all but indistinguishable in travelers' pastiches of sixteenth-century North American Indians.

Within a generation of initial European contact along the Caribbean, Atlantic, Pacific, and even Arctic shores, aboriginal societies living so far inland that they had heard of oceans only in legends had been irrevocably changed by the distant European presence. And just as encounters with Africans and Asians had changed European cultures before 1492, contact with American Indians changed them afterward. By the mid-seventeenth century, the third or fourth generation of enlightened western European explorers, divided by sect and section, were reporting differences among the tribes and chiefdoms of the mid-South river valleys and the Great Lakes. And beyond the first Spanish, Dutch, French, and English colonies, the clashes of legendary explorers, missionaries, and settlers with native groups of the great midcontinental forests, lakes, rivers, and grasslands—with Huron and Seneca, Shawnee and Ojibwa, Choctaw and Creek—became the mythic American frontier experience. The midcontinent was, in our nation's founding and again in the revival of native-federal conflict, the place where intellectual empires were forced to confront each other's raison d'être.

Despite the fragmentary nature of the written record, history, philology, and even theology have been invoked to explain American Indians' kaleidoscopic cultural patterns and their centuries of varied reactions as wave after wave of newcomers swept from the coasts, across mountains, and into the heart of the continent. This book offers the perspective that a generation of anthropological archaeological work brings to the understanding of the societies those Europeans first encountered.

As we are learning from anthropological archaeologists working among native people, the bases for ethnic inclusion often have more to do with allegedly shared languages and the relationships and spatial attribution of myths than they have to do with documented, shared material culture or site locations (e.g., Dongoske et al. 1997). To see how these divergent approaches relate the material aspects of group identity to the sociological aspects in historical perspective, David Hurst Thomas (Chapter 16) briefly synthesizes the politically volatile reinterpretations of exactly whose history this was or is to be. The engagement of American Indians with European Americans in the midcontinent has not ended, although the nature of the confrontation has changed.

The Character of Contact between Europeans and American Indians

From A.D. 1420 to 1760, a distinctive western European culture developed and expanded to every corner of the inhabited world. Those years also bracket the sweep of that culture across the last generations of American Indians to have lived life as their ancestors had, free of Europeans. Although Norse people from Iceland had spent several years around A.D. 1000 in feuds with "Skraelings," the aboriginal neighbors of their ill-fated Newfoundland settlement (Ingstad 1964), no evidence has yet been found for any real Norse impact on other American Indians' cultures.

But the next exotic influences were to change every American Indian culture, and they arrived in eastern North America only a few years after Spaniards first explored the Caribbean. Spain's presence was felt across the interior of the territory it termed La Florida, with Juan Ponce de León's brief exploration of 1513, the 1527–1569 treks by Narváez, de Soto, de Luna, and Pardo, and settlement of St. Augustine in 1565. English impact began with a colony at Roanoke in 1583, and Jamestown was founded in 1603. By the last third of the sixteenth century, Portuguese, Basque, and French whalers and fishermen were frequenting the Gulf of St. Lawrence. French exploration up the St. Lawrence began in 1585 with settlement of what would become Canada, dating from 1611. The Dutch established Fort Nassau in 1614, New England's northern colonies took root in 1620, and Swedish settlements along the mid-Atlantic coast began in the 1630s.

Some have imagined that the first decades were marked by pacific curiosity on both sides, tempered by the brief exchange of European goods for American Indian food or furs, after which Europeans reboarded their vessels and sailed away. But certainly, as contact became more frequent—as Europeans moved farther inland and stayed longer—curiosity and courtesy gave way to despair and violence. The story must have been more complicated than the historical documents tell us directly, for the European royal chronicles that followed Columbus's landfall by less than a decade are filled with references to American Indian men, women, and children who had been plucked off coasts from Baffin island to Yucatán. No doubt the flights and evasions described in early European accounts of encounters with American Indians reflect the wary natives' understandable reaction.

Some scholars have wondered what might have happened to American Indian societies if Europeans had not arrived, or if they had arrived at different times or places. Fischer (1970: 15–21) called this the "fallacy of fictional questions," noting that such fantasies can be useful for the ideas they raise and the inferences they help suggest, but that they can never be logically evaluated, much less "proven" in any meaningful way. Though we are resigned to the fact that we can never know what might have been, it is harder to live with the fact that we are none too certain about what actually did happen. Permanent European settlement resulted in substantial acculturation, and recognition of the mutuality of that acculturation and reactions to it differed dramatically among the various participants:

American Indian and European, visitor and immigrant, hunter and farmer, Catholic and Protestant, soldier and priest. Differing, too, were their descriptions.

The History of the Written Record

Huddleston's (1967) valuable study of European concepts of American Indian origins began with the observation that Columbus never questioned the existence of people in the New World because he did not believe it to be a new world. But Europe's intellectual confusion about American Indians has origins in its earliest propaganda. On his second voyage, Columbus forced his own crew to swear that Cuba was not an island but a mainland in which they would find civilized inhabitants (Todorov 1984: 4–7). Because he perceived the Indians of the Caribbean as too savage to know the truth (Todorov 1984: 24–27), Columbus felt obliged to give places, people, and things in the New World their true and rightful names, much as God did for Adam. Todorov noted that Columbus's journal descriptions of clothing, language, and so forth reveal a belief that because American Indians lacked proper material culture, they were without real spiritual or social culture as well (1984: 34). Equally lacking writing, North American Indians held a very non-European view of the importance of the speech of the ancients—making for past-oriented societies in which cyclicity prevailed over linearity and change (Todorov 1984: 80–84). The Christian Europeans saw the ease of their conquest as divine approbation, whereas American Indians initially sought to placate the spirits while awaiting the natural revolution that would rid the world of its newest pollution (Todorov 1984: 87).

Because Europeans had never been altogether ignorant of the existence of Africa, India, or China, Todorov (1984: 4) considered the European conquest of the Americas to be the perfect example of his thesis that the discovery of others is the key to the discovery of oneself. He argued that the conquest of the Americas heralded and established modern European intellectual identity. No date could be more suitable to mark the beginning of the modern era, Todorov argued, than the year 1492. As Columbus declared in 1503, "men have now discovered the totality of which they are a part whereas hitherto they formed a part without a whole" (Todorov 1984: 5).

Yet to imagine that both sides of the cultural coin might be so minted comes close to committing what Fischer (1970: 144–149) described as the "fallacy of false periodization"—assigning inappropriate temporal limits to a historical problem, chopping the spans of historical events into segments in ways that are irrelevant to the logic of what is to be studied. Although European intellectual horizons were changed almost immediately by the Columbian contact, describing eastern North American Indian societies as being pre- or post-1492 is not merely unhelpful but also misleading. As the chapters in this volume demonstrate, any single European object or action would fail as a conceptual fulcrum or hinge for discussing American Indian societies. The first scrap of brass kettle, the earliest extant written description, even the establishment of Jamestown—all have profound consequences for our current ability to study aspects of culture change, but they are likely to have had very different consequences and significance for the cultures that are the objects of our study.

By 1503 Amerigo Vespucci had seen enough of the coastline to call it Mundus Novus, and by 1530 the question of American Indian origins was current in European scholarly debate (Huddleston 1967: 3–14). Because sixteenth-century European theologies all espoused a restricted time scale for antiquity, the question of human origins and the question of American Indian origins became one and the same. The explanatory paradigm called for discovery of the Old World locations from which Indians had emigrated, so Classical authors and biblical passages were commonly studied for clues of missing or wandering peoples from whom American Indians might have descended—an ethnohistoric method exhalted to religion by Joseph Smith's *Book of Mormon*.

Although Hakluyt's story of the mythical Welsh prince Madoc did add local British flavor (Huddleston 1967: 53–93), by the seventeenth century Garcia's synthesis had redirected scholarly debate on American Indian origins from ancient writings to comparisons of Indian "names and words, arms, idols, insignias of the people and hair styles" with those of known Old World societies, many of more modern vintage (Huddleston 1967: 106–108).

We might suppose that, in a kind of ahistoric equity, few Europeans distinguished among the American Indian societies they encountered, and that Indians saw the Europeans as undifferentiated invaders, intruders, and usurpers—but the two suppositions would be equally incorrect. Among just the more structured native societies that first met Spaniards, the Inca believed them to be gods; the Aztec believed them such only for the first few weeks or months; and the Maya speakers of Yucatán thought them simply bearded strangers who did not know which fruits were good to eat. Of the three groups, only the last had experienced previous invasion by real foreigners—the Toltec in A.D. 1000 (Todorov 1984: 80–81).

How could the Spaniards have destroyed a civilization that their letters show them to have admired? Their letters show that they admired its objects and actions but never considered its actors to be on the same level as themselves (Todorov 1984: 129). Indeed, the possession of true culture by true savages would have been considered monstrous (H. White 1985a). The nobility esteemed by Rousseau was the American Indian's "simple and honest" life in the transcendent world of nature, not in the courts of Europe. Less intellectual but more personally involved, the French and British settlers continued the "deculturalization" of American Indians with whom they dealt—that is, perceiving them as having no real culture—often before they even arrived in North America (Forbes 1964: 10–16, 38–43). From Powhatan to Tecumseh, North American Indian leaders had their own interpretations of what was happening to them, often at considerable variance with the understandings of the European colonists who were involved in making it happen (Brown and Vibert 1996; Forbes 1964: 54–61). They learned late that the Reformation and Counter-Reformation had taught Europeans of the sixteenth and seventeenth centuries the existence of heterodoxy and the value of deception. To Europeans, a world without hierarchy was unimaginable, and a world without racial and religious polarities was unknown. Their narratives of American Indians did not neglect to imply the presence of these things.

Such scholarly European lenses, through which we must look at the anthropological and historical data on American Indians, colored not only the Spanish sources dealing with Latin America but also the earliest literary sources for the Eastern Woodlands: Marc Lescarbot's 1609 *History of New France,* Samuel Purchas's 1613–1617 *Pilgrimages,* and John Smith's *General History of Virginia* (Barbour 1986). Throughout the period that Huddleston (1967) saw lasting from 1492 until 1729, Euroamericans saw the broad comparison of cultural fragments from Indian societies with equally isolated fragments gleaned from the ancient writings of Old World peoples as the key to identifying the biological and thus cultural origins of the American Indian, granted some unknowable degree of antiquity.

In those early descriptions, from which we today would reconstruct the living biosocial systems of American Indians in the era of European contact, the cultural features discussed were those thought most likely to have been randomly concatenated from the detritus of some ancestral prototype. Controlled comparison of similarities and differences among groups' integrated cultural behaviors was irrelevant to the intellectual issues for which such data were collected.

Ethnohistoric and Archaeological Studies of Early Contact

Gruber (1985: 166–169) imagined that the 1814 founding of the American Antiquarian Society signaled a shift in the study of American Indians from the doomed peoples themselves to their imperishable artifacts. One might add that for the Eastern Woodlands, the rebellions, removals, and restrictions of American Indians in the 1830s and 1840s not only found reflection in the Smithsonian's publication of Squier and Davis's *Ancient Monuments of the Mississippi Valley* (1848) but were refracted in Longfellow's romantic writings about Hiawatha and in Cooper's *The Leatherstocking Tales,* in which Indian legends, myths, and history were equally artifacts to tell a non-Indian story.

Gruber (1985: 179–180) repeated Boas's statement that "while the archaeology of the Mediterranean country and a large portion of Asia deals with the early remains of people that possessed a literature, we find in America, almost exclusively, remains of a people unfamiliar with the art of writing and whose history is entirely unknown. . . . the problem . . . must be pursued in investigations in American archaeology." Unfortunately, neither Boas nor even Gruber was among the few historians or ethnohistorians who understood the limitations of data from which a socially relevant archaeological record could validly be constructed. But it does seem curious that neither Boas nor Gruber saw that the period of initial contact between Europeans and American Indians might be one for which, to paraphrase Boas, new insights might come partly from literary sources and partly from archaeology. One wonders why these anthropologists did not think that was so.

Galloway (1993:78) seems to have accepted Dunnell's informal suggestion that by the late nineteenth century many cultural anthropologists were distrustful of using the type of ethnohistory epitomized by J. R. Swanton's Bureau of American Ethnology reports to illuminate the archaeological record. Galloway (1993:86) seemed to feel that this had been true because few archaeologists understood the valid uses of historical documents, but she also appeared to agree that early ethnographers and historians did not collect the oral histories of living peoples because they believed those "savage cultures" had changed little over time, and so their pasts could easily be reconstructed from what could be observed in the present. To me, this overreaction to a dogmatic evolutionary perspective attributable only to a very few late nineteenth- and early twentieth-century anthropologists is an anachronistic fallacy. Whether true or not, it says nothing relevant about why records were or were not compiled by those historians and scholars whom we now recognize as the earliest anthropologists to have studied the American Indians of the eastern mid-continent in the late eighteenth and early nineteenth centuries.

It seems, rather, that for those such as Henry Schoolcraft, who lived among the American Indians of the Great Lakes, personal experience demonstrated that the histories they were able to record by the mid-nineteenth century were inapplicable to a past severed from the legends and myths they avidly collected. And that past had been severed deliberately by a practical society that in its eighteenth-century expansion displayed little interest in American Indians as sacred converts and necessary political allies and had not yet been taught to see them as fading bands of noble and romantic heroes—considerations that made the seventeenth-century encounters on the eastern coasts and late nineteenth-century encounters on the central plains quite different in terms of historical links to the archaeological past.

In an otherwise excellent overview of the historiography of the earliest societies encountered in the lower Mississippi Valley, Galloway (1993) failed to emphasize the profound role that the historian's sense of current issues plays in writing the history of any period—true equally of yesterday's business memorandum and Gibbon's (1777) study of the Roman Empire (see H. White 1974, 1985b). Fischer (1970:

4) called this professional oversight the "Baconian fallacy," noting that historians have frequently proceeded as if they could operate without preconceived questions, hypotheses, opinions, or theses of any kind. Fischer noted that this approach had spread into the other social and "hard" sciences, and I would add that it has been the theoretical leitmotif of the past half-century of American archaeology (Brose 1972, 1987a).

To further complicate the ethnohistoric record, as Todorov (1984: 62–77) noted, Spaniards' chronicles describing the complexity of the sociopolitical structures they encountered across the Caribbean, Mexico, and South America in the sixteenth century were strongly conditioned by the chroniclers' own positions vis-à-vis the hierarchy, cohesion, or disintegration of whichever ecclesiastical, military, or entrepreneurial expeditions they participated in. Perhaps only when historians have applied this perspective to French, English, and American observations of aboriginal societies in the trans-Appalachian woodlands will it be possible to reintegrate the historical documents with the archaeological evidence presented in this volume.

Societies in Eclipse

The introduction of current archaeological data into scholarly understandings of eastern American Indians seems a needed corrective to historically biased presentations. This book makes no attempt to disguise the biases inherent in archaeology but offers what are clearly other lines of evidence and other perceptions of how to study the past. Previous books (e.g., Fitzhugh 1984) have offered snapshots of early coastal contact or have been restricted to Spanish, British, or French colonial impact (e.g., Thomas 1990; Thomas, ed., 1989; Walthall and Emerson 1992; Washburn 1988). This book was conceived to follow Thomas's *Columbian Consequences* (1990) and to present new evidence on cultural changes that were well under way before Europeans ever encountered the indigenous peoples who claimed territories from the northeastern Appalachian forests to the southern trans-Mississippian prairies.

Among the original visions for this volume was the authors' hope to provide a better picture of American Indian demography before European contact. The maps by Milner, Anderson, and Smith (Chapter 2) reveal populations thinly and selectively distributed across the landscape between A.D. 1400 and 1650. Cowan, among others (Cowan and Watson 1989; B. Smith 1990), attributed this to the restriction of effective maize subsistence to the loamy terraces of rivers, and many of our chapters offer supporting data—except in places where littoral resources could support population concentrations (see Fitzgerald, Chapter 5; Marquardt, Chapter 12). Consequently, many areas devoid of prehistoric towns and villages were those where soils drained too fast or not at all and so were beyond the reach of primitive agriculture. And many areas between those occupied by agriculturalists acted as empty hunting territories, providing buffers between politically unstable neighbors. Mainfort (Chapter 13) and Williams (Chapter 14) show, however, that regional politics must have played a decisive role after 1450, when population declined precipitously in a "vacant quarter" of the central Mississippi Valley, despite its capacity to sustain many maize agriculturalists. An early concern regarding this vacant quarter phenomenon involved doubt that the effects of European pathogens were immediate and inevitable (see Blakely and Detweiler-Blakely 1989). Many chapters in the volume reveal that the archaeological detection of disease is difficult even where there is compelling historical evidence for it.

Another vision that all contributors had for this volume was that it might demonstrate the value of escaping particular methodological approaches, even though they are needed in order to analyze data. From the outset, Cowan, in organizing the volume, demanded that authors convey a regional approach encompassing the thousands of square kilometers over which aboriginal exchange and warfare had linked American Indian societies for millennia (Fig. 1.1). He supposed that cultural changes after 1450 took a pattern of "raiding and trading" (e.g., Trigger 1978) and dramatically intensified it as European goods entered circulation. Yet there seems to be little unambiguous evidence that this was, in fact, the case everywhere.

The contributions by Bradley (Chapter 4), Fitzgerald (Chapter 5), Brose (Chapter 6), Johnson (Chapter 7), and Drooker and Cowan (Chapter 8) document the movement of aboriginal and European materials and styles throughout the mid-Atlantic region, the Great Lakes, and the Ohio and upper Tennessee River valleys with no direct European involvement. Brown and Sasso (Chapter 15) show that societies on the prairies were engaged in largely east-west exchange, which, Cowan speculated, followed the eastward expansion of the range of the American bison (see Drooker and Cowan, Chapter 8). Hantman (Chapter 9), Ward and Davis (Chapter 10), Smith (Chapter 11), and Mainfort (Chapter 13) reveal a different system of frequent interaction in the Southeast, one that extended into the lower Mississippi Valley and the Gulf Coast but that only occasionally articulated with the systems of the prairies or the northeastern orbit. All of these articulations overlapped in the central to lower Ohio Valley before 1450, and all seem to have found alternative conduits to maintain interaction when the central riverine area from the mouth of the Wabash to the mouth of the Arkansas River was vacated of major protohistoric population centers (Green and Munson 1978; Mainfort, Chapter 13; Williams, Chapter 14).

Nearly every serious student dealing with the early contact period has recognized that European goods initially had limited effects on American Indian technologies or economies. Unfortunately, the evidence, often in the absence of any European record, consists of scraps of sheet brass and copper, which replaced native objects symbolizing prestige. Because these are the very items least likely to have had any significant economic value, they are the objects

Figure 1.1. General regions of the Eastern Woodlands covered by the authors of the chapters in this book.

most likely to have been taken out of use and therefore to have entered the archaeological record. Indeed, the initial "cargo cult" role of metal among the Onondaga (Bradley, Chapter 4) was almost certainly played out more broadly as satisfaction with ornamental scrap was replaced by a desire to acquire knives, kettles, and guns.

The varying roles European goods took on as curios, symbols of local prestige, badges of bargaining positions, and, finally, critical and scarce economic resources have been perhaps more fully explored in studies of Great Lakes Indian acculturation than in studies of other regions of interior eastern North America (see Brose 1978a, 1983, 1994a; Cleland 1971, 1992, 1999; Halsey 1999; Mainfort 1979, 1985; Martin and Mainfort 1985). Movement of European goods to the prairies, the region of Lakes Erie and St. Clair and the upper Ohio Valley, appears too politically complex for the kinds of simple exchange models that describe the movement of such goods into more directly accessible areas. Until 1625–1640, sites in the middle Ohio Valley (Drooker and Cowan, Chapter 8) produce European artifacts and scrap, as do contemporaneous villages on the south shore of Lake Erie west of Sandusky Bay—but at no time are such goods found at sites east of Sandusky as far as Niagara Falls (Brose, Chapter 6; Johnson, Chapter 7). Central Ohio appears to have been abandoned around 1450, and the routes bridging the lower Great Lakes and the middle Ohio Valley shifted dramatically for two centuries.

Though the various authors highlight local differences in their chapters, they were able to document few distinct regional patterns. In his original introduction, Cowan (along with Smith in Chapter 11), argued that southeastern trade patterns were quite distinct, with no early trade in furs or skins and no increase in European goods. Both saw early Spanish "wealth" (iron and metal objects) restricted to the burials of hereditary village elites in the complex agricultural chiefdoms visited by de Soto. No comparable northern expression of this pattern has yet been identified, but then no burial of an Iroquois sachem showered by Cartier has been excavated, nor have burials of Adawa lineage leaders who received largess directly from Champlain in the first decades of the seventeenth century (Brose 1994a; Cleland 1971, 1992, 1999). Indeed, as Cowan recognized, where there are comparable data—for the period following the founding of Charlestown in 1670—European goods at Ocaneechi in the Carolina piedmont generally followed the pattern that characterized the northeast (Ward and Davis, Chapter 10). And, as Cowan admitted, all broad generalizations about post-Columbian intensification of trade in the Southeast are challenged by Marquardt's claim (Chapter 12) that familiarity with Spanish shipwrecks and European technology were instrumental in elevating minor Calusa headmen to hereditary "kingship" long before Ponce de León set foot in agriculture-free southwest Florida.

The relationship between exchange and warfare is another topic addressed, in the belief that internecine conflict was widespread throughout the precontact East, with postcontact intensification. It seems that protohistoric warfare was a winter activity, motivated by the desire for revenge or prestige, in which small parties captured male prisoners (Brown and Sasso, Chapter 15). Historic warfare involved wholesale village destruction, capture of women and children, and adoption of war captives, all linked to acquiring European commodities or mitigating the impact of disease or warfare (Bradley, Chapter 4; Fitzgerald, Chapter 5; Snow, Chapter 3). Brose (Chapter 6), Johnson (Chapter 7), and Drooker and Cowan (Chapter 8) discuss the very different effects Iroquois warfare had on the people of northern Ohio, western Pennsylvania, and the central Ohio Valley.

In concert with these issues, most authors have tried to detail potential cultural changes or population movements triggered by the so-called Little Ice Age, the global cooling that characterized the Neo-Boreal climatic episode (A.D. 1550–1700). Cowan believed that Bernabo's (1981) estimated depression of summer temperature by 1.5–2.0 degrees Fahrenheit might have had little impact on the cultivation of the eastern eight-row or northern flint strains of corn, which were adapted to the short growing season of the Midwest and Northeast. Further, he cited Brown and Sasso (Chapter 15) for "rightly" implying that even if agricultural predictability were reduced, maize farmers could have altered the locations of their fields to take advantage of localized conditions in which the impact of late spring killing frosts was minimized. Yet unlike the situation in the broad and relatively homogeneous prairies, it was just such relocations to limited protected locations in southern Ontario (Fitzgerald, Chapter 5), northeastern Ohio (Brose, Chapter 6), and the western Pennsylvanian highlands (Johnson, Chapter 7) that triggered significant cultural changes, disrupting traditional resource procurement systems, altering exchange networks, and weakening social alliances just as such well-adapted survival strategies would be most sorely tried by foreign invaders.

In the letters he wrote initiating the publication of the symposium papers, Cowan expressed trust that *Societies in Eclipse* would demonstrate the enduring importance of the broad overview in an era when American archaeology had become atomized into particularistic or theoretical camps that were immersed in detail, and an era when more archaeologists were workers on projects than were scholars of a discipline. I now express the same hope, although I doubt that the profession as a whole has ever been much different—the scholars in the discipline simply refused to recognize the non-degreed project workers as real archaeologists until government regulations ensured that the public's archaeological interest and money would be popularized and privatized (see Brose 1985a; Brose and Munson 1986).

Like Cowan, I believe that *Societies in Eclipse* will be of great value to all archaeologists because the detailed literature of regional archaeology has grown so vast, and is growing so quickly, that no one can avoid some reliance on careful syntheses of data from other regions. I further believe that case studies of long-term cultural change in the face of environmental and social stress are relevant public issues as we begin a new millennium. The historical records of the Europeans who introduced many changes and exacerbated more, and the transmitted oral histories of the few American Indian societies that survived them, alike tell stories phrased in each culture's own sixteenth- to eighteenth-century explanatory paradigms. For North America, the anthropologically informed archaeology brought together in this volume provides an overview of the material precedents and consequences of such changes. While no one of these perspectives can be privileged, no one of them can be ignored if we are to understand how their interactions created the image and reality of politically formative American experience.

2

The Distribution of Eastern Woodlands Peoples at the Prehistoric and Historic Interface

GEORGE R. MILNER,
DAVID G. ANDERSON, AND
MARVIN T. SMITH

For the Eastern Woodlands as much as for the rest of the Americas, Columbus's landfall heralded the beginning of an era of Old and New World contact that ultimately devastated Native American peoples and their cultures (Cronon 1983; Crosby 1972; Dobyns 1983, 1993; Milanich 1992; Milner 1980; Ramenofsky 1987; M. Smith 1987, 1994; Thornton 1987). Despite a large body of scholarship on the postcontact period, there remains considerable uncertainty about the magnitude, timing, and causes of profound transformations in sociopolitical systems and population sizes. By A.D. 1700, the loss of people in eastern North America was so great that it was apparent to contemporary observers.[1]

A more precise understanding of postcontact changes in indigenous societies requires much work on two scales of analysis. First, fine-grained assessments of particular groups of people are essential for comparative studies of Native American responses to new political, economic, demographic, and ecological settings. Examples of such work, the focus of most archaeologists and historians, include the other chapters in this volume. Second, broader geographical perspectives are also necessary, because postcontact transformations in Native American societies—cultural upheaval, societal dissolution and realignment, and population loss and displacement—were played out across vast regions.

As an initial step toward the second goal, we present three maps (Figs. 2.1–2.3) that summarize what is known from archaeological remains about the distribution of Eastern Woodlands peoples. Regions where information is plentiful are apparent, as are those where data are limited or absent. While there are many inadequacies in existing data, which are as apparent to us as they will be to others, the maps illustrate how the collective efforts of many researchers can contribute to knowledge about the overall distribution of Native American peoples in the Eastern Woodlands.

The dates chosen for the maps—the early years of the 1400s, 1500s, and 1600s—provide distinctly different perspectives on population distribution. The maps show the Eastern Woodlands scarcely a century before Columbus's arrival in the New World; at the time of early Spanish penetrations deep into the interior, when indigenous societies were still populous and powerful; and a century after initial contact, a period of depopulation and cultural disintegration.

Despite an uneven and often inadequate spatial coverage, readily available information is sufficient to address several issues pertinent to hotly debated controversies about the late prehistoric to early historic periods. These topics include gross estimates of population size, the evenness of the spread of newly introduced infectious diseases into the continental interior, and the factors behind different postcontact cultural and demographic trajectories. We emphasize southeastern societies, but the general points we raise are equally applicable to ongoing debates over the timing and impact of epidemics in the northern Eastern Woodlands (Snow and Lanphear 1988, 1989; Snow and Starna 1989; cf. Dobyns 1983, 1989).

Plotting People

Figures 2.1–2.3 include an amalgam of archaeological phase limits, site concentrations, and individual settlements identified by many researchers. Shaded areas indicate places where there is a high likelihood of substantial occupation at particular times. It is also known that some areas lack evidence of occupation, despite considerable archaeological fieldwork. The maps, however, are intended to show only where researchers are reasonably sure people were present at a particular time, not to undertake the much more difficult task of indicating where they were absent or where archaeological work is too poor to tell.

Published information was supplemented by comments on drafts of these maps and by data generously provided to one of us (DGA) by more than 75 colleagues.[2] Earlier versions of two maps exhibited at regional conferences were based primarily on unpublished information from researchers across the region (D. G. Anderson 1989, 1991a, 1991b). They provided the impetus for developing the more detailed coverages presented here.

Although these maps represent crude approximations of regional population distributions, it does not follow that all shaded areas are equivalent in terms of population size and density.[3] Furthermore, we do not intend to imply that there is a one-to-one correspondence between illustrated phase boundaries or site concentrations and discrete societies such as historically known tribes or their immediate predecessors. Such attempts are futile exercises given current understandings of material culture variation, the low archaeological visibility of often ephemeral political relationships, and the highly volatile nature of social and demographic landscapes during the time periods of interest.

Where archaeologists have the advantage of documentary evidence, there are good reasons to believe that political formations sometimes encompassed more than one archaeological phase as defined by site distributions and artifact inventories. For example, the Coosa chiefdom that de Soto encountered in the early sixteenth century incorporated concentrations of sites known archaeologically as Barnett, Brewster, Dallas, Mouse Creek, and Kymulga (Hally, Smith, and Langford 1990; Hudson et al. 1985). Such constellations of affiliated groups seem short-lived when viewed from an archaeological perspective, in which even fine-grained temporal precision generally means that units of time span multiple generations. Certainly this interpretation is consistent with recently acquired evidence for unstable intergroup political relations and shifting patterns of regional occupation in the late prehistoric Southeast (D. G. Anderson 1990, 1994a, 1994b; DePratter 1991; Milner 1990; Peebles 1987; M. Smith 1987; Steponaitis 1991; Welch 1991).

Mapping Problems

Sources of error should be highlighted before covering what the maps can tell us about the distribution of past populations. Among the many difficulties with this sort of undertaking, four problems complicating the compilation of data and the use of these maps are worthy of special mention.

First, archaeological fieldwork has a spotty distribution. Some parts of the Eastern Woodlands are reasonably well known because they have been subjected to major surveys and excavations. For other areas, there is distressingly little information about the disposition of temporally secure sites. To some extent, intensive investigations mirror past cultural realities: big sites have attracted the most attention. Well-known areas elsewhere reflect the presence of nearby universities with active research programs or the requirements of cultural resource management (CRM) work. Thus it does not necessarily follow that regions with many, or few, places of securely dated occupation were more, or less, densely inhabited than other regions of equivalent size.

Second, the relative sizes of the mapped occupational areas do not necessarily reflect past patterns of human land use. In general, there appears to be an inverse relationship between the size of a shaded area and the precision of archaeological knowledge about the distribution and dating of sites within it. Crudely speaking, the smaller the shaded area, the better the data. For example, many parts of the mid-Atlantic states are covered by large shaded areas on the early 1500s map, whereas the separate components of the Coosa paramount chiefdom in Georgia, Alabama, and Tennessee appear as small and spatially discrete site concentrations. Large polygons are a function of great uncertainty about the actual distribution of contemporaneous sites. In contrast, intensive recent work has permitted the tight definition of spatially restricted site clusters representing separate elements of the Coosa regional polity (Hally and Langford 1988; Hally, Smith, and Langford 1990; Hudson et al. 1985; Langford and Smith 1990; M. Smith 1989a).

Third, an uneven reporting of information meant that different kinds of data had to be used for plotting purposes. The best data consist of site distribution information for well-defined and temporally narrow phases. Good examples of areas with solid site-distribution data include parts of the central and lower Mississippi River valley; the area encompassing northwestern Georgia, northeastern Alabama, and eastern Tennessee; the upper Oconee River valley of central Georgia; the Savannah River of Georgia and South Carolina; and the states of Alabama and Arkansas (D. G. Anderson 1994b; Anderson et al. 1986; Brain 1988: Fig. 192; Hally, Smith, and Langford 1990: Fig. 9.1; Knight 1988; D. Morse 1990: Fig. 5.2; Morse and Morse 1990: Fig. 13.1; Phillips 1970: Fig. 447; M. Smith 1989a: Fig. 1; Smith and Kowalewski 1980; Williams and Shapiro 1987).

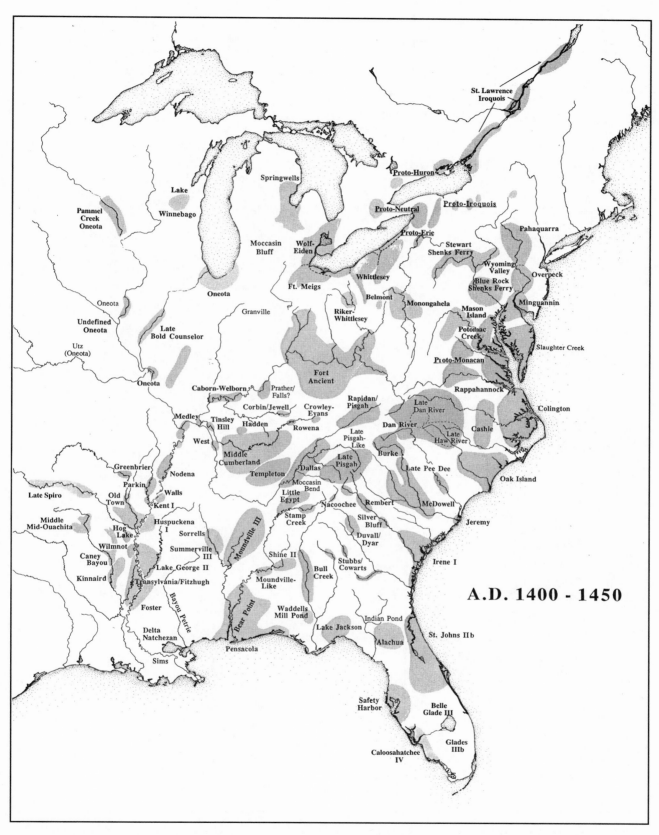

Figure 2.1. Archaeological phases during the early 1400s. Archaeological phases are labeled in boldface; names of groups are underlined. Modified from a map published in D. G. Anderson 1991a.

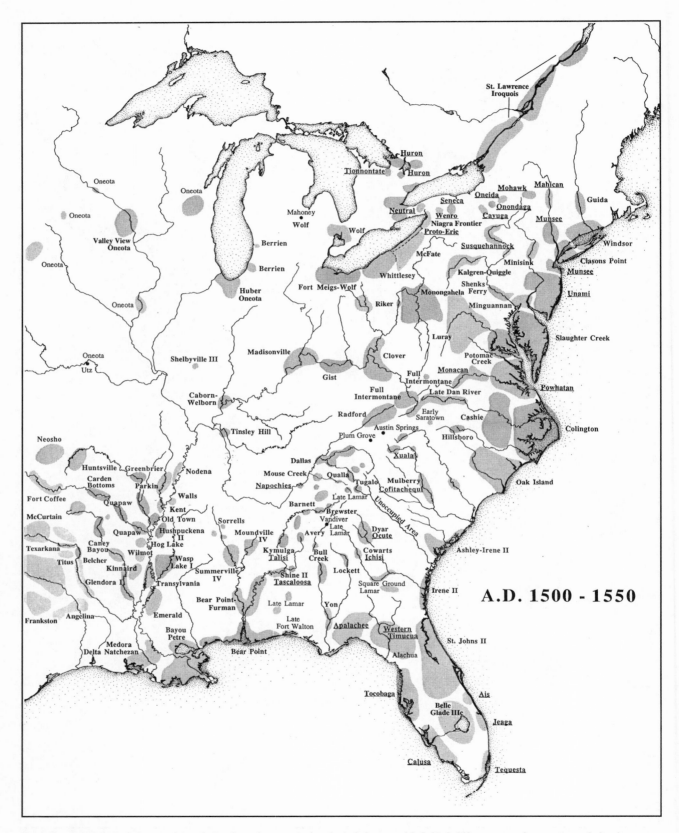

Figure 2.2. Archaeological phases and sites during the early 1500s. Archaeological phases are labeled in boldface; names of groups are underlined.

Figure 2.3. Archaeological phases and sites during the early 1600s. Archaeological phases are labeled in boldface; names of groups are underlined.

Most of the other shaded areas mark only the approximate boundaries of concentrations of roughly contemporaneous sites yielding more or less stylistically similar artifact assemblages.

Fourth, the archaeological visibility of people who lived in small, dispersed, or highly mobile groups is low. Although Europeans encountered such groups during the early historic period (e.g., Rogel 1570 in Waddell 1980: 147–151), archaeological evidence for their presence is often scanty.

Discontinuous Populations

All three maps indicate that people were irregularly distributed throughout the Eastern Woodlands. Although the quality of data is uneven and often poor, these distributions are not a function of sampling error alone. Large portions of the region were unoccupied or, at best, saw few permanent settlements.

Archaeologists have recognized for many years that late prehistoric populations tended to focus on areas with fertile and easily tilled soils accompanied by prolific, diverse, and readily acquired resources—that is, principally major river valleys and coastal settings (B. D. Smith 1978).[4] Even considering the significant strides made in upland-oriented research in recent years, there can be no doubt that highly productive zones, primarily river valleys and coastal settings, were especially favored places for settlement. More importantly, it is clear that not all prime resource zones were occupied to the same extent. Great gaps existed in the distribution of people, as shown by population concentrations scattered along principal rivers like so many beads on strings.

Blank areas, of course, often result from imperfect information. Nevertheless, there are enough unequivocal, archaeologically and historically known examples of places lacking evidence of occupation to support the general observation that settlement was discontinuous across even the most productive land.

One such example of a depopulated but resource-rich area is the Savannah River basin of Georgia and South Carolina. A recent study of more than 7,000 archaeological sites resulted in the identification of several Mississippian chiefdoms defined by the presence of mound centers and outlying support communities that postdated A.D. 1000 (D. G. Anderson 1990, 1994b). These societies experienced individualized histories of florescence and decline, and they were variously located at different times. Several centuries of local chiefdom rise and fall, however, came to an abrupt end at about 1450. At that point, most of the central and lower portions of the Savannah River basin were abandoned, an event caused by a combination of political and environmental circumstances.

Archaeological evidence for a late prehistoric depopulation of much of the Savannah River valley is supported by the experience of early Spanish adventurers. In 1540,

de Soto's expedition passed through this area while marching from Ocute in central Georgia to Cofitachequi in central South Carolina (Hudson, Smith, and DePratter 1984; Hudson, Worth, and DePratter 1990). When traveling between the domains of these traditional enemies, de Soto's army encountered no people, found themselves lost without the benefit of trails, and experienced great hardship from inadequate provisions.[5] The Spaniards' suffering was relieved only by their arrival at Cofitachequi, where they again discovered dense populations and, more significantly, large food reserves. Other such apparently depopulated areas include the central Tennessee River valley (Welch 1991: 195), the Mississippi Valley near St. Louis (Milner 1990), and much of the Ohio and Mississippi confluence region (Butler 1991; Mainfort, this volume; S. Williams 1990; cf. R. B. Lewis 1990).

The refinement of models concerning interpolity relations and demographic histories requires the determining of population dispositions at different times in the past. Despite many all too obvious imperfections, we believe Figures 2.1–2.3 provide a more accurate picture of human distribution than do most other portrayals of archaeological complexes and historical groups. The latter typically feature contiguous polygons that individually encompass vast areas and collectively blanket the entire Eastern Woodlands. Maps featuring contiguous polygons covering vast areas have had a long history in anthropology—for example, Swanton 1952: Map 5 for the Southeast, Kroeber 1939: Map 1b for all of North America, and, more recently, Dobyns 1983: Map 2 for Florida.

By combining the distributions of actual settlements, of sizable hunting territories, of largely ignored resource-poor areas, and of generally avoided buffer zones between hostile societies, these portrayals give the impression that regularly frequented areas covered all available land. We are reminded of sheets of postage stamps on which the stamps—representing multiple, well-defined social groups in this analogy—cover everything and join one another at well-defined borders, the perforations. Such maps convey little information, if any, on actual land-use patterns other than indicating the general parts of the continent once inhabited by particular groups of people. Furthermore, they give the false impression that people were once widely and uniformly distributed across the land, at least in prime areas. For example, Dobyns (1983: 294, 300), in a controversial but influential study, argued for enormous numbers of Timucuans—a population exceeding 700,000—in Florida during the early sixteenth century. He did so in part by viewing diverse natural habitats as being equally accessible to people distributed among a mosaic of societies filling peninsular Florida. Extrapolating from the Timucuan example, and taking into account gross ecological variation across the continent, Dobyns (1983: 42, 298) estimated that there were 18 million people in pre-Columbian North America. His total is much greater than other currently accepted figures.

For example, it is nine times the size of Ubelaker's (1988) 2 million people, the smallest and most carefully developed of recent authoritative estimates.

Dobyns's (1983) high estimate and the spotty distribution of archaeologically verifiable population concentrations cannot both be correct. If each of them accurately depicts prehistoric conditions, then occupied areas would have been saturated with people at impossibly high levels given available resources and technology. Such high population densities far surpass estimates for the inhabitants of organizationally complex late prehistoric societies in the Eastern Woodlands, including Coosa and Cahokia (Hally, Smith, and Langford 1990; Milner 1990), and those for tribal- to chiefdom-scale societies in general (Feinman and Neitzel 1984: 70).[6] Even if a considerable margin of error is allowed for missing data, the overall archaeological picture indicates that population levels fell far below Dobyns's figures.

The central to lower Mississippi River valley seems to be the only place in eastern North America where it might be argued that a sizable region was for the most part filled with clusters of sites representing a series of more or less discrete groups of people. Archaeologically speaking, relatively dense occupation is shown by numerous separable archaeological phases and site concentrations (e.g., Brain 1988:Fig. 192; D. Morse 1990:Fig. 5.2; Morse and Morse 1990:Fig. 13.1; Phillips 1970:Fig. 447). Even in the valley, however, buffer zones existed, though they appear to have been narrower than they were elsewhere, which is not surprising considering the area's topography and resource distribution.

It will be difficult to identify buffer zones consistently because of problems with ensuring adequate spatial coverage and developing sufficiently fine-grained temporal controls. Existing archaeological information, however, conforms to the experiences of early Spanish adventurers. De Soto and others encountered unoccupied, generally avoided, and frequently contested areas between polities in the sixteenth century Southeast (DePratter 1991: 30–32). Historical references to these areas often take the form of complaints about problems experienced in ensuring adequate provisions while traversing unoccupied, indeed avoided, areas.

Archaeologists should consider further the possible significance of the numerous archaeological phases or site concentrations in the vicinity of de Soto's path. If the overall pattern of archaeologically known early sixteenth-century population aggregates is merely a function of scholarly interest in de Soto, then it could be argued that the expedition-route sample is representative of what would be found in similarly sized areas if they were subjected to the same level of scrutiny. Thus, the great number and disposition of these archaeological complexes are not particularly interesting except as incentives for researchers to fill in the many gaps elsewhere in the Eastern Woodlands.

There is, however, an alternative interpretation. To a large extent, de Soto purposefully moved through the Southeast in directions that maximized his chances of finding large numbers of settled and hierarchically organized peoples (Hudson, Smith, and DePratter 1984). Spanish accounts show that de Soto's followers often were threatened by hunger, lived off the people they encountered, moved on when local stores were exhausted, and placed great emphasis on finding important towns with food reserves when they entered new provinces. Native American guides threatened with bodily harm for unsatisfactory performance were certainly motivated to lead the Spaniards to settled areas.[7] Leading figures were abducted to ensure the receipt of food from subsidiary towns along the route and sufficient numbers of porters to carry it (e.g., Bourne 1904, 1: 70, 83; Varner and Varner 1951: 307). Considering the generally oppressive behavior of the Spaniards, chiefs would have seen some advantage in sending the expedition along as quickly as possible to other settled areas, literally shifting the burden of their presence to other places.

New Infectious Diseases

Estimates of population distribution across broadly defined geographical areas represent an important source of information for studies of the effects of newly introduced Old World diseases on early postcontact period Native Americans. Dobyns (1983) has argued forcefully for the frequent and uniform diffusion of pathogens across vast regions from distant places such as Mexico. The sixteenth-century Indians of Florida, therefore, are said to have suffered from multiple high-mortality epidemics corresponding to known outbreaks of disease recorded by Europeans in far-off places. It is more likely, however, that physical and social barriers impeded the geographically broad dissemination of new diseases, including those passed directly between humans. As far as infections transmitted by human contact are concerned, including the great killers measles and smallpox, the spotty distribution of population aggregates, the common occurrence of infrequently traversed buffer areas separating often hostile societies, and the irregularity of communication among such groups would have interrupted their uniform dissemination among susceptible populations. Once a disease such as smallpox was introduced to eastern North America, the likelihood of its being passed from one group to the next, far into the interior, depended on the frequency of contacts among members of spatially separate and often culturally distinct populations.

The members of different sociopolitical groups in the Eastern Woodlands were certainly in occasional contact with one another. Such communication is shown archaeologically by the movement of distinctive artifacts across long distances. Exotic prestige goods that ended up in the hands of important people in southeastern chiefdoms are a particularly well-known component of the exchange of goods among pre-Columbian populations. Periodic elite-mediated transactions promoted the donor's prestige, solidified support constituencies, and fulfilled obligations to important people elsewhere. As noted in other chapters of this volume, during the early historic horizon European-produced items such as glass beads and metal objects moved into the interior far in advance of direct European occupation. The overall pattern, however, was one of sporadic movement through different populations of small amounts of material, much of it invested with some special significance and used to discharge social obligations on special occasions.

These intergroup communication networks served as avenues for the widespread transmission of human-borne diseases such as measles and smallpox only to the extent that contacts happened to bring sick people and susceptible people from separate populations together at the right time.[8] In contrast, Dobyns (1983: 324) argued that there was sufficient regularly occurring intergroup communication to characterize the entire Eastern Woodlands as a single "epidemic region."

There can be little doubt that during the early historic period new pathogens were transmitted to people in areas well beyond the territories of those who had direct face-to-face contact with Europeans (Dobyns 1983, 1993; Milner 1980; Ramenofsky 1987; M. Smith 1987, 1994). When a disease such as smallpox was introduced to a community or a group of affiliated settlements, it would have proved devastating to these unfortunate people. Physical and social barriers, however, separated individual communities and, especially, more inclusive social groups such as the southeastern chiefdoms. Such gaps in population distribution, including social impediments to contact among traditional enemies, produced something far less than Dobyns's (1983: 324) essentially uniform dissemination of diseases across vast regions—his single "epidemic region."

Differential Impact of New Circumstances

The irregular spread of deadly diseases would have resulted in a mosaic of affected and unaffected peoples, upsetting previous balances of power. Such situations would have provided ideal opportunities for traditional enemies to wreak vengeance on suddenly weakened foes, triggering movement to safer locales and prompting the formation of alliances among decimated groups desperately struggling for survival. Unpredictable and drastic shifts in the relative strengths of societies would have increased uncertainty about the intentions of neighboring groups in an already volatile sociopolitical arena. Unfortunately, archaeologists have directed only sporadic attention toward the role of warfare as a population spacing mechanism, its part in the development of social inequality, and its impact on the lives of Eastern Woodlands peoples, although hard-pressed communities suffered greatly in precontact times (D. G. Anderson 1994a, 1994b; DePratter 1991; Dye 1990; Gramly 1977; Larson 1972; Milner, Anderson, and Smith 1991;

Turner and Santley 1979). Nevertheless, it is clear that hostilities often erupted into outright warfare in late prehistoric times, and postcontact alliances and antagonisms were played out within the context of long histories of intergroup cooperation and enmity.

By the 1600s, major changes in the distribution of people had taken place. From this point forward, precise temporal controls become an especially critical element of attempts to trace patterns of occupation, because groups tended to move often and over great distances (Brain 1988; M. Smith 1989a, 1994).

From an archaeological perspective, a depopulation of the lower Mississippi River valley is one of the most readily apparent of the early postcontact discontinuities in regional occupational histories (Brain 1988; Mainfort, this volume; Williams 1990, this volume). From late prehistoric times well into the sixteenth century, archaeological sites corresponding to more or less contemporaneous phases were distributed throughout much of the wide valley. Yet occupation was sparse when Europeans again entered the area toward the end of the seventeenth century. When there is some reason to believe that continuities can be traced across the prehistoric-to-historic interface in the valley and elsewhere (Brain 1988; M. Hoffman 1986; M. Smith 1987, 1989a, 1994), it seems that surviving people moved in response to an opening of the land, to new pressures from antagonistic groups, and, eventually, to the opportunities and threats of unprecedented relationships with the newcomers to the Americas.

Many of the most organizationally complex chiefdoms those newcomers encountered early in the sixteenth century seem to have been among the first societies to collapse. This process is indicated by a depopulation of the central and lower Mississippi River valley, as well as the different experiences of the de Soto expedition and Spanish adventurers about a quarter century later at Coosa and Cofitachequi (Hudson 1990; Hudson et al. 1989; M. Smith 1987, 1994).

Formally established, elite-mediated links among spatially separate constellations of settlements, the principal components of paramount chiefdoms such as sixteenth-century Coosa, would have facilitated the spread of human-transmitted diseases through the periodic interaction of members of distinct population aggregates. Social ties enhancing a disease's chance of crossing sparsely occupied zones would have made paramount chiefdoms likely routes through which pathogens were transmitted to the continental interior from initial, and perhaps distant, foci of introduction.

Once a pathogen like smallpox was introduced to a multicommunity society, the likelihood of its spread from one settlement to another would have been greater in a close-knit chiefdom than in an atomized social system of loosely allied communities. Interruptions in disease transmission, which would have led to inadvertent containment, must have occurred more often in situations where linkages between settlements were weak than in tightly integrated societies featuring regular communication among villages.

Mississippian chiefdoms in the best of times were unstable, at least when viewed in terms of the several-generation-long periods that archaeologists typically use (D. G. Anderson 1990, 1994a, 1994b; DePratter 1991; Milner 1990; Peebles 1987; M. Smith 1987; Steponaitis 1991; Welch 1991; Williams and Shapiro 1987). In the postcontact era, such sociopolitical formations were highly vulnerable to collapse in the wake of disorder brought about by a sudden horrific loss of life from hitherto unknown and greatly misunderstood maladies (also see Zubrow 1990). The loss of leading figures would have left delicately balanced relations among powerful lineages in disarray. Inexplicable, uncontrollable, and demoralizing catastrophes would have seriously undermined the authority of surviving claimants to high-status positions. Many deaths, by disrupting ideal successional sequences and severely eroding chiefly authority, undoubtedly increased the likelihood of infighting among rival factions presented with unexpected opportunities to grab positions of influence.

The situation seems to have been different in other southeastern interior societies that initially were less populous or less hierarchically organized than those that so impressed de Soto's men. In the North Carolina piedmont, evidence for significant disruptions in earlier ways of life dates to the late seventeenth century (Ward and Davis 1991, 1993, this volume). These groups of people were initially smaller and more socially isolated than the powerful chiefdoms that existed elsewhere, including Coosa and the Mississippi River societies. Because of the nature of intercommunity ties among spatially separate population aggregates (represented archaeologically by discrete site clusters), the likelihood of disease containment would have been greater in places such as interior North Carolina than in areas dominated by large chiefdoms. Moreover, loose alliances among villages would have been more likely to survive high-mortality catastrophes or to be reestablished later in one form or another than would ranked social relationships featuring great inequalities in authority and prestige. It should also be noted that the loss of a few villages in tribal-scale societies would be much more difficult to detect archaeologically than would a disintegration of chiefdoms accompanied by an abandonment of mound centers and the disappearance of people with the trappings of high office.

Johnson's (1991a, 1991b) recent work in northeastern Mississippi is also consistent with the epidemic and social organization scenario presented here. During de Soto's time, this area was inhabited by people living in small and widely scattered settlements. By reducing the likelihood of interindividual contact, this settlement pattern, along with a more atomized society than the tightly integrated chiefdoms packed into the Mississippi River valley, would have put these people at an advantage when epidemics first arrived. Differential survival of various groups in this region presumably played a significant role in the eventual ascendancy of the historic Chickasaw, the descendants of people encountered by de Soto in this area. They became major players in the political maneuvering of the eighteenth century, a marked contrast to the situation in de Soto's day, when the most powerful polities were located in the Mississippi River valley to the west.

Conclusion

We close with a call for additional attention directed toward the study of human distributional patterns across vast areas and, furthermore, for a shift to the study of actual site distributions whenever possible (see Knight 1988; Morse and Morse 1990). During the 1960s, there was much talk in archaeological circles about changing research foci from single sites to what were called regional research universes. Yet the few completed studies have shown that even the latter are not large enough to capture much of the information about the behavior of prehistoric peoples that interests archaeologists (D. G. Anderson 1990, 1994a, 1994b; Peebles 1987; Steponaitis 1991). The problems posed by dealing with geographically broad expanses of land are admittedly immense—some will argue insurmountable—but immense, too, are the potential returns from such work. Stated differently, we can wring our hands and lament that geographically broad-scale perspectives on human occupation and interaction are forever beyond us, or we can initiate the first steps toward that admittedly distant goal.

Acknowledgments

We are grateful to our colleagues who kindly provided information and answered questions about the distribution of archaeological sites and phases; many of their comments were included. Those who reviewed the maps that appear in this chapter included James W. Bradley, James A. Brown, William C. Johnson, James B. Griffin, Robert C. Mainfort, William H. Marquardt, Robert Sasso, and Stephen Williams. Julie Smith drew the three maps.

Notes

1. The loss of life among the Indians of the mid-Atlantic states prompted one early eighteenth-century writer to note that "Small-Pox and Rum have made such a Destruction amongst them, that, on good grounds, I do believe, there is not the sixth Savage living within two hundred Miles of all our Settlements, as there were fifty Years ago. These poor Creatures have so many Enemies to destroy them, that it's a wonder one of them is left alive near us" (Lawson 1966: 224). Similar statements were made by other contemporary writers, and their comments are supported by archaeological findings (Ward and Davis 1993).

2. Specific information and source materials for the mapped

areas are available from the authors. The job of assembling distributional data is immense; therefore, we invite comments from regional specialists.

3. Future work with distributional maps could incorporate a ranking of areas by the numbers and kinds of sites or by other measures of population density and organizational complexity.

4. This pattern was recognized many decades ago during the first large-scale projects initiated during the New Deal, when many highly productive sites in river floodplains were selected for excavation (Milner and Smith 1986: 11, 30–32). The results from these early, and typically hurried, digs were used to bolster arguments for the initiation of post–World War II river basin salvage efforts that eventually matured into the CRM work of today.

5. At one point in their travels, the Spaniards recorded that the "Christians now were without provisions and with great labour they crossed this river and reached some huts of fishermen or hunters. And the Indians whom they carried had now lost their bearings and no longer knew the way; nor did the Spaniards know it, or in what direction they should go; and among them were divers opinions" (Ranjel 1922: 94). A description of the trip from Patofa to Cofitachiqui says: "He took maize for the consumption of four days, and marched by a road that, gradually becoming less, on the sixth day it disappeared" (Elvas's narrative in B. Smith 1968: 58). Biedma adds that the chiefs of Ocute and Cafaqui "said if we were going to make war on the Lady of Cofitachique, they would give us all we should desire for the way; but we should understand there

was no road over which to pass; that they had no intercourse, because of their enmity, except when they made war upon each other" (B. Smith 1968: 237).

6. We discount the greatly inflated and wholly unsupported population estimates for the Cahokia site in Illinois, as well as correspondingly high extrapolations from the major center to this sociopolitical system as a whole (see Milner 1990). Dobyns's (1983: 141, 183, 199, 205) estimates include a Florida town with 60,000 inhabitants, a figure half again as large as the most exaggerated claim for the number of people at Cahokia, 43,000 inhabitants (Gregg 1975). Cahokia, in contrast to Dobyns's (1983) settlement, was a large site with many examples of monumentally proportioned architecture, including huge mounds.

7. The Spaniards clearly threatened guides who gave false directions: "The Governor [de Soto] menaced the youth [their guide], motioning that he would throw him to the dogs for having lied to him in saying that it was four days' journey, whereas they had travelled nine" (Elvas in B. Smith 1968: 59). The same passage indicates that the expedition was then suffering greatly for lack of food; the "men and horses had become very thin, because of the sharp economy practised with the maize" (Elvas in B. Smith 1968: 59).

8. It could be argued that smallpox is an exception because the virus can remain viable for a time outside of the host. Indeed, infected goods were purposefully given to Native Americans by later colonists. Nevertheless, some form of contact was still necessary to transport such items among different groups.

3

Evolution of the Mohawk Iroquois

In the seventeenth century, the Mohawks were one of several surviving nations speaking northern Iroquoian languages (Fig. 3.1). Each of these nations lived in communities located amid named clusters of older, abandoned village sites. In addition to the named clusters, there remained in the region other clusters of sites representing groups that did not survive long enough to be observed and named in documents written by Europeans. This earlier, sixteenth-century reduction in the number of village clusters was not the product of overall population decline.

The Mohawks were just one of about two dozen northern Iroquoian nations living in a dozen village clusters in A.D. 1600. The precise numbers are still uncertain because of the confusion of names and places mentioned in early documents, but I estimate that there were about 95,000 northern Iroquoians in the early seventeenth century, 7,740 of whom were Mohawks (Snow 1995a: 4).

Geographic Area under Consideration

Discussion of Mohawk archaeology must begin at two scales. The northern Iroquoians lived on the glaciated landscape south of the edge of the Canadian Shield and west of the igneous New England uplands. They were settled north of the southern limit of Pleistocene glaciation, largely in the Lake Ontario drainage but extending partway around Lake Erie as well as down the St. Lawrence and Mohawk Rivers.

At a more local scale, the Mohawks lived at the core of the Mohawk drainage. All known Mohawk village sites are found within 7 kilometers of the Mohawk River between modern Amsterdam and Little Falls, New York. They clearly preferred locations on loamy soils overlying sedimentary bedrocks, and this was generally true throughout northern Iroquoia.

History of Investigations

People have taken archaeological interest in the Mohawks since at least the 1840s, when Ephraim Squier mapped Otstungo, the Mohawk site on which I have expended the largest fraction of my own energy (Fig. 3.2). Amateur interest remained high throughout the nineteenth and early twentieth centuries. Serious professional archaeology did not begin on Mohawk sites until after World War II, when William Ritchie moved from Rochester to his post at the New York State Museum in Albany. Ritchie, Robert Funk, James Wright, and others excavated several village sites in the 1960s. Mohawk archaeology was dormant in the 1970s but was revived by William Starna and me when new opportunities arose around 1980. I subsequently directed the Mohawk Valley Project until 1995.

A central organizing principal since 1952 has been Richard S. MacNeish's "in situ" hypothesis (MacNeish 1952). This model, which has become a controlling model over the past 40 years, resulted from a legitimate reaction to the freewheeling migration scenarios preferred by Arthur

DEAN R. SNOW

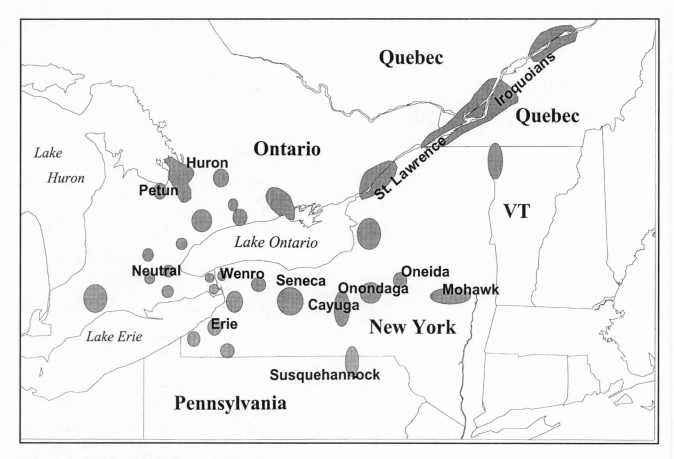

Figure 3.1. Seventeenth-century site clusters in northern Iroquoia.

Parker and others. James B. Griffin (1944) was really the first to call attention to the need to focus on the in-place development of Iroquoian culture—an early call, I judge, for an examination of processual issues. MacNeish initially treated only the Owasco and later Iroquois complexes, which dated to after A.D. 1000. Ritchie (1969) was also initially hesitant to extend the in situ hypothesis back to include the still earlier Point Peninsula tradition, but he had done so by the early 1970s, when he retired. Like most other specialists, I, too, thought then that northern Iroquoians had been in the Northeast for at least 3,000 years (Snow 1984). In recent years, however, various lines of evidence have converged in a way that has forced me to reconsider (Snow 1995b, 1996). The essentials of the new hypothesis are that northern Iroquoians originated in Clemson's Island culture in central Pennsylvania and spread northward into New York and Ontario after A.D. 900, bringing hallmark characteristics such as matrilocality, maize horticulture, longhouse settlements, and collared ceramics with them at the onset.

Cultural Chronology

The Point Peninsula tradition covers a variety of mainly New York phases dating to the period A.D. 100–1000 (Ritchie 1969: 205–208). Early Point Peninsula pottery is characterized by what Ritchie called the Vinette 2 series. Ceramics in this series exhibit pseudo-scallop-shell, dentate, and rocker-stamp decorative techniques. They mark the onset of the Middle Woodland period in New York. The classic description of Point Peninsula pottery types was written by Ritchie and MacNeish (1949: 100–107).

All Point Peninsula vessels tend to be elongated, with conical rather than rounded bases. Interior surfaces are often channeled (Ritchie and MacNeish 1949: 100). Sherds often show fracture planes indicating that the vessels were constructed from coils and fillets. In contrast, later Owasco vessels are rounder and show less evidence of coiling, implying very different motor habits in vessel construction. Owasco collars are never found on Point Peninsula vessels.

Early Owasco, which appears after A.D. 900, is universally acknowledged to have been produced by Iroquoians. I argue that there is a discontinuity between Owasco and the end of the earlier Point Peninsula tradition. Calibrations that I have carried out on published radiocarbon age determinations using CALIB 3.0 (Stuiver and Reimer 1993) indicate that the true dates of Owasco and later phases require some chronological revisions. The calendrical corrections for the few radiocarbon dates we have for the Early Owasco, or Carpenter Brook, phase should be set at around 1150

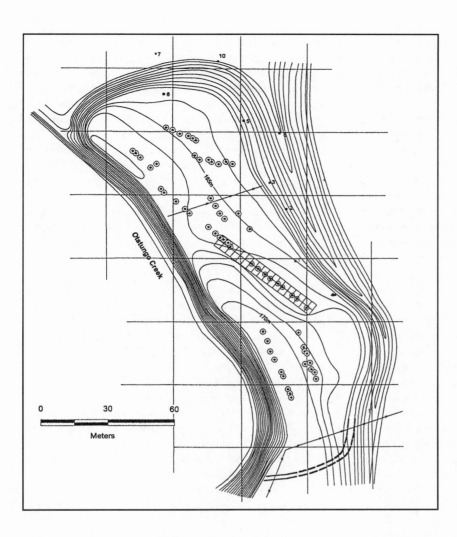

Figure 3.2. The Otstungo site. The small numbered squares indicate midden test pits. Circled dots indicate hearths. The diagonal grid of 3-meter squares shows the area in which all of one and a portion of a second longhouse were excavated. Other lines of hearths indicate unexcavated longhouses.

rather than 1000. I have argued elsewhere (Snow 1995a: 49–52) that the poorly dated Hunter's Home phase, the last of the Point Peninsula tradition, is in fact an artificial hybrid, designed to give the appearance of continuity where the evidence actually points to discontinuity. Its components are a mix of early Owasco villages that contain a few Point Peninsula sherds and late Point Peninsula sites having the remains of still later Owasco camps superimposed. The Hunter's Home phase should be dropped from the sequence. Future research probably will show that the earliest Owasco sites date to the period to which the Hunter's Home phase has been assigned in recent decades.

Middle Owasco (Canandaigua) dates indicate that Early Owasco was replaced by A.D. 1200. Middle Owasco was replaced almost as quickly, for Late Owasco (Castle Creek) sites have produced dates that cluster in the period 1275–1350.

Late Owasco was followed by the Oak Hill phase in New York, which lasted from 1350 to 1400. This was succeeded in turn by the Chance phase, 1400 to 1525. Ritchie and Funk (1973) suggested that a Garoga phase should be used to classify sixteenth-century Mohawk villages. Attempts to use this phase definition elsewhere have been unsuccessful, however (Bradley 1987a: 44), and even in Mohawk County

the phase appears to have been nearly squeezed out by the Chance phase and diagnostic trade goods that appear by the middle of the sixteenth century. In many ways, radiocarbon dating has made the whole phasing procedure superfluous, so there seems to be little reason to worry much more about it.

The National Science Foundation has supported my recent effort to clarify the latest part of the sequence by radiocarbon means. I have obtained nearly forty AMS age determinations on samples of charred maize. This project has resolved many lingering questions regarding the sequence of several dozen sixteenth- and seventeenth-century sites (Snow 1995c).

The Precontact Period

SETTLEMENT PATTERNS. The Point Peninsula tradition contrasts sharply with the Owasco complex in settlement and subsistence patterns. The subsistence systems of the people responsible for Point Peninsula culture appear to have been broadly based on hunting, foraging, and fishing. Point Peninsula sites are usually small camps sited at strategic places near where fish runs, waterfowl, passenger pigeons, or other naturally abundant resources would have been concentrated. Owasco villages were compact settlements built on bluffs. Their focus was not on lakes or streams but on good horticultural soils, which typically surround them.

Northern Iroquoians lived in compact settlements of longhouses from A.D. 900 onward. Longhouses started out as relatively short, unstandardized structures but evolved into large, multifamily residences that by the sixteenth century sometimes exceeded 100 meters in length. Later villages were palisaded, and in the sixteenth century they tended to be located in highly defensible places. Allied villages moved closer together, and village area per person dropped from 20 square meters to 12 square meters at the same time. Even though longhouses were larger than before, greater proportions of them were given over to residential use, and smaller proportions to food storage.

Regional settlement of Owasco and later villages was an artifact of the migration process. Initial community movements out of Pennsylvania occurred in leaps of up to 200 kilometers. Subsequent village relocations within each new area led to the accumulation of sites in clusters. As communities grew and fissioned, some daughter communities remained in the cluster, whereas others leapt to some new area to start clusters of their own. This accounts for both the spotty nature of regional Iroquoian settlement and the co-existence of two or more contemporaneous villages within some clusters. This is also consistent with documented village movements. Champlain (1907: 314) noted that villages moved only 1–3 leagues in a normal relocation but 40–50 leagues (over 200 km) when warfare forced relocation.

Demographic dynamics from the fifteenth century onward led to nucleation at three scales, those of the region, village, and household. Village clusters, individual villages, and households all became larger. This growth took place at a speed that outstripped endogenous population growth, so there was a concomitant reduction in the number of site clusters, villages, and longhouses. This consolidation sometimes has been mistakenly perceived as evidence of population decline. However, both my research in the Mohawk Valley and Warrick's (1990) work in Ontario have shown that even as the northern Iroquoians were drawing themselves into fewer but larger village clusters, villages, and longhouses, their numbers were initially still increasing. The overall population subsequently stabilized, but it did not decline in Ontario during the fifteenth century. The same probably occurred in New York, but abandonment of some village clusters led to rapid growth in others even as the overall population stabilized. Thus the Mohawks increased in numbers throughout the sixteenth century, at least partly because of the arrival of immigrants from village clusters that were being abandoned (Kuhn, Funk, and Pendergast 1993).

SUBSISTENCE.   Northern Iroquoians practiced shifting horticulture from the time of their first appearance in the region after A.D. 900. They grew maize, beans, and squash in clearings created by tree girdling and burning. Such plots usually wore out in about a decade, forcing new clearing, usually farther from the village. Settlements of up to about 200 inhabitants opened new fields slowly enough that the oldest of them could be reopened and used again before walking distance to the farthest fields reached 1 kilometer. Later and much larger precontact villages could persist for no more than about 50 years before walking distances to productive fields became too burdensome (Snow 1986).

Wild plants continued to be harvested for food and medicinal purposes until the Mohawks departed the valley in 1776. Deer were a critical resource, providing both meat and hides for clothing.

SOCIAL ORGANIZATION.   By the seventeenth century, the Hurons and Neutrals were each confederacies of five nations living in single clusters in southern Ontario. The Erie and St. Lawrence Iroquoians might have been three and two nations, respectively, living in equal numbers of small village clusters. The Iroquois proper, the League of the Iroquois, were by this time a confederacy of five nations—Mohawks, Onondagas, Senecas, Cayugas, and Oneidas—that continued to live in five separate village clusters strung out across upstate New York. The Mohawks lived in the easternmost of these (Fig. 3.1).

Longhouses were apparently always matrilocal residences presided over by senior women. Nuclear families lived as pairs sharing fires spaced along a central aisle. Each house was the domain of one or another of the three Mohawk matriclans, bear, wolf, and turtle. Only women and young unmarried males lived in houses of their own clans. Men's houses and other specialized men's structures, which are commonly found in matrilocal societies, are missing; the forest was the domain of men, and all but the very young and the very old spent much of their time there. Village affairs were managed by older men who were appointed by senior women from traditionally dominant clan segments. Household affairs were conducted by the women themselves. The shift from villages of only 200 inhabitants in A.D. 1400 to villages of 2,000 and individual longhouses of more than 200 residents a century or so later necessarily entailed some social and political innovations, but their precise nature has yet to be determined.

The League of the Iroquois was built upon the older clan system and funerary ritual. Fifty league chiefs, of whom nine were Mohawks (three from each clan), conducted league affairs. These chiefs were also appointed from dominant clans by senior women, and they were subject to recall. Condolence ritual served as a prophylactic against suspected witchcraft- and revenge-motivated internal warfare. Chiefly titles were hereditary, but only in the sense that chiefs were appointed (assigned the traditional name associated with the position) from specific clan segments. Although the organization did not have the economic characteristics of many chiefdoms, it did fit a political definition of chiefdom.

REGIONAL EXCHANGE. Commodities probably were seldom exchanged between village clusters, although there may have been more of it within clusters. Similarly, trace element analysis has indicated that pottery vessels did not move far from their places of manufacture. Prized items such as smoking pipes did travel great distances, however, probably as gift exchanges between wide-ranging male travelers.

Young men ranged over great distances and were often out of town for long periods. They carried out raids far from home, and more peaceful trading expeditions probably took them as far as Chesapeake Bay and the Gulf of St. Lawrence. Marine shell from the middle Atlantic coast began to appear in Mohawk villages in the fifteenth century. It became an important symbolic element in the League of the Iroquois, which also emerged at about that time.

WARFARE. External warfare was an aspect of northern Iroquoian expansion, and it intensified as the horizon of European contact approached. Most fighting took the form of raids by bands of young men far from home. Captives, especially women, often were brought back and incorporated as either adoptees or slaves. Female captives often made pottery from local clays in their native styles, so that although pots did not travel far, pot types did.

Male prisoners often were tortured and killed, a pattern that intensified until the Euro-American colonial wars changed the rules. Warfare occasionally took the form of pitched battles between large forces, in which armored participants dodged arrows until a few men were injured or killed.

As northern Iroquoian village clusters proliferated, warfare came to be waged between them as well as with non-Iroquoian Indians. Steep cliffs and palisades protected later settlements from attack. Successful attacks often led to premature abandonment and village relocation. Revenge-motivated attacks were endemic in the region by the fifteenth century. The League of the Iroquois formed as a political innovation designed to cut the cycle of revenge, at least between the Mohawks and the four other nations that composed the league. Thereafter they often operated as a confederacy, which made them militarily equal to the nucleated confederacies of the Hurons and Neutrals, and superior to all others. Even when cooperative warfare was not possible, the confederation allowed the Mohawks to face Mahican and other enemies to the east without concern for attacks from their rear.

MORTUARY BEHAVIOR. Precontact burials tend to be flexed primary interments with few or no burial offerings. Centralized cemetery sites are known for some western village clusters. Archaeologists' failure to find cemeteries with the large fifteenth- and sixteenth-century Mohawk village sites suggests that such a specialized central cemetery might exist undiscovered somewhere in the valley.

The Postcontact Period

SETTLEMENT PATTERNS. In the late sixteenth century, Mohawk villagers abandoned fortified hilltop locations in favor of more open sites nearer to the Mohawk River. The shift probably resulted mainly from increased security following the rise of the League of the Iroquois, coupled with a desire to live on better soils and, later, near trails leading to Dutch Fort Orange.

Villages continued to relocate periodically for other reasons, including pest infestation, exhaustion of firewood supplies, and cumulative social strains. Major attacks by Mahican forces in 1626 and French forces in 1666 and 1693 caused all villages to move first from the north bank of the Mohawk River to the south, then to the north again, and finally back to the south bank.

Settlement density on Mohawk sites relaxed once again to the 20 square meters per person standard that had been maintained prior to the period of nucleation. Smallpox and other epidemics reduced Mohawk population by 75 percent beginning in 1634. This led immediately to relocation and reconsolidation from four villages to three. Like other Iroquoians, the Mohawks stemmed declining population by incorporating captives and refugees, many of them non-Iroquoian. By 1675, longhouses had shrunk to standard sizes of three or four hearths each, and disconnected nuclear families were often arbitrarily assigned both fictive clan identities and new living spaces. French missionaries successfully converted many Mohawks and led them to new settlements in Canada, further reducing the Mohawk Valley population.

Settlement changed again in the eighteenth century, when even standardized longhouses were abandoned in favor of cabins built in a European style. The earliest of these retained central smoke holes and central hearths in the dirt floors. Later builders adopted fireplaces and chimneys. The Mohawks also abandoned compact palisaded villages when they gave up longhouses. After 1700 they lived in two very dispersed settlements of scattered cabins, one of them near an English fort built for their protection. These last two settlements were abandoned in 1776, when the Mohawks sided with the British. Nearly all of them resettled in Canada after the war.

SUBSISTENCE. The precontact subsistence pattern continued after contact, but European domesticates such as horses and pigs were added during the seventeenth century. Trade cloth, which was obtained with other goods in exchange for furs, replaced deer hides in the sixteenth century. This ended the importance of deer as a critical resource. Deer were replaced by beavers as the most critical natural resource with the rise of the fur trade.

Movement to site locations overlooking the Mohawk

River allowed the adoption of intensive river-flat horticulture in place of the more extensive upland pattern maintained earlier. For reasons mentioned previously, this did not increase village permanence, and relocations continued until a dispersed settlement pattern was adopted after 1700.

SOCIAL ORGANIZATION.   Ambitious men who could speak European languages gradually came to dominate political affairs from their positions as war chiefs and "pine tree" chiefs. Their increasing economic importance weakened the roles of both the traditional chiefs and women in village affairs. By the early eighteenth century, individual men were strong enough to insist upon neolocal residence after marriage, a major factor in the breakup of the traditional longhouse residence into individual nuclear family households.

With the adoption of cabins after 1700, settlements became dispersed collections of farmsteads on the river flats. Local affairs were run by self-made senior men, and the traditional chiefs faded in power and prestige. War claims filed after the American Revolution show that the traditional league chiefs no longer commanded the goods necessary to maintain their positions through gift giving (Guldenzopf 1986).

REGIONAL EXCHANGE.   As in precontact times, there was little exchange of commodities between village clusters, but there is evidence that Oneida women carried salmon from the Ontario drainage to the Mohawk, where waterfalls excluded migratory fish. Other commodities might have moved between village clusters under similarly asymmetrical circumstances. It is likely that much more such exchange occurred between allied communities within national territories.

Individual exchange of highly valued items continued, probably disguised as gift giving. Dutch, French, and later English trade items flowed rapidly into the system, and individual male entrepreneurs quickly learned to fend for themselves. As traditional league chiefs lost their ability to control the means of production and maintain their positions by redistributing goods, the entrepreneurs gained local supremacy.

Iron axes and copper pots were available in the late sixteenth century. Glass beads and brass pots appeared in large numbers early in the next century, and kaolin pipes appeared after 1624. Tubular shell wampum, much of it of Dutch manufacture, appeared after 1624, when the iron tools needed to make it became available in the region. Gun parts are nearly absent on sites dating to 1635 but are common on sites dating to 1645. By then the Mohawks were repairing their own guns and casting their own shot from lead bars purchased from the Dutch. From this time onward, the Mohawk economy was part of the world economy. During the seventeenth century, Mohawk and Dutch (later British) economic interests were interdependent in the region.

WARFARE.   Postcontact warriors abandoned slat armor and pitched battles. The pattern shifted entirely to swift raids by small, mobile, unarmored groups. The search for prisoners to replace losses due to warfare and epidemics increased in importance. The destruction of the Hurons and Neutrals was followed by wholesale incorporation of their remnants. Algonquian-speaking refugees from New England and elsewhere were similarly absorbed. By the eighteenth century, whole tribes such as the Delaware and Tuscarora were being incorporated into the League of the Iroquois. In this era, Mohawk warriors served mainly as irregular auxiliaries to French, British, and finally American armies.

MORTUARY BEHAVIOR.   At about the time of contact, Mohawks began burying their dead in cemeteries adjacent to their villages. Burial form did not change, but lavish grave offerings of trade goods characterize these cemeteries. Seventeenth-century Jesuit missionaries who inquired about this were told that European goods were new and not yet available in the next world; consequently, the dead (especially children) had to be supplied with the new goods that they would want to use there. This explanation, which is both plausible and consistent with all the evidence, will not be useful to archaeologists wishing to infer political rank, ethnicity, social standing, or other abstractions from such evidence.

Relation to Known Ethnic Groups

Mohawks currently live mainly on five Canadian reserves and two U.S. reservations. Two of these are actually a single community straddling the international boundary; it is known as Akwesasne or St. Regis. In all cases, the ancestry of these ethnic Mohawks is actually a mixture of many older Iroquoian and Algonquian heritages, with some Euro-American descent added. Thus, although the northern Iroquoians as a whole have probably not yet rebounded to their aggregate population size of 1600, the Mohawks, by virtue of their ability to absorb immigrants, are probably now more numerous than ever before.

Conclusion

Most of this brief summary should strike the reader as noncontroversial. However, my conclusions about (1) the intrusion of Iroquoians into the region after A.D. 900, (2) the delay in the onset of exogenous epidemics until the 1630s, and (3) revisions to the sequence based on radiocarbon calibrations are likely to provoke comment. Detailed arguments supporting all three of these points are in print (Snow 1995b, 1995c). A comprehensive synthesis of Mohawk archaeology can be found in *Mohawk Valley Archaeology: The Sites* (Snow 1995a). A comprehensive summary of the Iroquois can be found in a separate volume of that name (Snow 1994a).

Acknowledgments

I thank all the 26 graduate students, 154 undergraduate students, and more than a dozen Earthwatch and other adult volunteers who participated for one or more seasons in the Mohawk Valley Project over its 13-year duration. Special gratitude goes to William Starna, who was my co-director in the early years. Stanley Bond, Robert Kuhn, David Guldenzopf, and Susan Bamann wrote master's and/or doctoral theses based on the project. Special thanks are also due the National Endowment for the Humanities, the National Science Foundation, the National Geographic Society, Earthwatch, the Arkell Hall Foundation, the Lucius Littauer Foundation, the Wenner-Gren Foundation, the Evans Foundation, Hartgen Associates, the Rochester Museum and Science Center, and the J. M. McDonald Foundation.

Locations of Primary Collections

Primary repositories for Mohawk Valley collections are the New York State Museum, the State University of New York at Albany, Pennsylvania State University, the Mohawk Caughnawaga Museum, and the Fort Plain Museum. Summary descriptions of materials in these and many other minor repositories are available in *Mohawk Valley Archaeology: The Collections* (Snow 1995d).

4

Change and Survival among the Onondaga Iroquois since 1500

In a discussion of "societies in eclipse," the Onondaga Iroquois are an anomaly. Unlike most native groups east of the Mississippi, the Onondaga survived the trauma of European contact and remain to this day a distinct cultural entity. Moreover, they still reside within the boundaries of their traditional homeland in what is now central New York state. Archaeologically, the Onondaga can be tracked over a period of at least 600 years. During that time, all primary and most secondary Onondaga sites were situated within a well-defined region. Indeed, from the first antecedent groups to the establishment of the reservation south of Syracuse in 1788, Onondaga core villages moved within an area less than 60 kilometers across. The sixteenth and seventeenth centuries in northeastern North America were characterized by massive cultural displacement and demise. Against this backdrop, the Onondaga stand out as a remarkably stable point of reference on an ever-changing map.

Considerable archaeological and historical research has been done on the Onondaga since the late 1960s (Blau et al. 1978; Bradley 1979, 1987a; Tuck 1968, 1971). In addition, much important work on both prehistoric and historic period sites remains unpublished. The intent of this review is twofold. The first is to summarize recent work on the Onondaga without reiterating what is already in print. The second is to synthesize this body of work around a particular question: Why did the Onondaga survive? Rather than start with an answer, I would like to focus on three topics that provide a scale for both the continuities and the changes that occurred in Onondaga between 1500 and 1700. These topics are geography, identity, and meaning. For me, these are the factors that help to explain how the Onondaga accommodated changing circumstances and were, in turn, accomodated by them.

Geography

The primary criterion for what was "Onondaga" was location. Onondaga itself means "on the mountain." The Onondaga referred to themselves as "people of the mountain or great hill" (Beauchamp 1907: 147). This place, now known as the Pompey Hills, located south of Syracuse, New York, remained a fixed point of reference for the Onondaga throughout the period under discussion (the late fifteenth through the end of the seventeenth century). What changed was the radius of interaction, the arc of influence that swung from this point. To illustrate this changing scale of Onondaga activities and concerns, let us briefly examine four points in time: the end of the fifteenth century, the middle of the sixteenth century, the middle of the seventeenth century, and the end of the seventeenth century.

At the end of the fifteenth century (or the Chance phase), the Onondaga were one of several culturally distinct Iroquoian groups that resided along the margins of the Lake Ontario plain. The seminal work on Onondaga origins was conducted by James A. Tuck during the 1960s (1968, 1971).

JAMES W. BRADLEY

He argued that the Onondaga, as a tribal entity, formed late in the fifteenth century when antecedent groups from the Onondaga Hill cluster merged with those in the Pompey Hills (1971: 214–216) (Fig. 4.1). Although Tuck's work established the main outlines of Onondaga ancestry, three additional site clusters may represent other, less well-documented proto-Onondaga groups. These are the Baldwinsville cluster, a series of 6 to 10 sites along the Seneca River, most of which were palisaded and have produced Onondaga-like pottery (Beauchamp 1900: 115–116, nos. 20–23; M. Pratt, personal communication 1986; Tuck 1971: 136–137); the DeWitt cluster, a group of at least three poorly documented sites in the Butternut Creek drainage (Bradley 1987a: 28, 212, no. 28; Tuck 1971: 137–138); and the Cazenovia cluster, a dozen or more sites in the Chittenango drainage and possibly the Canaseraga drainage, both located around the southern end of Cazenovia Lake (Beauchamp 1900: 87–88, nos. 7–10; P. Pratt 1976: 93–95, 171; Weiskotten 1988: 14–17).

It should be noted that all these sites fit within an area 60 kilometers across, one defined largely by drainages and lakes. These include Oneida Lake on the north, Cross and Skaneatales Lakes on the west, and Cazenovia Lake on the east (Fig. 4.1).

Two additional things are important about this intra-tribal scale. The first is that most of the antecedent sites and all of the Onondaga sites are located close to the Onondaga Escarpment, a limestone outcrop that runs east-west across central New York, dividing it into two distinct topographical and environmental zones. Onondaga "territory" appears to have been defined largely by patterns of resource exploitation that encompassed both zones (Starna 1988). Second, during the late prehistoric period, the cognitive "world" of the Onondaga appears not to have extended very far beyond this traditional territory. Although hunting and raiding parties undoubtedly went farther afield, the archaeological record indicates that at this time the Onondaga world was small, self-contained, and self-sufficient (Bradley 1987a: 25, 34; Neumann and Sanford 1986).

By the mid-sixteenth century, the world of the Onondaga

Figure 4.1. Mid- to late fifteenth-century proto-Onondaga site clusters in central New York.

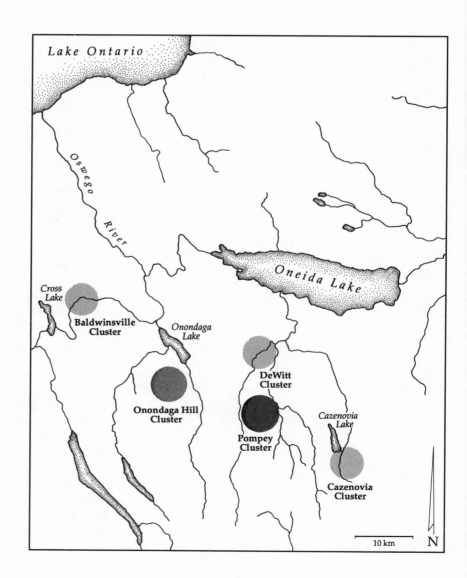

had expanded considerably, up to an intertribal scale, even if the actual size of their territory had not changed. At this point, not only had the Onondaga coalesced as a discrete tribal entity, but so had most of their neighbors, both within the emerging League of the Five Nations and beyond. The most important of these nonleague neighbors were the St. Lawrence Iroquoian people to the north (Engelbrecht et al. 1990) and the proto-Susquehannock people to the south (Kent 1984: 304–306). Each of these competing Iroquoian groups was located approximately 100 kilometers and a major watershed away (Fig. 4.2).

By the mid-seventeenth century, the scale had changed even more radically. Individual tribal territories had been subsumed into confederacies. This time, not only the sphere of Onondaga interactions had increased, but their territory had grown as well. With the disappearence of the St. Lawrence Iroquois and removal of the Susquehannock several hundred kilometers downriver, Onondaga territory expanded north and south into what had previously been buffer zones between adjacent tribes (Bradley 1987a: 83–

103) (Fig. 4.3). By this time, Onondaga territory fit the description recorded by Lewis Henry Morgan (1851: 43) and most subsequent authorities (Beauchamp 1900: 12 and accompanying map; Fenton 1940: 219–220).

By the end of the seventeenth century, although the same map can be used to show the world of the Onondaga, several major changes had taken place. Aside from the Five Nations, nearly all of the significant native participants—Huron, Neutral, Erie, Susquehannock—were gone. As sole survivors, the Iroquois were often given undo credit for their military prowess. "The Five Indian Nations are the most warlike people in America," reported Governor Thomas Dongan of New York in 1687. "They go as far as the South Sea, the North-West Passage, and Florida to war . . . [and] are so considerable that all Indians . . . are tributaries to them" (O'Callaghan and Fernow 1853–1887, 3: 393). Though Dongan's rhetoric was clearly self-serving, the scale of Onondaga affairs had, indeed, reached an imperial level. Even if the Five Nations were bit players, as revisionist historians have argued (Jennings 1984; Richter 1992), decisions made

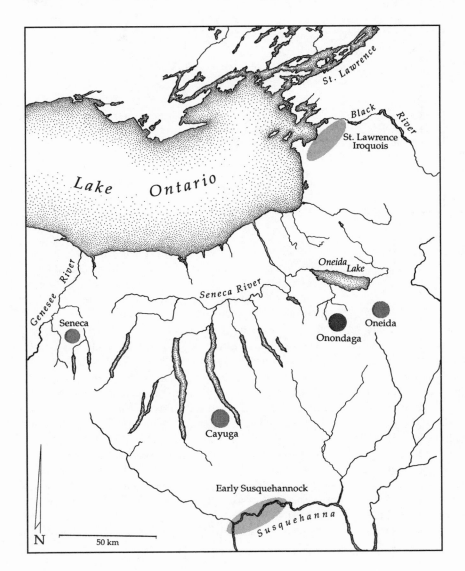

Figure 4.2. Mid-sixteenth-century tribal core areas.

Figure 4.3. Mid-seventeenth-century tribal and confederacy core areas.

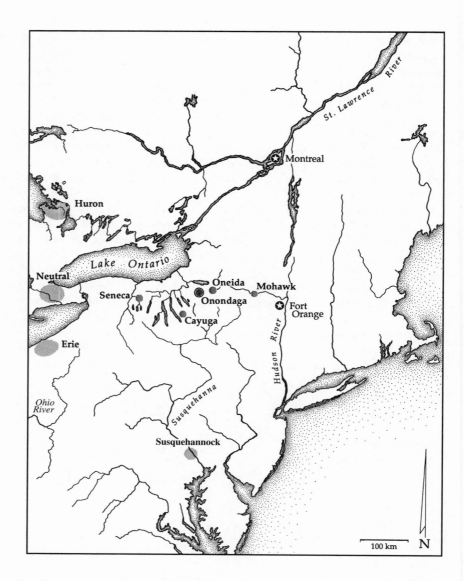

at Onondaga still had repercussions as far away as London and Versailles.

Identity

If location was a constant in defining who and what was Onondaga, then ethnicity was variable. One was considered Onondaga if one lived with, and was accepted by, the people of the great hill, regardless of one's origins. This meant that the definition of who and what was Onondaga changed considerably over the period under discussion. Using the same four time points, let us go back and examine this changing definition of Onondaga in terms of both population and material culture.

From the beginning, the Onondaga and their culture were an amalgam. As I noted earlier, Tuck has argued that the Onondaga came into existence through a process that merged several smaller, preexisting groups. Although there is at present no bioanthropological evidence to support this,

there is some oral tradition. Early in the nineteenth century, the Onondaga believed that their clans had different origins. Of the eight clans, some had sprung from the ground along the Seneca River, others originated on the shore of Lake Ontario, and still others had first come into existence in the hills of Onondaga (Clark 1849, 1: 34).

Tuck used archaeological evidence, particularly a set of settlement pattern and material culture (especially ceramic) preferences, to trace the formation of the Onondaga. These "microtraditions" were distinctive in each of the antecedent groups. The occurrence of traits from different groups in a new sequence of sites was, he argued, good evidence for the merging of these populations (Tuck 1971: 214–216). Although the archaeological record reflects the Onondaga's eclectic origins, it also demonstrates that by the end of the fifteenth century, a distinctive Onondaga settlement pattern and material culture were well established (Bradley 1987a: 34–42).

By the mid-sixteenth century, the Onondaga, archaeologically speaking, are relatively easy to track. Their sites are large, visible, and of fairly short duration, probably 10 to 20 years. Although population data remain difficult to reconstruct, the material culture record is substantial. We see clearly established traditions in ceramics (pottery and smoking pipes), as well as distinct preferences in raw material, implement form, and decorative technique. Against this uniform backdrop, exotic traits, whether material or stylistic, are hard to miss (Bradley 1987a: 48–69).

Onondaga received exotic traits from two sources during the mid-sixteenth century. The first was the St. Lawrence Iroquois, probably those from neighboring sites in Jefferson County. This foreign influence is most evident in ceramics and includes differences in vessel form and decorative treatment (Bradley 1987a: 56–57, 215, nos. 11–13, 15). Equally important are similarly derived traits in a wide range of other material and artifactual classes, including smoking pipes, lithics, and bone implements (Bradley 1987a: 63–64, 216–217, nos. 20–23, 29). During the last half of the sixteenth century, many of these traits vanished from the archaeological record. Others, however, were incorporated into and became a part of Onondaga material culture. Given the disappearance of the St. Lawrence Iroquois during the sixteenth century, a good case can be made that at least of portion of those people were assimilated by the Onondaga (Bradley 1987a: 83–87).

The second set of exotic traits is Susquehannock related, and again the evidence is primarily ceramic (Bradley 1987a: 58–59). Though it is less clear what cultural processes were at work in this case, the result was similar. By the end of the sixteenth century, the definition of Onondaga material culture had changed substantially, in part through the adoption of traits that previously were considered to be either St. Lawrence Iroquois or Susquehannock.

By the mid-seventeenth century, the cultural processes reflected in the archaeological record are more discernable. This is due in large part to the written accounts of French Jesuits who resided at Onondaga. It is clear from these documents that the Onondaga suffered considerable population loss during the seventeenth century, a result of both European-introduced diseases and the escalating scale of intertribal warfare. Assimilation of other cultural remnants had become a necessity for continued survival. The dispersal of the Huron in 1648 is a good case in point. The Onondaga did not play an active role in the assult on Huronia, but they were eager to adopt as many Huron refugees as possible (Thwaites 1896–1901, 41: 95–97, 193, 219, 42: 56). The archaeological evidence bears this out. By the mid-seventeenth century, Huron and Neutral material culture traits began to be a visible part of the Onondaga archaeological record (Bradley 1987a: 122–123, 125a and 125d).

The appearance of new material culture forms suggests that more fundamental changes also were taking place in Onondaga culture. It has been argued that many "traditional" Iroquois customs, especially those related to ritual healing, grew out of the ethnic mixing that occurred during this period (Fenton 1987: 75–92; Richter 1992: 73). It is also likely that the assimilation of captives brought about changes in the structure of the Onondaga clan and moiety system, as it did among the Seneca, adding new elements and changing the order of others (Fenton 1940: 227; Hamell and John 1987).

Throughout the remainder of the seventeenth century, the need to replenish population became increasingly urgent. In 1656, the Jesuits reported that the Onondaga had suffered nearly as many casualties as they had inflicted in defeating the Erie (Thwaites 1896–1901, 42: 177–183). A decade later, the Onondaga again incurred catastrophic losses in their war with the Susquehannocks (Thwaites 1896–1901, 54: 111). At the same time, new diseases continued to ravage the population, especially children (Thwaites 1896–1901, 49: 105–107, 60: 175). Shortly after mid-century, Paul LeJeune observed that "they have depopulated their villages to such an extent, that they now contain more foreigners than natives. . . . Onnontaghe counts seven different nations, who have come to settle in it" (Thwaites 1896–1901, 43: 256). By the end of the century, it is likely that a majority of the Onondaga were either adoptees or descendants of adoptees.

Not surprisingly, the archaeological record reflects the changing composition of the Onondaga population. Whether it is settlement pattern, mortuary treatment, artifact form, or stylistic preference, late seventeenth-century Onondaga sites—Indian Hill, Weston, and Jamesville/Pen—bear increasingly little resemblance to those of even 50 years before (Bradley 1987a: 205–206). Unfortunately, much of the specific information on sites of this period remains unpublished (P. Pratt n.d.; Sohrweide n.d.a, n.d.b).

The social implications of these changes must have been staggering. Although the goal of adoption was to remake foreigners into members of one's own family, clan, and village (Richter 1992: 69–70), the process had a reciprocal effect. With their ever greater numbers, adoptees accelerated the redefinition of what it meant to be Onondaga. As the scale of Onondaga interactions increased between 1500 and 1700, so did the cultural influences that helped to reshape their identity. By the end of the seventeenth century, the Onondaga were a different people from those they had been at the time of European contact.

Meaning

In discussing meaning, I would ideally like to revisit each of the four time points previously discussed and look at how traditional substances of power—copper in the sixteenth century, shell in the seventeenth, catlinite and silver in the eighteenth—evolved as media first of cross-cultural exchange and later of trade (Bradley 1987b). Unfortunately, this is too vast a subject for this review. I focus instead on the sixteenth century, the initial Onondaga response to European contact, and how that response changed over the first hundred years or so.

I want to preface this discussion with a comment about my own bias. What I believe is of interest is this: How can we understand the process of contact and response from a native, rather than a European, point of view? We certainly can do the latter—see native people as part of an emerging world system, or as protocapitalists in the nascent fur trade (Wolf 1982: 167). There is nothing wrong with this; it just is not the perspective pursued here. If we are ever to understand the archaeological record left by native people, then that record must be seen in the context of the people who created it. This is difficult, but as Hamell (1987, 1992; Miller and Hamell 1986), Simmons (1986), and others have demonstrated, it is also possible.

The goal is not simply to attempt a reconstruction of the native world but to develop hypotheses that are testable in the archaeological record. With this in mind, I offer two hypotheses about Onondaga behavior during the first century of contact and test them in a preliminary manner. Hypothesis 1 is that the initial Onondaga response to contact was essentially conservative—it was one in which traditional substances of power (native copper, marine shell, quartz and other crystalline minerals) and their ritual and mortuary uses were revitalized. Hypothesis 2 is that European materials were initially viewed as analogs for traditional substances of power, but that this perception diminished substantially as contact increased.

One way to begin testing these hypotheses is to look at the archaeological visibility of European contact. This is a deceptively simple issue. At the most straightforward level, an object of demonstrable European manufacture in an undisturbed context constitutes acceptable evidence for contact. A good example is a brass ring found at the base of a midden on the sixteenth-century Temperance House site (Table 4.1). For some 150 years, this site was considered prehistoric; now we know its occupation postdated European contact.

But is the evidence always so tidy? Consider the site that preceeds Temperance House in the sequence. Although there is no physical evidence of contact at the Barnes site, it is probably the most remarkable site in the entire Onondaga sequence, for several reasons: the sudden embellishment of what had previously been a very austere material culture; the renewed occurrence of exotic materials (marine shell, native copper, nonlocal lithics) after an absence of more than 700 years; and a concern for reserving some arti-fact forms and materials predominantly for use in ritual, a concern not evident on any of the preceeding Onondaga sites.

Something occurred while this site was occupied that profoundly changed the behavior of the people who lived there, and it seems plausible that these observable changes are appropriate archaeological corrolates of initial contact. How quickly would stories of strange, pale man-beings on floating islands travel 500 kilometers inland? Probably more

Table 4.1

Chronological Summary of Sixteenth- through Eighteenth-Century Onondaga Sites by Drainage

Date	Onondaga Creek	Butternut Creek	Limestone Creek	Chittenango Creek
16th Century				McNab
			Barnes	
			Temperance House	
			Atwell	
			Pickering	
			Quirk	
			Sheldon	
			Chase	
			Dwyer	
17th Century			Pompey Center	
			Pratt's Falls	
			Shurtleff	
			Carley	
			Lot 18	
			Indian Castle	
			Indian Hill	
		Weston		
		Jamesville/Pen		
18th Century		Sevier		
	Onondaga Castle	Coye		
	Reservation			

quickly than the actual objects. Although it may not be possible to prove that European contact was the cause of the changes observable at the Barnes site, for me this is the most parsimonious explanation.

Another way to test these hypotheses is to examine one of the "substances of power" and its patterns of use during the first century of contact. Let us take a brief look at copper. In northeastern North America, native copper has been strongly associated with ritual use and mortuary ceremonialism for more than two millennia (Tuck 1978). After the final florescence of Middle Woodland ceremonialism (ca. 1250 B.P.), native copper in central New York became conspicuous by its absence (Ritchie 1969: 258–261). No native copper had been found on any precontact Onondaga site until the Barnes site yielded two examples (Bradley 1987a: 42). The first European copper (this term includes both smelted copper and related alloys such as brass) occurs on the next sites in the sequence (Temperance House and Atwell), and then in increasing quantities throughout the rest of the sequence. The initial forms in which copper, native or European, appears are traditional Onondaga ones—disc-shaped pendants and tubular beads.

During the remainder of the sixteenth century, an interesting phenomenon occurred. In addition to traditional forms, copper began to occur in new, more elaborate forms. Two of the most distinctive of these have been termed spirals and hoops (Bradley and Childs 1991). These objects have a specific temporal and spatial distribution, occuring predominantly on late sixteenth-century Iroquoian sites. Though made from European materials, these objects are demonstrably the products of local native craftsmen. In terms of fabrication, Hopewellian earspools are the closest analog . Both spirals and hoops disappear from the archaeological record early in the seventeenth century. Whatever the specific meaning of these objects was, they were clearly

of great importance to the Iroquoian people who made and used them (Bradley and Childs 1991).

By the early seventeenth century, another trend becomes evident—the tendency to discard copper as waste. On sixteenth-century sites, there is no waste. Nearly all copper, whether native or European, occurs in the form of finished objects; the remaining 2 percent consists of partially completed objects. Virtually no "scrap" metal (cuttings, trimmings, etc.) occurs. This is consistent with a precontact style of fabrication that emphasized folding excess metal back into the piece rather than cutting it off (Childs 1994). During the first half of the seventeenth century, several changes take place. The percentage of completed objects drops to a fairly consistent 20 to 25 percent. The kinds of objects made shift away from traditional forms, such as pendants and beads, in favor of projectile points and other utilitarian objects. What changes most dramatically is the discard rate. Early in the seventeenth century, 73 percent of the copper takes the form of partially completed objects, and 6 percent is scrap. By mid-century, the percentage of partially completed objects has dropped to 31 percent while the discarded scrap has risen to 45 percent (Table 4.2). As a substance of power, copper appears to have undergone severe devaluation.

There are other ways to test these hypotheses. Let me briefly discuss one more: cross-cultural comparison. I have suggested previously (Bradley 1987a: 106–108) that the Onondaga (Iroquois) response to European contact shared many characteristics with that of Melanesian "cargo cults." Certainly such a comparison, like any other ethnographic analogy, must be used with care. Nonetheless, it can provide an extremely valuable guide if our goal is to understand contact from a native perspective.

About the same time my book on the Onondaga came out (Bradley 1987a), so did an excellent study on first con-

Table 4.2

Patterns of Onondaga Copper Use and Reuse

Site	Finished Objects		Incomplete Objects and Utilized Scrap		Unutilized Scrap		Total Number
	No.	%	No.	%	No.	%	
Barnes	1[a]	50	1[a]	50	—	—	2
Temperance House & Atwell	3	100	—	—	—	—	3
Quirk & Sheldon	6	100	—	—	—	—	6
Chase & Dwyer	100	90	8	7	3	3	111
Pompey Center	58	21	198	73	15	6	271
Pratt's Falls	—	—	—	—	—	—	0
Shurtleff	36	20	104	59	36	20	176
Carley	34	43	30	38	15	19	79
Lot 18	30	24	39	31	56	45	125

[a]Native copper.

tact between Europeans and the indigenous people of the New Guinea highlands (Connolly and Anderson 1987). There, too, the initial perception of Europeans was either as returning ancestors or as spirit beings of considerable power. With more prolonged exposure, it became clear that Europeans were men, not gods, but men with a special relationship to the spirit world, as evidenced by their enormous material wealth (Connolly and Anderson 1987: 115–116, 128). This belief, and how it subsequently changed, is exemplified by the following passage:

The next morning, the white man packed up and went, and we came back to where he had slept, and we searched. Our old men believed that these were lightning beings from the sky, with special powers, and they advised us to collect everything they had left behind. We swept the place and collected everything, tea leaves, matches, tin cans. . . . Then we put these special things in a string bag . . . and hung it on a post where everyone could see it. . . . Our old men said, "We will use these white man's things in the war against our enemies." And when we were successful we knew the white man's power was working with us. We held on to these beliefs for a long time, until more white men came. Then we realized these things were nothing special, just ordinary rubbish, so we threw them away. (Connolly and Anderson 1987: 55)

Change a few words—copper kettles for tin cans, glass beads for matches—and you could not find a more succinct description of the changing meaning of European materials among the Onondaga during the first century of contact.

Onondaga Survival

Let me return to the question posed at the beginning of this review: Why did the Onondaga survive, especially when so many other, comparable cultural groups did not? Perhaps it is premature, even presumptuous, to attempt an answer, but I want to try.

An initial explanation is grounded in the two concepts that defined what was Onondaga: locality and kinship.

As many previous scholars have pointed out, the Iroquois were favored by a series of locational and cultural factors (Richter 1992: 2–4). Many of these factors were especially applicable to the Onondaga. Not only was their location advantageous, but its advantages changed in tandem with the scale of Onondaga interactions. Prior to contact, the advantages were ones of environmental diversity; if resources in one zone failed, those of the other could be utilized. During the sixteenth century, the advantage was that of an interior position, which buffered the effects of European disease and gave the Onondaga time to absorb European materials on their own terms. By the seventeenth century, the advantage had shifted to one of access. Astride the boundary of the St. Lawrence and Susquehanna drainages, and a day's journey from both the Mohawk/Hudson and Delaware Rivers, the Onondaga were able to exert formi-

dable economic and political influence, first on other native groups and then on Europeans.

As the scale of the Iroquois world increased, so did the importance of a stable point at its center. That point was Onondaga. Whether it was "on the great hill" or along the shore of Onondaga Lake, as oral tradition states, this was where the Tree of Peace (the metaphor for society itself) was rooted. Onondaga was the center not only of the League of the Iroquois but of "this island, the Turtle's back," the world itself. Among a people who regarded metaphor as fact (Fenton 1962: 297), such sentiments were not just social and political rhetoric. Locality defined the Onon-daga as thoroughly as they defined it. As future events would demonstrate, this was a linkage that would not easily be broken.

If locality served as the tangible focus for Onondaga culture, then kinship bonds were the glue that held it together. Kinship operated at several levels—family, clan, moiety, and village—and provided the definition of a person's roles and responsibilities (Fenton 1951, 1987: 309–314). Taken together, these formed a social structure that was both flexible and resilient, one that was able to replenish itself through adoption and assimilation. As long as the structure of kinship was maintained, Onondaga culture could (and did) accommodate a great deal of biological, ethnic, linguistic, and even material diversity and still remain coherent and functional.

The ability to encompass such diversity was not without its price. With so many elements drawn from different sources, it was, and still is, difficult to know exactly what constituted "real" Onondaga culture. Nonetheless, the Onondaga survived because, beneath all those acquired traits, locality and kinship continued to serve as centripetal forces binding the pieces together. As long as this foundation remained in place, the rest of the definition of who and what was Onondaga could be quite flexible.

As definers of culture, locality and kinship were not unique to the Onondaga. These factors undoubtedly applied to the other Iroquois nations as well as to other Native American groups in the Northeast. What made the Onondaga different? I believe the key is that, in Onondaga, the advantages of geography and the flexibility of identity were infused with a unique sense of meaning. Onondaga became more than just a fixed place in a changing landscape; it was the central point in Iroquois ritual and tradition. If the Iroquois believed themselves to be "men preeminently," then Onondaga was the place where this was most real—where the league wampum belts were housed and displayed, where the pillar of smoke from the council fire touched the sky, where prestige was most concentrated and consensus could be achieved (William Fenton, personal communication 1993). This fusion of geography, identity, and meaning was reflected in the fact that, unlike comparable Mohawk and Seneca towns whose names change with location, the principal town in Onondaga was always known by that name (Bradley 1987a: 116, 205–207). Onondaga was more than the sum of its own traditions and rituals; it embodied those of the league as well.

By the end of the seventeenth century, many factors strained the fabric of Iroquois, and Onondaga, society. Caught between the increasingly aggressive imperial designs of England and France, the scale of Iroquoian influence began to contract. For the Onondaga, the destruction of their primary town by the French in 1696 was a humbling and painful introduction to the changing realities of a new century.

The first decades of the eighteenth century brought some respite as the Iroquois pursued a strategy of balance and peace rather than warfare. Yet although they retained their lands and autonomy, the Iroquois were increasingly a colonized people forced to live in a world no longer entirely their own (Richter 1992, 4: 255–256). Political intrigue and factionalism, ever greater economic dependence, and widespread alcoholism all took their toll. By mid-century, the once mighty Onondaga were a destitute and demoralized people who survived largely by digging and selling ginseng root (Beauchamp 1916: 173, 176, 188, 201; O'Callaghan and Fernow 1853–1887, 6: 808).

Worse was to come. The allegiances that pulled the American colonies away from England also had a devasting impact on the Iroquois. Unable to achieve one mind about which side to support, the league split asunder, uprooting the Tree of Peace (Graymont 1972). In April 1779, Onondaga was again burned, this time by an American raiding party, the advance guard of a campaign designed to destroy all the major Iroquois settlements. The Clinton-Sullivan campaign was a success. With their towns in ashes, most of the Iroquois chose to leave their ancestral lands. Although the Peace of Paris ended the war in 1784, it made no provision for the Iroquois. As for the league, the council fire that once burned at Onondaga was rekindled in two locations, Six Nations Reserve in Canada and the Buffalo Creek reservation in western New York (Tooker 1978a: 435).

Even in those darkest of days, the Onondaga survived, in large part because they did not abandon their land. Many did choose to go, some following Joseph Brant to Six Nations, others moving to Buffalo Creek. But a portion of the Onondaga decided to remain and to tend the site of the council fire in its traditional location. Although the Onondaga ceded most of their land in 1788, they retained the core of their territory, a 100-square-mile tract along Onondaga Creek, as the newly created Onondaga reservation (Blau et al. 1978: 495–496). True, significant portions of the reservation were sold in 1795, 1817, and 1822, but the Onondaga refused to give up their land completely. In contrast, the Mohawk never returned to their valley after the American Revolution, and the Seneca sold the last tract of land in the Genesee Valley in 1826 (Abler and Tooker 1978: 511). By 1840, the Onondaga were the only one of the Six Nations who remained on ancestral land.

This new shoot for the roots of the Tree of Peace manifested itself in other ways during the nineteenth century. Although other reservations, notably Tonawanda Seneca, also served as centers of traditional Iroquois practices, Onondaga increasingly regained its reputation as the custodian of league tradition and ritual. This position was greatly strengthened when the council fire of the league and many of its wampum belts were returned to Onondaga in 1847 after the Buffalo Creek reservation was sold (Blau et al. 1978: 496–497). Traditional practices manifested theselves in other ways. Early in the nineteenth century, Onondaga became a hotbed of support for the new religion of Handsome Lake. For the rest of the century, the majority of Onondagas were hostile or indifferent to the efforts of Christian missionaries (Blau et al. 1978).

The remainder of the nineteenth century brought a host of new challenges to the traditional way of life in Onondaga. Economic factors were a powerful force for change. Although many Onondagas continued to pursue seasonal activities such as hunting, collecting berries, and making baskets, brooms, and beadwork for sale, others increasingly chose to work off the reservation as day laborers (Tooker 1978b: 463). Other issues of contention included the teaching of native language and control over the education of children, proposals to divide the remaining tribally owned land into individual allotments, and whether tribal chiefs would be chosen through elections or traditional means (Connors et al. 1986: 6–10, 21–26; Hauptman 1981: 4–5). In spite of pressures to conform to mainstream culture, and the inevitable factions that resulted, Onondaga remained a stronghold of tradition. In 1888, the New York State Assembly appointed a special legislative committee to investigate the "Indian problem" and why assimilation of the remaining Iroquois was proceeding so slowly. The Whipple Report reserved its harshest words for the Onondaga, who were considered the most recalcitrant and resistant to change. "Just so long as they are permitted to remain in this condition," the report noted with asperity, "will there remain upon the fair name of the Empire State a stain of no small magnitude" (Connors et al. 1986: 9). For an entirely different set of reasons, the Onondaga might well have agreed with that assessment.

In the process of accommodating change, the Onondaga found that change accommodated them as well. At the time of European contact, they were one of dozens of similar Iroquoian groups. By the mid-seventeenth century, they had become the physical and spiritual center of the most powerful confederacy in the Northeast. That tradition sustained the Onondaga through the cataclysms of the eighteenth century and the pressures of assimilation during the nineteenth and early twentieth centuries. And today? Another generation has revived the traditions of the league, and Onondaga once again is the seat of an activist Grand Council (Hauptman 1986: 217–218). The rituals of thanksgiving and condolence continue to be observed, and the Gaiwiio (the Good Word) of Handsome Lake is spoken not only for the benefit of the Haudenosaunee (Six Nations) but for the whole world. Seen in an archaeological and historical perspective, the Onondaga continue to survive, in large part because the same factors that have defined them over the last 500 years continue to shape them now.

Acknowledgments

I am deeply grateful to William Fenton, George Hamell, and Daniel Richter for their comments, and to Marjorie and Peter Pratt as well as A. Gregory Sohrweide for permission to cite their unpublished work.

5

Contact, Neutral Iroquoian Transformation, and the Little Ice Age

The explanation of cultural developments among the Neutral Iroquoians of southern Ontario during the sixteenth and seventeenth centuries has been influenced largely by the fact that many of the changes occurred during the initial era of European presence in eastern North America. A reevaluation of the available archaeological, ecological, and climatic record, however, reveals other human and natural agents that contributed both directly and indirectly to those developments.

An underlying tenet of Iroquoian research as far back as the writings of Lewis Henry Morgan (1851: 144–146), and particularly following the work of Richard MacNeish (1952), William Ritchie (1969), and James Wright (1966), has been that Iroquoian culture was in a state of progressive development that reached its zenith during the seventeenth century. Exposure to Europeans, their material culture, and their diseases has traditionally been considered the dominant, if not the solitary, agent in the abrupt decline of Ontario Iroquoian societies (e.g., Warrick 1984: 131).

The profound effect of European contact on Ontario Iroquoian societies cannot be denied, but it has been proposed, upon a reappraisal of the archaeological evidence, that certain aspects of Iroquoian culture in Ontario had attained their cultural apogee by the fifteenth century. By the time European presence became an influential factor, Ontario Iroquoian society was already in the process of redefinition or, more precisely, devolution (Fitzgerald and Jamieson 1985), much like the contemporaneous chiefdoms of the southeastern United States (Peebles 1986; Smith 1987). The state of seventeenth-century Neutral Iroquoian society was the result of centuries of adaptations to a complex series of diverse circumstances and forces initially independent of, but later compounded by, the effects of European contact. Among trends observable in the archaeological record between the fifteenth and the seventeenth centuries are population contraction and dispersal, changing residential and subsistence patterns, a florescence of ritualism, and the adoption of foreigners and exotic material culture.

In 1615 Samuel de Champlain noted that the Iroquoian-speaking group concentrated around the western end of Lake Ontario was not involved in the hostilities between the Huron and the Iroquois (Biggar 1922–1936, 3: 99–100). That neutrality led Champlain and subsequent Europeans to refer to this group as the Neutral nation. To the Huron they were the Atiouandaronk (Thwaites 1896–1901, 8: 116). Although the devastating attacks of the Iroquois between 1647 and 1651 effectively extinguished this distinctive culture, the cumulative influences that had earlier molded it and other northern Iroquoian cultures also bore responsibility for their redefinition and ultimate demise.

History of Archaeological Research

The Neutral Iroquoians have been of interest to archaeologists, historians, and relic hunters since their villages and

WILLIAM R. FITZGERALD

cemeteries were first disturbed by forest-clearing activities in the early nineteenth century (see Lennox and Fitzgerald 1990: 405–408). In 1843 the American ethnologist Henry Schoolcraft was taken to the Dwyer cemetery west of Hamilton, Ontario, and he returned in 1844 and 1845 to collect additional artifacts. The first systematic archaeological investigations of Neutral sites were carried out in the late 1800s and early 1900s by David Boyle from the Royal Ontario Museum (Toronto). William Wintemberg from the Victoria Museum (Ottawa) conducted extensive surveys and excavations throughout Neutral territory during the first quarter of the twentieth century and was largely responsible for initiating chronological and classificatory studies for this group.

The 1950s and 1960s saw a florescence in Neutral research. Richard MacNeish, Norman Emerson, and James Wright incorporated Neutral data into broader Iroquoian developmental schemes, and Marian White undertook an intensive investigation of the Neutral in the Niagara region of New York and Ontario. During the 1970s and 1980s, substantial numbers of undergraduate and graduate theses from universities in Canada and the United States, as well as independent research projects and salvage excavations, added exponentially to our knowledge of the Neutral.

Neutral Distribution

Neutral Ontario Iroquoian occupations datable to the fifteenth century are dispersed in a broad band along the north shore of Lake Erie (Fig. 5.1), at the present northern edge of the Carolinian biotic province. During the first half of the sixteenth century a large tract of Neutral territory west of the Grand River was abandoned (T. Lee 1959). The ensuing compaction of Neutral groups around the southwestern corner of Lake Ontario led to the formation of the well-defined tribal territories of the late sixteenth and early seventeenth centuries, and the Neutral allied themselves into a seemingly loose confederacy that persisted until their dispersal (Fitzgerald 1990a: 252–404). It was also during the second half of the sixteenth century that other Iroquoian groups undertook long-distance relocations. Huron groups in the Trent Valley and around the northwestern corner of Lake Ontario were withdrawing into the confederated territory described initially by Champlain (Ramsden 1990). St. Lawrence Iroquoian groups were dispersed (Jamieson 1990), and the Susquehannock migrated southward toward Chesapeake Bay (Witthoft 1959).

Some believe that the migrations of the Huron, Neutral, and Susquehannock were motivated by the desire to relocate to areas where access to European goods was enhanced (Hunter 1959; Ramsden 1978; Trigger 1985, 1991). Even though Europeans had been in the Gulf of St. Lawrence since the end of the fifteenth century, they were there initially to fish, hunt whales, and explore, not to conduct commercial transactions with natives (Turgeon and Fitzgerald 1992). Although ceremonial exchanges and ancillary bartering did take place along the coast and the St. Lawrence River, the majority of European goods obtained in these limited activities would have become dispersed long before they filtered inland. Only after native groups could supply a

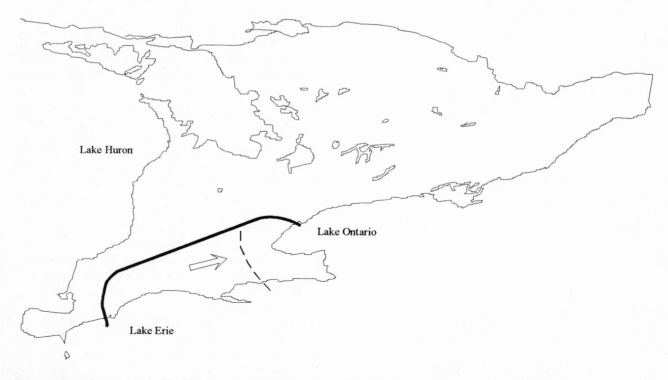

Figure 5.1. Neutral territory in the fifteenth century (south of the heavy line) and by the mid-sixteenth century (east of the dashed line).

commodity desired by Europeans might we expect an intensive commercial trade to have developed. Felt from beaver pelts became that commodity, but the French demand for non-Russian beaver did not become significant until the second half of the sixteenth century. It was not until the first years of the 1580s that the commercial fur trade commenced in northeastern North America, initially centered in the Gulf of St. Lawrence. Its onset is indicated by the dramatic increase of European goods of that era on native sites in the Canadian Maritimes, along the Saguenay River, and around the lower Great Lakes.

It is inconceivable that the incredibly small quantities of goods that did filter indirectly into southern Ontario prior to 1580 might have triggered population movements of such magnitude. That the migrations clearly preceded the commercial fur trade is especially evident in the Neutral situation, where well-defined sequences of site relocations document successive stages in the introduction of datable European commodities (Fitzgerald 1990a). Supporting the notion that these migrations were not a consequence of competition for European goods is the virtual absence of such commodities in St. Lawrence Iroquoian settlements. Martijn (1969) has suggested that the abandonment of the St. Lawrence lowlands was instead due to the failure of horticulture caused by the onset of the Little Ice Age.

On the basis of the presence of heavily fortified Neutral frontier settlements and foreign native ceramics on Neutral sites, it has been proposed that during the first half of the sixteenth century, Neutral groups in extreme southwestern Ontario were involved in hostilities with the neighboring Algonkian Fire nation (W. Fox 1980). The Neutral abandonment might be interpreted as a means of increasing the buffer zone between the combatants. The initial cause of these hostilities is unclear, but like their seventeenth-century manifestations, which have been ascribed to competition over beaver hunting territories (Fitzgerald 1982a: 100), they might have been related to competition over resources, not so much in a capitalistic sense related to fur trade activities but more basically for survival.

At mid-sixteenth-century settlements within the area of contraction, the presence of substantial house and village expansions (Fig. 5.2) and the continued practice of extensive settlement fortification indicate the incorporation of immigrants and the perception of an enduring threat (Fitzgerald 1991a). Similar expansions were occurring at contemporary Huron villages in the Trent Valley (Ramsden 1989).

The purported intensification of warfare in the lower Great Lakes throughout the precontact portion of the Late Woodland period has, since the 1950s, been linked to an increasing dependence on horticulture. Supposedly, warfare

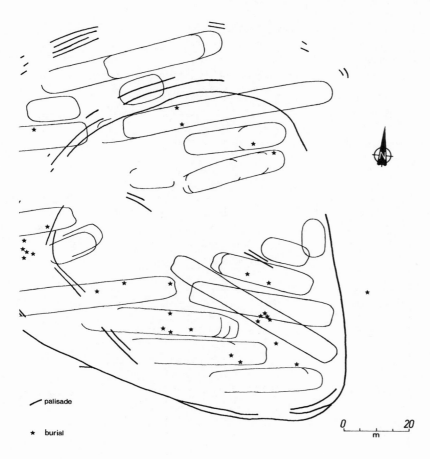

Figure 5.2. Plan of the MacPherson site, showing expansion of the palisaded village. The core village was surrounded by an original palisade that was partially replaced at least twice by new rows of palisades to the northwest as the village grew.

╱ palisade

★ burial

0 ___ 20
m

Table 5.1

Frequencies of Deer and Woodchuck Remains at Neutral Iroquoian Settlements

Period	Site	Mammal Sample Size	Deer %	Woodchuck %
1400–1500	Coleman	271	2.6	26.6
	Ivan Elliot	502	1.2	24.9
	Moyer	704	2.7	73.4
1500–1580	Buddy Boers	922	85.8	0.3
	Knight-Tucker	602	73.6	0.0
	MacPherson	291	78.4	0.3
	Raymond Reid	237	59.1	7.6
1580–1600	Cleveland	4,466	64.6	1.3
1600–1630	Brown	881	64.7	0.6
	Christianson	1,169	50.1	2.6
1630–1650	Hamilton	8,249	64.9	0.7
	Hood	2,250	75.2	0.4
	Walker	7,626	70.9	1.1

enabled the male members of society to continue to demonstrate their masculinity in some pursuit other than hunting (Engelbrecht 1987; Trigger 1981; Witthoft 1959). As faunal and carbon isotope evidence indicates (Table 5.1, Fig. 5.3), however, female-dominated farming activities never resulted in the abandonment of hunting.

The formulation in the 1950s and 1960s of the notion of males having to spend more time waging war in order not to feel emasculated is perhaps understandable in terms of a Cold War mentality. Yet the archaeological evidence implemented to propose an escalation of precontact warfare and cannibalism must be carefully scrutinized. "Brutalized"

human remains—interpreted as such because they been shattered, charred, or modified to produce artifacts—have been recovered in archaeological contexts that can just as convincingly be related to burial practices or the by-products of burial rituals (e.g., Spence 1992; Woodley, Southern, and Fitzgerald 1992). Cremated remains and discarded skeletal items not included in secondary reburials probably have been inappropriately attributed to hostile actions, especially if recovered from plow-disturbed contexts, and most certainly if the skeletal elements belong to very young individuals. In addition, shallow primary interments are commonly scattered by recent agricultural activities (e.g., Saunders 1989). The fabrication of gorgets and other items from human bone should not necessarily be perceived as evidence of mistreatment or disrespect of enemies. Ornately decorated Roman Catholic ossuaries contain small skeletal fragments of saints—hardly a situation to be construed as a display of interpersonal violence. Indeed, the Jesuits reported that the Neutral displayed the remains of family members within their longhouses, sometimes for prolonged periods, prior to final burial (Thwaites 1896–1901, 21: 199).

Intercultural feuding cannot be denied as a fact of Iroquoian life (e.g., Abler 1980; Jamieson 1983). But its impact on the formation of precontact Ontario Iroquoian culture should not be exaggerated on the basis of the present extent of archaeological evidence and Eurocentric interpretations of the treatment of Iroquoian dead.

Cultural Trends

A brief overview of major cultural trends for the Neutral reveal that their society underwent significant transforma-

Figure 5.3. Carbon isotope trends.

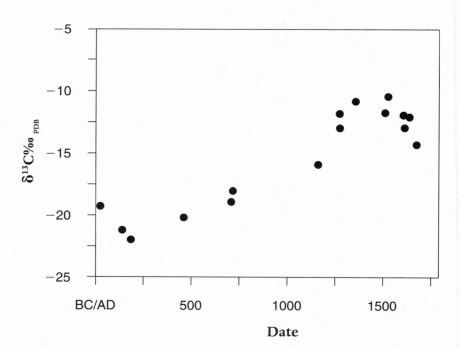

tion in the two centuries prior to its demise. These trends can be evaluated in terms of natural cultural evolution, foreign influences, and the limitations imposed on a society occupying a transitional biotic zone at the northern limit of productive horticulture during a period of worldwide climatic deterioration.

THE FIFTEENTH CENTURY. The widely distributed Neutral of the fifteenth century shared a number of traits that diverged from later expressions of Neutral culture. Longhouses attained their greatest lengths at this time—occasionally measuring more than 100 meters long (Table 5.2)—from which can be inferred a relatively complex social organization. The significant enlargement of house length at this time has been attributed to the desire of families to attach themselves to despotic military warlords (Finlayson 1985: 438; MacDonald 1986: 178; Warrick 1984: 65–68) or successful traders (Hayden 1978: 112–114). Evidence from twentieth-century New Guinea has been used to argue both scenarios for fifteenth-century Ontario, but perhaps an alternative explanation can be suggested on the basis of a more comparable situation from the Great Basin of the western United States. For that area, Larson and Michaelsen (1990) proposed that one result of an intensification of horticultural pursuits by the Virgin Branch Anasazi during the eleventh and twelfth centuries was the need to form larger social units in order to increase labor efficiency.

In southern Ontario, beans become increasingly visible in the archaeological record only after the beginning of the fifteenth century (Fecteau 1985: 171). This source of non-animal protein might have encouraged an intensification of horticultural pursuits and perhaps ultimately population growth. The mammal component of faunal assemblages from sites of this century (that is, sites possessing the cultural attributes to be listed later) is notable for its low representation of white-tailed deer (Fitzgerald and Jamieson 1985; Lennox and Fitzgerald 1990), a dietary mainstay both before and after the fifteenth century. Although deer appear not to have been exploited extensively, smaller mammal species such as the woodchuck, an edible nuisance in agricultural fields, are frequently represented in the faunal sample (Table 5.1).

Features associated with Ontario Iroquoian dwellings of this era are enclosed semisubterranean pits attached to longhouse exteriors. These have been interpreted as enclosed sweat lodges (MacDonald 1988) or storage structures (Fitzgerald 1991b). After the turn of the sixteenth century they are seen infrequently.

The pottery assemblage is characterized by a diversity of decorative motifs on the collar and neck areas of vessels and most notably by large, high-collared pots with elaborate decorations on the collars (Fig. 5.4). Chronologically and stylistically, the assemblage forms a distinctive pan-Iroquoian horizon considered to represent the zenith of Iroquoian pottery manufacture (Ritchie 1969: 313). Regional expressions include the Huron Black Creek–Lalonde, the "classic" St. Lawrence Iroquoian, and the Iroquois Chance cultural phases (Jamieson 1990; Ramsden 1990; Tuck 1971). Ceramic smoking pipes with flared or elongated barrel-shaped bowls predominate.

Although foreign links are evident in the presence of marine shell and copper ornaments, the rare occurrence of such artifacts indicates that long-distance, interregional contacts were intermittent and perhaps indirect. This situation seems to negate Hayden's (1978) model for increased house size. Species of marine shell recovered from Ontario have their origins along the Atlantic coast south of Chesapeake Bay and in the Gulf of Mexico (Pendergast 1989), and although New World copper from southern Ontario archaeological sites of this era has traditionally been assigned a Lake Superior origin, southern or eastern sources cannot be dismissed (cf. Rapp, Henrickson, and Allert 1990). Native copper outcrops have been noted in various places in the Appalachians from Georgia to New Brunswick since as far back as the 1560s, when Goulaine de Laudonniere, a Norman captain exploring the coasts of Georgia and Florida, referred to copper mines "in the mountains of Appalesse" (Sauer 1971: 206). Both Samuel de Champlain (Biggar 1922–1936) and Marc Lescarbot (Grant and Biggar 1907–1914) recounted explorations for copper in the Canadian Maritimes during the first decade of the seventeenth century.

THE SIXTEENTH CENTURY. The sixteenth century was a period of change and readjustment as the once widely dispersed Neutral consolidated into well-defined, confederated tribal areas around the southwestern corner of Lake Ontario. Changes in residential patterns are suggested by a trend toward reduction in longhouse size, a

Table 5.2

Trends in Neutral Iroquoian Longhouse Lengths

		Length (meters)	
Period	No. Houses	Range	Mean
1400–1500[a]	13	23–123	61.5
1500–1580[b]	33	12–78	29.5
1580–1630[c]	19	6–45	19.4
1630–1650[d]	18	6–28	15.3

[a] Sites: Coleman (MacDonald 1986); Ivan Elliot (Fitzgerald 1990b); Moyer (Wagner et al. 1973).

[b] Sites: MacPherson (Fitzgerald 1991a); Raymond Reid (Fitzgerald 1990b); Zap.

[c] Sites: Christianson (Fitzgerald 1982a); Cleveland (Noble 1972); Fonger (Warrick 1984); Thorold (Noble 1980).

[d] Sites: Bogle 1 and 2 (Lennox 1984a); Hamilton (Lennox 1981); Hood (Lennox 1984b); Walker (Wright 1981).

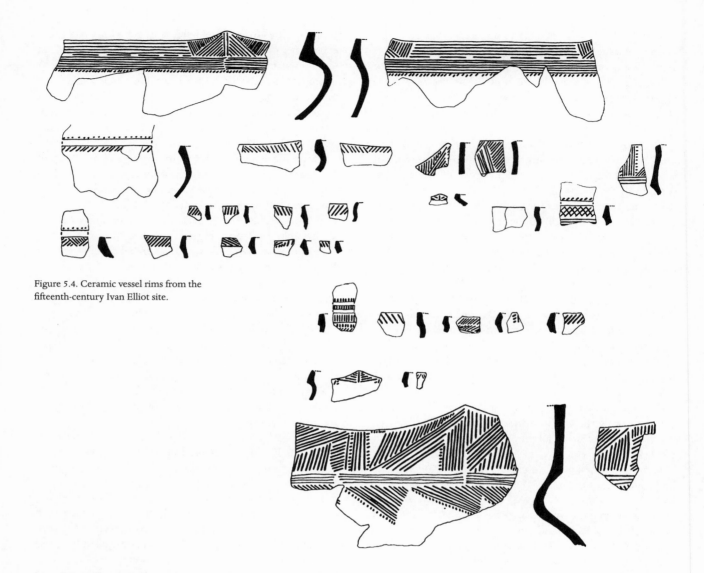

Figure 5.4. Ceramic vessel rims from the fifteenth-century Ivan Elliot site.

trend that becomes even more noticeable in the seventeenth century (Table 5.2). When under stress, societies at the confederacy level tend to fracture into components (Tooker 1963: 122).

Structural features of Neutral longhouse interiors also underwent change. Regularly spaced, large-diameter posts situated approximately 1.5 meters from the side walls served as roof supports and compartmentalized lateral storage and sleeping sections. Similarly, house end cubicles were defined by posts set in rows parallel to the end walls. This pattern has been observed in all northern Iroquoian houses. A shift from post to plank partitions (lateral "slash" pits and linear end features) began around mid-century, a technological phenomenon that has, with few exceptions, been observed only in Neutral structures (Fig. 5.5). If this shift was related to the appearance of European splitting implements, then adjacent groups might be expected to have adopted the practice, too. This change was under

way, however, before the post-1580 presence of substantial numbers of iron axes and chisels in the Northeast.

During the sixteenth and seventeenth centuries, the mammal assemblages recovered from Neutral settlements changed significantly, to domination by white-tailed deer (Table 5.1). The large amounts of animal protein that were again being procured presumably necessitated a return to traditional large-game hunting practices.

During the sixteenth century and continuing into the seventeenth, the decorative motifs on ceramic vessel collars became progressively simplified and homogeneous (Fig. 5.6). Pipe bowl shapes also shifted to short-barrel, collared, and coronet styles. In contrast to the apparent trend toward simplification of ceramic vessels and noneffigy pipes, during the sixteenth and especially the seventeenth century, zoomorphic and anthropomorphic effigies on ceramic and ground stone smoking pipes evolved rapidly (Mathews 1980; Noble 1979).

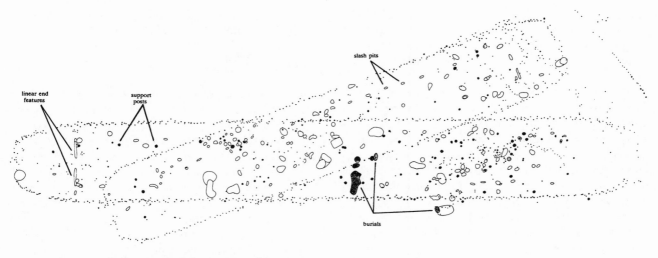

Figure 5.5. Houses 5 and 6 from the sixteenth-century MacPherson site.

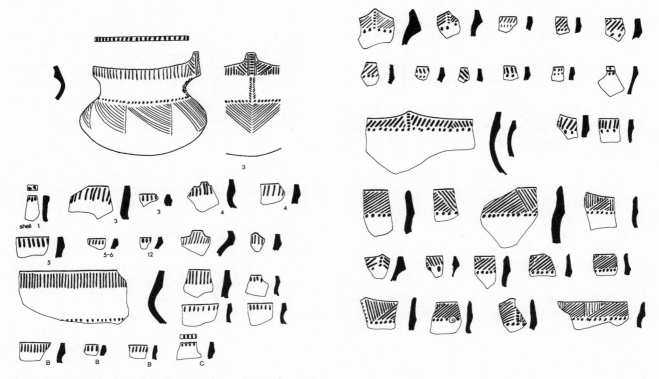

Figure 5.6. Ceramic vessel rims from the sixteenth-century MacPherson site.

Exotic goods on southern Ontario habitation sites and in burials remained scarce until the last quarter of the sixteenth century, when quantities of native marine shells and ornaments and European ornaments and utilitarian items suddenly exploded. Because the majority of these commodities were placed unaltered with the dead, the dramatic increase in the importation of such goods seems to indicate an intensification of ritualism and mortuary ceremonialism

(cf. Trigger 1991: 1204–1205). The onset of the intensified European commercial fur trade at this time appears to have been a fortunate event that provided the Neutral with yet another abundant source of goods with metaphorical associations.

Also indicating an increasing concern with ritual, just prior to the flood of European goods and marine shell, is the appearance on Neutral ceramic pipes and vessels of distinctively eastern Tennessee, Dallas phase, anthropomorphic falcon hunter–warrior icons (Fuller and Silvia 1984: 35–37; Lewis and Kneberg 1970: 96–97, pl. 54; Stowe 1989: 127).

THE SEVENTEENTH CENTURY. Even though Neutral tribal areas remained intact into the seventeenth century, there are numerous indicators of cultural instability and turmoil, especially during the quarter century prior to the Neutral's 1650 dispersal. Dwellings continued to decrease in length until, during the second quarter of the seventeenth century, they were shorter than any known from the previous two centuries (Table 5.2).

On the seventeenth-century sites of the Spencer-Bronte Neutral tribal grouping, a shell-tempered ceramic tradition suddenly appears (Fitzgerald 1982a; Lennox 1981, 1984a, 1984b; Lennox and Fitzgerald 1990; Stothers 1981). It is especially well represented on sites dating to the 1630s and 1640s, a time when European epidemics ravaged the Ontario Iroquoians. The presence of these ceramics is a manifestation of the massive, historically documented, nontraditional Neutral invasions against the Fire nation (Biggar 1922–1936; Thwaites 1896–1901), an Algonkian-speaking group situated around the western end of Lake Erie. In the early 1640s alone, more than 1,000 females—the pottery makers and their children—were brought back as captives to replenish a depleted Neutral population, something also practiced by the Iroquois during the 1650s (Engelbrecht 1987: 22–24).

During the 1630s and 1640s an assemblage of implements belonging to an extractive curing procedure appeared among the Neutral (Fitzgerald 1990a: 241–248). Among the items are long (generally greater than 100 mm) and frequently decorated animal bone "sucking" tubes, ceramic human effigy pipes that depict the practitioners of the procedure, and increasing frequencies of marine shell, copper, brass, and turtle shell rattles. Clearly, the devastating epidemics, compounded by famines, were having serious physical and psychological effects on the population.

Foreign goods continued to be present in significant amounts, but these French- and Dutch-supplied items in most instances supplemented rather than replaced native equivalents. The notable exception among the Neutral was the replacement of chipped stone cutting and ground stone chopping implements by iron knives and axes, respectively. The adoption of foreign material culture continued to be pragmatic and ritualistic. The deaths of large numbers of craftspeople during the epidemics did, however, accelerate the trend toward substitutions and dependence on European technology.

Additional Dallas phase artifacts appear on Neutral sites dating to the seventeenth century: marine shell masks and antler combs with forked-eye or Thunderbird motifs, and marine shell gorgets with Citico rattlesnake motifs (Boyle 1900; Fitzgerald 1982b; Kenyon 1972). These depictions and articles have hunting and warring associations (J. Brown 1989; Smith and Smith 1989; Strong 1989).

Agents of Change

In the two centuries prior to their extinction as a cultural entity, the Neutral underwent a series of dramatic transformations. The widespread fifteenth-century expression of Neutral culture was characterized by elongated, multifamily residential structures, an elaborate ceramic tradition, and a subsistence base whose mammal component was dominated by small animals. In the sixteenth century, long-distance relocations probably precipitated by conflicts with adjacent Algonkian groups led to the formation of a confederacy of Neutral tribes compacted around the southwestern corner of Lake Ontario. The number of families living in a single structure declined dramatically, the effort expended on ceramic decoration waned, and subsistence shifted significantly toward increased dependence on deer. In the second half of the century, the numbers of artifacts associated with ritual and ceremony suddenly rose. During the seventeenth century, increasing contact with Europeans and their diseases, as well as conflicts with other native groups, further stressed Neutral society. Longhouse fission accelerated, and the adoption of European technology, foreign captives, and curing cults characterized a rapid cultural breakdown.

Although the deleterious effects of contact with Europeans and their material culture are well documented, that vector of change in many instances only exacerbated developments that began before Europeans appeared in the Americas. The root cause of the Ontario Iroquoian demise remains perplexing. One explanation that requires greater scrutiny is that a sixteenth-century climatic deterioration severely weakened a society that had become increasingly involved in horticulture in a horticulturally marginal area.

For such a proposition to be supported, one must demonstrate, first, that significant climatic cooling took place and, second, that southern Ontario is a marginal horticultural zone. Climatic deterioration in a marginal agricultural area would have serious consequences, perhaps triggering the diverse yet interrelated chain of events in southern Ontario Neutral culture during the sixteenth and seventeenth centuries.

CLIMATIC DETERIORATION. From across the northern hemisphere, weather records, glacier movement data, pollen cores, wine harvest dates, and even paintings convincingly attest to the onset of a sixteenth-century cooling, a period referred to as the Neo-Boreal or Little Ice Age (Grove 1988).

Between 1350 and 1500, Alpine glaciers retreated moderately, but the climate did not return to the mildness that characterized the turn of the millennium (Le Roy Ladurie 1971: 264). Although researchers assign varying durations to the Little Ice Age, they agree that it encompassed the later half of the sixteenth century and the seventeenth century. Bryson and Wendland (1967: 296) suggested that the years between 1550 and 1850 saw cool summers and cold autumns, a climate that would have affected native farmers in the Northeast severely.

Hammer, Clausen, and Dansgaard (1980: 235) suggested a longer duration, from 1350 to 1900, divided by minor interstadials from 1500 to 1550 and from 1700 to 1800. This pattern corresponds to the acidity profile from the Crete ice core in Greenland, where greater amounts of volcanic aerosol acids were deposited during periods of large-scale volcanism—an occurrence that has been suggested to contribute to climatic cooling (Porter 1981: 141).

Sulman (1982, 1: 131–132) also suggested a longer span, 1430 to 1850, for the main phase of the Little Ice Age for most parts of the world. During the 1430s the first severe winters were recorded after the balmy Viking age. Rivers in Germany froze, many French vines were killed by frost, and cold winters began to grow common.

By 1500, in the lowlands of northwestern Europe, summers were on the order of 0.7 degrees Celsius cooler than the summers of the medieval optimum. This trend led to a shortening of the growing season by as much as five weeks by the seventeenth century (Ford 1982: 77; Grove 1988: 413–414). Throughout sixteenth-century Europe there was a notable cooling between 1550 and 1600 (Grove 1988: 193; Le Roy Ladurie 1971: 281–287). For example, tree rings in Switzerland indicate that during the early stages of the Little Ice Age, summer temperatures were about 2 degrees Celsius lower than those of the late nineteenth and early twentieth centuries (Grove 1988: 193). During the early seventeenth century, the glaciers of Europe advanced decisively, and the years between 1643 and 1653 were marked by the severest winters in western Europe since the end of the Pleistocene (Sulman 1982, 1: 131–132). Poor fishing and pestilence were among the consequences (Grove 1985: 149), and in marginal agricultural areas, where productivity depended on latitude and altitude, farmland became unproductive (Parry 1981; Pfister 1981).

This cooling period is also documented in the artwork of the period. The tradition of portraying winter landscapes, frozen rivers and harbors, abundant snowfall, and winter sports in Flemish paintings and prints was established by Pieter Bruegel the Elder (1528/30–1569) in the later half of sixteenth century. Flemish immigrant painters were largely responsible for introducing the subject into the Dutch repertoire in the first quarter of the seventeenth century (Bugler 1979: 59; Gaskell 1990: 414).

For the lower Great Lakes area of North America, Fecteau (1985: 98–99) proposed a sequence of climatic fluctuations. During the Pacific I stage (1250–1450), the climate was characterized by decreased rainfall and cooler temperatures. It was then that southern Ontario communities located on sandy soils were abandoned. The Pacific II stage

(1450–1550) was an era of climatic amelioration that permitted a northward movement of Carolinian biotic-zone fauna. During the Neo-Boreal (1550–1880), climatic deterioration included a cooling of temperatures by about 1 degree Celsius. The Recent stage (1880–present) has been marked by a general warming trend.

From Crawford Lake in southern Ontario, the fossil pollen record reveals that after 1360, pine and oak forests began to replace the previously dominant beech-maple forest (McAndrews 1988: 682). The presence of oak began to increase around 1370 and peaked around 1650, whereas white pine, a northern species near its southern limit at Crawford Lake, became more prevalent around 1390, peaking around 1860. McAndrews (1988: 683) attributed the south-ward advance of northern species to the cooler climate of the Little Ice Age. The establishment of white pine stands in the vicinity of Huron Iroquoian sites datable to the early sixteenth century (Bowman 1979) further supports the onset of cooler climatic conditions.

SOUTHERN ONTARIO AS A MARGINAL HORTICULTURAL AREA. Biotic boundaries are not static. When climate changes, the boundaries shift, and when boundaries shift, the subsistence base may be affected, especially in sensitive areas in high latitudes where conditions for plant growth and horticulture are marginal (Grove 1988: 1; Harding 1982: 3; Parry 1981).

In late twentieth-century Ontario, corn could be grown effectively only as far north as what was seventeenth-century Huron territory. This pattern is determined by criteria such as the number of frost-free days, the number of growing-degree days, "corn heat unit" (CHU) values, the length of the growing season, and soil conditions (Fecteau 1985: 102–108). Corn heat units (based on days with temperatures of more than 10 degrees Celsius and nights with temperatures over 4.4 degrees Celsius) are especially useful in determining the viability of corn. The Ontario Corn Committee (1992) publishes geographical ranges for corn hybrids adapted to the climate of Ontario.

Because corn is one of the few annual crops that uses the full frost-free period to complete its life cycle, varieties must be carefully selected to make optimum use of heat and to avoid frost damage. Tender crops such as corn and beans are damaged when air temperatures range between minus 1.5 degrees Celsius and the freezing point. In the late twentieth century, most shelled corn was grown in areas having CHU values of 2,900 or more, although some grain corn could be grown in areas that had as few as 2,500 CHUs (Fig. 5.7) (Brown, McKay, and Chapman 1980: 33, 37–38). Bean production is most efficient in areas with greater than 3,000 CHUs (Fecteau 1985: 32).

Though it is a reasonable assumption that climate-dependent agricultural factors were reduced in southern Ontario during the sixteenth and seventeenth centuries, it is difficult to determine confidently how much farther south

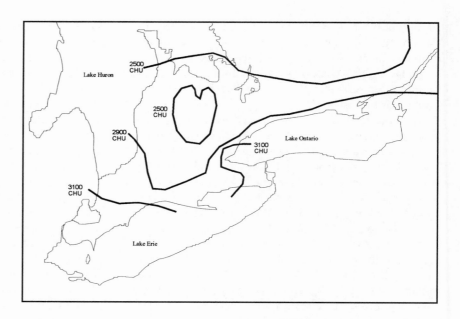

Figure 5.7. Corn heat unit values for southern Ontario.

the limits of effective aboriginal horticulture might have shifted. Historical accounts from seventeenth-century southern Ontario do, however, provide a notion of the extent of the climatic difference. On the basis of twentieth-century climatic conditions, Heidenreich (1971) suggested that one crop failure should be expected every 10 years. Between 1628 and 1650, however, when the Jesuits were among southern Ontario groups, severe winters, droughts, crop failures, and famines were documented almost annually (see Arès 1970; Thwaites 1896–1901). This undoubtedly reflected, in part, the climatic instability of the Little Ice Age: "Behold dying skeletons eking out a miserable life, feeding even on the excrements and refuse of nature" (Thwaites 1896–1901, 35: 89).

The Cultural Unsuitability of Marginal Horticulture

If not supplemented with other foods or prepared with certain additives, corn has marginal nutritional value. A dietary mixture of corn and beans produces a combination of amino acids that is a good source of protein (Fecteau 1985: 30). Soaking, boiling, or cooking corn with lime (calcium oxide) or alkali (potassium oxide) also releases the essential lysine and tryptophan amino acids and niacin, a member of the vitamin B complex (Katz, Hediger, and Valleroy 1974). In societies that depend heavily on corn, supplementing the diet with protein, treating the corn with alkaline substances, or both are essential to avoiding malnutrition.

Iroquoians of southern Ontario occupied the area in and immediately adjacent to the Canadian-Carolinian Transitional (Mixed Forest) and Carolinian (Deciduous) biotic zones at the northern limit of productive horticulture. It is in such marginal areas, especially those along the boundaries of biotic zones, that climatic variations have the great-

est potential for social and economic disruption. With the onset of climatic deterioration in the sixteenth century, the diminishing reliability and output of domesticated crops seems to have resulted in a return to a more traditional hunter-gatherer subsistence strategy (cf. Sioui 1992) that favored an intensification of large game exploitation.

The exponential increase in the proportion of deer remains on sixteenth- and seventeenth-century Neutral sites after a fifteenth-century lull suggests that hunting might have alleviated two climate-related stresses. In particular, if the reliability of the protein-rich but cold-sensitive bean was threatened by the colder climate of the Little Ice Age, an alternative source of dietary protein would have been required. Deer, being large, easy to capture, and especially abundant in areas of cedar swamps (Peterson 1966: 324), would have provided a ready supply. Another incentive for increasing deer procurement might have been a growing demand for warm winter clothing.

Analysis of stable carbon isotopes in human bone provides a ratio of carbohydrate to protein in the diets of past populations. Corn was the primary dietary source of carbohydrates for the Ontario Iroquoians, but bean protein cannot be distinguished from meat protein by this technique. Although it is clear that corn continued to be a significant contributor to the diet throughout this era, carbohydrate values were decreasing by the seventeenth century (see Fig. 5.3) (Katzenberg, Saunders, and Fitzgerald 1993; Schwarcz et al. 1985). If corn consumption was decreasing, so, presumably, was the consumption of beans. The dramatic increase in deer exploitation may represent a replacement of plant protein by animal protein.

Pressures on a population that had become increasingly dependent on horticulture, especially at a climatically unstable time and in a horticulturally marginal area, might have led to increased competition for deer hunting territories and thus to intercultural conflicts (Gramly 1977). Such conflicts might have been avoided when horticultural products constituted a greater proportion of the diet. In southern Ontario, land suitable for horticulture is much more abundant and widespread than are tracts that would support high densities of deer.

Summary

Late Woodland Ontario Iroquoian culture developed amid the uncertainty of northern horticulture. The widespread introduction of beans by the fifteenth century might have brought about a trend toward the substitution of plant protein for animal protein in a diet that included a substantial quantity of otherwise nutritionally poor corn. With this development, more effort might have been directed toward other aspects of society, if less time was spent on male-oriented subsistence pursuits. Cultural advancement and elaboration might have been related in part to the evolution of plant domestication.

Not only is northern horticulture an inherently unhealthy and hence maladaptive subsistence pursuit (see Patterson 1984; Pfeiffer and King 1983), but further stresses result when the stability of the horticultural base is undermined. Ontario Iroquoians attempted to adapt, a feat made easier by the flexibility of northern Iroquoian social organization. Like their hunter-gatherer ancestors and neighbors, during good times they were able to fuse into larger groups, whereas during lean and other stressful times they could split into smaller groups or move to areas of new resources. Although an increase in deer procurement might ultimately have become a successful subsistence adjustment to the restraints of a cooler and unstable climate, such an outcome was ultimately thwarted by the devastating effects of European epidemics. Native curing practices and the importation of captives to restock the population proved futile in the struggle to adapt to additional adversity. Attempting to combat famine, contagion, and Iroquois attacks while maintaining the basic necessities of life was too much to achieve, and by 1651 the decimated Iroquoian groups of southern Ontario succumbed.

Acknowledgments

Versions of this chapter were presented at a number of conferences in 1992: the Society for American Archaeology (Pittsburgh), Transferts Culturels en Amérique et Ailleurs (Québec), the Canadian Archaeological Association (London), and People to People (Rochester). Over the years, conversations with James Bradley, Shelley Saunders, Marvin Smith, and Bruce Trigger have provided valued insights. Bruce Jamieson in particular was instrumental in formulating a number of the notions that were developed. Paul Lennox, Rosemary Prevec, and Howard Savage generously provided access to unpublished faunal information. The chapter was largely written and revised while I was the recipient of a Social Sciences and Humanities Research Council of Canada Postdoctoral Fellowship.

6

Penumbral Protohistory on Lake Erie's South Shore

DAVID S. BROSE

Unseen by French explorers at the beginning of the seventeenth century, warfare rendered Lake Erie's south shore inaccessible to French and English exploration for generations. The Europeans' dim glimpses of the area's early historical inhabitants remind me of Churchill's view of Russia: a riddle shrouded in mystery wrapped in enigma. Since about 1990, it has become increasingly clear that along different environmental zones cross-cut and integrated by this littoral lived three or four aboriginal societies with markedly differing Late Woodland cultural trajectories. Equally different were their reactions to external economic and cultural influences and the diasporas the groups underwent soon after the arrival of Europeans.

With new investigations across the region reaching syntheses, the responses of these late prehistoric and early historic societies to environmental and social change can now be assessed. In retrospect, theirs may be considered a record largely of social misunderstanding and ecological misjudgment, at variance with the records of their aboriginal neighbors. In some scholars' interpretations, the indirect linkages that contact period societies in northern Ohio and Pennsylvania had to the larger world of the late sixteenth century seem nearly as dramatic as the interdependencies of linked world economies of the late twentieth century. The changes in our understanding may be similarly profound; in both cases, the homogeneity of ignorance yields to richer, albeit still indistinct, realities.[1]

Geographic Setting

From west to east, three environmental zones abut the southern shore of Lake Erie: the Glacial Lake Plains, the Central Till Lowlands, and the Glaciated Allegheny Plateau. Respectively, these correspond roughly to northwestern Ohio, north-central Ohio, and the narrowing strip from northeastern Ohio through northwestern Pennsylvania and northwestern New York state (Banks and Feldmann 1970; Braun 1950; Feldmann et al. 1977; Fenneman 1938; Gordon 1966, 1969). The aboriginal societies occupying these three zones display distinct prehistoric cultural trajectories, distinct reactions to external social influences, and distinct conclusions early in recorded history. In this chapter I review the record of late prehistoric and indirect historic response to environmental and social change for the social groups of northern Ohio and adjacent portions of the south shore of Lake Erie (Fig. 6.1). As I have argued elsewhere (Brose 1994b, 1997a, 1997b), several incompatible models of cultural traditions are currently proposed to account for the perceived archaeological interrelationships across this region.

Regional Environments and History of Research

The flat, poorly drained Glacial Lake Plains and sandy postglacial dunes and beach ridges bordering Lake Erie in

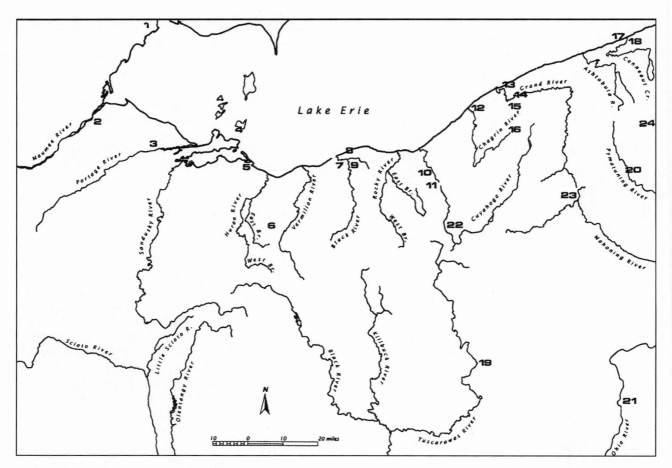

Figure 6.1. Northern Ohio, showing the locations of major sites in the region. 1, Springwells; 2, Indian Hills; 3, Libben; 4, Kelly's Island; 5, Harbor/Raintree; 6, Mixter; 7, National Tube; 8, Eiden; 9, Burrill Fort; 10, Tuttle Hill; 11, South Park; 12, Reeve; 13, Fairport Harbor/Grantham; 14, Lyman; 15, Vrooman Road; 16, Bass Lake; 17, Coneaut Fort; 18, Eastwall; 19, Riker; 20, Boice Fort; 21, Wellsburg; 22, Siebert Village; 23, Mahoning; 24, McFate Earthworks.

northwestern Ohio form a band 25 miles (40 km) wide at the St. Clair River on the west, narrowing to 2 miles (3 km) in width past the Cuyahoga River and fronting the northern edge of the Allegheny Plateau east as far as Niagara. This zone has a long growing season (180–200 days) and lake-associated weather patterns that buffer seasonal temperature changes but intensify differences between the lake-shore and the interior. Extensive marshes and elm-ash swamps with beech-maple forests along the shoreline give way to mixed mesophytic and oak-hickory forests inland and to grassland-oak openings on higher ground between rivers. Postglacial isostatic upwarping continues to inundate the shoreline, drowning islands and sand spits and constantly refreshing rich estuaries.

Archaeological studies began in the northern part of the Glacial Lake Plains with University of Michigan excavations (Greenman 1937, 1957, 1958) and later interpretation (Fitting 1965) of the Riviere au Vase and Younge sites as sequential phases in the Younge tradition. Subsequent Michigan students studied the areas around the west end of the lake (Brose 1976a, 1978a; Brose and Essenpreis 1973; Fitting

1970; Fitting and Zurrell 1976) and by 1972 were proposing a spatially and temporally expanded Western Basin (of Lake Erie) tradition, of which the Younge tradition was part (Prahl et al. 1976). Since 1972, archaeologists from Toledo, Heidelberg, and Ohio State Universities (Becker 1972; Bowen 1992; Graves 1984; Pratt 1981; Redmond 1984; Stothers 1978, 1981, 1995; Stothers and Abel 1991; Stothers and Graves 1978, 1983; Stothers and Pratt 1982; Stothers and Rutter 1978; Stothers et al. 1994) have excavated dozens of interesting sites and created dozens of incompatible models of cultural traditions, among which some see the Sandusky tradition as an eastern temporal equivalent of the later phases of the Younge tradition. Most of these cultural manifestations also occur in southwestern Ontario, where they are taken to denote different cultural phenomena (see Ellis and Ferris 1990).

The silty soils of the Central Till Lowlands mark a second environmental zone; it lies 25 miles (40 km) south of the Glacial Lake Plains in northeastern Indiana and 10 to 15 miles (16 to 24 km) inland in north-central Ohio. This major physiographic province disappears east of the Cuyahoga River. Its southernmost portions are characterized by moraines with rolling uplands, small lakes, bogs, and fens along the Great Lakes–Mississippi River divide. Precontact vegetation was predominantly beech-maple forest with chestnut, tulip, and pawpaw on interfluvial terraces and ridges, mixed oak-hickory forest on uplands, and ash and hemlock in the hollows.

Archaeological investigations of sites in the Portage, Sandusky, Huron, Vermilion, and Black River valleys of the Central Till Lowlands began with the speculative studies of Vietzen (1941, 1945, 1965), the largely unpublished work of A. G. Smith, and the unpublished field notes of E. F. Greenman (1930). These were followed by more systematic excavations and surveys, most by faculty and students from Case Tech (McKenzie and Blank 1976; McKenzie et al. 1973; Prufer and Shane 1976; Shane 1967, 1974), Kent State University (Neveret 1992; Romain 1979), Case Western Reserve University, and the Cleveland Museum of Natural History (Brose 1971, 1974, 1976a, 1978a, 1988a, 1993; Brose and Bier 1978; J. Scarry 1973). More recently, extensive studies of sites attributed variously to the early part of the Younge tradition and to later phases of the Sandusky tradition have been completed (Bier n.d.; Bowen 1994; Brose 1988b, 1993, 1997a; Brose, Arsenijevic et al. 1988; Brose, Weisman et al. 1988; Pratt and Brose 1992; Redmond 1999; Stothers and Abel 1991).

The glacially scoured and frequently exposed Paleozoic bedrock of northeastern Ohio's Allegheny Plateau forms the southeastern quadrant of this region. Its northwestern outliers are 15 miles up the east fork of the Black River but only 5 miles up the Cuyahoga. The steep, 150- to 250-foot-high Portage Escarpment of the Allegheny Plateau rises two miles south of the Lake Erie shore in East Cleveland and between one and two miles south of the lake from Ohio to New York. On the plateau, elevation, outcrop, exposure, topography, and drainage change significantly within short distances. Local flora form a mosaic of beech-maple forests on rolling uplands with elm-ash and hemlock bottomland facies and mixed tulip-oak-chestnut or oak-hickory-butternut facies on ridges. Numerous southern elements, such as rhododendron, occur. Seasonal variations are greater on the plateau than in the other environmental zones of the region, yet the plateau is everywhere cooler and wetter than the lakeshore, often dramatically so.

The earliest archaeological reports of fortified village sites along the Cuyahoga, Grand, and Ashtabula Rivers and the lakeshore of the glaciated Appalachian Plateau were by Charles Whittlesey (1851, 1871) and his Western Reserve Historical Society colleagues Judge D. Baldwin and Matthew C. Read (Flinn 1893; Fowke 1902). Later, Ohio Archaeological and Historical Society excavations at several sites (Greenman 1930, 1935a, 1935b, 1937; Morgan and Ellis 1943) identified the material culture of what became the Whittlesey focus, the temporal and spatial variations of which were isolated and studied (Fitting 1964; R. Morgan

1952). With Cleveland Museum of Natural History excavation and survey, these and new site data were organized into what is now the Whittlesey tradition (Belovich 1985a, 1991; Belovich and Brose 1992; Brose 1971, 1973, 1975, 1976a, 1976b, 1976c, 1978a, 1978b, 1985b, 1985c, 1987b, 1988a, 1992, 1997b; Brose and Pratt 1975; Brose and Scarry 1976; Brose, Belovich et al. 1981; Brose, Lee et al. 1985a, 1985b; J. Murphy 1971a, 1971b, 1971c, 1972a, 1972b). Recent studies in easternmost Ohio also reveal encroachment of the Iroquoian Allegheny Glen Meyer and McFate phases or traditions, which are related to (or derived from) groups in northwestern Pennsylvania (Brose 1976c, 1977a, 1988a; Brose, Johnson, and Hambacher n.d.; Brose, Lee, and Wolynec 1983; Bush 1984, 1990; Dragoo 1976; W. Johnson 1976, 1979; Lee 1981, 1988; J. Murphy 1971c, 1972b).

Northern Ohio's Late Woodland Background

The middle Late Woodland period (post–A.D. 800) began with adequate rainfall and relatively long, warm summers and cool, dry winters. After A.D. 1000, summers grew warmer and somewhat moister, and winters were increasingly dry, extending the agriculture season along the lakeshore (cf. Brose 1978a, 1994b). Although most Late Woodland sites are unspectacular and show similarities across northern Ohio, subtle differences in chipped stone points and significant differences in ceramic traditions correspond to the environmental zones described (Fig. 6.2).

For the coeval Late Woodland societies of northwestern and north-central Ohio, small, scattered, and probably seasonal camps, each of two or three circular houses, are found on river bluffs and old beach ridges inland and on islands, sand spits, and peninsulas across the western Lake Erie and Lake St. Clair drainage basins. After A.D. 750, burials were interred or reinterred in a small number of enormous regional cemeteries, accompanied by notched and triangular points, ceramic pipes, and the elaborately decorated Riviere au Vase and then Younge phase ceramics. I have argued that these Younge tradition styles derived from earlier Point Peninsula traditions that once spread from Minnesota across Ontario to New York (Brose 1988a, 1994b, 1997b). Fishing and gathering, with some horticulture, dominated the lake-plain sites' economies.

Coeval sites identified in upper portions of these drainages have cord-marked, often collared ceramics, a few of which bear incised guilloche designs or strap handles. Madison projectile points, often of southern Ohio chert, also occur. Although they have already been assigned to a number of phases (Bowen 1992), little is known about these sites, but their inhabitants seem to have shared a mixed horticultural economy, lithic sources and forms, and many functional and stylistic ceramic attributes with incipient Fort Ancient–like groups in the upper Miami, White, and Scioto River valleys (Prahl et al. 1976; Pratt and Brose 1992;

Figure 6.2. Late prehistoric phases in northern Ohio and northwestern Pennsylvania, approximately A.D. 750–1650.

Date	Northwestern Ohio	North-Central Ohio	Northeastern Ohio	Northwestern Pennsylvania
1650	Mascoutin	Pottawatomi? Indian Hills?	?	Neutral
	Indian Hills		Late Whittlesey	
1550		Fort Meigs		McFate
1450	Fort Meigs		Early Whittlesey	
1350	Eiden Wolf	Wolf		
1250				Glen Meyer
		Mixter		
1150	Younge		Allegheny Plateau Late Woodland	
1050		Younge		
950				Allegheny Plateau Late Woodland
850	Riviere au Vase	Riviere au Vase		
	Point Peninsula Middle Woodland		Scioto/Watson Middle Woodland	

Stothers et al. 1994). Most groups also carried out diffuse hunting and collecting, and people near the lakeshore and at the lower rapids of the major streams drew on spring-spawning walleye, white bass, freshwater drum, and redhorse sucker. In southern and eastern parts of the region, where lake-bottom conditions differ, deer, muskrat, raccoon, beaver, wild fowl, and nuts indicate more generalized foraging, although fish are present (Bowen 1992; Pratt and Brose 1992). Stable carbon isotope determinations on Younge phase burials (Crawford et al. 1997; Stothers and Bechtel 1987) suggest that maize was part of the diet.

In northeastern Ohio, most pre–A.D. 1000 Late Woodland winter sites are rockshelters or small hunting camps at upland bogs and springs. Larger, warm-weather fishing, gathering, and corn and squash horticultural camps occur along the lakeshore and in the middle and lower river valleys. Small, circular houses each contained one or two hearths and a few shallow storage pits. The rare burials in these sites show few differences in personal status or in the size or composition of the groups that occupied them. Points were usually notched (few were triangular), and a variety of tools and ornaments were made of antler and bone (Brose 1978b). The rather unimaginative early Late Woodland plain or cord-marked, grit-tempered ceramics of northeastern Ohio have straight or slightly curved rims with flat lips, some with interior cord-marking and some with fingernail impressions. Similar ceramics occur south and east on the Allegheny Plateau as far as the Ohio Valley, reflecting a ceramic tradition that even then went back a thousand years. By A.D. 1000, more vessels had plain interi-

ors, and rims were slightly incurving with folded collars. Decoration on the exterior neck and rim includes incising, and various stamped impressions resemble developing Iroquoian ceramic decoration in northwestern New York and Pennsylvania.

Northwestern and North-Central Ohio from A.D. 1000 to 1450

I have argued that late Younge and early Sandusky tradition societies in northwestern and north-central Ohio developed from a single late Riviere au Vase base. These traditions, at the point of differentiation, are visible in the Libben and Harbor site assemblages dating from A.D. 750 to 1250 (Bowen 1992; Brose 1988b, 1994b, 1997a, 1997b; Brose, Weisman et al. 1988; Murphy and Ferris 1990; Pratt and Brose 1992; Pratt et al. 1983; Prufer and Shane 1976; Romain 1979). Elongated, bag-shaped, grit-tempered, castellated, low-collared Younge ceramics with horizontal bands of linear cord-stamped impressions can be found from Ontario's Point Pelee around the St. Clair basin east almost to Sandusky Bay (Fitting 1965, 1970; Keenleyside 1977; Krakker 1983; Murphy and Ferris 1990). The more rounded Mixter vessels of the Sandusky tradition have high, scalloped (pseudo) collars covered with fields of simple and dentate tool stamps (Fig. 6.3). These occur from the Portage River east to the Cuyahoga River (Belovich 1991; Brose and Bier 1978; McKenzie and Blank 1976; Murphy 1972a; Prufer and Shane 1976; Redmond 1999; Shane 1967). The areas where these ceramics define discrete style zones, and the

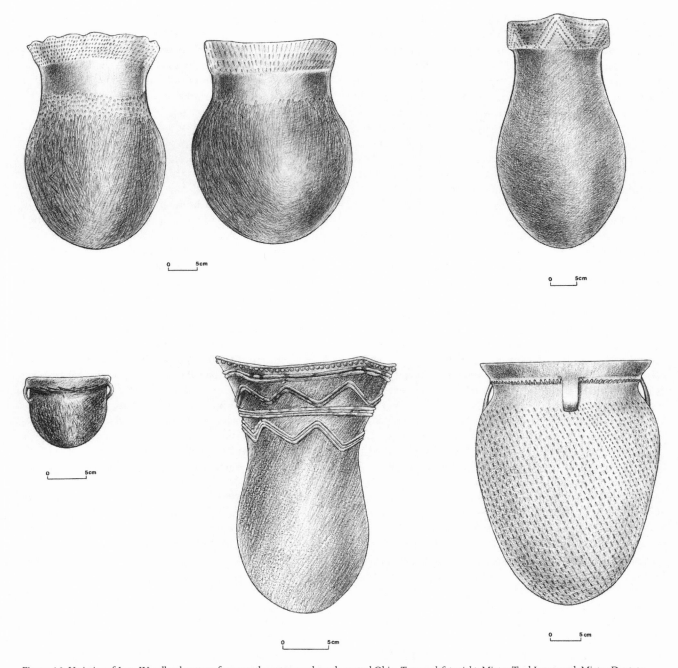

Figure 6.3. Varieties of Late Woodland pottery from northwestern and north-central Ohio. *Top row, left to right:* Mixter Tool-Impressed, Mixter Dentate, Springwells Interrupted Linear. *Bottom row, left to right:* Baum Cord-Marked, Parker Festooned, Fort Meigs Notched Appliqué. (Drawings by Emile Huston, Royal Ontario Museum.)

distinct Black Swamp environment where they overlap, display differing cultural trajectories.

Mississippian influence north of Fort Ancient first occurs in the early twelfth-century Oliver Complex of east-central Indiana (Griffin 1943), where ceramic traits of the Fort Ancient tradition and the Younge tradition appear mixed.[2] In this area, which heads the White, White Water, Miami, and Maumee Rivers, the major component of the large Bowen site was a multiseasonal squash and maize horticultural vil-

lage with rather focal hunting. The local Woodland Oliver ceramics, along with some Fort Ancient ceramics, are grit-tempered, round-bottom vessels with cord- and fabric-impressed bodies (rarely smoothed). Jar rims were everted, some with straight, low collars. Some rare vessel rims had "piecrust" (scalloped) lips with corded or tool-impressed lip and lip/rim exteriors. Some had trailed, curvilinear guilloche designs, and some vessels had an appliqué strip at the lip. Many had strap handles. After intensive analyses (Dorwin 1971; Redmond 1994), it is clear that Griffin (1943) was correct when he called this "a new cultural center from which would have developed other centers with more restricted range[s] of ceramics." These northern influences from Fort Ancient appear to correspond to a cooling trend that began about A.D. 1300 (cf. Keigwin 1996) and culminated in the post-Xerothermic low known in Europe as the Little Ice Age. Throughout what Fitting (1965) and Murphy and Ferris (1990) called the Wolf phase (too often defined by the mere presence of Parker Festooned pottery [T. Lee 1952]), significant ceramic, subsistence, and demographic changes across the entire western basin of Lake Erie reflected social responses to that climatic episode (Brose 1988a; Pratt 1981; Pratt and Brose 1992).

Some have argued that in the western portion of this region, late Younge phase settlements persisted, only to have their inhabitants forcibly displaced by "Mississippified" aggressors from the Sandusky River valley after 1350 or 1400 (e.g., Stothers 1978, 1995; Stothers and Able 1991; Stothers and Graves 1983; Stothers et al. 1994). Among others, I have argued that the significant settlement, subsistence, and demographic changes that appear to have accompanied this ceramic shift reflect geographically differing northward Fort Ancient influences that structured differing but similar social responses in the Maumee, Sandusky, and Black River valleys and around to the Ontario side of Lake Erie (Brose 1976c, 1978a, 1988a, 1994b, 1997b; Brose and Essenpreis 1973; Neveret 1992; Pratt 1981; Pratt and Brose 1992). The fact that Fitting's Younge-Wolf transition is not recovered in every site excavated in every region of the western basin is not a good argument that it did not take place in those regions where it has been recovered. And although the persistence of very late Younge phase sites peripheral to the lower Maumee River valley has been suggested several times (Stothers 1995; Stothers et al. 1994), and late Younge ceramics are documented from sites in Michigan (Fitting 1964, 1970) and Ontario (Murphy and Ferris 1990), not one such site has been reported from Ohio.

At some late Younge–early Wolf phase sites are found finely cord-marked and shell-tempered "Mississippian" vessels with outcurved rims and strap handles, some imported, some locally produced (Bowen 1992; Keenleyside 1977; Murphy and Ferris 1990; Pratt 1981; Stothers and Graves 1983). Many of these vessels display incised or trailed sublip curvilinear or rectilinear guilloches. Even sites in northwestern Ohio without imported southern vessels show obvious Oliver or Fort Ancient ceramic influence during the Wolf phase. From the Parker and Weiser sites at Lake St. Clair, the Williams, LaSalle, and McNichol sites in the Maumee Valley, the Pearson and Bloom sites at Sandusky Bay, and the Eiden site on the Black River come locally made shell-temper or mixed-temper Parker Festooned vessels with high everted rims, effigy adornos, lug handles, and decorative motifs executed in appliqué strips and/or by the various simple and complex tool stamping typical of the

earlier Mixter and Eiden, or Wolf, phases of the Sandusky tradition (Fig. 6.3) (Abel 1995; Bowen 1992; Brose 1976a, 1978a, 1987b; Prufer and Shane 1976; Shane 1967). As has long been noted (Brose 1978a, 1988a), these resemble the rectilinear guilloche designs of Cowan's (1987) Schomaker Fort Ancient phase (Drooker 1997a; Drooker and Cowan, this volume).

From Point Pelee north to Lake St. Clair, and south and east to the Portage River, Wolf phase sites appear by A.D. 1350 as small, seasonal, mixed-economy campsites but become larger (ca. 0.2 ha) by 1450. Near the lower rapids of the major river valleys of north-central Ohio, Wolf phase sites lie on sandy soils in oak-hickory forests adjacent to prairies. Where extensive excavations have been carried out, three Wolf phase sites are said to have had encircling ditches and at some time might also have had palisades enclosing large numbers of refuse pits and hearths. Several features had fired daub (Pratt and Brose 1992; Pratt et al. 1983). Although the claim that these were permanent agricultural villages remains unsubstantiated, they did yield remains of squash and maize, and at least one has yielded beans. Stable isotope determinations indicate significant use of corn, although large numbers of spring-spawning fish were also important (Stothers and Abel 1989; Stothers et al. 1994). From untested survey data, Bowen (1992) suggested that one or more late Wolf phase village groups of 180 people occupied each major river valley, moving one to four miles every 30 years. He further suggested that development of larger late Wolf phase sites was accompanied by abandonment of upper drainage basins, which were then used only for occasional hunting (cf. Bowen 1992, 1994; Pratt and Brose 1992). A few large cemeteries at the larger village sites yielded extensively mutilated bodies, some accompanied by Mississippian ceramic discs or stone discoidals (Bowen 1992; Pratt and Brose 1992).

Northeastern Ohio from A.D. 1000 to 1450

Before A.D. 1250, even the largest sites in northeastern Ohio consisted of two or three unfortified, oval, single-family houses, seasonally reoccupied. Remains of squash and corn are found only occasionally, and when present, they seldom equal the remains of local nuts. Fauna indicate a diffuse economy that exploited lacustrine and riparian environments and Allegheny Plateau catchments. Few burials occur in these microvillages, though some small separate sites with low family burial mounds are known (Belovich 1991; Belovich and Brose 1992; Brose 1985c; Brose, Belovich et al. 1981). By 1450 there were fewer such multifamily riparian camps, because populations concentrated seasonally in small villages on high river bluffs. These villages each had up to five subrectangular houses (some with partial wall-trench rebuilding). Corn and squash remains are ubiquitous, and a few sites yield beans. Hunting patterns shifted to focus on elk, raccoon, turkey, and then deer (Brose 1994b).

Northeastern Ohio potters, still working in an Appalachian Plateau tradition (Prufer 1967; Prufer and McKenzie 1966; contra Stothers et al. 1994), were making relatively thick, grit-tempered, coarse cord- and fabric-impressed open jars with rarely thickened or decorated vertical rims or notched lips (Belovich 1985a, 1985b; Bernhardt 1973; Brose 1973, 1976b, 1977b, 1983, 1988a, 1992, 1997a; Brose, Lee et al. 1985b; Brose and Scarry 1976; Lee 1986; Lee and Fienga 1982; Murphy 1971b, 1972b; Prufer et al. 1989). A few rare vessels had multiple horizontal lines incised below the lip or more finely incised chevrons and opposed triangular plats. Trade ceramics included both vessels and motifs of the Sandusky tradition types, especially in the Cuyahoga and Chagrin River valleys (Belovich 1991; Brose 1994b, 1997b; Brose, Lee et al. 1985a; Murphy 1972b).

Between 1250 and 1450, ceramic innovations created the Whittlesey tradition (Fig. 6.4). Shell temper, usually mixed with grit, appears in vessels with outcurved smoothed rims. Appliquéd strips have narrow tool impressions or incisions. Some vessels have quartered lugs with lip scallops (like those of the Philo phase [Carskadden and Morton 1977]). A band of trailed lines between the strip and the lip is common. Vessel bodies show fine vertical cord-marking or are smoothed or simple stamped. Most lips are plain, though tool notching occurs. During this period the few introduced grit- and shell-tempered Parker Festooned and Anderson Incised ceramics from southern or western Ohio were replaced by McFate and Glen Meyer or "Erie-type Lawson" (MacNeish 1952) vessels or motifs, especially east of the Grand River (Brose 1977a, 1994b; Dragoo 1976). Ceramics from small, seasonally occupied, inland rockshelters and from horticultural-gathering campsites on the shore and river bluffs stretching from Conneaut Creek in the extreme northeast into the upper Beaver drainage yield few Whittlesey modes and many Allegheny Valley Glen Meyer ones on rounded, smoothed, or fabric-marked bodies (Brose 1977a; Brose, Johnson, and Hambacher n.d.; Brose, Lee, and Wolynec 1983; Brose, Lee et al. 1985b; Brose, Wentzel et al. 1976; Dragoo 1976; W. Johnson 1976, 1979, this volume; Lee 1981; Murphy 1971b, 1972b; J. Wright 1966).

Northwestern and North-Central Ohio after A.D. 1450

For some archaeologists (Stothers 1978, 1991; Stothers and Abel 1991; Stothers and Graves 1978, 1983; Stothers et al. 1994), the late prehistory of northwestern and north-central Ohio is a tale full of sound and fury, replete with sweeping migrations of linguistic groups and what could be called ethnic cleansing from west to east by northeast. For others (Brose 1976a, 1978a, 1978b, 1994b, 1997a, 1997b; Murphy and Ferris 1990; Prahl et al. 1976; Pratt and Brose 1992), there is a gradual and varying shift and expansion of material stylistic influence from west to east, with little ev-

idence for population displacements. Some scholars unaccountably fail to take any clear position on the degree of population disjunction in portions of the region (Bowen 1992). All scholars do agree that by 1450 the Maumee River valley was characterized by a relatively rapid adoption of new types and styles in material culture and by accelerating changes in cultural geography. What are called Fort Meigs phase assemblages are marked by a series of shell- or grit-tempered globular vessels with fine cord-marked bodies. These jars have outflared flat rims and (rarely piecrusted) lips usually decorated with horizontal, vertical, or oblique rows of simple and complex tool stamping. Some vessels have appliqué rim strips with broad notching. Parallel-sided strap handles are common. Common, too, are the many and various bone and antler tools and the few lithic tool types characteristic of the Fort Ancient tradition (Drooker 1997a; Drooker and Cowan, this volume; Graves 1984; Griffin 1943; Prahl et al. 1976; Pratt 1981; Pratt and Brose 1992; Rutter 1984; Stothers 1995; Stothers and Graves 1978; Stothers and Rutter 1978).

In the middle and lower Maumee River valley, Fort Meigs populations appear to have been concentrated in a limited number of ovoid, wattle-and-daub houses at possibly permanent palisaded villages and at nearby seasonal campsites. At the larger sites, squash, maize, and bean agriculture was supplemented by hunting focused on small game (Graves 1984; Pratt 1981; Stothers 1995; Stothers and Abel 1991). Smaller Fort Meigs occupations were also established in the upper Portage and upper Maumee River valleys. Their characteristic points and endscrapers are reported to occur in a wide band to the south of the village sites, but the total region over which Fort Meigs phase sites occur seems to have decreased from its extent in earlier periods (Abel 1995; Bowen 1992).

After 1550, Indian Hills phase populations along the Maumee coalesced into a few large villages. Though similar to earlier Fort Meigs ceramics, wholly shell-tempered Indian Hills ceramics have smoothed or finely cord-marked globular bodies with flared rims, exterior impressions below the lip, and necks highly decorated with complicated patterns of stamping, punctation, trailing, and incising. Strap handles (tapered) and a single- or double-notched appliqué strip at the base of the rim are normal. Vessel bodies with flared rims and necks, along with a bone and antler industry that included bone beamers, flutes, and rasps similar to those at Fort Meigs sites, disappeared, whereas antler harpoons were added (cf. Graves 1984). The lithic assemblages are relatively generic for the Great Lakes–Midwest (cf. R. Mason 1981). Fishing and focused hunting supplemented a highly agricultural diet (Stothers and Abel 1991; Stothers and Bechtel 1987). All Indian Hills sites yield abundant fish, but in the Maumee Valley elk and raccoon were most abundant. Nonetheless, recovery of abundant charred maize, squash, and beans, together with stable isotope ratio values, indicates a highly agricultural diet for the occupants of

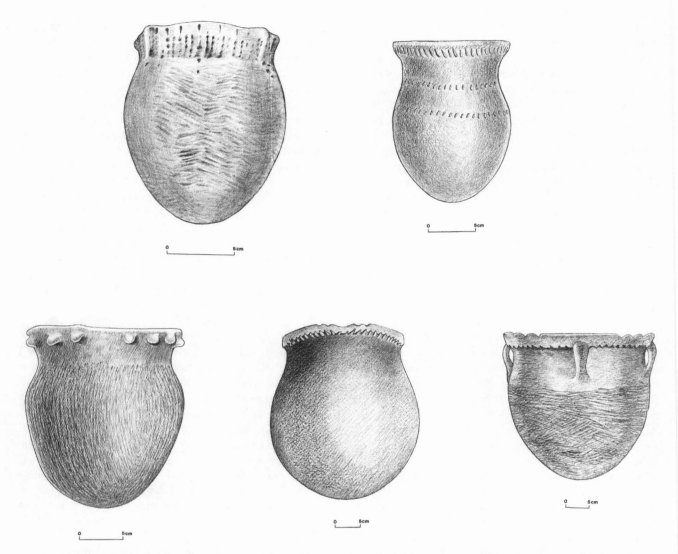

Figure 6.4. Varieties of Late Woodland pottery from northeastern Ohio. *Top row, left to right:* Fairport Harbor Cord-Marked, Allegheny Valley Glen Meyer Incised. *Bottom row, left to right:* Wellsburg Single-Stamped, Tuttle Hill Notched, South Park Notched. (Drawings by Emile Huston, Royal Ontario Museum.)

the Indian Hills site, the type site in the Maumee Valley (Stothers and Abel 1991).

That large, multicomponent type site with a central plaza (Fig. 6.5) occupies about 4 hectares on a peninsula formed by a sharp bend in an entrenched tributary, about 2 kilometers above its Maumee River junction (Becker 1972; Graves 1984; Prahl et al. 1976; Stothers 1978, 1995). A palisade and low linear mounds cut the site off from an up-land approach (Graves 1984). A second, smaller (seasonal?) group was living on a large island 15 kilometers up the Maumee in a village of as-yet-unknown morphology (Pratt et al. 1983). Indian Hills sites also lie near the forks of the Portage River, at the lower rapids of the Sandusky, and near the forks of Muddy Creek and on Green Creek (tributaries to Sandusky Bay). Despite the high frequency of fish re-

mains, large numbers of scraping tools and projectile points suggest that hunting remained important, with muskrat and beaver more common than elk and more important than maize in these sites (Bowen 1992; Pratt and Brose 1992). Except at the Sandusky rapids and Green Creek, these sites were downstream movements of earlier Fort Meigs sites (Bowen 1994; Pratt and Brose 1992).

Fort Meigs and Indian Hills styles influenced and then re-placed those of the late Wolf phase in the Maumee River to Sandusky Bay region (Bowen 1992; Brose 1988a, 1988b, 1994b; Pratt and Brose 1992) and on the Erie Islands (Davis et al. 1976) by the late fifteenth century. Fort Meigs sites in the Portage and Sandusky River valleys were similar to but much larger than those of the Wolf phase, and all appear to have been fortified. Maize consumption was less significant there than in the Maumee River valley. Bowen suggested that hunting increased during the local Fort Meigs phase and that inhabitants of these sites moved downstream to build the Indian Hills sites clustering at the lower rapids of many major rivers and on the Erie Islands and adjacent Sandusky Bay (Bowen 1992; Pratt and Brose 1992). At the Sandusky County Pearson site, along a tributary to Sandusky Bay, Bowen (1992) excavated a ring of 17 hearths, 30 meters in diameter, that he suggested marked the hearths and structures of perhaps seven extended families in a village whose population approached 400. Pearson is one of four sequential sites in a 9-square-kilometer area and may represent movement of a single group throughout the sixteenth century. Similar clusters are at the lower rapids of the Maumee, Portage, and Sandusky Rivers, and another group may be represented by coeval sites on Kelley's Island and adjacent Sandusky Bay.

Fort Meigs and Indian Hills cultural styles and patterns began to replace those of late Wolf phase sites in the Huron and Vermilion Valleys not long after A.D. 1500 (Brose 1997a; Neveret 1992; Pratt and Brose 1992; Redmond 1999; Shane 1974). Finally, Indian Hills material assemblages replaced the local Wolf–Fort Meigs assemblages in the Black River valley between 1550 and 1600. In the latest levels of the Eiden site (Fig. 6.5) and at the National Tube Company site,

fine cord-marked or smoothed globular jars (some vertically compound) with everted rims and dragged-stamp or notched appliqué strips and effigy adorno faces are replaced by shell-tempered Indian Hills linear stamped types and other vessels similar to plain Oneota globular jars with everted, piecrust lips and vertically finger-trailed necks (Bier n.d.; Brose 1976b, 1978a, 1978b, 1993; Brose and Bier 1978; Greenman 1930, 1935a; Pratt 1981; Redmond 1999; J. Scarry 1973; Vietzen 1941, 1945). Many sites also yield shell hoes, shell effigy masquettes, and weeping eye gorgets (Brose 1971, 1978a, 1993; Vietzen 1941).

The recovery of 4 glass beads, more than 50 brass and copper rings, bracelets, beads, and scraps, and 21 iron or lead artifacts (Graves 1984: 335–343) confirms the early seventeenth-century ^{14}C dates for the Indian Hills site, if not for the phase (Abel 1995; Stothers and Graves 1983). No such sites are known elsewhere, although what are said to be Indian Hills ceramic decorations (Murphy and Ferris 1990; Stothers et al. 1994; M. Wright 1981)—and what I believe to be a typically Indian Hills cultural practice of organizing ceramic decorative modes (Brose 1992, 1994b)—do occur after 1620 on protohistoric Neutral sites in southern Ontario. Further, I have seen virtually identical ceramic attributes and attribute clusters in sherds on what are said to be historic Wyandot sites in northern Wisconsin (R. Mason

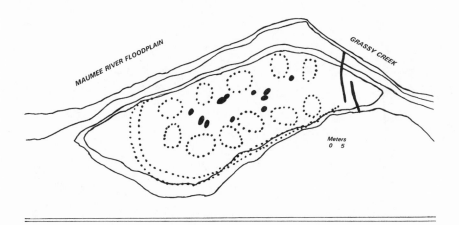

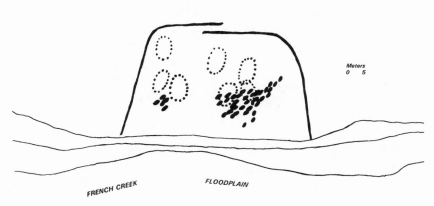

Figure 6.5. *Top:* Schematic reconstruction of houses, burials, embankment, and palisades at the Indian Hills site, Indian Hills phase occupation, A.D. 1500–1630(?); contour interval approximately 5 meters (after Graves 1984). *Bottom:* Schematic reconstruction of houses, burials, and ditches and embankments (heavy black lines) at the Eiden site, Eiden-Wolf phase occupation, A.D. 1325–1450; contour interval approximately 5 meters (after Bier n.d.).

1981, 1983) and on sites in northwestern Michigan occupied after 1670 by displaced aboriginal groups encompassing more than a single ethnolinguistic affiliation (Brose 1983; J. A. Brown 1990; Cleland 1992).

Northeastern Ohio from A.D. 1450 to 1625

Between the Black and Grand Rivers, summer agricultural villages occupied by Late Whittlesey populations grew larger after 1450 and were occupied for more of the year. Many sites on high dissected plateaus overlooking sheltered arable floodplains were cut off by palisaded ditches and embankments (Fig. 6.6) (Brose 1978a, 1994b; Greenman 1935a, 1937; Murphy 1971b; Whittlesey 1851), although not all of these earthworks were originally configured by their Whittlesey occupants (Belovich and Brose 1992). Squash, maize, and bean agriculture supported a dozen or more longish, one- or two-family houses of single post construction (cf. Baby 1971). Several villages had semisubterranean sweat lodges. Daub is not recorded, and mats or bark coverings were probably used. Small river hamlets were used in summer, whereas hunting camps and rockshelters in the uplands were occupied during the winter. Spring and fall fishing camps also existed along the lakeshore. Burials are usually encountered only at cemeteries located beyond village boundaries or on adjacent plateaus, although some cut and boiled or charred human remains have been recovered in a domestic trash pit at one site.

Late Whittlesey jars were tempered with grit or grit mixed with shell. Fine cord-marked, smoothed, and simple-stamped rounded bodies are nearly equal in frequency. Above smoothed outcurved rims, lips have quartered sets of scallops over parallel strap handles or lugs. Some vessels display notched and punctated vertical lugs below sharp but low castellations. Broadly notched appliqué strip and vertical finger-trailed necks are most common. Some small vessels appear to duplicate late fifteenth-century Riker ceramics in the Tuscarawas River valley (Vietzen 1972; Whitman 1975a), as well as pottery from coeval Wellsburg sites in the upper Ohio (Mayer-Oakes 1955) and from Neal's Landing phase sites (Hemmings 1977) in the upper Ohio valley dating to A.D. 1620/40 (cf. Graybill 1981, 1987) (Fig. 6.4, lower

Figure 6.6. *Top:* Schematic reconstruction of houses, burials, and palisade at the South Park site, South Park phase occupation, A.D. 1520–1640(?); contour interval approximately 5 meters (after Brose 1994b). *Bottom:* Schematic reconstruction of houses and burials at the Eastwall site, McFate occupation, A.D. 1530–1620(?); contour interval approximately 5 meters (after Brose, Johnson, and Hambacher 1979, n.d.).

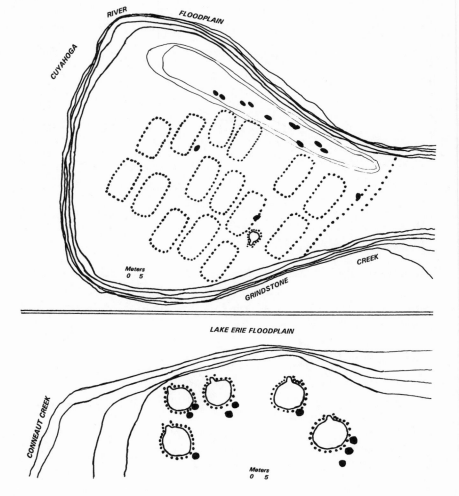

row). Exotic ceramics at Late Whittlesey sites in northeastern Ohio include Oneota, Indian Hills, and Eastwall Erie vessels (Brose 1994b; Greenman 1937; Murphy 1972a). Neutral/Huron-like ceramic smoking pipes are found, and although southern cult motifs occur, they are rare and show up on odd materials and strange artifacts. No stone discoidals or ceramic discs occur, and out of nearly 100 sites, only 2 have yielded shell hoes (less than the number of Iroquioan effigy phalli of antler and stone). Small lanceolate bifaces and bipointed drills, along with antler pipes, distinguish the Whittlesey industries from those of other late prehistoric cultures of the Northeast (Brose 1978b). These few sorts of diagnostic tools also occur at the Riker and Bosman sites along the Tuscarawas (Vietzen 1972; Whitman 1975a) and Muskingum Rivers, respectively (Carskadden 1992; Morton 1992), as well as at Madisonville horizon villages in the central and upper Ohio River valley (Cowan 1987; Drooker 1997a; Drooker and Cowan, this volume; Hemmings 1977; Henderson et al. 1992). Despite several historically irrelevant arguments, not one scrap of European material has yet been documented from any Whittlesey tradition context (Brose 1997a). This is what has led me to conclude that the lower corrected range of possible ^{14}C dates, A.D. 1570–1640, is more acceptable than the possible 1650–1680 or 1720 readings from the final Whittlesey site occupation in northeastern Ohio.

The only sites in Ohio north and east of the Grand River known to have been occupied after 1500 are small rockshelters on the Allegheny Escarpment or are palisade- and embankment-protected fishing villages such as those assigned to the Eastwall phase. The ceramics from the Eastwall site itself (Brose 1977a; Brose, Johnson, and Hambacher n.d.; Johnson, this volume) are shell-tempered McFate tradition vessels with fine cord-marked, badly smoothed, or simple-stamped bodies. These small jars have vertical to round or squared or pentagonal outcurved rims with high, thin collars. Lips are plain or have corded-stick or plain tool-impressed edges. Collars are decorated with Ontario Iroquois-like narrow notched/incised rim appliqués above triangular incised plats. Four or five castellations are common (Fig. 6.4), and spouts occur. Occasionally, Whittlesey vessels occur along with rare shell-tempered, finely cord-marked jars with pseudo-loop handles like those seen earlier at the Philo II and Richards sites in southeastern Ohio (Carskadden and Morton 1977). After 1550 this Eastwall complex spread west along the lakeshore, where it appears at the Grant-ham cemetery, overlapping the fourteenth-century Fairport Harbor village Whittlesey occupation at the mouth of the Grand River (Brose 1976a, 1976c; Bush 1984, 1990). By this time those few miles of Ohio east of Conneaut Creek had become the territory of the same protohistoric complex that extended eastward beyond Erie, Pennsylvania (Brose 1976b; Curtis and Hatch 1981; Johnson 1976, 1979; M. White 1978).

Sociocultural Consideration of the Late Whittlesey Tradition

Concomitant with the sixteenth-century concentration and reduction of Whittlesey tradition populations in northeastern Ohio, there seems to have been a Late Whittlesey cultural spread to the lower Tuscarawas River (Vietzen 1972; Whitman 1975a) and/or on down the lower Muskingum River (Carskadden 1992; Morton 1992; Morton and DaRe 1996) to its junction with the upper Ohio (e.g., Blennerhassett Island and Neals Landing [Hemmings 1977]). This was reflected as far upstream as the forks of the Allegheny and Monongahela (Buker 1968). Not only do ceramic and lithic styles suggest this emigrant movement, but dramatic changes in the settlement pattern and in faunal exploitation (Hemmings 1977) argue for the introduction of economic practices common to the Whittlesey tradition into the early seventeenth-century Madisonville horizon Fort Ancient sites of the upper Ohio River valley (Brown and Skinner 1983; Drooker and Cowan, this volume; Graybill 1981, 1987; Herbstritt 1981). It is difficult to imagine how such introductions might have taken place in the absence of real population movements, and this situation naturally raises questions about the social motives that might have underlain such abandonment of traditional territory. That any answers to such questions must be speculative psychohistory is certain.

Late Prehistoric Social Relationships in a Changing World

As a putative historical reality, the Whittlesey tradition displays a major failing. Unlike historic disruptions in areas around Georgian Bay farther northeast or even in areas farther southwest, the mid-seventeenth-century disruptions in the portion of the Great Lakes inhabited by Whittlesey people took place without European observers to record them, and so we have no secure information about the ethnosocial and ideational nature of Whittlesey culture. As an archaeological construct, however, the Whittlesey tradition is no more impaired than most other such archaeological cultures (cf. Brose 1988a, 1992).

Beyond any promise or pitfalls in the attempt to use ceramics to link the archaeological evidence for the Whittlesey tradition to historic Native American tribes and clans, the late cohesion of a decorative repertoire derived from the west and north, superimposed on an older technology derived from the southeast, in Whittlesey ceramic assemblages (see Brose 1992, 1994b) suggests a very open, if not fluid, Whittlesey female learning tradition. Indeed, the level of social information conveyed by Whittlesey ceramics is intermediate, in both time and space, between the levels observed in several adjacent traditions. One is that of the peripatetic or seasonally recombinant Late Woodland populations across the western basin of Lake Erie and along the western slope of the Appalachian Plateau, among whom economic stasis and low levels of social integration persisted for nearly a millennium (Brose 1987b; Brose, Weisman et al. 1988). The other is a pattern of repetitive ceramic types representing coeval clans and lineages from the large, permanent, riparian agricultural villages of the New York and Ontario Iroquois (Bradley 1987a; Heidenreich 1990; Lennox and Fitzgerald 1990; Snow 1994b; J. Wright 1972; M. Wright 1981) and, in the opposite direction, the coeval Madisonville horizon Fort Ancient agricultural societies along the Ohio River (cf. Drooker 1997a; Drooker and Cowan, this volume; Griffin 1943, 1978; Henderson 1992). Whittlesey ceramics offer more easily visible decorative variability than do these last. Perhaps, as I have argued elsewhere (Brose 1994b), Whittlesey societies' need for material identification of social relationships developed only partway along the path of material communication that characterized the shift to ranked societies. Beyond evidence for conservatism and an arrested social hierarchy, the distribution of ceramics suggests that Whittlesey tradition potters neither lived with nor made pottery with their mothers or sisters.

Similarly, I have argued (Brose 1978b, 1994b) that changing Late Whittlesey lithic and hunting patterns indicate culturally conservative and decreasingly opportunistic procurement strategies in response to a loss of traditional alternate resource catchments. This decreasingly opportunistic strategy seems matched by a preferential pattern in which males may have acquired stone and hunted with their fathers and brothers along networks and in territories that were long known, if not tightly controlled (cf. Brose 1992; Lenig 1977). Other locational changes in Whittlesey faunal exploitation (Brose 1992), partly due to changes in snowfall patterns favoring late winter and early spring group hunting, appear similar to the hunting practices that characterize nonhierarchical cultural systems under both economic and social duress.

Certainly, the way in which Whittlesey peoples used space suggests rather loose social cohesion, possibly reflecting a short historical trajectory. At no time do spatial archaeological data suggest a structurally complex or even partially hierarchical Whittlesey settlement system, as do data for some coeval upper Mississippian and Fort Ancient (Drooker 1997a) societies. Changes in house types through time indicate more extended family structures and more cohesive family relationships, and there is virtually no evidence for any seasonally differing structure types or economic differentiation, as has been suggested for the upper Ohio Valley (see Drooker and Cowan, this volume).

In all, the Whittlesey tradition represents the social cohesion of 20 generations of northeastern Ohio groups with economies that always relied on exploiting different habitats cut by riverine systems within a small region. The Whittlesey tradition groups' increasing economic dependence on agriculture corresponded to a period during which climatic conditions for agriculture became unreliable. Many similar late prehistoric groups that occupied less ecologically differentiated and less hydrologically partitioned habitats in the midcontinent developed cultural mechanisms promoting economic efficiency. In late Fort Ancient and Indian Hills societies to the west and south, there is evidence for increasing internal economic allocation and for the socially controlled redistribution of agricultural assets. This economic stratification paralleled the development of hierarchical structures for settlement, warfare, ideology, and social status (Drooker 1997a; Graves 1984). For the Iroquois of New York and Ontario, to the north and northeast, widely accessible aquatic resources provided a reliable substitute for intensive agriculture. Those groups redeveloped nonhierarchical social segments that formed strong but limited cooperatives with similar segments in diverse habitats. In response to the environmental pressures of the late prehistoric period, the increasingly centralized Madisonville Fort Ancient local economic organization, like the more regionally flexible organization of the Iroquois, promoted survival by either displacing or incorporating their neighbors from frontier zones.

The groups who had come to form the structurally loose and culturally conservative Whittlesey tradition and, in all probability, their Monongahela congeners on the other side of the upper Ohio River (Brown and Skinner 1983; Johnson, this volume) were different. Whittlesey regional groups appear not to have developed any internal mechanisms of social control or integration to buffer the river valley provincialism inherent in their briefly shared history. Nor did they reverse their deepening commitment to agriculture, a commitment that tied them to decreasingly productive areas and drew them inward economically, pitting them against their neighbors and eventually against each other. Not even demographic concentration and the adoption of defensive fortifications in the late fifteenth century could avert the consequences in store for an early seventeenth-century aboriginal group lacking either a history of social cohesion or friendly neighbors.

The End of Prehistory

The archaeological evidence suggests that four archaeologically distinct groups occupied northern Ohio at the beginning of the seventeenth century. Much of the littoral of western Lake Erie in present-day Michigan and western Ontario was unoccupied (Murphy and Ferris 1990; J. Wright 1972), but around the southwestern end of Lake Erie, in northwestern Ohio, are sites of the Indian Hills phase. Farther east, as far as the Black River, are Indian Hills–influenced late Sandusky tradition sites. From the Cuyahoga east beyond the Grand River were yet the final remnants of the Whittlesey tradition. And finally, from the Ashtabula River east into Pennsylvania was the Eastwall complex, either Iroquoian or strongly influenced by Iroquoian groups farther south and east. These distributions had been set in place by A.D. 1500, well into the paleoclimatologists' "Little Ice Age," when frost-free seasons were so short and irregular that an intensive agricultural economy had become a disadvantage (Brose 1978a, 1994b; Bryson and Murray 1977). Although summers around Maumee Bay and along the shoreline east of Cleveland remained warm and wet, late spring and early fall frosts must have placed a premium on well-drained and sheltered arable soils. It is not surprising that all of these latest aboriginal populations were tightly clustered into large, defended village sites located in the centers of their resource procurement regions. In each area there is biophysical evidence for increasing traumatic death, nutritional stress, and very limited ritual cannibalism, probably of war captives. Late prehistoric times along the southern coast of Lake Erie were indeed dark. Contrary to the popular adage, however, the coming dawn of colonization would be darker.

Possible Historic Connections

The earliest French documents, too, distinguish a number of aboriginal groups along the southern shore of Lake Erie between the Detroit River and Presque Isle (Erie, Pennsylvania) in the first half of the seventeenth century (cf. Brose 1978a, 1994b; J. Brown 1975, 1990; Heidenreich 1976, 1988; R. Mason 1981; T. Smith 1977; Stothers 1983; Temple 1975; Windsor 1894). Yet even with the discrimination gained from years of critical investigation, no scholar has been able to link any one of the archaeological complexes with any specific ethnic group mentioned in the early reports (Trigger 1969a). One of the more likely identifications is that the Indian Hills phase represents the "Nation of Fire," or Mas-

coutin. Some part of this aboriginal Algonkian-speaking group, the Attistaeronon or Assistaeronon, had been at war for a generation with the Adawa or Ottawa and the Neutral of southwestern Ontario, from at least 1635 to the Seneca's 1651 dispersal of the Neutral (Thwaites 1896–1901, 21: 195). By 1642, the Neutral had taken more than a thousand Mascoutin captives (Thwaites 1896–1901, 27: 10). The Fire Nation or Mascoutin appear rather consistently on early French maps to shift from northwestern Ohio in 1650 to southeastern Michigan in the early 1670s (Steckley 1985, 1990), and by 1680 they were found in eastern Wisconsin (Brose 1978a; Fitzgerald, this volume; R. Mason 1983).

The Iroquoian Eastwall complex group in the northeastern corner of Ohio barely lasted to the period of indirect European influence. The recovery of a single early red-glass stick bead from one of the latest McFate tradition trash-filled pits suggests that they may well have been some part of the Neutral group living southwest of Niagara whom Etienne Brule sought in 1618 as potential allies in Champlain's war against the Seneca (Fitzgerald 1982a; W. Fox 1990; White 1978). On an anonymous French map drawn between 1636 and 1642 (attributed to one Jean Bourdon in 1641 and relocated by Heidenreich [1988] in the British Hydrographic Office at Taunton, England) (Fig. 6.7), on maps published by Champlain from 1618 to 1632 and by Sanson in 1650 and 1656 (Fig. 6.8), and, apparently, on a lost map drawn by Ragueneau and described by Lejuenne in 1644 (Thwaites 1896–1901, 18: 233–235), one aboriginal group called Attiouendaronk is located between Lake Chatauqua, New York, and the upper Allegheny; another aboriginal group, called Attiouendarronen or Ationdaron, is located vaguely in the area drained by the upper Ohio, the Monongahela, and the upper Potomac. Both of these names, which are obviously the same (despite typically creative sev-

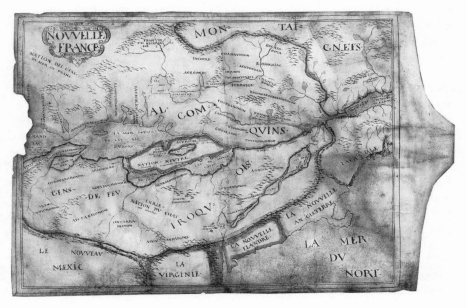

Figure 6.7. The Taunton map, *Novvelle France* (courtesy of the British Hydrographic Office, Taunton, UK).

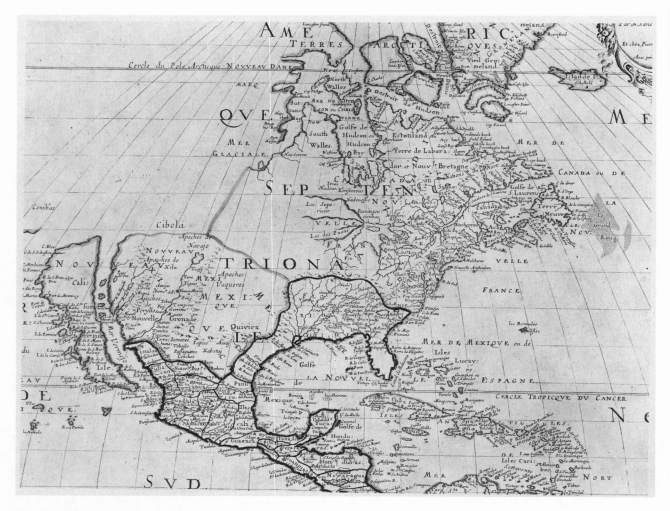

Figure 6.8. The 1656 Sanson map *America Septentrionale* (courtesy of Imprints from the Past, Gastonia, NC).

enteenth-century orthography), are Huron referents for the Neutral. I believe that some northern part of these Neutral were identified in the Jesuit Relation of 1639 as the Iroquoian-speaking Eriehronon (Erie) and Wenrohronon (Wenro) (M. White 1978). The archaeological referent for the southern group is likely some portion of the Susquehannock (Brashler 1987; Fowke 1894), although Johnson (this volume) suggests that the Monongahela complex is equally possible.

The Wenro may have been the western enemies who forced the Erie from their former locations along the lake near Buffalo to their inland location southeast of Lake Chautauqua after 1644 (Thwaites 1896–1901, 33: 63; cf. White 1961, 1976). This brought the Wenro closer to the Seneca, with whom they competed for fur (Hunt 1940). With Dutch firearms, between 1640 and 1644 the Seneca attacked and defeated the Wenro, who fled north as refugees with the Huron. In the winter of 1649–1650, the Seneca destroyed the Jesuit missions among the Huron, and in the fall and winter of 1650–1651, Seneca raids scattered the re-

maining Huron, the Petun, and the Neutral. The amalgamated refugees, called Wendat or Wyandotte, fled across the top of Lake Huron to Lake Superior, leaving southern Ontario abandoned (Fig. 6.9) and Quebec in a state of terror.

Belief that historical records show Erie Indians occupying the entire south shore of Lake Erie is both erroneous (Brose 1971, 1988a; White 1961, 1978) and so pervasive (e.g., Vietzen 1941, 1989) that it is worthwhile indicating what is known. In 1624 the Huron told Sagard of groups called Eriehronon or Eriquehronon who lived across the lake. Sagard's 1639 *Huron Dictionary* translated this as "Cat People." The Erie accepted some Wenro along with the larger number of Huron refugees after their dispersal in 1651 (Thwaites 1896–1901, 41: 83). These incited the Erie into war with the Seneca in 1654 (Thwaites 1896–1901, 42: 111–113, 179). Although Seneca hostility prevented the French from visiting, the Jesuit Relation of 1653–1654 noted that the Erie had taken arms against the Seneca, who claimed that an Iroquois town had already been destroyed

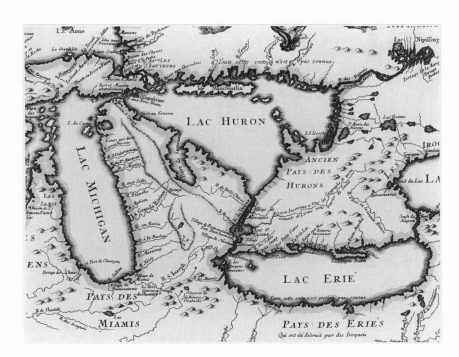

Figure 6.9. The Bellin map of 1755 (courtesy of Imprints from the Past, Gastonia, NC).

and, to repulse the enemy, the Seneca had issued a truce to the French. The Jesuit Relation of 1656 gave a vivid account of this short war, including ambassadorial treachery, several deaths by fire, heroic escapes, and the final Seneca blitzkrieg into Erie territory, resulting in

villages and dwellings [that] were abandoned to the mercy of the Conqueror, who after burning everything, started in pursuit of the fugitives. The latter numbered from two to three thousand besides women and children. Finding themselves closely followed, they resolved after five days' flight to build a fort of wood and there await the enemy. . . . The palisade was attacked on all sides; but the defense was as spirited as the attack, and the combat was a long one. . . . The besieging party . . . hit on the plan of using their canoes . . . to scale the large stakes built upon [the embankments] . . . as ladders. . . . their boldness so astonished the beseiged that, being already at the end of their munitions of war, with which, especially powder, they were but poorly provided, they resolved to flee. This was their ruin, for, after most of the first fugitives had been killed, the others were surrounded by [the Seneca] who wrought such carnage among the women and children that blood was ankle deep in certain places.

This is all that we have. After their disastrous war in 1656, the Erie were mentioned only as captives and refugees among the Seneca for a few years (White 1978). After the Seneca-French treaty of 1699, the record of the Erie per se is silent.[3]

The few seventeenth-century maps that locate the Erie show them along the southern shore of Lake Erie in an area east of a crescent-shaped lake draining north into Lake Erie and west of a second, fingered lake draining south to what appears to be the Allegheny River (cf. T. Smith 1977; Brose 1984; White 1978). Some modern authors equate this eastern, north-draining crescent lake with Lake Chatauqua (Bush and Callender 1984). But it is equally likely that those French maps accurately depicted Lake Chautauqua on the east, draining south to the upper Allegheny, and, farther west, the Waterford swamps from which Girard and Griswold Creeks flow north to Lake Erie at modern Erie, Pennsylvania. Across the low moraine bounding the southern edges of these swamps lay the traditional portage to French Creek, the Allegheny, and thence the Ohio River. If this interpretation is accurate, then some early maps place the Erie Indians from Erie, Pennsylvania, to Dunkirk, New York, whereas later maps show them between Lake Chautauqua and Niagara Falls. This is consistent with the hints in the early Jesuit Relations and matches archaeological investigations southeast of Buffalo.

Excavations east of Buffalo, between Cataraugus and Tonawanda Creeks, have revealed a series of tribal village sites, most surrounded by circular palisades and many with trade goods made around 1650 (Schock 1976; White 1976). The ceramic styles and house types indicate that the material culture of the aboriginal occupants was as closely related to the Iroquoian Seneca and Neutral as the Erie language was stated to have been (MacNeish 1952; White 1961). Several earlier sites of this archaeological tradition exist along Lake Erie between Presque Isle and Lake Chautauqua (Bill Englebrecht, personal communication; Sullivan and Coffin 1995; Sullivan et al. 1995), and European trade goods dating from the end of the sixteenth century to the early seventeenth century occur on the latest of those sites. These, then, are almost certainly some of the archaeological sites left by some part of those native groups whom the French called the Erie. The later seventeenth-century dislocation and southward movement across the Appalachians of at least some part of these peoples (and the cartographic recollection of their lacustrine culture) is documented by a series of French and English colonial maps (W. Green 1998).

The Identity of the Whittlesey and Sandusky Peoples of Northern Ohio

Late prehistoric materials found between Erie, Pennsylvania, and Dunkirk, New York, represent a culture quite distinct from that of the latest prehistoric occupations found between Sandusky and Cleveland, Ohio. There, on sites of the Indian Hills phase and the Eastwall complex, were the latest phases of the Sandusky and Whittlesey traditions. Because no archaeological material recovered from excavation at the sites occupied by these groups suggests even indirect contact with Europeans, it is unlikely that their occupations of the region lasted beyond 1650.

Although we have no firsthand, or even clear second-hand, historical accounts of northern Ohio, critical analyses of the early documents we do possess suggest that between 1640 and 1656 the area beyond the Wenro and Erie, between Sandusky Bay and Presque Isle, was occupied by three or four Algonquian-speaking groups whose names all end in an Iroquoian suffix meaning "the people" or "occupants of." These tribal names also have Iroquoian prefixes that refer to regional geographic detail (Steckley 1990). Recognizable versions of the same names reappear in southeastern Michigan, where at least some were included with the groups that were later called Pottowatomi and Kickapoo when the French again encountered them in eastern Wisconsin in 1678 (Brose 1978a, 1984, 1983, 1997a; Cleland 1992; Fitting 1970; Mason 1981).[4] By interpolating from contemporaneous French maps and accounts (cf. Heidenreich 1976, 1978), there was at least one group and possibly three groups whose names suggest that they were the local group's own name, that the group was not Iroquoian-speaking, and that the Huron knew nothing about the geography of the Whittlesey tradition people, many of whom appear to have moved into the upper Ohio valley about a generation earlier (cf. Brose 1997a).

But even this shrunken territory in northeastern Ohio cannot have been occupied for long. The Jesuit Relation for 1656-1657 claimed: "Our Iroquois have discovered beyond the Cat Nation other and numerous Nations who speak the Algonquian language. There are more than 30 villages whose inhabitants have never had any knowledge of Europeans, they still use only stone hatchets and knives. . . . our Iroquois carry fire and war thither" (Thwaites 1896–1901, 44: 49).

And sometime after 1658, an Onondaga captive in the area, Pierre Esprit Radisson (Radisson 1961), observed that the entire south shore of Lake Erie was unoccupied and used only seasonally as a hunting territory by New York Iroquois (Fig. 6.9).

Postscript

Since I first wrote this chapter, some long-awaited archaeological data from north-central Ohio have been presented (Able et al. 2000; Bowen 2000; Brose 2000; Redmond 2000; Stothers 2000; Stothers and Bechtel 2000). For the Ensign site, Bowen has described another late prehistoric, semi-subterranean sweat lodge, similar to that reported at the South Park site (Brose 2000). Despite Redmond's filial comment (2000: 432), there is little new in the current regional interpretations by Stothers and his colleagues. Stothers and Bechtel (2000) reassert an Iroquoian biolinguistic attribution for the Younge tradition, and their familiar charts still show it swept away by fourteenth-century invasions of exotic Sandusky tradition peoples. The biological evidence alleged for this "migration" consists of the kinds of morphological skeletal differences that are everywhere concomitant with agricultural intensification (Larsen 2000), and much the same is true of the schematized differences in seasonal settlement. As in the past, (cf. Brose 1994b; 1997a), the purported disjunction of traditions still appears to me to be an artifact of the analysts' taxonomic splitting, given their persistent misinterpretation of the transitional twelfth-century ceramic assemblages from the region.

Nor did the late 1990s bring many new perspectives on the late prehistory or early aboriginal history of northern Ohio, *sensu latu*. Stothers (2000) now identifies all early seventeenth-century Sandusky clusters (including Whittlesey tradition and McFate tradition sites as well) with specific Algonquian-speaking tribes scattered across the upper Great Lakes in the late eighteenth century. Those names are tied to Stothers's interpolations to a host of early maps and tenuous lists.

Stothers (2000: 71–76, 77) claims that Champlain suggested a route from Quebec to Lake Huron that avoided the Ottawa River. This is the way Stothers supposed European goods should have reached northeastern Ohio. That such a Lake Erie waterway physically exists is without debate. To show that it carried trade in the late sixteenth or early seventeenth century requires appropriate artifacts in situ at appropriately dated and located sites. Unfortunately, Stothers's (2000: 52) "protohistoric period" is less an archaeological taxon than an index of our collective historical ignorance: an aboriginal site is protohistoric only because we do not know who delivered some of its exotic artifacts. Ignoring the ambiguities in his initial formulation, Stothers (2000: 76, 77; Stothers, Prufer, and Murphy 1997; contra Brose 1994b, 1997a, 2000) persists in arguing that only the ineptitude of those who disagree with him explains the absence of early seventeenth-century European trade materials in "protohistoric" sites from regions not adjoining the lower Maumee River. Beyond illogic, this evinces a disregard for the role human societies play in creating the archaeological record. For even if the early seventeenth-century use of an eastern Lake Erie trade route were demonstrated by European goods at aboriginal sites elsewhere along the southeastern Lake Erie shore, it remains true that not a single Whittlesey site in northeastern Ohio has yet yielded documented European material (the McFate-affiliated Eastwall site has yielded no Whittlesey ceramics at all [Brose 1994b; Brose, Johnson and Hambacher 1979]). My parsimonious explanation, wholly consistent with the existing radiocarbon dates (Brose 1994b) and with Stothers's assumptions (but not his fallacious arguments), is that Whittlesey populations had largely abandoned northeastern Ohio before indirect trade of European artifacts penetrated the region in the early seventeenth century.

Notes

1. A great disappointment of Ohio archaeology is that even today we have virtually no reliable archaeological data for that fourth of Ohio lying just south of the Great Lakes–Ohio River divide. And we know of almost no late archaeological sites from another dozen counties surrounding this terra incognita. In only a few of these areas do we have enough information to suggest that there in fact may have been very little late prehistoric occupation in that region of short growing seasons.

2. Unfortunately, there is yet little agreement about how we might identify the Fort Ancient tradition. It would also be useful, before we attempt to investigate its northern influences, to know how early or how late were the various "Fort Ancient" architectural or settlement patterns, economic strategies, chipped stone or bone technologies, and ceramic styles when they occurred in the heartland of "Fort Ancient." This would certainly improve any discussion of how they relate to such phenomena in sites of the Younge or Western Basin or Sandusky tradition of northwestern and north-central Ohio and in sites of the Whittlesey tradition in northeastern Ohio. It is important to keep in mind the geographic and temporal variability within even the Ohio varieties of Fort Ancient. Developments in the Great Miami differ from those in the Little Miami, and these are quite different than Fort Ancient developments in the Scioto or the upper Ohio or the Muskingum. And, as Griffin (1943), Cowan (1987), Drooker (1997a; Drooker and Cowan, this volume), and Henderson (1992) have demonstrated, even within the Miami valleys, what existed at A.D. 900 is unlike what existed at 1200 or 1600.

3. Francis Jennings, in a rather unusual self-congratulatory footnote to his monograph on the French and Indian War (1988: 444 n. 16), suggested that he had a personal copy of a little-known (and currently unavailable) translation of Robert Navarre's journal showing that there were Erie Indians, along with their chief, at the 1763 attack on Fort Ponchartrain. Navarre was old enough to plan to retire from French service when he made his 1742 visit to Saguin's post on the Cuyahoga (Brose, Belovich et al. 1981). Perhaps he should have. No other account of the Detroit seige mentions this extraordinary native revival.

Yet there was, within a generation of their cultural demise, a kind of brief resurrection and a serious mislocation of the Erie Indians by cartographers. On a map that White (1961) attributed to C. Bernou in 1680 (allowing that it could have been by Van Der Liede in 1679), a note near modern Cleveland states, "Ce lac n'est pas le lac Erie, comme on le nomme ordinairement. Erie est un partie de la Baye de Chesapeack dans la Virginie, ou les Eriechronons ont toujours demeure." I have speculated (Brose 1992) that this remarkable claim was a lingering reflection of the fact that in 1656 some of the Susquehannock villages along the south branch of the Potomac (see Brashler 1987; Fowke 1894) accepted a small number of migrants whom the Tutelo called Richahecrian refugees (a probable Siouan mispronunciation of the Iroquoian name for the Erie, Riquehrronon). More recently, Green (1998) offered a strongly documented argument that after 1690 some portions of the Erie were to be found (along with cartographic referents for Lakes Erie and Ontario) in the upper North Carolina piedmont, where they were referred to as the Westo.

The French map-makers soon corrected these errors. On the 1680 map *Nouvelle France,* by Franquelin, the entire region bounded by Lake Erie and the Wabash, Ohio, and Allegheny Rivers is called "Ancien Pais de la Nation du Chat," and on the 1703 map *Canada,* by Guillaume Delisle, "N. du Chat" appears in the area south of the eastern half of Lake Erie and north of the forks of the Ohio. By 1744, Bellin's map *Carte de Louisiana* stated, in the area along the central south shore of Lake Erie, "ici etoient les ERIES qui ont ete d'truits par les Iroquois." Much the same appears on Bellin's 1755 map (Fig. 6.9), although along the south shore of the lake is written, "Tout cette coste n'est presque pas connue." Nonetheless, the Erie continued to flicker on and off secondary maps produced in Italy, England, and Holland until almost the nineteenth century. And they still reappear, sprawled across all of northern Ohio, in several popular twentieth-century publications.

4. Despite elegant theoretical models by Fitting and Cleland (see Fitting 1970; Cleland 1992), neither was able to find even one major winter site in Michigan that fit his proposed settlement model for the prehistoric Pottawatomi/Miami. Nor had such a site been found many years after the earliest of their papers appeared (John Halsey, personal communication 1990). I have already suggested that such ethnohistoric nineteenth-century models may be attributed to the prehistoric period only with the greatest caution (Brose 1983, 1984). Perhaps an equally good reason is that prehistoric Pottawatomi/Miami did not live in Michigan.

7

The Protohistoric Monongahela and the Case for an Iroquois Connection

The Monongahela culture was the dominant late prehistoric (ca. A.D. 1050/1100–1580) and protohistoric (1580–1635) manifestation in the lower portion of the upper Ohio River valley of southwestern Pennsylvania and adjacent portions of West Virginia, Maryland, and Ohio.

Early and Middle Monongahela community patterns, ceramic technological and decorative attributes, and maize horticulture reflect interaction with Fort Ancient societies in the middle Ohio River valley from the inception of the sequence. For the final late prehistoric decades, changes in ceramic decorative modes suggest a reorientation of Monongahela contacts toward Iroquoian groups in the Northeast. By the beginning of the protohistoric Late Monongahela period, "western Iroquoian" (i.e., Seneca and Ontario Iroquois tradition) ceramic attributes and items of native manufacture indicate that the Monongahela were drawn into a new trade axis with the lower Great Lakes. Documents and artifacts suggest that the Monongahela supplied furs to Iroquoian groups in the lower Great Lakes and acted as middlemen in the Neutral confederation–Chesapeake Bay whelk shell trade.

Early seventeenth-century cartographic and ethnohistoric sources suggest an identification of the protohistoric Monongahela variously with the Massawomeck, the Black Minqua, and a little-noted Atiouandaron group shown in the trans-Appalachian upper Ohio River valley. All three appellations refer to Iroquoian speakers and suggest that the protohistoric Monongahela might represent three (or all) of the tribes composing the Massawomeck nation. Archaeological and ethnohistoric data indicate the dispersal of the Monongahela by about 1635, almost surely at the hands of the Seneca, thus severing the Neutral's lower Great Lakes–Ohio Valley trade route.

Location and Environment

Monongahela sites are distributed in a broad, west-to-east-trending band across the unglaciated portion of the Allegheny Plateau and the adjacent Allegheny Mountain section of the Appalachian Plateaus physiographic province. Sites run from the Flushing Escarpment in east-central Ohio east to the Allegheny Front, on the edge of the Appalachian Plateaus province in south-central Pennsylvania. The core of Monongahela territory was the lower and middle Monongahela River basin from modern Morgantown, West Virginia, north to modern Pittsburgh, including the lower Youghiogheny River basin east to the foot of the first ridge of the Allegheny Mountain section (Fig. 7.1). Fifty-eight percent of the recorded Monongahela components are situated in this area (Johnson and Athens 1998). Other areas in the upper Ohio River valley displaying less intensive Monongahela occupation include the valley terraces of the Allegheny and Ohio Rivers; the Kiskiminetas River basin; major north- and west-flowing tributaries of the Ohio River from Pittsburgh downstream to the vicinity of modern Moundsville, West Virginia; and the middle Youghiogheny

WILLIAM C. JOHNSON

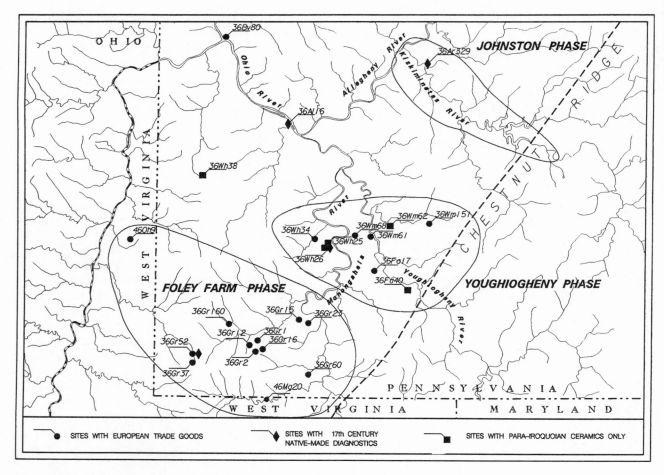

Figure 7.1. The Monongahela core area in the terminal late prehistoric and protohistoric periods. Map by Mark S. Fetch.

River basin in the Allegheny Mountain section, including the tributary lower Casselman River valley.

A single putative Monongahela village is recorded north of the mainstem Ohio-Allegheny River valley. Only two presumed Early Monongahela period sites are located east of the Ohio-Monongahela River drainage basin, in the Wills Creek–Potomac River drainage. A few possible Monongahela villages have been reported along the Cheat and Tygart Valley rivers, major north-flowing tributaries of the Monongahela River in West Virginia. Ceramics suggest village intrusions from the upper Potomac or James River drainages in the Ridge and Valley province. Finally, to the west, a few poorly known sites are recorded in the drainages of the east-flowing tributaries of the Ohio River in east-central Ohio (Morton and DaRe 1996; Whitman 1975b). An exception is a cluster of villages just west of the Flushing Escarpment in interior Belmont County, Ohio. Despite a general Monongahela settlement pattern, the ceramics from these Belmont County sites seem to represent a mix of Monongahela and Philo phase Fort Ancient and earlier Cole complex morphology, surface treatment, and decoration. These components are tentatively assigned to a distinct Belmont complex (see Johnson et al. 1989; Morton and DaRe 1996) and are not treated further in this discussion.

Monongahela sites are found within Braun's (1950) mixed mesophytic forest and Dice's (1943) Carolinian biotic province. A notable exception is the finger of the Canadian biotic province extending down the high Allegheny Mountain section from north-central Pennsylvania as far south as the Early Monongahela Somerset phase sites in the upper Conemaugh River drainage.

Monongahela sites generally are confined to the portion of the Ohio River valley that today has a mean frost-free growing season of more than 140 days. Notable exceptions are the Somerset phase sites and the later Middle Monongahela intrusion into the confluence area on the middle Youghiogheny River, a zone of slightly longer growing seasons in an otherwise 130 frost-free day area. Significantly, the Monongahela core area, including the immediate uplands, constitutes a microniche with a frost-free growing season averaging more than 170 days (see Johnson and Athens 1998; Johnson et al. 1989).

Settlement Pattern

It is perhaps the Monongahela culture's distinctive settlement pattern that most distinguishes it from other, contemporaneous horticulturists in the Eastern Woodlands. Of the 422 documented Monongahela components for which site function can be determined, 74 percent are villages. Smaller hamlets, isolated farmsteads, and perhaps other specialized sites make up the remaining habitation sites. Only 43 percent of recorded Monongahela components are situated on river or stream terraces; the remainder are in upland situations. The uplands include hilltop ridges and saddles as well as the generally slightly lower linear ridges with relatively level benches and saddles favored by the Monongahela for villages and maize fields. This class of landform includes river bluffs as well as hilltop situations ringing interior drainage basins. Seventy-seven percent of the upland sites are villages (Johnson and Athens 1998). Notable is the strong association of upland Monongahela site locations and higher-order tributary divides of the Monongahela, Youghiogheny, Allegheny, and Ohio Rivers. Of 239 upland components, 36 percent are located directly on tributary drainage divides, 48 percent are located within 300 meters of such divides, and 61 percent are within 600 meters of the interior heights of land (Johnson and Athens 1998).

Some archaeologists (e.g., George 1974, 1975, 1978, 1980, 1983; Mayer-Oakes 1955) have suggested that upland Monongahela villages were located on hilltops for defensive purposes, conjecturing that the more powerful village groups in the major valleys drove weaker communities from the better horticultural land into the less desirable interior uplands. Although some hilltops might have been selected with an eye to defense, and although some, presumably internecine, warfare did occur, I have argued that the Monongahela's choice of upland locales for seating their villages and maize fields seems to have been a deliberate proactive economic strategy (Johnson 1981; Johnson and Athens 1998; Johnson et al. 1989). Many upland Monongahela sites are located on or adjacent to extensive tracts of soils such as Westmoreland channery silt loam that are among the most productive soils for maize in the area (Johnson and Athens 1998; Johnson et al. 1989; Kopas 1973). Airflow patterns along the steep terrains adjacent to the villages would have reduced crop damage from late spring and/or early fall killing frosts (e.g., Adams 1979; Roberts 1990). King (personal communication 1989) has suggested that this same beneficial airflow pattern would also have buffered ridgetop nut crops from late killing frosts in the spring. Thus, the most reliable nut groves would have been along the upper slopes of the higher ridges. These stands would have attracted people to harvest nuts and to hunt the animals that came to eat them.

Cultural Periods and Phases

Following Mayer-Oakes (1955)—with some adjustments for period ranges—the Monongahela culture is divided into Early (ca. A.D. 1050/1100 to 1250), Middle (1250 to 1580), and Late, or protohistoric (1580–1635), periods. Each period is represented by one or more phases and addi-

tional complexes. Divisions are based almost exclusively on changes in ceramic temper, surface finish, vessel morphology, and decorative modes and on the presence of European trade goods in the latest period. Some changes in site distribution and size and in house and storage structure styles seem to parallel shifts in the ceramic industry.

THE EARLY MONONGAHELA PERIOD (CA. A.D. 1050/1100 – 1250). The Early Monongahela period includes three phases: Drew in the Allegheny Plateau section (Buker 1975); Somerset to the east in the Allegheny Mountain section (George 1983); and Kiskiminetas in the Kiskiminetas River valley in the Allegheny Plateau section, including its confluence with the Allegheny River (Johnson, Morgan, and Cholock 1991).

The Drew phase is characterized by varying proportions of plain-surfaced, generally shell-tempered ceramics that may have castellations, lugs, loop and occasionally strap handles, and rectilinear incising and/or horizontal bands of punctations on necks of vessels (e.g., Buker 1970; Eisert 1981). Kiskiminetas phase ceramics generally mirror Drew ceramics but are distinguished by very high frequencies of various pulverized rock tempering agents (Johnson, Morgan, and Cholock 1991). Somerset phase ceramics, however, are characterized by added-on collars or rim strips. George (1983) sees the Somerset phase ceramic assemblage as the northernmost extension of the central Appalachian Late Woodland ceramic tradition. Some Somerset phase sites also display Drew phase ceramic decorative attributes (e.g., M. Butler 1939; George 1983), reflecting a brief interlude when this stylistic horizon penetrated the Allegheny Mountain section.

Many Early Monongahela ceramic assemblages are also characterized by limestone and mixed limestone and shell tempering, particularly in Somerset phase components, where shell is absent or occurs in low frequencies (Butler 1939; Cresson n.d.; George 1983). The relative frequency of shell temper in initial Monongahela ceramic assemblages seems related to age as well as proximity to the middle Ohio Valley, the source for the new trait of baked mussel-shell temper. Thus, limestone is supplanted by shell increasingly later in time as one moves farther up the tributaries of the Ohio and Monongahela Rivers (Johnson 1981).

The Early Monongahela Drew and Kiskiminetas phase ceramic tradition likely was derived from the Early Fort Ancient Roseberry phase (ca. 1050–1250) of the middle Ohio River valley (Graybill 1981, 1986). Various changes in the local ceramic tradition, as well as those in projectile point forms, subsistence, and community pattern, probably diffused from the middle Ohio River, not as a coherent package but in a piecemeal fashion, and they seem to have been grafted onto an in situ Woodland base. Thus, changes in ceramic vessel shapes and forms of decoration outstripped the spread of shell tempering.

The predominance of final Z-twist cordage preserved as impressions on the exterior surfaces of Late Woodland and late prehistoric cord-marked pottery in the lower part of the upper Ohio River valley argues for population continuity during this rapid transition. Although another group characterized by final Z-twist cordage (e.g., a Roseberry phase Fort Ancient population) could have replaced the Late Woodland groups in the upper Ohio River valley, cordage impressions on Middle–Late Woodland cord-marked ceramics from a small area along the Ohio River around the confluence of the Beaver River are characterized by a final S twist, as are impressions on succeeding Monongahela ceramics from the same locale. When contrasted with the balance of the Late Woodland–Monongahela cordage twist pattern, this suggests diffusion of late prehistoric traits and population continuity rather than replacement (Johnson and Speedy 1993; Maslowski 1973, 1984a). By about 1250, smoothing of the exterior surfaces of vessels had dropped below 15 percent. Incised and punctated designs and ornamental appendages had similarly passed from vogue (see Johnson 1981). This shift signals the beginning of the Middle Monongahela period.

Early Monongahela people lived predominantly in nucleated, planned villages with relatively large, open central plazas encircled by a single ring of houses. Villages normally were surrounded by insubstantial wooden palisades. Stockades appear early in the late prehistoric period at all Drew and Somerset phase village sites where excavations have been sufficient to detect their presence. Drew phase village stockade dimensions range from 50 by 61 meters to a maximum of 67 by 91 meters, whereas those of Somerset phase villages range from a low of 37 meters in diameter to as much as 116 by 134 meters (see D. A. Anderson 1998; Boyce 1985; Cresson n.d.; Davis 1993; Dragoo, George, and Tanner 1964; Eisert 1981; George 1974, 1978, 1983; Herbstritt 1981; Johnson 1981; NPW Consultants 1983).

Early Monongahela houses are normally circular to oval; they range from 4 meters to 9 meters in diameter in Drew phase villages and 3 meters to 13 meters in Somerset phase settlements (see Archaeological and Historical Consultants 1990; Babich et al. 1996; Boyce 1985; Cresson n.d.; Dragoo 1955; Eisert 1984; Fields 1969; George 1974, 1978, 1983; George, Babich, and Davis 1990; Herbstritt 1981; Johnson and Babich 1992; NPW Consultants 1983). In the core lower Monongahela River valley area, post molds indicate structures with low, outsloping walls of wattle and daub associated with interior matched roof supports. The inclination of the post molds in this floor plan implies a pitched roof with overhanging eaves (Johnson 1981; Johnson and Babich 1992). Sites outside the core area display post-mold patterns suggesting circular, tension-pole, wigwamlike structures. Caching or storage seems to have been confined to semisubterranean, roofed structures that either occur randomly in the circular domestic zone of the villages (Drew phase) or are connected to the houses by a short, narrow, roofed and ramped passageway (Somerset phase).

The Early Monongahela mortuary pattern for infants and juveniles was normally interment within houses, whereas adults usually were buried in shallow pits in the domestic zone between the house ring and the palisade. Except for infants, inhumations were almost exclusively flexed, on their sides, with no apparent regular directional orientation. With the exception of items of apparel or adornment, inhumations generally are unaccompanied by artifacts (see Johnson 1981).

Carbonized cultigens from Monongahela sites are scarce for all time periods, but they include maize, beans, and squash (Adovasio and Johnson 1981). Despite the paucity of carbonized maize, studies of dental pathologies (Sciulli 1995; Sciulli and Carlisle 1977) and mass spectrometric analysis of human bone (Farrow 1986; Sciulli 1995) indicate a heavy reliance on maize. Large quantities of maize have been recovered from the Drew site and from the late Middle Monongahela period Kirshner site. Thus, preservation of carbonized maize on Monongahela sites may be a function of the method of storage employed and not of the importance of maize in the diet. The presence of relatively large quantities of carbonized nut hulls on Monongahela sites of all time periods suggests that these early sources of carbohydrates and fats continued to be exploited.

THE MIDDLE MONONGAHELA PERIOD(A.D. 1250 – 1580). The Middle Monongahela period is represented by the Campbell Farm phase (Johnson 1981) in the middle and lower Monongahela River valley. The Campbell Farm phase is an interpretive construct that incorporates all of the Youghiogheny phase sites shown in Figure 7.1 but extends north along the western shore of the Monongahela River as far as the Ohio River and south along both banks of the Monongahela to the vicinity of Morgantown, West Virginia, thus overlapping some eastern Foley Farm phase sites. The terminal Middle Monongahela and initial protohistoric Youghiogheny phase is present in the lower Youghiogheny River valley and adjacent portions of the Monongahela River valley (Fig. 7.1). A second terminal Middle Monongahela and initial protohistoric phase, the Johnston phase (George 1978, 1997), is generally restricted to the Kiskiminetas and adjacent Allegheny River terraces. Two successive undescribed and unnamed phases appeared in the Chartiers and Raccoon Creek drainages (Buker 1993; Dragoo, George, and Tanner 1964; Mayer-Oakes 1954).

The Middle Monongahela period began with a geographical contraction and the temporary abandonment of large areas on the eastern and northern margins of Monongahela territory, including the Allegheny Mountain section and the Kiskiminetas River valley. The upper reaches of the west-flowing tributaries of the Ohio River in the panhandle of West Virginia and adjacent Pennsylvania similarly appear to have been eschewed (Dunnell 1980; Fuller 1981). This apparent depopulation of the periphery and the more marginal horticultural areas of Monongahela territory, which today have relatively short frost-free growing seasons (i.e., 140 days), is correlated with the appearance of much larger villages in the central core area. The contraction seems correlated with the brief climatic decline of circa 1200–1250 that marked the end of the Neo-Atlantic climatic episode (Baerreis and Bryson 1965; Bernabo 1981; Bryson and Wendland 1967). The appearance of late Campbell Farm phase ceramic attributes and multiple, semidetached, pear-shaped storage structures at two village sites in the middle Youghiogheny River valley indicates a late Middle Monongahela intrusion into the confluence area, which enjoys a longer mean frost-free growing season than the rest of the Allegheny Mountain section.

Like Middle and Late Fort Ancient ceramic complexes in the upper middle Ohio River valley (Graybill 1981), Middle Monongahela ceramics are generally cord-marked and undecorated. Vessel lips infrequently are decorated by stamping, notching, or incising. Shallow bowls or dishes with appliquéd effigy heads have been recovered occasionally (e.g., Johnson 1981). In the Raccoon Creek valley during the late fifteenth to mid-sixteenth century, low molded collars, occasionally showing single horizontal bands of casually applied, oblique linear stamped or incised lines, appear in low frequency at the Scarem-Kramer site (Mayer-Oakes 1954) and more frequently at the later Moore-Olah site. Similar low to medium molded-collar vessels with similar decorations on the collars are recorded at the Portman site along Chartiers Creek (Buker 1993). These crudely rendered collared vessels suggest local imitation of post–Middleport horizon Ontario Iroquois tradition prototypes. This hints at the initiation of contacts between local Monongahela populations on the northwestern edge of Monongahela territory and Iroquoian groups around Lake Erie, and it signals the appearance of the terminal Middle Monongahela—tentatively, Scarem phase—in Chartiers and Raccoon Creeks.

The terminal Middle Monongahela Youghiogheny phase has 11 components, 4 of which have copper or brass artifacts indicating possible protohistoric occupations. These components are clustered in the lower Youghiogheny River valley and the adjacent Monongahela River valley (Fig. 7.1), and they were once assigned to the later Foley Farm phase (Johnson 1990, 1992). The Youghiogheny phase began approximately 50 to 80 years before European trade goods appeared in the region, but later sites yield small quantities of copper or brass artifacts and native artifacts dated elsewhere to the protohistoric period. None of the metal artifacts has been subjected to chemical analysis to determine whether it is of brass (European) or copper.

The Youghiogheny phase is also characterized by the appearance of para-Iroquoian ceramics with low to medium-high molded collars, occasionally with a poorly executed horizontal band of oblique punctates or incised lines on the collar, thus resembling the collared ware of the late Scarem phase. Some sites yield more elaborately decorated collared ware resembling Funk Incised ceramics from the lower Susquehanna River valley (see Adovasio et al. 1990). Lip decoration with a variety of stamped or incised impressions is present in high frequencies, particularly a scalloped or "piecrust" lip form. The orientation of cord-marked impressions on vessel rims approaches horizontal on many specimens. Shallow bowls are present in increasing frequencies.

Excavated Youghiogheny phase villages are surrounded by a stockade and ditch complex. Houses are associated with multiple pear-shaped storage pits, and multiple unattached storage pits are often scattered throughout the domestic zones of villages (Adovasio et al. 1990; Babich et al. 1996). The Sony site village includes two large, circular buildings encircled by multiple semidetached, semisubterranean, roofed, "flower petal"–shaped structures in the central plaza (Davis 1993). The elongated, semidetached appendages seem not to have functioned for communal storage, because many other domestic structures in the village display the single shorter and wider semidetached, roofed storage structures typical of other Youghiogheny phase sites. Indeed, some 60 percent of the houses at the Sony site have a semidetached storage structure, and several have two or three (Davis 1993, personal communication 1993). A greater emphasis on caching in terminal Campbell Farm and early Youghiogheny phase sites is suggested by the profusion of semisubterranean structures, perhaps as a response to a deteriorating climate (Adovasio et al. 1990; Babich et al. 1996; Cresson n.d.).

Very late in Middle Monongahela times a distinctive decorated pottery type, McFate Incised, appeared in the Kiskiminetas River valley along the northeastern margins of Monongahela territory. McFate Incised evolved after 1450 in the glaciated portion of the Allegheny Plateau of northwestern Pennsylvania and western New York. At least one variety of McFate Incised is a rather precise copy of a post–Middleport horizon, Ontario Iroquois tradition variety, Pound Blank, found on early Erie sites along the south shore of Lake Erie (Johnson 1994a, 1994b). Rim sherds identified as McFate Incised or the closely related and companion collared and pseudo-cord-decorated Conemaugh Cord-Impressed (Johnson 1994b) have been recovered from late prehistoric and protohistoric period Johnston phase village components in the Kiskiminetas River valley and adjacent mainstem Allegheny River terraces (Dragoo 1955; George 1978, 1997; Johnson, Morgan, and Cholock 1991; Robson 1958).

The presence of McFate Incised and Conemaugh Cord-Impressed ceramics defines the Johnston phase (George 1978, 1997). Johnston phase sherds have a frequency of impressions from final S-twist cordage ranging from 22 percent at the Huffman Farm–Cook Pacemaker Company site to 83 percent at the Johnston site. Sherds from other villages show approximately equal frequencies of final S- and Z-twist cordage (George 1997; Johnson 1994a). The predominant pattern of cordage displayed on Late Woodland Mahoning Cordmarked and succeeding Chautauqua Cordmarked and McFate Incised ceramics in northwestern Pennsylvania is final S twist, whereas that from contemporaneous Monongahela assemblages is final Z twist (Johnson 1994a; Johnson and Speedy 1993). This suggests that the Johnston phase represents a late amalgamation in the Kiskiminetas River valley of Monongahela populations from the Monongahela core area, with intrusive McFate phase populations from the glaciated Allegheny Plateau section in northwestern Pennsylvania. The cordage twist data indicate that the ratios of Monongahela and McFate phase people varied from village to village (George 1997; Johnson 1994a; Johnson, Richardson, and Bohnert 1979).

Many Middle Monongahela villages are surrounded by a stockade line or several concentric lines. Stockade trenches have been identified at Campbell Farm, Youghiogheny, and Johnston phase sites but have not been reported from sites in the Chartiers and Raccoon Creek valleys. These trenches probably were not defensive per se, as they are often shallow and noncontinuous and occasionally occur inside or between concentric palisade lines. Rather, the ditches seem to have been excavated to obtain dirt to heap up along the

bases of the wooden stockades to stabilize them. Palisade diameters range from 38 meters and 44 meters for the two late villages at the Bonnie Brook site to 137 meters at the Johnston phase type site.

Late Youghiogheny phase villages are associated with encircling stockades and ditches (Davis 1993; George, Babich, and Davis 1990). The terminal late prehistoric Sony village was surrounded with two concentric stockades bracketing the stockade trench; the diameter of the inner palisade was 597 meters, and that of the outer one, 615 meters. Within the stockades were two concentric rings or zones of houses (Davis 1993). The large size of this village relative to other Monongahela villages suggests population consolidation. Whether this was prompted by a desire to more efficiently exploit the resources of the adjacent Jacob's Swamp, by a need for mutual protection, or by some other cause is unclear.

Middle Monongahela villages have large, open, central plazas surrounded by a single ring of houses or occasionally two concentric rings (Fig. 7.2). Houses range in diameter from 3.4 meters at the initial Youghiogheny phase Kirshner site to 10.4 meters at the Johnson phase component of the McJunkin site. Campbell Farm, Youghiogheny, and John-

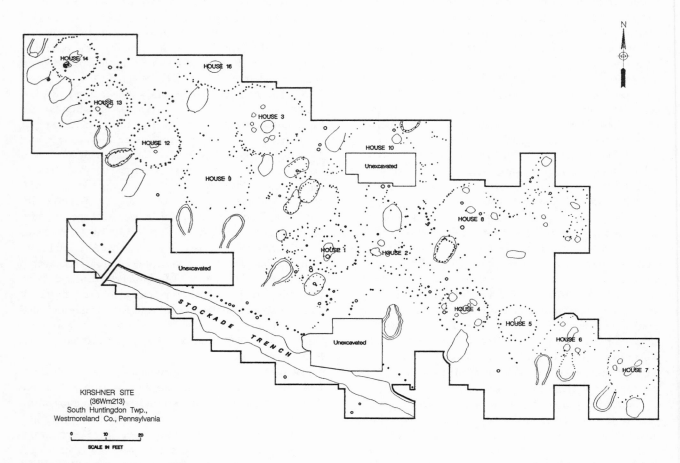

Figure 7.2. The excavated portion of the Kirshner site, showing parts of two rings of houses that surrounded the central plaza and were in turn encircled by a stockade and trench. Drawing by Mark S. Fetch.

ston phase houses continue to exhibit outsloping walls (Johnson and Babich 1992). Wigwamlike house structures, however, have been reported outside the Monongahela core area at two sites in the Chartiers and Connoquenessing Creek valleys (Richard L. George, personal communication 1992; James T. Herbstritt, personal communication 1978).

Caching in semisubterranean storage structures continued during Middle Monongahela times. These pits normally are connected to houses by narrow, roofed, ramped passageways, and they display two basic floor plans. The first is subrectangular with a short ramp or passageway connecting the pit to a house, whereas the second variety of pit is "pear-shaped" with a longer connecting ramp, a wall trench with vertically set posts around the outer edge of the pit floor, and smaller, more shallowly anchored posts encircling the periphery of the pit. Unattached pear-shaped storage structures with interior wall trenches also occur in the domestic zones of late Middle Monongahela Youghiogheny and Johnston phase sites such as Kirshner, Howarth-Nelson, Reckner, and Johnston (Adovasio et al. 1990; Babich et al. 1996; Cresson n.d.; Dragoo 1955; see Fig. 7.2).

Early Monongahela mortuary practices continued into Middle Monongahela times. Infants and juveniles normally were interred in house floors in shallow pits, either under the central hearth or just inside the exterior wall. Late in this period, graves often were covered with one or more sandstone slabs. Adolescent and adult inhumations are found in the domestic zone behind the house ring. A variation of this pattern is the interment of adolescents and adults along the floors of the stockade trenches at the Campbell Farm and Johnston sites (Dragoo 1955; Johnson 1981). All inhumations are flexed except for infants. Other than items of presumed personal apparel or adornment, grave inclusions are rare (see Johnson 1981).

Very different mortuary behavior was recorded at the Campbell Farm phase type site. There, the largest house contained five inhumations (adults and a juvenile) in specially excavated shafts around the interior of the wall. Although artifactual and ecofactual debris in the fill of these features suggested that this structure was a dwelling and that the interments might represent an extended family group (see Johnson 1981; Johnson et al. 1989), it could be an early example of a charnel house. Interment within a mortuary structure characterizes some Youghiogheny phase components in the Monongahela core area.

Such possible charnel houses are documented at the Youghiogheny phase Sony and Household sites. At the Household site, a structure 9 meters in diameter enclosed 16 graves. Although most of the burial features had been disturbed by earlier uncontrolled digging, all seem to have held adult inhumations, and most were originally slab covered (George, Babich, and Davis 1990). The structure at the Sony site is estimated to have contained about 24 adult inhumations. In both villages, however, interments occurred

elsewhere as well. One infant was buried in a house at the Household site, and excavation revealed that three infants/juveniles and a single adult were buried outside the Sony site charnel house, where many other similar but unexcavated features suggested additional interments between the domestic activity zone and the stockades (Davis 1993; George, Babich, and Davis 1990).

George and Scaglion (1992) have documented a general decrease in the size of Monongahela triangular projectile points through time. One apparent exception to this pattern is the long, narrow, isosceles-triangular, so-called Scarem arrow point (see Mayer-Oakes 1954). The Scarem point was long considered to be a local variant of the larger Early Fort Ancient triangular point type. Recent examination of post–Middleport horizon Nanticoke Triangular projectile points (Fox 1981) from southwestern Ontario suggests that the Scarem point is a local copy of this late Neutral form (cf. Buker 1993; Mayer-Oakes 1954). Importantly, the same sites that yield Scarem points in some frequency occasionally exhibit molded, low- to medium-high-collared vessels with single horizontal bands of oblique linear punctates or trailed lines. These suggest Neutral influence on northwestern Monongahela territory earlier than previously thought (Johnson 1990, 1992).

THE LATE OR PROTOHISTORIC MONONGA-HELA PERIOD (A.D. 1580 – 1635). The Late Monongahela Foley Farm phase (Herbstritt 1988) is centered on Greene County, Pennsylvania, and adjacent Monongalia County, West Virginia, including the Monongahela River drainages and Ohio River tributaries. The 12 components assigned to this phase (Fig. 7.1) are divided into an early Throckmorton subphase, with only copper or brass artifacts of European manufacture, and a late Foley Farm subphase, with the addition of iron artifacts and glass trade beads (Herbstritt 1988, 1993a).

The Youghiogheny phase in the adjacent Monongahela and Youghiogheny River valleys persisted into the early protohistoric period. Copper or brass beads and scrap have been reported at four components. No Youghiogheny components have glass beads or iron implements, indicating that the area was abandoned before the Foley Farm subphase began, around 1615. A native-made artifact that is generally dated elsewhere to the early seventeenth century was recovered from the Vesta site. Para-Iroquoian rim sherds have been recovered from the Fuller's Hill, Vesta, and Beazell School sites.

Youghiogheny phase populations may have sought refuge with the late Foley Farm phase villagers in the interior of Greene County. The high frequency (above 90 percent) of final Z-twist cordage impressions on sherds on most Youghiogheny phase sites and on some terminal Foley Farm sites strengthens this scenario. Four of the apparent terminal Foley Farm phase villages display a frequency of final Z-twist cordage greater than 95 percent, whereas the

Varner site, which also includes major Drew and Middle Monongahela components, has a frequency of Z-twist cordage of only 71 percent (Carr and Maslowski 1995; Johnson and Speedy 1993; Mayer-Oakes, personal communication 1993). This suggests that the indigenous Greene County Early and Middle Monongahela period villagers might have had a cordage-making tradition that featured a much lower preference for Z-twist cordage than that seen in the majority of terminal protohistoric villages in the same area.

In the Kiskiminetas River valley, the Johnston phase (George 1978, 1997) persisted into the seventeenth century. An Iroquois acorn/apple ring bowl pipe and a second imitation ring bowl pipe, both with local shell-tempered paste, were collected from the Huffman Farm–Cook Pacemaker Company site (Johnson 1994a; Johnson, Morgan, and Cholock 1991). Acorn/apple ring bowl pipes appear earlier, in the sixteenth century, in the Neutral sequence (Lennox and Fitzgerald 1990), but they do not occur on Seneca sites until around 1595/1600–1614 (Sempowski 1994; Wray, Sempowski, and Saunders 1991). Significantly, no artifacts of European manufacture have been reported from any Johnston phase village.

In addition to the named phases, three other components along the northern and western margins of Monongahela territory are assignable to the first half of the seventeenth century. The large, late sixteenth- or early seventeenth-century intrusive Riker-Whittlesey McKees Rocks Village site at the confluence of Chartiers Creek and the Ohio River yielded a para-Iroquois rim sherd and a fragment of an acorn/apple ring bowl pipe (see Buker 1968). A late protohistoric component at the Rochester site at the confluence of the Beaver and Ohio Rivers yielded glass beads and copper spirals during a salvage excavation (Alam 1957). Finally, 10 red-cored "cornaline de Alleppo" glass beads (Kidd and Kidd's [1970] type IVa1) and a cutout metal claw pendant were recovered in the backdirt of a burial excavated in the 1930s at the Drew phase Hughes Farm site in West Virginia (Dunnell 1962; Fisher n.d.). This component was previously assigned to the Foley Farm phase (Johnson 1992). The burial, however, was extended and was recovered in a loose cluster with four other extended interments (Dunnell 1962). Although red-cored IVa1 beads occur in small numbers on Seneca sites before 1625 (Sempowski 1994, personal communication 1992), they are far more common after that date. Extended interments are rare in Monongahela culture as a whole and are reported only from occasional Drew phase sites, suggesting that these supine, extended burials and their associated European artifacts might not be Monongahela. It may be significant that Kent (1984) reported that extended interments occurred with some frequency on the later Susquehannock Strickler and Oscar Leibhart sites, and 61 percent of the burials from the downstream, late protohistoric Neale's Landing site on Blennerhassett Island were extended (Hemmings 1977).

Protohistoric Monongahela site distribution represents a further contraction of settlement into the Monongahela culture core area, particularly into the interior of Greene County. This appears to have been a response to political pressure from Iroquoian groups to the north and east rather than to the onset of the Neo-Boreal climatic episode, for the longer growing season in the lower and middle Monongahela River valley (currently some 170 to 190 days [see Johnson and Athens 1998]) would have mitigated any effect of a shortened frost-free growing season on maize-based subsistence. Significantly, the late Foley Farm phase sites centered on the South Fork of Tenmile Creek and the Dunkard Fork of Big Wheeling Creek occupy an area that has only a 145-day growing season (see Johnson and Athens 1998).

No palisades were recorded at the extensively excavated Foley Farm phase Throckmorton and Foley Farm sites (Herbstritt 1984; NPW Consultants 1983). The diameter of the Throckmorton village is 42 meters, whereas that of the Foley Farm village (with at least three concentric rings of houses) is about 99 meters (Fig. 7.3). The earlier Throckmorton village site contained only 10 houses in a single ring around the central plaza. The crowding of three concentric house circles onto a small alluvial stream terrace at the Foley Farm site suggests the consolidation of several villages.

The contrast between the large, fortified, terminal late prehistoric, Youghiogheny phase villages and the smaller, unstockaded Foley Farm villages might reflect two successive strategies for confronting external military pressures. Like the people who followed the later unfortified and dispersed Fort Ancient Orchard phase community pattern (Graybill 1987), Foley Farm villagers might have coped with military pressure from Iroquoian neighbors to the north by avoiding concentration in fortified villages whose entire populations could be lost in an attack. In an unfortified village, some might perish, but others would escape. The *Jesuit Relations* testify to Iroquois warfare, which by at least the middle of the seventeenth century emphasized the siege of fortified villages (see M. White 1978).

At terminal late prehistoric and protohistoric villages where extensive excavations have been conducted, plaza areas are smaller than at earlier Monongahela sites. A large circular building with multiple semidetached, semisubterranean, roofed, "teardrop"-shaped structures was located in the plaza of each of the Throckmorton and Foley Farm villages (Herbstritt 1984; NPW Consultants 1983). As I noted earlier, two such houses were documented in the plaza area of the Sony site (Davis 1993). The elongated, semidetached appendages seem not to have functioned for communal storage. On the basis of clusters of thermally altered rocks on their floors, Herbstritt (1984) suggested that the "petal"-shaped appendages at the Foley Farm site might have served as sweat baths or as men's or council houses.

Circular structures with outsloping walls and pitched roofs persisted in the late Youghiogheny phase Household

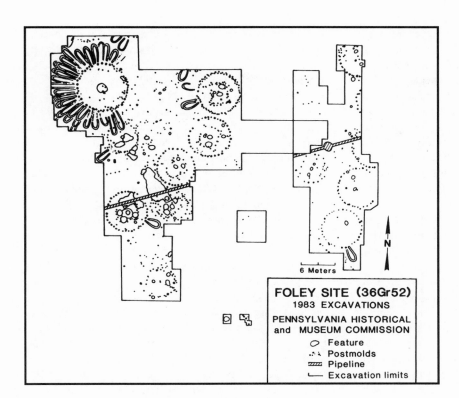

Figure 7.3. The Foley Farm site. Courtesy of
David A. Anderson.

and Mon City sites (Hart 1994; Johnson and Babich 1992).
West of the Monongahela core, house wall support posts at
the Foley Farm phase Throckmorton and Foley Farm sites
are vertical but seem too large to represent wigwamlike
tension-pole structures (Herbstritt 1984, personal communication 1984). Their centrally placed, matched interior
posts probably supported pitched, thatched roofs.

In both the Youghiogheny and Foley Farm phases, caching continued, within semisubterranean, roofed storage
structures generally attached to the house walls. Besides
the flower-petal structure, three houses at the Foley Farm
site exhibited multiple semidetached storage pits (D. A.
Anderson 1998). Limited excavation at the Household site
uncovered no evidence for detached storage structures
(George, Babich, and Davis 1990).

Foley Farm phase mortuary behavior deviated from the
earlier Monongahela pattern. Although most infants and
juveniles were interred in houses, no adult burials have
been found at either of the two thoroughly excavated sites,
Throckmorton and Foley Farm village (Herbstritt 1984;
NPW Consultants 1983). Antler and bone items accompanied an infant inhumation at the Foley Farm phase Ingra-
ham site, and ceramic vessels were associated with interments at the Foley Farm, Beazell School, and Fuller's Hill
sites. Copper or brass rolled beads, tinkling cones, animal
cutouts, and spirals and glass beads are common Foley
Farm and Youghiogheny Phase mortuary inclusions (Cottrell n.d.; Engberg 1930; George, Babich, and Davis 1990;
Gersna 1966; Herbstritt 1984; Mayer-Oakes 1955). This pan-
Northeast phenomenon, related to the initiation of the fur

trade and the influx of European trade goods, may reflect
an increase in personal disposable wealth.

Protohistoric Iroquoian Exchange and Interaction

Early and Middle Monongahela cultural patterns reflect
eastern Fort Ancient trends in the upper middle Ohio River
valley. Circular villages with a domestic area surrounding
a central plaza, early shell-tempered, plain-surfaced, and
elaborately decorated ceramics, and the ubiquitous discoidals and chunky stones are obvious shared traits. Vessels
with Roseberry phase strap handles and decoration on
Drew phase components in Chartiers Creek Valley (Eisert
1981; Nale 1963), as well as Clover-style bowls at the Campbell Farm site (Johnson 1981), reflect this downstream
Monongahela interaction.

During the later Middle Monongahela and the protohistoric Late Monongahela periods, broadly Iroquoian ceramic and other cultural influences penetrated the lower
portion of the upper Ohio River valley. Whether the contacts
were initiated by reintensification of earlier Middle Woodland networks in response to the European fur trade (as suggested by G. Wright [1967]) or whether they were directly
stimulated by competition for furs and European goods is
unclear. It is fairly certain that this movement of items of
native and European manufacture did not emanate from
one specific Iroquoian group or area. The Iroquoian morphological and decorative ceramic styles that might have
been prototypes for indigenous Monongahela types—the

para-Iroquoian styles—did not evolve until the late fifteenth or early sixteenth century. Presumed post-1450 Neutral-inspired ceramic and projectile point styles present in the Chartiers and Raccoon Creek valleys in the late Middle Monongahela period suggest that cultural exchange with Ontario Iroquois groups might have begun as early as the late fifteenth century. Although the presence of European artifacts on Monongahela sites is important, the Mononga-hela reorientation from Fort Ancient groups of the middle Ohio River valley to Iroquoian groups in the Susquehanna and St. Lawrence drainage systems is paramount.

CERAMICS. Like their earlier counterparts, most pro-tohistoric Monongahela ceramics are cord-marked and un-decorated. The increase in lip decoration (particularly notching with a smooth tool) and scalloping seen during the earlier Youghiogheny phase seems to peak and even de-cline, at least on some sites (e.g., NPW Consultants 1983). Cord-wrapped-paddle edge-stamped decoration appears for the first time on rim interiors at the Throckmorton site and increases in popularity at the Foley Farm site (NPW Consultants 1983; Herbstritt, personal communication 1989). At one Johnston phase site in the Kiskiminetas River valley, McFate Incised ceramics persisted into the early seventeenth century.

Monongahela Cordmarked "para-Iroquois" vessels—that is, vessels with low to medium-high, often bulbous molded collars displaying a horizontal band of parallel, usually oblique tool impressions or applied incised lines reflecting Iroquoian models—continued to be made in low frequen-cies on late Youghiogheny and Foley Farm phase sites (NPW Consultants 1983; Herbstritt, personal communica-tion 1989). The bulbous-collared vessels resemble some late Shenks Ferry Funk phase ceramics from the Locust Grove and Mohr villages (Adovasio et al. 1990; Kent 1974, personal communication 1988). Other vessels may be Monongahela copies of low-collared "western" Iroquoian prototypes, in-cluding varieties occurring on Seneca, Erie, and Neutral sites. Collars do not occur in Middle Monongahela assem-blages, and the only indigenous prototypes for this late sixteenth-century vessel form are contemporaneous Iro-quoian models. The valenced Monongahela Cordmarked vessels from protohistoric period sites in Greene County (see Mayer-Oakes 1955), possibly local copies of the early protohistoric Susquehannock ceramic type Blue Rock Va-lenced (Johnson 1972), also could be copies of the Seneca-Cayuga type Genoa Frilled.

Perhaps most diagnostic of the late protohistoric period and Neutral contact are the five so-called Madisonville Pedestaled vessels from the Foley Farm site (Ronald W. Eis-ert, personal communication 1993; Herbstritt, personal communication 1989) and a fragment of another from the Vesta site. Three or four of these distinctive vessels were re-covered from protohistoric graves and middens at the Fort Ancient Madisonville site (Drooker 1997a; Griffin 1943),

and one was recovered from the terminal Susquehannock Byrd Leibhart site in the lower Susquehanna River valley (Kent 1984).

Fragments from pedestaled vessels have also been recov-ered from seven Huron and Neutral sites in southern On-tario. Latta (1987, 1990) has argued that these could be copies of Recollet or Jesuit communion chalices in an in-digenous medium. Alternatively, they could be copies of Spanish chalices, knowledge of which moved from the Gulf coast to the Ohio River valley through the same conduit that moved Citico and Dallas "weeping eye"–style shell gor-gets and asymmetrical ear spools to the Fort Ancient area. There are no published references to this vessel style from Gulf coast or Tennessee Valley contexts, however, and their Ohio River valley occurrence could be the result of trade and/or alliances among Neutral-Huron-Petun, Mononga-hela, and Fort Ancient peoples.

METAL AND GLASS ARTIFACTS. Cut brass "lizard" or "salamander" effigies from a number of proto-historic Monongahela components are another key diag-nostic linking the middle and upper Ohio Valleys with the lower Great Lakes. These cutouts are most likely stylized beavers or beaver pelts. Eight have been recovered from four Foley Farm subphase sites (D. A. Anderson 1998; Bradley and Childs 1991; Herbstritt 1984; Mayer-Oakes 1955, 1993), and one specimen came from a Youghiogheny phase site (Eisert, personal communication 1993).

Single examples of beaver effigy cutouts have also been recovered from the downstream Fort Ancient Clover phase type site and from the Marmet site on the Kanawha River, both in southern West Virginia (Mayer-Oakes 1955; McMichael 1968). Another is reported from the Herman Barton site in western Maryland. The latter includes one of three Luray complex components along this stretch of the Potomac's north branch from which European trade goods have been recovered (Wall 1983, 1984, personal communication 1994).

The Monongahela, Fort Ancient, and Luray complex specimens closely resemble cut metal beaver effigies from the Eastern Seneca Cornish village midden (ca. 1635) and the Western Seneca Feugle village (ca. 1615). Beaver effigies in cut whelk shell have been recovered from the Eastern Seneca Steele village (ca. 1645–1655) and the Western Seneca Power House (ca. 1645–1655) and Dann (ca. 1655–1665) villages (revised dates after Wray, Sempowski, and Saunders 1991). Several effigies of cut and polished bone are reported from the Oneida Cameron village site (Whit-ney 1974), which dates to around 1609–1625 (revised dates after Kenyon and Fitzgerald 1986); they are recognized there as beaver or beaver pelt effigies.

The function of these artifacts is uncertain, but they might have served as counters in a beaver pelt trade. Their presence implies a network involving western or central New York and the upper and middle Ohio Valley. These distinctive cut metal effigies do not occur on contemporaneous Susquehannock sites in either the upper Potomac or the Susquehanna river drainage.

Another class of metal objects entered Monongahela territory by a different route. Using the distribution of native-made copper and brass spirals and hoops, Bradley and Childs (1991, n.d.) demonstrated a trade connection between the Five Nations Iroquois and the Susquehannock and the protohistoric Monongahela and Madisonville phase Fort Ancient people between about 1550 and 1640. Although Bradley and Childs argued for a primarily sixteenth-century distribution of these spirals and hoops, redating the Seneca Cameron, Dutch Hollow, and Factory Hollow villages (Wray, Sempowski, and Saunders 1991) and the Susquehannock Schultz village (Sempowski 1994) moves these and other sites with similar glass bead profiles into the first quarter of the seventeenth century.

Similar spirals from Foley Farm phase components include nine from the Ingraham-Spragg site and single specimens from the Foley Farm and LaPoe No. 2 sites. Four examples are reported from the Rochester site at the confluence of the Beaver and Ohio Rivers (Alam 1957; Bradley and Childs 1991, n.d.; Herbstritt 1984; Mayer-Oakes 1955). Thirty-eight tubular coils and rings were recovered from the protohistoric Fort Ancient Madisonville site (Drooker 1997a). Metal spirals also have been found at Susquehannock sites on the south branch of the Potomac, the pre–Schultz phase Pancake site (two spirals), and the Schultz phase Herriot Farm site (five) (Bradley and Childs 1991, n.d.; Brashler 1987; Manson and MacCord 1941, 1944). Herbstritt and Kent (1990) suggested an occupation of the Pancake site at about 1525–1550. Sempowski's (1994) reassessment of the Susquehannock's initial occupation of the Schultz site, circa 1595, implies that the occupation of the Pancake site was probably in the last quarter of the sixteenth century. Herbstritt and Kent (1990; contra MacCord 1952; Witthoft 1952) considered the Herriot Farm occupation to be contemporaneous with that of the Schultz village, about 1595–1615/20, following Sempowski's (1994) revised chronology.

Sempowski's (1994) limited documentation of differences between the techniques employed in the making of the spirals from the Seneca villages, on the one hand, and those from the Susquehannock Schultz site, on the other, suggests discontinuous artifact sets. If these differences are found on other Seneca and Susquehannock sites, an examination of Monongahela and Fort Ancient specimens might distinguish Seneca–Five Nations Iroquois trade from a Susquehannock trade, perhaps via the south branch of the Potomac River.

Glass beads from four Foley Farm phase sites—Foley Farm (2,300 beads), Ingraham-Spragg (601), Eisiminger (149), and Donley (84)—have recently been analyzed (Lapham 1995). Small numbers of glass beads have been recovered from the Varner, White, Delphene, Brave, and LaPoe No. 2 sites as well (Lapham 1995; Mayer-Oakes 1993). All four of the larger assemblages are dominated by the robin's-egg blue beads, Kidd and Kidd's (1970) IIa40 variety: Foley Farm, 28 percent; Ingraham-Spragg, 32 percent; Eisiminger, 91 percent; and Donley, 61 percent (Lapham 1995). The few beads from the Varner, White, and Brave sites also appear to be the robin's-egg blue or similar colored varieties (Lapham 1995; Mayer-Oakes 1993). The IIa40 and IIa40/41 bead varieties are present at the Seneca Cameron site, dating to about 1600–1610/14, at a frequency of 15.5 percent and at the slightly later Dutch Hollow site, approximately 1610/11–1625, at a frequency of 3 percent. They make up only 4 percent of the beads from the Susquehannock Schultz site, circa 1595–1615/20, but at the succeeding Washington Boro village site, they occur at a frequency of around 35 percent (Lapham 1995; Sempowski 1994; Wray, Sempowski, and Saunders 1991).

The next most frequently occurring bead type at the Foley Farm and Ingraham-Spragg sites, with frequencies of 26 percent and 27 percent, respectively, is a variation on Kidd and Kidd's (1970) IVa12* cored monochrome type, which has a transparent sky-blue outer layer and a middle layer of opaque shadow blue. Examples are reported at the Eisiminger and Donley sites (Lapham 1995). In contrast to the robin's-egg blue variety, the IVa12* variant is present at a frequency of 39 percent at the Seneca Dutch Hollow site but is absent at the earlier Cameron site. It represents only 1.3 percent of the beads at the Susquehannock Schultz site and is absent at the succeeding Washington Boro village site (Lapham 1995; Sempowski 1994). Significantly, this type or, rather, the related types IVa11–14 are present at the terminal western Niagara frontier Iroquois Kleis site at a frequency of 39 percent. Within this cluster, the blue-cored varieties are the most common (Stark 1995). Both Fitzgerald (1990a) and Stark (1995) assigned the Kleis village to the early part of Glass Bead Period (GBP) 3, circa 1625/30–1650. The IVa12* bead also occurs in low frequencies at the GBP 3 Neutral Burke (0.2 percent) and Port Colborne (9.6 percent) ossuaries. A IVa12/14 variety accounts for 17 percent of glass beads at the Neutral Daniels ossuary, which spans the GBP 2–3 transition (Fitzgerald 1990a).

Notably, the IVa12* is not documented among the cored monochrome beads from Fort Orange (Huey 1983), nor is it present in the Mohawk and Onondaga sequences (Bradley 1987a; Rumrill 1991). This implies the entry of the IVa12* bead into the upper Ohio Valley from the lower Great Lakes. Another interesting parallel between the terminal Foley Farm villages and the Kleis site is the occurrence at the latter of the robin's-egg blue beads (IIa40) at a frequency of 48 percent (Stark 1995). Red tubular beads are also present at the Kleis site, but in low frequencies. This suggests a close connection between the terminal Foley Farm villages and the Kleis and Dutch Hollow sites in western New York and certain Neutral sites in the Grand River valley and Niagara Peninsula of Ontario. The glass bead profiles of the terminal Foley Farm phase sites imply a trading relationship with groups at the end of the GBP 2 and Dutch Polychrome period and the initial GBP 3, when there was a brief influx of the IVa12* beads into a narrowly focused lower Great Lakes area. This connection appears to have been severed, however, before the characteristic GBP 3 red tubular beads entered both the French- and Dutch-supplied trade networks.

The frequencies of faceted chevron (IIIk3 and IIIm1) and tumbled chevron (IVk3 and IVk3*) beads vary between the Ingraham-Spragg and Foley Farm villages. The faceted types are present at Ingraham-Spragg at a frequency of 3 percent and at Foley Farm sites at 0.2 percent, whereas the tumbled variety is represented at the two sites at frequencies of 4 percent and 1 percent, respectively. Lapham (1995) suggested that these data indicate that the Ingraham-Spragg site is closer to the Susquehannock Schultz site, where the IIIk3 and IIIm1 varieties together make up 2 percent of the glass beads, and the IVk3/4 varieties, 7 percent. The Foley Farm village, on the other hand, is closer to the Dutch Hollow site, where the faceted varieties occur at a frequency of 0.1 percent, and the tumbled IVk3 variety at 4 percent (see Sempowski 1994). Lapham also suggested that although the Ingraham-Spragg and Foley Farm villages were roughly contemporaneous, Ingraham-Spragg exhibited this pattern and others indicative of a slightly earlier initial occupation. The percentages of the IVa12* cored monochrome beads from Ingraham-Spragg and Foley Farm are most similar to the percentage of this variety at the Dutch Hollow site. The frequencies of the faceted and tumbled chevron beads from Ingraham-Spragg most closely approximate those of the Schultz village, whereas the percentages of the same types from Foley Farm are most similar to the bead profile displayed by the Dutch Hollow village. The IVa12* and IVk3 tumbled chevron beads are absent at the slightly later Washington Boro village site, which was not occupied until after 1615/20. Few (less than 1 percent) faceted chevron bead types are present at the Washington Boro village (see Kent 1984). This suggests that the occupation of both sites overlapped that of the Schultz village, circa 1595–1615/20, and the Dutch Hollow village, circa 1610/11–1625. The differences in the relative frequencies of the chevron beads perhaps reflect, as Lapham (1995) suggested, different trading partners or different sources of European goods with which the two Monongahela villages were linked.

Kenyon and Fitzgerald (1986) emphasized the high frequency of blue spherical beads at the succeeding Susquehannock Washington Boro village compared with frequencies on contemporaneous New York Iroquois sites. They stressed that high percentages of spherical blue beads are diagnostic of English-derived, seventeenth-century trade assemblages, and the high frequency of occurrence of such beads at the Washington Boro village might indicate the initiation of trade with William Claiborne at Kent and Palmer

Islands in Chesapeake Bay. The high frequencies of the robin's-egg blue IIa40 beads at both the Monongahela Ingraham-Spragg and Foley Farm sites and the Washington Boro village reflect the beginning of the English fur trade in Chesapeake Bay in 1631/32. The abundance of spherical blue beads at the terminal Monongahela Foley Farm phase sites could indicate late contact with the Susquehannock during the early Washington Boro phase or, more likely, direct acquisition from Henry Fleet and the English at Anacostan at the falls of the Potomac River in the early 1630s. Further, Sempowski (1994) saw no convincing evidence for large quantities of Dutch-derived trade goods among the Susquehannock until the Susquehannock's mission to Manhattan in 1626, when they petitioned for direct trade with the Dutch, and the establishment of Fort Nassau on the lower Delaware River by the Dutch in the same year. This suggests that Fitzgerald's (e.g., Fitzgerald, Knight, and Bain 1995) GBP 2 and Dutch Polychrome period beads on Monongahela sites might have reached the upper Ohio River valley from Ontario and western New York, as did the aforementioned IVa12 cored monochrome beads.

Lapham (1995) also noted that the IIIc'3 blue twisted and squared beads from the Ingraham-Spragg site, while resembling a Nueva Cadiz variety (Herbstritt 1988), have also been recovered from the Seneca Dutch Hollow, Factory Hollow, and Warren sites, as well as from the Washington Boro village site. Significantly, she also reported no GBP 3 red straw monochrome or cored beads (Ia1 and IIIa1) from any Foley Farm phase sites. These varieties postdate 1625/30 in Ontario and the abandonment of the Washington Boro village in the 1630s (Fitzgerald, Knight, and Bain 1995; Kent 1984).

Finally, the four glass beads documented from the LaPoe No. 2 site in Monongalia County, West Virginia, suggest a slightly earlier occupation at the beginning of the Foley Farm subphase. The LaPoe No. 2 site has no IVa40 beads, but there are two chevron beads. There is also one white oval bead (IIa15), part of Fitzgerald's (Fitzgerald, Knight, and Bain 1995) GBP 2 and Sempowski's (1994) Indigo and White Bead Complex, which dates from about 1600 to 1625/30. This type also occurs in very low frequencies at the Ingraham-Spragg and Foley Farm sites (1 percent and 0.3 percent, respectively; Lapham 1995), suggesting a partial overlap in occupations.

SHELL ARTIFACTS AND CLAY PIPES.   The distribution of native-made whelk shell earspools or "spoons" and acorn/apple ring bowl ceramic pipes suggests that the Monongahela and downriver Fort Ancient people traded with groups in western New York and southwestern Ontario (see Drooker and Cowan, this volume). Whelk shell earspools have been recovered from protohistoric Madisonville horizon villages in West Virginia, Kentucky, and Ohio (Brashler and Moxley 1990; Drooker 1997a; Griffin 1943; Hanson 1975; Mayer-Oakes 1955; Moxley 1988a) as well as from the Western Seneca Power House and Dann villages in the Genesee Valley (Hayes 1989; Sempowski 1989). Such earspools also occur on historic Petun (Charles Garrad, personal communication 1987) and Neutral (W. Kenyon 1982) sites in southern Ontario. Although these distinctive artifacts have been documented from a number of sites in the mid-South and Southeast (Drooker 1997a), there is little question that they are the product of the Dallas phase people of eastern Tennessee. Their occurrence in west-central New York and southern Ontario may be due to the Fort Ancient trade or raiding.

An Iroquois acorn ring bowl pipe with a beaver incised on the underside of its stem was reported from the Clover phase Hardin Village site in Kentucky (Converse 1973), and several Iroquois pipes have been reported from the Madisonville site (see Drooker and Cowan, this volume). Acorn ring bowl pipes first appear in Seneca territory at the Cameron site (ca. 1595–1610/14), and they persist until at least the occupation of the Marsh and Dann sites (ca. 1645–1665) (Wray, Sempowski, and Saunders 1991). The acorn ring bowl pipe fragment from the Monongahela Huffman Farm–Cook Pacemaker Company site documents the persistence of the Johnston phase into the seventeenth century and the protohistoric period. A second fragment was recovered from the intrusive Riker-Whittlesey McKees Rocks Village site (Buker 1968). These rare artifacts also argue for a connection between aboriginal groups in the upper and middle Ohio River valley and Iroquoian groups dwelling around the lower Great Lakes.

Other evidence also suggests that the Great Lakes–St. Lawrence River system was the source of European goods and the focus of the fur trade for the upper and middle Ohio River valley before 1630. Pendergast (1989) has documented the large number of whole *Busycon* spp. whelk and columella beads on protohistoric and historic Neutral, Huron, and Petun sites. The two most common species are the sinistrally whorled *Busycon sinistrum* Hollister, 1958 (the lightning whelk), and the *Busycon laeostomum* Kent, 1982 (the snow whelk). Many of the columella beads collected from Ontario Iroquois sites, although not identifiable at the species level, are sinistrally whorled and likely derived from these *Busycon* species. The lightning whelk occurs from New Jersey southward to the Gulf of Mexico coast east of the mouth of the Mississippi River. The snow whelk is limited in distribution from the southern New Jersey coast to northern Virginia, essentially the Chesapeake Bay latitudes (Pendergast 1989).

Pendergast (1991) has argued persuasively that the middlemen in the Chesapeake Bay whelk shell trade with the Neutral were the Massawomeck, whom Captain John Smith encountered at the head of Chesapeake Bay in the summer of 1608. Pendergast believes that the Massawomeck dwelt essentially west of the Allegheny Mountains—at least in the 1620s and early 1630s—and were synonymous with one or more groups identified as the Atiovandaron on the 1641

Jean Bourdon map *Nouvelle France* (see Heidenreich 1988; Steckley 1990) and as the Attiouandarons on Nicholas Sanson's *Le Canada ou Nouvelle France* map of 1656.

A whole whelk shell and two large pendants cut from the walls of whelk shells came from the terminal Youghiogheny phase Beazell School site on a tributary of the Monongahela River (Cottrell n.d.). These artifacts may indicate that the terminal Youghiogheny phase sites equate with one of the four allied tribes that composed the Massawomeck nation enumerated by Henry Fleet's brother Edward in 1632 (see Hoffman 1964; Pendergast 1991).

Exchange with Chesapeake Bay Algonquians and Iroquois

Susquehannock villages along the lower Susquehanna River (Kent 1984) and the south branch of the Potomac River (Brashler 1987; MacCord 1952; Manson and MacCord 1941, 1944; Maymon and Davis 1998) could have been an even more convenient source of European goods for the Monongahela and Fort Ancient people than were western New York and southern Ontario. However, there is a paucity of such goods on aboriginal sites in the Chesapeake Bay Tidewater area before 1630, relative to the numbers reported at sites in the lower Great Lakes area. This is surprising, considering the number of Englishmen operating in the Chesapeake area from 1580 onward, but as Fausz (1984, 1985) noted, English trade from Chesapeake Bay did not begin until Henry Fleet's Potomac River expedition in 1631 and William Clairborne's establishment of trading posts on Kent and Palmer Islands. English trade prior to the 1630s was primarily for food surpluses to supplement shortfalls at the James River and New England settlements, so it is probable that little European trade material from Chesapeake Bay reached the Susquehannock before 1630. In fact, few robin's-egg blue beads, if any, apparently were recovered from the Moorefield village site, although several Dutch Polychrome period beads were found (Maymon and Davis 1998). This in turn suggests that the Moorefield village might have been abandoned before 1631, or if it continued to be occupied into the 1630s, then these Susquehannocks were temporarily cut off from access to Henry Fleet and his rivals on the Potomac River.

M. Smith (1988) has noted that the glass beads from middle and upper Ohio River valley protohistoric sites are (or could well be) those distributed through the French-Dutch-English fur trade. Bulbous collared and valenced para-Iroquoian ceramics, copper or brass spirals, and possibly the tumbled blue star and the round, uncored robin's-egg blue beads suggest contact between the Monongahela and the Susquehannock, yet the admittedly scanty evidence points to a northern terminus for the middle and upper Ohio Valley beaver pelt trade. Additionally, according to English sources, the early seventeenth-century Susquehannock appeared to be as intimidated by the periodic incursions of the trans-Appalachian Massawomeck as were their Algonquian-speaking neighbors in the upper Chesapeake Bay area (Pendergast 1991). Although I endorse Pendergast's (1989, 1991) arguments that the Chesapeake Bay fur trade was grafted onto the preexisting Neutral–Massawomeck–Eastern Shore Algonquian whelk shell trade network, present data do not suggest that Chesapeake Bay was a source of European trade goods for the interior tribal groups until after about 1630. Within five years of the initiation of the English trade out of Chesapeake Bay, the Monongahela had disappeared from the upper Ohio River valley as an identifiable cultural entity, and it is only the small, spherical, blue glass beads and tumbled blue star beads that hint at the late and fleeting Monongahela reorientation to the middle Atlantic.

Demise and Linguistic/Ethnic Identification

As a recognizable entity, Monongahela culture disappeared around 1635. Dutch documents and archaeological data suggest that the Monongahela were dispersed primarily by the Seneca. It is notable that the disappearance of the Monongahela corresponds to a drop in the quantities of European trade goods found on sites of Graybill's (1987) terminal Fort Ancient Orchard phase (ca. 1640–1690) in the middle Ohio River valley (see Drooker and Cowan, this volume). The paucity of European trade goods on such terminal Fort Ancient sites stands in marked contrast to the large volume of such goods at the Rolfe Lee Farm No. 1 site, the latest village of the earlier Clover phase.

This disruption of middle and upper Ohio River valley trade around 1635 is significant in light of Sempowski's (1989) recognition of fluctuations in the quantities of marine shell at protohistoric and early historic period Seneca villages. Between about 1570 and 1610/14, the incidence of marine shell in individual graves is between 15 and 20 percent. For the period 1610/14–1625/28, it ranges between 2 and 5 percent, and the frequency of marine shell in villages dating to circa 1625/28–1640/42 is similarly low. Yet at the same time, the frequency of European brass, copper, iron, and glass beads increases moderately, indicating that the Seneca were not cut off from access to other trade items. In succeeding Seneca villages, circa 1640/42–1655, both the frequency and quantity of marine shell exploded (Sempowski 1989). This suggests that after 1610 the Seneca were excluded from the Neutral-Massawomeck-Chesapeake Bay shell trade, but that shortly after they destroyed the Monongahela as a cultural unit or units (ca. 1635), their access to this valued commodity improved dramatically. Alternatively, it is possible that the Monongahela-Massawomeck were eliminated from their position as middlemen in the trade of the highly valued whelk shell, much as the Seneca destroyed or dispersed other groups who exercised control of the beaver resources in the upper Ohio Valley and the upper Great Lakes (Brose 1983; Hunt 1940; R. Mason 1981).

Herbstritt (1993b) believes that the large volume of whelk shell detritus at the Washington Boro village in the lower Susquehanna River valley implies that these Susquehannock were Pendergast's (1991) whelk shell trading Massawomeck. Reassessment of the age of the preceding Schultz village (Sempowski 1994) places the Washington Boro village occupation after 1620. Perhaps the Susquehannock took advantage of the dispersal of the Massawomeck-Monongahela middlemen in the whelk shell trade at the hands of the Seneca, or conspired with the Seneca. A legend regarding the Massawomeck–Black Minqua on the 1673 Augustine Herrman map reads: "Where formerly those Black Mincquas came over and as far as the Delaware to trade but the Sassquahana and Sinnicus Indians went over and destroyed that very great nation" (Hoffman 1964).

A final argument for placing the dispersal of the Monongahela before 1635 is the lack of Kidd and Kidd's (1970) red tubular beads (Ia1, IIIa1) from the terminal Foley Farm phase villages (Lapham 1995), although these sites do have other beads that seem to characterize some ossuary and village assemblages in Ontario and the Niagara frontier that span the GBP 2–3 transition (Fitzgerald 1990a; Stark 1995). The monochrome red tubular beads characterize Fitzgerald's (1982c, 1983, 1990a; Fitzgerald, Knight, and Bain 1995) GBP 3 assemblage, which spans the years 1625/30–1651. Fitzgerald has documented a distinct break in both the quantity and variety of glass beads entering the lower Great Lakes before and after the hiatus caused when English traders seized New France between 1628 and 1632. These same types occur in the lower Susquehanna River valley after the abandonment of the Washington Boro village and rise rapidly in frequency on later Strickler phase sites (Kent 1984).

These artifact changes take on new significance in light of a letter from Leonard Calvert, governor of Maryland, to his business partner in England in late May 1634. He noted that the Virginians (presumably Henry Fleet) apparently had been trading with the Massawomeck for beaver pelts on the Potomac River that spring. This is the last coeval reference to the Massawomeck (Pendergast 1991).

The linguistic ascription and tribal identify of the Monongahela may never be satisfactorily resolved. They have been variously ascribed to Central Algonquian (George 1994; McMichael 1968; Swauger 1974; Weslager 1948) and Siouan (George 1980, 1996) linguistic stocks. In spite of the Monongahela people's clearly non–northern Iroquoian material culture, some ethnohistorians hint at their having a vague Iroquoian linguistic affiliation, specifically an affiliation with the Black Minqua (Weslager 1948). I suggest that the Monongahela, rather than other previously identified tribal candidates (Fenton 1940; Hoffman 1964), were the Black Minqua referred to by the early seventeenth-century Swedes and Dutch, and that they perforce spoke an Iroquoian language.

Hoffman (1964) has clearly documented the Black Minqua's close relationship, if not synonymy, with the White Minqua or Susquehannock after about 1640. Although Hoffman (1964) argued that the Black Minqua–Massawomeck were the Erie, archaeological evidence—generally unavailable to him at the time—negates that argument. The protohistoric Erie, whether those in the Niagara frontier (e.g., M. White 1961, 1967, 1976) or those in Chautauqua County, New York, and Erie County, Pennsylvania (e.g., Carpenter, Pfirman, and Schoff 1949; Parker 1907), produced ceramics quite distinct from those manufactured by the late McFate and Chautauqua phase people who occupied the glaciated Allegheny Plateau section to the southeast and south (Johnson 1994a; Johnson, Richardson, and Bohnert 1979). Protohistoric and terminal Late Woodland period Erie pottery has been recovered exclusively from sites along the narrow Lake Erie Plain in Pennsylvania and New York. There is no archaeological evidence that the Eriechronon—at least as identified by post–Middleport horizon ceramics—ever operated in the Allegheny Plateau section of Pennsylvania.

It seems certain from Hoffman's (1964) argument that the Black Minqua and the Massawomeck were an Iroquoian-speaking group closely associated with, if not the same as, part of the post-1640 Susquehannock. Massawomeck is an Algonquian word applied by the Powhattan and other eastern Algonquians to the trans-Appalachian raiders and traders (to borrow Pendergast's [1991] appellation) who came down the Potomac during the first four decades of the seventeenth century. Pendergast (1991) indicated that three of the four names of the constituent Massawomeck tribes—Tonhoga, Usserahak, and Shaunnetowa—were probably Iroquoian words; these names were given to Henry Fleet in 1632 by the Massawomeck themselves. Only the fourth village or tribal name, Mosticum, apparently is not clearly an Iroquoian word.

References to the homeland of the Black Minqua–Massawomeck west of the headwaters of the Susquehanna and Potomac Rivers can be interpreted in two ways. The first scenario sees the Black Minqua as a division of the Susquehannock (as they were known to the Swedes, the Dutch, and, indeed, the Chesapeake Bay English) whose former homeland lay west of Blue/Great North Mountain and the Great Valley section of the Ridge and Valley province. They could be represented archaeologically by the Quiggle or Bell/McFate-Kalgren-Quiggle complex, the final prehistoric occupation in the west branch valley of the Susquehanna River (Herbstritt and Kent 1990; Matlack 1986, 1987; I. Smith 1984). Alternatively, they could be represented archaeologically by the occupants of the pre-Schultz and Schultz phase Susquehannock villages along the south branch of the Potomac River (Brashler 1987; MacCord 1952; Manson and MacCord 1941, 1944; Maymon and Davis 1998). Indeed, Herbstritt and Kent (1990) argued that at the Pancake site, the earliest site in this sequence, the mix of ceramic decorative styles and shapes suggested that popula-

tion amalgamation and intrusion into the south branch of the Potomac River might have preceded the initial Susquehannock incursion into the lower Susquehanna River valley. Although the south branch Susquehannock presumably were Iroquoian speakers, they seem to represent only a single, relatively small series of sequential village removals. This does not seem to equate with the four contemporaneous villages or tribes of the Massawomeck.

Yet the argument favored here is that the homeland of the Black Minqua–Massawomeck lay west of the Allegheny Front in the upper Ohio River valley. The glaciated Allegheny Plateau of northwestern Pennsylvania and southwestern New York, as well as the upper Allegheny River, seems to have been abandoned by village horticulturists around 1550 in response to the Neo-Boreal climatic episode, which shortened the growing season in an area that was marginal for prehistoric maize production (Johnson 1994a; Johnson, Richardson, and Bohnert 1979). The late migration of at least part of the McFate phase people into the lower Kiskiminetas River valley, where they mixed with indigenous Monongahela groups to form the Johnston phase after 1500/25, may reflect Pendergast's (1991) argument for an ultimate lower Great Lakes origin for the Massawomeck. After 1550/75, the only viable candidate for a trans-Appalachian Black Minqua is the protohistoric Monongahela.

If, after their defeat and dispersal by the Seneca around 1635, the majority of the Monongahela sought refuge with the White Minqua–Susquehannock on the lower Susquehanna River, then those refugees were the Black Minqua referred to in the Swedish and Dutch documents of the 1640s and 1650s. They still may have been sallying forth over the Alleghenies yearly to trap beaver in their former territory. The Black Minqua–Massawomeck could be one of the White Minqua nations enumerated as signatories to a treaty with the Swedes at Fort Trinity in Delaware in June 1655 and to another treaty with Maryland in 1661 (Becker 1987, 1991; Jennings 1978).

The large influx of nontraditional Susquehannock Strickler Cordmarked ceramics in post–Washington Boro village times may signal the arrival of the bulk of the Black Minqua on the Susquehanna River. Strickler Cordmarked ware first appears at the Washington Boro site village, which was occupied after 1615/20 (following Sempowski 1994), but it never exceeds 8 percent in any of the village cemetery assemblages. It reaches a frequency of 75–82 percent at the Strickler site village and cemeteries around 1645–1665 (Kent 1984; Kinsey 1959). Vessel rims of the rounded-collar variety of Strickler Cordmarked ware (Kent 1984; Kinsey 1959) are similar to vessel rims from several Youghiogheny and early Foley Farm phase sites. The "low collared" variant of Strickler Cordmarked figured by Kinsey (1959) resembles the valenced vessels recovered from Foley Farm sites in Greene County (Mayer-Oakes 1955).

Despite drastic population losses to the ravages of European-introduced epidemics among the Ontario and Five Nations Iroquois in the late 1630s and early 1640s (e.g., Trigger 1976), the estimated Susquehannock population increased dramatically between the occupation of the Washington Boro village (ca. 1,700 individuals) and that of the Strickler village (2,900 individuals). Humpf and Hatch (1994) suggested that migration might have played a significant role in this increase. I suggest that the majority of those immigrants were refugee Monongahelas.

An additional clue to the archaeological identity of the Black Minqua is found in a reference by a Dutchman, Adriaen van der Donk, in 1653 (cited in Hoffman 1964). Van der Donk noted that the Black Minqua were so identified "because they wear a black badge on their breast, and not because they are really black." P. Schuyler Miller (personal communication 1972) suggested that this was a reference to the cannel coal pendants common on Monongahela sites. Cannel coal pendants are rare to absent in Susquehannock assemblages (Kent 1984) and are also unreported from Mc-Fate and Chautauqua phase and Erie sites in northwestern Pennsylvania and western New York. They are also rare to absent in Monongahela Johnston phase component artifact inventories (Dragoo 1955; George 1997; Robson 1958).

Although cannel coal pendants are common on Fort Ancient sites, these villages are far removed from the lower Susquehanna Valley. Further, the protohistoric Clover, Madisonville, and Orchard phase Fort Ancient people are generally assumed to have been the Ontoagannha or Chiouanons, the Shawnee, who spoke a "corrupt Algonquin" language (Griffin 1943). These people could not have been the Iroquoian-speaking Black Minqua. The specific connection between an Iroquoian-speaking group and black badges can apply only to the Monongahela in this context.

This interpretation is congruent with a rarely noted second Attiouanderons tribal appellation on the 1656 Nicolas Sanson map *Le Canada ou Nouvelle France* (see Heidenreich 1971). The Huron referred to the Neutral as Attiouanderons, a reciprocal term that the Huron and Neutral assigned to each other, meaning "people who speak a slightly different language" (Trigger 1969b). The second Attiouanderons appellation appears south of the lands identified as those belonging to the "Eriechronons ou N. du Chat," west of the Appalachian Mountains and generally in the upper Ohio River valley. Significantly, what is essentially the same name, Atiovandarons, appears in the same area on the earlier Taunton *Novvelle France* map attributed to Jean Bourdon (see Fig. 6.7). The map was apparently drafted late in 1641 (Heidenreich 1988; Steckley 1990). This map and Sanson's 1656 map were arguably based on an earlier map acquired or compiled by the Jesuit Father Paul Ragueneau in 1639 or 1640 (Heidenreich 1988; Steckley 1990). This earlier map could not have followed the dispersal of the Monongahela by more than a few years at most, and it strongly suggests

the presence in the upper Ohio River valley of an Iroquoian group that spoke a dialect close to Huron.

George (1997) has argued that only the Johnston phase Monongahela in the Kiskiminetas River valley were the Massawomeck, on the basis of evidence there for the mid-sixteenth-century intrusion of people from northwestern Pennsylvania. He assigns the majority of the Monongahela—the Foley Farm and Youghiogheny phase population—to a Central Algonquian–speaking group (George 1998). The difficulty with this interpretation is that no European goods have been recovered from Johnston phase sites, and only the acorn ring bowl pipe from the Cook Pacemaker–Huffman Farm site demonstrates that at least one Johnston village persisted into the seventeenth century. This contrasts dramatically with the thousands of European goods recovered from Foley Farm and Youghiogheny phase sites. If the Johnston phase people alone were the Massawomeck, where are the trade goods, and who were the Foley Farm and Youghiogheny phase people?

Conclusion

The late prehistoric and protohistoric period Monongahela people were an Iroquoian-speaking confederation of tribes. They can be equated with the Black Minqua, who lived with the White Minqua–Susquehannock on the lower Susquehanna River in the 1640s and 1650s. They were termed Massawomeck and appeared on Chesapeake Bay and the lower Potomac River earlier in the seventeenth century as raiders and traders of whelk shell and beaver pelts. Some configuration of the protohistoric Foley Farm, Johnston, and Youghiogheny phase Monongahela constituted the four component tribes of the Massawomeck nation.

The Monongahela were dispersed, probably by the Seneca, around 1635, as much for their role in the Chesapeake Bay–Neutral whelk shell trade as for control of the beaver pelt trade in the upper Ohio River valley. Although a few Monongahelas may have been absorbed, willingly or otherwise, into the Seneca tribe, their presence at Seneca sites of the period is difficult to document. Although shell-tempered ceramics occur at the Eastern Seneca satellite Cornish village, they are uncommon, and the only diagnostic shell-tempered vessel fragments that are not renditions of traditional Seneca types are from a Fort Ancient Madisonville Cordmarked jar and a Susquehannock Washington Boro Incised pot. Cursory examination of ceramic assemblages from late eastern Fort Ancient sites also failed to identify any clearly Monongahela rim sherds or vessels.

After their dispersal, circa 1635, the bulk of the Monongahela refugees seem eventually to have sought refuge with the Susquehannock in the lower Susquehanna River basin, where they were later known to the Swedes and Dutch as the Black Minqua.

8

Transformation of the Fort Ancient Cultures of the Central Ohio Valley

For most of eastern North America, the seven centuries between A.D. 1000 and 1700 bracket the emergence, florescence, and radical transformation of societies whose economies were based primarily on field agriculture. In the central Ohio Valley, these agricultural people are known archaeologically as the Fort Ancient culture or tradition (Griffin 1943; Prufer and Shane 1970). Unlike many of the other regions discussed in this book, the central Ohio Valley did not enter the realm of recorded history until the later half of the eighteenth century, when settlers began arriving in what is now West Virginia, Kentucky, and Ohio. By then, Native Americans had abandoned much of the area. There are almost no earlier accounts of the region by European explorers, missionaries, or traders. None of the colonial powers had yet established a presence in the territory west of the Alleghenies and immediately south of the Great Lakes, although France, in particular, certainly attempted to collect information about the Ohio River valley and its inhabitants.

Although the early historical record is mute on the people who lived in the central Ohio Valley, their archaeological remains say a great deal. That unwritten record forms the basis for this chapter and provides a case study in the transformation of human populations in the face of developments far from their home territory, over which they exercise no control. Archaeologists and ethnohistorians have reached no consensus about which historically named group or groups might have been descended from Fort Ancient populations, although Shawnee and related Central Algonquian groups are most often suggested (see summaries in Callender 1978a: 630–631; Drooker 1997a: 103–105, 227–230; Griffin 1943: 11–35; Henderson, Jobe, and Turnbow 1986). Most of these groups were first met and described in historical documents at locations far from their original homelands, a century and a half after European powers began their encroachment in North America. Whoever the descendants of the Fort Ancient people might have been, the transformations that took place in the Ohio Valley during the seventeenth century marked the evolution of one society into another.

Fort Ancient Geography and Resources

Fort Ancient communities were all located within the drainage system of the central Ohio River valley (Fig. 8.1). The range of preferred settlement locations changed over time, and much of this territory might well have been utilized primarily for hunting after about 1450.

The region lay at a crossroads of water and land communication routes. The main southeastern portal through the Appalachians was via the New-Kanawha River valley, which gave access to the headwaters of a number of major rivers south of Chesapeake Bay. The Ohio River provided a major northeast-southwest communication axis. Northwestern Ohio and regions to the west could be reached

PENELOPE B. DROOKER AND
C. WESLEY COWAN

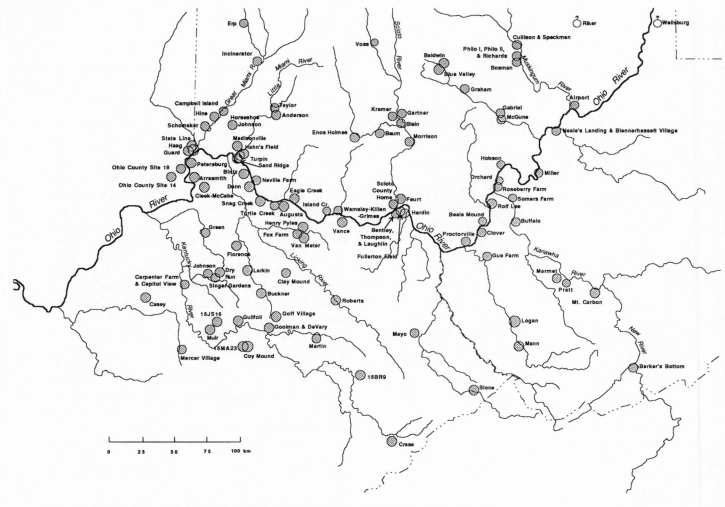

Figure 8.1. Important, currently recognized Fort Ancient and Wellsburg sites (after Drooker 1997a: Fig. 4-2).

readily via the Great Miami. Historically and probably prehistorically, an important system of trails led south cross-country from the Ohio River near Cincinnati to the Cumberland Gap and along the northern flank of the Appalachians.

Fort Ancient territory encompassed much geomorphological and biological diversity, including portions of three physiographic provinces (Church 1987: 40–60; Drooker 1997a: 70–72; Graybill 1981: 40–58; Henderson 1992: 23–27; Nass 1987: 15–27; Wagner 1987: 11–32). In all three zones, floodplains of the Ohio River and its major tributaries provide fertile agricultural soil today, whereas upland soils vary in their suitability for horticulture. Although this area is not on a major flyway for bird migration, the varied hydrology, topography, and plant cover once supported a broad range of edible wildlife. Large mammals included deer, elk, bear, bobcat, and, sometime after A.D. 1450, bison (Breitburg 1992; Tankersley 1986a; Tankersley and Adams 1991). Salt licks, attractive to large game animals, are common in northeastern Kentucky and southeastern Ohio.

History of Fort Ancient Research

Much of the basic research that defined the Fort Ancient culture took place in the last quarter of the nineteenth century and the first quarter of the twentieth. It was conducted by archaeologists from the Peabody Museum of Harvard University (Hooton and Willoughby 1920; Putnam 1886, 1973a, 1973b), the American Museum of Natural History (H. Smith 1910), and the Ohio Archaeological and Historical Society (Mills 1904, 1906, 1917; Shetrone 1926). Their excavation methods and documentation, though generally more than adequate by the standards of the time, leave much to be desired by the modern archaeologist. The materials excavated by these and other pioneers (e.g., Funkhouser and Webb 1928) formed the basis for James B. Griffin's massive *The Fort Ancient Aspect,* which organized collections from the central Ohio Valley into a McKernian classificatory scheme (Griffin 1943: 327–334) that remains largely intact.

Some of the first stratigraphically controlled excavations in the region took place in the lower Little Miami Valley during the late 1940s under the aegis of the Cincinnati Museum of Natural History, now the Cincinnati Museum Center, revealing the Late Woodland–Fort Ancient transition (Miller et al. 1997; Oehler 1950, 1973). Excavations from two important eastern Fort Ancient protohistoric sites that were published two decades later (Hanson 1966, 1975) were among the first to map the layout of structures within sites. Archaeological research in the central Scioto Valley in the

1960s produced an important volume (Prufer and Shane 1970) that reviewed Griffin's original framework in light of an emerging chronology made possible through radiocarbon dating. It replaced his geographically oriented "foci" (Griffin 1943: Map 1) with chronologically oriented "phases."

During the 1980s and 1990s, Fort Ancient archaeology witnessed a florescence as researchers throughout the central Ohio Valley devoted considerable energy to refining local and regional chronologies and investigating settlement and economic patterns and mortuary programs (Carskadden 1994; Church 1987; Cowan 1986, 1987; Cowan et al. 1990; Drooker 1997a, 1998; Essenpreis 1982; Graybill 1981; Heilman, Lilias, and Turnbow 1988; Henderson, ed., 1992; Maslowski 1984b; Nass 1987; Riggs 1986; Sharp 1990; Wagner 1987). Although most new excavations were small in scale—not extensive enough to reveal complete site layouts—the use of fine-grained stratigraphic excavation, radiocarbon dating by level, and flotation sampling, among other approaches, opened new windows to archaeologists. These studies have added tremendously to our knowledge about the late prehistory and protohistory of the central valley, and we now can better evaluate the concept of a Fort Ancient culture and its development.

Chronological Framework

Roughly speaking, the Fort Ancient tradition spans the eleventh through the seventeenth centuries. Fixing and ordering Fort Ancient occupations of the central Ohio Valley in time has been a focus of much of the recent research. Radiometric dating, thermoluminescence, seriation, cultural stratigraphy, and "index fossil" artifacts have all been used to define and temporally order sites and regional phases in sequence (Fig. 8.2). Although at least 150 radiocarbon dates from some 50 sites were available by 1996, coverage for Fort Ancient territory as a whole is still sparse. For example, there are no dates for a number of important sites with Late Fort Ancient components such as Hardin, Orchard, and Feurt, and many large, multicomponent sites have only one or two dates (Table 8.1).

Nevertheless, the available absolute dates have allowed archaeologists in the central Ohio Valley to sequence a

TIME SCALE, A.D.	ARCHAEO-LOGICAL SEQUENCE	HISTORICAL SEQUENCE	PHASES				
			Southern Ohio			Northern Kentucky	Western West Virginia
			Lower Miamis	Upper Miamis	Central Muskingum	& Lower Scioto	
1800		Historic Period					
	Contact Period						
1700						Montour (1550-1750)	
	Late Fort Ancient	Protohistoric Period					Clover (1550-1640)
1600			Mariemont (1400/50-1650/70)		Wellsburg (1500-1650)		
1500	(Madisonville Horizon)	(de Soto, 1540) (Columbus, 1492)				Gist (1400-1550)	Early Clover (1450-1550)
1400	Middle Fort Ancient		Schomaker (1250-1400)		Philo		Blennerhasset (1250-1450)
1300		Prehistoric Period		Anderson (1100-1400)		Manion (1200-1400)	
1200	Early Fort Ancient		Turpin (1000-1250)		Cole (1150-1250/1300)		Roseberry (1050-1250)
1100						Croghan (1000-1200)	
1000							
	Woodland						

Figure 8.2. Generalized Fort Ancient chronology and selected phases. Sources of phase designations are as follows: for the lower Great and Little Miami Rivers, Cowan 1986: 131, 143, 147, 1987; for the upper Miamis, Essenpreis 1982: 201–205; for the Central Muskingum with related Wellsburg phase, Carskadden 1994; for northern Kentucky, including the lower Scioto River, Henderson, Pollack, and Turnbow 1992: 255–278; for West Virginia, Graybill 1986: 1 and, for the Clover phases, Maslowski 1984b: 148. Graybill (1986, 1987) defined a Madisonville phase for the entire Fort Ancient region at circa A.D. 1450–1640. He later extended and divided it into the Clover (1450–1640) and Orchard (1640–1690) phases. See text for discussion.

Table 8.1
Radiocarbon Dates for Late Fort Ancient and Wellsburg Sites

	Sample No.	Years B.P.	Calibrated Date A.D., with 1-Sigma Range
Arrasmith, KY	RL 801	230 ± 100	1527 (1664) 1954
	UGA 5625	650 ± 60	1287 (1302, 1373, 1381) 1397
	RL 800	650 ± 100	1280 (1302, 1373, 1381) 1411
Augusta, KY	BETA 13365	210 ± 60	1650 (1669, 1783, 1797, 1948, 1952) 1954
	BETA 11855	470 ± 90	1408 (1437) 1490
	BETA 18183	470 ± 70	1412 (1437) 1481
Bentley, KY	BETA 18182	230 ± 50	1647 (1664) 1954
Big Bone Lick, KY	M 1352	500 ± 100	1330 (1429) 1480
	UGA 4291	530 ± 105	1318 (1414) 1447
Buffalo, WV	UGA 304	270 ± 120	1485 (1650) 1954
	UGA 303	780 ± 70	1212 (1263, 1273, 1275) 1289
Bosman, OH	I 16589	340 ± 80	1447 (1523, 1565, 1578, 1627) 1653
	I 16593	360 ± 80	1442 (1498, 1512, 1516, 1599, 1618) 1648
	I 16604	400 ± 80	1435 (1454, 1457, 1478) 1635
Campbell Island, OH	BETA 17995	440 ± 70	1424 (1443) 1610
	BETA 14222	540 ± 60	1330 (1412) 1436
Carroll-Oregonia Rd, OH	DIC 1042	480 ± 90	1406 (1436) 1486
Cullison, OH	I 16955	310 ± 80	1484 (1638) 1664
	I 16954	340 ± 80	1447 (1523, 1565, 1578, 1627) 1653
Clover, WV	DIC 3366	370 ± 45	1448 (1492, 1604, 1610) 1633
	DIC 3367	400 ± 50	1440 (1454, 1457, 1478) 1623
	DIC 3087, -88, -89	750 ± 190	1044 (1281) 1409
Fox Farm, KY	BETA 11856	390 ± 70	1439 (1486) 1635
	BETA 11857	530 ± 70	1330 (1414) 1440
	BETA 13364	590 ± 60	1302 (1332, 1342, 1395) 1416
	BETA 13363	790 ± 70	1209 (1261) 1287
Goolman, KY	DIC 2339	130 ± 55	1675 (1695, 1727, 1813, 1920, 1954) 1955
	DIC 2509	210 ± 50	1653 (1669, 1783, 1797, 1948, 1952) 1954
	DIC 2338	210 ± 100	1638 (1669, 1783, 1797, 1948, 1952) 1954
	DIC 2508	550 ± 40	1331 (1410) 1427
Hahn's Field, OH	AA 10223-2	285 ± 45	1527 (1646) 1660
	AA 10223-1	345 ± 45	1483 (1522, 1584, 1625) 1642
	AA 10222	375 ± 60	1443 (1491) 1637
Larkin, KY	BETA 19067	210 ± 70	1647 (1669, 1783, 1797, 1948, 1952) 1954
	BETA 19068	370 ± 80	1441 (1492, 1604, 1610) 1645
Madisonville, OH	BETA 51845	170 ± 50	1667 (1680, 1742, 1750, 1759, 1806, 1937, 1954) 1954
	BETA 45674	290 ± 45	1525 (1645) 1658
	AA-10220-2	292 ± 33	1529 (1644) 1653
	AA-10221-2	295 ± 50	1521 (1643) 1658
	BETA 45676	300 ± 60	1495 (1642) 1660
	BETA 51846	310 ± 70	1488 (1638) 1660
	AA-10217	315 ± 40	1502 (1534, 1539, 1637) 1649
	AA-10215	370 ± 45	1448 (1492, 1604, 1610) 1633
	AA-10220–1	392 ± 30	1445 (1485) 1619
	AA-10221–1	400 ± 55	1439 (1454, 1457, 1478) 1625
	UGA 5287	475 ± 95	1406 (1436) 1490
	AA-10219	485 ± 45	1413 (1434) 1444
	AA-10218	490 ± 55	1410 (1433) 1444
	AA-11774	514 ± 66	1333 (1423) 1442
	BETA 51847	690 ± 50	1282 (1292) 1386
	BETA 45675	710 ± 50	1278 (1288) 1376
	AA-10216–1	965 ± 110	987 (1033, 1143, 1147) 1212
	UGA 5285	985 ± 90	987 (1025) 1187
Morrison Village, OH	M 1761	260 ± 100	1496 (1653) 1954
	M 1760	290 ± 100	1485 (1645) 1954
	OWU 181	400 ± 115	1421 (1454, 1457, 1478) 1646

Table 8.1 *continued*

	Sample No.	Years B.P.	Calibrated Date A.D., with 1-Sigma Range
Neale's Landing, WV	UGA 955	365 ± 100	1438 (1494, 1601, 1616) 1651
	UGA 954	370 ± 155	1415 (1492, 1604, 1610) 1952
	UGA 951	430 ± 75	1426 (1445) 1620
	UGA 952	660 ± 135	1260 (1299) 1417
Petersburg, KY	BETA 46936	500 ± 50	1409 (1429) 1442
	BETA 46937	880 ± 60	1043 (1163, 1169, 1192, 1203, 1206) 1256
	BETA 46935	980 ± 50	1101 (1027) 1153
Riker, OH	OWU 175	390 ± 170	1408 (1486) 1667
Rolf Lee, WV	UGA 2638	220 ± 95	1534 (1667) 1954
South Fort, OH	BETA 74459	360 ± 80	1442 (1498, 1512, 1516, 1599, 1618) 1648
	BETA 74460	730 ± 60	1260 (1284) 1298
	BETA 74461	910 ± 70	1026 (1156) 1216
Speckman, OH	I 16953	230 ± 80	1638 (1664) 1954
	I 17358	300 ± 80	1488 (1642) 1667
	I 16952	400 ± 80	1435 (1454) 1635
Thompson, KY	BETA 11851	110 ± 60	1679 (1710, 1718, 1820, 1831, 1882, 1914, 1954) 1955
	BETA 11853	400 ± 70	1437 (1454, 1457, 1478) 1631
	BETA 13367	810 ± 60	1164 (1224, 1227, 1245, 1257) 1281
	BETA 13368	920 ± 100	1003 (1071, 1080, 1128, 1136, 1154) 1256

Sources: Data are from Cowan 1986; Drooker 1997a; Freidin 1987; Graybill 1981; Hanson 1975; Harper 1994; Henderson 1993; James Morton, personal communication 1994, 1995; Prufer and Andors 1967; Sharp 1990; Tankersley 1986b. Calibration is after Stuiver and Reimer 1993. See Drooker 1997a: Tables 4-1, 4-8, 6-1 for two-sigma ranges.

Note: **Boldfaced** site names indicate the presence of metal or glass artifacts (cf. Table 8.4).

host of time-sensitive classes of material culture (Fig. 8.3). These include projectile points (Church 1987; Graybill 1981; Railey 1992), ceramics (Baker 1988; Church 1987; Cowan 1986, 1987; Essenpreis 1982; Glowacki, Turnbow, and Fields 1993; Graybill 1981; Riggs 1986; Turnbow and Henderson 1992), and a large number of other objects, including pipes and a variety of tools, that can be thought of as markers of a particular cultural phase or temporal period (Cowan 1986, 1987; Drooker 1997a; Graybill 1981, 1987; Henderson, ed., 1992). Distinctive imports such as marine shell ornaments, certain pipe styles, and European metal and glass have their own chronologies, determined by archaeologists working in other regions (Fig. 8.4), and thus serve as valuable cross-checks for site dating.

By and large, before A.D. 1500, differences in Fort Ancient material culture (notably ceramics and house construction) seem to be expressions of the geographic isolation of local communities from other, contemporaneous villages. In Ohio, for example, the major tributaries of the Ohio River form a series of north-south drainage basins that probably separated largely autonomous cultural groups. In some cases, such as along the Great and Little Miami Rivers, material culture differed between upper and lower reaches within a single drainage (Cowan 1986). These variations have resulted in a proliferation of phase designations, some of which are diagramed in Figure 8.2, that have evolved over the years and are still in flux in a number of regions (cf. Drooker 1997a: 66–70; Henderson and Turnbow 1992).

Between 1400 and 1600, the regional diversity that characterized earlier material culture became far less apparent. At an informal meeting of Fort Ancient scholars in 1986, the term "Madisonville horizon" was proposed to recognize these pan-regional similarities (Cowan 1988; Essenpreis 1988; Griffin 1992: 54; Henderson and Turnbow 1987; Sharp 1990: 469–471). The most recent portion of this period is characterized by an abundance of useful horizon marker artifacts, particularly European goods such as glass bead types that are typical of relatively restricted time periods. The chronology of the Madisonville horizon will be discussed in more detail later.

In most regional Fort Ancient chronologies (Fig. 8.2), two pre–Madisonville horizon phases are recognized, which in general terms can be designated Early Fort Ancient (ca. 1000/50–1200/50) and Middle Fort Ancient (ca. 1200/50–1400/50). The Late Fort Ancient (Madisonville horizon) period (ca. 1400/50–1650/1750) is often divided into early and late phases, with the advent of European artifacts (ca. 1550) taken as the dividing point between them. This generalized terminology is used herein.

Pre-Columbian Developments in the Central Ohio River Valley

Over the course of five centuries, Fort Ancient people developed and sustained a way of life characterized by maize horticulture, nucleated villages, nonhierarchical settle-

Figure 8.3. Important locally produced artifacts that serve as horizon markers for the Early and Middle–Late Fort Ancient periods (after Drooker 1997a: Fig. 4-7).

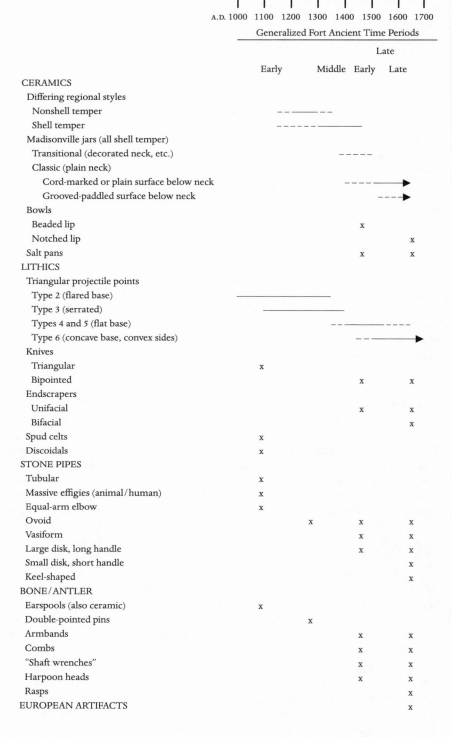

ment patterns, a social organization with a single level of achieved authority, and significant interregional interaction. The post–1400–1450 period, designated the Madisonville horizon, was characterized by less widespread settlement locations, probable increases in settlement and dwelling sizes, changes in burial practices and perhaps in social organization, less diverse pan-regional material culture, and intensified extraregional interaction. Although intraregional diversity declined over time, eastern and western Fort Ancient people still maintained some differences in mortuary customs, personal adornment, and extraregional areas of interest.

It is difficult to draw the line between prehistoric and protohistoric Fort Ancient times. Some of the most recent de-

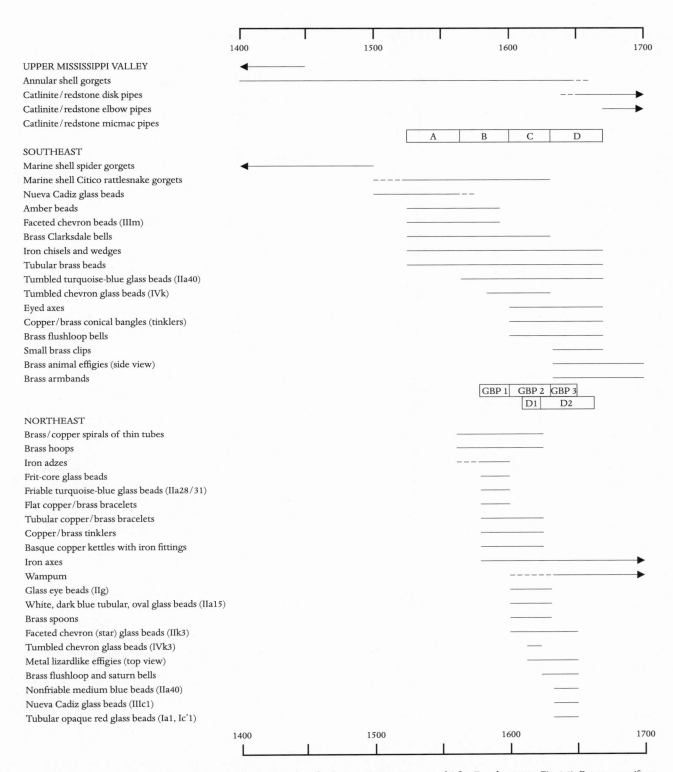

Figure 8.4. Important nonlocal artifacts that serve as horizon markers for the Late Fort Ancient period (after Drooker 1997a: Fig. 3-8). European artifacts from southeastern sites are related in time to assemblages A–D (Smith 1987; Waselkov 1989). Artifacts from northeastern sites are related in time to Glass Bead Periods 1–3 and Dutch bead periods 1 and 2 (Fitzgerald 1990a; Kenyon and Fitzgerald 1986; Kenyon and Kenyon 1983; see also Bradley and Childs 1991).

velopments noted in what follows might well have taken place after about 1550. New developments that definitely can be assigned to the protohistoric period are discussed in a later section.

SUBSISTENCE.   Maize can be recognized as an important dietary staple from Early Fort Ancient times onward, grafted onto an earlier tradition of horticulture based on plants such as maygrass (*Phalaris caroliniana*) and a domesticated goosefoot (probably *Chenopodium berlandieri* spp. *jonesianum*). With the exception of sunflower, by the seventeenth century all vestiges of the ancestral crops had disappeared.

Sometime between A.D. 800 and 1000, northern flint, or eastern eight-row maize, became the dominant variety in the central Ohio Valley. Although considerable speculation surrounds the ultimate origin of this cold-tolerant variety—was it introduced? did it evolve from an in situ gene pool?—there is little doubt about its ultimate impact.

At the Muir site in central Kentucky, the only single-component Early Fort Ancient site that has been subjected to large-scale flotation, carbonized maize was found in every sample collected from pits and house basins (Rossen 1988: Table 10.2). Large, shallow storage features were associated with every household. These factors suggest that maize was widely utilized and a surplus likely produced. On the other hand, the dispersed nature of this settlement and its apparently short duration imply that maize cultivation was not yet a factor in promoting population growth or coalescence into the sort of compact village typically associated with maize horticulture in eastern North America.

Fort Ancient people also cultivated beans, squash, sunflowers, and tobacco and utilized wild plant resources including fruits and nuts, with emphases somewhat different from those of Mississippian populations farther west (Rossen 1992; Rossen and Edging 1987; Schurr and Schoeninger 1995: 328; Wagner 1987). Regardless of local differences, the Fort Ancient subsistence system probably remained relatively stable over time (Dunavan 1991, 1993).

A summary of animal resource utilization data for 15 Fort Ancient sites (Breitburg 1992) concluded that four faunal resources formed the subsistence backbone: deer, elk, bear, and turkey. At most locations deer did not dominate the assemblage, but there was considerable variation among sites and subregions. Neither migratory birds nor aquatic resources appear to have formed a large part of the diet, in contrast to major Mississippian sites, the residents of which apparently relied more heavily on floodplain faunal resources (cf. B. Smith 1978: 480–488). After the early fifteenth century, there is evidence for bison use at the Madisonville site (Drooker 1997a: 109–110, 203–204).

The appearance and refinement of stone endscrapers during the Madisonville horizon (Fig. 8.3; Railey 1992) and a possible increase in numbers of bone beamers imply a heavier emphasis on hide preparation during that period.

A survey by Cowan (1992) of projectile points in 26 screened pit features at five Early, Middle, and Late Fort Ancient sites found a marked increase in points per cubic meter over time, implying an increase in hunting and/or warfare. At the Madisonville site, not only are stone and bone hide-working tools found in abundance, but so is red ochre (Drooker 1998: Photos 936, 939, 940), which is known to have been used widely in North America for hide processing (Walthall and Holley 1997: 158) as well as for ritual.

SETTLEMENT PATTERNS.   Within a century after eastern eight-row maize emerged, it had become the dietary mainstay of the central Ohio Valley populations (cf. Rossen 1992: Table XV-14). Like their counterparts everywhere in eastern North America, Fort Ancient farmers were tightly tethered to annually renewable tracts of rich, light-textured floodplain sediments. Although some good-sized settlements were maintained at upland locations (for instance, Fox Farm, situated near productive salt licks), the vast majority were located along the Ohio and its major tributaries (Fig. 8.1).

Contrary to the conclusions of some earlier publications (Essenpreis 1978; cf. Essenpreis 1988; Graybill 1980, 1981, 1984), Fort Ancient settlement patterns during all time periods display no obvious hierarchical relationships, although changes in settlement location and size did take place over time.

By the fourteenth century, Fort Ancient settlements were established 100 kilometers and more from the Ohio River along the Great Miami, Little Miami, Scioto, Hocking, and Muskingum Rivers in Ohio and the Kentucky, Licking, and Big Sandy Rivers in Kentucky (Fig. 8.5), almost to the hydrological divides with Lake Erie and the Cumberland-Tennessee River system. But during the fifteenth century, which apparently correlated with a climatic change to cooler, moister conditions (Graybill 1981: 57), many of these tributary valleys were virtually abandoned.

After the early fifteenth century, the majority of settlements were located within 20 kilometers of the Ohio River (Fig. 8.6). A number of these Late Fort Ancient villages were relatively large, both in area and in number of dwellings, and might represent the coalescence of formerly more dispersed populations (e.g., Buffalo [Graybill 1981: 168–169]). Others, although large in terms of numbers of burials, appear to have been occupied by smaller populations, on the order of 300 people, over a longer period of time (e.g., Madisonville [Drooker 1997a: 202–203]).

At least one upland hunting camp (Goolman, Kentucky) has been radiocarbon dated to the end of the Late Fort Ancient period (Table 8.1), so the "abandoned" regions away from the Ohio River most likely continued to be utilized for the procurement of animal and plant resources (see Brose and White 1983: 19–22). Graybill hypothesized that a shift from pithouses to surface dwellings in eastern Fort Ancient Madisonville horizon sites might signal a change

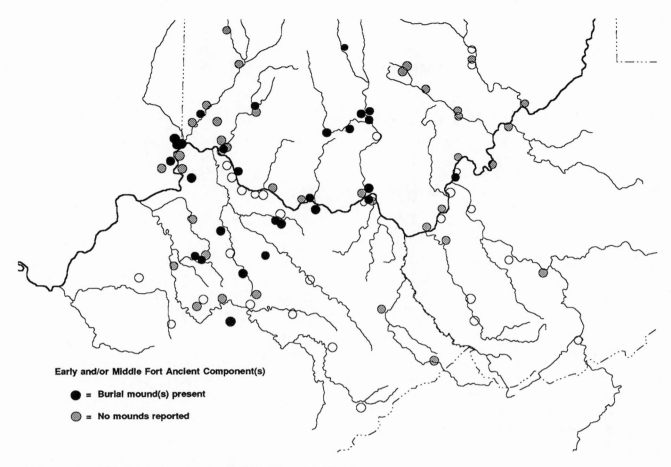

Figure 8.5. Early–Middle Fort Ancient components (after Drooker 1997a: Fig. 4-4).

Early and/or Middle Fort Ancient Component(s)

● = Burial mound(s) present

◍ = No mounds reported

from year-round habitation to winter dispersal for hunting and gathering (1981: 171–173).

SITE ORGANIZATION. The commitment to field agriculture, with its mutual labor requirements for clearing and planting the floodplain, provided the centripetal impetus for community aggregation, and scattered household clusters such as the eleventh–twelfth century Muir site (Turnbow and Sharp 1988) generally were replaced by compact, nucleated villages. Between A.D. 1100 and 1250, the basic pattern that was to typify Fort Ancient village arrangement for the next ten generations and more became established.

At the smallest scale, secular life centered on the single-family household with its attendant maize storage pits and other exterior features. Construction techniques and structure shapes, diverse before the Madisonville horizon, become more similar over time. Post construction was used during all periods, over the entire region. Wall trench construction is most evident at Early–Middle Fort Ancient components in southwestern Ohio (Drooker 1994, 1997a: 141–142). Rectangular semisubterranean structures are

found at Early–Middle Fort Ancient sites in many sub-regions, and circular ones at some sites in the west (Fig. 8.7; Drooker 1994, 1997a: 142; Graybill 1981: 143–154).

The general trend in structure size appears to have been from smaller to larger over time (Fig. 8.7). Data on structure sizes are available from only a few Late Fort Ancient sites, but two of them, Buffalo and Hardin, incorporated structures well over 150 square meters in area (Hanson 1966, 1975), implying co-residence of extended rather than nuclear family groups. From the diameters of isolated groups of post holes recorded at the Madisonville site, it too might have included some relatively large structures (Drooker 1997a: 133).

Many villages from all subregions and all time periods were organized around central plazas that served as focal points for communal activities (Church 1987: 218–220; Drooker 1994, 1997a: 119–133, Tables 4-2, 4-5, 4-11, Fig. 6-53; Essenpreis 1982; Graybill 1981: 136–139; Hanson 1975; Hawkins 1994; Henderson, Pollack, and Turnbow 1992: 265, 269; Nass and Yerkes 1995). At some settlements, a notably large structure adjacent to the plaza might have acted as a public building (Carskadden 1994; Church 1987:

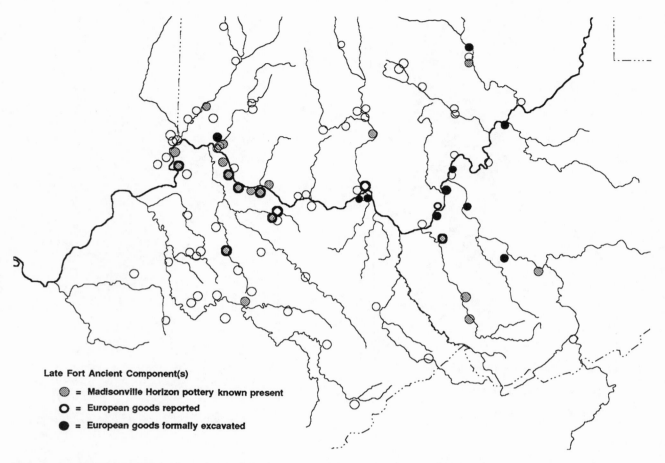

Figure 8.6. Late Fort Ancient and related components, defined on the basis of ceramics and European goods present (after Drooker 1997a: Fig. 4-5).

214; Hawkins 1994; Lileas 1988: 45–46; Nass 1987: 178–180, 255). At the Incinerator (Sunwatch) site near Dayton, Ohio (Fig. 8.8), the most completely excavated Early–Middle Fort Ancient settlement, the center of the plaza was occupied by an elaborate post complex that might have functioned to track seasonal changes in the position of the sun (Goss 1988; Heilman and Hoefer 1981). Sweathouses were also found there (Lileas 1988: 40–41, 43).

Exemplifying this circular pattern for Late Fort Ancient settlements is the much more densely populated Buffalo site on the Kanawha River in West Virginia (Fig. 8.9). Although both of these well-excavated sites (each located toward the edge of Fort Ancient territory) had palisades, most Fort Ancient sites have not been excavated thoroughly enough to reveal what proportion of them were stockaded. Although some earlier studies (e.g., Cowan 1992; Graybill 1987) hypothesized a trend in Late Fort Ancient times to a less coherent settlement plan, exemplified by the Hardin and Madisonville sites (Hanson 1966: Fig. 1; Hooton and Willoughby 1920: Pl. 30), the small number of broadly excavated Late Fort Ancient sites and the recent discovery of one or more plaza areas at Madisonville make this difficult to demonstrate (Drooker 1997a: 119–133, Table 4-10).

At many Early–Middle Fort Ancient villages, circa A.D. 1100–1300, burial mounds were located near the plaza (Church 1987: 220, 223; Graybill 1981: 149, 166–167; Henderson, Pollack, and Turnbow 1992: 261, 265; Mills 1904, 1906, 1917; Oehler 1950, 1973; Riggs 1977; H. Smith 1910). This practice was most common from the Scioto River westward (Fig. 8.5). Thereafter, and probably concurrently, burial took place within villages—around plazas and in and around houses. A number of sites with Middle Fort Ancient components have small numbers of graves lined with stone; at four western Fort Ancient sites (Anderson, Fox Farm, Incinerator, and Taylor) the proportion of stone-box graves was particularly high, as much as 50 percent or more of all graves (Drooker 1997a: Tables 4-6, 4-12).

Late Fort Ancient grave forms were less diverse, generally consisting of pits without stone linings. Data on intrasite burial locations are sparse, but some possible trends and subregional differences can be noted. At the Madisonville site, plaza-edge burials (early Late Fort Ancient) probably gave way over time to locations away from the plaza, near houses (Drooker 1997a: 192–196). Maps of burial locations relative to other site features are unavailable for many other Madisonville horizon components, but none of the pub-

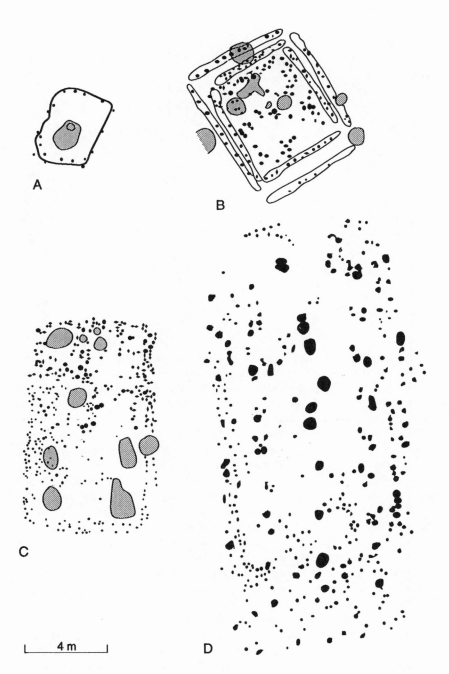

Figure 8.7. Examples of domestic structure plans from different Fort Ancient time periods. *A*, Early Fort Ancient. Muir, Kentucky. Single post structure with central hearth constructed in basin (redrawn from Turnbow and Sharp 1988). *B*, Middle Fort Ancient. Schomaker, Ohio. Wall trench structure in basin (Cowan et al. 1990). *C*, Late Fort Ancient. Buffalo, West Virginia. Post construction with some interior graves. This structure is about half the size of the largest building excavated at the site (redrawn from Hanson 1975: Fig. 14). *D*, Late Fort Ancient. Hardin, Kentucky. Post construction (redrawn from Hanson 1966: Fig. 4).

lished site plans shows plaza-edge cemeteries. At Hardin and at Neale's Landing, burials were near houses; at Buffalo Downstream Village, the majority were inside houses (Hanson 1966, 1975; Hemmings 1977).

SOCIAL ORGANIZATION AND INTRAREGIONAL INTERACTION. Only a few mortuary analyses have been carried out for Fort Ancient sites, but data from them, as well as from settlement patterns and intrasite organization, have extended our knowledge of Fort Ancient social organization. Increased regional social coherence over time may have been coupled with an increase in organizational complexity.

Although mound versus nonmound burial represents a potential marker for an elite class of Early–Middle Fort Ancient personages, excavation records for most mound sites lack the chronological control necessary to establish whether differing intrasite burial practices were contemporaneous. Mound burials did not necessarily have many grave goods; for instance, artifacts accompanied only 6 percent and 9 percent of individuals interred in mounds at the Turpin and Feurt sites, respectively, although Fox Farm mound burials "almost always" had them (Drooker 1997a: Tables 4-7 and 4-13). Ornaments and tools were the most common grave goods of this pre–Madisonville horizon period.

Figure 8.8. The Early–Middle Fort Ancient Incinerator (Sunwatch) site, Dayton, Ohio (redrawn from Heilman, Lilias, and Turnbow 1988).

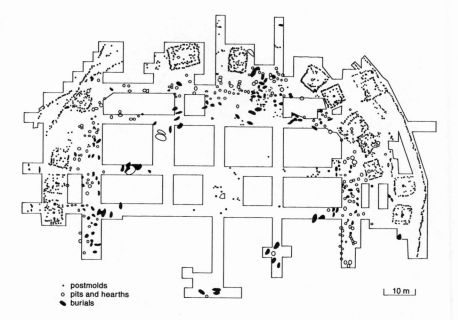

· postmolds
o pits and hearths
● burials

|___ 10 m ___|

Grave goods became more common over time, accompanying 20–60 percent of burials at Late Fort Ancient sites (see Table 8.3). The increases are more striking at eastern than at western Fort Ancient sites, because the former typically had had fewer grave goods during earlier periods. At a few sites across the entire region (e.g., Hahn's Field, Madisonville, Orchard), ceramic vessels accompanied up to 30–35 percent of burials. From evidence at Madisonville, this practice seems to have peaked toward the end of the early Madisonville horizon and then declined (Drooker 1997a: 174–196).

Pipes, which accompanied few Early–Middle Fort Ancient burials, became much more common as grave goods, as well as in general. At the Orchard site, a particularly high proportion of burials included pipes (Moxley 1988b: 4). At Madisonville, they constituted an adult male marker, probably an indicator of achieved status (Drooker 1997a: 230–233, 242–243). Historically, the exchange of pipe bowls often accompanied intergroup greeting ceremonies in the upper Mississippi Valley and surrounding regions, so these men, many of whom were buried with pipes of foreign materials and styles, might well have been directly involved in external interaction, functioning in a capacity of secular leadership.

Another statistically significant status marker at Madisonville was assemblages interpreted as "medicine bags." These were associated with teenagers and adult males, who were interpreted as ritual specialists (Drooker 1997a: Table 7-18). Similar assemblages were found with individuals at three eastern Late Fort Ancient sites (Broyles 1970; Hemmings 1977: 5.9–5.11; Holmes 1994: 164–165), as well as at western Early–Middle Fort Ancient sites (Essenpreis 1982).

In general, mortuary analyses for individual communities, both Early–Middle and Late Fort Ancient, have indi-

cated no more than one level of authority and no evidence for ascribed ranking, although horizontal differentiation perhaps associated with clans has been recognized at a number of sites (Drooker 1997a: 221–282; Essenpreis 1982: 54–135, 213–214, 237–239; S. Evans 1994; Griffin 1992; Holmes 1994; Nass and Yerkes 1995: 67). At least one type of artifact, however, might have served as a supralocal symbol, raising the possibility of a new level of complexity in late Late Fort Ancient society. Similarly shaped large barred copper pendants have been found with two important adult male burials at Madisonville and with a total of eight adults buried at Dunn, Fox Farm, and Hardin (Drooker 1997a: 273–275). Since no one site has a monopoly on them, they probably symbolize leadership at roughly the same level, as in an alliance or confederacy, not the apical level of a hierarchical complex chiefdom.

Although differences did persist (for instance, in some items of personal adornment and some mortuary customs) between western and eastern Fort Ancient people (Cowan 1992; Drooker 1997a: 327–329), intraregional interaction certainly increased after about 1450, with movement of people among settlements probably abetted by a less dispersed settlement pattern (Fig. 8.6). A primary marker for intraregional interaction is the development of increased similarity in ceramic styles (Cowan 1988: 8–9; Essenpreis 1988; Griffin 1992: 54; Henderson and Turnbow 1987: 220–221; Sharp 1990: 469–471). Middle Fort Ancient jars, often decorated with guilloche motifs around the neck, but in distinct subregional styles and a variety of tempers, gave way across the entire region to shell-tempered smooth (Madisonville Plain) and cord-marked (Madisonville Cord-marked) jars with undecorated necks and strap handles (for many examples, see Drooker 1998 and Griffin 1943). Inward-facing appliquéd lizards and other creatures peer

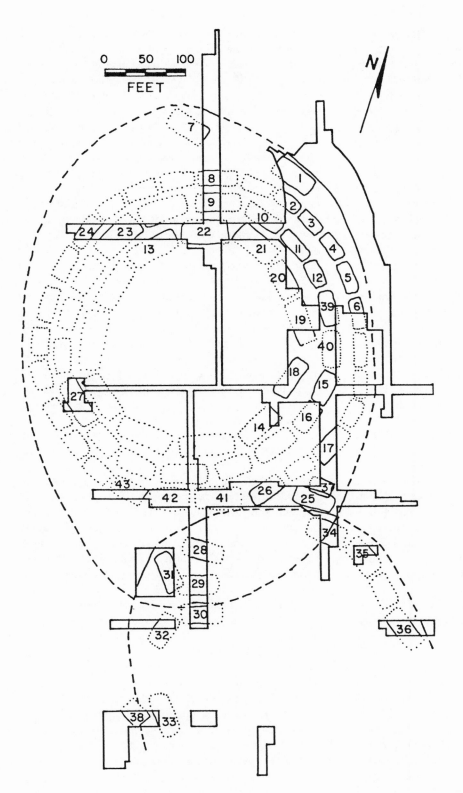

Figure 8.9. The Late Fort Ancient Buffalo site, West Virginia, showing sequentially occupied Downstream Village (*top*) and Upstream Village (*bottom*) (redrawn from Hanson 1975: Fig. 9)

over the rims of a distinctive minority of vessels from westernmost to easternmost Fort Ancient sites, starting in Middle Fort Ancient times but increasing in numbers at later components (e.g., Cowan 1987: 10–15; Drooker 1997a: 325–326, Figs. 4-13, 8-40, 8-41; Griffin 1943: Pl. 69; Mills 1917: Fig. 34). Since women almost certainly were the potters, these stylistic similarities imply increased female visiting or intermarriage among settlements along the entire central Ohio Valley.

INTERREGIONAL INTERACTION. Evidence for interregional interaction and exchange is present from Early Fort Ancient components onward, with different spheres of interaction persisting over time for western versus eastern settlements. Types and amounts of marine shell ornaments at different components have been particularly useful in tracing these interaction networks.

Middle Fort Ancient Anderson- and Baum-style ceramics excavated at northern Ohio sites (Bowen 1994: 62; Brose 1994b: Fig. 5.2) provide evidence of some contact between northern Fort Ancient settlements in Ohio and non–Fort Ancient groups near the Lake Erie shore. Early interaction between Fort Ancient people and Mississippian peoples to their west and south can be seen through a variety of foreign and foreign-influenced items from western Fort Ancient sites (Cowan 1986, 1992; Drooker 1997a: 89–95; Vickery and Genheimer 1994). These include both objects that were manufactured by Mississippian craftspersons, such as engraved shell gorgets, a few negative-painted ceramics and hooded water bottles, pipes, spud-shaped axes, and exotic flint knives, and objects that reflect knowledge of distant practices, such as wall-trench architecture, local copies of Ramey Incised ceramics, and ceramic adornos on vessels. Interment practices such as use of burial mounds (Fig. 8.5) and stone-lined graves also are congruent with contemporaneous practices among Mississippian groups (cf. I. Brown 1981). Large effigy pipes, including frogs and crouching humans, and marine shell ornaments such as annular gorgets (Table 8.2), reflect westerly interaction networks encompassing Illinois, with objects reaching Fort Ancient territory through its westernmost settlements (Drooker 1997a: 89–95, Fig. 8-20). This represents either an extension or a renewal of a strong interregional connection that had been present during earlier Hopewell times (Braun 1986). The relatively large numbers of marine shell beads and ornaments concentrated at Early–Middle Fort Ancient sites farther east, such as Fox Farm, Gartner, and Baum in the central part of Fort Ancient territory (Fig. 8.10), may mark a more southerly connection, with shell objects perhaps reaching northern Fort Ancient settlements via overland trails through Fox Farm (Drooker 1997a: 94–95, 301–303; Mills 1904, 1906; H. Smith 1910). This direction of interaction, too, had Hopewell period antecedents (Chapman and Keel 1979; Jeffries 1979).

Indigenous interaction networks continued into Madi-

sonville horizon times. Connections with northern Ohio are marked by the interchange of a variety of artifacts, including ceramics, bone items, and pipes. For example, Madisonville-style ceramics have been excavated at a number of northern Ohio sites; vessels and pipes of northern Ohio origin or influence were deposited as grave goods as well as discarded in pits at the Madisonville site; and upper Ohio Valley Wellsburg ceramics are a strong presence at a number of eastern Fort Ancient sites (Baker 1988; Drooker 1997a: 329, 331, 1997b; Moxley 1988a). Ceramics with notched appliqué strips, associated with a broad area south of the Great Lakes and considered a Central Algonquian marker, were present at the Madisonville site in mortuary and nonmortuary contexts (Drooker 1997a: Fig. 8-37, 1997b).

Westerly connections from the fifteenth century onward are strongly objectified by redstone disk pipes excavated in at least five Fort Ancient communities across the entire region, from Madisonville to Buffalo; their focus of origin is southern Wisconsin and adjacent areas (Drooker 1997a: Figs. 8-28, 8-29). Small disk pipes, often of limestone rather than redstone, also were common, occurring on at least 10 Fort Ancient sites; in the upper Mississippi River valley, this style is typical of protohistoric Orr Focus sites in northeastern Iowa (Wedel 1959: Fig. 11; West 1934: Pl. 257). Several were interred with adult males at Madisonville (Drooker 1997a: Figs. 7-5a, 7-6). Medicine bag assemblages with many congruences to Fort Ancient examples have been reported from late prehistoric and protohistoric sites in Illinois and Iowa (e.g., Bluhm and Liss 1961: 96–99; Bray 1961). Ceramics provide a more mundane link between Illinois and both eastern and western Fort Ancient sites. For example, two mortuary vessels from Madisonville, along with similar vessels from three eastern Fort Ancient sites, are virtually identical in form to a typical Keating Cord-marked jar from the Zimmerman site in Illinois (J. Brown 1961: Fig. 8.D; Brown and Willis 1995; Drooker 1997b). A variety of other artifacts and symbols, including bone rasps, grooved stone mauls, and the thunderbird motif, link the Madisonville site, in particular, to upper Mississippi Valley peoples (Drooker 1997a: 331–332).

Southwesterly connections to the central Mississippi Valley are exemplified by two unique artifacts from Madisonville: a locally made head pot with southeastern Missouri stylistic affinities and a square shell button that is a late prehistoric–protohistoric horizon marker artifact in the central Mississippi Valley (Drooker 1997a: 301, 332, Figs. 6-19b, 8-18, 8-39; S. Williams 1980: 106–108).

Southeasterly connections are typified by the presence of engraved marine shell gorgets in sixteenth- and seventeenth-century styles, including the Citico rattlesnake, mask, and maskette (Table 8.2; Cowan 1992). The Citico rattlesnake and mask styles are strongly associated with sites in eastern Tennessee and adjacent areas, with possible links to the historically known Coosa polity and Creek peoples

Table 8.2

Marine Shell Gorgets from Fort Ancient Sites

Site	Annular[a] Apex	Side	Circle-Cross	Spider	Rattlesnake Citico	Other[b]	Mask[c]	Maskette	Other[d]	Min. Total	Reference
West Virginia											
Buffalo					1?	1	1	2		5	Brashler and Moxley 1990; Hanson 1975
Clover					1					1	Brashler and Moxley 1990
Gue Farm							1			1	Brashler and Moxley 1990
Man									1	1	Brashler and Moxley 1990
Marmet							4			4	Brashler and Moxley 1990
Neale's Landing							P	1		1	Brashler and Moxley 1990
Orchard							1	3		3	Brashler and Moxley 1990
Pratt					1					1	Brashler and Moxley 1990
Rolf Lee				1	1		5	2		9	Brashler and Moxley 1990
Somers Farm			1							1	Brashler and Moxley 1990
Kentucky											
15JS16						1				1	Henderson et al. 1986
Augusta							2	P		3+	Henderson et al. 1986
Bracken Co. site				1						1	Wagers 1993
Clay Mound						1				1	Funkhouser and Webb 1928
Fox Farm	2		1	1	1	2	8	3		18	Glass n.d.; Griffin 1943; Smith 1910; Smith and Smith 1989
Hardin			1		1–3	0–2	4	5	1	14	Hanson 1966
Henry Pyles						2				2	Henderson et al. 1986
Larkin							2		1	3	Foley and Lipscombe 1961
Singer				1						1	Sharp 1990
Ohio											
Anderson		2–4	1							3–5	Griffin 1943
Baum		>2								2+	Mills 1906
Eagle Creek								2		2	Snider 1991
Feurt	P			1	1+					3+	Mills 1917
Gartner	1	>4								5+	Mills 1904
Madisonville		1			1			5–6		7–8	Drooker 1997a, 1998
Richards	P									1+	Carskadden 1994
State Line	1	1								2	Vickery and Genheimer 1994
Taylor	1	1								2	Griffin 1943

Note: For distribution maps of annular, circle-in-cross, selected spider, Citico rattlesnake, mask, and maskette gorgets, see Drooker 1997a: Figs. 8-15, 8-16, 8-17, 8-20, 8-21, and 8-22. For distribution of Brakebill rattlesnake gorgets, see Brain and Phillips 1996. *P* indicates "one or more present as unreconstructible pieces."

[a] These have a central hole plus two suspension holes. Two forms are reported, one cut from the apex of a *Busycon* shell, the other from the side.

[b] Includes non-Citico styles and rattlesnake gorgets of unknown type. The two rattlesnake gorgets from Buffalo include at least one Brakebill or Lick Creek; the other is a piece cut from what might have been a Citico-style gorget (Brain and Phillips 1996: 501; cf. Muller 1989: 21).

[c] Engraved, most with "forked eye" motif.

[d] Circular gorgets engraved with horned creature (Man site), "crane" (Hardin site), concentric circles and dots (Larkin site).

(Hally, Smith, and Langford 1990; M. Smith 1987; Smith and Smith 1989) and/or Cherokees (Muller 1989: 21, 1997: 371–372). The vast majority of such gorgets from Late Fort Ancient contexts, and of marine shell artifacts in general, have come from eastern, not western sites (Fig. 8.10). Judging from this and other evidence, eastern Fort Ancient people of this period appear to have had a stronger relationship with eastern Mississippian groups, and western Fort Ancient sites with western (Mississippi River valley) groups.

WARFARE. Possible indicators of warfare are present at both Early–Middle and Late Fort Ancient sites (Drooker 1994, 1997a: 204, 207–209, 213, Tables 4-5, 4-6, 4-11, 4-12). In western Fort Ancient territory, at least a few pre–Madisonville horizon sites, including Incinerator and

Figure 8.10. Distribution of marine shell ornaments in the central Ohio Valley at Early–Middle versus Late Fort Ancient sites (after Drooker 1997a: Figs. 8.23, 8.24a).

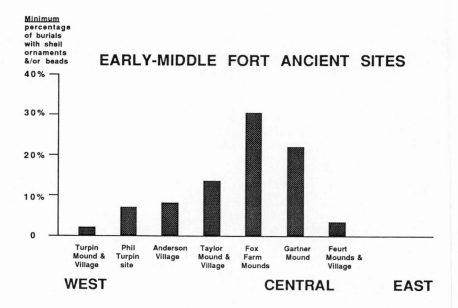

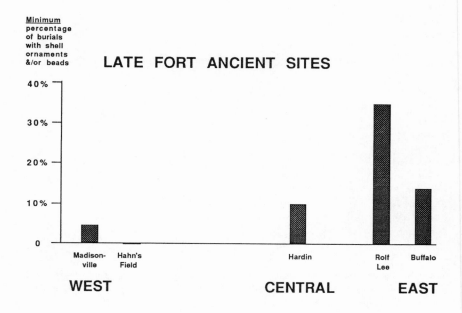

probably State Line, had palisades, and several sites of all time periods (e.g., the Early–Middle Fort Ancient Erp, Hine, Taylor, South Fort, and Sand Ridge sites, and the Late Fort Ancient Madisonville site) were located on defensible bluff tops. At least four, and possibly six or more, Late Fort Ancient sites from the Scioto River eastward were palisaded, Buffalo with at least two concentric stockades. Multicomponent Feurt is located on a bluff top.

Only spotty information is available on war-related traumas (projectile points in bone, crushing blows to crania, etc.). Among 10 sites with burial populations of around 100 or more, such traumas marked 1–2 percent of burials at most sites of all periods (Table 8.3) but considerably more

at some western sites: 6 percent at the Early–Middle Fort Ancient Anderson site and up to 7 percent (including all fractures) at the primarily Late Fort Ancient Madisonville site. One burial from the Larkin site, covered with limestone slabs, exhibited evidence of scalping (Pollack, Powell, and Adkins 1987). At no site did death by violence approach the magnitude of, for instance, the fourteenth-century Oneota Norris Farms 36 Cemetery, where 34 percent of the adults suffered traumatic death (Milner and Smith 1990: 148).

Among the sites summarized in Table 8.3, disarticulated burials (which might or might not be associated with warfare) generally are more prevalent at sites with later com-

Table 8.3

Proportions of Trauma and Disarticulation among Fort Ancient Burial Populations of Significant Size

| Site | Component | | | | | Burial Sample | Burials w/Trauma | Disarticulated Burials | Burials with Grave Goods |
	E–M	EL	LL	Palisade	Bluff Top				
Incinerator	X	—	—	X	—	145	?	3%	30%
Anderson	X	—	—	?	—	93 (of 125)	>6%	1%	28%
Taylor Mound	X	—	—	?	X	79	?	>22%	22%
Feurt	X	—	X	?	X	403	1%	3%	8%
Fox Farm	X	X	X	?	—	233	>2%	Common	Nearly always
Madisonville	X	X	X	—	X	591 (of 1447)	2–7%	25%	39%
Hardin	X	—	X	Perhaps	—	335–351	1%	>15%	47%
Buffalo	—	X	X	X	—	562	>2%	13%	22%
Orchard	?	?	X	?	—	>300	Several	~10%	>30%
Rolf Lee	?	?	X	?	—	101 (of 250–400)	2%	2%	53%

Source: Data compiled from Drooker 1997a:Tables 4-4 to 4-7, 4-10 to 4-13; see them for references.

ponents. At the Madisonville site, with the highest percentage of disarticulated burials, significantly more subadults than adults were disarticulated. However, three ritually arranged group burials containing the disarticulated remains of 6, 16, and 22 individuals, respectively, probably were war related; unfortunately, in the absence of associated horizon marker artifacts, their time period or periods are unknown (Drooker 1997a: 205–206). A mass burial of almost 40 individuals has been reported from the Orchard site, but without details of demography, trauma, or relative placement (Moxley 1988b: 4).

In Trenches 1–K at Madisonville, adults buried with weapons of war or hunting tended to be located on the same side of the plaza as those buried with pipes, the male status marker, and it was postulated that warfare and hunting were important social factors there during the Late Fort Ancient period. This pattern did not appear to be confined, however, to either the earlier or the later part of that period.

The Advent of Europeans in Eastern North America

Although intermittent contacts between Europeans and Native Americans in eastern North America took place along the Atlantic coast from 1497 onward, only during the early 1540s did sustained contacts take place at any distance into the interior. In the far northeast, these included Cartier's 1541–1543 attempt to establish a settlement on the St. Lawrence near the location of Quebec City; the establishment of a Basque whaling station on the St. Lawrence estuary near Tadoussac during the decades after that, with a significant trade for beaver pelts carried on between about 1580 and 1600; and the founding of Quebec in 1608. Missionaries began to live among the Huron of southeastern Ontario in 1634 (Fitzgerald et al. 1993; Trigger 1985: 129–135; 226–229). In the interior Southeast, the de Soto entrada of 1539–1543, which reached as far north as North Carolina, Tennessee, and northern Arkansas, along with a few other later sixteenth-century exploratory forays, introduced Spanish material culture, European plants and animals, and new, devastating diseases to the region (Hudson and Tesser 1994; M. Smith 1987).

Along the eastern seaboard, Spanish St. Augustine and a string of missions were established in Florida and Georgia starting in 1565; the failed English colony at Roanoke (1585–1587) was replaced by Jamestown on Chesapeake Bay in 1607; a Dutch trading fort was established near the location of Albany, New York, in 1614; the English trading center of Charles Towne, South Carolina, arose in 1670; and Pennsylvania was established in 1682 (Drooker 1997a: Table 3-1, Figs. 3-4, 3-5, 3-6). During the later half of the seventeenth century, the French continued to trade for furs, gradually established forts and missions in the upper Great Lakes, explored the Mississippi starting in 1673, and founded their first Lower Louisiana colony at Biloxi in 1699.

By the end of the seventeenth century, settlements, forts, and missions ringed the map of eastern North America but did not penetrate it (Drooker 1997a: Fig. 3-6). No documented visit by a Euroamerican to the central Ohio Valley occurred before 1674, when an illiterate English trader, Gabriel Arthur, was captured by Indians, with whom he probably visited the Kanawha–Ohio River confluence. An account written by his employer described the region as inhabited by people apparently with no iron tools or guns, members of a populous nation dispersed along the Ohio, 20 days' travel from end to end (Alvord and Bidgood 1912: 210–226). It is not known what they called themselves. The previous year, as Father Jacques Marquette passed the mouth of the Ohio on his way down the Mississippi, he obtained and recorded this description of residents in its upper reaches: "This river flows from the lands of the East, where dwell the people called Chaouanons in so great numbers that in one district there are as many as 23 villages, and 15 in another, quite near one another. They are not at all warlike, and are the nations whom the Iroquois go so far to seek, and war against without any reason" (Griffin 1943: 31).

Not until French expeditions took place in 1739 and 1749 were firsthand reports and reliable maps of the central Ohio Valley obtained (Drooker 1997a: 64). Records from the second expedition described a populous Euroamerican-Native trade center in the vicinity of Lower Shawneetown, at the mouth of the Scioto River, that at mid-century included Shawnee, Five Nations Iroquois, Delaware, and others—many of them known to have moved there fairly recently from Pennsylvania and New York (Henderson, Jobe, and Turnbow 1986: 21–40; Hunter 1978: 588; R. White 1991: 206–208). What had been happening in the Ohio Valley during the previous three-quarters of a century?

The conventional wisdom of historians has been that the Ohio Valley was virtually devoid of population by the last few decades of the seventeenth century, its residents having been "almost completely disrupted and evicted . . . in the so-called Beaver Wars of the Iroquois" (Hunter 1978: 588). Between the early 1640s and the late 1660s, a long series of attacks, first by Ontario Iroquoians and then by Iroquois Confederacy members, on people living to their west resulted in the depopulation of much of the area around the lower Great Lakes, with Eries, Hurons, Ottawas, Kickapoos, Fox, Sauk, Potawatomi, and others being displaced, many ending up by the 1660s between the western Great Lakes and the Mississippi (R. White 1991: 1–49). In the late 1660s, the French established an uneasy peace with the Iroquois, which extended to this region. According to the Frenchman Perrot,

The Iroquois could no longer make war with their neighbors (since the French had taken possession of the Ottawa country, 1669–1671). . . . they therefore sought to carry it into the country of the Andastes [Susquehannocks—finally dispersed in 1673 through the intervention of Maryland colonists] and Chaouanons, whom they routed in several encounters. From these tribes they considerably augmented their own forces, by the great numbers of children or other prisoners whose lives they spared (Griffin 1943: 30).

Shawnee and other captives probably from the general area of the Ohio Valley are known to have been brought back to Iroquoian territory in Ontario and western New York during the 1670s (e.g., Griffin 1943: 30, 31; cf. Richter 1983: 539–541). The wholesale devastation and forcible expulsion later claimed by the English as having been accomplished by their Iroquois League protégés, however, was never backed up by eyewitness accounts (see, for example, Jennings 1984: 16).

What can archaeology tell us about the nature and timing of actual events?

Protohistoric Developments in the Central Ohio Valley

As we have seen, the post-1450 Madisonville horizon is characterized by changes in settlement patterns, mortuary practices, and some aspects of material culture, greater intraregional interaction, and intensified extraregional interaction. Only a few of these changes can be correlated definitively with the advent of Europeans in North America.

CHRONOLOGY.   Sometime during the middle of the sixteenth century, members of Fort Ancient communities began to obtain small numbers of European-related artifacts (Drooker 1996, 1997a: 283–294). This marks the beginning of the protohistoric period in the region—the interval between the appearance of European goods and the earliest substantial European records (Trigger 1985: 116). In the central Ohio Valley, this interval extended for some two centuries, during which time residents experienced repercussions from events that took place hundreds of miles from their homeland and developed their own strategies of response.

Table 8.4 lists Fort Ancient sites from which metal and glass artifacts have been excavated or reported, organized in rough chronological order on the basis of datable artifacts (Fig. 8.4), along with five additional sites with seventeenth-century radiocarbon dates but no known European artifacts. Virtually all the European artifacts would have been available by 1640, which is why some Fort Ancient chronologies use 1640 or 1650 as a convenient terminal date (Fig. 8.2). The only significant exceptions are mid-eighteenth-century artifacts from a cluster of Kentucky sites (Bentley, Old Fort Earthworks, Laughlin) near Shawneetown, occupied around 1735–1758 (Henderson, Jobe, and Turnbow 1986; Pollack and Henderson 1984). Thus, although occupation of at least this portion of the central Ohio Valley *could* have been continuous until historical times, there is no positive, fine-grained artifactual evidence for it. European and aboriginal artifacts typical of the late seventeenth century, such as post-1650 glass bead types, Jesuit rings, types of bells other than Clarksdale, solid brass or iron wire, small-sized ax heads, gun parts, Micmac-style stone pipes, catlinite elbow pipes, and wampum, are not in evidence.

A few sites, including a number without European artifacts, have post-1650 radiocarbon dates. Dates with calibration intercepts in the 1650s include one of two from Buffalo and one of two from Morrison Village; in the 1660s, one of three from Arrasmith, one of three from Augusta, two of three from Speckman, and single dates each from Bentley and Rolf Lee; later dates include one of two from Larkin, one of eighteen from Madisonville, and three eighteenth-century dates from the Goolman hunting camp (Table 8.1).

Table 8.4

European and Other Important Exotic Artifacts at Late Prehistoric–Protohistoric Fort Ancient and Wellsburg Sites, and Associated Relative Chronological Placement

Site[a]	European and Other Exotic Artifacts	Artifact Dates[b]
SITES WITH DIAGNOSTIC ASSEMBLAGES FROM GOOD ARCHAEOLOGICAL CONTEXT		
Buffalo, WV	**Amber bead**, white glass seed bead; copper and brass tubular beads, **brass clips**, flat brass serpentine fragment, **serpentine thin copper tube**; redstone disk pipe; marine shell mask, maskette, and rattlesnake gorgets (1 Brakebill/Lick Creek, 1 Citico?), and "mushroom" earplugs	1525–1625
Hardin, KY	Copper and **brass** tubular beads, tubes, **clips**; **brass coil** made from thin tube and flat bracelet; copper pendant and tubular bracelet; redstone pipes incl. disk; marine shell Citico-style, mask, and maskette gorgets	1550–1625
(Reported)[c]	**Glass beads: tubular**, aqua blue spherical; iron celts; copper/brass pendants and "**salamanders**"	1600–1630
Neales Landing, WV	**Friable blue glass beads** (IIa31/28), **iron ax** (two type 4 maker's marks, 1225 g), marine shell mask and maskette gorgets	1580–1630
(Henry Stahl Collection)	Glass beads: white, blue; copper/brass "tinklers," tubular beads, pendants, tubular bracelets; iron ax	
Madisonville, OH	**Friable blue glass beads** (IIa31/28); **parts from Basque iron-fitted copper kettles; iron dagger guard; brass Clarksdale bell; thin copper/brass tubes in coil, ring, and serpent shapes;** copper and brass tubular beads, rings, and tinklers; copper and brass pendants; German silver ornament; redstone and non-redstone disk pipes; marine shell Citico rattlesnake gorget, maskettes, "mushroom" ear plugs, square "button"	1580–1630
Rolf Lee, WV	Glass beads: **white cored** (IVa11/13), turquoise blue (IIa31/40), **white and indigo tubular** (Ia5, Ia19), indigo (IIa52/55), **tumbled chevron** (IVk3), **blue and white striped** (IVb33), **black** (IIa7), white (IIa11), blue cored (IVa19); copper and brass tubular beads, brass strips, flattened **thin copper tube in spiral/C shape; large brass armbands;** marine shell Citico rattlesnake, maskette, and mask gorgets (one with copper eyes), "mushroom" earplugs	
(Reported)	Copper/brass spoons used as pendants, 2 flat metal serpents, **brass clips**, iron celts; spider gorget	
Clover, WV	Glass beads: **tumbled chevron** (IVk3), dark blue seed, turquoise blue (IIa31/40); **brass/copper kettle fragments**, tubular beads, **tinklers**, thin tube in C-shape, **lizard** (top view), button; **brass fish effigy** (side view); marine shell Citico rattlesnake gorget	1590–1700
Orchard, WV	Glass beads: turq. blue (IIa31/40), **red tubular twisted** (Ia1, Ic); **copper/brass** tubular beads, tinklers, arm bands (small); brass tubes, "dog head effigy"[d]; marine shell mask and maskette gorgets, and "mushroom" earplugs; disk pipes	1630–1700
Bentley, KY	Gun parts, gunflints, lead shot; iron nails, knives, shears, kettle fragments, key, etc.; brass Jew's harp, pendant, tinklers, etc.; glass beads; etc.	1700–1800
Old Fort Earthworks, KY	Iron axes, picks, gunbarrels, etc.; lead shot; silver crosses and buckles; brass kettles, Jew's harp; glass beads; etc.	1700–1800
SITES WITH FEW DIAGNOSTIC ARTIFACTS OR PROBLEMATICAL CONTEXT		
Pratt, WV (reported)	Marine shell Citico rattlesnake gorget	1500–
Eagle Creek, OH	Marine shell maskettes, non-redstone disk pipes	1500–
Dunn, KY, and vicinity (reported)	Copper/brass pendant, rolled copper tube	1500–
15JS16, KY	Tubular copper/brass beads, marine shell rattlesnake gorget, copper-covered earspool	1500–
Clear Creek, OH	Tubular copper bead	1500–
Riker, OH	Copper tubular beads and hair tubes	1500–
15MA23, KY (reported)	Light blue glass seed bead (surface)	1525–
Gue Farm, WV (reported)	Glass bead (surface); marine shell mask gorget	1525–
Logan, WV	Glass beads	
Larkin, KY	Rolled copper bead, lead shot (?)	
(Reported)	Tubular copper beads, piece of **brass**, marine shell mask and gorgets with dancing figures and concentric circles	1525–
Feurt, OH	Copper/brass tubular beads and conical "**tinklers**"; marine shell Citico rattlesnake gorget cut fragments; redstone pipes (not disk)	1580–

Continued on next page

Table 8.4 *continued*

Site[a]	European and Other Exotic Artifacts	Artifact Dates[b]
(Reported)	Glass beads: turquoise blue (IIa31/40), turquoise blue with **white stripes** (IIb56/57), tubular red with green cored	
Bosman, OH	Copper tubular beads and tinkler	1580–
Cullison, OH	Brass/copper tube, iron buckle	1580–
Snag Creek, KY (reported)	Copper/brass conical tinkler	1580–
Henry Pyles, KY (reported)	Copper/brass conical tinklers and tubular beads; marine shell rattlesnake gorgets; redstone items	1580–
Sandstone Shelter, WV[e] (reported)	**Amber bead**	1525–1600
Fox Farm, KY	Sheet lead pendant (surface); rolled copper beads; redstone pipes (not disk); marine shell mask and maskette gorgets	
Western edge (reported)	Melted **red glass bead**; copper pendant and tubular beads; redstone disk pipe; marine shell spider, mask, and Citico rattlesnake gorgets	1610–
Devary, KY	Red glass bead (surface)	1610–
Marmet, WV	Glass beads, including **friable blue beads** (IIa31/28); **brass spoon** and tubular bead	1580–1630
(Reported)	Glass beads: **Nueva Cadiz, non-red tubular**, faceted purple, **brass lizard effigy**; marine shell mask gorgets	(1525–1640/1675?)
Augusta, KY	Marine shell mask and maskette gorgets, disk pipe	
(Reported)	Light blue glass(??) beads; **iron bracelets**, tubular copper beads, "copper face mask," **copper tubular serpent pendant**	1550–1670
Beale Mound, OH? (reported)	**Brass animal** (bear?) **and fish effigies, brass/copper spiral**, copper tinklers	1550–1670
Arrasmith, KY	Hexagonal, cored blue glass bead (IIIf) (surface)	1700–
Laughlin, KY	Spall and blade gunflints (surface)	1640–1800+

SITES WITH SIXTEENTH- TO SEVENTEENTH-CENTURY RADIOCARBON DATES BUT NO DIAGNOSTIC ARTIFACTS
Hahn's Field, OH
Morrison Village, OH
Speckman, OH
Goolman, KY
Thompson, KY

Source: Compiled from information presented in Drooker 1997a: Tables 4-9, 6-5, 6-6, 6-7; see them for references. Bead type designations are from Kidd and Kidd (1983).

Note: Important diagnostic artifacts are **boldfaced**.

[a]Sites are in order by latest period represented by diagnostic European artifact.

[b]Time period(s) defined by diagnostic European artifacts; in no case do these assemblages rule out earlier site occupations. Date ranges encompass the entire period(s) represented by the diagnostic artifacts and thus give a maximum estimate of protohistoric occupation.

[c]Diagnostic artifacts reportedly excavated, but location not verified.

[d]Potential diagnostic artifact.

[e]Near Barker's Bottom, West Virginia.

Together with Gabriel Arthur's account of a well-populated central Ohio Valley in 1674, this evidence is congruent with Graybill's hypothesis that the central Ohio Valley continued as the home of Fort Ancient people at least until the 1680s, although direct pipelines to European goods broke down by 1640 (Graybill 1987; cf. Baker 1988: 48–51). Many of the material markers that he cited as evidence that a profound change took place in Fort Ancient society when these exchange networks broke down are not, however, consistent with recently analyzed data. Unfortunately, poor chronological control for seventeenth-century sites (many of which were multicomponent) still hinders complete understanding of this period, particularly in the eastern portion of the region. Nevertheless, additional useful information can be gleaned by considering the origins and contexts of European artifacts and materials.

SUBSISTENCE.   A number of lines of evidence for the increased importance of hunting during Late Fort Ancient times, including possible abandonment of villages during the winter hunting season, increased numbers and refinement of hide-working tools, and inferred status of adults buried with weapons, were discussed earlier.

Just one aspect of this shift can be tied definitely to the protohistoric period. Madisonville, the westernmost protohistoric site, is the only one where bison remains have been found, mainly in the form of thoracic vertebrae used for beamers (hide scrapers). Forty-seven extant examples represent over half of all beamers from the well-documented excavations in Trenches 1–K. Bison bone beamers from refuse pits were statistically correlated with the presence of metal, so the addition of bison to the subsistence menu, and probably an upswing in hunting and hide preparation, is taken as a protohistoric phenomenon (Drooker 1997a: 203, Fig. 6-54). Although bison are known to have visited Big Bone Lick, some 40 kilometers from Madisonville (Tankersley 1986a), a second source of bison products is possible. The long-established connection that Madisonville residents had with people of the Prairie Peninsula in Illinois and contiguous areas, an excellent hunting ground for bison, could have opened the door to either hunting parties from Madisonville or exchange for bison products, which is discussed further below.

The fact that huge numbers of skins were being supplied by Iroquoian middlemen to European traders—for instance, up to 20,000 per year through the Huron between 1615 and 1629—led Cowan (1992, citing Trigger 1978: 349) to explore the possibility that central Ohio Valley people might have participated in the early seventeenth-century beaver trade. Although no concrete evidence has yet come to light for that particular period, there is some evidence of earlier Iroquoian overtures that conceivably could have been connected with the potential for engaging in this exchange network.

SOCIAL ORGANIZATION. The trend toward larger dwellings (Fig. 8.9), and thus larger basic social units, during the Madisonville horizon seems to have been under way well before protohistoric times. For instance, the Buffalo site, with the largest measured structures, produced only a few, relatively early European goods (Table 8.4), and at least one of its rattlesnake gorgets is of an earlier style than Citico, which became prominent after 1525 (Table 8.2, Fig. 8.4). At the Madisonville site, structures might have diminished in size at the very end of the occupation, perhaps coupled with a trend toward a less horticulture-centered, sedentary way of life (Drooker 1997a: 203).

The possibility of an intraregional Fort Ancient alliance or confederacy, signaled by barred copper symbol badges worn by prominent adults at four Late Fort Ancient sites, is one that seems to span the prehistoric-protohistoric boundary, although future physicochemical testing of the artifacts could pin down the period more definitively. On one hand, badges of similar size and shape have been excavated from burials in the middle Cumberland Valley, a region that was depopulated by about 1500; on the other hand, a similar pendant made of brass was excavated with a subadult burial at Madisonville (Drooker 1997a: 160, 162, 170, 292–293). The relatively large sizes of the artifacts, surpassed in Fort Ancient territory only by brass armbands from the Rolf Lee site, argues for a European metal source, although the craft technology was well within local capabilities.

INTERREGIONAL INTERACTION. Interaction networks known prehistorically were all continued during the protohistoric period, with Fort Ancient groups in different locations accumulating distinctive assemblages from differing directions. In addition, new exchange partners, some of them surprising, were developed. All items of European derivation were small and easily portable. Down-the-line exchange, rather than face-to-face interaction with European traders, is strongly indicated.

Eastern Fort Ancient villages obtained more, and more diverse assemblages of, glass beads than settlements farther west (Table 8.4). Some types, such as the amber bead and white glass seed bead from Buffalo, are consistent with sixteenth-century types known from the interior Southeast (Fig. 8.4), but others probably mark a new direction of interaction. Those from Rolf Lee—the greatest number and variety known to have come from any Fort Ancient site— are a good match for Dutch bead period types known from early seventeenth-century Susquehannock settlements north of Chesapeake Bay (Graybill 1981: Table 19, 1987). The Susquehannock, who, during the late sixteenth century, migrated from the upper to the lower Susquehanna River, for a period of time maintained settlements as far west as eastern West Virginia (Brashler 1987; Drooker 1997a: 54; Kent 1984), which might have provided the opportunity for initial contacts with Fort Ancient people.

A few top-view and side-view brass animal effigies, associated, respectively, with Monongahela and Seneca sites to the north and interior Southeast sites to the south (W. Johnson 1992; Waselkov 1989), have come from eastern Fort Ancient sites such as Marmet and Clover, marking a protohistoric north-south exchange route (Drooker 1997a: 293, Figs. 8-12, 8-14). The large amount of marine shell at the Rolf Lee site, including thousands of beads, a Citico-style gorget, and five or more large masks (Table 8.2, Fig. 8.10), firmly establishes its residents' ties to settlements of the interior Southeast from eastern Tennessee southward. Evidence for a protohistoric connection in the same direction comes from the 13 or more large brass armbands worn by people buried at Rolf Lee, similar to examples found at Creek sites in Tennessee, Georgia, and Alabama dating to circa 1630–1650 (Drooker 1997a: 293, Fig. 8-14; M. Smith 1987; Waselkov 1989). The residents of this community, with the latest-dated large assemblage of European-derived items from any Fort Ancient site, appear to have been at the center of an exchange network stretching from New York to Alabama.

Residents of the western Fort Ancient Madisonville site also maintained far-flung communication networks. They began to obtain European goods almost as soon as they became available on the continent. Mid-sixteenth-century items that must have arrived from at least two different directions have been found (cf. Drooker 1996). A brass Clarksdale bell, a type associated with the de Soto *entrada* and other Spanish expeditions, probably was obtained from previously established exchange partners in the central Mississippi Valley. More surprising, because there is no prior evidence for interaction with northeastern peoples, is the assemblage connected to late sixteenth-century Iroquoian middlemen, most likely Neutrals or Senecas—Basque kettle parts, traded in from the lower St. Lawrence, an iron dagger guard, probably from the same direction, a brass spiral made from a thin metal tube, and friable blue glass beads of a type found at pre-1600 Ontario and New York sites. A variety of Iroquoian ceramic pipes, mostly broken, have come from Madisonville nonmortuary contexts (representing 6 percent of the pipes at the site, the most abundant foreign style after disk pipes), and one comes from the Hardin site; bulbous-tipped stems and other stylistic features mark at least some of them as coming from late sixteenth- or early seventeenth-century southern Ontario and Niagara frontier sites (Drooker 1997a: Fig. 8–27, 1997b). It is very likely that Madisonville and Hardin were visited by at least one group of Ontario Iroquoians, perhaps trying to extend their range for obtaining animal skins. If there was an extended relationship, it could have been the source of at least some of the copper and brass found at these sites, of which there was a particularly large amount at Madisonville. From the dates associated with European-derived artifacts at the two sites (Table 8.4), any such contacts appear to have ended by the 1610s, when the establishment of Dutch trading forts in eastern New York led to major alterations in exchange networks (Drooker 1996, 1997a: 333–335; cf. Sempowski 1994).

Another distinctive copper or brass artifact is a serpent shape made from a thin metal tube by the same methods as the spiral "Basque earrings," native-made from European metal, that are found throughout Iroquoian territory between about 1550 and 1625 (Bradley and Childs 1991). The serpent-shaped pendant has a map distribution linking Madisonville to prehistoric and protohistoric Oneota sites in Illinois and Iowa, and it may have functioned as a symbol badge at Madisonville and settlements such as Anker, Illinois (Bluhm and Liss 1961; Drooker 1996, 1997a: 284–287, 290–292).

Madisonville has produced far more metal than any other Fort Ancient site—including more ring, coil, and serpent shapes made from thin metal tubes than are known to be present at any other site in or out of Fort Ancient territory—as well as many other types of small artifacts, much scrap, and blanks for ornaments of various shapes. Over half of the more than 450 metal items at the site were discarded in pits and middens, not disposed of as grave goods (Drooker 1997a: Table 6-6). It seems likely that Madisonville people were manufacturing metal ornaments, including tubular beads and coils, rings, and serpent shapes made from thin metal tubes. Drooker (1997a: 335–337) has postulated that these might have been exchanged in connection with obtaining bison products and/or hunting rights among allies farther west.

WARFARE. Two vessels very similar in form to Late Fort Ancient Madisonville Plain jars (Drooker 1997a: Fig. 4-19) were excavated at the Seneca Dann site, which was occupied around 1655–1670. They could conceivably be connected to war captives from the Ohio Valley.

The possiblity of refugee groups at Fort Ancient sites, forced from territories farther north by Iroquoian depredations starting in the 1640s, has been investigated by a number of researchers. People from regions farther north definitely were present in Fort Ancient territory, but the major movements appear to have occurred before the accelerated Iroquoian warfare that is usually invoked to explain their presence. At Madisonville, the presence of small amounts of Indian Hills and related ceramics has been hypothesized to indicate the presence of refugees forced from northwestern Ohio during the early 1640s (Stothers 1994), but the metal and glass assemblages from the two site areas (apparently more recent in northern Ohio than at Madisonville, where no post-1600 "horizon marker" European artifacts have been excavated) do not clearly support this timing (Drooker 1997a: 329–331).

At eastern Fort Ancient sites, a long-term relationship with Wellsburg people from farther up the Ohio Valley is apparent. Although prehistoric Wellsburg settlements were located as far north as Pittsburgh, the mid-sixteenth-century Riker site and later protohistoric sites in the upper-middle Muskingum Valley (Fig. 8.1) were very close to Fort Ancient territory and have produced Madisonville-style ceramics (Drooker 1997a: 47; James Morton, personal communication 1994; Vietzen 1974). Wellsburg ceramics that occur in addition to Madisonville ceramics and locally developed styles at protohistoric Fort Ancient sites such as Neale's Landing and Orchard are strong evidence of groups of Wellsburg people at these settlements (Baker 1988; Moxley 1988a). Although it has not been firmly established that the Wellsburg groups arrived at Fort Ancient settlements on the Ohio River as late as the 1640s (for instance, European goods from the Neale's Landing site are typical of the pre-1630 period), southward movement due to Iroquois pressure remains a logical hypothesis.

Conclusion: Fort Ancient Peoples at the Dawn of History

The earliest firsthand descriptions of historically known Native American groups who might have come from the central Ohio Valley were based on observations made far from that region, beginning in the third quarter of the seventeenth century. Figure 8.11 shows the locations of Central Algonquian groups south of the Great Lakes at first documented European contact. No native settlements were visited by Europeans before the second half of the seventeenth century, when the French began to move into the upper Mississippi Valley, although individuals from some of these groups are recorded as having been met elsewhere.

Most groups mentioned by Nicolas Perrot and other Frenchmen in Wisconsin during the late 1660s, with the exception of the Menomini, had removed there within the previous few decades from homelands in Michigan and adjoining regions (from which came, archaeologically, items of material culture that have been found in small numbers at Fort Ancient sites such as Madisonville). Many of these people blamed Iroquoian depredations for their hegira. Illini bands such as the Kaskaskia and Peoria were first encountered by Marquette and Jolliet in Illinois, Iowa, and Missouri in 1673, within the same area they had inhabited for centuries.

No Shawnee groups were encountered then, but after Fort St. Louis was established on the Illinois River in 1682, not only large numbers of Illini but also groups of Miami, Shawnee, and others settled there at least temporarily (J. Brown 1961: 7–13). Earlier than that, members of one of the five Shawnee divisions, the Thawikila, settled on the Savannah River in South Carolina, soon after a 1674 encounter between the English trader Henry Woodward and two Shawnee men returning from the Spanish settlement at St. Augustine (Swanton 1946: 184). The Thawikila group was allied with the Upper Creeks and eventually moved

with them to Alabama in the early eighteenth century. In the early 1690s, Shawnee groups began to gather near the newly established city of Philadelphia, some traveling from Illinois, some from South Carolina, and some allegedly from Ohio territory. Pennsylvania is the region from which many of the Native Americans at Shawneetown in the mid-eighteenth century are known to have come (Callender 1978a; Hunter 1978; Jennings 1984: 223–274). Shawnee sites near Philadelphia have largely been destroyed or are inaccessible, but Savannah River Shawnee settlements might yet provide archaeological evidence to link these historically known people to the precontact residents of Fort Ancient territory.

If ancestors of historically known Shawnee groups were protohistoric residents of the central Ohio Valley, then this sequence of historical sightings, along with the lack of evidence for significant mass violence in Fort Ancient territory during the last half of the seventeenth century, would be consistent with people's having been drawn to newly established trading centers rather than having been forcibly expelled from their homeland entirely due to Iroquois depredations. Prehistoric and protohistoric connections between eastern Fort Ancient people and the interior Southeast, and

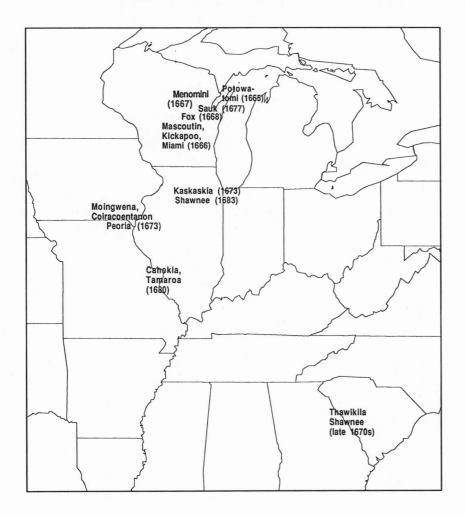

Figure 8.11. Locations of Central Algonquian groups from south of the Great Lakes at first European contact.

between western Fort Ancient people and the upper Mississippi valley, would have predisposed different Fort Ancient groups to travel in different directions. If the Thawikila Shawnees who settled near Charles Towne after 1674 came from the central Ohio Valley, it was probably from the eastern end. Shawnees were not among the Central Algonquian groups known to have taken refuge west of Lake Michigan between 1640 and 1670 due to Iroquoian attacks. Their appearence in large numbers only after the founding of Fort St. Louis in 1682 perhaps indicates that their homeland was less vulnerable to Iroquoian raids, which, when they did penetrate into Ohio country, probably affected eastern Fort Ancient territory first. Very likely, though, western Fort Ancient groups had been traveling to this vicinity long before they ever were sighted by Frenchmen.

The 1670s and 1680s mark the dawn of the historic era for Fort Ancient peoples, when increasingly direct contact with Euroamericans would result in profound changes to their precontact culture and way of life. But the archaeological record of the central Ohio Valley also reveals trends already under way long before the advent of Europeans. Evidence of population movements, subregional abandonment, and increasing intra- and interregional communication suggest that for whatever reason, the Ohio Valley was already in a state of flux at European landfall on the North American continent. For archaeologists interested in the transformation of the Fort Ancient societies, the dawn of history challenges us to explain these changes.

Locations of Primary Collections

Important collections pertaining to the Fort Ancient populations of the central Ohio Valley are located in the following institutions: (1) District of Columbia and Maryland. Smithsonian Institution National Museum of the American Indian and National Museum of Natural History, Washington, D.C.; (2) Kentucky. The William S. Webb Museum of Anthropology, University of Kentucky, Lexington; (3) Ohio. The Cincinnati Museum Center; the Dayton Museum of Natural History; the Ohio Historical Center, Columbus; (4) Massachusetts. The Peabody Museum of Archaeology and Ethnology, Harvard University, Cambridge; the Robert S. Peabody Museum of Archaeology, Phillips Academy, Andover; (5) New York. American Museum of Natural History, New York. (6) West Virginia. Grave Creek Mound Museum, Moundsville.

Note

This chapter grew out of an original manuscript by Cowan, incorporating additional data from Drooker's dissertation research.

9

Monacan Archaeology of the Virginia Interior, A.D. 1400–1700

An abundant and accessible ethnohistoric record and an increasingly well-synthesized prehistoric and contact-era archaeology make the Algonquian Powhatan people of coastal Virginia among the better-known tribal groups at European contact in eastern North America (Barbour 1986; Potter 1993; Rountree 1989; Turner 1985). The culture and history of native peoples of the interior, to the west of the fall line separating the piedmont from the coastal plain, is not nearly so well known, however. The same Jamestown colonists who created the rich ethnohistoric record of the Powhatans rarely ventured beyond the coastal plain prior to 1700. Thus, textual data are relatively sparse, and the interior cultures have remained largely in the historical shadows, although they were very much a part of the precontact and postcontact regional cultural matrix. As I have suggested elsewhere (Hantman 1990), understanding the interior cultures, particularly the Siouan-speaking Monacans of the Virginia piedmont, is essential to a full appreciation of late prehistoric regional interaction systems in Virginia and to understanding the uniqueness of the colonial encounter in the Chesapeake region and its effects on native history in the interior. In the absence of a rich documentary record, such an understanding must come largely from archaeological research and a careful reading of the historical sources. Further, such an understanding needs to move freely across the boundary typically established between history and prehistory.

Here I summarize what is known of the archaeology and ethnohistory of the central Virginia interior for the period A.D. 1400–1700. I specifically address the area principally along and between the Rappahannock, James, and Appomattox Rivers of the piedmont, between the fall line and the Shenandoah Valley–Ridge and Valley province. This was the area identified on historic maps of the Jamestown era as the "territory" of the Monacans and Mannahoacs, who most scholars today agree can be referred to collectively as Monacans (Figs. 9.1, 9.2). After reviewing the history of research in the area, I address the definition of chronological and cultural complexes, settlement patterns, subsistence, social organization, exchange, warfare, and mortuary behavior. For each category, I will be attuned to changes that occurred with the establishment of a permanent European presence in Virginia in 1607. There had been earlier colonization attempts in Virginia, such as the failed Spanish mission of 1570 (Lewis and Loomie 1953) and the failed Roanoke colony of 1585–1587 (Quinn 1984). Indirect effects probably were also felt from Spanish exploration to the southwest (Hudson 1990). As elsewhere, it is impossible to fix an absolute precontact-postcontact boundary after 1492, but the establishment of the Jamestown colony in 1607 clearly marks a fundamental change in the history of the region that demands particular attention.

JEFFREY L. HANTMAN

Figure 9.1. The Virginia interior. The hatched area shows the approximate extent of Monacan territory, circa 1600.

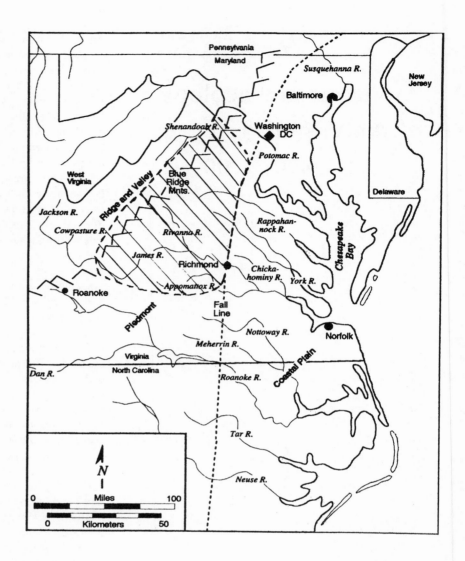

Archaeological Research in the Virginia Interior

Archaeological research in the Virginia interior had an auspicious beginning. Sometime between 1760 and 1781 (the exact year is uncertain), Thomas Jefferson excavated a burial mound in central Virginia (Hantman and Dunham 1993; Jefferson 1982 [1787]). The mound probably had been constructed by the recent ancestors of the Monacans and most likely was used well into the seventeenth century (Holland 1978). Introductory textbooks like to proclaim that it was at this mound that the first "scientific" archaeology was conducted in North America, and there that the principles of stratigraphy were first used. It was also to Jefferson's credit that despite common speculation concerning the mounds as burial grounds for ancient warriors who had died at the battle site, he tested that assertion and found that the skeletal evidence did not support it. The mound, Jefferson wrote, was the burial ground for more than a thousand individuals who had lived in the region. Though Jefferson did not assign the name Monacan to those Indians, he did describe a local group's paying a somber and mournful visit to the mound years before his excavation.

That mound appears in the first or second chapter of every "introduction to archaeology" or "history of archaeology" textbook published in recent years (e.g., Fagan 1991; Jennings 1974: 37; Thomas 1989: 27–31; Willey and Sabloff 1974: 28–29). Unfortunately, it is rarely mentioned again, even in discussions of Eastern Woodlands prehistory. This is not really surprising, since the mound was a 12-foot-high accretional burial mound, not a platform or temple mound, and although it contained an extraordinary quantity of human remains, it contained no grave goods. Interestingly, Jefferson also mentioned the presence of several other such mounds in the Virginia interior. Today we know there are at least 13 such mounds there (Dunham 1994; Gold 1998; Hantman 1990; MacCord 1986; Schmitt 1952), and their presence throughout the region raises questions of prehistoric regional cultural connections to other parts of the eastern United States that have not yet been systematically explored, more than 200 years after Jefferson's pioneering study.

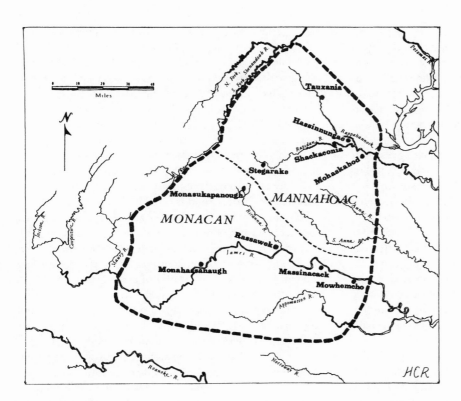

Figure 9.2. Villages and tribal names identified by John Smith in his 1612 *Map of Virginia* (Barbour 1986), placed in their approximate locations. The area within the dashed line is that of the hatched area shown in Figure 9.1. (Reproduced with permission from Rountree 1993: 97; copyright Helen C. Rountree.)

After Jefferson's work, little formal archaeological research was undertaken in interior Virginia until late in the nineteenth century, when Lucien Carr of the Harvard Peabody Museum excavated portions of the Ely Mound in southwestern Virginia (Carr 1877), and E. P. Valentine of Richmond published briefly on his mound excavations in Virginia and North Carolina (Valentine 1892). Smithsonian archaeologists Gerard Fowke (1894) and David Bushnell (1930, 1935) carried out surveys and excavations in the major river valleys of the Virginia interior and tested several mound sites in the central and west-central areas of the state. Bushnell conducted his surveys with an eye toward identifying sites that appeared on John Smith's 1609 map of Indian settlements.

In the later half of the twentieth century, surveys and excavations were conducted largely by the Archaeological Society of Virginia, under the direction of C. G. Holland or Howard MacCord. William Gardner conducted extensive surveys and excavations throughout Virginia and wrote an overview of the prehistory of the Shenandoah Valley (Gardner 1986). L. Daniel Mouer directed surveys and excavations in the James River piedmont in the 1970s and 1980s (Mouer 1983), and the University of Virginia has conducted archaeological and ethnohistoric research in the Virginia interior since 1984, under my direction. The survey data have been fruitful, but excavations of well-preserved piedmont sites have been few. Recent excavations in the Roanoke River drainage to the west and south of the study area, however, are offering dramatic new insights (Barber 1993; Barber, Barber, and Bowen 1998; Ward and Davis, this volume; Klatka and Klein 1993, 1998). An extremely complex geomorphological regime in the region (Hayes and Monaghan 1998), erosion, and plowing have created an archaeological record in the central Virginia piedmont that is challenging to reconstruct. Had Thomas Jefferson not published the results of his excavation, it is unlikely that his mound site would have been noticed in the twentieth century. Since Bushnell's time, archaeologists have looked unsuccessfully for traces of it at the place where it must have been located (Boyer 1982; Bushnell 1930). Such have been the destructive forces of farming and erosion.

Chronology and Cultural Complexes

In addition to site preservation, chronological control is a major problem for the Late Woodland (A.D. 900–1600) and early historic (1600–1700) periods in the Virginia interior, particularly in the James River and Rappahannock River areas of Monacan settlement. Ceramic stylistic and technological variation as recorded in series and wares (Evans 1955) is limited, and there are few radiocarbon dates, although this is changing rapidly. Table 9.1 lists radiocarbon-dated features from the Virginia interior; it is intended to be representative, not necessarily comprehensive (see also Gallivan 1999; Gleach 1985; Klein 1994a, 1994b). It divides dated sites in the central Virginia interior into two groups, first those of the Rappahannock and James River area of Monacan ethnohistoric territory, and then those in the surrounding areas of the upper James, the Shenandoah, the New, and the Roanoke Rivers, where the applicability of this ethnohistoric tribal name is less certain. As shown in Table 9.1, only two sites in the central Virginia piedmont have produced dates for the period 1400–1700 (550–250 B.P.), even though historic maps and texts suggest a denser settlement. Early Late Woodland sites are more frequent. In the surrounding territory of the Ridge and Valley and Mountain provinces, Late Woodland sites are equally common, but there are also many known sites with dated contexts in the 1400–1700 range. This geographic distinction will be explored later.

At the broadest level, archaeologists conducting research in the Virginia interior call the years from about A.D. 900 to 1607 the Late Woodland period and the years from 1607 to about 1700 the contact or ethnohistoric period. Most archaeologists refer to the years between A.D. 1400 and 1607 as the later part of the Late Woodland, or Late Woodland II (recognizing significant patterns of culture change that occurred at 1200 or so [e.g., Gallivan 1999]). Mississippian traits and "influence" have been noted in the extreme southwestern reaches of the state, where the Clinch and Powell Rivers flow west into the Mississippi drainage, but otherwise a "Mississippian" period is not traditionally recognized in Virginia's chronological framework (Egloff 1992).

Outside the piedmont, archaeologists have used the greater ceramic variation present as an opportunity to develop finer-grained temporal and cultural analytical boundaries. MacCord (1989, 1991) and Hodges (1993) have contributed models of the statewide distribution of cultures or archaeological foci for the period under study. Figure 9.3 illustrates the boundaries and temporal associations of the "cultures" as defined by MacCord. In this model, nine archaeological foci are defined for the Late Woodland, principally on the basis of ceramics but using other attributes, such as mortuary practices, as well. For the period of concern here, A.D. 1400–1700, MacCord distinguished between the Mason Island, Montgomery, and Luray foci of the interior Potomac, the Lewis Creek Mound culture in the Piedmont and Ridge and Valley provinces, the Dan River culture of the southern piedmont, and the Intermontane culture in the mountains of southwestern Virginia. For the coastal plain, he also marked the boundaries between the Algonquian Powhatan culture of the James, York, and Rappahanock Rivers, the Potomac Creek focus on the Potomac River, and the Nottoway-Meherrin culture of the river systems of the same names in southeastern Virginia (see also Turner 1992). Hodges (1993) offered a similar reconstruction but named the regions for which ethnohistoric records were lacking by reference to the dominant ceramic ware (Fig. 9.4).

In MacCord's model, almost all of these areas remain occupied after 1500, either through in-situ development or through migration and displacement, but they are occupied by vastly reduced numbers of people. The two exceptions are the northwestern and west-central regions of the state, where he suggests that the Lewis Creek Mound culture area was abandoned by 1450 and the Luray focus area by 1600. The other cultures or regions remain occupied until shortly after permanent European settlement began in the early

seventeenth century. It is the empty area in the center of MacCord's map (Fig. 9.3) that I am primarily concerned with filling here. I consider this central area of the state, along with some parts of what MacCord called the Lewis Creek area and some parts of the Dan River area, to have been Monacan territory in the early historic era *and* in the Late Woodland (as in Fig. 9.4). Although the Monacans were clearly part of a much larger Siouan landscape extending far north and south of Virginia (Hudson 1970; Merrell 1989; Mooney 1894), I propose the name Monacan as an explicitly archaeological complex based on prehistoric material culture patterns and as a name that allows recognition of continuity between prehistory and history. I realize that this label may be contested on the basis of ceramic variability, but there is a coherence to the region in mortuary practices and historical connections that is far more compelling than the markedly clinal patterns of ceramic variation (Klein 1994a) that regional studies reveal.

In the Rappahannock and James River region of central Virginia, the Late Woodland is defined by the dominant presence of Albemarle (crushed quartz temper) series pottery, with small amounts of Stony Creek (sand-tempered) series, Potomac Creek, and Dan River ceramics (see Evans 1955; Holland 1978). Fabric-impressed and simple-stamped surface treatments increased in frequency throughout the Middle and Late Woodland of central Virginia, but in general, decorative elaboration was less pronounced than in areas to the north. On the James River, simple-stamped ceramics suggest some connection to the south and east, and in the Rappahannock and James River drainages, some Potomac Creek sherds occur in the minority, suggesting ties to the north and east (Hantman and Klein 1992). Griffin's (1945) study of ceramics from the Virginia piedmont concluded with the observation that the ceramics of central Virginia bore a closer relation to the ceramics of the coastal plain than to those of the Fort Ancient area. I think that observation still holds, for the most part.

Archaeologists working in the adjacent regions of the Virginia interior have attempted to define shorter periods of time based principally on type and ware variations in ceramic assemblages. For instance, for the Shenandoah Valley to the west, Gardner (1986) and Walker and Miller (1992) broke the Late Woodland (A.D. 900–1700) into five stages, as follows:

Late Woodland I (900–1100): Albemarle crushed-quartz-tempered pottery

Late Woodland II (1100–1250): small percentage of limestone-tempered pottery

Late Woodland III (1250–1350): increasing percentage of limestone temper

Late Woodland IV (1350–1450): Page ceramics replace Albemarle

Late Woodland V (1450–1700): shell-tempered Keyser Cord Marked

Table 9.1

Radiocarbon Dated Sites of the Late Woodland–Contact Era in Interior Virginia

Site	Uncorrected Years B.P.	Site Name	Reference
Central piedmont, James and Rappahannock Rivers			
44 FV 19	920 ± 75	Point of Forks	Klein 1994a
44 FV 134	1050 ± 170	Spessard	Klein 1994a
44 FV 134	790 ± 80		Klein 1994a
44 FV 134	900 ± 80		Klein 1994a
44 FV 134	960 ± 80		Klein 1994a
44 FV 134	955 ± 55		Klein 1994a
44 AB 416	250 ± 60	Lickinghole Creek	Hantman et al. 1993
44 AB 416	370 ± 60		Hantman et al. 1993
44 NE 143	850 ± 80	Wood Site	Gallivan 1999
44 NE 143	910 ± 80		Gallivan 1999
44 NE 143	990 ± 100		Gallivan 1999
44 NE 4	1030 ± 80	Wingina	MacCord 1986
44 AH 193	980 ± 50	Partridge Creek	Klein 1994a
44 AH 193	890 ± 80		Klein 1994a
44 AH 193	910 ± 50		Klein 1994a
44 AH 193	930 ± 75		Klein 1994a
44 AH 193	820 ± 70		Klein 1994a
44 AH 193	870 ± 70		Klein 1994a
44 AH 193	950 ± 70		Klein 1994a
44 OR 1	510 ± 110	Rapidan Mound	Holland et al. 1983
44 OR 1	580 ± 35		Gold 1998
44 OR 1	590 ± 35		Gold 1998
44 GO 30	370 ± 40	Wright Site	Gallivan 1999
44 GO 30b	750 ± 60		Gallivan 1999
Upper James, Roanoke, New, and Shenandoah Rivers of interior Virginia			
44 SH 1	310 ± 120	Bowman	Hodges 1993
44 SH 1	240 ± 120		Hodges 1993
44 SH 3	500 ± 70	Quicksburg	Klein 1994a
44 WR 2	610 ± 50	Sauer	MacCord 1986
44 WR 3	260 ± 100	Cabin Run	Hodges 1993
44 WR 3	630 ± 50		Gleach 1985
44 WR 3	700 ± 60		Gleach 1985
44 WR 3	730 ± 80		Gleach 1985
44 WR 3	740 ± 120		Gleach 1985
44 WR 3	820 ± 80		Gleach 1985
44 WR 3	1030 ± 100		Gleach 1985
44 AU 20	580 ± 200	Lewis Creek	MacCord 1986
44 AU 20	810 ± 240		MacCord 1986
44 AU 20	865 ± 50		Gold 1998
44 AU 20	830 ± 55		Gold 1998
44 AU 20	850 ± 50		Gold 1998
44 AU 35	640 ± 150	John East Mound	Gleach 1985
44 AU 35	730 ± 90		Gleach 1985
44 AU 35	1050 ± 290		Gleach 1985
44 AU 35	900 ± 50		Gold 1998
44 BA 3	315 ± 60	Perkins Point	Klein 1994a
44 BA 3	440 ± 130		Klein 1994a
44 BA 3	435 ± 50		Klein 1994a
44 BA 5	730 ± 65	Huffman	Klein 1994a
44 BA 5	935 ± 75		Klein 1994a
44 BA 5	1065 ± 70		Klein 1994a
44 BA 15	645 ± 80	Noah's Ark	Hodges 1993
44 BA 15	675 ± 65		Hodges 1993

Continued on next page

Table 9.1 *continued*

Site	Uncorrected Years B.P.	Site Name	Reference
44 BA 15	725 ± 70		Hodges 1993
44 BA 15	920 ± 110		Hodges 1993
44 BA 35	880 ± 130	Hirsh Mound	MacCord 1986
44 BO 26	580 ± 50	Bessemer	Egloff 1992
44 BO 26	730 ± 70		Egloff 1992
44 BO 26	510 ± 50		Egloff 1992
44 BO 26	230 ± 60		Egloff 1992
44 BO 26	730 ± 90		Egloff 1992
44 BO 26	590 ± 50		Egloff 1992
44 BO 26	530 ± 50		Egloff 1992
44 BO 26	630 ± 50		Egloff 1992
44 BO 26	700 ± 50		Egloff 1992
44 BO 26	380 ± 70		Egloff 1992
44 BO 26	770 ± 50		Egloff 1992
44 BO 26	720 ± 70		Egloff 1992
44 BO 26	730 ± 50		Egloff 1992
44 BO 26	540 ± 70		Egloff 1992
44 PY 144	370 ± 60	Hurt Power Plant	Barber et al. 1998
44 PY 144	260 ± 80		Barber et al. 1998
44 PY 144	240 ± 50		Barber et al. 1998
44 PY 144	290 ± 70		Barber et al. 1998
44 PY 144	360 ± 60		Barber et al. 1998
44 PY 144	220 ± 70		Barber et al. 1998
44 PY 144	120 ± 60		Barber et al. 1998
44 PY 144	550 ± 60		Barber et al. 1998
44 PY 144	170 ± 60		Barber et al. 1998
44 PY 144	550 ± 50		Barber et al. 1998
44 RN 39	350 ± 90	Thomas-Sawyer	Egloff 1992
44 RN 39	320 ± 90		Egloff 1992
44 RN 21	250 ± 50	Graham-White	Klein 1994a
44 RN 21	180 ± 60		Klein 1994a
44 RN 21	360 ± 60		Klein 1994a
44 RN 21	460 ± 60		Klein 1994a
44 RN 21	570 ± 60		Klein 1994a
44 MY 3	235 ± 80	Trigg	Egloff 1992
44 MY 3	375 ± 60		Egloff 1992
44 MY 18	905 ± 60	Thomas	Egloff 1992
44 MY 11	700 ± 120	Ingles	Egloff 1992
44 MY 18	905 ± 60	Thomas	MacCord 1986
44 MY 33	680 ± 50	Hall	Egloff 1992
44 MY 33	740 ± 50		Egloff 1992
44 MY 33	740 ± 60		Egloff 1992
44 MY 37	420 ± 90	Mayre	Egloff 1992
44 MY 37	260 ± 60		Egloff 1992
44 FR 31	630 ± 50		Klein 1994a
44 CP 1	460 ± 50		Klein 1994a
44 HA 22	480 ± 60	Reedy Creek	Klein 1994a
44 HA 22	800 ± 65		Klein 1994a
44 HA 23	455 ± 80		Klein 1994a
44 HA 23	590 ± 50		Klein 1994a
44 HA 23	520 ± 70		Klein 1994a
44 HR 1	635 ± 60	Leatherwood	Gleach 1985
44 HR 4	205 ± 55	Philpott	Hodges 1993
44 HR 29	230 ± 40		Hodges 1993
44 PU 3	350 ± 200	Belspring	Egloff 1992
44 PU 9	620 ± 120	Fairlawn	Egloff 1992

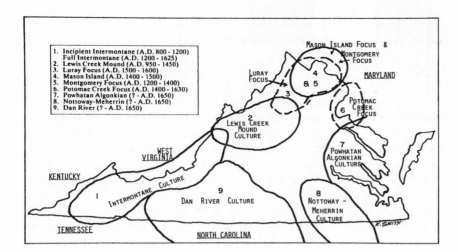

Figure 9.3. MacCord's construction of cultural and chronological complexes in Late Woodland and early contact period Virginia. (Reproduced from *Quarterly Bulletin of the Archaeological Society of Virginia*, vol. 46.)

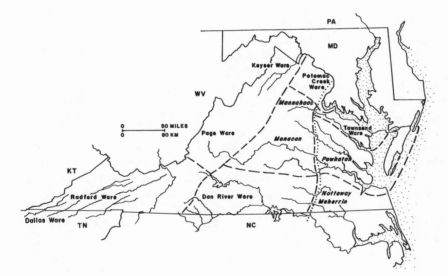

Figure 9.4. Hodges's construction of cultural complexes by ethnohistoric tribal name or dominant ceramic ware in seventeenth-century Virginia. (Reproduced with permission from Hodges 1993.)

To the east, for the coastal plain of Virginia, Turner (1992: 102) observed that shell-tempered, fabric-impressed, and incised Townsend Ware was the dominant pottery until about A.D. 1300, when sand- and crushed-quartz-tempered pottery with simple-stamping appeared. In the northern reaches of the Virginia coastal plain, these are called Potomac Creek wares (see Potter 1993), and in the southern area they are termed Gaston/Cashie Ware (Turner 1992: 103). A third ware found in addition to the common Townsend Ware is a shell-tempered, simple-stamped ceramic called Roanoke Ware (Egloff and Potter 1982: 109; Turner 1992: 104). Potter (1993) similarly broke the Late Woodland of the Potomac River area into two periods: Late Woodland I (A.D. 900–1300), with predominantly shell-tempered Townsend Ware, and Late Woodland II (1300–1500), marked by the introduction of new ceramic types such as Townsend Corded, Rappahannock Incised, and the crushed-rock-tempered Potomac Creek. Significantly, Potter (1993) added a subsequent archaeological period, the proto-historic (1500–1650), which he distinguished by the presence of a fine shell-tempered plainware called Yeocomico

Ware (see also Egloff and Potter 1982: 112–114). He also observed that the frequency of Potomac Creek and Moyaone Plain pottery increased during the early historic period. Both Potter (1993) and Turner (1992: 104) suggested that the distribution of these late (post-1300) Late Woodland wares reflected a pattern of increasing territoriality strikingly similar to that observed historically, around 1607.

For southwestern Virginia, Egloff (1992) described the pattern of change in ceramic wares over time, noting the common co-occurrence of sand-, soapstone-, shell-, or limestone-tempered pottery, but he did not propose a new periodization scheme. A prevalence of well-dated sites in the area would make such an effort worthwhile. Reliable radiocarbon dates from excavated sites in the region range from the tenth century A.D. to the early eighteenth century (Egloff 1992: Table 1). Egloff also observed that the "Appalachian Complicated Stamped Tradition" and the "Mississippian Shell Tempered Tradition" occurred in small amounts on the Late Woodland archaeological sites of southwestern Virginia (1992: 198).

Finally, in the Dan River area in the southern reaches of

piedmont Virginia, the University of North Carolina Siouan project has had great success in studying the late prehistoric–historic transition (Davis and Ward 1991a; Dickens, Ward, and Davis 1987). Because this project is discussed elsewhere in this volume, I note here only that where well-preserved sites can be located, fine-grained chronologies can be developed. The piedmont-interior region of Maryland has been best summarized by Kavanaugh (1983), but she treated the Late Woodland period as a single unit dating to A.D. 1000–1600, after which the area might have been abandoned. Several excavated sites in the region have yielded radiocarbon dates extending into the late fifteenth century (Curry and Kavanaugh 1991; Potter 1993), but the Maryland piedmont typically is argued to have been abandoned after that date.

Radiocarbon dating (see Table 9.1) and European artifacts (see Hodges 1993) provide clear evidence of post-fifteenth-century occupation in areas of Virginia west of the Blue Ridge Mountains and in some southwestern portions of the piedmont in that state. Key sites in this context are Bowman, Cabin Run, Perkins Point, and Keyser Farm—all in the northwestern part of Virginia—and the Trigg, Bessemer, Sawyer, Graham-White, and Hurt Power Plant sites in the Roanoke River drainage near the present-day city of Roanoke and farther southeast on the Virginia–North Carolina border in Pittsylvania County (Barber, Barber, and Bowen 1998; Egloff 1992; Hodges 1993; Klatka and Klein 1998). Postcontact radiocarbon dates and the presence and context of European trade items in the Virginia coastal plain have been described in publications such as those by Potter (1989, 1993) and Hodges (1993: 35–41).

For the central Virginia James and Rappahannock River piedmont—areas of particular focus in this chapter—radiocarbon evidence for occupation after A.D. 1200 is relatively scarce. Excavations at a small upland site with a burned structure on a small tributary in the James River drainage (44 AB 416) have produced the first radiocarbon dates for a postcontact period settlement (A.D. 1580 ± 60 and 1700 ± 60; Hantman et al. 1993). Artifacts were few but included Albemarle (crushed quartz temper) pottery and small, triangular projectile points—an inventory that, in the absence of radiocarbon dates, would have triggered a label of "Late Woodland" only. No European goods were found. At the Rapidan Mound site, one piece of human bone with a poorly recorded context produced a date of A.D. 1440 ± 110 (Holland, van Roijen, and Spieden 1983), but more recent and extensive dating by Gold (1998) from good mound contexts has confirmed fifteenth-century use of the mound and, by implication, contemporaneous occupation of the surrounding area. Artifacts, although scarce, included small triangular (Clarksville) projectile points and Albemarle series pottery. A very small amount of Potomac Creek pottery, diagnostic of the later Late Woodland period in the coastal plain, was also recovered. Preliminary testing by Gallivan (1999) at the Wright site on the eastern edge of the

piedmont identified at least one feature dating to the contact era. Given its apparent preservation and dating, this site holds the greatest promise as of this writing for future study of piedmont Monacans in the Late Woodland and early contact period.

Other than these dates, the latest radiocarbon date from a good context in the central James and Rappahannock River region of central Virginia is A.D. 1160 ± 80, from a feature at the Spessard site on the James River. Although excavations in the region have been few and preservation of sites there is poor, it is notable that so few later dates have been recorded. Excavations at the Wood site, once thought by many to be the Monacan village of Monahassanaugh identified on John Smith's map, have yet to produce a date later than A.D. 1130 ± 80 (Gallivan 1999; Hantman et al. 1993). The widespread effects of flooding and deep plowing may have eliminated later Woodland or contact era features, for seriations of ceramic surface collections produce later dates than do features (Gallivan 1999). Yet the archaeological record may reflect a historical reality; the region may have been largely abandoned after 1607 and sparsely settled in the years just before Jamestown. The presence or absence of diagnostic artifacts (indigenous ceramics or European trade goods) that can demonstrate a post-1400 to contact era occupation of central Virginia is obviously a critical issue. On the basis of limited archaeological and ethnohistoric information, I am optimistic that sites will be found in the James and Rappahannock River systems that were occupied after A.D. 1200 and until at least 1650, although I would not expect to see a significant change in ceramic production and decoration marking that time period. Certainly the demographic reconstruction based on the Rapidan Mound (see Gold 1998) indicates that village sites dating at least up to the fifteenth century existed but have not been preserved or discovered as of this writing.

Grumet (1990: 296), in his overview of the contact period in the eastern United States, observed:

Physical evidence of historic Indian occupation immediately west of the fall line [in Virginia] also is rare. The University of Virginia's multi-year survey of a 200 square mile area of the James and Rivanna River Valleys, for example, failed to find a single identifiably historic Indian site. . . . Many scholars believe that future research will uncover evidence of a 17th century Indian occupation in this and nearby areas. Others, however, believe that the absence of known archaeological and documentary evidence in piedmont Virginia indicates that most Indians moved away from the region sometime during the 1600s.

These comments are essentially on target (although 1997 tests at the Wright site [Gallivan 1999] proved a significant exception). Prior to 1993, the University of Virginia survey of the major river valleys of the central James and Rivanna Rivers did fail to find a single site that could be *definitely* attributed to the early seventeenth century (pre-1650), but I think this is a problem of chronological method rather than a reflection of settlement history. Both Holland (1978) and I (Hantman 1990) have suggested that village and mound sites along the James and Rappahannock Rivers were used until about 1650. This is not an untenable assumption and in fact is likely, considering that European settlement did not encroach in the area until after 1650, and villages are noted on early colonial maps.

Holland (1978) made his case for the post-1607 occupation of the village of Monasukapanough and the adjacent Jefferson Mound, and I make the same case for the Rapidan Mound in the Rappahannock River system (Dunham 1994; Gold 1998; Hantman and Dunham 1993). In addition to the fifteenth-century radiocarbon dates from the Rapidan Mound, the site produced six iron nails that were determined to have been in mound soils, though they were not associated with any bone features (Dunham 1994). Clearly, more data are needed. In addition, efforts to date features and sites using nontypological methods of ceramic attribute analysis hold great potential for improving chronological control in the region (Klein 1994a).

Settlement Patterns

More than 100 years of systematic and unsystematic archaeological surveys in central Virginia have led to a consensus description of the pattern of settlement during the Late Woodland period (A.D. 900–1600). Late Woodland sites are typically, though not exclusively, located on permanent rivers and streams, a pattern that contrasts with the earlier dispersed settlement of the Archaic through Early Woodland and early Middle Woodland periods (Hantman and Klein 1992; Holland 1978). Mouer (1983: 17) observed that "Piedmont Late Woodland settlements in the James River Valley are, for the most part, compact clusters or linear arrangements of houses along the banks of rivers near stream confluences and on large islands." Holland (1978) and I (Hantman 1985) both noted a striking correlation between Late Woodland villages and the soils of highest productivity. Klein (1986: 52) noted a distinction between the Middle Woodland period, when most permanent streams had sites on them, and the Late Woodland, when the settlement pattern was more intensively focused on the largest rivers. He suggested that this resulted more from issues of social interaction and trade than simply from the need for access to agricultural soils. A cultural resource management project in the region discovered some small Late Woodland sites on the floodplains of smaller, upland streams (Stevens 1989).

Late Woodland sites are densely distributed along major rivers. The banks of the James, Rivanna, Rappahannock, Rapidan, Roanoke, and Appomattox Rivers at times appear to hold nearly one continuous artifact scatter, with only occasional areas lacking settlement. Surveys in central Virginia have shown that "buffer zones" are located on the Hardware River and on the Rivanna; these empty areas help

put into some context the buffer zone described by Turner (1978) between the coastal plain Powhatans and the piedmont Monacans. That is, whereas archaeologists have examined many models to explain the empty region between the Powhatans and the Monacans in terms of hostility between the two groups, surveys in the piedmont show these kinds of buffer zones to have been the norm, even within Monacan territory. Social and ecological-agricultural factors are the most likely causes. At a finer spatial scale, Gallivan's (1999) intensive survey and subsequent excavation of one apparent "continuous artifact scatter" along the James River revealed that these scatters mask what are, upon excavation, more discrete, smaller villages, hamlets, or household clusters.

One record of settlement for the contact era (post-1607) in central Virginia is the famous John Smith map first published in Oxford in 1612 (represented in Fig. 9.2). Though the information on this map for the area west of the fall zone is, in Smith's words "by relation only," the pattern described to him by his Powhatan and Siouan informants shows the Monacans' exclusive use of the major rivers.

An important point must be made about this map and what it tells us of post-1607 settlement in the Virginia interior. The villages Smith put on his map are but a sample of those that existed even after 1607. Of the James River villages, Smith noted that four villages appearing on his map "pay tribute to Rassawek," and there were "*other nations* which do the same" (emphasis added). Of the Rappahannock River villages, Smith wrote that there were seven named villages "and divers others" (Barbour 1986; Hantman 1993). "Divers" in the early seventeenth century meant an unspecified number, and whatever that number might have been, the point is that for the interior of Virginia, unlike the coastal plain around which John Smith traveled directly, the villages appearing on his famous map should not be construed as representing the total number of villages that were in existence. As Grumet (1990) said, it is largely through archaeology that additional sites can potentially be located. The recent discovery of the seventeenth-century site in the uplands of the James River valley, described earlier, illustrates that potential (Hantman et al. 1993). In terms of ecological factors, then, there was little change in settlement pattern between the precontact and the postcontact world. The majority of the villages were on the major rivers, and some contemporaneous sites were in upland valleys where smaller patches of agricultural soil were found. There is little evidence for change in settlement prior to about 1650.

After that time, however, the political and economic geography changed dramatically. In 1646, the English signed a treaty with the coastal Powhatans that ended the chance of Indian sovereignty anywhere on the coastal plain (Rountree 1991). The treaty led to the creation of a series of forts and trading posts on the western edge of the coastal plain, facing into the interior. Perhaps the most important of these was Fort Henry, on the Appomattox River south of the James. Post-1650 archaeological sites in the central Virginia interior have been found only to the south and west of the central James River valley, with a concentration in the Roanoke and New River drainages. The James and Rappahannock River floodplains, which had been home to the Monacans, appear to have been largely abandoned at this time, as was the piedmont Potomac. The 1650 map made by Edward Bland (1651) identified the "Manikes" as being located somewhere south of the James River, toward the Roanoke or the Appomattox River (Fig. 9.5). The other sites in the Virginia interior that date at or after 1650 (Graham-White, Hurt Power Plant, Cabin Run, Bowman, Huffman, Keyser Farm; see Table 9.1) are in the Ridge and Valley province, the Shenandoah Valley, or the more southern Virginia piedmont.

In this context, it is striking to note that Tanner (1989) wrote of the trading paths in early colonial Virginia that "one branch diverted east, to the Catawba country near Roanoke Virginia, and followed the valley of the Shenandoah River" (Fig. 9.6). The allusion to Catawba country speaks mainly to the Siouan connection (Merrell 1989); the trail described in historic documents also corresponds to the archaeological pattern that has emerged for the late seventeenth century in the Virginia interior. It appears that participation in the interior deerskin trade accounts for those Indian communities in Virginia that we commonly recognize as making up the dominant pattern of late seventeenth-century settlement in the Virginia interior (i.e., sites with ^{14}C dates or European trade goods). Those who participated in this trade created the more permanent villages with European trade goods, which have come to typologically define Native American sites in the Virginia interior in the late seventeenth century.

I have suggested previously that for the most part, the Monacans (unlike the Powhatans) chose not to trade with the English in the first half-century following the James-town settlement (Hantman 1990). After 1650, the English intruded on the Virginia interior, and *some* Monacans likely relocated to the major rivers to participate in the trade. There they became a recognizable part of the archaeological record and are almost certainly a part of the groups referred to as Saponi and Tutelo, descended from a Monacan past (Hantman 1998; Merrell 1989). At the same time, some more obscure settlements may have been occupied away from the major rivers by those remaining Monacans who chose not to engage in the European trade (others presumably relocated elsewhere in the eastern United States [Hantman 1990; Hantman et al. 1993; Merrell 1989]). Although sites of this type are of the contact era, they may not contain European trade goods. Only improved ceramic and radiocarbon dating will enable archaeologists to find such sites, if they in fact exist in greater numbers.

Between 1650 and 1700, the area of the piedmont James and Rappahannock Rivers was largely, but not completely, abandoned. Some Indians remained in the hills above the James, where some were likely the ancestors of the Native American tribal group that lives today in this area and that recently revived the Monacan name and received state recognition in 1989 (Houck and Maxham 1993).

INTRASITE SETTLEMENT PATTERNS. Only two excavated Late Woodland sites in the piedmont of the Virginia interior have been sufficiently well preserved to allow the identification of house patterns. One of these is the early Late Woodland Wingina site, located on the James River floodplain, where MacCord (1974) identified post holes that formed the outlines of three houses. The most complete of these contained 44 post holes arranged in an elliptical pattern measuring approximately 6 meters by 5 meters. A possible door was identified on the east side, but no features were identified within the house. A single radiocarbon date from charcoal within a post yielded an age of A.D. 920 ± 80. The two other houses were identified by arcs

Figure 9.5. Edward Bland's 1650 map of the Virginia interior. Note the presence of the "Manikes" south of the James River, just north of the "Mangoakes." (Courtesy of the Special Collections Department, Manuscripts Division, University of Virginia.)

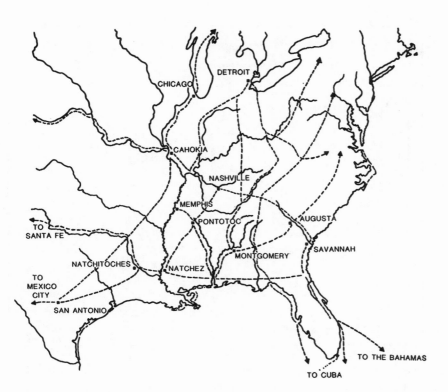

Figure 9.6. Tanner's approximation of the major trade routes of the early colonial era in the eastern United States. The routes marked in Virginia enter the southern piedmont and the Shenandoah Valley only. (Reproduced from Tanner 1989 by permission of the University of Nebraska Press. Copyright 1989 by the University of Nebraska Press.)

of postholes that suggested circular houses some 3 and 4 meters in diameter, respectively. Four storage or trash pit features and five rock-lined hearths also were identified in close association with the houses. It should be noted that surface finds at the site included Clarksville projectile points (late Late Woodland–early contact era) and that MacCord excavated less than 1 percent of the total site area.

Gallivan's research (Gallivan 1995, 1999) at the adjacent Wood site focused on the issue of internal house and community arrangements and has extended our knowledge dramatically on the question of Woodland site structure and settlement patterns. Though the houses dated prior to A.D. 1400, his results are worth reviewing briefly here because they may be pertinent to later Woodland settlement as well. At this site, Gallivan uncovered a dense scatter of 350 post molds, which, through statistical analyses (cf. Prezzano 1988), he grouped into seven clusters, five of which were clearly houses (Fig. 9.7). These houses are roughly analogous to historically described circular to elliptical domestic structures but date to the early part of the Late Woodland (ca. A.D. 900–1200) and are associated with at least one external storage pit. Analyses of other sites on the James and Dan Rivers in Virginia suggest that in the later Late Woodland period (ca. 1400 and afterward), storage pits were created within the house (Gallivan 1997, 1999). Although other sites in central Virginia have been studied that contain abundant feature remains, intrasite settlement patterns in interior piedmont Virginia are rarely observed in the archaeological record (see Gallivan 1999 for a comprehensive summary and interpretation of existing data). The one small contact era site identified in the central piedmont contained evidence of a burned structure that was roughly circular and measured approximately 10 by 14 meters (Hantman et al. 1993).

To the west in the Shenandoah Valley, circular houses are recorded throughout the Late Woodland period (Walker and Miller 1992). The Huffman site produced evidence of circular houses that measured more than 8 meters (25 feet) in diameter and dated to A.D. 1100–1250 (Geier and Warren 1982). The Noah's Ark site, dating to 1250–1350, had two houses with diameters of approximately 5 meters (16 feet) each. The Cabin Run, Miley, and Keyser Farm sites are palisaded villages that date between 1450 and 1700. Houses at these sites are circular and range in diameter between 3 and 8 meters (8 to 25 feet). The village at the Perkins Point site (in the Ridge and Valley province) measured some 113 meters by 100 meters (440 by 300 feet) within the palisade (Whyte and Geier 1982), and a 50-by-20-foot rectangular structure was identified inside the palisade line. Circular houses were located inside and outside the palisade (Walker and Miller 1992). Palisade lines are common at sites of this time period in the Shenandoah Valley, and other sites contain both rectangular and circular houses (Walker and Miller 1992).

Several postcontact villages have been excavated in the Roanoke and New River drainages toward the southwest. Perhaps the best documented village plan is that of the Trigg site, which includes both Late Woodland and contact period components. Excavations there revealed two palisade lines, 29 circular or oval houses, and 762 features in-

Figure 9.7. Houses and village plan of a
portion of the Wood site (44 NE 143), a
Woodland era village in the Virginia
piedmont. (Reproduced with permission
from Gallivan 1999.)

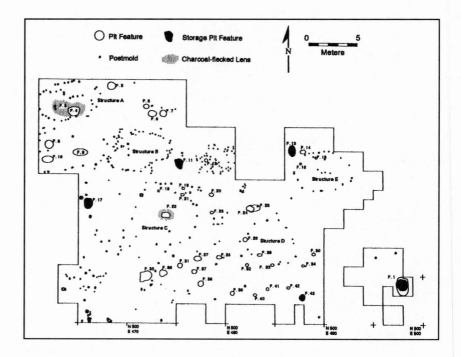

cluding storage pits and burial pits (Boyd 1993; Buchanan 1984; Sternheimer 1983). In contrast, Barber (1993: 2) interpreted the Hurt Power Plant site as "a series of dispersed households as opposed to a nucleated palisaded village complex," although this interpretation was based on feature distributions in the absence of discernible house outlines. In the far southwestern reaches of the state, several palisaded Late Woodland and contact era villages have also been excavated (see Egloff 1992 for a comprehensive review). These typically consist of a majority of circular or oval houses of varying size, with one or more larger, rectangular structures. Palisaded Late Woodland–early historic era villages also occur in the Dan River drainage in the southern Virginia piedmont, as described elsewhere in this volume.

Subsistence

The Late Woodland economies of central Virginia included gathering and horticulture. Despite a common misreading of the ethnohistoric record on this point to suggest an absence of agriculture in the region (see Hantman 1990, 1993), the archaeological record is fairly clear. The evidence includes (1) settlement patterns that show a clear selection of high-yield agricultural soils for village location; (2) macrobotanical remains of domesticated corn and cucurbits found at two sites in the central James River piedmont (Point of Forks, Spessard) with radiocarbon dates of A.D. 1030 ± 75 and 1160 ± 80 (Hantman and Klein 1992); and (3) stable carbon isotope studies of skeletal remains from Monacan-area mound sites showing mean delta carbon 13 ratios analo-

gous to those of other maize agriculturalists of the Southeast and Midwest (Trimble 1996) (Table 9.2). An analysis of caries rates by Gold (1998) provides another line of evidence confirming the carbon-isotope interpretation. If corn was a major component of the starchy diet reflected in these results, then the Monacans in the Late Woodland and early historic era were eating a great deal of it. Rapidan Mound, the subject of the most systematic excavation (Dunham 1994), provides limited evidence of increase in the consumption of maize through time.

Identification of three large, empty storage pits at the Spessard site on the James River, which were dated to circa A.D. 900–1000, may suggest the storage of surpluses, but this is conjectural. Ethnobotanical studies show clearly that chenopodium and nuts were also significant parts of the diet, as were deer and small game. Fish bones were noticeably rare at the site, despite careful recovery methods (Barber 1991; Butler 1988; Hantman 1990).

Evidence for the post-1607 period suggests that agriculture continued to be a primary contributor to both subsistence and trade. Louis Michel (1916), a French Huguenot in Virginia in 1705, gave an account of corn traded by the Manakins (Monacans) to Huguenot settlers who, intriguingly, settled what appears to have been a recently abandoned Monacan village site on the eastern edge of the James River piedmont. Excavation of the Graham-White site provides the best information currently available for the Virginia interior (Klatka and Klein 1993, 1998). Gremillion's (1993a) analysis of 35 features there showed that maize and hickory nuts were the dominant plant food remains, though beans, squashes/gourds, and sunflowers were also

Table 9.2

Mean Delta Carbon 13 Ratios for Monacan Mound Sites (in Boldface) and Other Eastern Sites

Site or Area	Delta C13	Source
Illinois Woodland	−21.0	Kidder 1992
American Bottom Woodland	−21.0	Kidder 1992
Caddoan Woodland	−21.0	Kidder 1992
Mississippi Valley Woodland	−21.0	Kidder 1992
Emerg. Mississippi–Mississippi Valley	−21.0	Kidder 1992
Caddo I–Caddoan	−20.0	Kidder 1992
John East Mound	**−19.6**	Trimble 1996
Emerg. Mississippi–Illinois Valley	−19.0	Kidder 1992
Rapidan submound burials (ca. A.D. 1000)	**−18.1**	Trimble 1996
Cahokia, Mound 72	−17.6	Buikstra and Milner 1991
Helton (A.D. 1150–1250)	−17.5	Buikstra and Milner 1991
Ledders (A.D. 1000–1100)	−17.4	Buikstra and Milner 1991
Rapidan Mound burials (ca. A.D. 1200–1450)	**−17.0**	Trimble 1996
Mississippi–American Bottoms	−16.8	Kidder 1992
Fingerhut (A.D. 1000–1050)	−15.6	Buikstra and Milner 1991
Illinois Valley–Mississippi	−14.8	Kidder 1992
Hayes Creek Mound	**−13.4**	Trimble 1996
Caddo II	−13.5	Kidder 1992
Mississippi Valley–Mississippi	−13.3	Kidder 1992
Dickson Mounds LW (A.D. 1000–1175)	−13.3	Buikstra and Milner 1991
Lewis Creek Mound	**−12.4**	Trimble 1996
Norris Farms (ca. A.D. 1300)	−12.6	Buikstra and Milner 1991
Schild (A.D. 1100–1200)	−12.3	Buikstra and Milner 1991
Dickson Mounds, Miss. (A.D. 1000–1175)	−10.9	Buikstra and Milner 1991
Dickson Mounds, Miss. (A.D. 1250–1350)	−10.8	Buikstra and Milner 1991
Dickson Mounds, Miss. (A.D. 1175–1250)	−10.4	Buikstra and Milner 1991
Kane Mounds (A.D. 1150–1250)	−10.3	Buikstra and Milner 1991
Orendorf (A.D. 1175–1250)	−9.2	Buikstra and Milner 1991

noted. The maize was predominantly 8-row, with smaller percentages of 6-row and 10-row cobs. In addition, 11 varieties of fleshy fruits were recorded, but these did not include peaches (Klatka and Klein 1993: 4–5).

Social Organization

Opinions about the social and political organization of precontact and early contact era groups in the Virginia interior are markedly diverse. Interpretations range from that of an essentially egalitarian organization (Holland 1978) to scenarios of temporary hierarchies (Mouer 1981) and chiefdoms (Hantman 1990). All interpretations are based on severely limited data. For instance, Holland (1978, 1983) saw the mass secondary burials of the burial mound complex of the piedmont as representing an unrestricted mortuary ritual, thus implying an egalitarian society, whereas I have argued (Hantman 1990) that the mound features themselves may suggest the presence of an elite. It should be noted that these mounds contain secondary burials; social distinctions probably were manifested in the primary ritual acts that

preceded final deposition. A typological debate centering on "chiefdom" versus "egalitarian" organization is not fruitful to pursue. Political systems are fluid and can shift among different forms without difficulty, as Leach (1954) elegantly described some decades ago. My point for the Late Woodland of the Virginia interior is to suggest the possibility of the temporary presence of "chiefs" in the piedmont. The tenure (and authority) of individual chiefs may have been short-lived, but considering the permanence and duration of the mounds and the mound complex, I suggest that the institution of chiefly leadership itself was long-lived.

Postcontact evidence comes primarily from documentary data, which must be viewed with caution. On his 1612 map of Virginia, John Smith used the same symbol for Monacan "King's Houses" that he used for Powhatan "King's Houses." The villages marked by king's houses were those that housed the "werowances," or petty chiefs, of the Powhatan chiefdom on the coastal plain. They were distinguished from villages that lacked king's houses and from "Hunting Townes." Smith's map suggests that a similar settlement hierarchy existed for the Monacans. A rare instance of direct contact between John Smith and an Indian from the Virginia interior supports this conclusion. In his discussion with Amoroleck, a piedmont Indian he captured for a brief time on the falls of the Rappahannock River, Smith was told of tributary relations among the villages of the James River piedmont and the Rappahannock River piedmont. In the James River area, the village of Rassawek, at the juncture of the James and Rivanna Rivers, was identified as the central village to which all others paid tribute (Barbour 1986; Hantman 1990, 1993).

For the post-1650 world, documents note the presence of people in the Virginia interior who continued to be identified as kings and chiefs, but their actual roles remain ambiguous. Nevertheless, it must be noted that the Treaty of Middle Plantation was signed in 1678 by Shurenough, the "King of the Manakins," as well as by "a young king" and "a chiefe man" (note the distinction) of the Sappone, who are thought by many to be descendants of the James River Monacans (Hantman 1992). Boyd (1993) analyzed the distribution of European trade goods in burials at the contact era Trigg site and concluded that there was no evidence for status differences. He observed that most of these goods were in the graves of subadults, so alternative interpretations are feasible.

Exchange

Exchange is central to understanding the history of intertribal and European-Indian relations in Virginia between 1400 and 1700. I suggest that prestige trade relations, particularly those relating to native and European copper, were of primary importance in this period. Ethnohistoric and archaeological sources reveal that among coastal plain Algonquians (Powhatans), copper was a prestige item, available only to a chiefly elite. Potter (1989) illustrated how copper as a prestige item among the Powhatans was devalued by the increasing and freer flow of European copper into the coastal plain area after 1607. Copper is not native to the coastal plain. Prior to 1607, Powhatan and his "werowances" obtained their copper from sources to the west. That copper either came from the native copper sources of the Blue Ridge Mountains of the interior or passed through the piedmont while coming from farther west. In either scenario, the Monacans of the Virginia interior were likely involved. The Mangoak, typically considered an Iroquoian group to Powhatan's southwest, are noted as an alternative source of copper. Interestingly, several lines of evidence suggest that the Monacans and the Mangoaks might have been closely related. The similarity of the name and the *man/mon* prefix common to Siouan groups, the Bland map of 1650, and DeMallie's suggestion that the Mangoak were, in fact, Siouan speakers (see Merrell 1989: 11) all should force a reconsideration of a possible Monacan-Mangoak connection. Accepting this interpreta-

tion, it follows that prior to 1607, Siouan speakers of the Virginia interior (Monacans) controlled access to and trade of native copper. Powhatan was dependent on the interior groups for the very prestige item upon which he established his power (steatite and puccoon root also were traveling from west to east).

This prestige exchange system could well have functioned smoothly and cooperatively throughout much of the Late Woodland period. But around the time of contact (1607), animosity between coastal and interior groups began to be felt (Hantman 1993). In this context, Powhatan negotiated trade with the Jamestown colonists, which emphasized corn for copper (Hantman 1990; Potter 1989), and Powhatan's need for or interest in a native copper source was eliminated.

In the interior of Virginia, evidence for the exchange of lithics shows an interesting pattern that fits with what Stewart (1989) has called a "focused" exchange typical of the Late Woodland. Focused exchange is not necessarily elite exchange, though it would encompass that category; it refers to the exchange of certain exotic goods on a seasonal basis or as negotiated between individuals. It is distinct from a broader-based exchange. Parker (1989) analyzed lithic distributions across the Piedmont and Ridge and Valley provinces and observed that cherts, which are native to the mountains and valley but not to the piedmont, were distributed prior to the Late Woodland in a fairly general and widespread manner. In the Late Woodland period, however, chert appears predominantly as projectile points, and little debitage is found on piedmont sites. Twelve percent of all projectile points found in the Late Woodland piedmont are made of chert, up from a high of 4 percent in earlier time periods. Furthermore, although the geographic pattern of chert use follows a generally even fall-off from the Blue Ridge sources, a few piedmont sites deviate significantly from this pattern and have large quantities of chert in the Late Woodland (Parker 1989: 14), suggesting some local control over the distribution of these nonlocal materials.

Discussion of the post-1607 world must shift to a consideration of the deerskin and fur trade (Merrell 1989). Archaeological data are not presently available to enable me to comment on this trade, but it should be noted as having been a tremendously important force in relations between interior tribes and between Indians and colonists. The post-1650 shift in settlement toward the trading paths of the Roanoke and Shenandoah Valleys reflects the overwhelming importance of this exchange sphere. Though they are absent in the central Virginia James and Rappahannock River drainages, European copper, glass beads, and other metal artifacts moved deep into the Virginia interior along the Roanoke and Shenandoah Rivers (e.g., Barber, Barber, and Bowen 1998; Boyd 1993; Klatka and Klein 1993, 1998; Lapham 1998; Manson, MacCord, and Griffin 1944).

Mortuary Behavior

Mortuary behavior in the Late Woodland Virginia interior was characterized by three modes of burial. First, throughout the region individual extended burials were located in and adjacent to villages (Barber, Barber, and Bowen 1998; Holland 1963; Sternheimer 1983). Second, small rock-cairn burials also occurred in both the Piedmont (Bushnell 1914) and the Ridge and Valley provinces (Gardner 1986). Third was the use of accretional burial mounds. Thirteen such mounds have been recorded in central and northwestern Virginia (Fig. 9.8). MacCord (1986) grouped these as the "Lewis Creek Burial Mound Complex." I agree that the mound complex has a historical coherence, but I see no reason not to attribute the mounds to the Monacans who resided in this territory at contact. As I mentioned previously, there is evidence to suggest that they were in use into the seventeenth century.

Dunham (1994) and Gold (1998) recently summarized available data for all 13 of the mounds of central and northwestern Virginia. Among the many insights of their studies, I can note here only some of the most pertinent:

1. Although there is a coherence to the mound complex, there are also patterns of historical change, both in burial practices and in mound locations. One sees a shift over time from individual burials to mass, secondary burials (up to 50 individuals per burial feature). A pos-

sible return to individual interments in the historic era may have occurred, as suggested by nineteenth-century descriptions.

2. Most mounds were built over submound burial and habitation features.

3. Some mounds (especially the Jefferson and Rapidan Mounds) contain an extraordinary number of individuals—between 800 and 2,000. Estimates vary depending on how extrapolation was made from the excavation sample to the postulated size of the original mound.

4. Placement of the bones in accretional mounds was the result of many burial episodes, each involving approximately 30–50 individuals, and the bones were placed into the ground in a very programmatic manner—not in the random jumble that previous trenching excavation strategies suggested (Dunham 1994).

5. Mounds are situated within the regional settlement system in a way suggesting that they were placed to emphasize some form of political or ritual centrality.

6. There is an apparent historical trajectory of west-to-east movement in the placement of mounds. Before around A.D. 1400, the actively used mounds were located in Virginia west of the Blue Ridge Mountains. After 1400, the three that were in most active use (Rapidan, Jefferson, and Leesville) lay east of the Blue Ridge Mountains. Thomas Jefferson described a visit of "sorrowful" Indians to a mound in the Virginia piedmont, a visit that must have taken place in the 1750s (Jefferson 1982

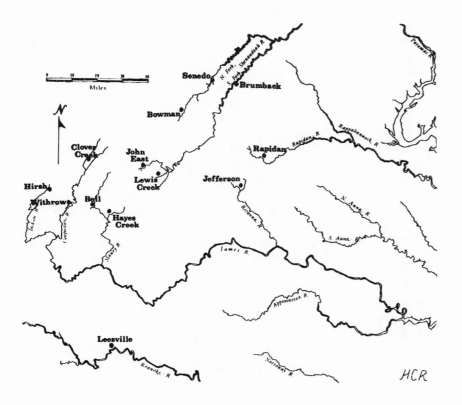

Figure 9.8. Locations of accretional burial mounds of the Virginia interior during the Late Woodland period and possibly the early contact era. (Reproduced with permission from Roundtree 1993: 108; copyright Helen C. Roundtree.)

[1787]). Finally, Holland (1983) and I (Hantman 1998) have each noted that the Leesville mound is located far south of the others, in the Roanoke River drainage, where we have suggested many of the "prehistoric" Monacans moved in the early contact period.

Warfare

Historic texts from the Roanoke and Jamestown colonies refer to an enmity between the coastal Algonquians and the piedmont and mountain Siouans (Hantman 1993), but both groups are portrayed at times as together fearing the northern Iroquoians. I believe the archaeological record shows a shifting relationship between coastal-plain Algonquians and piedmont Siouans (Hantman 1993). Lithic and copper exchange occurred between the two regions, and the minority appearance of Potomac Creek pottery at some piedmont sites hints at patterns of alliance. Even as colonial documents refer to an ancient enmity between the two regions, Powhatan himself repeatedly told the English that he sought no help in fighting the Monacans, and at one point he directly denied that the Monacans were his enemy (Barbour 1986; Hantman 1993). It is not hard to see that this was an on-again, off-again relationship. By 1611, the Monacans and Powhatans were allied against the English (Hantman 1993). Finally, it should be noted that John Smith was told, regarding Indian warfare in Virginia, that they "seldom make warre for land or goods, but for women and children, and principally for revenge" (Barbour 1986: 166). With respect to the Iroquoian enmity, similar questions arise from Lapham's demonstration of north-south movement of European trade goods along the western edge of the Virginia piedmont, linking Monacans to northern (Iroquoian?) groups in the early colonial period. Clearly the boundary between trading and raiding, enmity and alliance, was a shifting and fluid one in the Virginia interior.

Archaeologically, at village sites where flooding has not destroyed the overall village pattern (as it has done so widely throughout the James and Rappahannock River area), palisade walls are known at many sites, but not all. As discussed earlier, many sites in the Ridge and Valley province, southwestern Virginia, and the coastal plain are palisaded (Potter 1993).

Two pieces of archaeological evidence are relevant here, and these take us back to the mounds. Jefferson has always been respected for demonstrating that burial mounds were not final resting places for warriors on the battlefield. His excavation demonstrated the lack of physical evidence for armed warfare, as well as the presence of children. Rapidan Mound has offered some potentially conflicting data. At least one skull and possibly seven others (all dating to the Late Woodland period) showed evidence of having had the skull cap intentionally taken off (Hantman and Dunham 1993; Hantman, Dunham, and Olsen 1990). Olsen conducted scanning electron microscopy studies and determined that

the removal of the skull tops was a cultural process involving a sharp tool. Several skulls showed evidence of devastating blows from a blunt weapon; the damage was located in parts of the skull typically associated with intentional and often lethal blows to the head (Gold 1998). That some of these bones represent the remains of enemies captured in war is an interpretation supported by ethnohistoric analogy, but other interpretations must be considered as well.

Conclusion: On Geographic Centrality and Cultural Continuity

The interior of Virginia, including the James, Rappahannock, Roanoke, and Appomattox River areas, was occupied during the Late Woodland period, up to and including the early contact era in Virginia. I have suggested that by A.D. 1000 this area can be referred to as an archaeological complex by the historic name Monacan. I think this name can be used confidently any time after about A.D. 1000, when the cultural form that is Monacan appears in Virginia. It remains to be determined whether this was a local development, a migration from the west, or some combination of the two. The Monacans lived in villages along major rivers, grew corn and other domesticates, hunted game and collected wild foods, made pottery with locally available tempers and decorated it with fabric and cord impressions, and engaged in mortuary rituals involving mound construction. Their territory historically included the Virginia piedmont and both sides of the Blue Ridge Mountains. After about 1450, I believe the Monacans were living largely on the east side of the Blue Ridge in the Virginia piedmont, and after contact they were located in trading villages in the Roanoke Valley, with smaller refuge hamlets dispersed throughout the uplands of the region.

Ethnohistoric evidence suggests that the Monacans were either the source of copper, the primary elite exchange item that moved through Virginia, or a conduit for copper coming from the Great Lakes area. Prior to 1607, the Monacans lived in central Virginia, and their burial mounds marked a territory flanking the Blue Ridge Mountains and their known copper mines (Allen 1964; Hantman 1990). This territory was central to the continent-wide trade in copper that ran from the Great Lakes to the coastal plain. A working hypothesis is that they were in a position to be middlemen in trading with the Powhatans on the coast. In that context, their centrality afforded them a potential position of power in regional intertribal relations in Virginia. Recent studies (Lapham 1997, 1998) have shown that some (but not all) Monacans living on the western edge of the piedmont were active participants in a north-south trade in deerskins and European trade goods.

The arrival of Europeans on the Atlantic coast, at Roanoke and Jamestown, reordered native positions of economic and political centrality. Now Europe was on one side of the geographic equation and the Virginia piedmont and mountains, and the continent beyond, were on the other. In the middle, beginning in 1607, were the coastal plain Algonquians—the Powhatans. Theirs became the position of power where the new prestige item, European copper, entered the continent, and this is the position that historic texts and history itself have given to them. At this key point in time, when Captain John Smith created the historic "snapshot" that would affect their place in documentary histories, the Monacans became peripheral. We cannot know exactly what impact this change had on regional trade spheres, but it appears that the Monacan villages began to dissipate at this time.

Powhatan control of the prestige exchange link was, however, short-lived (Potter 1989). Forty years later, when the deerskin trade was initiated into the Virginia interior following the 1646 treaty and fort construction, some remaining Monacans may have moved off the James and Rappahannock Rivers to join or found villages on the Shenandoah and the Roanoke River trade routes, once again to become middlemen in a trade network. That is where they are picked up by historic texts and archaeological sites bearing European trade goods, but now they were known by a plethora of names such as Manakin, Saponi, Totera, Tutelo, and Nahyssan (see Merrell 1989 on the reorganization of Siouan groups in the Virginia and Carolina interior). As Merrell (1989) suggested, this was a "new world" for Native American and European alike, and the cultural geography of the Virginia interior between 1650 and 1700 was redefined largely by the demands of participation in the interior trade. The James and Rappahannock River drainages of the central Virginia piedmont appear from that point on to have been largely abandoned by Native American groups. Yet Jefferson's mid-eighteenth-century observation of mournful Indians making their way through the forest to a burial mound near his piedmont Virginia home serves as a reminder of some cultural continuity. In that group must have been some who remembered the ancestors who constructed those monuments, marking an indigenous cultural and political landscape no longer intact but only recently lost.

10

Tribes and Traders on the North Carolina Piedmont, A.D. 1000–1710

Because of their small sizes and their location, the "Siouan-speaking" tribes that dotted the North Carolina piedmont managed to avoid the first waves of disease and disruption ushered in by the Spaniards during the sixteenth century. Even the creation in 1607 of a permanent English colony at Jamestown had no immediate impact upon these piedmont Siouans. Although word of the light-skinned foreigners and occasional trinkets almost certainly made their way to the interior through Indian intermediaries, it was not until 1646, following two Indian wars and the establishment of Fort Henry at the falls of the Appomattox River, that Virginia was in a position to develop a trade with tribes to the southwest (Merrell 1989: 28).

Interest in exploiting the newly opened frontier was almost immediate (see Bland 1651), and during the last half of the seventeenth century numerous traders and explorers turned their attention to the Carolina "backcountry" and began to venture into the heart of the North Carolina piedmont. Some, like John Lederer in 1671 (Cumming 1958), searched for the "Indian Sea," while others looked for the quickest passage through the Appalachian Mountains. Most, however, sought new suppliers of deerskins and pelts, and markets for their "edged tools" and ornaments.

Unlike their European rivals in the New World, these early Englishmen did not come to conquer or to proselytize the natives but to establish commercial relationships. Their motives seemed harmless enough. Yet the arrival of foreign traders presaged a tidal wave of cultural and biological devastation. By the end of the seventeenth century, the piedmont tribes had felt the full sting of disease, depopulation, and social upheaval. In this chapter, we review some of the consequences of this clash of cultures in light of recent archaeological studies conducted as part of the University of North Carolina's Siouan project.

History of Siouan Project Research

Although a North Carolina Siouan project was organized in 1938 by Joffre Coe (Coe and Lewis 1952; Lewis 1951) and reported on in 1945 by James B. Griffin (Griffin 1945), the current project traces its roots back only to 1972. In January of that year, Bennie Keel and Keith Egloff, both of the university's Research Laboratories of Archaeology, made a routine visit to the purported site of Upper Saratown, a seventeenth-century Siouan village on the Dan River in North Carolina (Fig. 10.1). They happened upon a relic collector who had just dug into one of the few undisturbed burials among the many that had been looted there since the early 1960s. With some persuasion, they convinced the pothunter to leave, salvaged the exposed grave, and returned to Chapel Hill to report to Coe, the Research Laboratories' director (Keel 1972). Because of the extensive looting, it was decided to begin full-scale excavations at Upper Saratown the following summer. Archaeological investigations

H. TRAWICK WARD AND
R. P. STEPHEN DAVIS JR.

at the site continued every summer until 1981 (Ward 1980; Wilson 1983).

While excavations were being conducted at Upper Sara-town, many of the staff and students associated with the Research Laboratories developed a strong interest in culture change on the piedmont during the contact period. When Coe retired as director in 1982, he was replaced by Roy Dickens, who also was very interested in contact period archaeology. Soon after his arrival, a long-term program of research was formally organized as the "Siouan project" (Dickens, Ward, and Davis 1987).

The first phase of the project involved reviewing the Upper Saratown materials and other collections thought to date to the contact period. One of these was from the Wall site near Hillsborough, North Carolina, which was extensively excavated by Coe and Robert Wauchope between 1938 and 1941 (Fig. 10.2). This site was thought to represent the remains of the Occaneechi village that the English surveyor John Lawson visited in 1701 (Coe 1952, 1964; Lefler 1967). After a casual appraisal of the pottery and historic artifacts, the archaeologists raised questions regarding the date of the Wall site occupation. A comparison of the site's pottery with pottery from Upper Saratown suggested that

the Wall site predated the contact period. Furthermore, the few historic artifacts recovered by Coe and Wauchope were primarily from the plow zone and appeared to date to the late eighteenth century, the period following the settlement of nearby Hillsborough.

To clarify the timing of the Wall site occupation, excavations were resumed there during the summer of 1983. It quickly became apparent that Wall was occupied too early to be the site of the 1701 Occaneechi village. Field reconnaissance of the area around the Wall site revealed another village site—the Fredricks site—that contained conclusive evidence of a late seventeenth- to early eighteenth-century occupation. This small village was completely excavated between 1983 and 1986 and is now believed to represent the remains of the Occaneechi village described by Lawson (Dickens, Ward, and Davis 1987; Lefler 1967: 61).

In 1987 and 1988, Siouan project excavations were expanded to include late prehistoric and contact period sites in the Haw River drainage to the southwest and along the Dan River to the north. In 1989, work resumed on the Eno River in the same field that contained the Wall and Fredricks sites. These data, in conjunction with previous research, provide an almost continuous view of the northeast

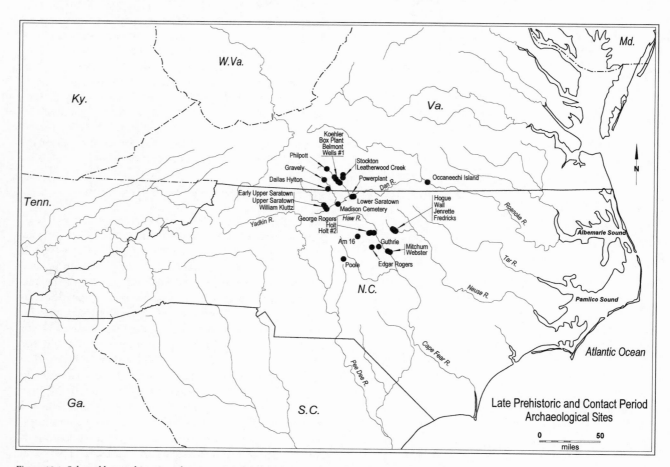

Figure 10.1. Selected late prehistoric and contact period sites in the Siouan project area. (Map by R. P. Stephen Davis Jr.)

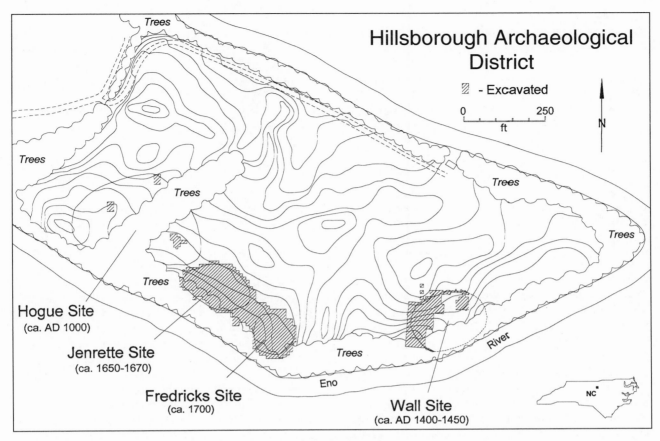

Figure 10.2. Excavated late prehistoric and contact period sites near Hillsborough, North Carolina, showing areas excavated through 1990. (From Ward and Davis 1999:238. Copyright 1999 by the University of North Carolina Press. Used by permission of the publisher.)

piedmont tribes from the eleventh century until the area was abandoned shortly after 1700 (Ward and Davis 1993) (Table 10.1).

Culture Chronology of the Haw and Eno River Drainages

HAW RIVER PHASE (A.D. 1000 – 1400). The early end of the late prehistoric cultural sequence in the Haw and Eno River drainages is defined by the Haw River phase. Dating of this phase is based on several radiocarbon assays obtained from sites in both drainages (Table 10.2). Most Haw River phase sites represent small settlements of widely dispersed households with associated storage pits, hearths, and burials. Archaeologically, such sites are recognized by very light concentrations of debris—mostly net-impressed potsherds of the Uwharrie and Haw River series, triangular projectile points, and stone flakes. Although some sites are located along the banks of the Haw and Eno Rivers, many are situated on ridges and knolls that border the smaller tributary streams. A few late Haw River phase sites seem to reflect more compact settlements

and are situated on the floodplain of the Haw River, but none of these evidences an intensive or long-term occupation comparable to those of the succeeding Hillsboro phase.

Typical features on these sites are fairly large, cylindrical storage pits that were refilled with soil and refuse. Pit hearths and small, shallow basins also occur. Haw River phase features are usually widely scattered, and post hole patterns representing house structures have not been identified.

Subsistence remains include evidence of cultivated plant foods, including maize, beans, squashes, and sunflowers. Wild plant food remains are dominated by acorn and hickory nutshells (Gremillion 1993b). In addition, a wide range of faunal resources was exploited (Holm 1993). The subsistence picture is one of diversity, based on a mixed hunting-and-gathering strategy with some reliance on domesticated plants.

Burials have been found at only two Haw River phase sites. At the Guthrie site, both burials and other pit features were widely dispersed across the site. In contrast, the Hogue site contained a cluster of eight or more graves in a small cemetery-like area. In most cases the bodies were flexed and

Table 10.1

Chronological Framework for the Late Prehistory and Early History of the North-Central North Carolina Piedmont

Drainage	Period	Archaeological Phase	Estimated Time Range (A.D.)	Primary Sites Sampled by the Research Laboratories of Archaeology
Haw River	Late prehistoric	Haw River	1000–1400	Holt, Guthrie, Webster, Mitchum
	Protohistoric	Hillsboro	1400–1600	Edgar Rogers, George Rogers
	Contact	Mitchum	1600–1670	Mitchum
Eno River	Late prehistoric	Haw River	1000–1400	Hogue
	Protohistoric	Hillsboro	1400–1600	Wall
	Contact	Jenrette	1600–1680	Jenrette
	Contact	Fredricks	1680–1710	Fredricks
Dan River	Late prehistoric	Dan River	1000–1450	Powerplant, William Kluttz
Saratown	Protohistoric	Saratown (Early)	1450–1620	Early Upper Saratown, Powerplant
	Contact	Saratown (Middle)	1620–1670	Lower Saratown
	Contact	Saratown (Late)	1670–1710	Upper Saratown, William Kluttz

placed in simple pits. Grave goods were lacking, although several burials contained large stones that were placed near the feet of the deceased.

HILLSBORO PHASE (A.D. 1400–1600). Although this phase encompasses the period during which initial contacts were made between Europeans and southeastern Indians, there is no evidence of such contacts in the North Carolina piedmont. European goods are totally lacking, as are indications of disruptions caused by epidemic diseases and depopulation.

The settlement pattern of the earlier Haw River phase continued, but a few Hillsboro phase sites represent compact, nucleated villages with circular houses that were enclosed by multiple palisades. The best known example of this community type is the Wall site (Fig. 10.3). It is estimated that the Wall site was occupied for less than 20 years by a population of 100 to 150 people (Ward and Davis 1991).

Later Hillsboro phase sites, and in fact most habitation sites that can be attributed to this phase, are small and are situated along the valley margins or adjacent uplands of small tributary streams—a pattern of settlement that also typified the earlier Haw River phase. However, artifact and pit feature densities at Hillsboro phase sites usually are much greater, and remains of circular wall-post houses are now present. Evidence for increased intensity of occupation is particularly noticeable during the later half of the Hillsboro phase.

A new kind of pit feature—large, refuse-laden shallow basins—also appears during the Hillsboro phase. Such features are filled with rich deposits of food and other domestic refuse, and they frequently contain ash, charcoal, and fire-cracked rocks. These basins are interpreted as roasting pits, or "earth ovens," that were used in the preparation of large amounts of food, probably associated with community-wide ceremonies. Storage pits, though present, are overshadowed by these large food preparation facilities.

Although the stone tool technology of the Haw River phase, based on small, bifacially chipped triangular projectile points and ad hoc flake tools, continued into the Hillsboro phase, other aspects of native technology underwent substantial change. Unlike the net-impressed pottery of the preceding Haw River phase, Hillsboro series pottery has either simple-stamped, smoothed, or check-stamped surfaces and exhibits much greater diversity in vessel size, form, and decoration. Widespread use was made of bone and shell to manufacture tools and ornaments during the Hillsboro phase. Awls were made from deer and turkey bones, beamers from deer metatarsals, flakers from antler, and polished pins and needles from a variety of bone splinters. Shell artifacts include serrated mussel shell scrapers and a variety of marine shell ornaments, including circular shell pendants, large columella beads, large and small disk beads, and marginella beads (see Hammett 1987). These items indirectly reflect a subsistence base balanced between hunting and gathering and crop cultivation—an intensification of the pattern seen during the earlier Haw River phase.

Hillsboro phase burials were placed in shaft-and-chamber pits. At the Wall site, graves were widely dispersed and usually were placed inside or adjacent to houses. Some burials contained rich, middenlike deposits of fill in their upper zones and resembled trash pits when first encountered at the base of the plow zone. Grave goods, when present, consisted of pottery vessels and shell ornaments. It appears that children and some adult males received the most elaborate treatment at death, a pattern that continued into the contact period in the Haw and Eno River drainages (Ward 1987: 107).

MITCHUM PHASE (A.D. 1600–1670). The Mitchum phase is represented only by the Mitchum site and is attributed to the Sissipahaw tribe, which lived along the Haw River. This phase reflects the first contacts between Indians and Europeans in the Haw drainage. The Mitchum

Table 10.2

Calibrated Radiocarbon Dates from the Haw, Eno, and Dan River Drainages

| Archaeological Phase, Site, and Context | Uncalibrated Age | | Calibrated Dates (Years A.D.) | | | | |
| | Sample No. | (Years B.P.) | Lower Limits | | Intercepts | Upper Limits | |
			2 Sigma	1 Sigma		1 Sigma	2 Sigma
Haw River Phase (Haw and Eno Drainages)							
Hogue (31Or231b/233), Feature 108	Beta-36096	1790 ± 200	350	15 (B.C.)	231	526	640
Fredricks (31Or231), Feature 30	Beta-20378	1030 ± 60	890	978	997	1026	1156
Hogue (31Or231b/233), Feature 1	Beta-20380	920 ± 70	980	1020	1044, 1090, 1122, 1139, 1152	1209	1260
Holt (RLA-Am163), Feature 1	Beta-20379	900 ± 100	904	1003	1133, 1136, 1156	1256	1280
Guthrie (RLA-Am145), Feature 3	Beta-23507	620 ± 70	1260	1281	1315, 1369, 1386	1408	1430
Webster (31Ch463), Feature 1	Beta-23506	510 ± 70	1280	1329	1418	1440	1490
Holt (RLA-Am163), Feature 2	Beta-23508	480 ± 50	1328	1411	1429	1442	1486
Hillsboro Phase (Haw and Eno Drainages)							
Wall (31Or11), Sq. 350R620, PH #3	GX-9834	495 ± 120	1280	1317	1424	1485	1650
Wall (31Or11), Sq. 340R640, PH #1	GX-9719	395 ± 140	1280	1410	1453	1650	1955
Edgar Rogers (RLA-Am162), Feature 1	Beta-23509	350 ± 50	1440	1450	1494, 1502, 1506, 1605	1637	1650
George Rogers (RLA-Am236), Feature 7	Beta-23510	350 ± 50	1440	1450	1494, 1502, 1506, 1605	1637	1650
George Rogers (RLA-Am236), Feature 1	Beta-20381	230 ± 60	1494	1639	1656	1955	1955
Wall (31Or11), Bu. 1-83	GX-9718	220 ± 145	1420	1490	1659	1955	1955
Mitchum Phase (Haw Drainage)							
Mitchum (31Ch452), Feature 7	Beta-23505	101.2 ± 1.0	1690	1700	1711, 1717, 1884, 1914, 1955	1955	1955
Dan River Phase (Dan River Drainage)							
Powerplant (31Rk5), Feature 18	Beta-36094	1480 ± 90	390	432	578	645	690
Leatherwood Creek (44Hr1), Feature 3	UGa-565	1370 ± 80	540	602	652	759	851
Clark (44Pk11), Feature 1	UGa-1363	935 ± 55	990	1020	1038, 1101, 1117, 1141, 1150	1186	1220
Stockton (44Hr35), Feature 27	UGa-617	925 ± 60	990	1021	1042, 1093, 1121, 1139, 1152	1191	1256
William Kluttz (31Sk6), Feature 15	Beta-36091	780 ± 70	1041	1194	1259	1280	1383
Lower Saratown (31Rk1), Feature 41	Beta-36092	750 ± 60	1161	1222	1264, 1268, 1276	1282	1386
Koehler (44Hr6), Feature 56	UGa-1364	645 ± 70	1260	1279	1298, 1374, 1378	1394	1420
Dallas Hylton (44Hr20), Feature 52	UGa-566	635 ± 60	1260	1281	1302, 1372, 1382	1394	1420
Box Plant (44Hr2), Feature B-15	UGa-619	620 ± 60	1280	1282	1315, 1369, 1386	1405	1420
Koehler (44Hr6), Feature 106	UGa-1365	610 ± 70	1264	1282	1321, 1367, 1388	1410	1430
Upper Saratown (31Sk1a), Feature 18	Beta-36089	590 ± 60	1280	1285	1328, 1350, 1391	1413	1430
Wells No. 1 (44Hr9), Feature 15	UGa-2831	570 ± 55	1280	1305	1332, 1343, 1394	1417	1440
Koehler (44Hr6), Feature 122	UGa-1366	545 ± 55	1280	1325	1409	1427	1440
Gravely (44Hr29), TP-2	UGa-2832	230 ± 70	1490	1532	1656	1955	1955
Philpott (44Hr4), Refuse Pit	UGa-2830	205 ± 55	1526	1647	1664	1955	1955
Saratown Phase (Dan Drainage)							
Early Upper Saratown (31Sk1), Feature 2	Beta-36090	600 ± 80	1260	1282	1323, 1353, 1363, 1365, 1389	1415	1440
Lower Saratown (31Rk1), Feature 46	Beta-36093	420 ± 60	1410	1428	1443	1492	1640
Powerplant (31Rk5), Feature 27	Beta-36095	970 ± 80	893	988	1025	1159	1230

site probably was occupied shortly after 1650 and consisted of a 1.5-acre palisaded village. A single house structure measuring 20 feet in diameter has been uncovered along with several pit features and two burials (Petherick 1987; Ward and Davis 1993).

Interaction with European traders had negligible effects on the lives of the Mitchum site inhabitants. Subsistence practices changed little from the preceding phases. Deer were the most important meat source, and the Haw River contributed fish, turtles, and mussels to the diet. Old World animals were not used, nor is there any indication that the peltry trade had a significant impact on the exploitation of animal resources (Holm 1987). Charred peach pits are the only dietary evidence of contact between Indians and foreigners (Gremillion 1987). Likewise, the ceramic and stone tool technologies of the Mitchum phase show clear continuities with those of the preceding Hillsboro phase and are remarkably similar to those at the roughly contemporaneous Jenrette site, discussed in the next section.

Mitchum phase features are poorly known. Because of

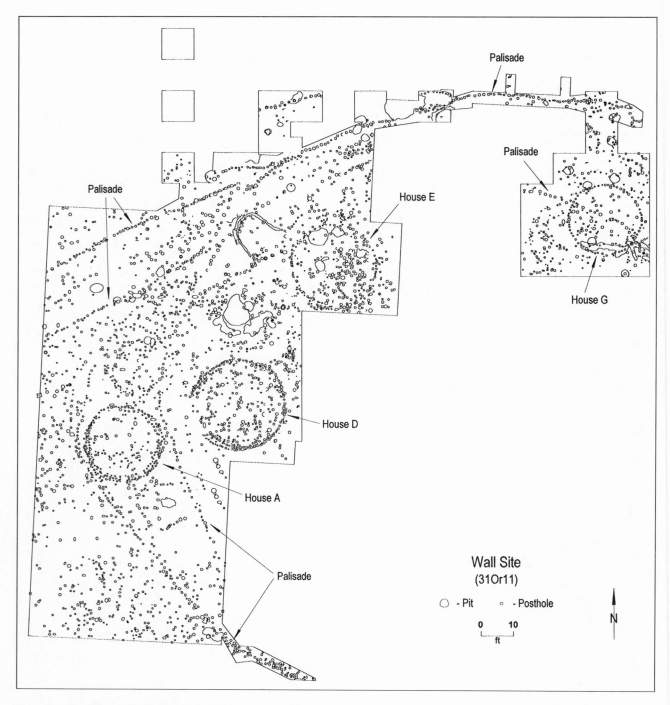

Figure 10.3. The Hillsboro phase village at the Wall site, as exposed by excavations conducted in 1938–1941 and 1983–1984. (From Ward and Davis 1999:114. Copyright 1999 by the University of North Carolina Press. Used by permission of the publisher.)

the sandy soil at the Mitchum site, most pit features were vague and poorly defined. Storage and smudge pits were the only functional categories that could be identified with confidence.

Like subsistence, mortuary practices seem to have changed little from those of the preceding phases. Shaft-and-chamber pits were dug near the houses, and flexed (perhaps

wrapped) bodies were placed in the burial chambers. The only noticeable difference seen during the Mitchum phase was the substitution of glass trade beads and brass ornaments for those of shell and bone used earlier.

These ornaments—brass bells, rolled brass and copper beads, and small white and blue glass beads—represent most of the trade goods found at the Mitchum site. The lack of gun parts and other iron tools suggests that the Sissipahaw were not yet fully engaged in the European trade network that was being established after 1650 along Virginia's southwestern frontier. This lack of direct contact with the Virginia traders may also explain the absence of evidence for disease epidemics during the Mitchum phase.

JENRETTE PHASE (A.D. 1600 – 1680). Like the Mitchum phase, the Jenrette phase is currently defined by excavations at a single site, the Jenrette site. It is attributed to the Shakori tribe and may be the village of Shakor that John Lederer visited in 1670 (Cumming 1958: 27–28). It is located on the Eno River, adjacent to the Fredricks site, which represents the 1701 Occaneechi village visited by Lawson (Lefler 1967). Between 1989 and 1998, the entire palisaded village was excavated, exposing wall-trench houses, numerous pit features, and five Jenrette phase burials. The area enclosed within the palisade is approximately 0.5 acres in extent (Fig. 10.4).

Wall-trench structures have been found in the Siouan area only at the Jenrette and Fredricks sites. The Jenrette houses were slightly the larger. All structures excavated at sites in the Siouan area reflect a common "bower" or "wigwam" type of construction. Whether the wall posts were set in individual holes or in trenches, their upper portions were bent and their tops tied together to create a framework for the roof. The entire structure was covered with thatch, bark, or wattle-and-daub, depending on the season.

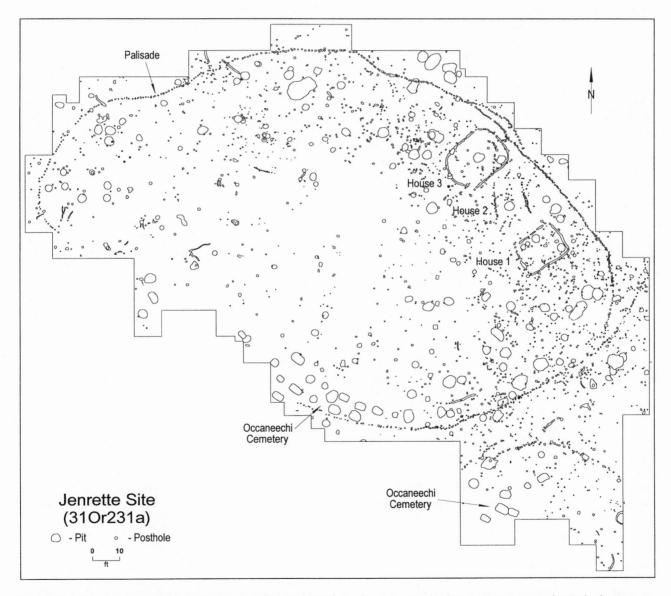

Figure 10.4. Archaeological plan of the Jenrette site near Hillsborough, North Carolina. (From Ward and Davis 1999:239. Copyright 1999 by the University of North Carolina Press. Used by permission of the publisher.)

In plan, the houses ranged from nearly circular at the Wall site and Upper Saratown to nearly rectangular at Jenrette. Contrary to Petherick's (1987: 48) suggestion, we see no evidence for separate summer and winter houses.

Large quantities of faunal and botanical remains were recovered from the Jenrette site, but they show no pronounced differences from the preceding phases in terms of the relative importance of plant and animal species. The presence of cultivated sumpweed at Jenrette, however, is the most recent occurrence of this domesticate in the eastern United States (Gremillion 1989).

During the Jenrette phase, storage pits and food preparation facilities described as roasting pits or earth ovens made up the majority of the subsurface features. Most storage facilities were located near houses and in some cases were dug into the house floor. The large, shallow roasting pits, like those described for the late Hillsboro phase, usually were located near the palisade. Similar facilities have been found at sites on the Dan River dating to the early contact period, but they have not been found on later sites in either the Haw, Eno, or Dan River drainage. This may reflect a breakdown in community celebrations brought on by disease and depopulation during the last quarter of the seventeenth century.

Simple pit and shaft-and-chamber burials are represented at the Jenrette site. Burial associations reflect the beginnings of trade with the English and consist primarily of small glass seed beads that probably were sewn on garments. Contacts between natives and Europeans were probably both indirect and intermittent, which may explain the lack of evidence for epidemic diseases during the Jenrette phase.

FREDRICKS PHASE (A.D. 1680–1710). The Fredricks phase defines the archaeological remains of the Occaneechis after they moved from the Roanoke River to the Eno River following Bacon's Rebellion in 1676. At present, the Fredricks site is the only site assigned to this phase (Davis and Ward 1991b). We believe this is the site of the "Achonechy Town" visited and briefly described by Lawson in 1701 (Lefler 1967: 61). The small, palisaded village was completely excavated between 1983 and 1986 (Dickens, Ward, and Davis 1987; Ward and Davis 1988) (Fig. 10.5).

By the time of Lawson's visit, European diseases and warfare had decimated the Occaneechis and other piedmont tribes. Archaeologically, this decimation is indicated by the small size of the settlement and a very high crude mortality rate. A single palisade of small posts, some placed in wall trenches, enclosed no more than 10 to 12 houses of wall-trench and single-post construction. Probably fewer than 75 people lived in the village at this time (Davis and Ward 1991a; Ward and Davis 1991). Based on a detailed analysis of the burials in a cemetery located just outside the palisade, Hogue (1988: 99) calculated a crude mortality rate of 57 (per 1,000). This compares with a crude mortality rate of 38 computed for the late prehistoric Shannon site

on the Roanoke River in southwestern Virginia, and a rate of 48 for the Upper Saratown site (Hogue 1988). These data, in conjunction with the historic record (e.g., Merrell 1989), leave little doubt that by the time of Lawson's visit, the northern piedmont tribes had suffered severe depopulation.

Although the Fredricks phase represents a time of dramatic disruption and upheaval, a surprising degree of continuity is reflected in the subsistence data. As seen during the Mitchum and Jenrette phases, the peltry trade and the introduction of European tools and trinkets seem to have had minimal impact on the Occaneechis' day-to-day subsistence. Deer, turkey, fish, turtles, and numerous small mammals were hunted and trapped. Only one bone each of pig and horse attest to the European presence (Holm 1987: 245). The only evidence of the use of Old World plants during the Fredricks phase consists of two watermelon seeds and numerous peach pits (Gremillion 1988).

Although most aspects of Occaneechi technology and tradition appear to have remained relatively intact, there is clear evidence that the trade between Indians and Virginians intensified considerably during the last quarter of the seventeenth century. This is seen primarily in the grave goods associated with the Occaneechi burials. Knives, hoes, kettles, and guns were added to the beads and brass ornaments that appeared during the Mitchum and Jenrette phases. Shaft-and-chamber burial pits were abandoned in favor of rectangular, straight-sided graves dug with metal tools. Bodies were still flexed, but burial pits no longer were placed in and around dwellings. The Fredricks site burials were carefully aligned and interred in at least two cemeteries adjacent to and outside the village palisade. The existence of separate cemeteries might reflect the amalgamation of different ethnic groups forced to band together as a consequence of depopulation, or, more likely, they might reflect episodes of epidemics and a recognition of the contagiousness of Old World diseases (Ward 1987; Ward and Davis 1991).

Cultural Chronology of the Upper Dan River Drainage

DAN RIVER PHASE (A.D. 1000–1450). The cultural pattern that emerged after about A.D. 1000 in the upper Dan River drainage is recognized as the Dan River phase and is coeval with the Haw River phase to the south. Its chronological position is reasonably well established by radiocarbon dates from both Siouan project excavations and several sites excavated by Richard Gravely in southern Virginia (Table 10.2).

Throughout the late prehistoric and contact periods, the upper Dan River drainage supported a much larger population than the Haw and Eno River drainages. Still, early Dan River phase (A.D. 1000–1300) settlements apparently consisted of scattered household clusters with associated features, similar to the small communities of the Haw River

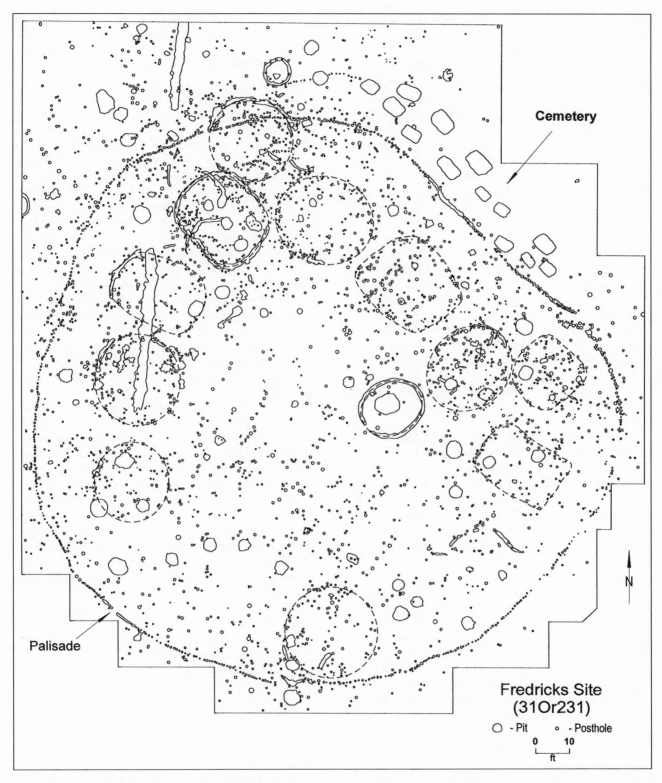

Cemetery

Palisade

**Fredricks Site
(31Or231)**

◯ - Pit   ◦ - Posthole

0   10

ft

N

Figure 10.5. Archaeological plan of the Fredricks site (Occaneechi Town) near Hillsborough, North Carolina. (From Ward and Davis 1999:243. Copyright 1999 by the University of North Carolina Press. Used by permission of the publisher.)

phase. Like Haw River phase settlements, these sites are characterized by relatively sparse artifact densities.

Subsistence remains suggest a mixed economy of hunting, gathering, and agriculture. At the Powerplant site, evidence of maize was found in almost every feature. Other cultigens included beans and sunflowers, clearly indicating the importance of agriculture during the early Dan River phase (Gremillion 1993b).

Typical features are large storage pits and large, shallow basins that usually contain secondary deposits with modest amounts of cultural material. Feature contents suggest less intense activities, perhaps lacking the ritual component indicated by the large quantities of food remains found in many pits from later sites.

The single early Dan River phase burial excavated at the Powerplant site was a flexed individual who had been placed in a simple oval pit without grave goods. This interment was similar to early Haw River phase burials at the Hogue site in the Eno drainage, although many more graves were clustered together at the Hogue site.

The late Dan River phase is known primarily from isolated pit features found during excavation of later site components, from survey collections, and from excavations in southern Virginia on the Dan River. The combined evidence suggests that by A.D. 1300, Dan River phase populations began to coalesce into larger, more nucleated villages enclosed by palisades.

One of the most interesting aspects of Dan River material culture is the variety of bone, shell, and clay tools and ornaments that were used. Most information about bone working, shell working, and ceramic art comes from various sites in the Smith and Mayo River drainages of southern Virginia that were investigated by Gravely during the 1960s and early 1970s (see Gravely 1983). Most were habitation sites or villages that spanned the duration of the Dan River phase.

Bone artifacts include awls, pins, needles, fishhooks, beamers, gouges, antler flakers, antler picks, turtle carapace bowls and cups, and a variety of beads. Mussel shells were fashioned into serrated scrapers; shell from the marine whelk was used to make long columella beads, shorter barrel and disk beads, circular gorgets, and pendants; and a variety of other beads were made from marginella and olive shells. Clay, in addition to being used for well-made Dan River series pottery, mostly net impressed and often highly decorated, was also employed to make numerous other items, including beads, dippers or spoons, cups, disks, and elbow pipes.

EARLY SARATOWN PHASE (A.D. 1450 – 1620). The processes of coalescence and amalgamation begun during the later half of the Dan River phase intensified during the early Saratown phase. Site size and occupational intensity increased, although the overall number of sites appears to have decreased. Many early Saratown

phase sites are located along the Dan River near the mouths of the major tributaries (i.e., the Smith and Mayo Rivers and Town Fork Creek). Although overall site numbers decreased from those of the Dan River phase, the population of the Dan River valley appears to have increased. One of the largest, richest, and most intensively occupied sites in the entire region, Early Upper Saratown, was occupied during this phase (Davis and Ward 1991a; Wilson 1983).

The most characteristic features of the early Saratown phase are large, straight-sided or bell-shaped storage pits. Roasting pits, or "earth ovens," are also common. These facilities are similar to those of the Jenrette phase and the middle Saratown phase. The large storage pits suggest curation and village abandonment during part of the year (DeBoer 1988; Ward 1985), whereas the large cooking pits suggest feasting and community-wide celebrations.

Analysis of faunal remains reveals the exploitation of a variety of resources from varied habitats. White-tailed deer and black bear provided the bulk of the usable meat, followed by raccoon, beaver, turkey, and mountain lion; turtles also were an important meat source. Wilson (1983: 531–542) suggested that this variety reflected a shift from a focal, specialized subsistence orientation during the Dan River phase to a more diverse utilization of animal resources during the early Saratown phase.

Plant food utilization during the early Saratown phase cannot be directly assessed because no botanical samples have been analyzed. Given the results of the analyses of Dan River and middle Saratown phase samples, there is no reason to suspect that early Saratown phase samples would present drastically different patterns of plant food use. The only difference that might be hypothesized is an increase in the importance of agricultural production. The relatively large size of the settlements and the apparent intensity of their occupation suggest that agriculture might have been more important than it was during the preceding and succeeding phases. There is little doubt that this was the case when early Saratown phase sites are compared with the hamletlike communities of the early Dan River phase. Current data indicate that a process of agricultural intensification that began during the Dan River phase probably reached its peak just prior to the first contacts with Europeans. A similar trend toward increasing agricultural production is seen during the Haw River and Hillsboro phases.

Mortuary behavior during the early Saratown phase is known only from the excavation of six graves at the Early Upper Saratown site. Four individuals were placed in shaft-and-chamber pits, whereas the other two were interred in simple pits. The most interesting characteristic of these burials, particularly those in shaft-and-chamber pits, was the large quantity of associated grave goods. Hundreds of bone and shell beads, along with bone awls, shell hairpins, three conch-shell rattlesnake or Citico-style gorgets, serrated mussel shells, and a burnished Oldtown series pot, accompanied these individuals (Wilson 1983: 379–385).

The richness of these burial offerings stands in sharp contrast with that of the earlier Dan and Haw River phases, and the absence of European trade materials contrasts markedly with the quantities of trade goods (primarily glass beads) found in the late Saratown phase burials at Upper Saratown, located only a few hundred yards away. The mortuary complex also reinforces the changes suggested by shifts in settlement, community pattern, and subsistence. That is, during the early Saratown phase, people living in the Dan River drainage were integrated into relatively large, nucleated villages with some degree of specialization and sociopolitical stratification. This may represent the apogee of Siouan cultural development in the Dan River valley.

MIDDLE SARATOWN PHASE (A.D. 1620–1670). The middle Saratown phase is represented at Lower Saratown, located on the Dan River just below the mouth of the Smith River. This phase marks the first arrival of European trade goods in the northern North Carolina piedmont. Although Spaniards supposedly traveled through the region several decades earlier (Hudson 1990), their visits left no discernible traces in the archaeological record. Even the early seventeenth-century English settlements on the James River meant little to the piedmont tribes. It is doubtful that many natives living along the Dan River during the middle Saratown phase ever laid eyes on a European or felt the deadly sting of their diseases. The few beads and trinkets that found their way into native villages probably were passed along through traditional trade networks.

Survey data suggest that settlement patterns during the middle Saratown phase changed little from those of the preceding phase. Most people continued to reside in large, palisaded villages, and the population of the Dan River valley seems to have stabilized. Limited excavations just inside the palisade at Lower Saratown uncovered two superimposed, single-post structures similar in size and shape to wall-trench and single-post structures on the Eno and Haw Rivers.

Middle Saratown phase features are very similar to those found on other protohistoric and contact period sites on the piedmont. Large, shallow roasting pits are common and usually are located around the periphery of the village. These appear not to have been recycled and normally are filled with food remains and cooking debris. Circular storage pits and small, cob-filled smudge pits also characterize the middle Saratown phase. The large storage pits, like those on other piedmont sites, were quickly filled with soil and refuse after they were no longer suited for their primary purpose.

Although contact with Europeans is indicated by the presence of a small number of glass and brass beads, European influence is not seen in the food remains. Data from Lower Saratown point to a varied diet balancing wild plant and animal resources with indigenous crop production. As

in the early Saratown phase, turtles, mussels, and fish from the Dan River provided important supplements to the diet of terrestrial deer, turkey, and bear. Maize was both abundant and ubiquitous. Beans also were grown, along with squash, but sunflowers and other common eastern North American cultigens were not harvested (Gremillion 1989).

The single middle Saratown phase burial excavated at Lower Saratown points to a continuation of the shaft-and-chamber type of grave. A relatively small number of grave goods, mostly rolled copper or brass beads, may contrast with the extensive use of shell beads and ornaments during the early Saratown phase.

LATE SARATOWN PHASE (A.D. 1670–1710). By 1670, the flow of English goods reaching the inhabitants of the Dan River valley increased dramatically. It was also during the late Saratown phase that European diseases struck with devastating force, making many of the excavated villages appear more like cemeteries than habitation sites. The most extensive investigation of this phase has taken place at the Upper Saratown site. Excavations there between 1972 and 1981 uncovered several houses, numerous pit features, and 111 burials (Ward 1980; Wilson 1983) (Fig. 10.6). At another late Saratown village site—the Madison Cemetery site located near the confluence of the Mayo and Dan Rivers—an amateur archaeologist uncovered graves so tightly packed that he thought he was working in a cemetery rather than a habitation site (Gravely 1969: 11).

The end of the late Saratown phase is represented by the William Kluttz site, located just downstream from Upper Saratown. This site was occupied between 1690 and 1710, probably by the former inhabitants of Upper Saratown. Here, numerous shallow graves clustered in a cemetery area attest to the continuing devastation of alien diseases.

As evidenced at Upper Saratown and the William Kluttz site, community patterns changed drastically during the short time span of the late Saratown phase. At Upper Saratown, occupied during the first half of the phase, the community consisted of a palisaded village occupied by 200 to 250 people living in circular houses. Although no structures were found at the William Kluttz site, the distribution of artifacts and features suggests a very different community pattern by the turn of the eighteenth century. By this time, the communities no longer consisted of compact, palisaded villages but rather of widely dispersed households. Ceramic evidence further indicates that remnants of neighboring tribes that survived the onslaught of epidemic disease may have merged with the Saras to form dispersed refuge communities such as the William Kluttz site.

The most characteristic late Saratown phase features are large, deep, almost perfectly circular storage facilities. These pits usually measure over 3 feet in diameter and often as deep. Typically, they contain stratified deposits that are rich in food remains and other domestic refuse. Large roasting pits are also frequently encountered; they are identical

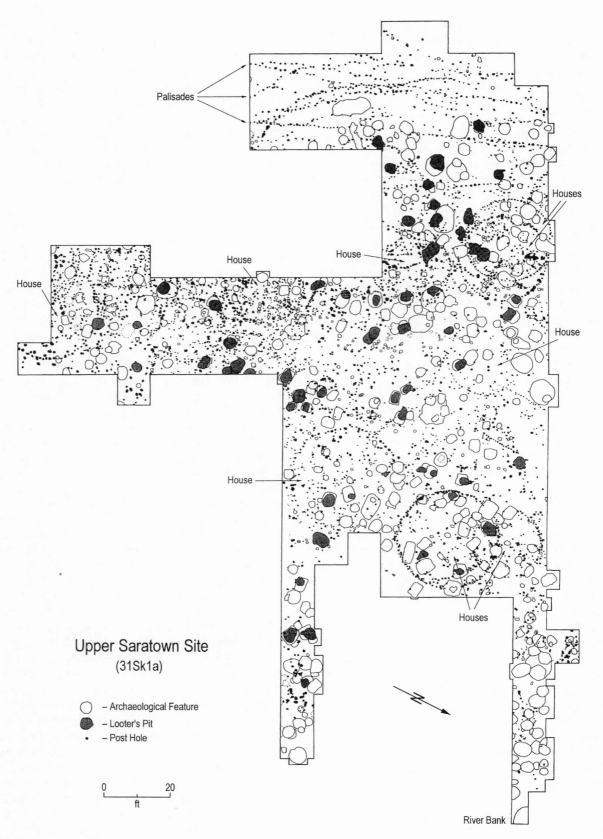

Upper Saratown Site

(31Sk1a)

○ – Archaeological Feature

● – Looter's Pit

• – Post Hole

Palisades

Houses

House

House

House

House

Houses

River Bank

0 ___ 20
ft

Figure 10.6. The late Saratown phase village of Upper Saratown, excavated between 1972 and 1981. (Courtesy of the Research Laboratories of Archaeology, University of North Carolina.)

to those described for the late Hillsboro, Jenrette, and middle Saratown phases. Usually these large cooking facilities are located around the edges of the villages and near the palisades, and they probably were used to prepare large amounts of food that were consumed during ritual celebrations (Ward 1980; Wilson 1977).

The subsistence pattern described for the earlier protohistoric and contact period Siouan phases continued into the late Saratown phase. A balance appears to have been struck between wild and domestic food resources. Corn, beans, squashes, and gourds were cultivated, and peaches were a popular Old World addition (Wilson 1977). As in other contact period Siouan phases, there is no evidence that European animals played any role in the subsistence cycle during the late Saratown phase.

Like community patterns, mortuary patterns reflect dramatic changes during the late Saratown phase. At Upper Saratown and the Madison Cemetery site, graves were placed within and around domestic structures. Usually these were deep shaft-and-chamber pits, with the "central chamber" type occurring most frequently. Bodies were flexed and often were accompanied by large numbers of European ornaments, particularly glass beads and copper trinkets (Navey 1982). Toward the end of the late Saratown phase, however, a drastic change took place.

Excavations at the William Kluttz site uncovered a cemetery that contained numerous, shallow pit burials (Ward and Davis 1993). Most were subadult interments with no associated artifacts. The implication is that the community could no longer muster sufficient energy to continue its traditional mortuary practices. The isolation of the dead in a cemetery might also indicate a growing understanding of the contagiousness of alien microbes, a lesson perhaps learned earlier at Upper Saratown. That most of the dead were subadults points to their deaths having resulted from a single epidemic, since adults who survived earlier epidemics at Upper Saratown would have developed some immunity to new waves of European diseases.

In addition to the cemetery burials, two individuals were placed in traditional shaft-and-chamber pits. One of these was a young adult male outfitted in European attire, with a pistol in his belt. Although most of the dead in the cemetery received comparatively little attention, this grave suggests that some individuals warranted special treatment. And the fact that this person was a young adult male reinforces the pattern of differential status identified for the Occaneechis during the Fredricks phase (Ward 1987).

Contact, Interaction, and Change

Using the chronological framework just presented, we now synthesize and review some of the more specific consequences of the interaction between the piedmont Siouans and the English. The discussion focuses on four different but in most cases related topics: trade, intertribal relations, subsistence, and disease.

TRADE. During the Jenrette and middle Saratown phases, only a few glass and copper beads found their way into the piedmont villages. The scarcity of trade goods suggests that these items were exchanged through native intermediaries operating within traditional trade networks. During the 1670s, this picture changed abruptly and dramatically when Virginia traders began making regular trips into the "backcountry" searching for new markets.

The intensification and spread of the peltry trade is directly reflected during the late Saratown and Fredricks phases. Thousands of glass beads, copper bells, and other ornaments—but very few tools and weapons—have been recovered from Upper Saratown. At Occaneechi Town, guns, iron knives, and hatchets were popular items, along with beads and trinkets (Table 10.3). The Occaneechis' role as middlemen in the Virginia trade allowed them to control the flow of goods to more remote groups like the Saras. And by controlling access to firearms and using intimidation when necessary, the Occaneechis were able to maintain their dominant position (Davis and Ward 1991b; Merrell 1987). The Virginia trader Abraham Wood noted that the Occaneechis' supply of arms and ammunition made them "the Mart for all the Indians for at least 500 miles" (quoted in Merrell 1982: 91).

The Occaneechis' stranglehold was broken by Bacon's Rebellion in 1676, and groups like the Saras began receiving the full inventory of goods offered by English traders (Davis and Ward 1991b). The young adult male from the William Kluttz site was buried with a 1680 British military-issue pistol, tucked in a leather belt with a brass buckle that was used to hold up cloth trousers. After 1676, the Saras were no longer satisfied to deal in glass beads and copper trinkets but had gained access to weapons and other utilitarian goods offered by the Virginia traders.

The introduction of iron tools and firearms, however, had no major impact on the traditional technologies of the piedmont tribes. They were used alongside, not in place of, their aboriginal counterparts. At Occaneechi Town, lead shot and gunflints were recovered from almost every excavation unit, but so were stone arrow points. Clay pots were still being made, although copper kettles were available, and while glass beads were worn and sewn on garments, shell beads also continued to be used. Perhaps the only new technology introduced by the traders is represented by the numerous pairs of scissors needed to cut and shape the bolts of cloth that were used to make clothing, bags, and other items that animal skins had provided in the past.

The peltry trade probably had a greater impact on traditional Siouan social structure than it did on technology. Among the piedmont tribes, individuals who could deal most successfully with the Virginia traders might have gained a level of prestige and influence impossible within

Table 10.3

European Trade Artifacts from Feature and Burial Contexts at Upper Saratown and Occaneechi Town (Fredricks Site)

Artifact Type	Material	Upper Saratown	Occaneechi Town
Awls	Iron	—	2
Axes	Iron	—	5
Beads	Copper/brass	519	3
Beads	Glass	324,779	11,790
Bell fragments	Copper/brass	—	2
Bells	Copper/brass	149	33
Bottle fragments	Glass	28	48
Bottles	Glass	—	2
Bracelet	Copper/brass	—	2
Buckle fragments	Copper/brass	—	6
Buckle tang	Iron	—	1
Buckles	Copper/brass	—	3
Buckles	Pewter	—	9
Button	Copper/brass	2	1
Buttons	Glass	—	11
Buttons	Lead	—	3
Buttons	Pewter	—	6
Cones	Copper/brass	18	—
Cut ornaments	Copper/brass	5	—
Cooper's tool	Iron	—	1
Ember tenders	Iron	—	2
Fishhook	Copper/brass	1	1
Fishhook	Iron	—	1
Flakes	Glass	9	6
Gorgets	Copper/brass	6	—
Gun	Iron	—	1
Gun springs	Iron	—	2
Gunflints	Flint	10	47
Hoes	Iron	1	5
Hook	Iron	—	1
Indet. fragments	Copper/brass	—	3
Indet. fragments	Iron	34	98
Jew's harps	Iron	—	3
Kettle	Copper/brass	—	1
Kettle fragments	Copper/brass	—	1
Knife blades	Iron	—	8
Knife handles	Bone/wood	—	9
Knives	Iron	1	14
Lead shot	Lead	26	410
Lead sprue	Lead	—	27
Mirror fragment	Glass	—	1
Nails	Iron	8	39
Pendant	Copper/brass	1	—
Pin	Copper/brass	—	1
Pipe fragment	Kaolin clay	—	146
Pipes	Kaolin clay	—	4
Pipes	Pewter	—	4
Porringers	Pewter	—	3
Projectile point	Glass	1	—
Rings	Copper/brass	30	—
Scissors	Iron	2	6
Scrap	Copper/brass	6	—
Scrap	Lead	—	8
Scrap	Pewter	—	2
Sheet/strip	Copper/brass	74	22
Sheet/strip	Indeterminate	1	—

Table 10.3 *continued*

Artifact Type	Material	Upper Saratown	Occaneechi Town
Sheet/strip	Iron	3	85
Snuff box	Copper/brass	—	2
Snuff box	Iron	—	1
Spoons	Copper/brass	1	3
Tack	Copper/brass	1	—
Tack	Iron	—	1
Thimble	Copper/brass	—	1
Wire coil	Copper/brass	—	2
Wire fragments	Copper/brass	—	12
Total		325,716	12,911

the traditional social structure. For the Fredricks and late Saratown phases, mortuary data from Occaneechi Town and the William Kluttz site suggest that these individuals were young adult males (Ward 1987). Earlier, during the middle Saratown phase, mortuary evidence indicates that adult females rather than young adult males might have occupied positions of highest prestige (Navey 1982). These differences in status recognition appear to reflect the relative impact of trade on the social structures of the Saras and Occaneechis at the beginning and end of the contact period (cf. Davis and Ward 1991b).

The ethnohistoric documents point to comparable differences. John Lederer observed in 1670 that kinship was traced through the female line and that among the "remoter" tribes, such as the Eno, the government was democratic. However, a "democratic" social order seems not to have been the norm among the tribes that had been heavily engaged in trade with the English. The Occaneechis were said to have had two "kings" governing them when they lived on the Roanoke River, astride the main trading path from Virginia to the Carolina piedmont. The nearby Saponis were ruled by an "absolute monarch," according to Lederer (Cumming 1958).

EUROPEAN PLANTS AND LIVESTOCK. The Europeans not only brought new tools and strange weapons to the New World but also filled their boats with horses, pigs, chickens, and other creatures unknown to Native Americans. They packed seeds of wheat, barley, and peaches to be planted in the fertile soils of their new home. Surprisingly, archaeological evidence has shown that most piedmont Indians virtually ignored these new plants and animals. They planted peaches and watermelons, but the traditional trinity of corn, beans, and squash remained the mainstay of the diet (Gremillion 1989).

Old World animals were even less popular than Old World plants. The only evidence of their use comes from the Fredricks site, where one bone each of pig and horse was recovered (Holm 1987). As was the case with tools and trinkets, only those items that did not require a reorganization of traditional ways of doing things were incorporated,

and these were used alongside, not in place of, familiar native resources (Gremillion 1993b).

INTERTRIBAL RELATIONS. Palisaded villages such as the Hillsboro phase Wall site attest that conflict was not unknown before the arrival of Europeans. Hostilities increased dramatically, however, during the contact period, when Indian slaves and stolen deerskins could be traded for the prized guns and kettles of the foreigners. The knife-scarred skull of a scalp victim and a lead ball flattened against the fibula of a young woman in the Occaneechi cemetery at the Fredricks site are clear evidence of such hostilities. And often these conflicts took the form of raids by larger, well-armed groups from as far north as Pennsylvania and New York. In 1701, John Lawson was forced to turn off the main trading path to Virginia after being warned of a "Sinnager" (Seneca) raiding party in the vicinity of Occaneechi Town (Lefler 1967: 61).

Not only did the infusion of European goods and arms increase external threats, but the competition for foreign trade and a market for native slaves heightened hostilities among the North Carolina piedmont tribes themselves. Whereas in the past, blood feuds and revenge fueled the fires of conflict, the European presence introduced new motives and new ways of conducting warfare.

At different points during the later half of the seventeenth century, groups such as the Wainokes, Occaneechis, and Tuscaroras gained unprecedented opportunities, through trade and the acquisition of firearms, to obtain and exert economic and political power. All of these groups lived along the ever-advancing colonial frontier and thus were in a position to control, or at least influence, contacts with more remote tribes. The Occaneechis, located astride the principal trading path out of Fort Henry, achieved particular success in this respect. By controlling access to firearms and using intimidation when necessary, the Occaneechis were able to maintain their dominant position as middlemen. Significantly, when their downfall came in 1676, it was at the hands not of their deprived "trading partners" but of the superior forces of Nathaniel Bacon and his well-armed militia.

DISEASE.   Without a doubt, the most devastating result of the European arrival on the North Carolina piedmont was the introduction of new diseases to which the native people had little or no immunity. Smallpox, measles, and other viral infections swept across the region, killing and disabling thousands. Their devastation was enhanced even further by increased movements of people during the contact period. The intensification and spread of traditional trade networks to accommodate the flow of European goods and deerskins also facilitated the rapid spread of deadly pathogens (Wood 1987: 31).

There can be no argument over the final, devastating result of the introduction of foreign diseases, although scholars debate the timing and spread of those diseases into the interior Southeast. Many researchers (e.g., Ramenofsky 1987; Smith 1987) generally support the position taken by Henry Dobyns (1983), who believes that waves of pandemics swept through the interior Southeast soon after the arrival of the first Spanish explorers. According to Dobyns (1983: 13), diseases spread from population to population on their own momentum, without the necessity of face-to-face contacts between natives and foreigners. Others (e.g., Blakely and Detweiler-Blakely 1989; Henige 1989; Milner 1980; Snow and Lanphear 1989) have suggested that, rather than continent-wide pandemics on the heels of the Spanish *entradas,* the spread of Old World diseases depended on a number of local and regional factors. Population densities, community size, and the degree and nature of the contacts between natives and foreigners all affected the timing, speed, and scope of the devastation of diseases such as smallpox, measles, and influenza. Both of these positions depend heavily on historical and ethnographic data.

In the Siouan project area, there is neither ethnographic nor archaeological evidence of epidemic diseases until the arrival of the Virginia traders in the last half of the seventeenth century. In 1670, John Lederer passed through southern Virginia and central North Carolina visiting the villages of the Saponis, Occaneechis, Enos, Shakoris, Saras, and others without mentioning any signs of population disruption or decline (Cumming 1958). Three years later, James Needham and Gabriel Arthur traveled through the north-central piedmont without reporting any evidence of depopulation. Even John Lawson in 1701 was impressed with the numbers of people he encountered during the middle leg of his journey through Catawba country (Lefler 1967: 46). As he moved northeastward and began to visit groups that had been intensively engaged in the Virginia deerskin trade, however, his observations changed. There, Lawson described large vacant areas and small towns of "not above 17 houses." At Sapona, he mentioned for the first time the amalgamation of once-distinct tribes into single villages as a consequence of depopulation (Lefler 1967: 50–53). It was these more northern piedmont groups that caused Lawson (Lefler 1967: 232) to observe: "The Small-Pox and Rum have made such a Destruction amongst them, that, on good

grounds, I do believe, there is not the sixth Savage living within two hundred Miles of all our Settlements, as there were fifty Years ago."

The archaeological record also points to a late arrival of epidemic diseases in the Siouan area. Late Hillsboro phase sites (1500–1600), which were occupied during the time of the initial arrival of Spaniards in the Southeast, consistently have low burial densities and show no evidence of increased mortuary activity. Despite extensive testing, few burials have been found. Nor is there any evidence of a breakdown or disruption of other cultural components during the Hillsboro phase. On the contrary, settlements became more densely populated, subsistence practices became more intense and diverse, and ceramic and lithic technologies became more elaborate.

It could be argued that cemeteries were located away from the habitation areas, and we simply failed to find them. Or, as some have suggested, the living were so weakened that they were unable to bury their dead (Ramenofsky 1987; Smith 1987). The first argument can never be completely dismissed because of the nature of archaeological data. However, the typical pattern of Siouan burial from the late prehistoric period until the close of the seventeenth century was to place graves in or near domestic structures. These are the site areas that were intensively tested and excavated during the Siouan project. Evidence from the Fredricks and William Kluttz sites indicates that this pattern did change by 1700, when both the Occaneechis and the Saras began to bury their dead in cemeteries. Still, using the same subsurface testing strategy as that employed at earlier sites, we were able to locate cemeteries at both sites (Davis and Ward 1987; Ward and Davis 1993).

There is also ample archaeological evidence that the dead were buried even during the most virulent epidemics. At Upper Saratown and the Madison Cemetery site, two Sara villages that were decimated by diseases during the late seventeenth century, individuals were buried in traditional shaft-and-chamber pits with appropriate ritual. Even at Occaneechi Town, where probably fewer than 50 souls survived, deep graves were arduously dug into a stiff subsoil clay, and the dead were laid to rest with full, traditional ceremony.

Only at the William Kluttz site, which represents the last desperate gasp of the Saras on the Dan River, is there evidence that the decimation had become so great that it affected the burial of the dead. There, children and subadults were interred in shallow pits within a cemetery, apparently with little attendant ritual. Adult graves, however, were placed away from the cemetery and displayed traditional deep pit forms. Burial goods indicate that those individuals were given their last rites in a traditional manner. Even during the worst of times, the dead were still buried, and more often than not, with full ceremony.

Further evidence for the late arrival of epidemics on the Carolina piedmont comes from excavations at sites occupied during the Mitchum, Jenrette, and middle Saratown phases (ca. 1600–1680). At the Jenrette site, more than 14,000 square feet of the palisaded village have been excavated, exposing more than 75 pit features but only two graves. Extensive auger testing and excavations at Lower Saratown have revealed only a single burial among more than 40 pit features. And both of these sites contained trade materials suggesting only indirect contacts with European traders.

These data alone may not be entirely convincing, and contrary arguments could still be made about the reliability of the excavation samples and the possibility of drastically altered mortuary patterns. Yet when the burial density data from sixteenth-century and early seventeenth-century sites are compared with those from late seventeenth-century sites, the differences are so striking that they cannot be explained away by sampling error. At Upper Saratown, the graves were so dense that it was difficult to dig a 10-by-10-foot excavation unit without uncovering the top of at least one burial pit. At the Madison Cemetery site, the number and density of graves led an avocational archaeologist to mistakenly assume the site was a cemetery (Gravely 1969). The sheer numbers and concentrations of burials on sites postdating 1670, compared with earlier sites, make it clear that diseases, not sampling error or burial practices, were the culprits responsible for the dramatic differences in mortuary evidence.

Summary

By viewing the archaeological data of the Siouan project against the background of the ethnohistoric record, it is possible to create a composite picture of life on the Carolina piedmont during the seventeenth century with a great degree of clarity and focus. At first glance, this picture appears to be one of explosive and dramatic change. It cannot be disputed that the Indian societies that entered the eighteenth century were vastly different from those of 1600 or even 1650. From the native perspective, the ultimate consequence of Indian-European contact was both devastating and irreversible. Yet as one moves in for a closer look, it becomes clear that change was tempered by stability and that many native traditions persisted in the face of the devastation brought on by disease and depopulation. The Siouan peoples of the piedmont were not simply passive observers of their own demise; rather, they were active participants

trying in their own culturally prescribed ways to adjust to and even benefit from the emerging new world order. Although change brought short-term success for some groups, such as the Occaneechis, their ultimate fate was the same as that of their neighbors. By 1714, the Occaneechis had removed to Fort Christanna, under protection of the Virginia colonial government, while other groups, including the Saras, Shakoris, and Sissipahaws, drifted southward, where they eventually joined the Catawbas (Mooney 1894). Although some families might have remained in their ancestral homeland, and others returned from Virginia in small numbers throughout the later half of the eighteenth century (Hazel 1991), the English, German, and Scots-Irish immigrants who first settled the North Carolina piedmont during the 1730s and 1740s found only abandoned villages and vacant fields.

Acknowledgments

This chapter summarizes Siouan project research conducted since 1983. During that time, generous support was provided by the National Science Foundation, the National Geographic Society, the North Carolina Division of Archives and History, and the University of North Carolina. Many students and colleagues associated with the Research Laboratories of Archaeology contributed to the success of the project. In particular, we would like to thank Jane and Joe Eastman and Randy Daniel for supervising the NSF-sponsored fieldwork, and Kristen Gremillion and Mary Ann Holm for their analyses of the paleoethnobotanical and faunal remains, respectively. We are also indebted to Vincas Steponaitis, Richard Yarnell, and the late George Holcomb for their helpful comments and encouragement. Finally, we would like to acknowledge the early direction of the project by the late Roy S. Dickens Jr. Roy's dedication and enthusiasm had an enduring effect upon our own research and helped propel the Siouan project to a point where this synthesis became possible.

Location of Primary Collections

All artifact collections and associated records of the Siouan project, as well as Richard Gravely's collections and notes, are curated at the Research Laboratories of Archaeology, University of North Carolina, Chapel Hill, North Carolina.

11

The Rise and Fall of Coosa, A.D. 1350–1700

When encountered by the Hernando de Soto expedition in 1540, Coosa was one of the largest complex chiefdoms in eastern North America, controlling a vast area of present-day eastern Tennessee, northwestern Georgia, and north-eastern Alabama (Hudson, Smith, and DePratter 1984). Recent research into Coosa suggests that this polity was a relative newcomer on the scene, probably rising to power no earlier than about A.D. 1350–1400. Within 50 years following the de Soto *entrada*, Coosa had lost much of its power, its population, and its territory. By 1700, most of its original territory had been abandoned, and remnants of its many towns were concentrated in just a few villages.

Throughout much of its history, the Coosa polity was restricted to the Coosawattee River valley in present north-western Georgia. At its height in the mid-sixteenth century, however, the complex chiefdom of Coosa controlled much of the Ridge and Valley physiographic province from the upper Tennessee River drainage (French Broad River) in eastern Tennessee southwest to include the Coosa River drainage of northwest Georgia to east-central Alabama (Fig. 11.1). During its decline, many of the people of the present northwestern Georgia area moved down the Coosa River into present-day Alabama. This chapter focuses on the Coosa River drainage, with only passing reference to the Tennessee River drainage to the north.

Both the Tennessee and Coosa drainages consisted of fertile river valleys with nearby mountains and ridges. Most major towns were located at the contact point between the Blue Ridge province to the northeast or the Piedmont province to the southeast and the Ridge and Valley province to the west. These settings were locations where streams left the mountains to drop fertile soil as the valleys opened up and stream gradient changed. They were also shoal areas where fishing was excellent and river crossing was easy. Resources such as suitable stone for ground stone tool production and mast-producing hardwood stands were available in the Blue Ridge and Piedmont provinces to the east, while rich farmlands and sources of chert were available in the Ridge and Valley province to the west (Hally and Langford 1988; Hally, Smith, and Langford 1990; Larson 1971a). Subsistence, of the sort typical of most horticultural Mississippian societies, was based on maize, beans, and squash with additional reliance on native nuts, fruits, and seeds. Fishing and hunting for deer, bear, turkey, and other, smaller game provided animal protein.

History of Archaeological Research

Archaeological research in the Coosa province has a long history. In the nineteenth century, investigators from the Smithsonian Institution investigated sites such as Etowah and many sites in eastern Tennessee (Thomas 1894). In the 1920s, Warren K. Moorehead excavated at Etowah and the Carters Quarters site (now known as Little Egypt) (Moorehead 1932), and J. C. Harrington (1922) worked in

MARVIN T. SMITH

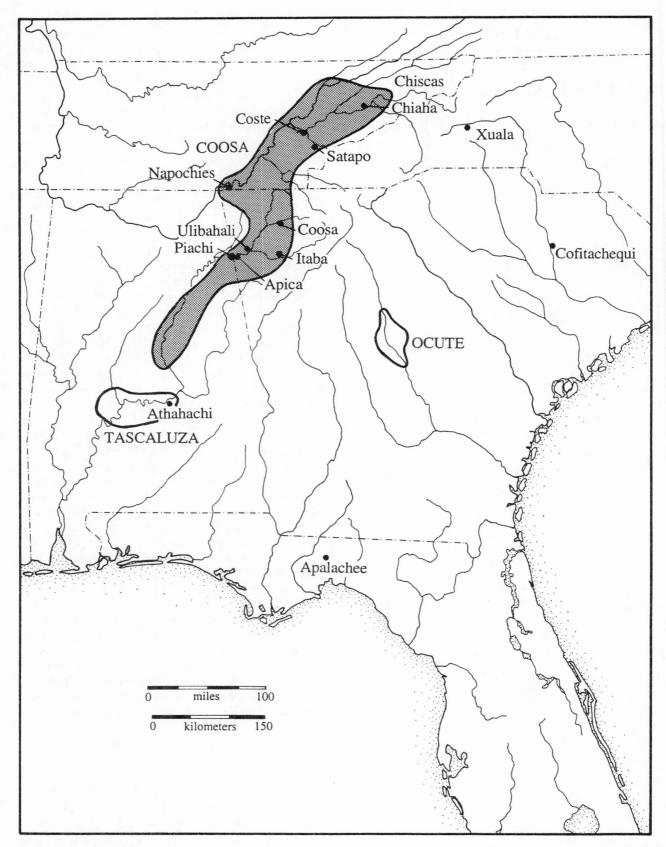

Figure 11.1. The chiefdom of Coosa at its greatest extent (after Hudson et al. 1985: 733). The towns and villages labeled are those known archaeologically and from the Spanish chronicles.

eastern Tennessee for the Museum of the American Indian. During the 1930s, large WPA teams examined sites in eastern Tennessee under the direction of William S. Webb, T. M. N. Lewis, and Madeline Kneberg (Lewis and Kneberg 1941, 1946; Webb 1938). At the same time, WPA work, primarily survey, was conducted in northern Georgia under the supervision of Robert Wauchope (1966).

During the 1950s, Lewis Larson and A. R. Kelly excavated at the famous Etowah site (Kelly and Larson 1956; Larson 1971b, 1989), and in the 1960s, reservoir construction on the Coosa River prompted considerable salvage work under the direction of David L. DeJarnette (University of Alabama 1963, 1964, 1965; DeJarnette, Kurjack, and Keel 1973; Graham 1966). Further excavations in the 1960s and 1970s for the Carters Lake reregulation project on the Coosawattee River by A. R. Kelly and David J. Hally yielded much valuable information (Hally 1979; Kelly 1970, 1972; Kelly et al. 1965). Work by Patrick Garrow and David Hally at the King site has provided excellent data on community plan and mortuary practices, and Hally has continued to work in the region up to the present (Hally 1988, 1993). Keith Little and Caleb Curren (1981, 1990) have salvaged a good deal of information on looted sites in northern Alabama, and the present author has worked with previously unreported collections, both private and professionally excavated, to further unravel the story of the Coosa River people (Smith 1977, 1987, 1989a, 1989b, 2000).

Thus, data range from early excavations for museum specimens to large-scale survey efforts, reservoir salvage, and major problem-oriented excavations and surveys. In sum, the present study area is one of the most thoroughly investigated regions in eastern North America.

Cultural Chronology

Cultural chronology for the upper Coosa drainage has evolved over the last 50 years. Pioneering efforts by Willey, Fairbanks, Sears, and Caldwell have been fine-tuned recently by David Hally and his associates (Hally and Langford 1988; King 1997). It is now possible to divide the Mississippian period into several periods and phases, beginning with Etowah at around A.D. 1000 (Fig. 11.2). Despite several early attempts to divide the Etowah period into as many as four subperiods, recent syntheses have found it prudent to divide the continuum into Early Etowah and Late Etowah, ending about A.D. 1200. The Middle Mississippian period, circa 1200–1350, can be divided into several phases in the Coosa region, including the Wilbanks phase on the Etowah River (a branch of the Coosa) and an unnamed phase on the more northerly Coosawattee River, homeland of the Coosa proper. This unnamed phase has ceramic attributes comparable to those of the Dallas phase of eastern Tennessee. Following this unnamed phase on the Coosawattee River come two sequential Lamar period phases, Little Egypt (ca. 1350–1475) and Barnett (ca. 1475–1575). The sixteenth-century Barnett phase is contemporaneous with late Dallas on the

Little Tennessee River and the Mouse Creek phase on the Hiwassee River in Tennessee, and with the Brewster phase on the Etowah River to the south. This is the period of initial Spanish contact.

Following the Barnett phase in the Coosa drainage, northwestern Georgia appears to have been abandoned, but later phases are known from the Coosa in Alabama. Although Cherokee groups moved into northwestern Georgia during the eighteenth century, the focus of this chapter is on Muskoghean peoples, and their story continues in Alabama. The early seventeenth-century Weiss phase (Holstein et al. 1990), named for a cluster of sites in the Weiss Reservoir, was succeeded by mid-seventeenth-century occupation downstream labeled the Whorton's Bend phase after the location of the major towns (Smith 1989b). The final seventeenth-century Coosa settlement was on Woods Island. Knight (1985: 13) suggested the name Woods Island phase for this period; the phase as he defined it overlaps temporally with the Whorton's Bend phase as I use it here. Numerous radiocarbon determinations from the region (see Hally and Langford 1988) seem to be particularly unreliable. Phase dates are determined largely by cross-dating, by judiciously using the available radiocarbon determinations, and by using datable European trade objects after European contact.

PRECONTACT PERIOD. About A.D. 1300, the Bell Field Mound site (Hally and Langford 1988; Kelly 1970, 1972) was the dominant town on the Coosawattee River (Fig. 11.3). Bell Field was not the capital of the first chiefdom in the valley—the early Etowah period Sixtoe Mound site and the late Etowah Baxter Mound site had held sway during earlier centuries. Before it was flooded by Carters Lake, the Bell Field site consisted of a single, 4-meter-high platform mound with dual summit levels and at least four single-post structures on the top. A series of log tombs held the remains of elites, along with exotic grave goods such as a bipointed stone sword of Tennessee chert, a copper headdress and earspools, a shell cup, a sawfish bill, a negative-painted dog pot, an anthropomorphic stone pipe, and a negative-painted water bottle with two modeled skulls alternating with two faces. The sumptuary ceramics document an eastern Tennessee Dallas connection and might well have originated there. The flint sword also suggests northerly connections, although the sawfish bill and marine shell clearly came from the south. The elaborate mound construction, elite burials, and evidence of long-distance trade clearly indicate that a chiefdom type of organization was present.

The size of the Bell Field village was not determined, because most of the archaeological work centered on the mound and because the village was covered with a blanket of alluvium. Only one other village site of this period is known from the Coosawattee Valley, despite much survey effort. This site, the Poarch Farm, has not been excavated.

Although Bell Field was undoubtedly the principal town

Figure 11.2. Cultural chronology of the Coosa region.

Years A.D.	Coosa Drainage	Etowah River	East Tennessee
1700	Childersburg	Abandoned?	?
	Woods Island		
	Whorton's Bend		
1600	Weiss		Dallas/ Mouse Creek
1500	Barnett	Brewster	
1400	Little Egypt	Early Lamar?	Dallas
1300	Unnamed (Dallas Related)	Wilbanks	
1200	Late Etowah	Late Etowah	Hiwassee Island
1100			
1000	Early Etowah	Early Etowah	

of a minor polity, the main power center of this period, circa A.D. 1200–1350, was the Etowah site, located about 35 miles to the south at the point where the Etowah River flows out of the piedmont into the Ridge and Valley province (Fig. 11.3). At its height, Etowah had six mounds and a village area of 21 hectares, and it was surrounded by a fortification wall with towers and a large ditch, 9 meters wide and 3 meters deep (Larson 1989). The richly accompanied burials of Etowah Mound C are well known (Larson 1971b). The elites were buried in log tombs, stone box graves, or simple pits and were accompanied by copper, shell, mica, pottery, and exotic chipped and ground stone artifacts. The copper and shell in particular show evidence of an elaborate art style depicting a rich iconography. By

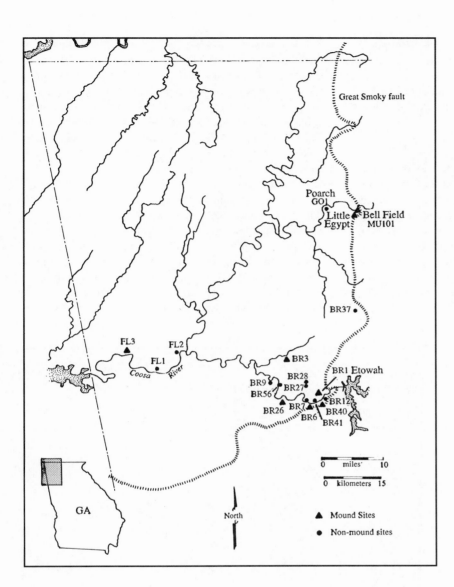

Figure 11.3. Middle Mississippi site distribution (after Hally and Langford 1988: 58).

about 1350, Etowah was abandoned, and presumably the Etowah polity collapsed. From this point, we may begin our discussion of the Coosa chiefdom with the founding of the Little Egypt site on the Coosawattee River just across from the earlier Bell Field site.

The collapse of Etowah produced a power vacuum in the Ridge and Valley province, and the chiefdom centered at Little Egypt gradually filled this void. It is worth noting that Little Egypt was the fourth mound center since A.D. 1000 in the Coosawattee Valley, suggesting that political power had been unstable there. Whereas other southern Appalachian Mississippian groups often chose to reuse mound centers, sometimes intermittently, for hundreds of years (Williams and Shapiro 1987) the Coosawattee situation was marked by serially occupied new centers, presumably ruled by different lineages.

During the early Lamar period Little Egypt phase (ca. 1350–1475), the capital of the new chiefdom was the Little Egypt site. Early in its history, the town had one plat-

form mound and a sizable residential area. At least one and perhaps two other single mound centers were located in the Coosawattee Valley within 20 miles of Little Egypt (Hally and Langford 1988). These three villages may indicate some population growth at this time, although internal site chronologies are not secure enough to demonstrate absolute contemporaneity. Perhaps these sites struggled for control of the valley, but subsequent events suggest that the Little Egypt site became the dominant center.

During the succeeding Barnett phase (ca. 1475–1575), Little Egypt grew to have three mounds and a village of approximately 5 hectares, which was large in relation to the sizes of other, contemporaneous sites in the region. Furthermore, population growth clearly took place at this time. Besides the paramount center at Little Egypt, six other villages and at least three smaller settlements are known for the valley. This cluster of towns and settlements was the largest population concentration in the Ridge and Valley province in the sixteenth century, and this growth may explain the rise of Little Egypt as the dominant power in the region. Given this population base, conquest of neighboring chiefdoms might have been relatively easy, and as more groups were incorporated, the military advantage grew. Thus was formed the paramount chiefdom of Coosa visited by Spaniards.

CONTACT PERIOD. With the Hernando de Soto expedition of 1540, Coosa entered the historic period (Fig. 11.4). Reconstruction of de Soto's route by Charles Hudson and his colleagues indicates that the Little Egypt site was the capital town of the Coosa chiefdom visited by the Spaniards (DePratter, Hudson, and Smith 1985; Hudson 1997; Hudson, Smith, and DePratter 1984). This reconstruction also indicates that Coosa held sway from the French Broad River in northeastern Tennessee down the valley well into central Alabama (see Fig. 11.1). The archaeologi-

cally known settlement pattern of this period, as detailed by Hally, Smith, and Langford (1990), consists of seven clusters of 5 to 13 villages each. Five of the clusters are located at the ecotone between the Blue Ridge–Piedmont and the Ridge and Valley provinces, and two lie to the west near, respectively, present-day Rome, Georgia, and Chattanooga, Tennessee (Fig. 11.5). Each cluster is approximately 20 kilometers in diameter. Sixteenth-century European artifacts have been recovered from each of them.

At the individual site level of settlement, there is some evidence of the plan of the capital, the Little Egypt site (Fig. 11.6) (Hally 1979, 1980), which consists of two large mounds surrounding a low, central, rectangular area that was probably the plaza. A third mound, described by Moorehead (1932), may have been in the area of the site investigated as XU-3. Domestic structures were excavated in XU-4 and XU-5, and it is assumed that additional structures surround the plaza. Excavations in Mound A yielded a rec-

Figure 11.4. The routes of the Hernando de Soto and Tristán de Luna expeditions (after Hudson 1990: 9).

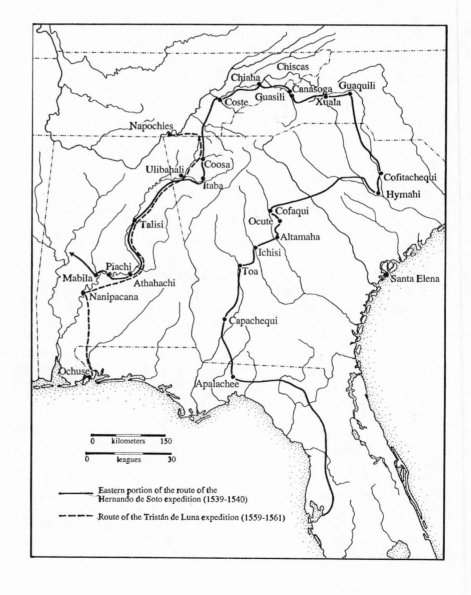

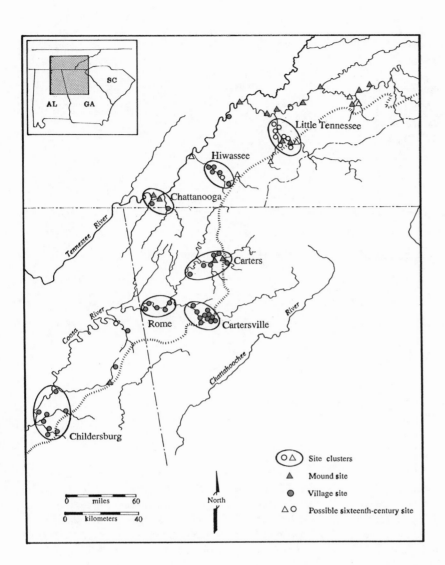

Figure 11.5. Archaeological site clusters in the Coosa region, around 1540 (after Hally, Smith, and Langford 1990: 125).

tangular summit structure and numerous burials. It was there that Moorehead recovered iron sword fragments and other European items. Excavations in Mound B were quite limited, and the XU-3 area produced many burials and evidence of structures.

The King site, on the Coosa River in Floyd County, Georgia (see Fig. 11.8), may be taken as a typical village of the mid-sixteenth century (Hally 1988, 1993). The town consisted of a ditched and palisaded enclosure approximately 2 hectares in extent (Fig. 11.7). More than half the site has been excavated, allowing an estimate of 47 structures and a population of 250 to 475 people. Nearly square winter houses with interior partitions and central hearths were constructed over house pits using single set posts. Work areas were clearly delimited within each house, and burial of the dead under the floor was common. Summer houses consisted of ground-surface rectangular structures of widely spaced posts, and burials were found inside these houses as

well. A large, square council house, 48 feet on a side, dominated the northeastern side of the plaza.

More than 200 burials were recovered from the King site, accompanied by somewhat less spectacular grave goods than those found at earlier centers—but some perspective must be kept. According to reconstructions of the de Soto route, King would have been a village down the hierarchy of political authority, a village subject to Ulibahali, which was in turn subject to Coosa (DePratter, Hudson, and Smith 1985; Hudson 1997; Hudson, Smith, and DePratter 1984). Forty-eight percent of the burials at King had grave goods (Seckinger 1977), including native pots, rattlesnake and mask shell gorgets, shell beads, chipped flint knives and arrow points, discoidal stones, spatulate and plain celts, and European metal chisel or celt blades and a sword (Little 1985). The limited distribution of European metal objects and their association with known markers of elite status such as shell cups, embossed native copper, and spatulate celts sug-

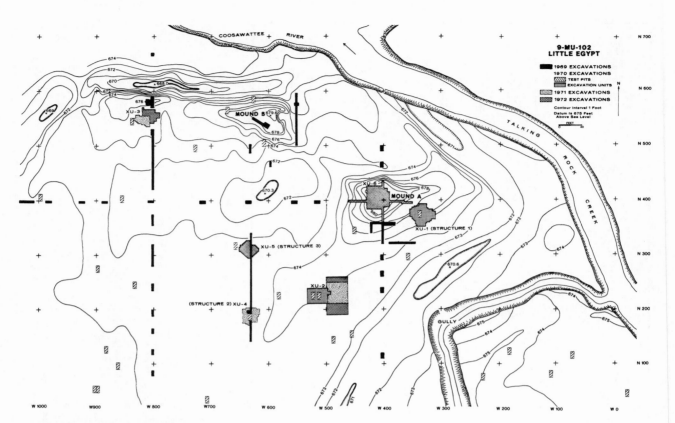

Figure 11.6. The Little Egypt site (source: Hally 1980).

gest that iron was an exotic material hoarded by the elites (Smith 1987). Grave goods excavated from Little Egypt, the presumed capital of the paramount chiefdom of Coosa in the sixteenth century, are virtually identical to those from King, seemingly showing little social differentiation. The major difference is the locations of burials. The Little Egypt elites were buried together in a mound, whereas the most richly accompanied burials at King were scattered across the site. The former pattern suggests a ruling lineage, whereas the latter suggests an equitable distribution of prestige goods, perhaps to lineage heads.

A site of short occupation, King clearly shows evidence of the outcome of European contact. Several burials consist of multiple individuals, suggesting that European disease epidemics might have ravaged the population (Smith 1987). According to one analysis, some people represented in the multiple burials had wounds inflicted by Europeans (Blakely and Mathews 1990). Both healed and fatal wounds are said to be present in the multiple burials, however, so not all such interments were victims of a European battle, presumably with members of the de Soto expedition. Milner (1992; Milner et al. 1994) has questioned Blakeley and Mathews's interpretation of the high level of violence at the King site. Milner's reanalysis of the King site skeletal series has demonstrated conclusively that there is no firm evidence for a massacre. The interpretation of a "King site massacre" should be put to rest forever.

Following the de Soto expedition, other Spaniards created additional historical documentation about Coosa. In 1560 a detachment from the expedition of Tristán de Luna visited Coosa (Fig. 11.4), apparently in the same place where de Soto had found it 20 years earlier (Hudson et al. 1989). Some of Luna's men had been with de Soto, and they could not believe the changes in Coosa. In de Soto's day, Coosa was said to have consisted of eight towns in an area about 11 kilometers long, and this description fits the cluster of known archaeological sites in the Coosawattee Valley. But by 1560 Coosa was clearly in decline. The villages of Luna's day were smaller than those the men remembered. The chronicles specifically mention a smaller population and a general lack of land under cultivation, and their description of thistles and weeds evokes images of abandoned fields.

During the mid-sixteenth century, there were 18 known village sites on the upper Coosa drainage in northern Georgia (and more are suggested by Spanish documents), but by the late century, only one or two sites on Terrapin Creek in extreme northeastern Alabama are known. It seems unlikely that depopulation by introduced disease pathogens following European contact was so severe that only one town remained, but the present archaeological evidence suggests this.

Following the mid-sixteenth century, northwestern Georgia (three large clusters of sites near Carters Lake,

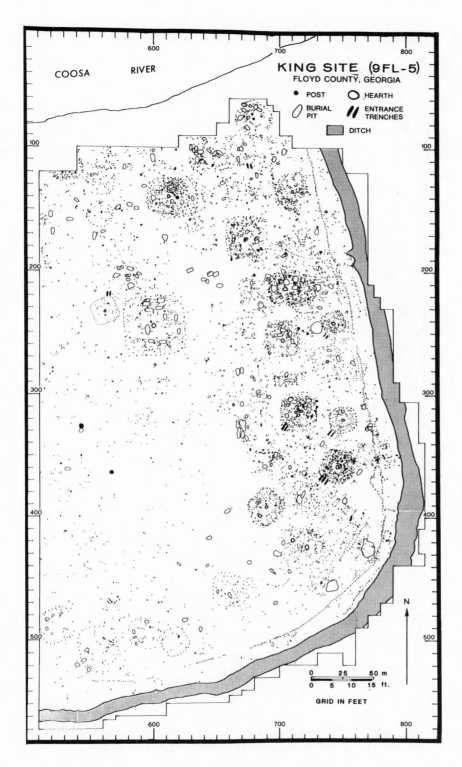

Figure 11.7. The King site (reproduced from Hally, Garrow, and Trotti 1975: 56, courtesy of the Southeastern Archaeological Conference and David J. Hally).

Etowah, and present-day Rome, Georgia) was abandoned. The exact timing of this move is unclear, but it appears to have taken place before 1600, perhaps as early as 1575. It marked the end of mound building on the upper Coosa. With northwestern Georgia abandoned, the Coosa people moved downstream into present-day Alabama. Two villages on Terrapin Creek, a tributary stream of the Coosa River in northeastern Alabama, appear to have been sequentially occupied during the last third of the sixteenth century. These are the only villages of this period known in the upper Coosa drainage (Fig. 11.8). One of the two, the Polecat Ford site, had a long prehistoric occupation that began hundreds of years prior to the Barnett phase and continued, perhaps intermittently, to the end of it (Little and

Figure 11.8. Contact period settlement along the upper Coosa River

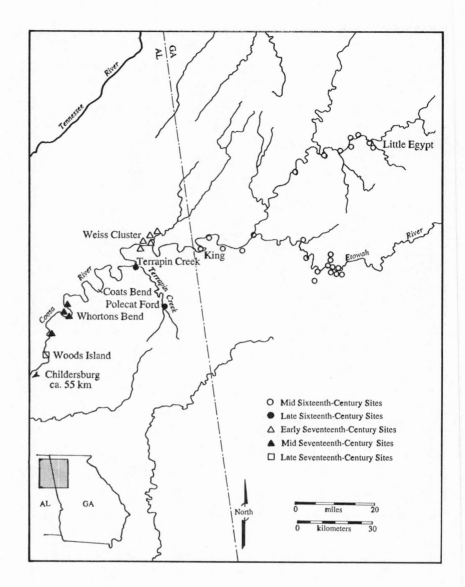

Curren 1981; Smith 1989b). European trade material and a reconstruction of the de Soto route suggest at least one occupation between 1540 and 1575. This site has been ravaged by relic hunters, and details about its occupancy are now lost.

The other of the two villages, the Terrapin Creek site, is located downstream from Polecat Ford at the junction of Terrapin Creek with the Coosa River (Holstein et al. 1990; Smith 1987). Again, little is known of this village, but European trade items suggest a date of about 1575–1600. Its size has been reported as less than 2 hectares. Artifact collectors report that European goods are uncommon at the site; nearly all objects purportedly came from one household. Native shell beads were commonly found strung with glass beads, and European copper or brass ornaments were common in the area that produced the other trade goods. It could be suggested that the European items were being hoarded by one village lineage or family, but considering

the hearsay nature of the data from Terrapin Creek, such an interpretation would probably exceed the reasonable. The ceramic collection from Terrapin Creek differs from that of the Barnett phase, showing a preponderance of shell-tempered types and the relative loss of grit-tempered Lamar types compared with the earlier Barnett phase (see Holstein et al. 1990: Table 36).

By the beginning of the seventeenth century, the archaeological picture comes into better focus. There is a distinct cluster of early seventeenth-century sites in and around Lake Weiss on the Coosa River near the Alabama-Georgia border (Fig. 11.8; DeJarnette, Kurjack, and Keel 1973; Smith 1987, 1989b). This cluster consists of at least 4 village-size sites and 14 smaller hamlets or farmsteads (Holstein et al. 1992; Smith 1989b). It might be suggested that the four villages are the remnants, respectively, of the people from Terrapin Creek in Alabama and people from the three sixteenth-century site clusters found on the Coosawattee, the Etowah, and the head of the Coosa River in Georgia. The change in settlement is noteworthy: before this period, small hamlets or farmsteads are virtually unknown. These sites form a cluster approximately 13 kilometers in maximum extent—that is, smaller than the sixteenth-century clusters. Three villages, including the largest, are located at the junction of the Little River–Chatooga River system with the Coosa River, and their inhabitants clearly took advantage of this strategic setting. Although this location is not on the Cartersville Fault, which separated the Ridge and Valley province from the Piedmont–Blue Ridge province, it is on a similar ecotonal boundary near the junction of Lookout Mountain with the Ridge and Valley province.

Little is known of Weiss phase sites except for burials and pit features. No houses have been reported, nor have mounds (almost certainly absent) or palisades. Recent research (Holstein et al. 1992) suggests that one house was excavated at site 1Ce137, but this site has not been reported. Virtually no subsistence data were recovered. The use of refuse-filled pits at this time is a radical departure from behavior in the sixteenth century, perhaps suggesting people's increased absence from the village during winter hunts (cf. Ward 1985: 99). Ceramics also are much different from those of the earlier Barnett phase. Weiss phase ceramics are almost entirely shell tempered, with a plain or incised surface finish. The Lamar tradition grit-tempered and complicated stamped ceramics virtually disappear, but continuity is seen in incised motifs (Smith 1989b).

Burial data are available for 47 Weiss phase interments, and 66 percent of the graves contained European items, especially ornaments such as glass beads and brass discs, bells, and bangles. A total of 76.6 percent of all burials contained some form of grave goods, including the 38 percent that contained aboriginal grave goods (Smith 1987: 106–107). Children often were accompanied by the largest quantities of European materials. Iron tools, although present, were relatively rare. Native manufactures were less abundant than previously, and materials such as shell gorgets, shell beads, and stone axes were absent, having been replaced by glass and metal counterparts. Clearly these people had trading contacts with Spaniards to the east, although no known Spanish records suggest European expeditions into the interior. Waselkov (1989) has suggested that the deerskin trade might have begun this early, but the earliest historic sources place it nearer mid-century (Bushnell 1986). The abundance of European items far into the interior supports Waselkov's earlier trade scenario. Pottery vessels, projectile points, pipes, and red ocher were still placed in graves, however. At the Bradford Ferry site, although burial clusters were present—presumably representing family groups—there was no apparent clustering of richly accompanied burials, and no cluster appeared to have greater access to European or native goods than any other. Thus we might infer that by the early seventeenth century, the system of social ranking so evident in the sixteenth-century mound centers was no longer in operation. There were two instances of multiple burial, again perhaps reflecting limited disease or warfare episodes.

Twenty-three kilometers downstream, at Coats Bend (Fig. 11.8), is a cluster of three small sites known only from surface collections (Harry Holstein, personal communication 1992). The ceramic sample suggests possible assignment to the Weiss phase or perhaps the end of the sixteenth century, and a glass bead from the surface demonstrates historic age. Little can be said about these sites until more work is done, but their small size indicates that there was no real population concentration in this area.

By about 1630, the Coosa River population had again moved downstream, to Whortons Bend near present Gadsden, Alabama (Fig. 11.8). In 1948 DeJarnette and Wimberly excavated five burials and two midden-filled pits at Milner Village (Smith et al. 1993). This portion of the Coosa River became part of the Neely Henry Reservoir in the 1960s and was investigated by archaeologists from the University of Alabama and a local chapter of the Alabama Archaeological Society prior to and following inundation. The professional work was limited to moderate testing, but the amateurs excavated and subsequently reported on numerous burials at the Cooper Farm site during removal of construction fill and following shoreline erosion after the lake was completed (Battles 1969, 1972; Lindsay 1964). Given the limited nature of these excavations, data on settlement pattern, houses, and subsistence are virtually absent. Even the sizes of the sites are unknown; some were recorded as extraordinarily large (but are multicomponent), whereas others, such as Cooper Farm, were listed as quite small, although numerous burials were later salvaged from them. There appear to have been three village-size sites and three smaller sites on Whorton's Bend, and another possible village of this period is located downstream 11 kilometers straightline distance. Perhaps the pattern of four main villages was carried on from the earlier Weiss phase settlement.

The Whorton's Bend phase is characterized by the appearance of brushed pottery (nearly a third of the sherds), while incised and plain surface treatments continued to be in vogue. Tempering remained exclusively of shell. Burials were excavated at the Cooper Farm, Whorton's Bend, and Milner Village sites. European trade material was abundant, although aboriginal goods such as pottery vessels, flint arrow points, pipes, discoidals, and pigments such as red ocher and galena were still placed in graves. Of particular interest was a large copper celt, a so-called Tukabahchee plate, that was recovered from the Whorton's Bend site (Greer 1966; Smith 1989b). This sociotechnic artifact type perhaps signals a revitalization of native values, a trend also seen in the reappearance of native-made shell beads and earpins in the Whorton's Bend phase. European grave goods included glass beads, brass discs, armbands, neck collars, animal effigy pendants, bangles, and cast brass harness bells. Iron knives and eyed axes (largely replacing earlier iron celt blades by this time) were common. Gun parts and glass bottles were absent. Sixty-four percent of the 25 burials reported from Cooper Farm contained European artifacts, and 68 percent contained aboriginal grave goods (Smith 1987: 106).

Although little village excavation has been conducted on sites of this period, one important change in subsistence can be noted. At the Milner Village site, excavated by DeJarnette and Wimberly in the late 1940s and recently analyzed for the first time by my colleagues and me (Smith et al. 1993), the remains of two bison were found (Susan Scott, personal communication 1993), suggesting changing hunting patterns. Bison bones are also known from early seventeenth-century sites in the Chattanooga, Tennessee, area, and Rostlund (1960) has suggested that bison migrated into the Southeast to occupy old field environments of abandoned Indian towns as depopulation due to European diseases took its toll. Other animals utilized by Milner Village inhabitants included deer and bear. Data on plant remains are lacking.

Sometime around 1670, the Coosa people again moved downstream, this time to settle on Woods Island (Fig. 11.8). Although the entire stretch of the Coosa River from Whorton's Bend to Logan Martin Lake below Woods Island is now a series of reservoirs that received archaeological salvage work in the 1960s, no other site of the late seventeenth century is known in this region except for a small hamlet located near Woods Island on the mainland. The founding of the Woods Island settlement seems to indicate that the villages and scattered farmsteads of the Whorton's Bend phase had amalgamated into one large village around 1670. Indeed, the Woods Island settlement is the largest historic site of the upper Coosa River, measuring some 10.4 hectares in extent. This large size may be misleading, however, if used as a population measure. Excavated houses at Woods Island are considerably smaller than those documented for the sixteenth-century King site (199 square feet vs. 684 square feet), and the houses are much more widely spaced (King, 35 feet apart, vs. Woods Island, 81 feet apart). Projecting from the distribution of houses in a block excavation, there were only about 46 houses at Woods Island altogether (Smith 1995). Information on community pattern is generally lacking.

Ceramics of the Woods Island phase are almost completely shell tempered. Brushed pottery continues to be important but drops to only 12.3 percent of the total assemblage. Shell-tempered, cord-marked ceramics appear (3.5 percent of the total), perhaps signaling the immigration of Tennessee River Koasati-speaking groups into the area from the Guntersville basin region of the Tennessee River. The Spaniard Marcos Delgado documented the southern movement of northern Muskoghean groups fleeing armed Indian slave raiders in the 1680s (Boyd 1937). The sudden appearance of cord-marked pottery probably reflects this

migration, since cord-marking was a common decoration on pottery at seventeenth-century archaeological sites in the Guntersville Reservoir (Smith 1989b: 9; Webb and Wilder 1951). The naturally fortified island location of the Woods Island site, the fact that the populations of many towns amalgamated there, and the presence of firearms in the deposits for the first time all suggest that the Coosa people were forced into a defensive position by historical events such as the English-backed slave trade.

Forty-eight burials were excavated during investigations at Woods Island (Morrell 1965; Smith 1989b, 1995). Some burials were largely destroyed by heavy equipment, but data on the presence or absence of grave goods are available for 41 interments. Ten burials contained no grave goods, but the manner of burial (extended) and the presence of stone box graves suggest that several of these belonged to the Etowah phase component of the site (Smith 1989b). Graves with European artifacts contained flexed burials. Of the 30 burials with grave goods that appeared to date to the historic period, only 2 had no European trade objects. Native-made goods continued to be included in graves occasionally. Four graves contained pottery vessels, stone projectile points, or steatite and ceramic pipes. In general, the use of native goods in graves seems to have been on the decline. European goods were numerous, including glass beads, brass harness bells, brass disc and crescent neck collars, armbands, iron axes, buttons (perhaps indicating European-style clothing), and knives. New types of European goods included a brass kettle, iron hoes of the Spanish lugged type, gun parts in at least two burials, an English sword, scissors, and many new styles of beads.

The Woods Island site probably was occupied until around 1715, and it shows definite contact with English traders, as well as continuing Spanish and possible French trade. It is likely that Englishmen such as Thomas Nairne visited the Abihka people at this location (see Moore 1988; Smith 1989b, 1995), although no known account mentions an island town. Woods Island lies at a natural crossing point on the Coosa River and was probably on the English path to the Chickasaw. The Barnwell map of circa 1722 shows "Habiquechee" (Abihkutci, or "Little Abihka") at a place where the trading path crosses the river that could be Woods Island (Smith 2000). Subsistence remains have not been studied in detail for Woods Island, but maize, beans, squash, and the introduced peach have been identified. Animals identified include deer, turtle, and small mammal (Morrell 1965).

Following settlement on Woods Island, the Coosa people moved farther downstream to the Childersburg site area in the early eighteenth century (DeJarnette and Hansen 1960). Crane (1981: 169) mentioned that the Abihka killed their English traders in 1715 as part of the general uprising known as the Yamassee War, and Swanton (1922: 253) noted that the Abihka suffered a severe defeat by the Cherokee in 1716. Either or both of these events might have caused the Woods Island site to be abandoned. Although the Childersburg site, the eighteenth-century location of Coosa, is the best known settlement of this time, many other sites are located in the region, including Abihkutci, or Little Abihka. It was there that historical documents again pinpoint the Coosa and Abihka Indians' home, from which they were to be removed to Oklahoma in the 1830s—but that part of the story is beyond the scope of this chapter.

Relation of Archaeological Data to Historically Known Tribes

The people of this region were known as the chiefdom of Coosa to mid-sixteenth-century Spaniards. The main town of Coosa was located on the Coosawattee River, but in addition, the de Soto accounts mention Itaba on the Etowah River, the Luna accounts mention Apica on the Coosa, and both expeditions record Ulibahali on the Coosa (Hudson, Smith, and DePratter 1984; Hudson et al. 1989). Itaba and Ulibahali disappear from the historic record prior to the eighteenth century, but Coosa was still an important entity, and the small Luna village of Apica returned to history as the powerful Abihka of the eighteenth century. It is my thesis that the archaeological sites described in this chapter represent the settlements of the Coosa and Abihka, with the remnants of the Itaba and Ulibahali amalgamated into these groups (Smith 2000).

Conclusion

The powerful, complex chiefdom of Coosa, known to sixteenth-century Spanish explorers, began as a small chiefdom on the Coosawattee River. Following the collapse of the Etowah chiefdom in the mid-fourteenth century, Coosa began its ascent to power. Though its elites seem not to have been as rich as their earlier Etowah counterparts—judging from grave goods, village size, or mound construction—Coosa nonetheless controlled a vast territory and was clearly a powerful polity. It was at its height when Hernando de Soto found it in 1540. Following European contact, Coosa began to disintegrate. European diseases, famine caused by the theft of stored food surpluses by the Spaniards, and perhaps a change in the aboriginal balance of power all combined to shatter the population base of Coosa. Survivors began a steady migration downriver and a constant regrouping during the seventeenth century. By the eighteenth century, towns known as Coosa and Abihka were still viable entities, but many other towns had ceased to exist.

Acknowledgments

My perspective on Coosa came from many field seasons with David Hally and Patrick Garrow at the Little Egypt and King sites. Years of collaboration with Charles Hudson and Chester DePratter led to an understanding of the Spanish presence. Vernon Knight has been a most generous colleague in my search for the Coosa-Abihka into Alabama, and Carey Oakley and Eugene Futato have opened the Alabama site files on many occasions. James Langford, Keith Little, Caleb Curren, and Harry Holstein have freely shared the results of their investigations. I am also indebted to many collectors who have shared what they know and allowed me access to their materials. Greg Waselkov has freely shared his perspective on Creek archaeology, and Wes Cowan provided much editorial assistance. A grant from the Alabama de Soto Commission supported a segment of my research on collections at Moundville. This chapter represents a condensed version of a forthcoming book, which was written during research time supported by the University of South Alabama. Figures 11.1, 11.3–11.5, and 11.8 were drafted by Julie B. Smith.

Locations of Primary Collections

Primarily data utilized for this chapter are curated at the University of Georgia, West Georgia College, Moundville Archaeological Park, and Jacksonville State University and in several private collections.

12

The Emergence and Demise of the Calusa

In early sixteenth-century southwest Florida, Europeans encountered a complex and powerful society known as the Calusa. Divided into nobles and commoners, the Calusa supported a special military force and collected tribute from throughout south Florida. Their belief system encompassed daily offerings to their ancestors and a concept of afterlife. Elaborate rituals included processions of masked priests and synchronized singing by hundreds. They painted, engraved, and carved wooden objects (Fig. 12.1; see Fontaneda 1944; Hann 1991; Solís de Merás 1964).

Because the Calusa raised neither maize nor manioc, they are often cited as an enigma, or an exception, because they were *complex* fisher-gatherer-hunters. A dominant, nonproductive nobility and the apparatus of rulership were supported by extracting labor and products from kin-ordered communities. Historically documented "kings," such as Carlos and Felipe, controlled vast territories and had far-reaching power. Their authority was based on sacred knowledge and broadly recognized royal ancestry (Hann 1991: 246; Marquardt 1988: 170–185).

What is not known about the Calusa is their place of origin, the mechanisms by which they became so extraordinarily complex, and the timing of the transformation. On the positive side, we know a great deal more about the area's material culture, subsistence, and environment than we did 15 years ago (Marquardt 1996). Some of the new knowledge is surprising. For example, it is now apparent that sedentary habitation on the southwest Florida coast dates to the fourth millennium B.C. and that mound building had begun well before the advent of pottery making (Russo 1991, 1994). We have also learned that environments long thought to have been the source of Calusa prosperity were as heterogeneous and dynamic as they were rich and sustaining (Walker 1992; Walker, Stapor, and Marquardt 1994, 1995).

In this chapter I first provide an introduction to south Florida's environmental and cultural history, concentrating on the Calusa domain of southwest Florida. Then, in keeping with the theme of this book, I focus on the period from around A.D. 1450 to 1750 and report what we know and do not know about the rise and fall of the Calusa.

Environmental Setting

"South Florida" means simply the southern half of the Florida peninsula. For most considerations, this includes everything south of a line drawn from Sarasota on the west coast to Fort Pierce on the east, approximately the route of Florida Highway 70. For other purposes, south Florida extends as far north as a line running from Tampa Bay on the west to Lake Kissimmee in the central area and to Vero Beach on the east, approximately the path of Florida Highway 60. In this discussion, the terms "southwest Florida" and "Calusa region" are used informally to mean the southwestern Gulf coastal zone from Charlotte Harbor south to

WILLIAM H. MARQUARDT

Figure 12.1. Wooden artifacts discovered in the 1890s at the Key Marco site, Collier County, Florida, attributed to the prehistoric Calusa (see Gilliland 1975). Photographs of watercolors by Wells Sawyer, courtesy of the National Anthropological Archives, Smithsonian Institution; photograph of feline figurine (center left), Smithsonian Institution catalog number 240915, courtesy of the Department of Anthropology, Smithsonian Institution.

the Ten Thousand Islands (Fig. 12.2). The term "Caloosahatchee area" is used more restrictively to refer to an archaeological zone between southern Sarasota County and an east-west line drawn about 40 kilometers north of Marco Island in Collier County and between the barrier islands on the west eastward to a north-south line approximately 90 kilometers in from the coast. The physiography, ecology, hydrology, and culture history of south Florida are summarized in publications by Widmer (1988) and Griffin (1988); see also Gleason et al. 1984.

South Florida straddles temperate and tropical biomes, fostering rich and intergrading plant communities (Scarry and Newsom 1992). In the sixteenth century, the zone of Calusa influence stretched across the vast wetlands and flatlands of the southern Florida peninsula from the Gulf to the Atlantic coast and south to the Florida Keys. The Calusa heartland centered on Charlotte Harbor, near present-day Fort Myers. In Charlotte Harbor the combination of river

outflow from the interior and the enclosing barrier islands furnished a protected, shallow, grassy estuary of extraordinary year-round productivity.

Climate and sea-level fluctuations must have affected past peoples in southwest Florida. Fluctuations in past environmental conditions are becoming better understood. Long-term wet and dry cycles are known with some assurance (Gleason et al. 1984; Marquardt 1992a; Perry 1948; Watts and Hansen 1988). Generally speaking, when rainfall increases, estuaries become fresher, moving the salinity gradient oceanward and altering fish and shellfish distribution. At a broader scale, long-term warming leads to higher ocean levels, which bring saltwater closer to, and sometimes inundate, coastal settlements. At a limited temporal scale, disastrous storms can cause short-term interruptions in staple food supplies, and inlet openings and closings can cause medium-term fluctuations in salinity, affecting the abundance and spatial distribution of food (Walker

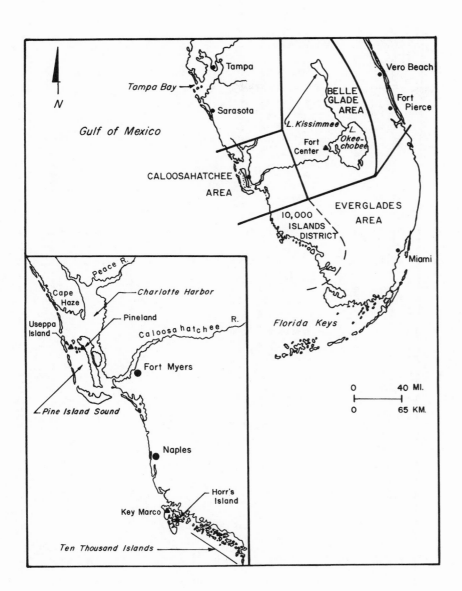

Figure 12.2. South Florida archaeological zones and sites discussed in this chapter.

1992). To understand such processes and how they interact, one must obtain reliable data on both cultural and noncultural phenomena at multiple scales. Such interdisciplinary research is ongoing (Marquardt 1996; Marquardt, ed., 1992, 1999).

Precontact Cultural Chronology and Culture History

The history of archaeological research in south Florida has been summarized comprehensively by Widmer (1988: 36–54) and Griffin (1988: 48–65). Additionally, Griffin (1988: 111–142) provided a history of archaeological culture concepts for south Florida that is indispensable for anyone who hopes to comprehend the rationale for regional chronologies. In earlier publications (Marquardt 1987a, 1988, 1991), I summarized what is known of the postcontact Calusa social formation and of transformations that were taking

place at and just prior to European contact. Essential ethnohistoric documents for southwest Florida have been translated by Hann (1991), who also provided background information for documents of the sixteenth, seventeenth, and eighteenth centuries. The 1697 Franciscan mission to the Calusa, on which Hann (1991: 3–216) primarily focused, is the best documented of all the Spanish mission efforts in the southeastern United States. Important firsthand historical accounts are those of Fontaneda (1944; see also Worth 1995) and Solís de Merás (1964) for south and southwest Florida and Dickinson (1985) for southeast Florida.

South Florida's cultural history has been reviewed by Widmer and Griffin. Griffin's (1988) study is a synthesis of work in the Everglades area but includes reviews of previous research, cultural chronologies, and sociopolitical interpretations relevant to south Florida as a whole. Widmer (1988) provides a synthesis of environmental information

Figure 12.3. Generalized chronologies for South Florida from 5000 B.C. Sources: Cordell 1992, 1994; Griffin 1988; Marquardt 1992a, 1992b, 1999; Sears 1982; Widmer 1988.

Date	Caloosahatchee Area	Everglades Area	Belle Glade Area
A.D. 1600–1763	Caloosahatchee V	Glades IIIc	Belle Glade IV
A.D. 1500–1600	Caloosahatchee V	Glades IIIc	Belle Glade IV
A.D. 1400–1500	Caloosahatchee IV	Glades IIIb	Belle Glade III
A.D. 1300–1400	Caloosahatchee III	Glades IIIa	Belle Glade III
A.D. 1200–1300	Caloosahatchee III	Glades IIIa	Belle Glade III
A.D. 1100–1200	Caloosahatchee IIB	Glades IIc	Belle Glade III
A.D. 1000–1100	Caloosahatchee IIB	Glades IIb	Belle Glade II
A.D. 900–1000	Caloosahatchee IIB	Glades IIb	Belle Glade II
A.D. 800–900	Caloosahatchee IIA	Glades IIa	Belle Glade II
A.D. 700–800	Caloosahatchee IIA	Glades I late	Belle Glade II
A.D. 600–700	Caloosahatchee IIA	Glades I late	Belle Glade II
A.D. 500–600	Caloosahatchee IIA	Glades I late	Belle Glade II
A.D. 400–500	Caloosahatchee I	Glades I early	Belle Glade I
A.D. 300–400	Caloosahatchee I	Glades I early	Belle Glade I
A.D. 200–300	Caloosahatchee I	Glades I early	Belle Glade I
A.D. 100–200	Caloosahatchee I	Glades I early	Belle Glade I
A.D. 1–100	Caloosahatchee I	Glades I early	Belle Glade I
100–1 B.C.	Caloosahatchee I	Glades I early	Belle Glade I
200–100 B.C.	Caloosahatchee I	Glades I early	Belle Glade I
300–200 B.C.	Caloosahatchee I	Glades I early	Belle Glade I
400–300 B.C.	Caloosahatchee I	Glades I early	Belle Glade I
500–400 B.C.	Caloosahatchee I	Glades I early	Belle Glade I
600–500 B.C.	Terminal Archaic	Transitional	Belle Glade I
700–600 B.C.	Terminal Archaic	Transitional	Belle Glade I
800–700 B.C.	Terminal Archaic	Transitional	Belle Glade I
900–800 B.C.	Terminal Archaic	Transitional	Belle Glade I
1000–900 B.C.	Terminal Archaic	Transitional	Belle Glade I
1100–1000 B.C.	Late Archaic	Late Archaic	Late Archaic
1200–1100 B.C.	Late Archaic	Late Archaic	Late Archaic
1300–1200 B.C.	Late Archaic	Late Archaic	Late Archaic
1400–1300 B.C.	Late Archaic	Late Archaic	Late Archaic
1500–1400 B.C.	Late Archaic	Late Archaic	Late Archaic
1600–1500 B.C.	Late Archaic	Late Archaic	Late Archaic
1700–1600 B.C.	Late Archaic	Late Archaic	Late Archaic
1800–1700 B.C.	Late Archaic	Late Archaic	Late Archaic
1900–1800 B.C.	Late Archaic	Late Archaic	Late Archaic
2000–1900 B.C.	Late Archaic	Late Archaic	Late Archaic
3000–2000 B.C.	Late Middle Archaic	Middle Archaic	Middle Archaic
4000–3000 B.C.	Early Middle Archaic	Middle Archaic	Middle Archaic
5000–4000 B.C.	Early Middle Archaic	Middle Archaic	Middle Archaic

and sets forth a cultural-evolutionary model to explain the emergence of the Calusa social formation. Several papers by me (Marquardt 1987a, 1988, 1991) provide a critique of Widmer's model as well as further information on Calusa political economy and social relations.

CHRONOLOGY AND SETTLEMENT. The maritime adaptation of southwest Florida becomes archaeologically visible in deposits that began to accumulate between 5000 and 4000 B.C. (Marquardt 1992a; see Fig. 12.3). Shell middens began to amass on the Pleistocene-era dune ridges of Horr's Island, near Marco Island, at about 5000 B.C., judging from dates near the bottom of oyster shell middens, and on Useppa Island as early as about 4500 B.C. Settlement was undoubtedly not limited to the tops of dunes; rising seas have inundated any low-lying coastal sites of the Middle Archaic and earlier periods.

Russo (1991) has shown that by about 2800 B.C. a site on

Horr's Island was occupied year-round by people who exploited a variety of fish and shellfish. They lived in small, circular houses made of poles and thatch, and they constructed a 6-meter-high conical sand mound that was used at least in part for human burial (Marquardt, Payne, and Walker 1992: 1–2; Russo 1991).

Useppa Island, located in Pine Island Sound, has extensive Archaic period shell middens, including one occupied circa 2000–1860 B.C. showing evidence of the manufacture and use of large gastropod columella hammers (Marquardt 1992c: 204–205, 208, 1999; Marquardt, Payne, and Walker 1992: 5; Torrence 1999) and another containing fiber-tempered pottery of the Orange series (Marquardt 1992b: 25–29). A distinctive *Busycon sinistrum* shouldered adze (Marquardt 1992c: 207–208, 210) is limited to the Middle and Late Archaic periods. Fiber-tempered pottery has been found at several locations in Pine Island Sound; it is also known from several sites in the Marco Island area (Widmer 1988: 70–72). Excavations at Heineken Hammock (Lee 1993), an interior site in Collier County, suggest that plain sand-tempered pottery without fiber tempering may date as early as 2000 B.C.

Coastal middens of the Late Archaic (2000–1200 B.C.) and Terminal Archaic (1200–500 B.C.) periods are known from Useppa Island (Marquardt 1992b: 25–29), Calusa Island (Edic 1992), and Galt Island (Austin and Woods 1991), but excavations and collections at these sites have been limited. Little is known of settlement characteristics.

The Caloosahatchee I period (500 B.C.–A.D. 500) is defined traditionally by the appearance of thick, sand-tempered plain pottery, not by any known change in settlement or subsistence. Middens continued to accumulate at Cash Mound, Useppa, Galt, and—beginning by at least A.D. 100—Pineland (see Marquardt 1992b: 29–55). The Type E gastropod cutting-edged tool (Marquardt 1992c: 197–198) occurs in the Caloosahatchee I period and may date somewhat earlier. The later half of the Caloosahatchee I period, circa A.D. 200–500, is marked by a higher sea level stand, rising from a point about 0.6 meter below today's level in A.D. 100 to a point as high as 1.2 meters above today's level by A.D. 250 (Stapor, Mathews, and Lindfors-Kearns 1991; Walker, Stapor, and Marquardt 1995).

The Caloosahatchee II period is divided into IIA (A.D. 500–800) and IIB (A.D. 800–1200). Caloosahatchee IIA is marked by the rapid accumulation of middens at Useppa Island, Galt Island, Pineland, Josslyn Island, and a number of other coastal sites. The period A.D. 500–600 coincides with a lowering of the sea from a high point about 1.2 meters above today's level to a point about 0.6 meter below it (Stapor, Mathews, and Lindfors-Kearns 1991; Walker 1992: 277–290; Walker, Stapor, and Marquardt 1995: 215–216). Shell artifacts became more diversified during Caloosahatchee IIA. Various "Woodland" hafted biface types, such as Broward, Columbia, Duval, and Sarasota, are firmly dated to the Caloosahatchee IIA period at the Pineland site complex.

The Caloosahatchee IIB period is thought to have been a stormy and warmer climatic episode, with a corresponding sea-level rise (Gleason et al. 1984: 321; Walker, Stapor, and Marquardt 1995). Ceramic markers include minor amounts of Belle Glade Red, Weeden Island pottery, Pasco limestone-tempered pottery, and micaceous paste pottery and a further increase in the popularity of Belle Glade Plain. Belle Glade Plain pottery, introduced into the region by A.D. 500, became ubiquitous by A.D. 800 during a period of intensive midden accumulation (Cordell 1992: 165–168). The possibility of significant migration from the Belle Glade area (near Lake Okeechobee) to the southwest Florida coast cannot be ruled out.

Midden accumulation continued throughout Charlotte Harbor during the Caloosahatchee IIB period. At Big Mound Key, an extensive shell-midden site near Cape Haze, two of the principal midden mounds accumulated between A.D. 800 and 1000 (Luer et al. 1986: 103). Belle Glade Plain pottery is prominent in the Big Mound Key site deposits located south of the main elevated "mounds" and north of the so-called finger ridges (Marquardt 1992b: 44–47; Upchurch, Jewell, and DeHaven 1992; Weisman 1991: 3–4).

Knowledge of dwellings during this period is scant, due to the spatial limitations of excavations, but it seems evident that hundreds, if not thousands, of people lived in the Charlotte Harbor–Pine Island Sound area. By A.D. 800, the settlement pattern in Charlotte Harbor included several large and small villages and probably a number of temporary camps or fishing stations (Widmer 1988: 255–260). Widmer (1988: 260) estimated the Caloosahatchee area's population at 4,800, and that of the Ten Thousand Islands area at 4,250.

The Caloosahatchee III period (ca. A.D. 1200–1350) is prominently represented at Big Mound Key and Pineland, as well as at Buck Key, Josslyn Island, and other Charlotte Harbor sites. A sea level on the order of 30 centimeters or more higher than today's is thought to have prevailed between about 850 and 1400 (Stapor, Mathews, and Lindfors-Kearns 1991; Walker, Stapor, and Marquardt 1995), probably a response to a global warming episode called the Neo-Atlantic (e.g., Bryson, Baerreis, and Wendland 1970). By A.D. 1200, the Neo-Atlantic warm period had been superseded by the cooler Pacific episode, and by 1550, the even colder Neo-Boreal, or "Little Ice Age." These global cooling events eventually resulted in a lower sea-level stand in southwest Florida by the fifteenth century A.D. (Walker, Stapor, and Marquardt 1995).

The appearance of St. Johns Check Stamped pottery marks the beginning of Caloosahatchee III, but no dramatic changes in site characteristics are evident. Although Widmer (1988) correctly noted that no *new* sites are known to have been established after A.D. 800, I would add that modern development has removed many sites from examination, that survey coverage of both coastal and riverine areas is anything but complete, and that landforms that did not exist at A.D. 800 but were later inhabited must be excepted. A number of sites occupied since at least A.D. 500 continued to be occupied into the Caloosahatchee III period and sometimes into Caloosahatchee IV.

Caloosahatchee IV (A.D. 1350–1500) is traditionally recognized by the appearance of Glades Tooled pottery, the diminution of Belle Glade Plain, and the increase of Sand-tempered Plain pottery, possibly signaling political realignments or a reorganization of trade relationships. Certainly Belle Glade Plain pottery continued to dominate in the Belle Glade area itself, even as it diminished in importance on the southwest coast relative to Sand-tempered Plain.

The origin of Glades Tooled pottery is poorly understood. Widmer (1988: 86) believed it came into the Caloosahatchee area from the south, but he presented no data to substantiate his claim. Evidence from the Buck Key Shell Midden site suggests that Glades Tooled dates to about 1350 or earlier in Pine Island Sound (Marquardt 1992b: 34–40), and Cordell noted that tooled and indented lips similar to those of Glades Tooled might be as early as Caloosahatchee IIA at the Pineland site complex (Cordell n.d.). The south Florida tooled and indented lips resemble the Suazey ceramics of late pre-Columbian Grenada and St. Vincent islands of the Lesser Antilles (Bullen 1964: 50–51; Bullen and Bullen 1972: 144–145), but the pastes are very different. According to Cordell (1992: 131–132), Glades Tooled pottery of southwest Florida is similar in paste to local Sand-tempered Plain. There is no evidence for communication with Antillean groups prior to European contact (Marquardt 1987b).

Pinellas Plain and Safety Harbor incised and punctated wares, common in west-central Florida, occur in Caloosahatchee area midden and burial contexts. Widmer (1988: 86) and Mitchem (1989: 595–598) discussed several possibilities by which they might have arrived there. If pots were people, one might suggest a new political alignment that saw closer relationships (alliance or possibly conquest) among the Tampa Bay, Charlotte Harbor, and Ten Thousand Islands areas and less contact (or perhaps more hostility) between the Florida Gulf coast and the Belle Glade area. Our collective knowledge of the Safety Harbor culture is derived primarily from ceramics found in mortuary contexts. As Mitchem (1989: 567–578) noted, regional variability in Safety Harbor material culture is recognized but poorly understood. The fact that Safety Harbor pottery is associated with Pinellas Plain pottery at its northern geographic limit and with Sand-tempered Plain and/or Belle Glade Plain at its southern extent is not surprising. It is premature to infer, as Mitchem (1989: 575) did, that the presence of Belle Glade Plain in southwest Florida sites indicates significant trade with the interior, that is, the Belle Glade area. Until ceramic technology researchers succeed in identifying the raw materials used to make Belle Glade Plain, we will not know whether this common plainware was imported to southwest Florida or made locally in the late precontact period.

SUBSISTENCE. Over the past 15 years, great strides have been made in characterizing and quantifying southwest Florida subsistence data (Milanich et al. 1984; Quitmyer and Massaro 1999; Russo 1991; Scarry 1999; Scarry and Newsom 1992; Walker 1992). The overwhelming impression is that southwest Florida people were fisher-gatherer-hunters who depended primarily on estuarine fish and shellfish and a variety of wild plant foods (Marquardt 1988: 164–169; Widmer 1988: 224–255). There is no evidence for broad-scale agriculture, but there is good evidence that small house gardens were being cultivated by A.D. 100 (Newsom and Scarry n.d.).

Maritime fishing-gathering-hunting was in place by 4000 B.C., and it was maintained with modest technological modifications for many hundreds of years thereafter. Net fishing is at least as old as 3500 B.C., judging from net mesh gauges and faunal remains found at Useppa Island (Torrence 1999). More than 30 different fish species and more than 50 kinds of mollusks and crustaceans were gathered for food. Although the occasional large shark, grouper, jewfish, or sea turtle is represented in the archaeological record, the fishing strategy seems to have been aimed mainly at capturing large numbers of small fish, probably in nets and tidal traps, rather than angling for large fish. Pinfish, pigfish, and hard-head catfish are consistently among the most prominently represented fish in the middens. Deer, ducks, land turtles, small rodents, and other animals were occasionally eaten, but fish were the main dietary staple (Walker 1992).

Plants used for food and firewood included saw palmetto, cabbage palm, cocoplum, seagrape, pepper, mastic, papaya, hog plum, acorns, red mangrove, black mangrove, buttonwood, pine, red cedar, wax myrtle, goosefoot, sea purslane, prickly pear, grapes, hackberry, talinum, mallows, grasses, water lilies, rhizomes, and tubers (Newsom and Scarry n.d.; Scarry 1999; Scarry and Newsom 1992). In addition to food and fuel, plants provided many raw materials for the manufacture of tools, containers, clothing, shelter, watercraft, weapons, and fishing gear, including nets (Marquardt 1988: 169). Both cucurbita gourd (*Cucurbita pepo*) and bottle gourd (*Lagenaria siceraria*) may have been used for containers and net floats; the seeds of these small, wild gourds are nutritious and yield a high-quality vegetable oil as well.

SOCIAL ORGANIZATION. Calusa social organization, first brought to the attention of anthropologists by Goggin and Sturtevant (1964), was one of obvious complexity and hierarchy after contact with Europeans. But when did the Calusa achieve this level of complexity, and what was the nature of the transition? Advancing a cultural-evolutionary model, Widmer (1988: 263–265) suggested that the carrying capacity of the Charlotte Harbor–Pine Island Sound area was reached by about A.D. 800. Critical resources would have required management. For example, the inshore fishing grounds must have been corporately owned and managed by lineages. Sources of freshwater and raw materials for manufacturing fishing gear (e.g., palm and yucca fiber) would have also been at a premium and hence subject to control or management. Widmer hypothesized organization of the area by A.D. 800 according to a ramage system, wherein groups split off but maintained close kin ties and reciprocal relations with the parent group. Warfare would have been endemic by 800 because of competition for scarce resources and the difficulty of further fissioning due to the population's having reached the environmental carrying capacity (Widmer 1988: 266–269).

Widmer's model may be correct, but the burden of proof still rests with those who would argue for an evolutionary trajectory ending at A.D. 800. One would have to demonstrate that carrying capacity was reached or exceeded, perhaps by showing that overexploited species diminished in size or number or by showing from analysis of burial populations that nutrition or health deteriorated. Such has not been established. There is as yet no evidence for endemic warfare, nor has it been shown that freshwater or plant fiber resources were as limited as Widmer believed. Naturally flowing wells were plentiful in the area until modern well drilling lowered local water tables; sturdy fibers are easily gathered from several native plants that are abundant in the area even today (Brown 1994: 85–91).

The assessment of complexity is an old and vexing problem, and one that requires an especially critical commitment if we are to avoid projecting our own cultural biases onto the past. Are we to believe that southwest Florida Indians achieved complexity by A.D. 800 because they built mounds, causeways, and other earthworks? In fact, one could make a better case that Mound A on Horr's Island, dating to circa 2800 B.C., was a purposely constructed mound than one could make for most of the midden mounds of the Caloosahatchee I, II, III, and IV periods in Charlotte Harbor (see Russo 1994).

Widmer's argument for hierarchical political organization by A.D. 800 hinges on demonstrating platform mound and causeway construction, as exemplified by the Wightman site (Widmer 1988: 93–94). Supporting Widmer's "mound-building" hypothesis are dates obtained by Fradkin (1976) and Wilson (1982) from Wightman's so-called mound deposits. They are not in stratigraphic sequence, which could indicate episodes in which a mound was built higher by using older midden materials (Walker, Stapor, and Marquardt 1994: 172–174). Test excavations at the Wightman site show that a shell midden dating to about 250 B.C.–A.D. 400 is overlain by a layer of naturally deposited shell and sand probably associated with a higher-than-present sea-level stand (Walker, Stapor, and Marquardt 1995). A later midden began to accumulate on top of the naturally deposited zone at about A.D. 650–750 (Walker, Stapor, and Marquardt 1994: 173–177). Some mound building may be indicated at Wightman, but a great deal of accumulation seems to be simple midden accretion and

episodes of storm deposition. In any case, there are enough documented Archaic period earthworks in the Southeast (see Russo 1994) to cast doubt on a necessary association between mounds and complexity.

REGIONAL EXCHANGE.   That the Caloosahatchee area people were recipients of Belle Glade pottery—or at least the idea of Belle Glade pottery—by A.D. 500 is clear, though it is not known whether these ceramics were accompanied by migrations of people to the coast. Certainly the Belle Glade area itself (near Lake Okeechobee) was not abandoned. The well-known linear earthworks in the Belle Glade area were constructed during the Caloosahatchee II period (Carr 1985; Griffin 1988: 134; Hale 1984). Midden mounds accumulated rapidly in the years following A.D. 500 throughout Charlotte Harbor and Pine Island Sound.

Present, though infrequent, in Caloosahatchee II middens are sherds characteristic of Weeden Island, an archaeological culture associated mainly with northern Florida and dating from about A.D. 300 to 900. At one Charlotte Harbor site, Boggess Ridge (Luer and Archibald 1988), human burials were interred with whelk-shell vessels and intentionally broken and often carefully arranged and stacked potsherds. Most of these sherds are plainwares, and they include sand-tempered, chalky, and Belle Glade pastes, but Weeden Island pottery is also represented. In southwest Florida, Weeden Island pottery is found in Caloosahatchee II–III contexts (500–1350) (Cordell n.d.).

Cherts probably originating in the Tampa Bay area were made into bifaces, probably in their area of origin. Lithic manufacturing debitage is uncommon in the Caloosahatchee area, and even sharpening flakes are rare. A ground stone celt found at the Pineland site probably came from the piedmont of Georgia. At the same site, two lumps of galena, each less than 10 millimeters across, were found in midden deposits dating to late Caloosahatchee II–early Caloosahatchee III times. Analysis by R. M. Farquhar of the University of Toronto shows that the source of the galena was southeastern Missouri (Farquhar correspondence with K. J. Walker, 1993).

St. Johns Check Stamped pottery, which may have originated in northeastern Florida, appears in both the Everglades and Caloosahatchee areas by A.D. 1200. It may have appeared "in small quantities" in the Belle Glade area somewhat earlier (Griffin 1988: 126), and it is known at the Jupiter Inlet I site on the east coast by about 1000 (Kennedy et al. 1993: 175). Again, the interpretation of this new addition is unclear. Chalky plain wares had been present, and probably manufactured locally, for many centuries. No obvious changes in settlement or subsistence systems took place at around 1200, though by this time Safety Harbor pottery, generally associated with the central western Gulf coast, occurs in mortuary contexts, as I discuss later.

By about 1350–1400, Belle Glade Plain, the dominant plainware in the previous Caloosahatchee III period, had waned in importance in the Caloosahatchee area, though it still dominated in the Belle Glade area itself. Also about 1400, incised pottery ceased to be manufactured in the Everglades area, and the only decorations were the lip and rim treatments known as Glades Tooled. Some have interpreted the abrupt cessation of incising and the spread of tooled rims to represent the expansion of Calusa influence up and down the coast (Griffin 1988: 142). Certainly it can be said that in Caloosahatchee IV (Glades IIIb) times, the Everglades and Caloosahatchee areas were ceramically more homogeneous than ever before.

WARFARE. There is little evidence for warfare in pre-contact times, and no evidence for violent death, mass graves, trophy skulls, or defensive structures such as palisades. Again, such statements must be tempered with the observation that little extensive excavation has been done in south Florida. Not even one unambiguous house structure is known for the central Gulf coast, Caloosahatchee, Belle Glade, or Everglades area, so any generalizations about village layout or defensive structures would be premature.

MORTUARY BEHAVIOR. Information on most burial mounds and other mortuary sites is sketchy because they have been either looted or excavated with inadequate control. The first period for which a discernible pattern can be seen in south Florida is the Middle to Late Archaic. At Little Salt Spring (Clausen et al. 1979), Republic Groves (Wharton, Ballo, and Hope 1981), and Bay West (Beriault et al. 1981), Archaic cemeteries were located next to or in ponds or springs. Similar patterns are known from the east-central Florida wet sites Gauthier (Jones 1981; Maples 1987) and Windover (Doran and Dickel 1988). Young and old, male and female were buried together, though it is not certain whether the known cemetery sites represent entire populations; perhaps people of special status were buried elsewhere. Burial goods include baskets, clothing, and tools.

Mound A on Horr's Island, dating to about 2900 B.C. (Russo 1991: 387–443), apparently was purposely built up in layers of white sand, charcoal-stained sand, and oyster shell to a height of some 6 meters above the island's surface. Two flexed burials were found near the mound's periphery, one of which was dated to 2130–1790 B.C. (Beta-35344). The flexed burial of an adolescent was discovered in each of two late Middle Archaic shell middens on Useppa Island dating to about 2800–2400 B.C. (Hansinger 1992; Marquardt 1992b: 27–29, 1999; Marquardt and Wallace 1995).

At the Fort Center site near Lake Okeechobee, Sears (1982) excavated a mortuary pond with charnel house and a nearby flat-topped mound apparently used for preparation of the dead for interment. Within the artificial mortuary pond, a wooden platform had been constructed at roughly A.D. 200–600/800, incorporating carved bird and other animal effigies into the pilings. Some 300 bundle buri-

als were apparently placed on the platform, which eventually collapsed into the water, leading to extraordinary preservation of the bones and some of the wooden carvings (Sears 1982: 145–169, 186–189).

Just under the present-day ground surface near the Collier Inn on Useppa Island, a number of burials were discovered dating to the Caloosahatchee II period. Only two complete individuals were removed, but more remain unexcavated. The burials, both young adults, had been haphazardly placed in quasi-flexed postures in an earlier midden of the Caloosahatchee I period (Hansinger 1992; Marquardt 1992b: 26–29). Fragments of several Sand-tempered Plain and Belle Glade Plain ceramic vessels had been placed on top of the burials, being especially concentrated near the crania. Bones in direct association with the pottery dated to A.D. 610–670. An apparently isolated, semi-flexed burial of an adult male, without artifacts, dating to 640–770 was also found on Useppa Island, intruding deeply into a late Middle Archaic midden (Hutchinson 1999).

In the central Gulf coast and Caloosahatchee areas, a preference for burial in sand mounds or in easily excavated natural sand hills characterized the Caloosahatchee II period (ca. A.D. 500–1200). At the Palmer site, near Sarasota, Bullen and Bullen (1976) excavated more than 400 burials from a sand mound dating to about 850–1100. Three-quarters of the burials were flexed, with others being bundles or isolated skulls. No ceramic vessels were buried with the human remains. Collins (1929: 151–153) excavated a small burial mound on Captiva Island, again finding flexed and bundled burials. As at Useppa, sherds were placed around the skulls; a layer of marine gastropods was found encircling the mound at its base.

The Weeden Island–related interments accompanied by stacked sherds at the Boggess Ridge site (Luer and Archibald 1988), a natural sand ridge near Cape Haze, were mentioned earlier. The Buck Key Burial Mound, although severely disturbed, yielded one flexed and four associated, articulated, fragmentary burials placed in a sandy matrix without grave accompaniments about A.D. 1000–1160. At least three of the four fragmentary burials appear to have been placed surrounding the flexed individual, an adult female. The central individual and three of the four surrounding burials—a child four to six years old, an adult male, and an adult female—were excavated (Hutchinson 1992; Marquardt 1992b: 41–44). At the Smith Mound, part of the Pineland site complex, limited investigation indicates scattered inclusion of potsherds with burials, though there is no evidence of stacking. Not only common wares such as Sand-tempered Plain, Belle Glade Plain, and St. Johns Plain but also decorated pottery such as Weeden Island Punctated, Weeden Island Red, Papys Bayou Punctated, Little Manatee Zoned Stamped, St. Johns Check Stamped, and various Safety Harbor–related types are found. Sixteenth-century Spanish materials are known from disturbed contexts in the upper levels. The time range of the Smith Mound is probably Caloosahatchee IIB to Caloosahatchee V (Cordell n.d.).

In sum, the Caloosahatchee II mortuary pattern can be described as interment in sand mounds, natural sand ridges, or abandoned shell middens, with both flexed primary and fragmentary and bundled secondary burials. Except at the Weeden Island–related Boggess Ridge site, there were no whole ceramic accompaniments, but stacks or layers of pottery sherds were sometimes placed near the skulls.

Sand burial mounds continued into the Caloosahatchee III period, with Safety Harbor pottery accompanying some of the burials. For DeSoto County, Willey (1949: 346) reported Safety Harbor bottle and collared jar vessels from the Arcadia site. The Keen Mound was characterized by an initial layer of yellow sand, partially covered by a white/gray sand layer, and that layer was covered by a white sand cap. Englewood and Safety Harbor pottery vessels were reported (Willis and Johnson 1980), as were glass beads, showing a Caloosahatchee V component. The Galt Island Burial Mound was characterized by prone burials interred in layers of alternating white, reddish brown, and black sand. In addition, bundle burials, or possibly cremations, were interred in small intrusive pits. Dates of A.D. 1160–1260 and 1020–1220, as well as European artifacts, suggest a time range of Caloosahatchee III to V.

Some sand burial sites in Sarasota County contained Weeden Island, Englewood, and Safety Harbor pottery. For example, the Englewood sand mound contained burials in a submound pit covered with red ocher, with additional burials in subsequent layers of variously colored sand (Willey 1949: 128). Artifacts included sherds, perforated vessels, and perforated whelk-shell drinking cups; Weeden Island, Englewood, and Safety Harbor pottery was present. The stratified Laurel Mound (Luer and Almy 1987) also contained red ocher over a submound feature and Safety Harbor pottery. Seven extended burials were arranged in a circle, their skulls meeting in the center, legs projecting outward. This pattern has been noted at least five other times in south Florida (Luer and Almy 1987: 306–311), all instances dating to the late precontact period and possibly to the postcontact period.

In southwest Florida, sites such as the Aqui Está Mound in Charlotte County (Mitchem 1989: 252–253), a burial mound on Pine Island excavated by Moore (1900), a badly disturbed sand mound on the island of Cayo Pelau (Mitchem 1989: 232–236), a mound near Punta Rassa (Moore 1905), and the Blue Hill Mound on Horr's Island (Moore 1905) fit the pattern of isolated sand mounds with Englewood and/or Safety Harbor pottery. Burial mounds at Pineland, Galt Island, and Mound Key were sand mounds located in wet areas, and all have Caloosahatchee III, IV, and V components, including European goods of the sixteenth century.

Special mortuary ware was sometimes buried with individuals in late pre-Columbian times, especially after A.D. 1000 in southwest Florida. Judging from the presence of perforated ("killed") pottery and whelk drinking vessels, consumption of the ritual emetic known as "black drink" is probable (Luer and Almy 1987: 317). Many mounds continued in use into the postcontact period.

The Postcontact Period

SETTLEMENT AND ARCHITECTURE. For southwest Florida, the "postcontact" period effectively began by 1500. Every Florida schoolchild is taught that Juan Ponce de León "discovered" Florida in 1513, but Ponce was met by hostile natives, some of whom knew Spanish and possessed gold (Weddle 1985: 45). This suggests that native south Floridians were aware of the Spaniards long before the arrival of Ponce de León, in part because they had salvaged Spanish wrecks in the Florida Keys. Moreover, freelance European merchants and slavers had undoubtedly visited the peninsula prior to 1513 (Marquardt 1988: 178).

The Calusa and their neighbors principally inhabited the coastal zone, though modern road building, land leveling for agricultural purposes, and housing development have probably masked many inland sites from our view. Spanish missionaries and explorers found people in south Florida mainly on the coast, though there were interior villages, probably of smaller size, the residents of which were said to pay tribute to the coastal Calusa.

Calusa houses were said to be on little hills, which might indicate that huts were situated on top of midden mounds or ridges (Hann 1991: 287–288). The missionaries who visited the Calusa in 1697 remarked that they were allowed to sleep in thatched huts. There were 16 "houses" in the king's village, probably large communal structures, each accommodating several dozen people (Hann 1991: 41–42).

In 1566 it was noted that the Calusa king's "house" was large enough for 2,000 people to stand in it "without being very crowded" (Solís de Merás 1964: 145). This may have been a community lodge rather than the domicile of the king himself. To accomodate 2,000 people requires an area of approximately 625 square meters. This translates into a circular building 28 meters in diameter or a square structure 25 meters on a side. For comparison, the circular council house of the postcontact Apalachee (in present-day Tallahassee, north-central Florida) measured 36 meters in diameter (Hann 1988: 113), encompassing about 1,018 square meters of interior area.

Some Calusa rituals were performed in a special building, replete with masks covering the walls; benches and an altar or central mound are also mentioned (Hann 1991: 159–160, 195–196). In 1697 the temple in the king's village was said to be a "very tall and wide house with its door and . . . in the middle a hillock or very high flat-topped mound, and on top of it a sort of room made of mats with seats all closed" (Hann 1991: 159).

In Dickinson's (1985: 11, 32) 1696 account of southeast coastal Florida, the Indians lived in circular huts with poles tied together at the top, covered with thatch. The houses stood on hills of oyster shells. Dickinson (1985: 23) noted that one village chief's house was 40 by 25 feet, "covered with palmetto leaves both top and sides." This would be 1,000 square feet, or 93 square meters, room for perhaps 300 persons to stand in, if one estimates that 20 percent of the interior area was taken up by furniture, containers, hearths, and so forth.

SUBSISTENCE. The postcontact period Indians of southwest Florida continued to subsist mainly on products of the sea, although they were said to be fond of Spanish food and drink (Hann 1991: 161–210, 425–426; Solís de Merás 1964: 148). On more than one occasion they resisted tilling the soil, telling the Spaniards they did not need the tools offered them or implying that digging in the dirt was beneath their dignity (Hann 1991: 184–185, 329–330, 428). We must remember that the Spaniards almost always conversed with men, either because native women avoided the Spaniards or because of the Spanish expectation that men were the makers of decisions. If gardening was women's work, then the Calusa men may have responded correctly—that horticulture was not for them—but this need not mean that there was no plant husbandry at all. What information we have for protohistoric sites, however, includes no evidence for farming.

SOCIAL ORGANIZATION. The aforementioned dearth of data on house structures prohibits our making inferences of social inequality on the basis of house size, preferred foods, or special artifacts. European observers noted that the Calusa were divided into two estates. The Spaniards explicitly referred to nobles and commoners and at other times to "leading men." Whether the Spaniards witnessed an actual class or estate system or simply misperceived a dominant clan or lineage from which leaders and priests were chosen is impossible to tell from the records. Apparently the privileged group was not expected to work, nor were warriors at the command of the king.

The king, a head priest, and a war captain were the three primary leaders, and a significant part of the king's authority rested on his ability to mediate between the secular and sacred realms (Hann 1991: 246–247; Lawson 1992: 90). The king sat on a special stool and was greeted with deference. Processions of masked priests, accompanied by singing women, were mentioned, and masks were said to cover the inner walls of the "temple" (Hann 1991: 44, 159–160, 195–196, 287–288). Whether the masks were meant to represent clans, animal spirits, mythical or real ancestors, or some combination of these may never be known.

The only documentary references to kinship pertain to the royal family. The king was expected to marry his own sister (possibly a classificatory sister rather than a blood sibling), and his son was expected to succeed him in office. Women were not inconsequential in such issues; we know that King Senquene's widow's permission was required for the divorce of her adopted son, Felipe (Hann 1991: 269; Marquardt 1988: 182). It is entirely possible that the Calusa reckoned descent matrilineally even though males were commonly the leaders. One documentary reference to a queen (cacica) among the Calusa is contained in an abstract discussion of what happened when a member of the royal family died:

Those [Indians] of Carlos firstly have as custom [that] each time a child of the cacique dies, each resident sacrifices his sons or daughters who go in company of the death of the child of the cacique./ The second sacrifice is that when the cacique himself dies, or the cacica, they kill his or her own servants, and this is the second sacrifice./ The third sacrifice is that they kill each year a Christian captive in order to feed their idol which they adore, and which they say eats the eyes of the human male and eats the head. They dance each year, which they have for custom./ And the fourth sacrifice is that after the summer come some sorcerers in the shape of the devil with some horns on their heads, and they come howling like wolves and many other different idols which yell like animals of the woods, and these idols stay four months, in which they never rest night or day, running so much with great fury. What a thing to relate the great bestiality that they do!—Escalante Fontaneda, 1569 (Worth 1995: 344; emphasis added by WHM)

The role of women is an intriguing and important issue pertaining to the question of whether the Calusa social formation was hierarchical, tributary, and male dominated before European contact. Throughout the southeastern United States, native societies were predominantly matrilineal and matrilocal, and most are still so today. Generally speaking, women own the household, the means of production, and other aspects of the secular world, accomplish farming or gardening and gathering tasks, and process, cook, and distribute food. Men hunt, wage war, communicate with the sacred realm, and often (but not always) handle trade and diplomatic activities. The documented Calusa practices of polygyny and royal sibling marriage among the ruling lineage are unusual for a southeastern U.S. society, especially for a fisher-gatherer-hunter society (Goggin and Sturtevant 1964: 189–190).

Let us suppose that the Calusa social formation was at one time typical of the broad southeastern U.S. pattern, and that at some point the roles of men in warfare, diplomacy, trade, and religion became more prominent while those of women as owners of property and houses and providers of food became less important. What events and processes might lead a culture in this direction?

First, if there is an increased need for organized defense against a formidable military threat, then men's roles come to the fore. In some circumstances, such as the transition in ancient Mesopotamia from temporary war chiefs to petty kings in response to threats from neighboring cities (see Frankfort 1956: 78–79), periodic wartime leaders can become institutionalized dictators. In the southeastern United States, among Muskogee-speaking Indians, *henihas* (advisors) and *tustunnuggee* (war leaders) could exercise unusual power to meet the exigencies of war. War captains were specifically documented among later Creek Indians (*tustunnuggee tlucco,* "great warrior"), as well as among the Tocobaga in the Tampa Bay area and the Ais of the Florida east coast (Hann 1991: 227). Second, if there is a perceived need for increased intercession with the spirit world, either to ensure success in war or to propitiate spirits of ancestors, then men's roles can become more central. Third, if the flow of essential goods is interrupted due to a breakdown in relations of reciprocity and redistribution, or if there is a failure of alliances that had guaranteed the services of warriors in time of need, then men's roles in diplomacy and exchange might become more prominent.

Now consider that by the early sixteenth century, Spaniards had swept into the Caribbean and Florida in amazing sailing vessels, bringing with them metal tools and deadly blades, muskets and cannons, never-before-seen animals, exotic foods, inebriating drink, colorful cloth, glass beads and metal trinkets, and an aggressive, proselytizing religion that offered an alternative worldview (Marquardt 1988: 176–179; Weddle 1985: 13–50). There was an immediate need for organized defense in response to this new and strange threat, a need that quickly became a perpetual state of emergency and vigilance.

Skirmishes with the Spaniards soon proved them to be formidable enemies, and this might have led to increased interest in seeking the assistance of the Calusa god of war. And as Spanish priests came among the Calusa—Jesuits in the sixteenth century, Franciscans in the seventeenth—their competing ideologies might have elevated the need for consultation with the Calusa spirit world, including the ancestors. Finally, as European-introduced diseases took their toll and relations of production and authority became strained, there might have been further impetus to search for answers in the sacred realm, by performing more rituals and feeding the spirits of the dead ancestors. The commentaries on the Calusa belief system by the Jesuits Juan Rogel and Joseph Javier Alaña are relevant here:

The oneness of God and his being the creator of every good, they admit to. They also believe those who govern the world to be three persons, but in such a manner that they say that the first one, who is greater than the other two, is the one to whom the universal government of the most universal and common things belongs, such as the heavenly movements and seasons, etc. And

that the second one is greater than the third, that to him belongs the government of the kingdoms, empires, and republics. The third one . . . is the least of all and the one who helps in the wars. And to the side to which he attaches himself, they say that that one gains victory.—Juan Rogel, 1568 (Hann 1991: 239)

They have a great fear of the dead and its effect appears [in] their not suffering their being named; their daily offering to them of foodstuffs, tobacco [and] plants[?]; the covering of the graves with reed mats and the bestowing of gifts on the graves. They maintain a guard in the cemetery, which they frequent with pilgrimages, and they keep it somewhat distant from the village, fearing the dead should do them harm.—Joseph Javier Alaña, 1743 (Hann 1991: 423–424)

One can readily cite examples of tribal societies that did not transform into petty kingdoms as a result of serious military threats, so we know that men's roles need not become dominant in all such cases. And it must be stated that the Spaniards who wrote of the Calusa may have dealt almost exclusively with men, so the accounts may exaggerate men's roles and diminish the importance of women's. But more than a few independent historical sources from the 1500s through the 1700s describe royal polygyny, royal sibling marriage, sacrifice of retainers, a nobility, lordship over dozens of towns, tribute taking, and a standing military force under the command of the king. We must conclude that during the sixteenth through eighteenth centuries, the Calusa social formation was a male-dominated kingdom, perhaps a weak, tribute-based state (see Gailey and Patterson 1988: 79). Whether the Calusa were a weak state or a complex chiefdom/kingdom is a less important question than that of how their sociopolitical organization became so centralized, hierarchical, and tributary, even as it was plagued by endemic factionalism (Marquardt 1987a: 104–110).

I have hypothesized (Marquardt 1987a: 103–110, 1988: 187, 1991: xvi–xvii) that in the sixteenth century, European goods (food, drink, and clothing, as well as items of metal and glass) acquired high value and came into exchange and trade networks that were outside the bounds of the normal redistributive network. Such goods found their way to one or more of the competing paramount chiefs, such as Tocobaga, Tequesta, and Serrope in south Florida. Faced with challenges to his authority to collect and redistribute the new exotic goods—from both upstart town chiefs and his old rivals—the Calusa chief responded by imposing sanctions and enforcing his will by military force. To support this new power structure, he ensured the loyalty of other chiefs by intermarriage, thus extending his family to a broader scale (see Brumfiel 1989: 128–132 for an example from the pre-Aztec Valley of Mexico in which political competition within and between towns led to military alliances through intermarriage). Ultimately, the Calusa kingdom proved short-lived, unable to withstand a suite of challenges that included interpolity competition, intrapolity factionalism, social disruption due to the depredations of disease, and the military superiority of first the Spaniards and then armed Indian invaders from present-day Georgia and South Carolina.

REGIONAL EXCHANGE. Regional exchange took the form of "tribute," according to Spanish accounts, but the Spaniards were unimpressed with the items actually brought to the king—foods, mats, hides, and feathers (Hann 1991: 237). Captives also were delivered to the king, and sometimes these people were sacrificed; others were made to work. That not all captives were killed is obvious from reports that in 1566 some Spanish women elected to stay with their children rather than be rescued by other Spaniards (Solís de Merás 1964: 151). These women and their children may have been the same ones referred to by the Spaniards interviewed in 1564 by Laudonnière:

I questioned them about the places they had been and how they came. They answered that fifteen years ago three ships, including one they had been on, were wrecked across from a place named Calos, in the shallows called The Martyrs, and that the King of Calos had recovered most of the treasure in the ships and saved most of the people, including several women. Among them were three or four young married gentlewomen who with their children were still staying with this King of Calos.—René de Laudonnière, 1564 (Lawson 1992: 88–89)

What the Spaniards called tribute may have been nothing more than symbolic gifts proffered in consideration of the prestige and spiritual authority of the king. It is known that the king sometimes personally supervised the salvage of Spanish shipwrecks, and he sometimes redistributed booty to town chiefs loyal to him (Fontaneda 1944: 34–35).

Exchange requires travel. South Florida natives had several different kinds of watercraft, including seagoing vessels, small cargo canoes, and barges made of platforms connecting two canoes. There is also empirical evidence of artificially constructed canals that connected major coastal towns, such as Pineland, with interior Florida by way of the Caloosahatchee River and that connected interior settlements to one another (Luer 1989; Luer and Wheeler 1997). The paths of these canals are visible on aerial photographs of the area taken prior to modern development, and they were described in detail by explorers of the late nineteenth century (e.g., Anonymous 1875; Douglass 1885; Kenworthy 1875, 1883). In 1896, when Cushing visited the Pineland site, then known as Battey's Landing, the canal still measured 9 meters wide and 2 meters deep (Cushing 1897: 342).

Most who have studied the canals believe them to be pre-Columbian, but dating them is difficult. They might have been dug during a time when sea level was higher than today, perhaps about A.D. 150–450 or 850–1400 (Walker, Stapor, and Marquardt 1995: 215), then made wider and deeper as the water level fell. Luer speculated that the Pineland canal might have been built around 1000, because this was the time when Belle Glade Plain pottery became predominant in southwest Florida, perhaps indicating well-developed trade between coast and interior (Luer 1989: 124, personal communication 1991; see Luer and Wheeler 1997 for further discussion).

WARFARE. Warfare certainly existed in postcontact times. Not only did the king have a subsidized corps of warriors, but he could command that his people produce bows and arrows and other weapons of war and could call warriors from subject towns into his service (Hann 1991: 254, 266). Warfare was likely waged to gain prestige, seek revenge, humiliate an enemy, bolster population, or maintain boundaries, rather than to annihilate one's neighbors. (Bradley [1987a: 81–82, 109] made a similar argument for the historic Onondaga Iroquois.) It was said that Carlos was "at war with" Tocobaga of Tampa Bay when Pedro Menéndez de Avilés arrived in 1566. Hostage taking is known from the account of Tocobaga's holding of 12 of Carlos's kinspeople (Solís de Merás 1964: 225).

In postcontact times the bow and arrow was a principal weapon, but clubs and throwing sticks were also used. Cushing (1897: 372–373, 422–423) interpreted a carved wooden implement inset with shark's teeth found at Key Marco as a saber-club, though we cannot be certain that this was its intended use. That the Calusa were able to muster numerous warriors on occasion is certain; warriors in 80 canoes are said to have shot arrows at Ponce de León's ship in 1513 (Weddle 1985: 45).

The political system of the natives was in upheaval in the 1560s. The authority and legitimacy of the Calusa king himself had been called into question more than once, and the ambitious Tocobaga had claimed some Calusa towns (Marquardt 1987a: 106, 1988: 184). The Calusa king Carlos and his successor, Felipe, allied themselves with the Spaniards in the hope of enlisting their aid against Tocobaga.

I doubt that warfare of this sort was common before Spanish contact in the 1500s. Centrifugal tendencies in the 1500s were probably the result of the presence of Spanish goods and competing religious ideas. So long as the king's authority was beyond question, Spanish goods came to the king to be redistributed at his will. But as Spanish artifacts came increasingly easily into the hands of peripheral chiefs, the latter might have begun to question their need for allegiance to a king in southwest Florida who could not offer them the metal, cloth, and wine that they could obtain for themselves by salvage, trade, or thievery (Marquardt 1988: 187, 1991: xvi–xvii).

The gold, silver, and copper-alloy medallions sometimes found in postcontact period sites may bear on the issue of political hierarchy. The carvings vary, but the overall shapes of the medallions are quite similar (Allerton, Luer, and Carr 1984). Some have interpreted the designs as symbolizing spiders or jaguars. They may also represent stylized faces of masks. Whatever the carvings on these metal objects mean, they had precedents in carved wooden and stone forms. The spatial distribution of the metal versions is consistent with the known Calusa domain (McGoun 1993: 36). If the Calusa king controlled the salvage of Spanish metals, it may be that he presented the medallions to town chiefs in order to reinforce bonds of sacred trust and relations of patronage and clientage. Luer (1994: 181–184) believes that most, if not all, of the medallions date to the 1600s and 1700s, but there is an explicit statement from the 1560s that a gold ornament worn on the forehead, along with leg beads, constituted the royal insignia of the king's successor (Hann 1991: 268). One can speculate that similar ornaments were given to town chiefs to symbolize and legitimate their sacred connection to the king and the spirit world.

MORTUARY BEHAVIOR AND BELIEFS. In postcontact times, people continued to be buried individually in sand mounds, sometimes with European goods. These mounds are the contexts most likely to have been disturbed over the past century by explorers and looters, and so the contextual evidence that might help bridge the gap between precontact Safety Harbor–related patterns and those of the postcontact period is lacking.

Among the sixteenth-century Tocobaga, when a principal chief died, his body was dismembered and boiled until the flesh separated from the bones. In a temple the bones were joined together, and following this ritual the people fasted for four days. Finally, "all the Indian town," "making much reverence," joined in a procession honoring the bones (Worth 1995: 344).

Sixteenth-century records say that when a Tequesta chief died, his larger bones were separated out and kept in a box in the chief's house, to be venerated by the whole village, whereas the smaller bones and flesh were buried. In the same box were placed bones obtained from the heads of whales captured communally in the winter (Worth 1995: 344–345).

The Calusa greatly feared the dead (Hann 1991: 329, 423–424). Further, they believed that a person's soul could become separated from the living body. When this happened, a shaman was summoned to locate and reinstall it. A fire was built outside the hut to discourage the soul from venturing out again (Hann 1991: 238). Another recorded belief is that each person had three souls: one in his shadow, another in his reflection, and a third in the pupil of the eye. The last of the three lived on after death. Offerings to the departed were placed on mats at grave sites (Hann 1991: 237–238, 423).

From Archaeological Remains to Known Ethnic Groups

It is not known when the Calusa social formation that we know from Spanish accounts began to exist as such. I feel confident in attributing Calusa ethnicity to occupants of the Caloosahatchee culture area by A.D. 500, the beginning of the Caloosahatchee II period. As discussed earlier, Widmer (1988: 261–276) believes that a full-fledged Calusa chiefdom existed by A.D. 800.

Only a few dozen words of the Calusa Indian language were recorded, mostly place names. Spanish translations exist for only one dozen words. Granberry (1995) concluded that the Calusa language most closely resembled Gulf coast languages; specifically, sixteenth-century Calusa forms were most similar to those of the twentieth-century Tunica of southwestern Mississippi. Taking as a starting point Widmer's model of Calusa society being in its mature form by circa A.D. 700–800, Granberry speculated that the sixteenth-century Calusa "may have been the descendants of the last Tunica-stock migrants to settle Florida," having migrated into south Florida by 500–800 (Granberry 1995: 170).

Granberry's hypothesis aside, we can infer that the Belle Glade pottery tradition that originated in the Lake Okeechobee area around A.D. 200 exerted increasing influence in southwest Florida by A.D. 500. It reached the Charlotte Harbor area by that date and increased significantly until the beginning of the Caloosahatchee IV period, when Sand-tempered Plain pottery increased in importance at the expense of Belle Glade Plain (Cordell 1992). The Caloosahatchee IV period was also the first time a single decorated pottery tradition characterized both the Caloosahatchee and the Ten Thousand Islands areas (Griffin 1988: 135–142). The latter is associated with the Everglades area, the vicinity of Key Marco. This phenomenon might represent a spread of Calusa influence or even the first crystallization of a Calusa complex chiefdom–kingdom at about 1400.

I assume, but cannot prove, that the Indians of south Florida heard about Columbus's first landfall in the late fifteenth century and that they had firsthand knowledge of Spanish merchants or slavers, possibly by 1500 and certainly by 1510. The native population of Cuba was devastated between 1510 and 1514 (Sauer 1966: 181–189). Some native Cuban refugees resettled in southwest Florida under Calusa control (Fontaneda 1944: 29), probably before Ponce de León's first visit in 1513. The site of this settlement has never been conclusively identified. Ponce de León's visits to Calusa territory in 1513 and 1521 were uniformly hostile encounters (Weddle 1985: 38–54).

Certainly the Calusa would have learned of the expeditions of Narváez in 1528 and de Soto in 1539 (see Milanich 1995: 115–136). Some Dominican missionaries blundered into Charlotte Harbor in 1549, where they encountered hostile natives who knew Spanish and recognized the crucifix (Weddle 1985: 242). Shipwrecks in the 1540s and 1550s brought Spanish captives into Calusa hands, including the boy Escalante Fontaneda, who would live among the Calusa for 17 years and play a pivotal role in the encounters between Spanish governor Menéndez and Calusa king Carlos in 1566 and 1567 (Lyon 1983: 148, 177; Solís de Merás 1964: 139–152).

In March 1567, Spanish Jesuits established a mission at the Calusa capital town of Calos and attempted to convert the Calusa to Christianity. They failed, and abandoned the mission in 1569. During their encounter with the Calusa, the Spaniards killed a number of people, including two Calusa kings—Carlos and his successor, Felipe—but the Spanish presence in 1566–1569 did not spell the end of the Calusa social formation.

During the time of first intensive European-Calusa contact in 1566–1569, the Calusa king's domain included at least 50 towns, some of which Fontaneda (1944: 30–31) enumerated by name. But in October 1612, Governor Fernández de Olivera reported to the king of Spain that a King Carlos had "more than 60 villages of his own not to mention the other very great quantity that pay tribute to him" (Hann 1991: 11). The governor based his report on a recent diplomatic expedition to Carlos (Hann 1991: 9–11), which had apparently had salutary results.

To my knowledge, no one commented further on Calusa politics until 1680. Nor was any resolution of the documented sixteenth-century hostilities between the Calusa and the Tocobaga chronicled. At some point during the 1600s, however, the Tocobaga moved north to settle on the Wacissa River under the dominion of the Apalachee (Hann 1991: 23, 332, 347).

An abortive voyage commissioned by Governor Pablo de Hita Salazar in 1680 to ransom Spanish captives held by the Calusa is instructive of late seventeenth-century Calusa control in southwest Florida, which can be gauged by the reactions the party experienced as it moved southward along the Gulf coast. Led by Juan Bautista de la Cruz, a small crew of soldiers and Indian guides made its way down the coast, passing through the villages of Alcola, Pojoi, Elafay, Apojola Negra, and Tiquijagua. At each successive village the local natives begged the expedition to turn back for fear that the Calusa king would have them executed if he learned that they had allowed the expedition to pass beyond them. Finally, at Tiquijagua the Indian guides fled and the expedition was aborted (Hann 1991: 23–30). From this one can infer that as late as 1680 the Calusa were protected by buffer zones of client communities who were bound under penalty of death to turn back strangers approaching Charlotte Harbor. It also suggests that the Calusa were purposefully isolating themselves from the prolonged hostilities between the Spanish and English that were bringing chaos to the northern Florida missions and independent native settlements in northwestern Florida (see Hann 1996).

Unlike many north Florida Indians, who were devastated by diseases and forced to live in missions throughout the seventeenth century, the Calusa managed to remain in their precontact territories for nearly 200 years after European contact, with a population estimated at 2,000 people in the late 1690s (Hann 1991: 165, 168). The Calusa still inhabited their coastal towns as late as 1697, when Franciscan missionaries from Cuba attempted unsuccessfully to establish the mission of San Diego de Compostela in southwest Florida (Hann 1991: 157–161). The Franciscans were repulsed when they insisted that the Calusa give up their rituals, which were said to have taken place in a temple structure with masks on the walls. The Indians would discuss becoming Christians only when given Spanish goods, and lots of them. Apparently the novelty of Europeans and their manufactures had worn off since the sixteenth century. The Franciscan friar Feliciano López noted that the Calusa king spoke to him in both the Timucuan and Apalachee languages (Hann 1991: 160), suggesting that the Calusa knew north Florida Indians, perhaps refugees from Spanish missions in north Florida. Leon-Jefferson pottery, associated with the mission period in north Florida, has been found at sites in northern Charlotte Harbor (Bullen and Bullen 1956: 50–51). It is known that the Calusa king's son journeyed to north Florida in 1688 and that the king himself visited Cuba in 1692, reportedly to request that missionaries be sent to his realm (Hann 1991: 121–140).

By 1704 the British had effectively breached the line of Spanish missions and garrisons that had once stretched across northern Florida (Arnade 1996). Lands abandoned due to depopulation and forced missionization lay open to other Native American groups displaced from their own territories, and these groups began to move into the Florida peninsula. By processes that are not well understood, the Calusa and neighboring groups became displaced from their traditional lands in the first few years of the eighteenth century. Lower Creek–related Indians known as Uchise, loosely allied with the British, and Yamassee Indians bent on enslaving south Florida Indians for sale in the Carolina colony, overran south Florida (Hann 1991: 325–333). These Indians had been themselves displaced by the slave raiding, colonization, and military activities of the English and Spanish (Hann 1996).

European-introduced diseases, militarism, slavery, and displacement eventually took their toll on the Calusa. By 1711, remnants of Calusa and other groups were living in the Florida Keys under continuing pressure from Uchise and Yamassee people. Feeling some responsibility to offer refuge to Indian people who had professed an interest in Christianity, Spaniards living in Cuba tried belatedly to rescue some of the beleaguered Indians (Hann 1991: 334–335, 380–382), but most of those transported died en route of infectious diseases. A few remnant Indian groups living in the Florida Keys were later contacted by Jesuits in 1743 (Hann 1991: 399–431; Parks 1985: 56–65), and some south Florida Indians may have returned to Florida in the 1770s (William Bartram, quoted in Sturtevant 1953: 38).

Although the Calusa successfully resisted conquest for over 200 years, ultimately they fell victim to political struggles that derived from European colonialism (Marquardt 1987a). By the 1750s their culture had been essentially erased. An account published in 1775 says that the last remnants of the south Florida native coastal Indians departed for Cuba in 1763 (Parks 1985: 69). It is possible that some of the so-called Spanish Indians who inhabited the southwest Florida coastal area in the late eighteenth and early nineteenth centuries and worked for the Cuban mullet fishermen were related to the Calusa and other south Florida natives, though most scholars believe it is more likely that the "Spanish Indians" were descended from Creeks and other northern groups (Covington 1959; Hammond 1973).

The Seminole and Miccosukee people who live in south Florida today are not directly descended from the indigenous Calusa. They descend from Creek-related groups from north of present-day Florida who began to live in northern Florida as early as the early eighteenth century and especially following 1814, in the aftermath of the Creek War (Weisman 1989: 37–81). The First Seminole War began in 1817, while Florida was still nominally under Spanish control but was coveted by the United States (Mahon 1998). When Spain ceded Florida to the United States in 1819, the Seminoles withdrew eastward and southward, deeper into the peninsula. In 1823 the Treaty of Moultrie Creek gave them perpetual rights to a reservation that extended from Fort King near Ocala south to Lake Okeechobee. But in the 1830s the United States sought to force removal of the Florida Indians to west of the Mississippi River. Resistance to removal led to conflict and the 1835–1842 Second Seminole War (Mahon 1985). Many Native Americans were ultimately removed to the West, but several hundred retreated into the Everglades and Big Cypress Swamp. In 1855 a band of surveyors in Big Cypress Swamp destroyed agricultural fields belonging to Chief Billy Bowlegs, starting the Third Seminole War. Despite a massive effort by the U.S. Army, the Seminoles were never conquered. Some Seminoles agreed to move west, but many more remained in Florida, where their descendants continue to live (Seminole Tribe of Florida 1998).

Conclusion

The postcontact Calusa social formation was hierarchical and tributary, and it functioned intermittently as a weak tribute-based state between 1500 and 1700. I agree with Gailey and Patterson (1988) that state formation is best understood as a process rather than as an inexorable climb up a ladder toward complexity. State formation is an ebb and flow of accommodation, imitation, and encapsulation. It is a *dynamic* process of regional definition and redefinition that may have operated in postcontact Florida just as rapidly as the regional dynamics we observe today (e.g., central and eastern Europe in the 1990s).

The Calusa were a chiefdom, possibly as early as A.D. 800, but their degree of organizational complexity before contact is still an open question. I believe that the intensely hierarchical, tributary, and androcentric political organization described by the Spaniards was a direct response to the Spanish invasion. Southwest Florida's precontact and postcontact periods show far more continuities than discontinuities in basic fisher-gatherer-hunter subsistence, settlement, and ideology (Hann 1991; Marquardt, ed. 1992). The Calusa accomplished much, but I am not convinced that their social formation was intensely hierarchical and tributary before the arrival of the Spaniards.

Acknowledgments

I appreciate Wes Cowan's invitation to summarize the archaeology of southwest Florida in this book and David Brose and Robert Mainfort's efforts in bringing the volume to press. I am grateful for critical comments on an earlier draft by Claudine Payne, Ruth Trocolli, and Karen Walker.

Locations of Primary Collections

The major south Florida collections under professional curation and available for study are located at (1) the Bureau of Archaeological Research, Division of Historical Resources, Department of State, Tallahassee, Florida; (2) the National Park Service's Southeastern Archeological Center, Tallahassee, Florida; (3) the Florida Museum of Natural History, Gainesville, Florida; and (4) the Historical Museum of Southern Florida, Miami, Florida. South Florida collections excavated in the late nineteenth century, including materials from Key Marco and Mound Key, are located primarily at the University of Pennsylvania Museum, Philadelphia, Pennsylvania; the National Museum of Natural History, Smithsonian Institution, Washington, D.C.; and the Florida Museum of Natural History, Gainesville, Florida.

13

The Late Prehistoric and Protohistoric Periods in the Central Mississippi Valley

Although stripped of its mantle as the "heartland" of the Mississippian cultural tradition (B. Smith 1984), the central Mississippi Valley remains essential to any attempt to understand the societies and dynamics of the late prehistoric and protohistoric periods in eastern North America. The richness of the late period archaeological record of this region was recognized in the 1800s (e.g., Holmes 1886; Thomas 1894), but it was the landmark survey of Phillips, Ford, and Griffin (1951) that surely drove the point home.

Following Morse and Morse (1983), I use the term central Mississippi Valley to refer to that portion of the Mississippi River meander belt and immediately adjacent areas between the mouth of the Ohio River to the north and the St. Francis River near the terminus of Crowley's Ridge to the south (Fig. 13.1). The area so encompassed is slightly more restricted than that discussed by the Morses, and this region is perhaps more properly referred to as the northern portion of the lower Mississippi alluvial valley (cf. Phillips, Ford, and Griffin 1951).

Within the study area, the east and west sides of the Mississippi River presented significantly different adaptive opportunities and challenges to aboriginal populations. To the west are the broad (often greater than 60 kilometers wide) Eastern and Western Lowlands of Arkansas and the Cairo Lowland of southeastern Missouri, much of which lie within the modern Mississippi River meander belt. Major drainage is provided by the St. Francis River and its larger tributaries, which roughly parallel the Mississippi. In Kentucky and Tennessee, however, the floodplain is generally quite narrow and is flanked on the east by an extensive system of loess bluffs that provided the setting for several important Mississippian towns.

The alluvial soils of the central Mississippi Valley, highly valued today for their agricultural productivity, were prized by prehistoric farmers as well. Virtually all of the study area enjoys a growing season of at least 200 days, with relatively mild winters and hot summers. Heavy rainfall, especially in the spring, often floods the bottomlands and produces severe soil erosion. Within the last century most lowland areas have been cleared, drained, and put into agricultural production. Today it is difficult to envision the vast stands of cypress, ash, hackberry, gum, and, in slightly higher areas, oak and hickory that once covered much of the landscape (Fisk 1944; Shelford 1963).

Following publication of the 1951 report by Phillips, Ford, and Griffin, major professional investigations in the central Mississippi Valley were limited until the late 1960s (a notable exception is S. Williams 1954). The intervening years saw a marked increase in pothunting, as well as the initiation of large-scale, mechanized land leveling, resulting in damage to the archaeological record of the Mississippi alluvial valley on an extraordinary scale. In many instances, virtually nothing more is known about recorded sites than the information reported by Phillips and his colleagues, because many large sites have essentially been obliterated.

ROBERT C. MAINFORT JR.

Figure 13.1. The central Mississippi Valley, showing archaeological sites discussed in the text and related sites.

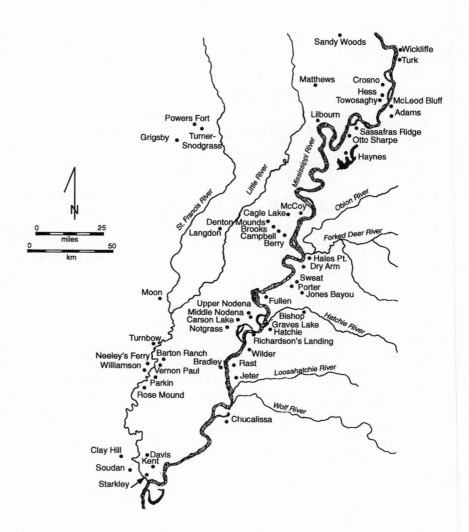

Moreover, the relative density and large sizes of late period sites in the region simply exceed the ability of professional archaeologists to adequately investigate all but a small fraction of them. The long-term research projects needed to extensively investigate large, multimound towns have rarely been feasible. Few systematic surveys have been conducted in the vicinity of the large recorded Mississippian towns (but see P. Morse 1981), and data about small hamlet or farmstead sites simply do not exist for much of the study area, greatly limiting inferences about settlement patterns.

This admittedly depressing state of affairs notwithstanding, the last quarter of the twentieth century saw major advances in our knowledge of the late prehistoric and proto-historic periods in the study area. Phillips's (1970) synthesis provided a typological and temporal framework that remains highly influential. During the late 1960s and early 1970s, the University of Michigan Powers phase project (Price and Griffin 1979) generated an unparalleled data set pertaining to Middle Mississippian period settlements. At the same time, the University of Missouri conducted large-scale excavations at several roughly contemporaneous towns (Chapman et al. 1977) and recorded an impressive amount of data from numerous sites threatened with land leveling (e.g., R. Williams 1968, 1972).

In 1983, the University of Illinois began a multiyear investigation of the long-neglected Mississippian towns in western Kentucky (e.g., Lewis 1986), and shortly thereafter the Tennessee Division of Archaeology initiated intensive research in the Reelfoot Lake basin (Mainfort 1996a) and systematic study of floodplain Mississippian sites to the south (Mainfort 1996b; Mainfort and Moore 1998). The efforts of the Arkansas Archeological Survey have been instrumental in advancing our understanding of late period societies in the study area. The syntheses of the Nodena (D. Morse 1989), Parkin (P. Morse 1981), and Kent phases (House 1991) are noteworthy in this regard, and the Morses' (1983) overview will be cited repeatedly in this chapter.

Of Vacant Quarters and Depopulation

In this chapter I address two critical questions regarding the aboriginal people of the central Mississippi Valley. The first is the "vacant quarter" hypothesis set forth by Stephen Williams (1983, 1990). Briefly stated, Williams called attention to the apparent abandonment of the large Mississippian civic-ceremonial centers throughout an area that encompassed sizable portions of the Mississippi (including the northern half of the study area), Ohio, and Tennessee River valleys during the fifteenth century—that is, prior to de Soto's *entrada*. Importantly, this phenomenon was posited to be the result not of drastic population reductions but rather of changing sociopolitical structures (Morse and Morse 1983; S. Williams 1990). What factors might have been responsible for such widespread population relocation? Perhaps it was no coincidence that after several hundred years of warm, dry summers between A.D. 1250 and 1450, around 1450 the climate rapidly became cooler and wetter, marking the beginning of the Little Ice Age (Baerreis, Bryson, and Kutzbach 1976). But the timing and effects of this event in the study area require finer resolution, and it is extremely unlikely that a single cause can be implicated. A search for multiple factors in specific regions seems a more productive research pursuit.

The study area is central to assessing the vacant quarter hypothesis not only because the original formulation drew heavily on data from southeastern Missouri but also because the greatest criticisms of the hypothesis have employed data from the same area (e.g., Lewis 1986, 1990). The vacant quarter hypothesis has not previously been formally evaluated from a broad, regional perspective with reference to specific data sets. Such an evaluation is presented in what follows.

A recurrent theme of this volume is that aboriginal populations in eastern North America were significantly reduced by European diseases (Dobyns 1983; M. Smith 1987; Ramenofsky 1987). Direct contact with Europeans clearly was not required for the rapid spread of disease. Populations in the Midwest, for example, evidently were ravaged by epidemics during the mid-sixteenth century, more than a century before the first Europeans arrived in the area (e.g., Green 1984). Prior to the late seventeenth century, societies in the central Mississippi Valley had minimal contact with Europeans.

It seems unnecessary here to recount the numerous and often arcane discussions concerning the specific route of the de Soto expedition in the Mississippi Valley. All researchers seem to agree that the Spaniards spent a fair amount of time trudging through portions of eastern Arkansas (e.g., Morse and Morse 1983; Young and Hoffman 1993). More than 130 years then passed before Father Jacques Marquette descended the Mississippi River to the mouth of the Arkansas, followed shortly by LaSalle and various missionaries.

The early French accounts of Native American societies in Arkansas differ dramatically from the descriptions in the de Soto chronicles. Gone were the large flotillas of war canoes and the sumptuary pomp of Casqui and Pacaha, as were the large towns and large populations reported by the Spaniards. By roughly 1700, the population of eastern Arkansas may have been no more than one-fifth its size in 1541.

Epidemics ravaged the region, and the French accounts provide some insights into a process that may have been under way for well over 100 years. An example is provided by St. Cosmé, who in 1699 wrote:

We were greatly consoled at seeing ourselves at the seat of our missions [at the mouth of the Arkansas River], but we were deeply afflicted at finding this nation of the Acanscas, formerly so numerous, entirely destroyed by war and disease. Not a month had elapsed since they had rid themselves of the smallpox, which had carried off most of them. In the village are now nothing but graves, in which they buried two [i.e., two tribes of the Arkansas/Quapaw] together, and we estimated that not a hundred men were left. All the children had died and a great many women. (Kellogg 1917: 359).

From our twentieth-century perspective, it is nearly impossible to grasp the magnitude of epidemics among Native Americans. An account by Denig (1961: 71–72), who was an eyewitness to a smallpox epidemic among the Assiniboine in 1837–1838, is chilling:

This disease made its appearance in Fort Union when the steamboat arrived in the month of June with the annual supplies of the post. No Indians were then near except the wives of the engagees of the Fur Company in the fort, every one of whom caught the infection. In a short time 30 persons were laid up. When the first band came in, they were met a mile from the place by good interpreters who represented to them the danger of going near and goods were brought out with the view of trading with them at a distance. All efforts of the kind, however, proved unavailling. They would not listen, and passed on to the fort, and 250 lodges or upwards of 1000 souls contracted the disease at the same time, which during the summer and fall reduced them to thirty lodges or about 150 people old and young. Other bands coming in from time to time caught the infection, some of which remained at the fort where the dead were daily thrown into the river by cart loads. Others attempted to run away from it. The different roads were dotted with carcasses and occasionally lodges standing in which whole families lay dead.

The second major question addressed in this chapter, therefore, is the timing and extent of aboriginal depopulation in the central Mississippi Valley. This and the vacant quarter hypothesis are investigated by examining evidence from four subareas within the study area: southeastern Missouri, western Kentucky, much of eastern Arkansas, and western Tennessee. Discussion of the subareas is preceded by the development of a chronology for the late period archaeological record.

Establishing the Chronological Framework

Although a number of distinctive ceramic vessel forms and decorated types, as well as lithic artifacts, are consistently associated with late period occupations in the central Mississippi Valley (e.g., Morse and Morse 1983; Phillips 1970; Phillips, Ford, and Griffin 1951), more precise dating of the sites or components that produced this material culture remains largely unaccomplished. Much of our knowledge of the material culture is derived from surface collections of pottery sherds (Mainfort 1999) and amateur excavations that emphasized collection of mortuary ceramics (e.g., Hathcock 1988). A dearth of radiocarbon dates (a consequence of limited professional excavations) compounds the problem (e.g., D. Morse 1990), although this situation is improving (Mainfort 1996b).

As noted by D. Morse (1993), identification of late period (A.D. 1400–1650) sites in the study area is usually based on the presence of Nodena ("willow leaf") points and the ceramic types Parkin Punctated and Barton Incised. In contrast, the immediately preceding middle period Mississippian assemblages are characterized by relatively small notched points and a scarcity of decorated ceramics; the type Matthews Incised is often associated with this period. More extensive discussion of artifact types and styles appears in the Morses' 1983 synthesis.

The data presented in this section largely corroborate and refine the Morses' interpretation of regional chronology, but several issues remain unresolved. First, it is important not to view the appearance and subsequent distribution of various artifact types and styles as strictly unilineal phenomena, even within the confines of the relatively small study area. The pitfalls of such thinking are well illustrated by Phillips's (1970: 933) interpretation of the Walls and Nodena phases as being "later" than the Parkin phase, an assertion disproved by the Spanish artifacts recovered from the Parkin site itself (e.g., Mitchem 1996a, 1996b). I note later that there is some evidence to suggest that Nodena points and endscrapers, both important temporal markers, appear somewhat later in the southern part of the study area than in the north. It would be remarkable if some temporal variability did not occur, but specific timing should not invalidate the sequential trends discussed here.

A second problem, related to but more specific than the first, is that the date of 1350–1400 used for the start of the Late Mississippian period in the study area, though likely to be generally correct, presently is not well supported by radiometric assays and stratigraphy (Mainfort 1996b). This situation largely reflects a lack of attention to middle period Mississippian sites in much of the study area. I provide here only a brief summary of data on the middle period Mississippian, specifically focusing on artifacts and chronology.

The Moon site, a middle period Mississippian palisaded town, was completely excavated during the winter of 1989–1990, and more than 30 domestic structures were exposed (Benn 1998). The site, located in Poinsett County, Arkansas, produced a fairly large artifact assemblage that represents the best-documented material culture for this time period in the study area. Of almost 25,000 ceramic sherds, only 35 exhibited surface decorations; fine-paste Bell Plain was very scare (37 sherds). Vessel forms included 20 percent plates and 2 percent bottles. The number of plates (including some

O'Byam Incised, as well as painted examples) is presently without parallel in the study area; in the American Bottom area, this vessel form became prominent during the Moorehead phase (circa 1150–1250; Holley 1989). Notched, scalloped, and noded rims were not reported, nor were rim effigy elements. Of the Mississippian points recovered from feature contexts, about 75 percent were notched forms (Lander, Scallorn, Reed, Schugtown), and the remainder were small, triangular (Madison) points (Benn 1992).

The Moon site was destroyed by fire, save for the surrounding palisade, so it is not unreasonable to treat its eight radiocarbon assays (Table 13.1) as the products of a single event, at least as a point of reference. The resulting calibrated average is A.D. 1276 (1291) 1303.[1] How long the Moon site community actually existed can only be conjectured, but the 200-year estimate proposed by Benn (1998) probably is overgenerous.

Another completely excavated, burned Mississippian town, the Snodgrass site, is located in southeastern Missouri about 90 kilometers north of the Moon site. Numerous radiocarbon determinations from Snodgrass and the adjacent and similar Turner site suggest occupation between 1300 and 1400 (calibrated) (Table 13.2). Both towns were occupied for short periods (Price and Griffin 1979). The 208 points recovered at Snodgrass exhibit a fair amount of variation. Nearly half are notched forms, one-quarter are stemmed, six are triangular, and two appear to be atypical variants of the willow-leaf Nodena type. Ceramics at Snodgrass exhibit a number of contrasts with those from Moon, including the occurrence of several rim treatment modes (notching, nodes, effigy elements), incised chevron motifs (Matthews Incised) on the shoulders of a number of jars, and an absence of plates.

Data from Moon and the somewhat later Snodgrass site contribute the best contextual evidence for middle period Mississippian material culture in the study area. But although these sites are informative about when late period artifacts and decorative motifs were *not* present, we still lack hard evidence for when most late period material culture did appear.

I recently presented data (Mainfort 1996b) from the western Tennessee portion of the central Mississippi Valley that provide the best available contextual and chronometric control for late prehistoric–protohistoric occupations in the study area. Most of the discussion immediately following is drawn from that publication, which contains many details (including all radiocarbon assays) omitted here.

Located about 10 kilometers south of downtown Memphis, the Chucalissa site (also known as Fuller and Shelby) encompasses a 3-meter-tall substructural mound, the remains of a substructural and burial mound, a plaza surrounded by a ridge of house mounds, and various residential loci within an area of about 6 hectares (Lumb and McNutt 1988). Radiocarbon determinations and stratigraphy indicate that the site was occupied for at least 100 years,

Table 13.1

Radiocarbon Dates from Eastern Arkansas

Sample ID	Provenience	Uncorrected Years B.P.	Calibrated Date A.D. (1 Sigma)
M-385	Upper Nodena	630 ± 125	1280 (1310, 1350, 1390) 1429
Beta-34405	Moon	870 ± 60	1051 (1200) 1248
Beta-43957	Moon	780 ± 60	1221 (1280) 1288
Beta-43958	Moon	780 ± 50	1225 (1275) 1286
Beta-43954	Moon	730 ± 50	1271 (1286) 1298
Beta-43956	Moon	670 ± 60	1285 (1300) 1393
Beta-35402	Moon	660 ± 60	1287 (1300) 1396
Beta-35403	Moon	610 ± 60	1299 (1320, 1340, 1390) 1408
Beta-43955	Moon	600 ± 50	1304 (1328, 1333, 1395) 1408
TX-846	Hazel	370 ± 180	1407 (1490, 1610) 1954
TX-847	Hazel	370 ± 70	1445 (1490, 1610) 1641
TX-848	Hazel	600 ± 90	1294 (1330, 1400) 1426
TX-877	Hazel	500 ± 80	1400 (1430) 1454
TX-700a	Hazel	1120 ± 70	880 (900, 910, 960) 1005
TX-844	Hazel	860 ± 60	1063 (1210) 1255
TX-878a	Hazel	760 ± 60	1228 (1280) 1293
TX-845	Hazel	870 ± 100	1031 (1200) 1278
TX-704	Hazel	840 ± 80	1051 (1220) 1278
TX-848	Hazel	600 ± 90	1294 (1330, 1400) 1426
TX-786	Hazel	690 ± 70	1278 (1300) 1391
TX-750	Hazel	690 ± 70	1278 (1300) 1391
DRI-3213	Neeley's Ferry	532 ± 116	1305 (1410) 1457
DRI-3218	Neeley's Ferry	293 ± 54	1516 (1640) 1660
Beta-57266	Parkin	290 ± 60	1515 (1640) 1663
Beta-44560	Parkin	630 ± 60	1294 (1310, 1350, 1390) 1403
Beta-44559	Parkin	180 ± 60	1659 (1680, 1770, 1800, 1940, 1950) 1954
Beta-63086	Parkin	750 ± 50	1250 (1282) 1293
Beta-66948	Parkin	980 ± 70	1004 (1030) 1162
Beta-70355	Parkin	840 ± 80	1063 (1220) 1280
Beta-70356	Parkin	460 ± 80	1409 (1440) 1483
Beta-72283	Parkin	490 ± 60	1407 (1430) 1449
DRI-2888	Parkin	381 ± 30	1458 (1482) 1621
Beta-59969	Parkin	280 ± 90	1487 (1650) 1954
Beta-61438	Parkin	620 ± 60	1297 (1320, 1350, 1390) 1405
Beta-59968	Parkin	180 ± 70	1656 (1680, 1770, 1800, 1940, 1950) 1954
Beta-61439	Parkin	300 ± 70	1487 (1640) 1663
Beta-61440	Parkin	330 ± 50	1481 (1525, 1558, 1631) 1647
Beta-61964	Parkin	610 ± 100	1290 (1320, 1340, 1390) 1426
Beta-70357	Parkin	350 ± 60	1459 (1520, 1590, 1620) 1644
Beta-70358	Parkin	300 ± 60	1510 (1640) 1660
Beta-72284	Parkin	330 ± 50	1481 (1525, 1558, 1631) 1647
Beta-72285	Parkin	690 ± 60	1281 (1300) 1386
Beta-57266	Parkin	290 ± 60	1515 (1640) 1663
SMU-2099	Clay Hill	240 ± 40	1644 (1660) 1953
SMU-2100	Clay Hill	230 ± 120	1515 (1660) 1955
SMU-2101	Clay Hill	390 ± 40	1448 (1478) 1621
SMU-2102	Kent	600 ± 115	1289 (1330, 1400) 1435
SMU-2103	Kent	310 ± 90	1472 (1640) 1666

Note: Calibrations were performed with CALIB 3.0 (Stuiver and Reimer 1993).

Table 13.2

Radiocarbon Determinations from Southeastern Missouri

Sample ID	Provenience	Uncorrected Years B.P.	Calibrated Date A.D. (1 Sigma)
M-2276	Powers Fort	540 ± 100	1307 (1410) 1446
M-2277	Powers Fort	660 ± 100	1279 (1300) 1405
M-2278	Powers Fort	590 ± 100	1294 (1400) 1433
M-2279	Powers Fort	660 ± 200	1213 (1300) 1441
M-2280	Powers Fort	650 ± 100	1281 (1300, 1370) 1408
M-2135	Snodgrass	630 ± 100	1285 (1310, 1350, 1390) 1416
M-2432	Snodgrass	660 ± 100	1279 (1300) 1405
M-2430	Snodgrass	790 ± 100	1167 (1260) 1295
M-2185	Snodgrass	810 ± 100	1161 (1250) 1290
M-2182	Snodgrass	620 ± 100	1287 (1320, 1350, 1390) 1421
M-2181	Snodgrass	730 ± 110	1221 (1290) 1391
M-2275	Snodgrass	620 ± 100	1287 (1320, 1350, 1390) 1421
M-2181	Snodgrass	620 ± 100	1287 (1320, 1350, 1390) 1421
M-2274	Snodgrass	560 ± 100	1302 (1410) 1441
M-2183	Snodgrass	560 ± 100	1302 (1410) 1441
M-2134	Snodgrass	560 ± 150	1290 (1410) 1463
M-2137	Snodgrass	520 ± 100	1315 (1420) 1454
M-2433	Snodgrass	540 ± 100	1307 (1410) 1446
M-2133	Snodgrass	470 ± 100	1402 (1440) 1611
M-2136	Snodgrass	430 ± 100	1414 (1450) 1631
M-2184	Snodgrass	410 ± 100	1425 (1460) 1638
M-2180	Snodgrass	400 ± 100	1430 (1470) 1641
M-1957	Turner	500 ± 100	1327 (1430) 1473
M-1958	Turner	570 ± 100	1299 (1400) 1439
M-1959	Turner	720 ± 100	1229 (1290) 1391
M-1960	Turner	560 ± 100	1302 (1410) 1441
M-1961	Turner	810 ± 110	1063 (1250) 1293
M-1962	Turner	560 ± 100	1302 (1410) 1441
M-1963	Turner	560 ± 100	1302 (1410) 1441
M-1964	Turner	730 ± 100	1225 (1290) 1385
DIC-171	Lilbourn	690 ± 120	1241 (1300) 1403
DIC-178	Lilbourn	580 ± 100	1297 (1400) 1436
Avg. DIC-171/8	Lilbourn	625 ± 77	1291 (1310, 1350, 1390) 1408
DIC-182	Lilbourn	500 ± 170	1299 (1430) 1631
DIC-191	Lilbourn	710 ± 90	1251 (1290) 1391
DIC-204	Lilbourn	1010 ± 140	890 (1020) 1197
N-1232	Lilbourn	855 ± 90	1043 (1220) 1279
N-1233	Lilbourn	860 ± 90	1041 (1210) 1278
Avg. N-1232/3	Lilbourn	858 ± 64	1061 (1210) 1260
N-1490	Lilbourn	580 ± 75	1303 (1400) 1429
N-1491	Lilbourn	650 ± 75	1286 (1300, 1370) 1402
N-1493	Lilbourn	595 ± 75	1299 (1400) 1421
N-1495	Lilbourn	590 ± 75	1301 (1400) 1424
Avg. N-1491/2/5	Lilbourn	608 ± 44	1304 (1322, 1339, 1393) 1404
N-1492	Lilbourn	795 ± 75	1191 (1260) 1288
N-1494	Lilbourn	780 ± 75	1215 (1280) 1292
Avg. N-1492/4	Lilbourn	788 ± 55	1220 (1270) 1286
DIC-189	Lilbourn	790 ± 60	1217 (1260) 1286
N-1496	Lilbourn	560 ± 75	1308 (1410) 1435
N-1497	Lilbourn	760 ± 75	1223 (1280) 1297
Avg. N-1496/7	Lilbourn	658 ± 54	1289 (1300) 1395
DIC-518	Lilbourn	1150 ± 50	870 (891) 973
DIC-519	Lilbourn	510 ± 60	1402 (1430) 1444
DIC-520	Lilbourn	870 ± 140	1019 (1200) 1286
DIC-521	Lilbourn	1080 ± 70	890 (980) 1020
DIC-638	Lilbourn	880 ± 100	1028 (1180) 1276

Table 13.2 *continued*

Sample ID	Provenience	Uncorrected Years B.P.	Calibrated Date A.D. (1 Sigma)
DIC-639	Lilbourn	1000 ± 65	992 (1020) 1155
UGa-147	Hess	355 ± 75	1448 (1510, 1600, 1620) 1647
GaK-1309	Hess	350 ± 90	1445 (1520, 1590, 1620) 1654
UGa-145	Callahan-Thompson	480 ± 65	1408 (1440) 1458
UGa-148	Callahan-Thompson	570 ± 90	1302 (1400) 1436
M-2217	Denton Mounds	660 ± 100	1279 (1300) 1405

Note: Calibrations were performed with CALIB 3.0 (Stuiver and Reimer 1993).

and the vertical distribution of decorated ceramics suggests that the late period occupation began around 1400 (Mainfort 1996b; see also Lumb and McNutt 1988; G. Smith 1972; Smith and McNutt 1991). The penultimate structure of the substructural mound is dated to circa 1435 (calibrated), with use of the site continuing into the early 1500s (Mainfort 1996b; Smith and McNutt 1991).

The Chucalissa ceramic assemblage is noteworthy because of its unusually high frequency of decorated types relative to assemblages from most other sites in the study area (Mainfort 1996b, 1999; contra G. Smith 1990). All of the "classic" Late Mississippian types are represented (Parkin Punctated, Nodena Red and White, Rhodes Incised, Walls Engraved, etc.; see Phillips 1970), and stratigraphic evidence suggests that many of these types persisted throughout the major occupation of the site (see Lumb and McNutt 1988). Of note are five helmet-shaped bowls, which are typically found in post–de Soto contexts, such as the examples from the Oliver (Starr 1992) and Kinkead-Mainard (Hoffman 1977) sites; all four excavated vessels from Chucalissa were associated with the upper occupation stratum (Mainfort 1996b). Also present are examples of Leland Incised, *var. LeFlore,* and a Parkin Punctated, *var. Castile,* helmet jar with vertical appliqué strips. No gadrooned bottles or painted head pots have been reported (Childress 1992; Mainfort 1996b). Nodena points may have been associated primarily with the uppermost occupation levels (Lumb and McNutt 1988), although the lithic assemblage has not been systematically studied. Neither snubnosed endscrapers nor large, well-made triangular points have been reported (Mainfort 1996b).

Data from the Graves Lake site in Lauderdale County, Tennessee, complement the evidence from Chucalissa (Mainfort 1996b; Mainfort and Moore 1998). Covering an area of approximately 2 hectares, the site is located at the southern terminus of the First Chickasaw Bluff system. No mounds are present, and occupation deposits are relatively shallow.

Parkin Punctated is the most common decorated ceramic type in the Graves Lake assemblage. Barton Incised is less numerous, with nearly equal numbers of *var. Barton* and *var. Kent;* Ranch Incised, defined on the basis of "fish-scale" curvilinear designs, outnumbers Barton Incised. Minority types include Vernon Paul Appliqué, Campbell Appliqué, Nodena Red and White, Rhodes Incised, and Walls Engraved. The presence of the vertical appliqué types is noteworthy, as they are characteristic of post-1500 assemblages in the study area.

A number of whole or partially restorable ceramic vessels were recovered during test excavations, including two helmet-shaped bowls, which seem to be excellent late period markers (see S. Williams 1980). Other vessels included a pair of Bell Plain bird effigy vessels, a Barton Incised, *var. Kent,* jar with symbolic punctated handles, and a fragment of a gadrooned bottle. Two fragmentary Barton Incised, *var. Kent,* jars were associated with a non-wall-trench house that had been rebuilt several times (Mainfort 1996b).

All identified projectile points were subtriangular to triangular types (i.e., Madison and Nodena). Several long triangular points classified as Madison are similar to specimens from the Otto Sharpe site (Lawrence and Mainfort 1995). A single snubnosed endscraper fragment also was collected; only two other sites in western Tennessee have yielded examples of this distinctive artifact type (Mainfort 1996b). Fifteen specimens of Mill Creek chert, including two Nodena points and a hoe rejuvenation flake, were recovered.

Seven radiocarbon determinations may define two distinct periods in the occupational history of the site, though all of the dates overlap at approximately A.D. 1450 at two sigmas. Four calibrated dates cluster tightly around the mid-1400s, which is a reasonable age for the surface-collected ceramics. The three remaining dates provide evidence of occupation during or after the de Soto horizon, and several artifact types are consistent with this interpretation—namely, the gadrooned bottle, the appliqué sherds, the large triangular points, and the snubnosed endscraper fragment (Mainfort 1996b; Mainfort and Moore 1998).

The Richardson's Landing site, in Tipton County, Tennessee, lies on a major bend of the Mississippi River several kilometers west of the Second Chickasaw Bluff system and covers approximately 1 hectare. Ceramic counts from surface collections are similar to those from the Graves Lake site, but decorated types such as Parkin Punctated and Barton Incised, *var. Barton,* are relatively low in frequency. Barton Incised, *var. Kent,* Vernon Paul Appliqué, and Campbell Appliqué have not been found at Richardson's Landing. Lithics include Nodena and Madison points, flaked adzes or gouges, and a ground basalt celt. Three calibrated radiocarbon dates suggest an age comparable to that of the inferred earlier occupation at Graves Lake, circa 1440 (Mainfort 1996b; Mainfort and Moore 1998).

The latest aboriginal occupation in western Tennessee was documented by excavations at the 4-hectare Otto Sharpe site, near Reelfoot Lake (Lawrence and Mainfort 1995; Mainfort 1996b). Limited testing produced a large artifact assemblage, most of which was associated with a single depositional event. Recovered artifacts included snubnosed endscrapers, large triangular projectile points, and numerous examples of Campbell Appliqué and Campbell Punctated, most of which represented helmet-shaped jars. Four European artifacts also were recovered—a small sheet-brass tinkling cone or bead and three badly corroded iron objects. Two radiocarbon determinations from the deposit that yielded most of the artifacts produced a calibrated average of A.D. 1649 (1658) 1661.

The lithic assemblage is virtually identical to what Brain (1988: 277–280) called the "Oliver lithic complex." Many triangular points exhibit excellent workmanship, including fine secondary flaking along blade edges (see Price and Price 1990). Most specimens are 30 to 40 millimeters long, and some grade into the smaller size range typical for Madison points. Less numerous are Nodena points, most of which are of the contracting, truncated-base form (see D. Morse 1989: 20). Small snubnosed endscrapers, characterized by a steep, unifacially worked surface along one lateral edge, are the most distinctive lithic artifacts. Brain (1988: 279) and others have suggested that endscrapers represent a response to the European stimulation of the deerskin trade. No nonlocal cherts are present in the lithic assemblage.

Mississippi Plain (coarse shell-tempered ware) is the dominant ceramic type at the Otto Sharpe site, with a low frequency of Bell Plain (fine shell/grog-tempered ware). Campbell Appliqué and Campbell Punctated are the most common decorated ceramic "types," and these decorative modes frequently occur in combination on the necks and shoulders of helmet-shaped jars. Surface treatment consists of vertical appliqué strips on the neck, with a relatively narrow band of punctations around the vessel shoulder. There are possible parallels between Campbell Appliqué and the protohistoric type Alabama River Appliqué of the central Alabama region (Curren 1984). Kent and Barton Incised, Walls Engraved, and Fortune Noded are present in small quantities.

Of critical importance is the unequivocal association of vertical appliqué ceramics, snubnosed endscrapers, large triangular points, and European objects. The Otto Sharpe assemblage thus provides an important baseline for the early to mid-seventeenth century in the central Mississippi Valley. As discussed later, several sites in the Missouri bootheel have produced artifact assemblages that are generally similar.

Lewis's (1990, 1991, and elsewhere) oft-cited radiocarbon determinations for the Callahan-Thompson and Hess sites require some discussion. The dates and associated artifact assemblages are of considerable relevance to both southeastern Missouri and western Kentucky because Lewis's interpretation of the chronological position of several decorated ceramic types, and hence his assertion that some large sites in western Kentucky remained major centers well after 1400, apparently stems from data derived from these two sites, which lie only about 5 kilometers apart.

Testing at Callahan-Thompson and Hess exposed the remains of typical Mississippian wall-trench houses. Portions of at least five partially superimposed structures were exposed at Callahan-Thompson; two building episodes were represented by the Structure 4 area at Hess (Lewis 1978). Radiocarbon determinations suggest an age of approximately A.D. 1400 for Callahan-Thompson and 1500–1600 for Hess (see Table 13.2). Lewis (1990: 54) considered these to be "particularly strong" dates.

Artifact assemblages from the sites (particularly those from Hess) are not consistent with the radiocarbon determinations. Decorated ceramics from the immediate vicinity of the excavated structures are limited to Kimmswick Fabric Marked, Matthews Incised, vars. Beckwith, Manly, and Matthews, and O'Byam Incised; Wickliffe Thick is present at both sites. Neither Nodena points nor endscrapers are reported for either site. The artifact assemblages are characteristic for the period around A.D. 1250–1350, as discussed earlier; artifacts indicating post-1450 occupation are absent. Presumably this was why Lewis (1990: 54–55) stated that the "material culture . . . at the Callahan-Thompson and Hess sites shows no changes from . . . older Mississippi period occupations." In fact, the material culture of these sites is that of older (i.e., pre-1400) Mississippian occupations. The radiometric assays and associated material culture from Hess make no sense with regard to any other archaeological data in the central Mississippi Valley, whereas the calibrated dates from Callahan-Thompson are not entirely inconsistent with a pre-1400 middle period Mississippian occupation (see also Wesler 1991a: 113–114).

A summary of late period diagnostic artifacts, time periods, and key sites is presented Table 13.3, which owes much to S. Williams's (1980) formulation of the Armorel phase, in which he called attention to a number of protohistoric horizon markers. The absence of certain Armorel horizon markers from the table is not meant to suggest that these items are unimportant. Although artifacts such as nonrepouseé copper eagles and engraved shell buttons are valuable for linking sites across great distances, they are quite rare, making them somewhat less useful when viewing a restricted geographic area. In the discussion that follows, I have generally refrained from referencing the Armorel phase, primarily because I believe that we are now in a position to refine and strengthen it—but that task lies beyond the scope of this chapter.

Table 13.3

Summary of Horizon Markers for the Central Mississippi Valley

Date	Horizon Markers and Key Sites
A.D. 1600–1650	Artifacts: Decline of "classic" decorated types and exotic vessels toward end of period; appearance of French artifacts (notably beads and brass); endscrapers and large triangular points. Key sites: Otto Sharpe, Campbell
A.D. 1541–1600	Artifacts: Appearance of snubnosed endscrapers; significant amount of Campbell Appliqué; proliferation of exotic vessel forms (compound vessels, teapots, stirrup-necked bottles); rare occurrence of Spanish artifacts. Key sites: Graves Lake, Campbell and other Pemiscot County, Missouri, sites
A.D. 1500–1541	Artifacts: Appearance of Campbell Appliqué, large triangular points, helmet-shaped vessels, burial urns, gadrooned bottles (at or just prior to the de Soto horizon). Key sites: Chucalissa, Graves Lake
A.D. 1400–1500	Artifacts: Appearance of most Late Mississippian decorated ceramic types (especially Parkin Punctated, Barton Incised, Nodena Red and White, Rhodes Incised, Ranch Incised, Walls Engraved; Barton Incised, *var. Kent*, Ranch Incised, Rhodes Incised, and perhaps several other type-varieties probably do not appear until A.D. 1500 or later) and apparently sudden appearance of Nodena points. Key sites: Chucalissa, Graves Lake, Richardson's Landing

Source: Modified from Mainfort 1996a.

Using the foregoing chronology for the study area, I now turn to developments in the four selected subareas within the central Mississippi Valley.

Assessing the Evidence

SOUTHEASTERN MISSOURI. Southeastern Missouri is an appropriate starting point for a discussion of late period developments in the central Mississippi Valley, not only because of the richness of its archaeological record but also because data from this subarea form the basis for the vacant quarter hypothesis (Price, Price, and Harris 1976; S. Williams 1983, 1990), which posits the abandonment of the large Mississippian civic-ceremonial centers throughout a broad area of the midcontinent by about A.D. 1450.

Excavated data from Lilbourn (Chapman et al. 1977) and several sites of the Powers phase (Price and Griffin 1979) support the hypothesis. Lilbourn is one of the few adequately studied large, fortified towns that compose the Cairo Lowland phase (Phillips 1970); it includes at least 10 mounds and covers more than 16 hectares. Other notable sites of the phase include Sandy Woods (9 mounds, 22 hectares), Matthews (7 mounds, 9 hectares), Towosaghy (at least 7 mounds, more than 10 hectares), and Crosno (4 mounds, 7 hectares).

Lilbourn produced a number of radiocarbon dates indicating that the site was occupied for about 200 years between A.D. 1200 and 1400 (Table 13.2), and the site is an important benchmark for the material culture of this time period. Bottles and plates were added to the ceramic inventory; decorated types include Matthews Incised, Kimmswick Fabric Impressed, O'Byam Incised, and Nashville Negative Painted. These vessel forms and types are horizon markers for the middle period Mississippian in the study area.

Investigations at sites of the Powers phase, centered roughly 100 kilometers west of the Cairo Lowland phase, provide insights into settlement patterns. Powers phase material culture is generally (but not specifically) similar to that of the Cairo Lowland phase. Powers Fort, probably the apical site, includes four mounds surrounded by a fortification ditch that encloses an area of about 4.5 hectares (Pertulla 1998). The locations of 10 associated villages, ranging in size from about 0.5 to 1.3 hectares, indicate a preference for easily tilled soils. Approximately 70 small hamlets or farmsteads also have been located.

The adjacent and apparently sequent Turner and Snodgrass sites were completely excavated (Price and Griffin 1979). Snodgrass, the larger and later of the two, was surrounded by a ditch with associated bastions and included 90 dwellings. Much of the western portion of the community was enclosed by a wall; houses within the wall were generally larger than those outside. All structures at the site had been burned intentionally, as was the case at Turner. Nearly 30 radiocarbon assays were obtained from Powers Fort, Snodgrass, and Turner. Calibrated averages of the dates from each site (see also Table 13.2) indicate that the Powers phase existed between approximately 1300 and 1400.

A recent description of the multimound town of Langdon, located in Pemiscot County, Missouri, suggests that the abandonment, or vacant quarter, scenario may require reconsideration (Dunnell 1998). Data derived largely from surface collections (and unfortunately not quantified) suggest a predominance of Nodena points over middle period Mississippian notched forms; no comparable assemblage has been reported in the study area. Examples of Campbell

Appliqué and Campbell Punctated ceramics are reported but not illustrated; surface decoration occurs infrequently, and Late Mississippian types such as Parkin Punctated and Barton Incised are not mentioned. My guess—and the scant published data permit no more than a guess—is that the primary occupation of Langdon was partially contemporaneous with but extended somewhat beyond the Powers phase, and that the Campbell Appliqué/Punctated sherds represent reuse of the site roughly 100 years after major occupation had ceased.

A cluster of sites in Pemiscot County, Missouri, provides one of the best windows on protohistoric occupation in the study area. It includes Campbell, Denton Mounds, Cagle Lake, McCoy, Berry, Brooks, Holland, and a number of virtually unreported localities in the vicinity. Most of the sites occupy natural levees along Pemiscot Bayou, which meanders in a generally east-west direction across the county.

Several of these sites, especially the extensively excavated (albeit by an amateur) Campbell site (O'Brien and Holland 1994), provided the basis for S. Williams's (1980) definition of the Armorel phase. Diagnostic artifacts include snub-nosed endscrapers, large triangular points, and vertical appliqué ceramics. Based on the chronology proposed earlier in this chapter, major occupation at all of these sites postdated A.D. 1500. Late period ceramic vessel forms, including gadrooned bottles, various effigy forms, and painted head pots, abound. Relic hunters have plundered literally thousands of vessels from this mere handful of sites (see Hathcock 1988). European artifacts (glass beads, brass, and iron) are documented at Campbell (O'Brien 1994; Price and Price 1990) and Brooks (O'Brien 1994). Although detailed descriptions are not available for some sites, the available data are impressive and demonstrate that in extreme southeastern Missouri, large towns with one or more mounds were established and/or continued to function into post–de Soto times.

The Campbell site covers an area of approximately 15 hectares and includes the remains of a possible platform mound (perhaps a large levee remnant; O'Brien 1994: 198). No evidence of fortifications has been reported (Chapman and Anderson 1955; O'Brien 1994). More than 200 burials were excavated under fairly controlled conditions, and many (perhaps hundreds) of additional graves have been looted (Holland 1991). No readily identifiable sociotechnic items have been reported from mortuary contexts.

Spanish artifacts, including a number of chevron and clear-glass beads, a Clarksdale bell, and iron beads, have been found at the site (O'Brien and Holland 1994); most were excavated by looters, and no reliable provenience information is available. The quantities and kinds of European artifacts led Morse and Morse (1983: 312) to propose that Campbell was visited by two members of de Soto's expedition who ventured north from Pacaha. In this regard, it is interesting to note that Campbell has produced more six-

teenth-century Spanish artifacts than any recorded site in Arkansas, where the provinces of Casqui and Pacaha probably were located (e.g., D. Morse 1990; Morse and Morse 1983; P. Morse 1990). It is possible, but as yet undemonstrated, that some of the European artifacts from the Campbell site are of French origin. If true, this would indicate that occupation at Campbell extended into the early seventeenth century (see D. Morse 1990), but the lack of brass tinklers and iron gun parts like those recovered from the circa-1700 Grigsby site (D. Morse 1992) near Pocohontas, Arkansas, militates against this interpretation.

Holland (1991; O'Brien and Holland 1994) analyzed the available skeletal remains from the Campbell site (138 individuals). Because some interments at Campbell postdated the de Soto *entrada,* the Campbell site population might be expected to exhibit clear indications of high stress induced by European diseases. Not only is this not the case, but the incidence of linear enamel hypoplasia at the Campbell site is substantially lower than that observed by Powell (1989) at the late prehistoric Upper Nodena site. As Holland (1991: 180) stated: "The picture presented by the analysis of the Campbell skeletons is one of a maize-reliant population with marked sexual dimorphism and a relatively light disease load."

Perhaps the most architecturally impressive of the Pemiscot County sites, the Denton Mounds site (also known as Rhoades; Hathcock 1988) encompasses an area of approximately 6 hectares within which five mounds are located (R. Williams 1972). Most of a large, roughly square structure measuring 8 meters on each side was disclosed during limited testing. The walls were constructed with individually set posts. Its lack of a hearth and its large size indicate that this was a special purpose structure (see R. Williams 1972: 155–156). The radiocarbon determination obtained for this feature is not credible (Table 13.2). Eleven burials were excavated at Denton Mounds; of the 15 associated ceramic vessels, 2 were Campbell Appliqué jars with outflaring rims. A fairly large ceramic sherd assemblage was obtained, much of it from a single pit that also contained Nodena and large triangular points, providing useful contextual data.

The McCoy site, with an area of roughly 3 hectares and a single mound, was briefly examined after it had been chisel plowed. Thirty-eight house stains were recorded, of which the 22 measurable examples averaged about 3.6 meters by 5.5 meters. Locations of 48 burials were noted; both single interments and clusters of two to five individuals were represented (O'Brien and Williams 1994). The small artifact assemblage included Campbell Appliqué ceramics, Nodena and large triangular points, and endscrapers.

R. Williams (1968) also conducted limited investigations at Cagle Lake, located about 12 kilometers west of the McCoy site in Pemiscot County, Missouri. The site covers at least 2 hectares, and a 2-meter-tall mound once was present (O'Brien and Williams 1994). The artifact assemblage is comparable to those of the other Pemiscot Bayou area sites, although projectile points and endscrapers seem to be especially numerous.

The Holland site, 7 kilometers west of Campbell, at one time had at least five mounds. Lithics are reportedly plentiful on the surface, and a large, pierced, spatulate celt is known from the site (S. Williams 1954, 1980). Brooks, with a single mound, was the source of numerous head pots illustrated by Hathcock (1988), and several European artifacts have been reported (O'Brien and R. Williams 1994). The Berry site, less than 4 kilometers east of Campbell, has produced more than 1,000 ceramic vessels, many of them decorated (O'Brien and Williams 1994).

There are a number of parallels in material culture between the Pemiscot County, Missouri, sites and the Caborn-Welborn complex centered at the mouth of the Wabash River (Green and Munson 1978; S. Williams 1980). Ceramic vessels that undoubtedly were made in Pemiscot County (and/or northeastern Arkansas) have been recovered from Caborn-Welborn sites, as have endscrapers, large triangular points, Nodena points, and European artifacts. It is important not to overstate the similarities, however, because most of the Caborn-Welborn ceramic assemblage has a decidedly local flavor referable to the Angel phase.

The Pemiscot County sites probably offer a firmer basis for positing occupation by a single cultural or ethnic group during the years from about 1500 to 1600 than any other group of sites discussed in this chapter. Yet linking these sites to a historically identified cultural group remains problematic at best. For example, the Marquette map of 1673 recorded no villages in the vicinity, which, considered in light of the paucity of European artifacts (recovered only from the Campbell and Brooks sites), hints that by the time of Marquette's voyage, the protohistoric towns of Pemiscot County had ceased to exist.

WESTERN KENTUCKY. The Mississippian towns in the western Jackson Purchase of Kentucky produced a considerable amount of data during the 1980s and 1990s, largely owing to a research program by the University of Illinois (e.g., Lewis 1986). This subarea has figured prominently in discussions of the vacant quarter hypothesis (e.g., Lewis 1990; S. Williams 1990).

Investigations at Wickliffe Mounds, located 6 kilometers south of the mouth of the Ohio River on the Mississippi River bluffs, yielded a series of relatively homogeneous ceramic assemblages and consistent radiocarbon dates from a variety of well-controlled contexts (Table 13.4). At least six mounds are present at this 2-hectare site. Although the onset of the Mississippian occupation that produced this compact town has not been securely dated, radiocarbon evidence and the artifact assemblage indicate that use of the site had largely terminated by the early to mid-fourteenth century (Wesler 1991b).

Another blufftop town, the Turk site, lies approximately 8 kilometers south of Wickliffe and includes at least three mounds within an area of about 2.5 hectares (Edging 1990). Very limited subsurface investigations produced nine radiocarbon assays which suggest that major occupation at Turk occurred after the apparent abandonment of Wickliffe, circa A.D. 1325. Nodena points are not reported, implying that intensive occupation did not extend much beyond 1400 (see Edging 1990: 31, but contra Edging 1990: 105).

Some 25 kilometers south of Turk is the McLeod Bluff (O'Byam's Fort) site (Phillips 1970; Thomas 1894; Webb and Funkhouser 1933), which has received paltry attention from professional archaeologists. No accurate site map is available, but field inspection suggests an area of at least 3 hectares. Surface-collected ceramics, a majority of which are grog tempered, include fairly high frequencies of Kimmswick Fabric Marked, O'Byam Incised, and Wickliffe Thick, as well as Bell Plain plate rims. On the basis of published and unpublished ceramics, maximum use of the site probably occurred between A.D. 1150 and 1250, with no *major* occupation at McLeod Bluff after about 1300.

The largest Mississippian town investigated by Lewis and his associates was the 7-hectare Adams site, which is located about 8 kilometers south of McLeod Bluff and includes at least seven mounds, the largest of which is over 6 meters tall. Fieldwork included five test pits and a large, controlled surface collection (Lewis 1986). None of the ceramics or lithics is indicative of a post-1400 occupation. Rather, the assemblage is characteristic of the middle period Mississippian in the northern portion of the central Mississippi Valley. Notable in this regard is the occurrence of O'Byam Incised, Kimmswick Fabric Marked, and Matthews Incised, *vars. Beckwith* and *Manly*. Major use of the site between approximately 1200 and 1400 is also supported by five radiocarbon dates (Lewis 1986). Stout (1987: 32–33, 39) reported nine Campbell Appliqué sherds in a surface collection of more than 76,000 sherds, but neither the single illustrated rim profile nor the description of the sherds strongly supports this identification; at least some sherds probably are rims with vertical appliqué handles (see Lewis 1986: 142). Neither Nodena points nor endscrapers were reported from Adams.

Post-1500 occupation clearly is present within the limits of the Sassafras Ridge site, judging from the occurrence of snubnosed endscrapers (Lawrence and Mainfort 1995; see Lewis 1986: 142, 148). Given the relatively meager published information about the site, however, it is difficult to use these artifacts as evidence that Sassafras Ridge continued to function as a large town during the protohistoric period. Site boundaries have not been adequately defined, but artifacts are scattered over an area of at least 10 hectares. The associated substructural mound is approximately 6 meters tall. From published surface collections as well as comments from people engaged in systematic looting of the site

Table 13.4

Radiocarbon Determinations from Western Kentucky

Sample ID	Provenience	Uncorrected Years B.P.	Calibrated Date A.D. (1 Sigma)
ISGS-1143	Wickliffe	830 ± 77	1162 (1230) 1282
ISGS-1156	Wickliffe	765 ± 76	1220 (1280) 1296
Beta-25217	Wickliffe	1030 ± 90	897 (1010) 1153
Beta-25216	Wickliffe	430 ± 60	1432 (1450) 1611
Beta-31520	Wickliffe	620 ± 50	1299 (1315, 1347, 1390) 1403
Beta-31833	Wickliffe	1060 ± 70	895 (1000) 1026
ISGS-1171	Wickliffe	728 ± 76	1247 (1290) 1372
Beta-25911	Wickliffe	770 ± 60	1225 (1280) 1290
Beta-25219	Wickliffe	740 ± 70	1240 (1280) 1300
Beta-25220	Wickliffe	730 ± 50	1271 (1286) 1298
Beta-27506	Wickliffe	750 ± 60	1239 (1280) 1295
Beta-27507	Wickliffe	580 ± 60	1307 (1400) 1421
Beta-33584	Wickliffe	760 ± 80	1221 (1280) 1298
Beta-33585	Wickliffe	760 ± 90	1217 (1280) 1300
ISGS-1288	Turk	710 ± 90	1251 (1290) 1391
ISGS-1289	Turk	700 ± 70	1276 (1290) 1385
ISGS-1323	Turk	910 ± 70	1028 (1160) 1222
ISGS-1324	Turk	710 ± 70	1272 (1290) 1379
ISGS-1724	Turk	490 ± 70	1404 (1430) 1454
ISGS-1725	Turk	630 ± 70	1292 (1310, 1350, 1390) 1405
ISGS-1734	Turk	630 ± 70	1292 (1310, 1350, 1390) 1405
ISGS-1735	Turk	590 ± 120	1290 (1400) 1438
ISGS-1736	Turk	1090 ± 150	782 (980) 1153
ISGS-1141	Adams	610 ± 70	1297 (1320, 1340, 1390) 1411
ISGS-1149	Adams	700 ± 70	1276 (1290) 1385
ISGS-1150	Adams	820 ± 70	1167 (1230) 1282
ISGS-1151	Adams	610 ± 70	1297 (1320, 1340, 1390) 1411
ISGS-1161	Adams	900 ± 70	1031 (1160) 1226
ISGS-1172	Adams	810 ± 80	1167 (1250) 1286
ISGS-1142	Sassafras Ridge	660 ± 80	1283 (1300) 1400

Note: ISGS-1724 (Turk site) was composed of charred maize and apparently was not corrected for ^{13}C (Edging 1990: 31). Calibrations were performed with CALIB 3.0 (Stuiver and Reimer 1993).

in the 1970s, it appears that major occupation at Sassafras Ridge took place between approximately A.D. 1200 and 1400. As at the Adams site, major decorated types include Kimmswick Fabric Marked, Matthews Incised, *vars. Beckwith* and *Manly*, and O'Byam Incised. A radiocarbon determination from near the top of the large mound is consistent with these types (Table 13.4).

Lewis (1990: 55) stated that the material culture (particularly ceramics) of his protohistoric Jackson phase (A.D. 1500–1700) was "quite similar" to that of his Late Mississippian Medley phase (1300–1500). Further, he suggested that the failure of other researchers to recognize this alleged continuity in material culture had resulted in the mistaken impression that the post-1500 occupation of western Kentucky and the Cairo Lowland was very sparse.

This view was based largely on the questionable radiocarbon dates from the Hess site, discussed earlier. Data from the Otto Sharpe site, located just south of the Kentucky state line, provide forceful evidence to the contrary (Lawrence and Mainfort 1995; Mainfort 1996b). Although some decorated types (Nodena Red and White, Walls Engraved, etc.) continued into the sixteenth century, closely spaced vertical appliqué strips (Campbell Appliqué) are demonstrably associated only with post-1500 (or 1550) contexts, and the Late Mississippian decorated types became very infrequent by about 1650. Endscrapers and large triangular points are unique to protohistoric sites such as Otto Sharpe.

There are no clear indications that any of the large Mississippian towns in the western Jackson Purchase continued to function after about 1400. Arguments to the contrary (e.g., Edging 1990: 103) presently lack substantive evidence. Western Kentucky was not totally uninhabited, however, as is shown by the endscrapers from the Sassafras Ridge site. Endscrapers, as well as large triangular points, also were recovered from site 15FU119, just north of the Kentucky state line in Bessie Bend (Lawrence and Mainfort 1995). European artifacts, including firearms, reportedly were collected from the site by amateurs. No comparable assemblages have been recorded elsewhere in the subarea, suggesting that the region was very sparsely inhabited in the late sixteenth and seventeenth centuries.

WESTERN TENNESSEE. Data about middle period Mississippian occupation in this subarea are paltry, but sites comparable to the fortified towns of southeastern Missouri have not been recorded. The DeSoto Park mound group in Memphis may represent the largest western Tennessee site during this period, but little is known about it (G. Smith 1990). Two sites with more than 10 mounds each (40LK33 and 40LA6) seem, on the basis of limited investigations, to be of middle period Mississippian age. The only published data come from the Haynes site, near Reelfoot Lake, where the remains of a large wall-trench structure were exposed on the summit of a substructural mound. Two calibrated radiocarbon determinations date the structure to approximately A.D. 1280. Associated ceramic vessels include examples of O'Byam Engraved and Matthews Incised (Lawrence and Mainfort 1993).

Also in contrast to southeastern Missouri, there are actually more Late Mississippian sites recorded in western Tennessee than there are for the preceding period, but the Reelfoot Lake basin, just across the Mississippi River from some of the Cairo Lowland phase sites in Missouri, may have been largely abandoned during Late Mississippian times (Mainfort 1996a).

The bottomlands in Lauderdale County, Tennessee, were occupied extensively during the Late Mississippian period. The largest site, Dry Arm, consists of a 5-meter-tall substructural mound and over a dozen smaller mounds in an area of approximately 2 hectares (contra G. Smith 1990: 153–154). Collections from the site are quite limited, but the occurrence of a burial urn and vertical appliqué ceramics establishes a Late Mississippian–protohistoric age.

The Porter, Jones Bayou, and Sweat sites probably represent sequent occupations by the same political group, with Porter the earliest and Sweat the latest (Mainfort and Moore 1998). A single sherd of Campbell Appliqué and two fairly large triangular points were found at the latter site. Porter and Jones Bayou each cover at least 5 hectares, and each has an associated substructural mound and cemetery (Mainfort 1991), whereas the area of the later Sweat site is less than 2 hectares. Two smaller sites (40LA17 and Fullen), each with the remains of a single mound, are situated about 10 kilometers west of the Jones Bayou cluster.

South of the Fort Pillow ridge are the Graves Lake site (discussed earlier) and the Hatchie site, both of which lack associated mounds. The latter is only 3 kilometers south of Graves Lake and is probably the earlier of the two; it is also the larger, with an estimated area of at least 5 hectares. Proceeding south approximately 10 kilometers brings us to the previously discussed Richardson's Landing site, located just south of part of the Nodena plantation in Arkansas (Mainfort 1996b; Mainfort and Moore 1998).

With an area of approximately 2 hectares, the Wilder site is situated along a meander scar about 7 kilometers south of Richardson's Landing; a mound was reported by a former landowner (G. Smith 1990), although no traces of it remain. This site apparently produced a number of vessels in the collection of the amateur archaeologist James Hampson, and the "teapot" vessel illustrated by S. Williams (1980: 107) probably was obtained from Wilder as well. Hampson also visited the Rast site, 8 kilometers to the south, but obtained little material there. The site has an area of 1.5 hectares and includes an associated mound of unknown function. Some 15 kilometers to the south, the Jeter site is a blufftop town with a single mound and a cemetery within an area of about 2 hectares; this site may represent a relatively early Late Mississippian occupation (Mainfort 1991). Judging from frequencies of decorated ceramic types, all of the recorded Late Mississippian sites north of the Loosahatchie River (just north of Memphis) appear to be closely related to sites of the Nodena phase in northeastern Arkansas (Mainfort 1999).

Chucalissa, located in south Memphis, was described earlier. Radiocarbon determinations and stratigraphy indicate that the site was occupied for at least 100 years, with most occupation occurring during the Late Mississippian period (Mainfort 1996b). More than 100 burials have been excavated (Nash 1972). Adult males are overrepresented in mound burials, with children virtually absent; adult males from mound contexts also exhibit a higher incidence of traumatic injuries than other subpopulations. No evidence of epidemic disease has been reported (Nash 1972; Powell 1992).

Few sites in western Tennessee have produced evidence of post-1500 occupation. Vertical appliqué ceramics have been reported from Otto Sharpe, Dry Arm, Sweat, Graves Lake, Bishop, and Chucalissa, but the absence of endscrapers and gadrooned bottles suggests that Chucalissa probably was abandoned prior to the arrival of de Soto. The Dry Arm and Sweat sites may have persisted into post–de Soto times, but larger artifact samples will be required to confirm this possibility.

Both the artifact assemblage and radiocarbon determinations indicate that the Graves Lake site was occupied into the mid-sixteenth century. Bishop, a site of at least 1 hectare on the Hatchie River, approximately 22 kilometers east of its mouth, also was excavated by Hampson (see S. Williams 1980). The Roper collection at the Memphis Pink Palace Museum includes a number of vessels from the site, including a Campbell Appliqué jar, several helmet-shaped vessels, and fragments of a burial urn; many vessels exhibit vertical appliqué handles. Hampson collected several endscrapers (Peabody Museum, Lower Mississippi Valley Survey files). Presence of a large cemetery is indicated by the numerous ceramic vessels, but nothing is presently known about the associated habitation area. The Bishop site undoubtedly was partially contemporary with Graves Lake and continued to function well into the late 1500s.

The Hales Point site, formerly located about 8 kilometers north of Dry Arm, might also have dated to the late sixteenth century (Williams 1980). Unfortunately, most, if not all, of this large site has been claimed by the Mississippi River.

As discussed previously, the Otto Sharpe site represents the latest aboriginal occupation in the subarea. Two radiocarbon determinations place its occupation in the mid-seventeenth century. The association of European artifacts with the distinctive late lithic complex and vertical appliqué ceramics lends the site considerable significance.

Even allowing for the likelihood that several sites dating between 1400 and 1500 represent sequent occupations of a single sociopolitical group, it seems apparent that the number of occupied sites in western Tennessee dropped markedly prior to de Soto's *entrada*. Current interpretation of the temporal relationships among several sites in this subarea indicates that later sites tend to be smaller, adding support to this argument. Only two west Tennessee sites can be assigned confidently to the period between 1541 and 1600. In the early to mid-seventeenth century, the Otto Sharpe site may have been the only sizable Native American site in western Kentucky or western Tennessee.

EASTERN ARKANSAS. According to Morse and Morse (1983), between A.D. 1200 and 1400 the Mississippian societies inhabiting eastern Arkansas were characterized by a dispersed settlement pattern, with only a single multi-mound town associated with each polity. This view is contradicted by data from the completely excavated middle period Mississippian Moon site (Benn 1992, 1998), discussed earlier. The postulated shift in settlement pattern around 1400, coincident with the appearance of Late Mississippian material culture (D. Morse 1989, 1990), may not have occurred. A date of 1400 traditionally is used for the onset of the Nodena phase, which the Morses (1983) viewed as lasting for approximately 250 years and which D. Morse (1990) equated with the province of Pacaha in the de Soto chronicles.

The material culture of Nodena phase sites is very similar to that described earlier for other post-1400 sites in the study area; it includes typical Late Mississippian decorated ceramic types, Nodena points, chert adzes, and ground basalt celts. Extensive excavations at Upper Nodena by James Hampson, the University of Arkansas Museum, and the Alabama Museum of Natural History have provided some insights into the organization of one of the largest (greater than 6 hectares) centers of the phase. Three substructural mounds partially surround a plaza area; the existence of two smaller mounds has yet to be confirmed. Hampson excavated more than 60 houses, but descriptions have never been published. Limited professional excavations disclosed the remains of a rebuilt wall-trench house measuring approximately 5.5 meters square. The sharply defined margins of the site imply the existence of a moat or palisade, but no evidence of such a structure has been identified archaeologically (D. Morse 1989, 1990). No head pots or snubnosed endscrapers have been recovered at Upper Nodena; two relatively late artifacts, a burial urn and a catlinite disk pipe, have been found (Morse and Morse 1983).

At least 1,755 skeletons were excavated at Upper Nodena under controlled, albeit primitive, circumstances; numerous others have been destroyed by plowing and relic hunters. The extensive collections and burial records at the Arkansas and Alabama museums remained virtually unstudied for over half a century, but recently an excellent summary of the mortuary data was completed by Fisher-Carroll (1997), who found minimal evidence for the marked social differentiation often associated with "chiefdoms." Most burials occurred in small groups throughout the town, but excavation of a small burial "mound" (Mound C) exposed about 345 interments. Originally, all but two of these were reported to be adult males, but analysis of 18 individuals from this locality by Powell (1989: 70) identified 2 children, 5 adult females, 8 adult males, and 3 adults of indeterminate sex. The aberrant demography described by the excavators thus appears to be the result of misidentification. Mortuary ceramics were fairly common at Upper Nodena, but shell, bone, and lithic artifacts were rarely found in graves. No clear examples of sociotechnic items such as spatulate celts or large copper ornaments were recovered from any burials (Fisher-Carroll 1997).

Analysis of the extant skeletal collections by Powell (1989, 1990) found no evidence for death linked to epidemic diseases. Indeed, the examined remains suggested relatively good nutrition and the typical Mississippian pattern of dental caries associated with corn agriculture. The excavated skeletal remains obviously represent an undefined fraction of the total number of interments at the site. Moreover, the age and sex distribution falls far outside the parameters for a normal living population and therefore is unsuited for the generation of life tables and living population estimates. Nonetheless, it is instructive to note that a living population of 1,000 could produce as many as 5,000 individual interments within a period of 100 years, assuming an annual death rate of 5.0 percent, as computed by Howells (1960) for Indian Knoll, Kentucky. Using Buikstra's (1976: 24–25) calculated death rate of 2.5 percent, the same number of interments would be produced in 200 years.

As Fisher-Carroll (1997) pointed out, the Nodena phase concept is in serious need of refinement (see also O'Brien 1995). Data about most sites are limited to those from surface collections and sketch maps, and the few sites that have produced relatively large, published ceramic samples vary considerably (see Mainfort 1999; Phillips 1970). The geographical clusters of Nodena phase sites proposed by D. Morse (1989, 1990) may potentially represent distinct cultural entities. An adequate understanding of the Nodena phase settlement pattern will require systematic surveys (see P. Morse 1981), data from controlled excavations, and radiocarbon dates from good contexts.

Clearly, all of the major Nodena phase sites were not strictly contemporaneous. Morse's observation that occupation at Upper Nodena ceased prior to de Soto's arrival in Arkansas is supported by the chronology presented earlier in this chapter. The inhabitants of Upper Nodena probably relocated to the smaller Middle Nodena site, which has produced endscrapers but lacks mounds (D. Morse 1989, 1990; cf. S. Williams 1980). Nine head pots reportedly were found at Pecan Point, implying an occupation that continued later than the one at Upper Nodena. Two sites on Bradley Ridge have produced European artifacts, including brass and iron beads, brass scrap, and glass beads. D. Morse (1990) has proposed that one of the Bradley Ridge sites is the town of Pacaha mentioned in the de Soto chronicles. In light of the length of the Spaniards' stay in Pacaha, the paucity of Spanish artifacts recovered from this cluster of sites is curious. Regardless of specific historical ties, it is clear that some large sites of the Nodena phase not only cross the de Soto time line but may have continued into the seventeenth century.

The Grigsby site, near Pocohontas, Arkansas, has produced more than 100 European artifacts, including glass and copper beads, gun parts, iron ax and knife fragments, and a glass mirror fragment (D. Morse 1992). A number of large triangular points and several endscrapers were also recovered. No comparable sites have been identified in northeastern Arkansas, and D. Morse (1992) equated Grigsby with the Michigamea village noted by Marquette in 1673. Although ethnic affiliation cannot be substantiated, a late seventeenth-century age is plausible for the small sample of European artifacts.

If D. Morse's interpretation of the relationship between Upper and Middle Nodena is correct (and it is quite plausible, insofar as endscrapers have been collected from Middle but not from Upper Nodena), then we have at least one instance of a major town's being abandoned prior to 1541, with the surviving population founding a significantly smaller new town. Such a scenario is plausible in light of some of Father Gravier's (1900) comments about a potentially comparable situation that he observed among the Quapaw in 1700. That the pre–de Soto abandonment of Upper Nodena was not an isolated event is suggested by the lack of diagnostic artifacts such as endscrapers at many (perhaps most) of the larger Nodena phase sites. This points to the likelihood of significant population decline preceding or immediately following the arrival of the Spaniards. The extremely limited distribution of early French artifacts at Nodena phase sites provides a fairly firm basis for inferring catastrophic population decline between 1541 and 1650. By the 1670s, the Michigamea, recent arrivals in the region, may have occupied what is presently the only known Native American village of that age in northeastern Arkansas (Bauxar 1978; Callender 1978b; D. Morse 1992).

The region immediately west of the Nodena phase, along the St. Francis and Tyronza Rivers, was inhabited by societies of the contemporaneous Parkin phase, which has been equated with the province of Casqui mentioned in the de Soto chronicles (P. Morse 1981; Morse and Morse 1983). As in the case of the Nodena phase, sometime prior to 1400 populations became concentrated into large, often fortified towns; small farmsteads are not known to have been part of the settlement system. The Parkin phase appears to be an in situ development, since many Parkin phase sites were occupied during the Middle Mississippian period (P. Morse 1981). The Moon site (Benn 1992, 1998) may represent a society ancestral to the Parkin phase; it is located about 20 kilometers from the Parkin phase Hazel site. Archaeologically, the Parkin phase is distinguished primarily by a high ratio of coarse-shell-temper (Mississippi Plain) to fine-shell-temper (Bell Plain) wares (Phillips 1970; see also Mainfort 1999).

A systematic survey of a substantial portion of the Parkin phase area by P. Morse (1981) yielded valuable data on site size and location, but use of these data to examine the settlement system is complicated by a lack of radiocarbon dates and published artifact counts from the relevant sites. With an area of 6.9 hectares, the Parkin site itself covers an area twice as large as any other site of the phase and may be confidently viewed as the paramount town. Four sites, each with an area of at least 2.8 hectares, may represent secondary centers, but there are 10 additional sites ranging in size from 1.6 to 2.4 hectares, including some with multiple mounds, and some of these might also have been of considerable political importance.

P. Morse (1981) seems to imply that most, if not all, of the larger Parkin phase sites were contemporaneous. Though this may be the case, the close proximity of some sites (e.g., Vernon Paul and Neeley's Ferry, which are only 1.7 kilometers apart) raises the possibility of sequent occupations at nearby sites. Sherd counts are not terribly instructive in this regard, but the absence of Kent Incised in the large (greater than 3,000 sherds) ceramic collections from Barton Ranch, Turnbow, and Williamson (see Mainfort 1999), as well as the lack of Vernon Paul Appliqué at the first two sites, may hint that these sites date early within the Parkin phase.

The Parkin site clearly was occupied at, and subsequent to, the de Soto baseline, and it may actually have been visited by the Spaniards (Mitchem 1996a, 1996b; Morse and Morse 1983). Major features include a 6.5-meter-tall platform mound, at least six smaller mounds, and a well-preserved moat surrounding the central portion of the site on three sides. The Clarksdale bells and chevron bead from Parkin are unquestionably linked to the brief Spanish presence, and the occurrence of endscrapers is also noteworthy

(P. Morse 1981; S. Williams 1980). The remains of a large wooden post exposed atop the large platform mound yielded a calibrated radiocarbon date range of 1515–1663, raising the possibility that the post might represent the remains of the large wooden cross erected at Casqui by de Soto in 1541 (Mitchem 1996b). A number of radiocarbon assays have recently been published for the Parkin site (Table 13.1), as has an overview of excavations there (Mitchem 1996a, 1996b).

There is presently no evidence of pre–de Soto depopulation within the Parkin phase. Indeed, accepting the equation of the Parkin phase with the province of Casqui as correct, a vigorous polity with settlements ranging in size from 20 to 400 houses is described by the chroniclers (P. Morse 1981). Unfortunately, the large fortified towns of the Parkin phase would have provided an ideal setting for the spread of epidemic disease. The occurrence of endscrapers at only two Parkin phase sites (Parkin and Rose Mound) suggests a major population decline in the wake of the de Soto expedition, and the lack of reported French trade goods probably reflects the passing of the Parkin phase and its people by the early seventeenth century.

Occupying a roughly triangular area extending northward from the mouth of the St. Francis River, the Kent phase is the final Late Mississippian–protohistoric cultural manifestation treated in this chapter. Here I use the Kent phase concept in the more restrictive geographic sense employed by House (1991), wherein "Kent" is used simply to refer to a group of 19 Late Mississippian–protohistoric sites in Lee County, Arkansas. As with the other subareas discussed here, interpretation of the Kent phase is hindered by the very limited extent of professional excavations (as well as extensive depredations by commercial collectors), but House (1991, 1993) has done a commendable job of synthesizing the available data.

Defining attributes of the Kent I period (A.D. 1350–1450) include many of the typical Late Mississippian ceramic types and varieties mentioned earlier, as well as the absence of triangular strap, triangular appliqué, and vertical appliqué handles. Only a single large site (Davis) is presently assignable to the Kent I subphase (1350–1450); it includes two mounds in an area of 1 hectare. Eleven other sites, most of them less than 0.5 hectare in size, may also date to this period. Thus, there is a suggestion of some form of dispersed settlement system.

During the Kent II period (1450–1550), population levels seem to have peaked, and the greatest number of towns was occupied. This period is characterized by the appearance of Barton Incised, *var. Kent,* the ceramic handle styles noted previously, and rims with beveled interiors. Kent III (1550–1600) is marked by the addition of Nodena points and endscrapers to the cultural inventory of Kent II; as already discussed, Nodena points have been documented in good fifteenth-century contexts elsewhere in the study area. A Clarksdale bell was collected at the Clay Hill site, re-

portedly in association with a non-repouseé copper eagle, and glass beads were reported with a burial at the Kent site. Kent III, therefore, represents a local equivalent of the Armorel phase (S. Williams 1980). Only four sites have components that can be confidently assigned to this time period, supporting an interpretation of population reduction (House 1991, 1993).

Occupation and mound construction at many of the largest Kent phase towns occurred after 1450. These include such "classic" St. Francis–type settlements as Soudan (2 mounds, area of 2 hectares), Kent (6 mounds, 6 hectares), Clay Hill (2 mounds, 2 hectares), and Starkley (1 mound, 3 hectares). The apparent lack of small sites datable to this period is consistent with population nucleation; House (1993) is appropriately cautious in his interpretations due to limitations of the data base. One major shortcoming is the lack of conclusive chronometric evidence from the Kent site itself. This 6-hectare site has an associated platform mound 5 meters tall, making it an obvious candidate for a paramount regional site. Until events at Kent come more clearly into focus, settlement models for the region cannot be robust. Significantly, radiocarbon evidence suggests that initial occupation (and hence mound construction) at Clay Hill did not occur until sometime after 1500 (House 1993; see Table 13.1).

The apparent late florescence in the Kent phase area, as expressed at Clay Hill and perhaps several other sites, evidently was of short duration. No early seventeenth-century artifacts have been reported from Kent phase sites, providing compelling evidence of a drastic reduction in population and/or virtual abandonment of the lower St. Francis drainage by about 1650.

Summary and Discussion

Between approximately A.D. 1000 and 1500, the central Mississippi Valley supported what must have been among the largest populations of Native Americans in eastern North America. By the beginning of the eighteenth century, the region was sparsely populated, the only well-documented settlements being those of the Arkansas/Quapaw near the mouth of the Arkansas River.

In attempting to document and chronicle these aboriginal population changes during the period 1400–1700 in the traditional Mississippian "heartland," I have focused in this chapter on two critical issues. The first is the vacant quarter hypothesis, which states that the large Mississippian towns in the northern subareas of the study area were abandoned before 1500 and probably almost a century sooner (S. Williams 1983, 1990). I assessed this hypothesis using specific data sets, including radiometric and artifactual evidence. Although the hypothesis cannot be definitively regarded as validated, examination of the data relied upon by critics (e.g., Lewis 1986, 1990) does not support claims that large civic-ceremonial centers in southeastern

Missouri and western Kentucky continued to flourish into the sixteenth century. Recent data from the Langdon site (Dunnell 1998), however, hint that the postulated abandonment was not universal or that it occurred only farther to the north.

Second, although the precontact demise of major centers in the northern subareas of the central Mississippi Valley may not have been linked to population reductions, it is apparent that aboriginal population declined dramatically throughout the study area between approximately 1500 and 1700. The large towns and complex political organizations described in the de Soto accounts no longer existed by the later half of the seventeenth century. Yet depopulation appears not to have been uniform in its effects. For example, the Nodena phase may have been on the wane prior to 1541, but major post-1500 occupation and mound construction seem to be fairly securely demonstrated for the nearby Kent phase. The lack of French trade goods at sites in the Kent and Parkin phase areas provides strong evidence that post-1600 populations were sparse.

That major population declines occurred in the central Mississippi Valley is supported by evidence from all of the subareas discussed in this chapter, but establishing causality remains an elusive goal. In this regard, Hoffman (1993) has called attention to several matters of potentially crucial importance to unraveling the complexities of protohistoric population dislocations and decline in the study area, specifically eastern Arkansas. First, since the de Soto narratives do not mention the outbreak of an epidemic during the Spaniards' lengthy stay in the town of Pacaha, there is a strong possibility that the Spaniards did not introduce smallpox into the region. Smallpox symptoms typically appear within a few days of exposure, as was graphically reported in the eyewitness account presented earlier. Hence, invoking epidemic disease (particularly smallpox) in the wake of the de Soto *entrada* as a major cause of depopulation during the late sixteenth and early seventeenth centuries in the central Mississippi Valley may be unwarranted.

Moreover, intimations of drought recorded by the chroniclers (especially in Casqui) are supported by dendrochronological evidence indicating that the "worst June drought period for Arkansas in the past 450 yr." occurred between approximately 1549 and 1577 (Hoffman 1993; Stahle, Cleaveland, and Hehr 1985). Repeated crop failures would, of course, have been extremely disruptive to the agricultural populations described by the Spaniards, not only by causing dietary stress but also by undermining the basis of political and ideological power. Compounding this situation, de Soto's political machinations involving Casqui and Pacaha effectively demolished long-standing political and social relationships between these groups and quite possibly instigated widespread warfare throughout eastern Arkansas.

The conclusions presented here are necessarily tentative. Despite significant advances in recent decades, the available data are not yet adequate to definitively answer the critical questions I have discussed. Throughout the chapter, I have stressed the need for additional fieldwork and published results. The interpretations offered are surely but a pale reflection of the complex social, political, and biological processes that operated during the late prehistoric and protohistoric periods in the central Mississippi Valley. Adoption of a multicausal framework will be essential to delineating these processes.

Acknowledgments

Investigations in western Tennessee were funded by the Tennessee Division of Archaeology. Mitch Childress and Gerald Smith provided unpublished data from Chucalissa. Michael O'Brien shared his knowledge of Pemiscot County, Missouri, sites. Discussions with Dan Morse and Stephen Williams greatly assisted preparation of this chapter; neither is accountable for any errors and misinterpretations contained herein. Earlier versions of this chapter were reviewed by Wes Cowan, Mary Kwas, Bill Lawrence, and Charles McNutt, all of whom offered helpful substantive and editorial advice.

Locations of Primary Collections

Most artifacts and field records for the referenced sites in southeastern Missouri are housed at the University of Missouri. The Murray State University research center at Wickliffe Mounds, Kentucky, curates materials from the Fain King explorations, as well as those from the systematic investigations that began in the 1980s. Data generated by the Western Kentucky Project are housed at the University of Illinois. Field stations of the Arkansas Archeological Survey in Jonesboro and Pine Bluff maintain collections from the Nodena and Parkin and the Kent phase areas, respectively; several large collections from southeastern Missouri are also located in Jonesboro. Most of the western Tennessee material discussed here is curated by the Tennessee Division of Archaeology at Pinson Mounds State Archaeological Area. Other western Tennessee artifacts and records, particularly those from Chucalissa, are housed at the C. H. Nash Museum–Chucalissa, University of Memphis. Data from the Lower Mississippi Valley Survey files were obtained from copies housed in the Department of Anthropology, University of Memphis.

Note

1. Two assays were not used in computing this value. Using the "test" option in CALIB, Beta-34405 was revealed to be a statistical outlier, and it was excluded from averaging. Beta-43955 was run on a sample of red cedar; evidence from the American Bottom demonstrates that conifers should not be used for radiometric dating (Holley 1989).

14

The Vacant Quarter Hypothesis and the Yazoo Delta

This chapter encompasses a 450-year period (A.D. 1400–1850) in the Yazoo Delta, a physiographic region in the southern part of the Mississippi Valley (Fig. 14.1) for which I trace the known Indian occupation against the background of current archaeological and historical data.

It was during a 1978 field trip through the northern end of the lower Mississippi Valley that the notion came to me that there were some anomalies in site occupations during Late Mississippian times (Williams 1980: 105). It seemed that the Cairo Lowland, adjacent to the confluence of the Mississippi and Ohio Rivers, was virtually devoid of late period sites, whereas the southern part of the Missouri bootheel held a cluster of components closely related to those found in the heavily occupied middle reaches of the St. Francis River in northeastern Arkansas (Morse and Morse 1983: Fig. 12.1). Some of these latter sites lasted into historic times, whereas all the sites farther north lacked late time markers (Williams 1962).

From that perception came the "vacant quarter" hypothesis (Williams 1983, 1990; see also Mainfort, this volume), which suggested that the once-populous major Mississippian centers such as Cahokia, Kincaid, and Angel, as well as a whole host of minor sites in the Ohio-Mississippi confluence area, were essentially vacant some time after 1400–1450. The concept grew to include the Nashville basin on the Cumberland River and also the Tennessee River drainage north from Shiloh. There were, of course, some notable exceptions, such as the Caborn-Welborn phase sites on the lower Wabash River (Green and Munson 1978) and the now infamous Slack Farm site just across the Ohio River in Kentucky (Munson, Pollack, and Powell 1988). Even the great Alabama center at Moundville was sparsely occupied after 1450 (Steponaitis 1983: 160, 168–174), and such also seemed to be the case for the two major Yazoo Delta centers of Lake George and Winterville (Brain 1988: Fig. 194, 1989: 125–128; Williams 1983, 1990).

It should be emphasized, since misunderstandings have already occurred (Telster 1992: 14, 28), that the vacant quarter hypothesis did not suggest *total* absence of human occupation (see, for example, Mainfort, this volume). Instead, it highlighted the demise of the major "ceremonial" centers. The hypothesis has been briefly discussed favorably in some regional syntheses (Butler 1991: 272–273; B. D. Smith 1986: 58–60) and even in some popular accounts (Nabokov and Snow 1992: 140; National Geographic Society 1988: 33). There has been some dissent elsewhere (Lewis 1988: 766, 1990: 42, 53–55).

It is within such an intellectual framework that I review "late times" in the Yazoo Delta.[1] The lower Mississippi Valley, of which the Yazoo Delta is one of the most clearly defined subregions, was encountered repeatedly in early North American history by European explorers and, later, settlers. The Spanish explorer Hernando de Soto crossed it first, in 1540–1541, and found major centers of Native American occupation on both sides of the river he called

STEPHEN WILLIAMS

Figure 14.1. The lower Mississippi Valley, showing the Yazoo Delta region.

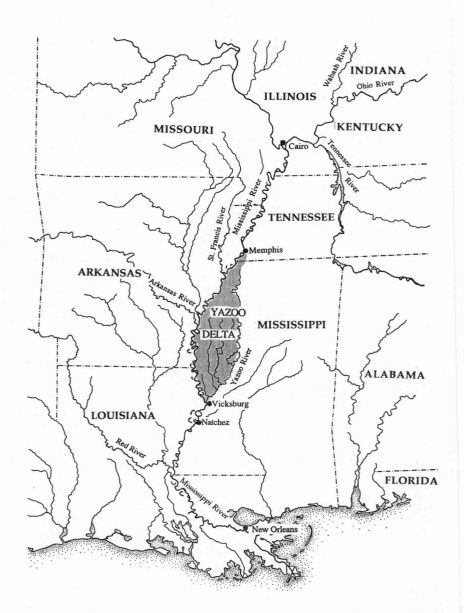

the Espirito Santo. The exact route taken by his plunderous *entrada* is still debated, but it no doubt traversed the Yazoo Delta somewhere in its northern half (Brain 1985; Hudson, Smith, and DePratter 1990).

Marquette and Joliet, on their much later adventure down the Mississippi (1673), found an "echoing stillness" (Bakeless 1950: 327). They saw few, if any, major *occupied* village sites. In the past, many scholars, myself included, have interpreted this finding as indicative of a very low Native American population in the lower valley in the 1670s and afterward. Although a careful review of a number of eighteenth- and nineteenth-century narratives and maps does, in fact, seem to reveal such a situation, in this chapter I reach a rather different conclusion.

It now seems apparent that in the entire lower valley, only a few major sites remained on the banks of the Missis-

sippi after about 1670; those were on the bluffs near Memphis, Vicksburg, and Natchez. Indeed, a review of early European settlement in this area shows the folly of locating too near the meandering river. Dozens of short-lived Euroamerican towns appear on eighteenth- and nineteenth-century maps of the region but have since vanished. It took land speculators and other entrepreneurs some time to learn the lesson that the "ancients" knew quite well: do not build your hopes and dreams directly on an active Mississippi River bank.

The message is that repeated reports of only a few occupied sites in the lower valley, whether Indian or European, actually say little about the true nature of the population, if the area was traversed by boat alone. In fact there were many Indian villages in the valley at this time. De Soto could have testified to that; for the most part his ill-fated expedition took the land routes and encountered many inhabited sites, except on its final escape route down the Mississippi at the disastrous end of its mission.

Population estimates unsupported by intensive ground surveys are notoriously inaccurate. Moreover, a common misconception needs to be addressed: in ethnographic and archaeological studies, maps showing tribal distributions tend to fill all the geographic space completely (see Milner, Anderson, and Smith, this volume). There are no "voids." When one gets to the ground truth in archaeology, however, that is seldom the case.[2]

Thus one must be careful to delimit two kinds of space: (1) that covered by artifactual debris—sites and their adjacent "used land"—and (2) tribal "territory"—space between chiefdoms or polities. The latter is both a resource area for various extractive needs and an "empty" buffer between polities. Such space has recently been shown to have existed in the Savannah River region of Georgia (Anderson and Joseph 1988: 314–320, Fig. 72; DePratter 1989: Fig. 7.3). As Milner and his colleagues rightly point out in Chapter 2, understanding these two kinds of space allows the "filling up" of phase distribution maps without overestimating population size by employing large-scale map areas containing only a few sites or by using a simplistic area-multiplied-by-carrying-capacity formula.

On that cautionary note, what follows is a detailed review of the Yazoo Delta from A.D. 1400 to 1850 using a seven-part sequence chart (Fig. 14.2). Unfortunately, space limitations allow for only cursory discussion of the adjacent areas shown on the distribution maps.

A.D. 1400–1500: The Late Prehistoric Period

This period was one of climax in the Yazoo basin. It began with both of the major centers, Winterville and Lake George (Fig. 14.3), in full flower and with many secondary mound centers and towns dotting the landscape (Brain 1988: Fig. 190; Williams and Brain 1983: Figs. 10.7, 10.15, 11.19, 11.20). By the end of the period, both Winterville and Lake George were essentially abandoned (Brain 1988: Fig. 194; Williams 1983, 1990). Especially in the southern half of the delta, the number of sites, and presumably the population as well, was much reduced. The Haynes Bluff site, at the extreme southeastern bluff edge (just above Vicksburg), became the major center, judging from known mound-building activities there (Brain 1988). An empty buffer zone lay between the two main phases in the delta (Brain 1988: Fig. 190).

This decline of the largest Mississippian centers is the linchpin of the vacant quarter hypothesis. In broad perspective, on the basis of current evidence, this vacancy seems to have begun earliest at the northern central Mississippi Valley site of Cahokia (circa A.D. 1250–1350) (Emer-

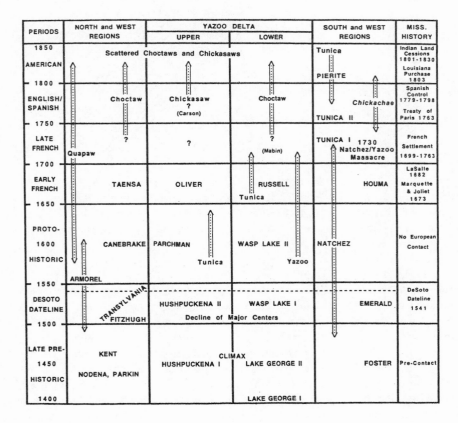

Figure 14.2. Culture history in the Yazoo Delta and adjacent regions, A.D. 1400–1850.

Figure 14.3. Phases and sites in the Yazoo
Delta, A.D. 1400–1500.

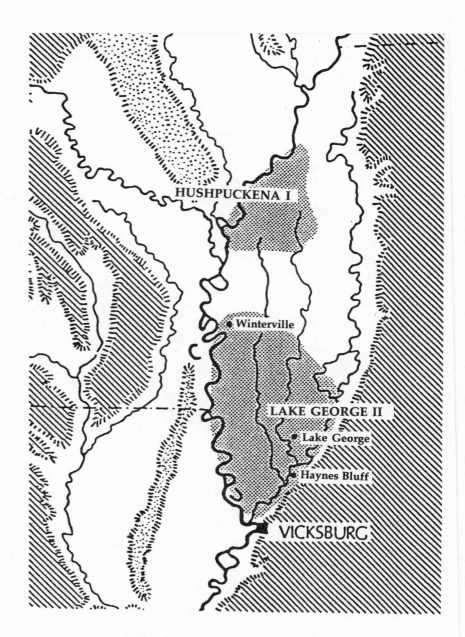

HUSHPUCKENA I

• Winterville

LAKE GEORGE II

• Lake George

• Haynes Bluff

VICKSBURG

son 1991: Fig. 12.1; Hall 1991: 33; Milner 1991: 30, Fig. 2.1).
Moundville, on the Black Warrior River of Alabama, seems
to have been the longest-lasting of the mega-centers in the
Southeast; major occupation there extended until about
1450–1500 (Peebles 1987; Steponaitis 1983: 160, 168–174).

While these major ceremonial centers and surrounding
support-villages were falling into disuse, other, nearby regions were well populated, including the region of the
St. Francis River in northeastern Arkansas (Morse and
Morse 1983: 280) and the Coosa mega-polity of northern
Georgia and Alabama and southeastern Tennessee (De-
Pratter 1983; Smith, this volume). The cause of the decline
of the major Mississippian mound centers remains unresolved; climatic changes (Griffin 1961; Smith 1986) and the
effects of warfare (Larson 1972) seem not to be viable ex-
planations, and the case for disease, of either the human or

the plant variety, so far lacks evidence. Socioeconomic and
political change also has received some well-deserved consideration (Peebles 1986), but it is likely that any search for
a *single* explanation for the decline will prove unfruitful.

A.D. 1500–1550: The de Soto Dateline

De Soto's arrival in the lower Mississippi valley in 1540
changed things forever. The event produced a few well-
known archaeological horizon markers—Clarksdale (or
Oliver) bells,[3] along with beads of cut crystal and glass—
that allow us to set our "timepieces" with some accuracy.
The northern Yazoo was heavily occupied, whereas the
southern half was quite empty save for a few sites along
the bluffs. In the south, only at the site of Satartia (Fig. 14.4)
has a solitary de Soto marker been found—a fragment of

one of the distinctive sheet-brass bells (Brain 1975: 132)—and occupation continued at Haynes Bluff (Brain 1988: 196). In the north, a number of finds and radiocarbon dates confirm that activities were taking place at sites around A.D. 1540, when de Soto would have been crossing the area (Childress 1992; House 1987; Mainfort 1991, 1996b, this volume; Smith and McNutt 1991).

The data seem clear concerning a significant differential of activity in the northern and southern areas of the delta; one cannot fault the evidence. Again, no specific causal factor can be invoked; these regional differences surely existed well before Spanish arrival. Therefore, one can generalize and say that virtually empty regions really did occur, as exemplified by the distribution of the (late protohistoric) Armorel phase in eastern Arkansas and the spottiness of

sites and phases of this period in the lower Ohio Valley (Muller 1986: 184; Williams 1980) and in the Southeast in general (DePratter 1983: Table 2; Smith 1987: 72).

A.D. 1550–1650: The Protohistoric Period

More than 100 years elapsed between the de Soto encounter and the next historic dateline, the French exploring expeditions of 1672–1700. This gap (Brain 1988: 18) remains hard to fill, so the 100-year period is appropriate. Mapping of sites at the midway point (1600) shows a period of profound change (Brain 1988: 272), with the first obvious signs of tribal amalgamation and movement that would characterize the Southeast for much of the next 200 years.

The Quapaw were by this time at the mouth of the

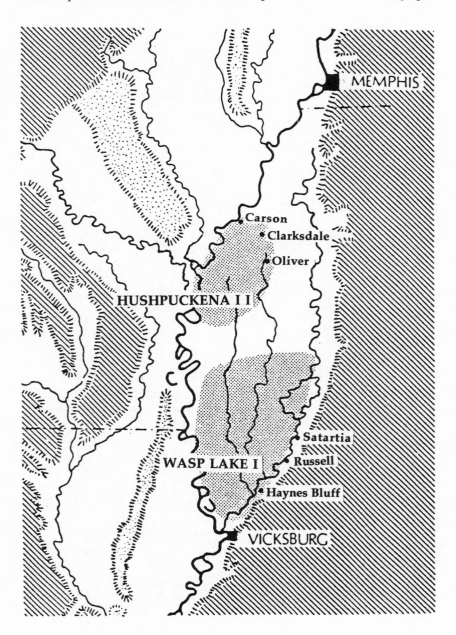

Figure 14.4. Phases and sites in the Yazoo Delta, A.D. 1500–1550.

Arkansas (Fig. 14.5)—their exact origin is still a matter of great discussion (Brain 1988: 281–283; Jeter 1989)—and the Ofo may have arrived on the Yazoo, possibly from the north. Archaeologically, the Armorel phase (ethnically unattributed) held a position to the north of Memphis, while the northern end of the Yazoo basin is thought to have included Tunican speakers who may have come from west of the Mississippi along with numerous Parchman phase residents (Phillips 1970, 2: 939), whose ethnic affiliations are not surmised even today.

The Yazoo (unfortunately little known despite the tribe's strong influence on subsequent cartography) seem also to have been in place near the mouth of the river that bears their name. At this period much less than 50 percent of the Yazoo Delta seems to have had any native occupation, but large bodies of data do not yet bear on that proposition. There is a real gap in knowledge, but it is reasonable to postulate the onslaught of European-introduced epidemic diseases and the consequent decline of native populations into small remnant groups (Brain 1988: Fig. 213).

Figure 14.5. Phases and ethnic groups in the Yazoo Delta, A.D. 1550–1650.

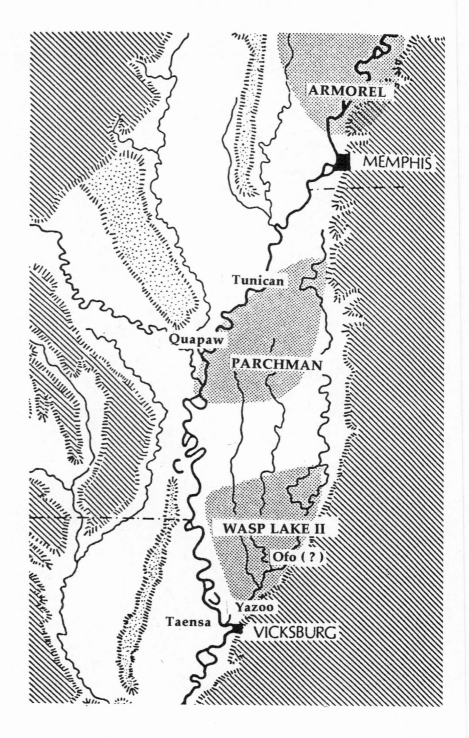

A.D. 1650–1700: The Early French Period

Things seem very different in this period as we begin to get historical documentation for the area again. Not that the data are plentiful or complete; they are in fact quite weak, with some very sketchy maps. The earliest expedition, that of Marquette and Joliet in 1673, was ill recorded, but LaSalle (in 1682) and some subsequent missionary work, especially around the turn of the century (1690s–1710), added much.

Populations seem to have been greatly reduced, with only two areas having measurable groups (Fig. 14.6): those living opposite the mouth of the Arkansas (Oliver phase; Brain 1988: Fig. 198, 277–280), who likely were Quapaw, and those living along the bluffs on the lower half of the Yazoo (Russell phase; Brain 1988: Fig. 198; Williams and Brain 1983: 382–386), probably including the Yazoo and Ofo and possibly the Ibitoupa. The Tunica appear to have trekked south from the northern Yazoo (Brain 1988: 294–297) and were by now resident at the Haynes Bluff site.

The enigmatic Chakchiuma, likely the ancestors of the

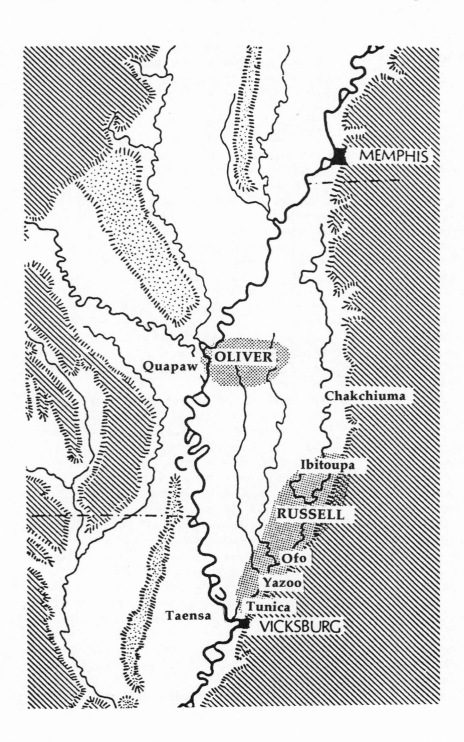

Figure 14.6. Phases and ethnic groups in the Yazoo Delta, A.D. 1650–1700.

Houma of southern Louisiana, seem cartographically to be only on the very eastern edge of the Yazoo Delta, possibly at the Leflore site (Brain 1988: Fig. 203, 284). Otherwise, they remain little known archaeologically.

French cartographic evidence is precise enough to lend these statements some certainty, but the empty wastelands of the interior of the Yazoo Delta are of real concern. Granted that the French were around (Brain 1988: Fig. 214) and that their presence increased markedly in the next decades, the fact is that *none* of the Europeans is known ever to have penetrated the center of the delta region. Our maps and theirs continue to show blank spaces. At present, historical archaeological finds, too, occur only at the delta edges. Is this confirmation of a historic reality or simply fulfillment of prior expectations?[4]

A.D. 1700–1750: The Late French Period

During this period the data bank at last begins to get rich. French cartographers, aided by intrepid surveyors such as Pierre Charles Le Sueur (1700), took seriously the curves and meanders of the great Mississippi from its headwaters to the Gulf. Of course, political machinations had briefly caused the the Mississippi to be rerouted cartographically far to the west, in order to intercept the eastward movement of the Spanish (Franquelin 1684), but from this point onward latitude can usually be discerned from the major bends of the great river and the debouchment of its tributaries.

Literate explorers and missionaries give us, for the first time in the Yazoo area (1698–1730), descriptions of tribes and their customs, including the Tunica, Yazoo, Ofo, and Koroa (Brain 1988: Fig. 203, 294). Little could they have known that it would be over so quickly (Brain 1988: Fig. 215). The Natchez and Yazoo uprisings of 1729 were followed by the virtual extermination of both tribes in the succeeding years.

The Tunica abandoned the Haynes Bluff area in 1702, so they escaped the Yazoo's fate, but they were then attacked in their new southern home by the refugee Natchez. Fortunately, some Tunica survived far to the south (Fig. 14.7); along with (possibly) the Ofo, they were the only original Yazoo Delta groups left (Brain 1988: Fig. 204).

The Quapaw, though reduced in numbers, remained on the lower Arkansas, and the Choctaw and the Chickasaw were waiting in the wings in the east (Brain 1988: Fig. 204; Kenneth Carleton, personal communication 1993). The unanswered questions now are, exactly where were the Choctaw and Chickasaw at 1750, and how much land did they really control and put to use?

In the southern portion of the delta, one bit of enigmatic archaeological data is so far unexplained—namely, materials from the Mabin site, which rests on an anciently occupied part of the east bank of the Big Sunflower River. This rather modest site has produced a fair number of glass beads dating to the eighteenth century (ca. 1720–1760). Phillips

(1970, 1: 325) knew of these historic items, but none of the ceramics now known from the site seems to date to this period. There are also some nineteenth-century remains: a clay pipe and reportedly a burial in a wooden casket (Greengo 1955). Were Choctaw or Chakchiuma here? That question cannot yet be answered.

A.D. 1750–1800: English and Spanish Control

Change of ownership of the territory under consideration was significant during this 50-year period. With the Treaty of Paris in 1763, the English took control of the Mississippi sector of the area, but only until 1779, the end of the American Revolution. In the nearby Louisiana sector, Spanish control ran from 1763 until 1803, the advent of the Louisiana Purchase.

The British, who had early (1700–1715) been pushing trade westward out of the southern coastal colonies, especially trade with the Chickasaw (Brain 1988: Fig. 215), now threw resources and men—surveyors and census takers—at the Mississippi Valley in the first years of the peace. A British cartographic survey of the Mississippi, led by Lieutenant Ross in 1764, compares with that of Le Sueur, and the British also mapped the Indian tribes from the Creeks west to the Mississippi River. John Stuart, the superintendent for Indian affairs, was given the task of obtaining census figures of all the Indians in his southern district, presumably for trading purposes (Alden 1944: 7). His researches have not been published in detail, but maps of the period, especially that by de Brahm in 1766, depended heavily on the survey work of men under Stuart's direction. In many cases the information seems extraordinarily detailed, including census figures on all the known tribes in this large southern department.

A splendid example of British exploration is to be found in the infrequently referenced journey of Captain Harry Gordon, a British officer who descended the Mississippi following the Treaty of Paris in 1763 (Gordon 1766). Gordon was a keen observer and in touch with Native American informants on his way west from Pittsburgh. His journey south, however, from the Illinois country to Natchez in mid-summer of 1766, was a nightmare. The river was low, and he traveled down a "gorge" with high mud walls that were forever crumbling and crashing down. He recorded only the Quapaw at the mouth of Arkansas. Were other tribes present, especially in the Yazoo Delta? He saw none.

But is that really the "ground truth?" Only the Quapaw, Chickasaw, and Choctaw are thought to have been in the area (Fig. 14.8). The English census clearly shows the Choctaw settlements in eastern Mississippi, their fictive homeland. Some scholars suggest that by 1800 the Choctaw were indeed using the Yazoo, but mainly as a hunting ground for deer (White 1983: 10–13).

For the entire 100-year period from 1750 to 1850, it re-

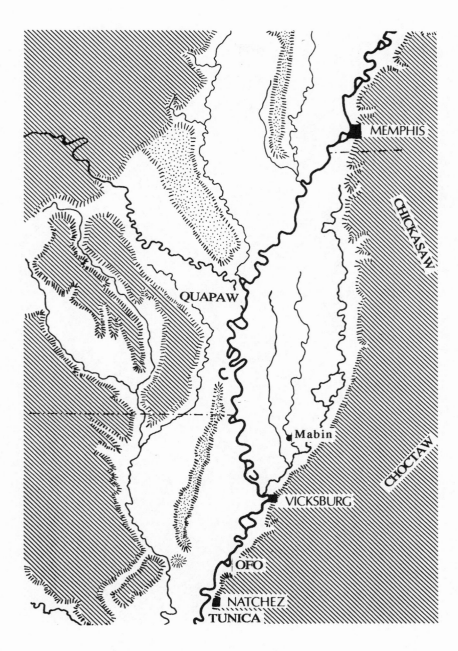

Figure 14.7. The Yazoo Delta after A.D. 1730.

mains uncertain how and to what extent the Choctaw "used" the Yazoo Delta. Conventional history, beginning with Bowman (1904) and Halbert (various) in the 1900s, suggests that the Choctaw hunted and fished in the delta during the nineteenth century. Patricia Galloway (personal communication 1992) believes this scenario is probably accurate, although she admits the data are few. She thinks that the whole area was freed up by the 1730s–1740s, when the former residents (from north to south, the Chakchiuma, Yazoo, Ofo, and Tunica) are known to have left their locations in the southeastern corner of the delta next to the Yazoo River.

The exact nature of the Choctaw's use of the Yazoo Delta for the period 1750–1800 seems not to be well documented, even with regard to their hunting in the region.

Galloway feels, however, that long-term hunting use was sufficient to provide the Choctaw with detailed knowledge of the area, and thus it provided the basis for the post-1800 European settlers' having picked up the Choctaw place names that are now part of the cartographic record.[5]

What is the meaning of the discovery of typical late eighteenth- and nineteenth-century Choctaw "Chichachae Combed" pottery at the Carson site (Clarksdale Library Collection [Penman 1983])? At a minimum, it indicates trade; at most, it signifies resident Choctaw in western Coahoma County, Mississippi. Did the Choctaw have specific hunting grounds? Territorialism would seem quite natural with the divisons of the Choctaw and their different places of access to the delta from north to south. More questions than answers will exist until we acquire more data.

Figure 14.8. The Yazoo Delta, A.D. 1750–1800.

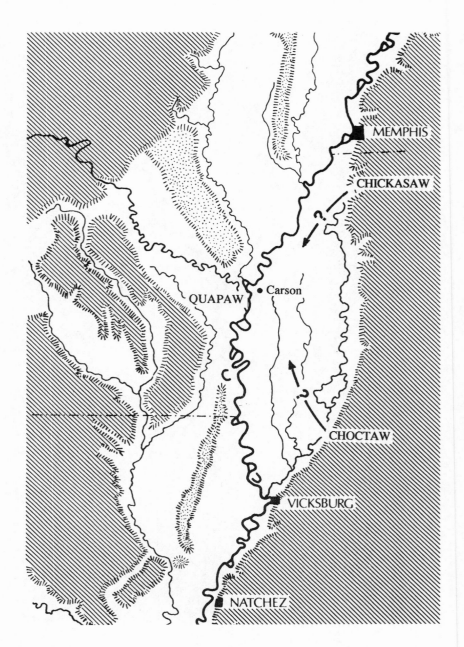

Because in the next century the land of the Yazoo Delta was divided under treaty by the Choctaw and the Chickasaw, perhaps it had indeed been theirs earlier. Information from the Spanish period (1763–1803) throws some light on this topic; a document dated 1793 confirms that Choctaws were hunting on the west side of the Mississippi River (Kinnaird 1946: 114). At this point we can only hope that new data will be forthcoming.

A.D. 1800–1850: The American Period

During this period, a number of significant land transactions took place, involving especially the Choctaw, that should help to clear up the matter of the territory held by that tribe (Fig. 14.9).[6] In 1792, just before the start of the

American period, Spain obtained the land at Vicksburg from the Choctaw for its Fort Nogales (Kinnaird 1946: xv). In 1820, the U.S. Treaty of Doak's Stand with the same tribe transferred much of the southern half of the Yazoo Delta to American ownership and thus opened it for legal occupation. There is some cartographic support, too, for the notion that the so-called Western Division of the Choctaw reached as far west as the Mississippi River (Riley 1915: 150). A good example is "Charlie's Trace" in the northern part of the delta, which was named for an Indian who ran a fueling station for steamboats near Clarksdale in the 1820s and 1830s. He certainly sounds like a resident of some permanence, not a wandering hunter.

Mainly Choctaws and Chickasaws were seen in various parts of the lower valley during the 1830s. We can docu-

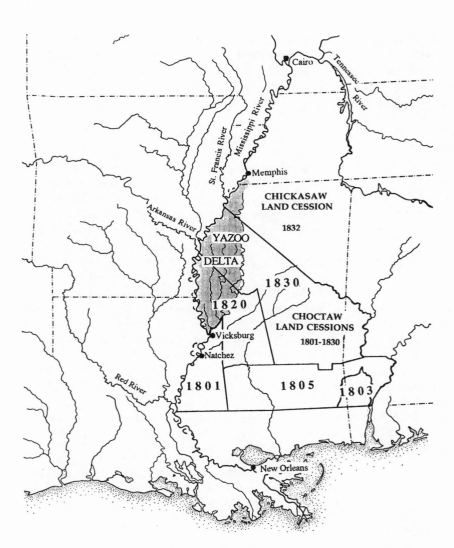

Figure 14.9. Choctaw land cessions, A.D. 1800–1830.

ment Choctaws near Memphis, Natchez, and New Orleans at this time, thanks to two western travelers who were also artists. Karl Bodmer (Joslyn Art Museum 1984: Pl. 113–115), the Swiss artist for Prince Maximilian de Wied, made a little-known trip to New Orleans in January 1833, which has not been completely published.[7] Charles Alexandre Lesueur, the French artist and naturalist, traveled up and down the Mississippi six times between 1817 and 1838 (Fundaburk 1958: Pl. 181–183; Hamy 1968; Leland 1924). Both men identified and drew members of the Choctaw and Chickasaw tribes during their trips.

It is also known that a number of Native Americans who were removed west to Indian Territory returned some years later to their former eastern homelands. South of the delta there were resident Choctaws in Louisiana in the 1850s, especially north of Lake Pontchartrain, as depicted in paintings by Francois Bernard (1846) and Alfred Boisseau (1847) (see Brain 1988: Fig. 209).

These Choctaws would be located and studied by anthropologists, including Swanton (various) and Bushnell (1909), in the first decades of the twentieth century. According to

some scholars (Ken Carleton, personal communication 1993), these Louisiana Choctaws may have been descendants of the southernmost of the three original groups of Choctaws that came together during the eighteenth century as a tripartite confederation in central Mississippi.

The conventional wisdom on Choctaw use of the delta was codified as early as 1900 by Bowman (1904), who saw the Choctaw only hunting there in small migrant groups, but I am not impressed by this hypothesis. The facts are that the Western Division of the Choctaw was well in place before 1830. Greenwood LeFlore, a powerful Choctaw leader, established a plantation on the very edge of the delta in the early 1830s and built his mansion, Malmaison, there in 1854.

It is hypothesized here that Choctaw use of and modest settlement in the Yazoo Delta may have begun no later than shortly after the final abandonment of the southern sector of the Yazoo Bluffs near Haynes Bluff before 1750. Thus the Choctaw would have been familiar with the delta for more than 50 years at the time of the Louisiana Purchase, and they would have had, quite reasonably, their own names for watercourses and locations when the first American settlers came into the area in force in the 1820s.

Certainly it appears that in the nineteenth century, settlers called all Indians in the delta generically "Choctaw." Their reminiscences make reference to encounters with the "Choctaw" and include accounts of the Indians' use of the mounds as "places of resort" during floods (McCain and Capers 1954: 147, 350). That few archaeological finds convincingly document such a Choctaw presence in the delta can be considered a matter of little weight, given the difficulty of "seeing" such a Native American presence during this time period (1800–1850) in any part of the lower Mississippi Valley (Morse and Morse 1983: 324–330; Neuman 1984: 325–327; Price 1976).

Conclusion

Overall, the story of the Yazoo Delta for the period A.D. 1400–1850 is one mainly of movement, dislocation, and reduction of native population until the Choctaw became almost invisible. That major mound centers were deserted before 1500 seems to be confirmed, and large portions of the delta were quite empty in many of the succeeding centuries. Much research remains to be done to ensure that those last important centuries from 1650 to 1850 are properly understood—a statement that applies, unfortunately, to most of the other geographical areas of North America as well.

Coda

In 1994, about a year after making the original presentation on which this chapter is based, I made some changes to it at the suggestion of Wes Cowan, then editor of this volume. Having since then done considerably more research on the later periods of the lower Mississippi Valley, I have found nothing that measurably contradicts my expressed views of the great demographic changes throughout the whole Southeast from 1700 to 1900. Because I felt the manuscript was generally correct in most areas, I declined the opportunity Brose and Mainfort presented to rewrite this chapter in 1998. However, one new fact relating to the lower Yazoo region deserves publication. That is the reassignment of the temporal position of the Edwards, *var. Sunflower,* point referred to as a late protohistoric derivative of a Gary-type point in the Lake George site report (Williams and Brain 1983: 225–227, 325, Table 9.22, 327, Table 9.23). As Vin Steponaitis noted in 1997, a non-arrow projectile point thought to date to A.D. 1400–1500 would be quite an anomaly. Though complex, my immediate analyses of proveniences detailed in the Lake George report (Williams and Brain 1983) make it clear that the published cultural and temporal assignment was wrong. All of the variety Sunflower points were in mixed secondary deposits and should not

have been dated by the most recent ceramics in those levels. The Edwards, *var. Sunflower,* projectile point should date a thousand years earlier than defined at Lake George, just where other scholars find such points, in Deasonville–Bayland contexts. Mea culpa.

Acknowledgments

I wish to thank my Lower Mississippi Survey staff members Michael O'Grady, for his extensive research assistance on this project and its graphics, and Brian Geon, for his editorial help. I gratefully acknowledge Patricia Galloway's generous tutorial on matters concerning the Choctaw and the very helpful consultation of Kenneth Carleton, archaeologist for the Choctaw Tribe of Mississippi. I received valuable research aid from my archaeological colleagues of the Yazoo Delta area: John Connaway, Janet Ford, Jay Johnson, and Robert Thorne. The staff of the Museum of the Mississippi Department of Archives and History in Jackson have been uniformly helpful and interested in my research objectives for the past 30 years.

Notes

1. The research behind this paper started some 40 years ago, when, following three field seasons at Lake George (1958–1960), I happened upon data relating to the historic period (Williams 1988). With that start (Williams 1962), I then searched for the Taensa tribe (Williams 1966, 1967); work on the Tunica began in 1969 (Williams 1981a, 1988). The Lower Mississippi Survey (LMS) research culminated in two major volumes (Brain 1979, 1988). Other, broader perspectives for late times in the lower valley were also set forth during this period: the vacant quarter hypothesis (Williams 1983, 1990) and the definition of the Armorel phase (Williams 1980) and its ethnographic connections (Williams 1981b). Detailed discussions of tribal distributions, especially in the Yazoo Delta, are to be found in the Lake George report (Williams and Brain 1983) and in the Tunica volume (Brain 1988). The views set forth here follow in the main those two summaries, but new conclusions, especially for the period 1700–1850, are presented that reflect my own reassessments of both old and new data.

2. Estimates of land use have a special "fudge factor" in the Mississippi alluvial valley. Quite some time ago (Williams 1956), I pointed out (in what others now call my "dry foot hypothesis" [Lafferty and Sierzchula 1989: 42–43]) that only a small proportion of this bottomland was really habitable in the preindustrial era. My current best estimate is that this proportion averages about 20 to 25 percent of a county or parish located wholly within the "true alluvial valley" (Phillips, Ford, and Griffin 1951: 7). I would definitely include in such a characterization the American Bottom in East St. Louis, Illinois, and the lower Ohio "Black Bottoms" of southern Illinois.

3. These distinctive copper bells were first studied in 1971 by Ian Brown, as a Harvard undergraduate (cited in Brain 1975: 132). He called them "Oliver" bells, since the Peabody sample was from that site. Later, Jeff Brain (1975) referred to them as

"Clarksdale" bells, despite the fact that none is known from that specific locality. Interestingly, a member of the Clark family, responsible for the name of the town, has objected to Brain's terminology. He prefers the term "Oliver"; that type site, which produced the first bells studied, was also owned by his ancestor.

4. A recent review of LMS data suggests that my earlier statements concerning the protohistoric period in the Yazoo Delta need further revision. The distribution of the marker type Fatherland Incised (dating quite clearly after 1500), some late lithic forms (pipe drills), sherd disks, and even blue glass beads clearly show a light but recognizable historic presence at Lake George and other Yazoo basin sites. Ethnic affliation can not be ventured at this time.

5. Another heretofore unused source of information on the situation in the Yazoo Delta has been a modest LMS study of Indian place names in the region. Choctaw names abound, from counties such as Coahoma and Issaquena and streams like Bogue Phalia and Hushpuckena to places such as Itta Bena and Nitta Yuma. Earlier studies (Gannett 1902; Halbert 1899a) are of general help, though they also include some doubtful linguistic "guesses."

6. During this period some major U.S. governmental actions also took place that would have as great an effect on the native populations as anything so far discussed. I refer to the "resettlement program" passed by President James Madison but put into effect by the "enforcer," President Andrew Jackson. This taking of Indian land by the government in 1831–1833 meant major movement, or at least regional relocation, for most of the southern Indians, who were so carefully documented first by the English and later by the Americans on the so-called Armstrong rolls. In the aftermath of the more than five "trails of tears" to the Indian Territory (Oklahoma), scattered fragments of tribal entities were left all over the Southeast, including the area around the Yazoo Delta. The Choctaw had a treaty right to remain in Mississippi, but only a small number of them (29 families) seem to have tried to remain behind legally. Many more, however, did indeed stay (see White 1983).

7. I became aware of Bodmer's southern trek through the work of my old friend William C. Sturtevant of the Smithsonian Institution. I am grateful to Marsha V. Gallagher, curator of material culture at the Joslyn Art Musuem, for allowing me access to a portion of the unpublished translation of Maximilian's field journal by Emery C. Szmrecsanyi.

15

Prelude to History on the Eastern Prairies

At the time of European contact, Indians of the eastern prairies possessed a cultural life that was organized around an economy divided between long-distance upland hunting of bison or elk and localized hunting and mixed agriculture. The semisedentary settlement practices associated with this economy were markedly different from those that had existed 500 years earlier. Then, the interior of eastern North America was populated by concentrated settlements supported by floodplain agriculture and localized foraging. Principle among these settlements was that of the American Bottom in East St. Louis, Illinois, with its great social, economic, and political center of Cahokia, which is commonly regarded as the archaeological key to the upper watershed of the Mississippi and the eastern prairies (Fowler and Hall 1978). As important as Cahokia once was to the area, by the time of European contact this site and similar towns were no longer occupied, and throughout colonial times it rested in complete obscurity. Except for a single instance in the early nineteenth century, resident native people laid no claim to the massive earthworks of Cahokia or its neighbors.[1] Outside the greater Cahokia area, residence was so transient that by 1800 the distribution of cultures bore little connection to the cultural and political map of 500 years earlier.[2]

What happened to have led to such a change? Since the heyday of the Mound Builder myth there has been no lack of solutions posed for the apparent discontinuity between precontact and postcontact cultures in this part of the Midwest. Historians have offered their perspective, but largely from an eastern standpoint, and long after fundamental changes were well under way (e.g., Hunt 1940). Comparative ethnology has challenged the historian's perspective by pointing to aboriginal culture geography as indicating an earlier, more complex way of life identified with Central Siouan–speaking peoples that was overlain by cultures of simpler eastern Algonquian societies (Howard 1965; Kroeber 1939). The details of this implied shift in culture type must rely on an archaeological perspective. The importance of historic textual and comparative ethnological sources of information notwithstanding, only archaeology identifies the principle events and places them in their proper sequence together with the cultural, biological, and natural contexts critical to any understanding of the dramatic changes that took place in late precontact times (Emerson and Brown 1992).

Although each of these perspectives makes the contrast between precontact and postcontact patterns more, rather than less, complex, advances in the acquisition and analysis of archaeological information offer promising avenues for bridging the gaps between the perspectives offered by divergent fields of inquiry. Although the contribution of archaeology is just beginning to achieve its potential, certain patterns have emerged that make a review of our knowledge useful at this time.

JAMES A. BROWN AND
ROBERT F. SASSO

The Three Faces of the Past

Comparative ethnology indicates that at the dawn of European penetration, the eastern prairies were inhabited by both Siouan- and Algonquian-speaking tribes who were identified with a distinct set of common economic and social practices (Eggan 1952; Kroeber 1939). The French identified the region as the "Illinois country" (Le Pays des Illinois) and characterized it as a populous one in which settled village life alternated twice a year with wide-ranging upland big game hunting. Although corn, bean, and squash agriculture was fundamental, subsistence was broadly based, with large-scale cooperative hunting of elk and bison along with wetland plant and animal exploitation (Brown 1991). A distinctive social organization was based on moieties of internally ranked patrilineal clans employing Omaha kinship terminology (Brown 1991; Murdock 1955). Although the cultures of this region were characterized by a mixture of traits common to groups in the Great Plains and the Eastern Woodlands, nonetheless a regional integrity did exist (Brown 1991). The antiquity of this pattern is only now becoming clear, although many unresolved problems remain. Archaeological evidence points to a long historical development in which the shift to the postcontact pattern to took place definitively around A.D. 1450.

Historical perspectives have been influenced by the large-scale migrations that characterized the eastern prairies from the outset of recorded history. As early as 1655, depredations by the Iroquois had forced resident peoples to flee west of the Great Lakes and the Mississippi River (White 1991; Wilson 1956). Although the presence of French logistical networks within the region stabilized the tribal composition at first, westward expansion of Euroamerican settlement, coupled with changes in French policy, led to periodic population disruptions (Bauxar 1978; White 1991). The record of postcontact migrations has predisposed many to believe that the same pattern of westward intrusion extended into prehistory.[3] Thus, the cultural picture of the eastern prairies is one in which the original Siouan-speaking peoples were supplanted by Algonquian-speaking newcomers of Eastern Woodlands and Great Lakes affiliations (Kroeber 1939: 91). When this scenario is spelled out in terms of the distinctive traits of the two groups, the history of the eastern prairies takes on the simplistic picture of an earlier, more complex Central Siouan past being replaced by or intermixed with various socially and politically simpler eastern Algonquian cultures.

Two consequences emerge from this picture of cultural displacement. The first is to expect radical changes between the archaeology of the precontact period and that of the contact period. The second is to conceive of the Iroquois as the prime stimulus behind events surrounding the eastern prairie tribes (e.g., Jennings 1984). The ongoing migration of certain tribes into the region lends an air of credibility to the portrait of the region as one filled with the destabilized descendants of long-term inhabitants and more recent refugees who flowed into the area well before European contact.

Archaeologists customarily have identified the cultural disjunction in terms of the relationship between two major types of prehistoric agriculture—one a relatively intensive expression represented by the Middle Mississippian Cahokian tradition and the other, identified with the Oneota tradition, having less investment in agriculture. Essential to this formulation is the relative geographic distribution of the two cultural types. The former is largely (but not entirely) concentrated in the broad alluvial valleys of the Mississippi River and its chief tributaries, whereas the latter is found in both upland and lowland settings (Stoltman and Baerreis 1983). Most significantly, Oneota sites are concentrated at the northern edges of the Mississippi watershed, where corn growing is tenuous relative to the American Bottom area, with its longer and warmer growing season. The relationship between the two traditions is customarily conceived in terms of adaptive fit (Brown 1991; Gibbon 1972). How each type has been fostered or constrained by the environment has loomed large, a consequence of the search for the origins and limits of dependence on agriculture (Hart 1990).

At first, archaeologists believed that the Oneota tradition originated out of the gradual attenuation over time of Middle Mississippian cultural forces at the edges of viable agriculture (Griffin 1960a; McKern 1945). But with increased recognition that the Oneota tradition had an independent history, the grip of the "cultural diaspora" perspective gradually lessened (Hall 1962). This shift in thinking is reflected in the significance attributed to the occupation of Aztalan, Wisconsin, in the northerly spread of Middle Mississippian cultural "influences." At first, the date of Oneota emergence was set at the end of the Aztalan site occupation, when Middle Mississippian influences were held to have declined to the point of insignificance (Brown 1991; Gibbon 1972; Griffin 1960b). But as the history of Oneota pottery has been clarified, the date of its emergence has come to be placed significantly earlier, and the tradition's history has come to be visualized independently of the abandonment of Aztalan. Early Oneota can be placed sometime around A.D. 1000, well before the town of Aztalan was established (Goldstein and Richards 1991).[4] Developments within the Oneota tradition were first formulated by Robert Hall (1962). The shift from early Oneota to classic Oneota was first dated around 1300 (Gibbon 1972; Overstreet 1978), and after extended experience with isotopic dating this development has been raised to 1400–1450 (Boszhardt 1989).

Ethnic identifications of archaeological complexes have been based on the continuity-of-place argument, with the latest known prehistoric cultural assemblage representing the material trace of the earliest tribal entity that texts place in the area. But this logic assumes a geographical (and political) stability of tribes over many generations that is unwarranted for the Midwest (R. Mason 1976). In the first decades of European contact, frequent and sometimes long-distance migration of communities brought about a fluidity of residence that, coupled with a rapid loss of distinctive native crafts, has deprived archaeologists of the markers that would have facilitated ethnic linkages with material assemblages (Emerson and Brown 1992). Together these factors have undermined the argument based upon continuity of place. The more interesting problem that emerges from this generalization is why local continuities remained in some areas, such as central New York and the middle Missouri River, but not over much of the eastern prairies. Archaeologists have responded with the thesis that one or more exogenous factors led to the instability of local continuities in the eastern prairies prior to the advent of the fur trade. These factors have included epidemic diseases, warfare, climatic deterioration, and (in the case of the immediate precontact period) Iroquois raiding.

In sum, the picture that has slowly materialized from archaeological evidence points to a basic continuity of subsistence and settlement. Although changes took place in degree of social complexity, those of greatest magnitude clearly happened in the precontact past, at a time significantly earlier than the penetration of Europeans into the Midwest. In this land where the fluidity of tribal location has been held to be the norm, one of the important contributions of archaeology has been to demonstrate the kinds and degrees of change that have transpired in the context of subsistence and settlement continuity.

Geographic Area

The geographic scope of this chapter is the eastern part of the Prairie Peninsula (Brown 1991; Transeau 1935). Within this extension of western grasslands into eastern woodlands, the eastern prairies region makes up the part of the Prairie Peninsula that extends from the western edge of the Mississippi Valley to an apex in southwestern Michigan. This area was dominated by prairie vegetation intermixed with woodland in the stream valleys and in fire-protected positions, particularly along the northern borders with the mixed hardwood and coniferous forest. It lies south of the mixed hardwood-coniferous forest of Wisconsin and north of the dissected, unglaciated plateaus of southern Illinois and Indiana (Fig. 15.1).

Although tall grass prairie dominated the uplands, other features of the landscape were of equal, if not greater, importance to human occupation, notably the aquatic habitats and adjacent terrestrial environments. The area contains major rivers (e.g., the Mississippi, Illinois, Wisconsin, Rock, Fox, and Kankakee) and large shallow lakes and major wetlands (Lake Winnebago, Lake Koshkonong, Lake Calumet, and the Kankakee Marsh). Bottomlands rich in forest resources and easily tilled soils, however, are not evenly distributed. The richest waterways, riparian resources, and fer-

tile soils are properties of the slow-moving rivers of the Midwest, located outside of the most recently deglaciated terrain of the Woodfordian Till Plains. These waterways abound in fish, shellfish, and aquatic mammals and are attractive to migratory waterfowl (Gallagher and Stevenson 1982; Kay 1979: 110). In contrast, streams in the Woodfordian Uplands, created after the last glaciation, occupy youthful, steep-gradient drainages with relatively narrow bottoms. Before modern flood control, not only were these upland prairie rivers periodically dry, but also their bottomland resources were relatively meager. The division of the eastern prairies between the Woodfordian Uplands and the older land surfaces is one that has been employed fruitfully by Douglas (1976), Goldstein (1991), and Jeske (1989, 1990) in portraying cultural developments in the eastern Prairie Peninsula.

History of Investigations

The two cultural traditions have attracted correspondingly different approaches to research. Investigation of Middle Mississippian cultural manifestations has been guided by research in the American Bottom and the Cahokia site. Archaeologists have discovered that changes in ceramic attributes in the American Bottom sequence provide useful guidelines for the sequencing of ceramics throughout the eastern prairies. Although Middle Mississippian manifestations outside of Cahokia drew upon local antecedents, the degree of synchronism in changes to the common stock of ceramic attributes (largely rim form) indicates strong social interaction between the American Bottom and the eastern prairies as far north as south-central Minnesota (Brown 1991; Stoltman 1991). Therefore, Middle Mississippian manifestations have readily responded to chronological ordering. Quite the opposite obtains for the Oneota tradition. Symptomatic of its organizational simplicity, Oneota ceramic rim form is quite insensitive to attribute constraint. Owing to the confusion caused by mixed assemblages from unstratified middens at multicomponent sites, it is not surprising that until recently, students of Oneota archaeology commonly distinguished only two prehistoric subperiods for the past millennium (see Brown, ed., 1990; Emerson and Lewis 1991; Gibbon 1970a; Griffin 1943; Harn 1990; Milner 1990).

After many years of extensive field investigation, examination of the issues of cultural change addressed here has emerged only since about 1970. A shift in attention toward the cultural and environmental contexts of the regional traditions began after the true temporal relationships between Oneota and Middle Mississippian manifestations were revealed by the widespread application of isotopic dating. The first effect of this chronometric revolution was to extend the range of the Mississippian period back in time. Middle Mississippian cultures that once were compressed into the late sixteenth and seventeenth centuries must now be placed within a four-century span (Wray and Smith 1944:

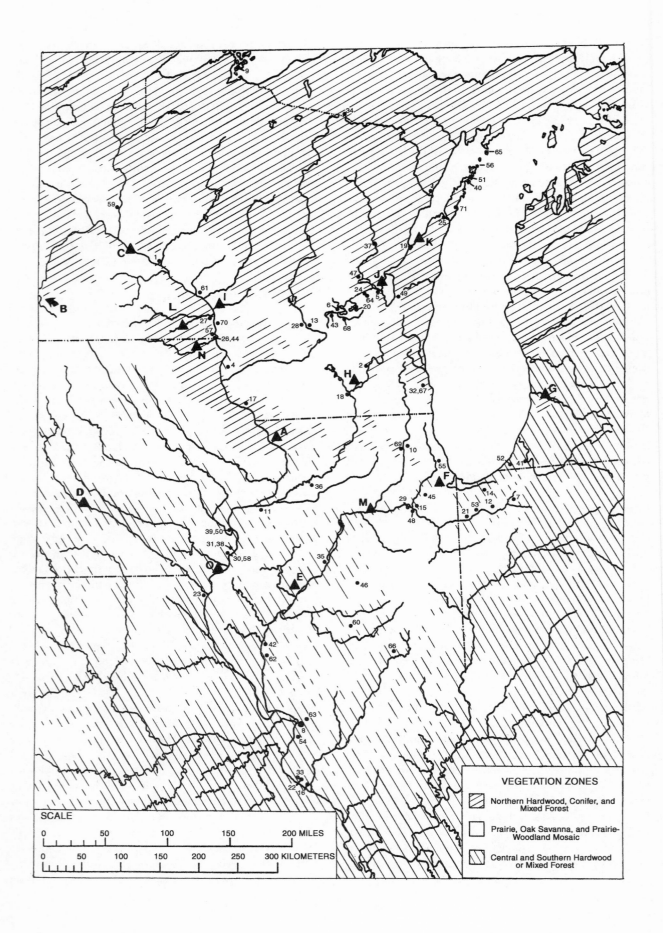

24). Hence, manifestations once thought to be near contemporaries have been thrown into entirely different centuries, forcing old causal models to be discarded and new ones to be set in place. For instance, the site of Aztalan can no longer be thought of as the way station of a group migrating from Cahokia to the north before dispersing to become the Oneota (Griffin 1946).

These developments fostered the resurgence of an adaptationist perspective. Interest focused on the correspondence between climate and Oneota subsistence and settlement patterns. Climate either dampened agricultural success (Baerreis and Bryson 1965; Griffin 1960b) or stimulated communal hunting of upland game animals through the movement of bison east of the Mississippi (Brown 1991; Gibbon 1972). Thus, mechanisms had to be considered that were more causal than merely the attenuation of high cultural influences on the northern frontier.

Recent advances in our knowledge stem from changes in the way archaeology is conducted in both the field and the laboratory. First, the broad exposure of sites by surface stripping has revealed village and cemetery layouts that would have gone undetected in small-scale block excavations (e.g., Arzigian et al. 1994; O'Gorman 1995; Santure,

Harn, and Essary 1990). Second, flotation and other fine-scale recovery methods have led to important refinements in the study of food remains.

The development of Mississippian period archaeology has been hampered by relatively small-scale excavations and by meager stratigraphy. This often has produced uninterpretable settlement patterns and collections of mixed components. Two developments have led to major changes in our perspective of the eastern prairies. First has been the widespread application of radiocarbon dating to large numbers of unmixed samples. Physical stratification has played only a minor role in chronology building. In sites such as the Fisher site in northeastern Illinois, the stratigraphic sequence of burial layers in two of the mounds contributes to our understanding of the pre-1300 period but not of later centuries (Brown 1991). At the Zimmerman site in north-central Illinois, the separation of storage pits merely helps us distinguish a middle historic period component from a prehistoric one, although it took the implementation of flotation and fine screening to accurately discriminate between the two (M. Brown 1975). The colluvial fan at the Sand Lake site in southwestern Wisconsin has provided an important instance of physical stratification. The strati-

Figure 15.1 (*opposite*). Vegetation zones and archaeological sites in the eastern prairies region.

1. Armstrong	13. Dells Enclosure	25. Hanson	37. Leeman	48. Osborne/Kankakee Refuse Heap	60. Shire
2. Aztalan	14. Fifield	26. Hayes Enclosure	38. Malchow Enclosure	49. Pipe	61. Shrake-Gillies
3. Backland Mound Group	15. Fisher	27. Hokah Enclosure	39. McKinney Enclosure	50. Poison Ivy	62. Slim Lake
4. Becwar I	16. Fort du Chartres	28. Hulbert Creek	40. Mero	51. Porte des Morts	63. Sponemann
5. Bell	17. Fred Edwards	29. Jehalo	41. Moccasin Bluff	52. Preserve Sites	64. Springview
6. Bornick	18. Fulton Earthwork	30. Kelley	42. Naples-Tabbycat	53. Rader	65. Summer Island
7. Brems	19. Green Bay (La Baye)	31. Kingston	43. Neale Enclosure	54. Range	66. Sweat Bee
8. Cahokia	20. Green Lake Enclosure	32. Kinnickinnic Enclosures	44. New Albin	55. Robinson Reserve	67. Tiffany Enclosure
9. Chequamegon Bay	21. Greismer	33. Kolmer	45. New Lenox	56. Rock Island II	68. Walker-Hooper
10. Cooke	22. Guebert	34. Lac Vieux Desert	46. Noble-Wieting	57. Ruined Fort	69. Washington Irving
11. Crawford Farm	23. Haas-Hagerman	35. Lake Peoria	47. Old Spring	58. Schmeiser	70. White Camp II
12. Davidson	24. Hamilton-Brooks	36. Lawrence		59. Sheffield	71. Whitefish Bay View

A. *Apple River area:* Aiken Elliptical Enclosure, John Chapman Village, Lundy, Mills Village, Mills Group Circle, Savannah Proving Ground

B. *Blue Earth–Cambria area:* Cambria, Humphrey, Poole, Price, Rynearson, Vosburg

C. *Cannon Junction:* Bartron, Bryan, Diamond Bluff–Mero 1, Double, Energy Park, Silvernale

D. *Central Des Moines Valley:* 13PK46, Christianson, Clarkson, Cribb's Crib, Dawson, Howard Goodhue, Mohler Farm–Colter, Norman Dille, Wildcat Creek

E. *Central Illinois Valley:* Charles W. Cooper, Crable, Dickson Mounds, Emmons, Eveland, Larson, Morton Village, Norris Farms No. 36, Orendorf

F. *Chicago area:* Anker, Higginbotham–Comstock Trace, Hoxie Farm, Huber, Knoll Springs, Oak Forest, Palos Hills

G. *Kalamazoo Valley:* Allegan Dam, Elam, Nordhof, Schwerdt

H. *Koshkonong area:* Carcajou Point, Crabapple Point, Crescent Bay Hunt Club

I. *La Crosse area:* Brunson's Enclosure, Farnam Street Cemetery, Filler, Firesign, Gunderson, Herbert, Jim Braun, Keppel Enclosure, Krause, Lower Sand Lake, Midway Village, North Shore, Olson, OT, Overhead, Pammel Creek, Sand Lake, State Road Coulee, Trane, Tremaine, Valley View

J. *Oshkosh area:* Baer I, Karow Village and Cemetery, Lasleys Point, McCauley, Overton Meadow, Sauer Resort

K. *Red Banks area:* Beaumier Farm, Point Sable, Red Banks Enclosure, Red River

L. *Root River:* Dahl, Farley, Hahn, Hogback, Hokah Enclosure, Jore, Riceford Creek, Wilsey, Yucatan Fort, Yucatan Village

M. *Starved Rock area:* Gentleman Farm, Hotel Plaza, Material Service, Plum Island, Starved Rock–Fort St. Louis, Zimmerman–Kaskaskia

N. *Upper Iowa:* Burke Cemetery, Elephant Cemetery, Flatiron Terrace, Flynn, Grant Village, Hartley Fort, Hogback Cemetery, Kumpf Circle, Lane Enclosure, Lane Farm Mound Group, Lane South Enclosure, Lyons Enclosure, Malone Cemetery, Malone Terrace, Malone II Shelter, New Galena Enclosure, New Galena Mound Group, O'Regan, Ratcliffe Enclosure, Simonson Enclosure, Spike Hollow Rockshelter, Woolstrom

O. *Wever Terrace:* Lost Creek, Median, Morrow, Wever

graphic layering of the Rock Island II site at the tip of the Door Peninsula in extreme northwestern Wisconsin is helpful in distinguishing various historic components from one another. In short, despite the stratigraphic information contributed by a few sites, the main role in chronology building for the years before European contact has been shouldered by radiocarbon dating.

Expectations about subsistence patterns derive largely from ethnohistoric information concerning tribal economies in the early contact period. That these economies differed from earlier patterns in their heavy reliance upon bison raises the question of the timing and circumstances surrounding the emergence of the bison-hunting pattern. Were all the features of historic subsistence practices present in antiquity, or only some of them? How is long-distance hunting to be evaluated archaeologically? When did the historical pattern of the maize-beans-squash agricultural triad arise? And what impact, if any, did the "Little Ice Age" have on subsistence practices?

Subsistence studies have played a strong role in the development of archaeological research in the eastern prairies. Cleland (1966), Shay (1978), and others have contributed to uncovering the age and evolution of the communal bison-hunting practices after contact (Griffin and Wray 1945; Lehmer 1963; Tankersley 1986a). The evolution of agricultural systems and the role of nondomesticated plants in the collecting systems have also emerged as important research foci (Arzigian 1989; Asch and Asch 1975; Asch and Sidell 1990; Cremin 1980, 1983). Despite the contributions of these studies, many old questions remain unanswered. Principal among these is just how different were Oneota and Middle Mississippian levels of investment in maize agriculture at any point in time.

For most areas of the upper Midwest, systematic settlement data are lacking, but several systematic surveys offer useful information, even in areas that were not conspicuously settled in late precontact times (Goldstein 1987; Hart and Jeske 1991; Sasso 1989; Trow 1981). Surveys in heavily settled areas typically have devoted attention entirely to large village sites without incorporating smaller, specialized procurement sites (Overstreet 1978). The La Crosse region of the upper Mississippi Valley is one place where systematic settlement data exist for areas in or near clusters of major Oneota villages, largely due to research conducted in the Coon Creek watershed of western Wisconsin (Sasso 1989, 1993). A systematic sampling of survey units in this tributary to the Mississippi has helped to identify a core-hinterlands pattern of Oneota settlement clearly related to land use practices. Major habitation sites, palisaded villages and enclosures, agricultural sites, and cemeteries have so far been identified only in core areas of settlement: on and adjacent to the terraces in the vicinity of La Crosse, and in select portions of the upper Iowa and Root River valleys to the west. Smaller habitations occur there as well. Away from the core areas, the relatively few identified habitation

sites are typically small and appear to represent seasonal camps. Several small Oneota habitation sites were located at the mouth of the Coon Valley—for example, the White Camp II site (McKern 1931, 1945; Sasso 1987). Farther up-valley and in adjacent upland zones, the only evidence for Oneota occupation exists in the form of small, limited activity sites—that is, extractive sites, procurement sites, and/or bivouacs (Sasso 1989, 1993).

The study of mortuary practices in the eastern prairies is relatively undeveloped. Most known cemeteries predate 1450 (Brown et al. 1967; Dirst and Kreisa 1982; Harn 1990; Kreisa 1986, 1993; Rothschild 1979; Santure, Harn, and Essary 1990). Among the few within our timeline, scattered burial plots are the rule, as at Hogback (Wilford and Brink 1974) and Flynn (Bray 1961); the earlier mounded cemeteries appear to have been replaced by other practices. The more substantial Tremaine series documents the placement of interments beneath the floors of longhouses during the 1400s (Grauer 1995). The Tremaine series points to practices that may have been more commonplace during the classic Oneota period. Although these studies represent only a beginning, variable patterns of health and nutrition can already be detected (Grauer 1995; Sullivan 1990; Vradenburg 1993, 1998).

Cultural Chronology

INDIGENOUS PERIODS. The chronological framework adopted here was developed for Oneota cultures in the upper Mississippi Valley, but it has wide applicability throughout the eastern prairies region. Boszhardt (1989, 1994, 1997) proposed five periods—Emergent (A.D. 1000–1150), Early Developmental (1150–1300), Late Developmental (1300–1400), Early Classic (1400–1625), and Late Classic (1625–1750). This represents an expansion of the threefold chronology advanced by Hall (1962), with horizon style refinements recommended by Stoltman (1983, 1986). Although the boundary between the Late Developmental and Early Classic periods has been set differently by various students, the periodization that has come out of the La Crosse area is preferred here because it is based on the largest series of well-controlled ^{14}C dates (Table 15.1). Of these periods, it is the Early and Late Classic that concern us directly.

There is general agreement that the Classic periods are set off from the Developmental ones by the different patterns of punctation use (if they are present at all) deployed on ceramics (Boszhardt 1994, 1997; Henning 1995). A signature ceramic feature during the Early Developmental period is the domination of the dot- or punctate-bordered line motif embodied in the type Perrot Punctate and widely identified with the Blue Earth pottery style. With the Early Classic period, closely spaced vertical-line shoulder decorations prevail, typified by Allamakee Trailed in Iowa and identified with an Orr or Allamakee style. The transition

Table 15.1

Model of Oneota Chronology

Phase (Component)	Ceramic Type
Emergent period (A.D. 1000–1150)	
Silvernale (Silvernale, Bryan, Mero, Bartron)	Armstrong Trailed
Koshkonong (Carcajou Point, Crabapple Point)	Carcajou Curvilinear
Fisher (Fisher A)	Fisher Trailed
Developmental period (A.D. 1150–1400)	
Brice Prairie (Olson, North Shore, White Camp II, Grant, Tremaine)	Perrot Punctate
Bold Counselor (Norris Farms, Crable)	Diamond Bluff Trailed
Blue Earth (Sheffield, Humphrey, Vosburg)	Blue Earth Trailed
Grand River (Grand River)	Grand River Trailed
Burlington (Schmeiser)	Fifield Trailed
Langford (Fisher B, Zimmerman)	Langford Trailed
Developmental/Classic period (A.D. 1400–1500)	
Pammel Creek (Pammel Creek, Jim Braun, Sand Lake, Tremaine)	Perrot Punctate
Early Orr (McKinney)	
Kelley (Kelley, McKinney?)	
Vulcan?	
Huber (Huber)	Huber Trailed
Early Classic period (A.D. 1500–1600)	
Valley View (Valley View, OT, Tremaine, Overhead)	Allamakee Trailed
Lake Winnebago (Lasley's Point, Overton, McCauley)	Lake Winnebago Trailed
Berrien (Mocassin Bluff, Schwerdt)	Berrien Trailed
(Late) Orr (McKinney)	Midway Incised
Oak Forest (New Lenox, Oak Forest, Palos Hills)	Huber Trailed
Late Classic period (A.D. 1600–1750)	
Orr/Yucatan (Lane Enclosure, Farley, Yucatan Village)	Allamakee Trailed

Source: Expanded on the basis of Boszhardt 1989.

between the two style horizons in the Late Developmental period is well defined by the Pammel Creek and Sand Lake sites in the La Crosse area. During this period Perrot Punctate declines in favor of Allamakee Trailed. Corresponding changes in native technology are less well defined. Even the Late Classic, which is conventionally placed in protohistoric times, is probably better defined as a period in which European trade goods began to replace native crafts. Throughout the Developmental and Classic periods the average width of incised lines steadily declined (Boszhardt 1994: 207–209; Brown, ed., 1990; Henning 1995: 82–83).

The Late Developmental period was one of resurgence in southeastern interaction as witnessed by an influx of southeastern prestige goods into the eastern prairies. Exotic pottery, marine shell, and chipped stone items appear at the Crable site in central Illinois during the Oneota Bold Counselor (1300?) and Crable (1375–1450) phases. In apparently contemporaneous Oneota contexts in the Chicago area, the Anker site has yielded marine shell artifacts.[5]

EUROPEAN PERIODS. Frequently, the mere presence of European items is used as an indicator of a "proto-historic" period. This poses a problem, because initially European goods were treated (for all intents and purposes) as new items in an aboriginal prestige system. They might as well be classed together with other exotics of native manufacture, and as exotics they appear to have been spotty in their archaeological distribution. Hence, the simple presence of European goods by themselves says nothing about the native system, which is presumably the focus of classification.

To compound these difficulties, the initial presence of European goods is timed very differently from place to place. Contact was much earlier in the lower Great Lakes than in the upper. In the Prairie Peninsula, European goods were theoretically available as early as Nicolet's famous landfall at Green Bay or the Cal-Sag area in 1634 (Hall 1993, 1995). In fact, small amounts of brass and glass beads trickled into the Chicago area at the New Lenox, Oak Forest, and Palos Hills sites in the 1620–1630 period (Brown, ed., 1990; Emerson and Brown 1992; R. Lurie 1994). In northeastern Iowa and southeastern Minnesota, the initial European trade influx came several decades later. But whatever the date, the initial appearance of trade goods in each of these early contexts appears to have had little impact on the character of locally produced crafts.

Segmentation of this block of time in the seventeenth century is to some extent arbitrary because time-sensitive features other than chronologically controlled European trade goods have yet to be formulated. For our purposes, 1600 will be used to end the Early Classic, since there is little basis for dividing what was obviously a slowly changing cultural continuum. Much more precise for the purposes of chronology is the sequence of glass beads imported into the Americas from 1580 to the end of the fur trade in the Midwest. The glass bead chronology that has won wide acceptance in Ontario archaeology (Kenyon and Kenyon 1983) has the potential for extension into the eastern prairies.[6] When this bead sequence is dovetailed with the ceramic chronology, the resulting composite has the potential for use as a framework covering a period in which native cultures came into increasing contact with Europeans in the entire Great Lakes and upper Mississippi watershed.

RADIOCARBON CHRONOLOGY.   Ceramic assemblages show mutually exclusive distributions of shoulder decorations belonging to each of the style horizons, with changes in lip decoration leading the way by about a half century (Boszhardt 1997). Assemblages of sherds from each site or site level have distinctly different distributions of radiocarbon dates as well. Boszhardt, Holtz, and Nienow (1995) have published the most complete list of dates. The Blue Earth sites date to the fourteenth century, whereas the Orr sites date after the fifteenth (Boszhardt 1997; Sasso et al. 1985: 99). The transition from predominantly Blue Earth to Orr ceramic attributes is documented in the colluvial stratigraphy of the Sand Lake site. Percentage shifts in lip treatments on Perrot Punctate from the lowest Horizon V stratum to the topmost Horizon I stratum place the beginning of this transition between 1400 and 1450 (Boszhardt 1997).[7] Replacement of the Blue Earth–type (Perrot Punctate) shoulder motifs was complete by 1500. Therefore, it can be reasonably concluded that a substantial presence of punctate-bordered lines is indicative of a pre-1400/1450 age in the eastern prairies. After 1500 such line treatments appear to be completely absent throughout the eastern prairies.

A problem that has beset the use of ^{14}C dating for this period is the non-monotonic relationship between atmospheric radiocarbon levels and calendrical dates (Asch and Brown 1990; Hall 1991). Irregularities in the curve describing this relationship raise difficulties in translating radiocarbon dates into calendrical ones. Indeed, the flatness of the radiometric curve during the sixteenth century seriously lessens the value of radiocarbon dates in this critical period (Asch and Brown 1990). However, a rapid rise in the atmospheric concentration of ^{14}C after 1640 does help to distinguish samples postdating that year from those predating it (Brown, ed., 1990: Fig. 4.1). As a consequence of this technical problem, the distribution of uncalibrated dates becomes a poor means for inferring differences in the relative densities of sites from one century to another (e.g., Green 1993). Nevertheless, central tendencies in large suites of ^{14}C dates help to confirm and anchor a chronology based on other lines of evidence.

SUMMARY.   The most archaeologically visible time of cultural change in the eastern prairies took place around A.D. 1400–1450, with two developments. First, the Middle Mississippian cultures of the middle Illinois and upper Kaskaskia Rivers were no longer present. After 1450, connections into central Ohio and the Southeast declined as well. Neither the Crable nor the Bold Counselor phase was succeeded by any detectable Middle Mississippian occupation in the middle Illinois Valley. Second, a major ceramic horizon style, of which Allamakee Trailed is the principal type, appears to have dominated the eastern prairie region. This new horizon style represents a stylistic simplification of its long-established predecessor. Presumably, these two events were connected, since the temple-town communities of the Middle Mississippian culture and the simple upper Mississippian communities had an intense and complicated interrelationship characterized by patterns of trade, strife, and cultural emulation. One can conclude that the absence of Middle Mississippian culture representatives in the Illinois River valley (and probably the American Bottom) had removed the intergroup dynamic between societies at different levels of cultural complexity that had been in existence since A.D. 1000. After 1500, cultures of the eastern prairies took on a relative uniformity in material culture that was to characterize them until the seventeenth century.

Relation of Archaeological Evidence to Known Ethnic Groups

PROBLEMS AND ISSUES.   Although numerous Siouan- and Algonquian-speaking peoples have been closely associated with the eastern prairies, ethnohistoric investigation has shown that only a portion of each of these linguistic families resided in the area before contact. The Ioway, Winnebago, and Illinois appear to have the best credentials. Related tribes (e.g., Miami, Oto) also had connections, but these were of uncertain duration. For this reason, the former three will be used in support of cultural practices most closely associated with the area.

Documenting the historical time depth of all tribes present in the area during the seventeenth century has been a slow process. In the Midwest, few tight associations between aboriginal remains and ethnohistoric peoples have been advanced convincingly. The issues involved have been widely recognized for some time (Emerson and Brown 1992; C. Mason 1976; R. Mason 1976). First, the abrupt decline in aboriginal crafts—particularly pottery, with its all-useful stylistic features—upon involvement with the fur trade reduces the number of promising associations between aboriginal culture and native tribal habitations to a very small number of archaeological sites of early contact time (Walthall 1992).

Second, the earliest French written accounts coincided with a period of widespread tribal movement in response to the threat of Iroquoian raiding. Hence, geographic continuity of ethnic groups is difficult to demonstrate. There remains only a small window of opportunity for excavating the pottery of a single, accurately placed ethnic group (Emerson and Brown 1992). Nor can one rely on general geographic arguments to advance a case of ethnic affiliation for a specific archaeological manifestation. Tight historical association means everything in a highly fluid cultural geography. Just because a tribe occupied a particular river valley or lake basin in the decades after first contact does not mean that it was there *at* first contact, or that its residence extended into late prehistoric times (Brown, ed., 1990).

Third, the Algonquian-speaking villages were customarily multiethnic, including individuals and households from different tribes (e.g., the well-known late seventeenth-century "Mascoutin village" in east-central Wisconsin, with Miami, Kickapoo, and other groups). Thus, the presence of multiple ceramic types at a single site points in conflicting directions, and the record from a single site is insufficient to provide a conclusive connection. Only the patterns of many sites can overcome the confusing signals that a multiethnic community could potentially offer. Hence, a substantial number of sites—much larger than the number at hand—is required to build confidence in our reconstruction of ethnic connections. Although research to date has provided fruitful leads, many alternative reconstructions remain possible.

Tribes placed in the eastern prairies between the time of first contact until 1700 include the Algonquian-speaking Illinois, Miami, Fox, Sauk, Kickapoo and Mascoutin, and Potawatomi. Siouan-speaking groups are the Winnebago, Ioway, and Oto. The Missouri and Osage were located to the west during this period. In general, most of the documented eastern prairie tribes had been drifting westward during or just before contact. Some of these, such as the Potawatomi, Fox, Sauk, Kickapoo, and Mascoutin, appear to have been recent migrants into the area, probably in the seventeenth century. Others, such as the Winnebago and Ioway, were well established. As for the remainder, the matter is an open question. It is noteworthy, however, that the remaining Algonquian-speaking Illinois and Miami tribes possessed strong affinities to the east.

In contrast, Siouan-speaking tribes appear to have had a long-term connection with the Mississippi Valley (Springer and Witkowski 1982). In the Springer-Witkowski historical linguistic model, all of the Siouan-speaking tribes maintained their positions with respect to each other since the time when they were undifferentiated. The model argues for long-term geographic stability in the relative position of each of these tribes. Because some were found much farther west than others at the time of European contact, this model tells us that these Siouan-speaking peoples were the first to have undertaken a westward migration that later became a general movement, presumably from a previous location in the Mississippi Valley.

If Algonquian-speaking peoples were in the process of moving into the eastern prairies from the Great Lakes and central Ohio Valley areas when Siouan-speaking tribes were moving into the plains, several questions arise. Is it possible to detect these movements archaeologically? And can it be determined when they took place? Archaeology has yet to provide clear answers, but available information points to certain possibilities. These can be examined in the context of the specific connections proposed between early historic tribes and protohistoric archaeological ceramic assemblages.

PROPOSED IDENTIFICATIONS. The most successful ethnic identification has been the equation of the upper Iowa and Root River valley sites of the Orr phase with the Ioway. M. Wedel (Mott 1938) advanced this identification first, and subsequent fieldwork and revisions in the chronology of European trade goods have reaffirmed the connection (Wedel 1986). Trade goods of the Glass Bead Period 3 have been found consistently at the O'Regan Cemetery, Hogback Cemetery, Wilsey Cemetery, Lane Enclosure, Farley, Flynn, Malone, Woolstrom, and Yucatan Village sites (Gallagher 1990; Wedel 1959; Wilford and Brink 1974; Withrow 1988), all known to have been occupied by the Ioway at that time. This ethnic connection has contributed in an important way to viable approaches to the history of populations in the upper Mississippi valley.

Far less successful has been the proposal that the "Lake Winnebago focus" represents the Winnebago tribe (McKern 1945). This tie was asserted on the basis of weak evidence for geographical continuity, without firm archaeological associations of aboriginal pottery with European goods of the proper age (C. Mason 1976, 1993; R. Mason 1976, 1986, 1993; Spector 1975). It remains controversial (Overstreet 1992, 1993, 1995). There is probably a gap of at least 100 years between the Lake Winnebago phase proper and Glass Bead Period 2, when European goods probably first entered Wisconsin.[8] No consistent pattern of European trade materials in clear association with Lake Winnebago phase artifacts has been demonstrated.

The ethnic identification of the Oak Forest phase has had a more contested history. Material evidence for contact period associations has been slow to accumulate (Brown, ed. 1990), but even before firm evidence had been marshaled, this phase had been assigned either to the Miami (Faulkner 1972) or to one of the Central Siouan tribes (Hall 1993; Quimby 1960: 105). The related Berrien phase has been tentatively related to the Potawatomi (Cremin 1996). French trade goods associations offer no immediate help in resolving the historical identity of the Oak Forest phase. At the three sites with European trade goods (New Lenox, Oak Forest, and probably Palos Hills), the French items belong to Glass Bead Period 2, at least 50 years before Marquette's appearance in the area. Because of a gap in the archaeological record for the succeeding half-century, it appears likely that Oak Forest phase occupants had departed the Chicago area well before European contact in 1673. Hence, the absence of cultural continuity in the crucial period between the first appearance of European items and the first Frenchman renders pointless any argument based on geographical continuity.

The Danner phase is known from the Glass Bead Period 3 occupations at the Zimmerman site (1673–1690) and the Haas-Eckles site (Iliniwek Village State Historic Site) near the mouth of the Des Moines River (Grantham 1996). Other Danner components have been identified in the Fort St. Louis area at Starved Rock (Schnell 1974). Both sites, visited by Marquette within a year's time, are dominated by Danner Cordmarked and Keating Cordmarked pottery. Association of the Zimmerman site with the Kaskaskia division of the Illinois and the Haas-Eckles site with the Peoria has eliminated a competing assignment of the Danner phase to the Shawnee (M. Brown 1975; Orr 1949). Anyway, the tie to the Shawnee rested primarily on the supposed similarity of Danner Cordmarked to Madisonville Cordmarked. But the notched fillet on Danner Cordmarked lies too low on the neck to fall within the recognized limits of Madisonville Cordmarked, and the Danner companion type Keating Cordmarked points to a source outside of the Madisonville area altogether. In short, the two pottery types indicate an origin near to and probably north of Madisonville, rather than to this phase (contra Tankersley 1992). Intrusion into the area begins as early as Glass Bead Period 2, since a handful of Keating sherds have been recovered from the New Lenox and Oak Forest sites (Brown, ed., 1990). Further complicating matters, the aboriginal ceramics found in the fill of the abandoned French Fort St. Louis atop Starved Rock belong to the related but readily distinguishable LaSalle series (Keller 1949). Moreover, attempts to trace the archaeology of the Illinois to their subsequent villages in the Fort du Chartres area have failed to discover useful examples of aboriginal ceramics (M. Brown 1973; Walthall 1992).

The Bell site, occupied by the Fox between 1680 and 1730, yielded mainly two distinct pottery types (Wittry 1963). Glass beads of the pigeon egg and faceted types of the early middle historic period were also present. The majority Type I pottery was a smoothed-surface, grit-tempered ware that Wittry (1963) identified with Fox culture. Type II was a cordmarked, grit-tempered ceramic that Wittry originally assigned to another, unspecified Algonquian-speaking group. On the basis of the Rock Island work, it can be assigned more specifically to the Potawatomi. Two LaSalle Filleted/Danner rimsherds represent contact with northern Illinois.

Rock Island II site is a partly stratified multicomponent site with postcontact tribal documentation (R. Mason 1986). The four early contact components are (1) an early Potawatomi occupation (post-1641 to pre-1650); (2) a Huron-Petun-Ottawa or proto-Wyandot occupation (1650/51–1653); (3) a later Potawatomi occupation (1670–1730); and (4) an Ottawa occupation (1760–1770). Of these, the first three are of interest here. The earliest component contained Bell site Type II pottery and some nondescript shell-tempered body sherds in association with a type IIa40 glass bead and various brass scrap probably belonging to Glass Bead Period 2. The second component, associated with the construction of the first palisade, included Bell Type II pottery, Huron Incised, one vessel combining attributes of the two types, and a Huron Incised–like Michipicoten Stamped rim. Eastern prairie connections are indicated by one Allamakee Trailed vessel (possibly Winnebago; C. Mason 1976: 343) and Danner Cordmarked pottery ("LaSalle Filleted"). The third occupation produced largely Bell Type II pottery. Associated European goods included Jesuit rings, gunflints, and a variety of iron weaponry. Although each component records the impact of eastern Algonquian- and Iroquoian-speaking newcomers on the eastern prairies, the 1650–1653 occupation, at least, records interaction with groups having older connections with the area.

ETHNIC PATTERNS.   The predominant regional pattern seems to be that of Oneota continuity into the 1680s in the upper Mississippi Valley but only to the 1630s in the Chicago area. By the late seventeenth century, after increasingly numerous intrusions, four new ceramic complexes had become established in the eastern prairies. The most ubiquitous was the Danner-Keating ceramic complex, which dominated the Hass-Eckles site and the Danner component of the Zimmerman site and had a minority presence at other sites (e.g., Oak Forest, Rock Island).

Other exogenous ceramics were more closely associated with tribal groups of relatively recent involvement with the eastern prairies, namely, Bell Type I with the Fox, Bell Type II with the Potawatomi, and Huronian types with the Huron-Petun. The directions in which these stylistic newcomers seem to point are compatible with the presumed prehistoric home of each. The Bell types have close analogs with pottery produced for centuries in Michigan's Lower Peninsula (R. Mason 1986: 217). The Danner complex (including La Salle Filleted) has analogs with pottery from northern Ohio. The Huronian types are derived directly from southwestern Ontario. In sum, all of the pottery with non–eastern prairie roots is associated with Algonquian- and Iroquoian-speaking peoples. The single established ethnic connection of indigenous Oneota pottery is with the Central Siouan-speaking Ioway. This pattern is one that makes general geographic sense, but whether the implied equation of Oneota pottery with Central Siouans will hold in every instance is quite another matter. For instance, Cremin (1992, 1996) saw in the mixture of Bell Type II–like pottery with shell-tempered Berrien ware the possibility of a Potawatomi identification with the prehistoric Berrien phase. This case hints at the possibility that migrants might have adopted the regional Oneota style upon entering the region (Brown 1991).

All told, the geographic patterns of the most stylistically sensitive items of material culture betray very distinct affiliations. The Oneota pottery associated with the Ioway has a historical connection with the eastern prairies. Danner pottery, which is probably associated with the Illinois (and possibly other related groups), betrays connections with the upper Ohio Valley. Bell Type I and Type II pottery, associated with the Fox and Potawatomi, respectively, has clear antecedents in the lower peninsula of Michigan, though probably not in the Oneota ceramic tradition. Thus, the pottery associated with Algonquian speakers comes from two different source areas to the east, whereas the long resident Oneota pottery is connected with a Siouan-speaking tribe.

Economy and Society from 1400 to 1700

SOCIAL ORGANIZATION. On this topic the principal research questions have revolved around the problem of how the politically decentralized early contact tribal social systems arose from their more complex Middle Mississippian ancestors (Brown 1991; Griffin 1960a). Gibbon (1972: 176) expressed a commonly held idea when he characterized the transition from early Oneota societies as a process of "factionalization into smaller economic units" that was no less than "a cultural-ecological re-adaptation in a marginal area to environmental change and the appearance of a new food source [bison]." Thus, social and political change was tied to subsistence and settlement change. The appearance of Oneota culture and the eventual replacement of Middle Mississippian material cultural have been regarded as marking the cultural transition (Gibbon 1972; Griffin 1960a; Stoltman 1991). The applicability of the early contact social organization to the precontact Oneota has, however, remained problematical (Benn 1989; Brown 1991; Gibbon 1972; Hollinger 1995; Michalik 1982; Staeck 1993).

Ethnohistoric sources provide, nonetheless, a richly documented baseline applicable to nearly all of the protohistoric inhabitants of the eastern prairies.[9] A high degree of local lineage autonomy existed among village-level representatives of pan-tribal patrilineal clans organized into earth and sky moieties (Callender 1962). Moiety affiliations structured village-level governance, ritual observance, and marriage. Households consisted of extended polygynous families, and archaeological evidence appears to fall in line with the large size of the co-resident household. Larger dwellings possess multiple hearths. Housing continued the prehistoric pattern of domed, mat-covered dwellings framed by arched saplings.

Comparative ethnology suggests that the degree of authority vested in clan and village leaders was somewhat greater for the Central and Chiwere Siouan than for the Central Algonquian newcomers (Brown 1991). Furthermore, rank and wealth appear to have been more firmly embedded in the social organization of Siouan groups than in that of the Algonquians. What little comparative data exist, however, reveal no obvious expression of differences in material wealth. For the precontact past, there is evidence that authority structures and social hierarchies were stronger (Staeck 1993).

With stepped-up intertribal competition for European goods came social stresses connected with greater settlement nucleation. Not only was the resource base strained, but native political organizations also found difficulty in coping with unaccustomed close contact (J. Brown 1975; Peckham 1947: 8–9; Temple 1958: 60, 86). From the impact of these and other developments arose new forms of political integration in societies generally organized for local-level autonomy and expansion through warfare.

A major development in response to indirect European pressures was the widespread acceptance of the Calumet dance, from the Great Plains to the upper Ohio Valley. Drawing upon the preexisting Hako ceremony of the Pawnee, the Calumet ceremony used the conferral of sacred kinship for safeguarding travelers, conciliating hostile parties, concluding peace, and forging alliances (Hall 1997). A central artifact was the calumet pipe (or rather its staff), which embodied the essence of good on behalf of which the dance was performed. Since the pipe bowl commonly used in the ceremony was the disc bowl form known earlier, elements of the Calumet ceremony evidently were drawn from important rituals of long standing.

SETTLEMENT PATTERNS. Two changes took place in housing and settlement layout that point to important social and economic developments. The more dramatic of these was an expansion in house size that took place by around A.D. 1400—followed by a contraction almost to preexisting sizes sometime before 1600 (Hollinger 1995).

During the period under consideration, structures appear to have belonged to a single constructional type. The square or rectangular post-and-beam form of construction (probably earth lodges) of the thirteenth century appears to have fallen into disuse (Brown 1961; Griffin 1946; Santure, Harn, and Essary 1990). Later, construction was of the arched sapling type, sometimes augmented with interior supports (e.g., the Anker and Overhead sites). Whatever the type, pre-1400 structures were of single-family size, with a mean floor area of 29.6 square meters. For Early Classic period Oneota sites (A.D. 1400–1600), Hollinger (1995) showed that the average floor area jumped to 171.6 square meters, with an upper limit of 380.9 square meters. The Tremaine (O'Gorman 1995) and Anker (Bluhm and Liss 1961) sites contain good examples of longhouse structures of this size. By protohistoric times, floor plan sizes had dropped back to an average of 62.5 square meters. Simple oval-plan structures are evident at Oak Forest (Bluhm and Fenner 1961) and Zimmerman (M. Brown 1975).

Hollinger (1995) cited the cross-cultural analyses of Ember (1973) and Divale (1977) in support of his argument that the Early Classic longhouse development signified a switch away from patrilocal residence to matrilocal. The changes in the late sixteenth century pointed to a return to the pre-Classic patrilocal pattern. This pattern was compatible with the patrilineal descent recorded historically for all of the eastern prairie tribes. Hence, archaeology cautions against undue extrapolation of ethnohistoric conditions back in time, even into the previous century.

The other change was a shift in settlement locations from the major channels to the mouths of peripheral valleys and the bases of bluffs (Boszhardt 1991; Sasso 1993; Stevenson and Boszhardt 1993: 17–22). Probably related to this was the greater visibility of palisades and embankments—for example, at the small, palisaded Valley View village of the Early Classic period. Whether surrounded by embankments or not, settlements varied greatly in size. Large base camps had areas of scatter of up to 40 hectares. As for Oneota village layouts, little information is available, although the Tremaine site, the eight-structure cluster found at the Oak Forest site, and possibly the four-structure cluster at the Grant site offer some insights (Bluhm and Liss 1961; McKusick 1973; O'Gorman 1995).[10] Houses were not uniformly oriented. Instead, dwellings were clustered into relatively compact groups in a manner reminiscent of contemporaneous longhouse villages of the lower Great Lakes.

Specialized camps are also known. The Slim Lake site may represent a small protohistoric bison kill site in the lower Illinois Valley (Stafford 1989). An Illini winter hunting camp has been found nearby (Walthall, Norris, and Stafford 1992). The many lithic scatters with triangular projectile points and endscrapers discovered in the Coon Creek drainage survey suggest similar procurement sites in the uplands of southwestern Wisconsin (Sasso 1989).

After European contact, dramatic aggregations of population were recorded, albeit they were observed for only brief periods of time. French trade depots exercised a strong pull on Native Americans (J. Brown 1975; Peckham 1947: 8–9; Temple 1958: 27; Thwaites 1899, 59: 221). Large populations were attracted to the early, successful trade depots to the point of outstripping local resources. Ten thousand people were counted within 2 leagues of the Starved Rock fortified post in the 1680s. But after 10 years time, complaints about firewood exhaustion were followed by native pressure to relocate downstream. An earlier aggregation in the region of Green Bay during the 1660s led to repeated brushes with wintertime starvation (Wilson 1956: 1060–1062).

Although the intrinsic demand for firearms and other trade goods was high, the opportunities for also using European goods, particularly firearms, as tools in intertribal politics were too good for native people to pass up. European goods allowed well-positioned tribes to dominate a tribal hinterland by several means—through control of scarcity, through intimidating use of superior firepower, and by extracting slaves and certain prestige goods that were difficult to acquire by other means. The French tolerated intertribal competition for middleman domination until challenges by the Fox led them to reverse their policy (White 1991). In the aftermath of the Fox War of 1734, the French imposed an entirely colonial logistical system upon the Midwest.

At the end of the seventeenth century, native settlements tended to be compact and frequently but not always surrounded by a palisade. Representative of stockaded settlements of this period is the Bell site (Wittry 1963). Although Wittry reported an enclosure of one-half acre, subsequent and more comprehensive fieldwork has disclosed multiple expansions, one of which included at least 6.4 hectares (Behm, personal communication 1999). Where settlements were unfortified, as at the Zimmerman site, historic descriptions emphasize their vulnerability to surprise attack from Iroquois raiders (J. Brown 1975; Stout, Wheeler-Voegelin, and Blassingham 1974: 16). The reasons for the inconsistency in fortification are probably related to settlement size. Whereas the Bell site measures less than 0.5 hectare in a rea, the Zimmerman site covers at least 27 hectares. Moreover, the latter lay within a protective radius of Fort St. Louis on top of Starved Rock.

Leaving aside the attractions of controlling access to European trade goods, historic settlement patterns appear to have continued the trend toward greater emphasis upon defense already expressed many centuries before. Largely concealed in ethnohistoric accounts was a brief, century-long prehistoric development toward a means of community organization entirely different from that of later times. Although intertribal warfare probably increased the use of stockades, defensive works had a long history of development in the region.

SUBSISTENCE.   Ethnohistorical accounts provide a rich picture of a mixed subsistence system revolving around communal bison hunting, field agriculture, and exploitation of wetland farinaceous tubers (Blair 1911, 1: 119; Pease and Werner 1934: 345). Most food was either produced or extracted within a small radius of permanent settlement. Fields were planted with maize, squash, beans, and watermelons (Blake and Cutler 1975). Deer and other woodland game were hunted locally. Tubers of the wild sweet potato (i.e., macoupin, *Ipomoea pandurata*), lilies, and other plants were collected from wetlands (*Nelumbo lutea* and *Nymphaea tuberosa* [Cremin 1980: 28, 1983: 99, 1996: 404; Faulkner 1964: 94, 1972: 112–3; Jeske 1990: 225]). Stands of wild rice were harvested from large lakes and streams, including the upper Mississippi River. Bears were the objects of specialized hunts in late winter. The major exception to this localized pattern of exploitation was communal hunts, which regularly took all able-bodied persons out of the village and onto the upland prairies in pursuit of bison. These parties spent several weeks twice yearly, during midsummer and early winter, ranging as far as 60 miles away from the village settlement.

One trend identified in different parts of the area was an increasing use of maize over time, although locally the picture may have been more complicated. The La Crosse area (Arzigian et al. 1994; Egan and Brown 1995), the Starved Rock area (Brown et al. 1995), the Illinois Valley (F. King 1993), and northeastern Illinois (Markman 1991) are places where this trend has been empirically recognized.

A second trend was the decline in the economic use of the small seed-bearing plants of the eastern agricultural complex (King 1993). The *Chenopodium* and *Polygonum* from Pammel Creek were of nondomesticated types, and those from Oak Forest were probably that as well (Arzigian 1989; Asch and Sidell 1990). The historic component at Zimmerman disclosed a far greater proportion of domesticated seeds relative to small starchy seeds, even when certain unclassified seeds (now identifiable as little barley) were taken into consideration (Asch and Sidell 1990: 257).

Some of the best information on agricultural field systems comes from the early fifteenth-century Sand Lake site near La Crosse, where ridged fields were constructed repeatedly in the same location. Remains of maize, beans, and squash cultigens and a number of commensal plants were present in sediments from the fields. The Sand Lake fields were constructed first in organically rich marsh soil and subsequently in organically poor colluvium as earlier plots were covered by slope wash from adjacent bluff slopes. Heavy domestic occupation (and possibly deforestation for firewood) by Oneota inhabitants is strongly implicated as the cause of the erosion of uplands adjacent to the Sand Lake site during a time when regional climate was generally dry but characterized by somewhat more intense and frequent summer storms (Gallagher et al. 1985; Sasso et al. 1985: 55).

Although Sand Lake represents one of the latest dated ridged field systems, agricultural fields probably existed in similar wet locations at other sites (Sasso and Brown 1987). Later postcontact fields are likely to have been prepared by hoeing separate hills rather than trenching continuous ridges, although these two patterns of cultivation might have coexisted in certain areas (Sasso 1992). Riley (1994) observed that although ridged fields were documented earlier than at Sand Lake, in the historic period fields were simply cultivated everywhere as isolated cornhills. The difference between the two field preparation patterns probably reflects changes in the organization of labor, not differences in the agricultural systems themselves. Riley observed that ridged fields presuppose gang-organized labor that prepared each field as a single communal operation. In contrast, hilling connotes the opposite—the preparation of fields in separate, uncoordinated operations. Thus the shift from communal, coordinated field preparation to atomistic, uncoordinated preparation signals a weakening of community-level organization and perhaps says something about community size. The timing of this shift in the organization of labor, which appears to have been complete by the middle historic period, has yet to be elucidated (Gallagher 1992; Moffat 1979; Sasso 1992).

The timing of the influx of bison herds east of the Mississippi remains elusive. The movement of bison across the Mississippi represents the beginning of the integration of this major source of meat into regional subsistence. By the late seventeenth century, eastern prairie groups had organized their subsistence pursuits to include major communal bison hunts. The benchmark description of an Illinois village hunt was provided by Deliette, a French participant (Pease and Werner 1934).[11] Bison probably were available west of the Mississippi well before the Mississippian period. Small quantities of bison remains dating somewhat later have been found on the east side. The earliest site in Illinois to produce bison remains is the Lundy site in the Apple River valley (Table 15.2), where unifacial chipped-stone endscrapers and bison bones were found in a context dating around A.D. 1100 (Coburn 1989). Only after 1400, however, are bison otherwise recorded east of the Mississippi (Purdue and Styles 1987). All of the bison remains Shay (1978) reported from sites preceding 1400 in the Mississippi Valley corridor are either without reliable context or consist of token teeth and bones incorporated into personal jewelry, costumery, or headdresses (Purdue and Styles 1986, 1987).

A list of bison food remains and bone artifacts indicates that the processing of bison carcasses was undertaken away from the base settlements (Cardinal 1975; Styles and White 1995). Presumably as a consequence, only certain bones were retained for further use at the village, notably scapulae for manufacture of hoe blades and other useful tools. A more sensitive indicator of an upland large-mammal component in the diet lies in the ratio of endscrapers to projectile points (Hall 1962). Endscrapers are regarded as defleshing tools geared to the removal of fatty substances adhering to the undersurfaces of bison and elk hides. According to Hall (1962), the presence of these lithic artifacts in Oneota assemblages provides a graphic measure of the growing role of heavy hide preparation in the economy of the eastern prairies.

MORTUARY PRACTICES. Available burial data from unmounded cemeteries point to poorly defined mark-

Table 15.2

Presence of Bison Remains and Bison Bone Tools on Selected Eastern Prairie Sites

Site Name and Number	Bison Elements Present	Bison Tools Present
Aztalan 47JE1	*	—
Carcajou Point 47JE2	X	—
Bell 47WN9	X	—
Karow 47WN57/198	?	X
Lasleys Point 47WN96	*	X
Overton Meadow 47WN106	*	X
Sauer Resort 47WN207	—	X
Shrake-Gillies 47TR44	?	X
Olson 47LC76	X	?
Jim Braun 47LC59	X	?
Overhead 47LC20	—	X
Pammel Creek 47LC61	X	X
Sand Lake 47LC44	X	X
Krause 47LC41	X	X
Midway 47LC19	*	X
Herbert 47LC43	X	—
Valley View 47LC34	X	X
Ot 47LC262	X	X
Filler 47LC149	X	X
Tremaine 47LC95	—	X
Gunderson 47LC394	X	X
State Road Coulee 47LC176	X	X
Trane 47LC447	—	—
Armstrong 47PE12, 7	X	X
Diamond Bluff (Mero 1) 47PI2	X	—
Bryan 21GD4	X	X
Silvernale 21GD3	X	X
Bartron 21GD2	—	X
Energy Park 21GD158	*	X
Cambria 21BE2	X	X
Sheffield 21WA3	X	*
Humphrey 21FA1	—	X
Vosburg 21FA2	X	X
Farley 21HU2	X	X
Grant Village 13AM201	—	X
Lane Enclosure 13AM200	X	X
Hartleys Fort 13AM103	n/a	n/a
McKinney 13LA1	X	X
Kingston 13DM3	—	X
Poison Ivy 13LA84	X	X
Lundy 11JD140	X	—
Jehalo 11GR96	X	—
Zimmerman 11LS13	X	X
Gentleman Farm LS°1, LS^v2	X	—
Hotel Plaza 11LS36	*	—
Plum Island 11LS2	X	—
Fisher 11WI5	X	—
Huber 11CK1	X	X
Robinson Reserve 11CK2	X	—
Hoxie Farm 11CK4	X	X
Knoll Springs 11CK19	—	X
Anker 11CK21	—	X
Oak Forest 11CK53	*	X
Clear Lake 11T—	X	—
Crable 11F249	?	?
C. W. Cooper 11F249/11F891	?	?
Slim Lake 11ST107	X	—

Table 15.2 *continued*

Site Name and Number	Bison Elements Present	Bison Tools Present
Naples/Tabbycat Area 11ST121	X	—
Shire 11LOᵛ117	X	—
Crawford Farm 11RI81	⋆	—
Moccasin Bluff 20BE8	⋆	—
Griesmer 12LA3	—	X
Fifield 12PR55	X	X
Madisonville 33HA36	X	X

Note: An asterisk denotes tentative identification.

ing of individual status (Benn 1989; Kriesa 1993). These flat cemeteries appear to have been small plots, if interments were concentrated at all. They replaced the low-mounded cemeteries of the pre-1400 period identified with the Fisher, Grand River, and Langford complexes. Benn (1989) argued that the change toward cemetery organization was due to a reduction in recognized status positions. He and Kriesa (1993) identified a trend toward decreasing quantities of grave goods through time, with grave goods being concentrated with a minority of the dead. These were preferentially male as well (Kriesa 1993). At the Tremaine site, burial occurred in the floors of habitations (O'Gorman 1995). The Gundersen site and other, less adequately examined sites (e.g., Overhead) suggest that this pattern was more general, at least for the Pammel Creek phase. Clusters of burials, whether under dwelling floors or in isolated locations, are uniformly small, indicating household or lineage segment associations at most.

Archaeological information concerning historic burial treatment coincides with literary sources in essential features. These sources indicate differentiation in the treatment of the dead by place of interment (Brown et al. 1967: 42–43). The elite dead were reduced to cleaned bones and stored in special places. The Illinois had the bones of their chief placed in a "granary" on Starved Rock. Other dead were interred as articulated burials under small wooden lean-tos that served as covers until the burial cavity filled in naturally (Brown 1961). Still others were stored temporarily as flexed bodies in sacks until they could be placed in the ground. The Zimmerman site suggests an additional detail: the placement of most individuals beneath dwellings in the same pattern seen at the precontact Gundersen and Tremaine sites (Arzigian et al. 1994; O'Gorman 1995). Further, one area seems to have been set aside as a small cemetery; this could have been reserved for elites and persons of other special statuses. Other cemeteries with historic goods include Hogback and Wilsey in southeastern Minnesota, the Hanson cemetery site near Sturgeon Bay in northeastern Wisconsin (Overstreet 1993), and O'Regan, Flynn, Malone, and Woolstrom in northeastern Iowa.

REGIONAL EXCHANGE. Patterns of interregional trade changed during the three centuries we are concerned with here. During the Late Developmental period, exchange was particularly pronounced to the south and southeast. The Crable site (A.D. 1375–1450) yielded a wide range of prestige goods, including elongate ceremonial bifaces ("dance swords") and shell gorgets (locally made spider motifs, the "stepped cloud" design, and a large number of small annular or cruciform gorgets). Cross-in-circle motifs are found incised or painted on a number of bowls and jars. Trade pottery from the lower Mississippi Valley is also present (Conrad 1991; Smith 1951).[12] Export of disc bowl pipes (sometimes of catlinite) and perhaps copper ornaments to the south and the lower and central Ohio Valley was well established in the fifteenth century (I. Brown 1989; J. Brown 1991). The Huber phase Anker site in the Chicago area produced an olivella shell bead, small marine shell gorgets, and an example of the square-jawed type of mask gorget (Bluhm and Liss 1961: Fig. 70). Smith and Smith (1989) regarded this gorget type as a Fort Ancient specialty of the central Ohio Valley.[13]

The interaction between groups at the Middle Mississippian and Oneota levels of social organization was complex. Not only did relations of trade and warfare exist between them, but relations of emulation seem to have obtained as well (Benn 1989; Conrad 1991; Emerson 1989). Furthermore, rituals binding the two appear to have existed that had as their material embodiment bowls decorated with cross-and-circle motifs (Conrad 1991). These vessels were descendants of a line of similar ritual objects going back to the cazuella bowls of Ramey Incised (Pauketat and Emerson 1991).

After European contact, well-delineated networks of long-distance exchange developed, which upon involvement with the French trade became strengthened through greater activity. G. Wright (1967) summarized the diversity of trade in the Great Lakes area. In the eastern prairies the sites yielding evidence of the most important relations were aligned east-west rather than north-south (Table 15.3).[14] Whether this arrangement was due to the overwhelming attraction of European trade goods emanating from the east is uncertain.[15] The availability of European hardware stimulated trade between the Illinois and the Ottawa. Marquette recorded that the Illinois enslaved many Pawnees in order to trade them to the Ottawa for muskets, gunpowder, kettles, hatchets, and knives (Thwaites 1899, 54: 191). Away from the source of French goods, Illinois became middlemen in the trade of "hatchets, knives and awls" to the Osage (Pease and Werner 1934: 389).[16] The eastern prairies became home to middleman traders (White 1991).

This east-west axis may have built upon a more southwesterly trade connection. A connection to the turquoise trade from the Spaniards occupying the Southwest was well established by 1700 via the Pawnee and Wichita (Pease and Werner 1934: 388). Evidence for this trade comes from an isolated disk-shaped turquoise bead found at the Hogback Cemetery (Table 15.3; Wilford and Brink 1974: 38). Examples of glass versions of this highly valued mineral have

been recovered at Zimmerman, Hotel Plaza, and other sites in the form described by Deliette and having an obvious southwestern prototype (M. Brown 1972). Glass pendants imitating turquoise were fabricated by the Illinois, and perhaps others, by fusing crushed and ground blue glass trade beads, sometimes with white glass frit veining to simulate the impurities commonly present in the real thing. The production of fake turquoise constitutes our best evidence of the preexisting esteem in which southwestern elite goods were held in the Midwest.

Sometime during the precontact period, trading connections to the south and southeast declined in favor of southwestern and eastern orientations. This shift may have been

Table 15.3

Postcontact Exotic Goods from La Crosse–Region Oneota Sites

Site Name and Number	Catlinite/ Pipestone	Marine Shell[a]	Copper	Galena Cubes	Miscellaneous (Including European Trade Goods)
Farnam St. Cemetery 47Lc12	X	—	—	—	—
Midway Village 47Lc19	X	1	X	X	Obsidian
Overhead 47Lc20	—	1–2	X	2	—
Valley View 47Lc34	X	—	X	11	Seed jar, 19th-century glass beads
Herbert 47Lc43	X	—	—	—	—
Sand Lake 47Lc44	X	2	X	1	1 obsidian chip
Pammel Creek 47Lc61	X	—	X	1	—
Tremaine 47Lc95	X	—	X	—	—
State Road Coulee 47Lc176	—	—	—	—	—
Trane 47Lc447	X	—	X	—	—
Hogback Cemetery 21Hu1	X	X	X	—	Obsidian flake; turquoise bead; calcite pipe fragment; brass tubes; glass beads
Farley Village 21Hu2	—	—	X	—	Iron, brass artifacts; glass beads
Wilsey Cemetery 21Hu4	X	—	?	—	Copper/brass tubes
Yucatan Village 21Hu26	—	—	?	—	Brass artifacts; glass beads
Jore 21Hu33	—	—	—	—	Mica
Riceford Creek 21Hu39	—	—	X	—	—
Hahn 21Hu63	X	—	—	—	—
Dahl 21Hu75	X	—	—	—	—
Flatiron Terrace 13Am1	—	—	—	—	(Brass and/or iron?)
Malone Terrace 13Am6	—	?	X	—	(Brass and/or iron?)
O'Regan Cemetery 13Am21	X	—	X	—	Iron, brass artifacts; glass beads
Flynn Cemetery 13Am43	—	—	X	—	Copper/brass artifacts; glass beads; iron artifacts
Spike Hollow Rockshelter 13Am47	?	X	—	1	—
Malone II Rockshelter 13Am50	—	—	X	—	(Brass and/or iron?)
Elephant Cemetery 13Am59	X	—	X	—	—
Malone Cemetery 13Am60	X	X	—	—	Iron, brass artifacts; glass beads
Woolstrom Cemetery 13Am61	—	—	X	—	Iron, brass/copper artifacts
Burke Cemetery 13Am67	X	—	X	—	—
New Albin Village 13Am85?	X	—	—	—	—
Hogback Cemetery 13Am86	—	—	X	—	—
Lane Farm Md. Group 13Am104	—	—	X	—	—
New Galena Md. Group 13Am108	X	—	X	—	—
Lane Enclosure 13Am200	X	—	X	—	Iron knife blade; brass fragment; sheet-metal ring

Sources: Arzigian et al. 1989; Boszhardt 1985, 1987, 1989, 1992; Boszhardt et al. 1984, 1986; Bray 1961; Clark 1971; Gallagher 1990; Gallagher et al. 1981, 1992; Gibbon 1970b; Henning 1957; Logan 1953, 1976; McKern 1945; McKusick 1973; Orr 1922; Rodell 1989; Sanford 1914; Sasso 1984; Sasso et al. 1985; Stevenson 1984, 1994; Wedel 1959; Wilford and Brink 1974; Withrow 1988, personal communication 1988, n.d.; Withrow and Rodell 1984.

[a]All whelk, with the exception of two marginella shells from Sand Lake and one or two marginella shells from Overhead.

stimulated primarily by the availability of European goods in those two directions after the appearance of the Spanish and French, respectively, in the early sixteenth century.

WARFARE. Warfare presumably had a long history in the area, though it escalated in intensity with European contact. A large number of defensive enclosures distributed throughout the area probably date to prehistoric times. Because the small numbers of them investigated so far have Oneota occupations, the actual number of Oneota earthworks is probably far greater.

At the Valley View site in 1885, T. H. Lewis recorded a modest-sized, "horseshoe-shaped" embankment enclosing 0.65 hectares (Fig. 15.2; Stevenson 1994). Lewis described the embankment as composed of midden. Although no trace of an embankment has survived into recent times, a stockade trench was discovered in its approximate location when the site was partially stripped and cleared of features in 1979 (Stevenson 1994). Two ditches flanked the outside of the north side where the embankment would have stood. Embankments at the Keppel (McKern 1931) and

Higginbotham–Comstock Trace (Kullen 1994) sites demonstrate an even wider distribution of fortifications. Other embankments that can be reasonably attributed to an Oneota component are generally small in size. Three-quarters of the known enclosures surround 1 hectare or less. In shape they tend to be circular (more properly "C-shaped"), although a few with simple geometries are known (Fig. 15.3). Presumably these fortified places were strongholds belonging to a dispersed population scattered nearby. A large portion of all such small enclosures were probably Oneota, since many small, low-banked earthworks of simple geometry have been recorded in areas where late prehistoric habitation sites are found (e.g., Kullen 1994; Potter 1988; Sasso 1989: 247–248; Trow 1981; Wedel 1959). A distinctive feature of the Valley View site is the continuous ring of large borrow pits on the inside of the palisade line (Stevenson 1994). A similar ring of pits was mapped for the Lane Enclosure in northeastern Iowa (McKusick 1973: Fig. 24).[17] The stockade wall was set inside the embankment, with a large borrow pit located to one side.

Direct evidence of deadly conflict is less obvious. Several

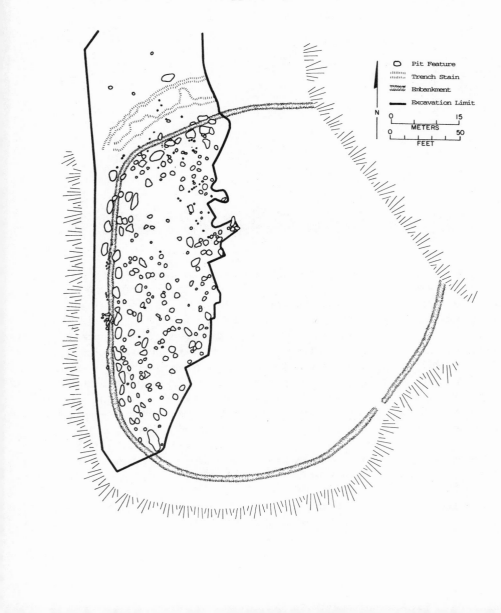

Figure 15.2. The Valley View site. Excavated features and trenches are shown against the alignment of the embankment drawn by T. H. Lewis in 1885 (after Stevenson 1994: Figs. 4 and 5).

Pit Feature
Trench Stain
Embankment
Excavation Limit

N

0   15
METERS
0   50
FEET

Figure 15.3. The Yucatan Fort site (21Hu18)
(after Trow 1981: Fig. 7).

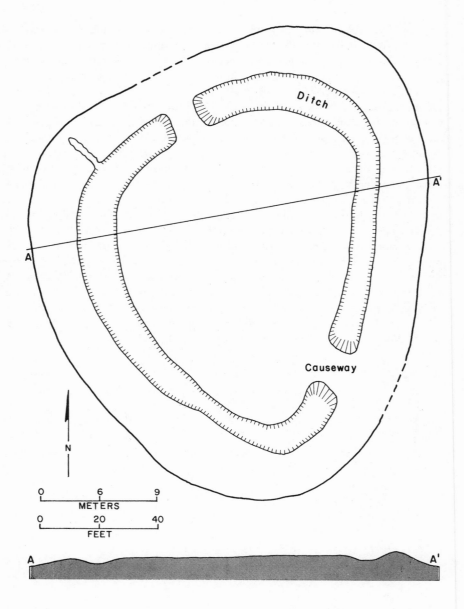

skeletons found in the cemetery at the Tremaine site show evidence of violent death (Grauer 1995; Vradenburg 1993).[18] Although skeletons with arrowpoints and lesions are found throughout the eastern prairies, the remarkable Norris Farms 36 cemetery in the middle Illinois Valley provides the best systematic information (Santure, Harn, and Essary 1990). There, an Oneota Bold Counselor phase cemetery of the late thirteenth century was located close to Middle Mississippian temple towns. A substantial number of both utilitarian trade goods and prestige goods were recovered from this compact burial ground. Milner and his associates (Milner, Anderson, and Smith 1991; Milner, Smith, and Anderson 1991) concluded that the skeletal sample exhibited a high level of violent death. The pattern was attributable to small-scale killing, presumably through surprise attacks that left many bodies on the field, exposed to carnivores, before they were retrieved and buried. The dead were often mutilated for trophies or to signal disdain for the enemy. A surprising feature of the Norris Farms population was the proportion of adult females killed, which reinforces the serious impact of the raiding.

Although it would be presumptuous to extrapolate from the Norris Farms case to the eastern prairies as a whole, this case indicates that no cultural barrier prevented vicious fighting. Furthermore, it makes raiding all the more likely as a general pattern, although the level visited on the Norris Farms population might have been extreme. Perhaps it reflects the competition implied by the immediate juxtaposition of Oneota people with a Middle Mississippian community. In this light, the widespread distribution of palisaded villages and strongholds is all the more suggestive of an elevated level of deadly conflict, albeit on a local scale.

Possible casualties of warfare were the temple-town societies that existed up to 1400 or 1450. Although this change is incompletely understood, population attrition from warfare was undoubtedly one of its components. Reproductive decline is logically another, since the well-studied Dickson Mounds skeletal population reveals greater disease loads than those of comparable Middle Mississippian populations (Goodman et al. 1984).

With the advent of European intrusion, new strategic considerations seem to have led to a diversification of preexisting patterns of intergroup raiding and warfare. Among the Illinois, raiding was undertaken by small, fast-moving war parties to capture male prisoners (Hauser 1973: 363–364). The preferred season for such raids was late winter, when hunting was typically poor. With the rise in demand for slaves by Ottawas and Frenchmen, entire villages came to be mobilized for capturing females and children who would become currency in procuring European trade goods (e.g., Hyde 1962: 222; Pease and Werner 1934: 10; Shea 1903: ii, 1, 25, 35; Wiegers 1988).

The response to this pattern of raiding and captive taking was an even greater visibility of defensive works. Archaeologically, we see the commonplace, though not ubiquitous, construction of embankment enclosures during the early historic period, as at the Bell site (Wittry 1963), Leeman (Fox 1916: 18; Wittry 1963: 42), and the Lane Enclosure (Wedel 1959: 9–12) (Figs. 15.4 and 15.5).[19]

Fortification of villages was certainly a response to vulnerability to attack, which led to a shift in settlement locations and probably encouraged the development of communal hunting. The settlement location practices of the

Illinois point to fear of surprise attack, and the Raudot memoir indicates that even while away from their main villages during their winter communal hunt, the Illinois occupied camps on the open prairie, far from the cover of woods (Kinietz 1940: 407). Such a practice served both to prevent sneak attacks and to permit easier pursuit of their enemies (Kinietz 1940: 407).

The military organization that late seventeenth-century accounts indicate was important in readying a group for either defensive or offensive fighting was also beneficial to the success of communal large-mammal hunting (e.g., Blair 1911, 1: 119–126; Hennepin 1938: 59; Kinietz 1940: 173–174, 407; Pease and Werner 1934: 307–320, 339–351). Later eighteenth- and nineteenth-century accounts for the Winnebago, Ioway, Oto, Sauk, and, by extension, other groups indicate people's expectation and even hopeful anticipation of engaging in conflict with enemy groups while on communal hunts (Blaine 1979: 12, 18–21; Jackson 1964: 93; Markman 1991: 114; Radin 1923: 64–66; Sasso 1993: 340–341; Skinner 1926: 288–295; Thwaites 1895: 450–451; Whitman 1937: 7–10).

Out of the ascendancy of the Iroquois and the deployment of firearms in intertribal conflict came the development and spread of the Calumet ceremony (Brown 1991: 93; Turnbaugh 1979). By cementing alliances and providing safe passage to otherwise defenseless strangers, the ceremony established an institutional framework that offset the hardships of increased warfare. We can conclude from this ceremony's rapid rise in importance that a high pre-

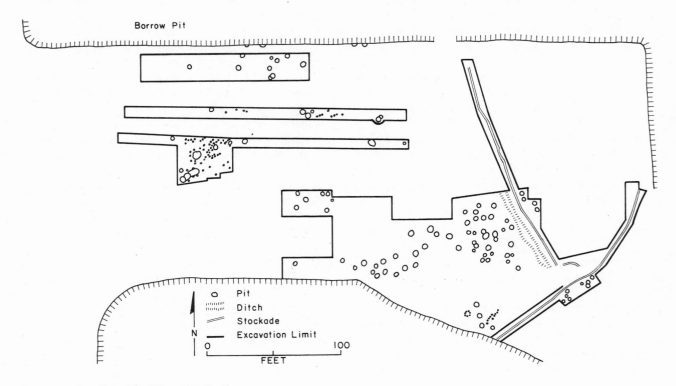

Borrow Pit

Pit
Ditch
Stockade
Excavation Limit

N

0   100
FEET

Figure 15.4. The Bell site (after Wittry 1963: Fig. 1).

Figure 15.5. Leeman earthworks and nearby garden beds (reproduced from Fox 1916: 18).

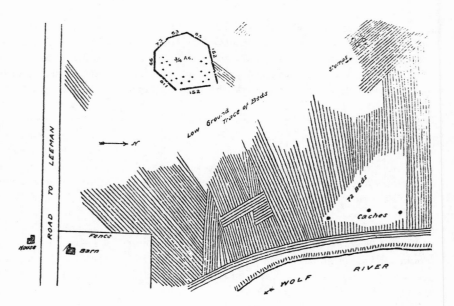

mium was placed on dampening the effects of worsening intertribal strife.

Climate, Disease, and Depopulation

Although single factors operating at decisive moments in time dominate the literature on the causes of change in subsistence and settlement, we have emphasized the interrelationship of social, settlement, and subsistence factors over the duration of many centuries. Of central concern to the focus on single causes has been the replacement of "intensive" agriculture in stable, permanent villages with communal bison hunting and "less intensive" agriculture based in seasonally occupied villages. At first this replacement was conflated with the disappearance of the temple towns. Since relatively intensive agriculture was thought necessary to support temple-town societies, any shift toward less intensive agriculture presumably undermined the production of agricultural surpluses that supported the Middle Mississippian lifeway. Gradually, the two processes have become dissociated. As a consequence, the problem of subsistence change in the late prehistoric period has shifted toward other factors such as climatic cooling and the ravages of European disease.

CLIMATIC DETERIORATION.   Interest in the rise of the historic subsistence-settlement pattern on the eastern prairie has led to a search for reasons behind its emergence (Gibbon 1972). Dominating these reasons has been climatic cooling during the Neo-Boreal period, or Little Ice Age (Baerreis and Bryson 1965).[20] This cooling has assumed the role of a forcing function, whereby a drop in summertime temperature has been postulated to have cut the productivity of maize and thereby undermined full-time reliance upon agriculture (Gibbon 1972; Harvey 1979; Hen-

ning 1970; Penman 1988; Riley and Friemuth 1979). The same cooling has been implicated in a shift toward greater reliance on communal bison hunting through its hypothesized effect in extending the range of bison into the eastern prairies (Brose 1978a: 582; Shay 1978). The presence of bison east of the Mississippi encouraged a shift away from agriculture. Either way, climatic cooling has been argued to have been a major driving force behind cultural change.

The strength of the climatic deterioration argument rests largely upon the effects the Little Ice Age had on simple hoe agriculture. Throughout the Northern Hemisphere, climate during the growing season was cooler and somewhat moister from 1550 to 1700 (Baerreis, Bryson, and Kutzbach 1976; Bernabo 1981; Green 1993; Howe and Webb 1983; King 1993; Swain 1978; Webb 1981; Webb and Bryson 1972).[21] A reduction of as much as 1–2 degrees Fahrenheit in mean July temperature has been adduced from quantitative data from several pollen cores in Minnesota, Wisconsin, and Michigan. Beyond these general observations, opinions have diverged widely on the impact these patterns had on human and other organic life.

Just how was this climatic episode expressed from year to year? Was the drop in average temperature sufficient to affect agriculture as it was then practiced? These are questions for which we have only incomplete data. Green (1993), using palynological data from Minnesota, hypothesized extreme effects, under the assumption that the average daily drop in temperature during the growing season was 2 degrees Fahrenheit. He cited a loss of 34 days to the frost-free season, which would have depressed the northern limit of agriculture far south into the eastern prairies. The few clues we have about the northern limit of effective maize agriculture, however, indicate a far more modest depression—to a limit well north of the eastern prairie area (Larsen 1985a). Hence, such an extreme summertime cooling is unlikely. In a review of the climatological record on the Great Plains, Bamforth (1990) discovered little to suggest that the Little Ice Age had a strong effect on carrying capacity. Tree-ring records on the Great Plains reveal great differences in the severity of winter temperatures since 1602 (Fritts, Lofgren, and Gordon 1979: 33–34). Bamforth argued that interannual differences in temperature, and probably precipitation as well, characterized the period. He cited the variation in the varves deposited at the Vore site in Wyoming in support of this interannual variability. The mid-1500s were conspicuous in this respect (Bamforth 1990: 364). Such variation would have reduced agricultural predictability more than anything else might have done.

Bamforth's study (1990) casts serious doubt on the severity of cooling that Green (1993) read into the Minnesota palynological record. Not only were the effects of the period milder than the estimated 2-degree Fahrenheit drop in average daily temperature during the growing season, but characterizing the period as one of consistently cooler and wetter climate seems questionable. For central Europe, where the Little Ice Age is routinely cited in terms of the seriousness of its economic impact, analysis of monthly records discloses the period to have been very mixed. In a pattern congruent with the Great Plains data, the only consistent features were a March that was cold and a June that was cool and wet (Bamforth 1990: 359–360).

Irrespective of the effects of the Neo-Boreal pattern, there remains the issue of the degree to which contemporary hoe cultivation systems were vulnerable. On this matter opinion is divided. Brown (1982), Hart (1992), Moffat (1979: 242–245), and Sasso (1993: 335–340) have argued that agricultural techniques might have been sufficient to overcome the effects of small environmental downturns, particularly if those downturns did not persist over long sequences of years. Anfinson and Wright (1990) have criticized the climatic model in general, arguing that on-the-ground effects were rarely the same from place to place under the same climatic regime. Hence, even under adverse climatic fluctuations, the availability of wide choices in where to locate fields would have offset the worst of the fluctuations.

EPIDEMIC DISEASE. Recent attention to the historic importance of epidemic diseases in reshaping cultures through dramatic population shrinkage has raised the possibility that the native experience of European diseases was a potent force in the eastern prairies as well as in other parts of the Americas. Dobyns (1983) has advocated the position that European diseases had a ripple effect on populations deep within the northern continent. He regarded eastern North America as having been severely afflicted by European diseases, starting with the smallpox epidemic of 1520–1524. Repeated pandemics ensured that even the relatively remote populations of the eastern prairies underwent serious population reductions. Green (1993) agreed, arguing that trade contacts between midwestern groups and peoples of the Mississippi Valley and the Southwest, via the Great Plains, made early exposure to Old World pathogens possible. This explained a drop in his count of dated archaeological sites for the early sixteenth century. This count, however, has serious deficiencies (to be discussed later) and should not encourage uncritical acceptance of European-introduced diseases as shapers of culture history in the absence of more direct information.

Reevaluation of evidence from throughout the Americas has led to a very different picture of the impact of European diseases on Native American populations (Larsen 1994; Thornton 1997). Certain populations declined little until after they had come into direct, sustained contact with Europeans (Ramenofsky 1987; Snow 1995c). Larsen (1994) pointed out that Indian populations also suffered losses in pre-Columbian times that reflected the ongoing impact of non-European vectors.

The case for European disease as a likely factor in population reduction has frequently been made in the case of the Winnebago (e.g., N. Lurie 1960: 795–802). La Potherie mentioned this factor in describing the supposedly large-scale changes in Winnebago population during the mid-1600s, when they were reduced from legendary dominance to a more diminutive role in eastern Wisconsin (Blair 1911, 2: 293–301). Although Winnebago contact with the French was limited mainly to Nicolet until the 1670s, his visit in 1634 may have set off the same disease effects that Champlain's meeting had on the St. Lawrence Iroquois a century earlier. After the 1700s, a population decline was recorded for the people of the eastern prairies that was basically similar to those recorded elsewhere in the East (Blassingham 1956; Thornton 1987; Zitomersky 1994). For times prior to Nicolet's visit, however, insufficient evidence has been gathered to demonstrate that populations in the eastern prairies were depressed on a scale of epidemic proportions and, by implication, dropped to new levels of cultural simplification. Perhaps the changes in social organization implied by the decrease in house floor size from the height of the longhouse period of the sixteenth century were the result of sudden population loss (Hollinger 1995), but a comparable change in average house size among the Iroquois did not accompany evidence of a pandemic (Ramenofsky 1987; Snow 1995c).

TIMING OF CRITICAL CHANGES. Distinguishing among the various factors proposed to account for settlement and subsistence change in the eastern prairies poses major problems, owing largely, but not entirely, to the coarse-grained chronology that has prevailed until recently (Ramenofsky 1987). For example, Baerreis and Bryson (1965: 217) observed that the relative roles of cultural and climatic factors were obscured by what they thought was the coincidental timing of the Neo-Boreal episode with the beginning of European contact.

Building on patterns noted earlier by C. Mason (1976: 338) and Dobbs (1982: 93), Green (1993: 291) identified the sixteenth century as the period during which depopulation changed the cultural situation in the upper Midwest. He argued that "a gap in calibrated radiometric dates between the early 1500s into the mid 1600s" indicated a period of reduction in occupational intensity. He asserted that the sample of 39 dates from 24 sites available in 1984 was large enough and sufficiently unbiased to be useful empirically. Green thought that any deliberate bias was offset by the relatively impartial distribution of research in the Oneota, Late Woodland, and historic periods.

In the sixteenth century, however, sites were concentrated differently from the way they had been in previous periods. The Cal-Sag area of Chicago witnessed a relative boom in population, corresponding to an observed decrease elsewhere (Brown, ed., 1990). Further, the literal interpretation of radiocarbon date distributions on which Green's inference rests has many pitfalls (Shott 1992). Asch and Brown (1990: 184) have pointed out that large changes in the atmospheric concentration of ^{14}C between 1400 and 1700 significantly affect the extraction of chronological information.

The problem with scenarios that emphasize population reduction as either a cause of cultural changes or a proxy variable for either climatic deterioration or pandemic onslaughts is that the most specific changes identified or even guessed at took place in the fifteenth century rather than the sixteenth. Village layout, bison exploitation, and endemic warfare were features of the social landscape for which an earlier rather than a later context can be supported by the admittedly small amount of archaeological evidence available. Thus, climate and pandemics would have played either reinforcing or other roles, and not the role of primary agent.

Conclusion

Archaeological research into the precontact period in the eastern prairies has disclosed broad continuities in social and economic organization from 1400 to 1700. Many of the cultural features distinctive to the eastern prairies in the early historic period appear to have become established by 1450. With the disappearance of the Middle Mississippian cultural formation, the eastern prairie archaeological cultures assumed the basic form that persisted into the historic period. The final changes took place within a century of initial contact.

Details of this development remain meager, in spite of the assumptions that archaeologists, ethnologists, and historians have readily made about the prairie cultural type. A particular blank is the history of bison hunting, which has

been held for over a century to show western connections that marked a discontinuity with the surplus-producing maize farmers of the Middle Mississippian cultural tradition living east of the Mississippi River. Available information indicates that notions of a replacement of maize-intensive Middle Mississippian societies by more mobile hunter-farmers of the historic type are oversimplistic. This warmed-over version of the Mound Builder myth needs serious reconsideration.

Accumulating archaeological evidence supports the thesis that the eastern prairies had long-term cultural integrity. The ethnic migrations typical of the contact period did not fundamentally alter the area's cultural distinctiveness. Immigrant groups quickly adapted to long-entrenched cultural forms. There is even some question about the antiquity of the immigration of the eastern Algonquian-speaking tribes. Whatever their influence was, it was minor in comparison with the basic developments in material culture achieved by peoples of Siouan-speaking ancestry.

The major impact of events in the historic period was the escalation of warfare in which captives acquired new uses. A Calumet ceremony arose to cope with this rise in intertribal warfare. At the same time, eastern and southwestern trade connections were strengthened, and from time to time groups experimented with large-scale settlements. Although these and other cultural features either intensified or developed in response to factors generated upon contact with Europeans, the basically offensive patterns of warfare of relatively mobile farmers had developed at least a century before Europeans set foot on the continent.

Acknowledgments

A version of this chapter prepared in 1993 was circulated widely for critical review. In addition to comments received from our readers, this version has benefited greatly from the spate of articles published since the earlier version was written. We wish to acknowledge the assistance of many individuals who graciously provided data, comments, and suggestions. In particular, we wish to express our gratitude to the following colleagues: Adrian Anderson, Jeffrey Behm, Robert Birmingham, Robert F. Boszhardt, William Cremin, Victoria Dirst, Clark A. Dobbs, Thomas Emerson, Kenneth Farnsworth, Fred Finney, Guy E. Gibbon, Larry Grantham, R. Eric Hollinger, Lynne Goldstein, William Green, Robert Jeske, Noel Justice, Thomas Kehoe, Paul Kreisa, Rochelle Lurie, Charles Markman, Terence Martin, Carol I. Mason, Jodie O'Gorman, David F. Overstreet, Roland L. Rodell, Lynn Rusch, Barbara Stafford, James Stoltman, Bonnie Styles, James L. Theler, Joseph Vradenburg, Mike Wiant, Randall Withrow, and James Yingst. Any shortcomings in our use of this information rest with us. We also wish to thank Donald Lintner and Kim Avery of the Graphics Division of Media and Duplicating Services of the University of Wisconsin–Parkside for their assistance in the development of Figure 15.1.

Locations of Primary Collections

Major collections pertaining to the Oneota tradition and related late prehistoric populations of the eastern prairies are located in the following institutions: (1) Illinois. Illinois State Museum, Springfield; Dickson Mounds Museum, Lewiston; Northwestern University, Evanston; Field Museum, Chicago; University of Illinois, Champaign-Urbana; and LaSalle County Historical Society, Utica; (2) Wisconsin. Great Lakes Archaeological Research Center, Inc., Milwaukee; Lawrence University, Appleton; Logan Museum of Anthropology, Beloit College; Public Museum of the City of Milwaukee; Neville Public Museum of Brown County, Green Bay; Oshkosh Public Museum; State Historical Society of Wisconsin, Madison; University of Wisconsin–La Crosse (Mississippi Valley Archaeology Center); University of Wisconsin–Madison; University of Wisconsin–Milwaukee; and University of Wisconsin–Oshkosh; (3) Iowa. Luther College, Decorah; Office of the State Archaeologist, Iowa City; and University of Iowa, Iowa City; (4) Missouri. Missouri State Parks, Columbia; and University of Missouri, Columbia; (5) Minnesota. Houston County Historical Society, Caledonia; Institute for Minnesota Archaeology, Minneapolis; Minnesota Historical Society, St. Paul; Science Museum of Minnesota, St. Paul; and University of Minnesota, Minneapolis; (6) Michigan. Western Michigan University, Kalamazoo; (7) Indiana. Glenn A. Black Laboratory, Indiana University, Bloomington; (8) District of Columbia. National Museum of Natural History, Smithsonian Institution, Washington, DC.

Notes

1. According to George Rogers Clark, this single claim was made by Chief Baptist Ducoign of the Kaskaskia (James 1928: 497; Schoolcraft 1851–1857, 4: 135).
2. An excellent case in point is the migration history mapped in the Ioway land claim (Green 1995).
3. For the Great Lakes area, Cleland (1992) showed that substantial continuity existed in some parts but not others.
4. The date for the beginning of this cultural tradition remains hotly contested.
5. The small ceramic collection is insufficient to place the Anker site unambiguously into present-day conceptions of the Fisher-Huber tradition. The mixture of cord-marked surface treatment (12 percent) and wide-line decoration (58 percent, distributed on smoothed and cord-marked surfaces) points to an age between the twelfth and sixteenth centuries (Bluhm and Liss 1961). According to criteria developed in the LaCrosse area, the two sherds with punctates are compatible with a fifteenth-century age. The length of the Anker house may point to a later date (Hollinger 1995).
6. See also Brain 1979; Quimby 1966; Wray 1983.
7. Lake Winnebago Trailed was present in Horizon I; a similar dated context for this type is documented for the Pammel Creek site (Arzigian et al. 1989).
8. As Cleland (1992) noted, the diagnostic pottery type Lake Winnebago Trailed is present at numerous fifteenth-century sites in the upper Great Lakes.

9. Brown (1991) and Lehmer (1963) have summarized the first-hand reports of Perrot (Blair 1911), Raudot (Kinietz 1940), and Deliette (Pease and Werner 1934).
10. The radiocarbon dates point to an early twelfth-century date for the Grant site, somewhat earlier than the decorated sherds seem to indicate.
11. A comparable description made more than 100 years later among the Pawnee of the Great Plains was recorded by Dunbar and analyzed by Roper (1991, 1992).
12. The attribution of the Arkansas vessels to the Anker site by Bluhm and Liss (1961: 106–107) rests on the uncorroborated testimony of private collectors.
13. Before 1400, the stream of pottery and other objects made its way up the Illinois as far as the Osborne site (Kankakee Refuse Heap) (Conrad 1991: 153). Prestige goods in the form of copper repoussé objects entered the Illinois Valley (e.g., Material Service and Gentleman Farm sites) and elsewhere in the eastern prairies (Hall 1962: Pl. 81; Sampson and Esarey 1993).
14. The Illinois, however, received their porcupine quills from the Potawatomi and Ottawa to the north (Pease and Werner 1934: 339).
15. According to G. Wright (1967: 192), the idea that the direction of trade arose from the attraction of European goods "is illustrated by the comments of Perrot (Blair 1911, 1: 88) that the hosts lavished 'all that they possess in trade goods or other articles; and they reduce themselves to such an extreme poverty that they do not even reserve for themselves a single hatchet or knife.' In this context, even French kettles, 'used until they were past service' (Blair 1911, 1: 173), were traded to groups not in direct contact with the French, where they became status items."
16. Raiding, hunting, and trading expeditions often covered great distances. For instance, the Illinois traveled to Chequamegon Bay to trade with the French in the late 1660s (Hunt 1940: 123), and seventeenth-century Iroquois raids were made deep into Illinois country (Hunt 1940). Hennepin (1938: 145) commented that members of Louisiana tribes not uncommonly covered 300 to 400 leagues as long-distance hunters. Sauk traveled far to the southwest to get horses from Spanish settlements, reportedly going to "St. Fee," and Pawnees conducted long-distance hunts ranging from 400 to 900 miles in distance (Roper 1991: 198). Charlevoix mentioned that at La Baye in 1721, a Winnebago chief showed him various European items, including a Catalán pistol, a container of ointment, and a pair of Spanish shoes obtained in 1719 by the Oto in an ambush raid on a Spanish group to the southwest in the Missouri Valley, subsequently traded to the Ioway and then to the Winnebago (Thwaites 1902: 413–414).
17. Radiocarbon dates support the position that the Lane Enclosure embankment belongs to the Classic period, not the contact period, although contact period pits intrude into the earthwork (Hollinger 1995: 163).
18. Hall (1993) reported skeletal dispositions at the Crable site that suggested casualties from violent conflict.
19. In addition, Rusch (1985) tentatively identified a stockade line on a 1936 aerial photo of the Springview site in east-central Wisconsin. This site may represent the well-described, often-

discussed, but archaeologically elusive "Mascoutin village" near the Fox River. The village was reputedly occupied around 1650–1680 by numerous groups besides the Mascoutin, including the Miami and Kickapoo (Rusch 1985).

20. The temporal limits placed on the Neo-Boreal have differed widely. Although Emerson and Brown (1992) considered the onset to wetter and cooler conditions to have started around 1450, other sources have placed it around 1500 (Bamforth 1990).

21. Vegetational effects are noted north of one area of intense Oneota occupation: the "Big Woods" of east-central Minnesota apparently expanded as a result of the Neo-Boreal shifts of around 1550 (Grimm 1983). King (1981) also noted roughly contemporary effects on the vegetation in northeastern Illinois. The water level of Lake Michigan responded to this regime of increased moisture by rising approximately 3 meters (Larsen 1985a, 1985b). High levels began in the sixteenth century and declined mainly in the early eighteenth century.

16

Postscript

The chapters in this volume provide a badly needed synthesis of archaeological research on aboriginal people living in eastern North America at the time of European contact. Chapter 2, by Milner, Anderson, and Smith, offers a valuable set of first-level approximations of how people distributed themselves across the Eastern Woodlands. As the other chapters then clearly set out, some of the precontact societies survived; others did not. Some archaeological complexes have clear-cut affiliations with modern tribal groups; others do not. The contributors have provided a real service to the archaeological profession. We are all too specialized these days, and none of us can hope to know the primary literature beyond our own narrow focus.

But the value of these contributions goes well beyond the world of professional archaeology. In this concluding essay, I wish to situate them within the shifting political landscape of contemporary American archaeology.

Archaeologists long held a monopoly on the pre-Columbian past of native America. The discipline arose when eighteenth- and nineteenth-century intellectuals decided it was important to gather facts and artifacts before the Indians vanished completely. Thomas Jefferson, America's first scientific archaeologist, argued that Indians could—and really should—be studied as part of the rest of nature. Jefferson defined American Indians, like the mammoth bones and fruit trees in his own garden, as specimens to be empirically investigated and objectively understood.

A century later, American Indians seemed to be vanishing as surely as the American bison, and so too were the archaeological vestiges of Indian history. As museum anthropologists hurried to document the remaining Indian culture and collect its artifacts, pothunters plundered one archaeological site after another. Many Americans worried that foreigners were exporting the best of America's ancient past.

Congress recognized the threat of uncontrolled excavation of archaeological sites and in 1906 passed the Antiquities Act. The bill reflected President Theodore Roosevelt's passion for conserving and studying natural history, protecting America's past, and ensuring continued access for a fast-growing scientific community. The new law made looting of Indian sites on federal land a felony, established a regulatory framework to restrict research permits to professionally trained archaeologists, and empowered the president to designate key archaeological sites as national monuments. Congress asked the Smithsonian Institution to identify America's most important archaeological sites and to issue permits to those archaeologists properly qualified to work on them.

By criminalizing the unauthorized removal of antiquities from federal lands, the 1906 law effectively quashed amateur access, Indian and non-Indian alike, to the remote American past. The archaeological record became part of America's greater national identity because it documented its progression from savagery to becoming the most civi-

DAVID HURST THOMAS

229

lized place on earth. In 1906, this heritage was formally entrusted to science. The Antiquities Act never acknowledged that Indian people might have their own religious, spiritual, or historical connections to it, in large part because American Indians were seen as representing an earlier, archaic stratum of ancient America, destined to pass gracefully into oblivion. Whatever Indians had to say about their past was defined as irrelevant to the greater American narrative.

A series of antiquities-related acts followed over the next half century or so: establishment of the National Park Service in 1916, the National Environmental Policy Act of 1969, the Archeological Resources Protection Act of 1979, and so forth. In light of this comprehensive federal mandate, it is small wonder that professional archaeologists came to view the archaeological record of the United States as their exclusive intellectual property—because by law, it pretty much was.

American Indians, of course, refused to vanish. Their numbers bottomed out in the 1890s and have dramatically increased ever since. Twentieth-century Indian people survived their predicted extinction and began exploring non-Indian America on their own, applying their "ancient ways" to fresh pursuits including art, politics, medicine, the law, sports, and even anthropology. They began to create their own reality, defining pathways distinct from the mainstream American values that had nearly destroyed them.

Especially since the 1960s, Indian people have stepped up their fight to reclaim and reinforce their treaty-guaranteed sovereignty. Native Americans realized that achieving power over their own history had tangible payoffs in their everyday lives, which were still subject to long-conflicted federal policies. Economic development in Indian country remains integrally connected to politics—intertwined with issues of sovereignty, tribal identity, access to resources, cultural issues, and ideology. In seeking identities independent of the notions of them held by non-Indian historians and anthropologists, many Native Americans came to resent the appropriation of their ancient artifacts and ancestral bones by "experts" who claimed an authority denied to the Indians themselves. As native people across the land tried to recapture their own language, culture, and history, they became increasingly concerned with recovering and taking control of tribal heirlooms and human remains.

Congress responded to these sensitivities in 1990 by passing the Native American Graves Protection and Repatriation Act ("NAGPRA" for short). NAGPRA protects newly discovered Indian graves, but it also mandates that America's universities and museums audit their Indian collections and return inappropriately collected materials to affiliated tribal representatives. This legislation marked a significant shift in the federal stance toward the rights of Indian people and a sea change in the perception and practice of American archaeology. As in 1906, the federal government asserted its right to legislate access to the American past. But the

1990 law explicitly acknowledged that Indian pasts are relevant to the American present. This public and visible benchmark reflected a deep-seated shift in thinking, emphasizing America's self-perception as a multifaceted, pluralistic society (McLaughlin 1998a, 1998b). The American creed shifted away from that of the time-honored melting pot to newer perspectives recognizing the merits of a multicultural society.

Such an interpretation of the American character was unimaginable in earlier decades. The Antiquities Act of 1906, which legally transferred the Indian past to the American public domain, was crafted without Indian involvement and with no suggestion that Indian people might have spiritual affiliations with that past. In 1990, for the first time, native people were empowered to question mainstream American ownership of the Indian past, both literally and metaphorically. No longer were Indian bones found on public land automatically defined as natural resources, as federal property to be safeguarded in scientific custody. No longer did science have a monopoly on defining the meaning of archaeological sites; instead, native groups were invited to assign their own spiritual and historical meanings to archaeological sites and their contents.

A key provision of NAGPRA requires that certain artifacts and human remains held in America's museums be returned to the people who are "culturally affiliated" with those objects. In the language of NAGPRA, the critical question of cultural affiliation is to be decided by "a preponderance of the evidence based upon geographical, kinship, biological, archaeological, linguistic, folkloric, oral tradition, historic, or other information or expert opinion." No priority was assigned to these very diverse criteria.

In instances where a court is called upon to adjudicate the issue of cultural affiliation, the judge will listen to all sides and make a determination based upon the weight of evidence. Although archaeologists and historians have traditionally enjoyed priority over native people in giving "expert testimony," NAGPRA shifts the balance. No longer is the scientific position privileged by the courts—the equivalent of "beyond a reasonable doubt" or "scientific certainty." Preponderance, involving as it does only 51 percent confidence, has opened up the dialogue on establishing cultural affiliation, paving the way for oral tradition and native perspectives to weigh in more heavily than before.

By not specifically defining "Indian," NAGPRA implies that the term designates anyone who has been accepted as a member of a federally recognized Indian tribe. In this way, NAGPRA reinforces the sovereignty of tribal authority, basically defining as "Indian" anybody who belongs to an "Indian tribe." The law thus places a tremendous burden on that deceptively simple word "tribe," which itself has multiple definitions and shades of meaning.

The term "tribe" had been troublesome for anthropologists long before the passage of NAGPRA. In a classic study, Morton Fried (1968) defined tribes as loosely organized sets of villages or migratory camps with some central leadership but with little or no coercive power. So viewed, members of a tribe commonly speak the same basic language, share an ideological unity, and use a distinctive name for themselves. Tribes generally have a cultural network that includes common ritual and religious beliefs, a subsistence network linking economic production, distribution, and consumption, and a kinship network stipulating that people marry within the tribe. Fried believed that tribes were secondary phenomena resulting from contact with more powerful societies. "So-called tribal groups . . . are not social organizations whose integrity receded into a remote past," he argued. Rather, "the tribalism displayed is a reaction to more recent events and conditions. . . . What it amounts to is [that a tribe is] created by governmental action, its members showing considerable diversity in culture, language, and in physical type" (Fried 1968: 17). But this forces one to ask: If "tribes" resulted only from Euroamerican contact, what went before? What about the Mississippian chiefdoms discussed in several chapters of this volume?

Fried's definition also caused considerable trouble because, as William Sturtevant (1983) pointed out, it is almost impossible to determine the existence of a tribe from documentary evidence; we simply know too little about the various cultural, economic, and kinship networks to make an informed decision. And if it is difficult for an ethnohistorian to infer tribal structure from documents, how likely is it that archaeologists can define such "tribes" on the basis of excavated remains? How do you dig up "the same basic language," an "ideological unity," or a "distinctive name?"

These problems notwithstanding, it is hard to overemphasize the importance of "tribe" to generations of attorneys, judges, juries, lawmakers, and bureaucrats. As Felix Cohen (1982) stressed in his classic *Handbook of Federal Indian Law,* the notions of tribe and tribal status have been critical in establishing relations between the United States government and Indian communities. The legal concept of tribe derives from a 1901 Supreme Court decision, *Montoya v. United States,* which defined an Indian tribe as "a body of [1] Indians of the same or a similar race, united in [2] a community under [3] one leadership or government, and [4] inhabiting a particular though sometimes ill-defined territory" (Sturtevant 1983: 10). In this and subsequent decisions, the court clearly distinguished tribe from band and nation, concluding that "the word 'nation' as applied to the uncivilized Indians is so much of a misnomer as to be little more than a compliment."

So, unsatisfactory though the term might be, "tribe" remains the fundamental unit of Indian law. Congress has long insisted that federal agencies are not allowed simply to overpower Indian tribes; they are mandated to sign treaties with tribes, as they would with any other sovereign power. The term "tribe" is common in the pre-1871 treaties that effectively chartered modern Indian societies and established the basis for treaty-guaranteed rights. The Indian Reorganization Act of 1934 established various political entities known as "tribes" throughout the United States.

Then there is the common-sense definition of tribe, the meaning of the term as used by Indian people. "As I use it and as I understand other Indian people using it," wrote Vine Deloria Jr., the word tribe "means a group of people living pretty much in the same place who know who their relatives are. I think that's the basic way we look at things" (Deloria quoted in Bordewich 1996: 68).

In practice, each of these definitions is difficult to apply to modern issues of cultural affiliation because, in large part, today's tribal governments are the product of lobbying by John Collier, commissioner of Indian affairs under Franklin D. Roosevelt, and the subsequent Indian Reorganization Act, in the 1930s. To complicate matters still further, each Indian tribe is entitled to establish its own membership requirements. The great range in tribal self-definitions has become a major issue in NAGPRA cases because the very concept of tribal sovereignty assumes that tribes have remained in the same place over long periods of time.

Sometimes historians can trace tribal roots back for centuries; sometimes they cannot. Sometimes archaeologists can find material residues tracking tribal histories well back in time; sometimes they cannot. Sometimes archaeological and historical research confirms Deloria's assumption of tribes "living pretty much in the same place"; sometimes it does not. Sometimes, in the language of NAGPRA, the "geographical, kinship, biological, archaeological, linguistic, folkloric, oral tradition, historic, or other information or expert opinion" leads to a single verdict on cultural affiliation based on "preponderance of the evidence"; sometimes it does not.

The specifics of NAGPRA highlight the differing histories that have evolved for ancient Native America. One was written down in books, taught in schools, and exhibited in museums—this is mainstream history, reflecting the perspective of the outsider, the conqueror of continents. An entirely different history existed in Indian country, a history handed down by Indian people from elder to child as tribal tradition, language, spirituality, ritual, and ceremony—even as jewelry and personal ornamentation.

Federal law now recognizes the validity of both historical pathways, triggering significant changes in American archaeology in recent years—from the scientific study of ancient things toward the systematic study of people and their history. Archaeologists no longer conduct their inquiries in a vacuum; archaeologists today actively consult and involve Indian people.

Archaeology and oral tradition differ, of course, in the ways observations are made and interpreted. Western science relies on discrete observational units and measurable variables that can be combined analytically and/or held constant. Native observations arise from people who view themselves within a holistic environment and societal framework. These are separate ways of knowing the past, but they tend to converge in a broad sense because certain important issues tend to dominate both realms—migrations, warfare, land use, ethnicity, and so forth. But because different standards apply to the ways relevant information is collected, evaluated, and used, the two ways of knowing will never completely coincide.

Like most of the other archaeologists contributing to this volume, I was trained under the old, pre-NAGPRA rules, which invested archaeologists with the primary authority to protect, excavate, curate, and interpret the archaeological record. NAGPRA broke archaeology's long-standing monopoly on the ancient American past, and contemporary Native Americans now have a legally defined stake in the archaeological record of their ancestors. Since 1990, archaeology has become only one of the multiple stewards of America's remote past. American archaeology is trying to reinvent itself, and the process is not an easy one.

Many native people are encountering archaeology for the first time, and reactions are typically mixed. Whereas some see archaeology as increasingly relevant to their interests, others see a distinct limit to that relevance. A number of Native Americans have said publicly that they already know their past from traditional sources; they don't need archaeologists to tell them about their origins. For many other Indian people, archaeology holds great interest, with the potential for contributing important historical information. On many issues, archaeologists and Indians find themselves in complete agreement: The past is important—we should attempt to understand it and preserve whatever remains of it. Many tribes have long-standing archaeology programs, employing both Indian and non-Indian archaeologists. Several tribes sponsor their own museums that display archaeological materials. The Society for American Archaeology presently sponsors a Native American scholarship fund to encourage Indian people to become qualified professional archaeologists; it is funded, in large part, from royalties earned on books written by archaeologists discussing the Native American past. Indian people are increasingly involved in archaeological meetings and publications—not merely as "informants" but more often as participants and collaborators.

Archaeologists have provided evidence in support of litigation for land claims, evidence that sometimes turns the tide in a tribe's favor. Some tribes have used their archaeological record to promote tribal sovereignty, an important social and political issue throughout Indian country. For some tribes, archaeology has important financial consequences.

I recap this background to ask how the contributions to this volume fit into the political landscape of modern American archaeology. The answer to this question is not easy, because archaeologists no longer speak just to one another. For better or worse, others are listening, and larger issues are involved. I believe that a useful direction might come from an unlikely source. In quite another context, Vine Deloria Jr. has suggested that the modern social sciences need to define for others the "acceptable" beliefs to which a majority of the discipline subscribes (Deloria 2000). He suggests that the legal profession might provide a useful model for such summaries with its periodic "Restatements," through which a number of prestigious scholars and practicing attorneys summarize current thinking on important topics such as contracts, torts, and so forth. These Restatements provide judges, lawyers, and interested lay people with authoritative and concise interpretations of the current state of law and doctrine. Deloria suggests that the social sciences might adopt a version of this practice, to inform nonspecialists about doctrines that have changed over time, the development of new theories, and the relevance of new kinds of evidence.

It is critical today that archaeologists translate the minutiae of their research into human terms, that they bring the products of their painstaking work to a broader audience. The chapters in this volume address a level of detail virtually incomprehensible to outsiders—nuances of Z-twist and S-twist cordage, mind-numbing details of ceramic and glass bead typology, a welter of confusing terms for archaeological horizons and traditions. If we are to be taken seriously, archaeologists must interpret the specifics of paleoenvironmental data, artifact typology, settlement patterning, demographic shifts, evidence of warfare, changing social organization, mortuary patterns, and so forth in a way that interested nonprofessionals can understand. I think the chapters in *Societies in Eclipse* do this quite well.

Archaeologists no longer enjoy the cultural and political clout of pre-NAGPRA days. Archaeology in the early twenty-first century serves multiple publics, and if the profession is to survive, it must make archaeological results available in more readily accessible ways. Viewed as "Restatements" in Deloria's sense, the chapters published here provide nonspecialists with concise and up-to-date summaries of what modern archaeologists think, and why they think it.

If archaeologists cannot adequately explain such things, why should anybody else care?

References Cited

Abel, Timothy
1995   The Petersen Site and New Perspectives on the Late
        Prehistory of Northwestern Ohio. Master's thesis,
        University of Toledo.

Able, Timothy J., J. Mark Koralewski, and George B. DeMuth
2000   Cemetery Ridge: An Early Village Site Located in San-
        dusky County, Ohio. In *Cultures before Contact: The
        Late Prehistory of Ohio and Surrounding Regions,* edited
        by R. A. Genheimer, pp. 384–403. Ohio Archaeologi-
        cal Council, Columbus.

Abler, Thomas
1980   Iroquois Cannibalism: Fact Not Fiction. *Ethnohistory*
        27 (4): 309–316.

Abler, Thomas S., and Elisabeth Tooker
1978   Seneca. In *Handbook of North American Indians,* vol. 15,
        Northeast, edited by Bruce G. Trigger, pp. 505–517.
        Smithsonian Institution Press, Washington, DC.

Adams, E. Charles
1979   Cold Air Drainage and Length of Growing Season in
        the Hopi Mesas Area. *Kiva* 44 (4): 285–296.

Adovasio, J. M., and W. C. Johnson
1981   The Appearance of Cultigens in the Upper Ohio Val-
        ley: A View from Meadowcroft Rockshelter. *Pennsyl-
        vania Archaeologist* 51 (1–2): 63–80.

Adovasio, J. M., K. J. Shaunessy, W. C. Johnson, W. P. Athens,
A. T. Boldurian, R. C. Carlisle, D. C. Dirkmaat, J. Donahue,
D. R. Pedler, and E. J. Siemon III
1990   Archaeology at the Howarth-Nelson Site (36FA40),
        Fayette County, Pennsylvania. *Pennsylvania Archaeolo-
        gist* 60 (1): 32–68.

Alam, Emil A.
1957   A Preliminary Report on the Rochester Site. *Section of
        Man, Carnegie Museum, Newsletter* 12: 3–7.

Alden, John Richard
1944   *John Stuart and the Southern Colonial Frontier.* University
        of Michigan Press, Ann Arbor.

Allen, Rhesa M. Jr.
1964   Geology and Mineral Resources of Greene and Madi-
        son Counties. *Bulletin of the Virginia Division of Min-
        eral Resources* 78: 81–85.

Allerton, David, George M. Luer, and Robert S. Carr
1984   Ceremonial Tablets and Related Objects from Florida.
        Florida Anthropologist 37: 5–54.

Alvord, C. W., and L. Bidgood (editors)
1912   *The First Explorations of the Trans-Allegheny Region by
        the Virginians, 1650–1674.* Arthur H. Clark, Cleveland.

Anderson, David A.
1998   Elites among the Monongahela? An Examination of
        the Late Prehistoric/Protohistoric Period in South-
        western Pennsylvania. Paper presented at the annual
        meeting of the Society for Pennsylvania Archaeology,
        New Cumberland.

Anderson, David G.
1989   Late Prehistoric Phases in the Eastern Woodlands.
        Poster presentation at the annual meeting of the
        Southeastern Archaeological Conference, Tampa, FL.
1990   Stability and Change in Chiefdom-Level Societies. In
        *Lamar Archaeology: Mississippian Chiefdoms in the Deep
        South,* edited by Mark Williams and Gary Shapiro,
        pp. 187–213. University of Alabama Press, Tuscaloosa.

1991a   Examining Prehistoric Settlement Distribution in Eastern North America. *Archaeology of Eastern North America* 19: 1–22.

1991b   Paleoindian and Early Archaic Settlement in the Southeast: Inferences from the Primary Record. Paper presented at the annual meeting of the Middle Atlantic Archaeological Conference, Ocean City, MD.

1994a   Factional Competition and the Political Evolution of Mississippian Chiefdoms in the Southeastern United States. In *Factional Competition and Political Development in the New World,* edited by Elizabeth M. Brumfiel and John W. Fox, pp. 61–76. University of Cambridge Press, Cambridge.

1994b   *The Savannah River Chiefdoms.* University of Alabama Press, Tuscaloosa.

Anderson, David G., David J. Hally, and James L. Rudolph

1986   The Mississippian Occupation of the Savannah River Valley. *Southeastern Archaeology* 5: 32–51.

Anderson, David G., and J. W. Joseph

1988   *Prehistory and History along the Upper Savannah River: Technical Synthesis of Cultural Resource Investigations, Richard B. Russell Multiple Resource Area,* vol. 1. National Park Service, Interagency Archeological Services, Atlanta, GA.

Anfinson, Scott F., and H. E. Wright Jr.

1990   Climatic Change and Culture in Prehistoric Minnesota. In *The Woodland Tradition in the Western Great Lakes: Papers in Honor of Elden Johnson,* edited by Guy E. Gibbon, pp. 213–211. Publications in Anthropology no. 4. University of Minnesota, Minneapolis.

Anonymous

1875   Ancient Canals in Florida. *Forest and Stream* 5 (8), August 12, 1875.

Archaeological and Historical Consultants

1990   Archaeological Data Recovery at Site 36Fa368, Grays Landing Lock and Dam, Fayette County, Pennsylvania. Report. Contract no. DACW59-88-C-0036. E.R. no. 81-1120-051. Archaeological and Historical Consultants, Inc. Submitted to the US Army Corps of Engineers, Pittsburgh District, Pittsburgh, PA.

Arès, Richard

1970   Les Relations des Jésuites et le climat de la Nouvelle-France. *Memoires de la Societé Royale du Canada* 8: 75–91.

Arnade, Charles W.

1996   Raids, Sieges, and International Wars. In *The New History of Florida,* edited by M. Gannon, pp. 100–116. University Press of Florida, Gainesville.

Arzigian, Constance M.

1989   The Pammel Creek Site Floral Remains. In *Human Adaptation in the Upper Mississippi Valley: A Study of the Pammel Creek Oneota Site (47Lc61), La Crosse, Wisconsin,* by Constance M. Arzigian, Robert F. Boszhardt, James L. Theler, Roland L. Rodell, and Michael J. Scott, pp. 111–156. *Wisconsin Archeologist* 70.

Arzigian, Constance M., Robert F. Boszhardt, Holly P. Halverson, and James L. Theler

1994   The Gunderson Site: An Oneota Village and Cemetery in La Crosse, Wisconsin. *Journal of the Iowa Archeological Society* 41: 3–75.

Arzigian, Constance M., Robert F. Boszhardt, James L. Theler, Roland L. Rodell, and Michael J. Scott

1989   Human Adaptation in the Upper Mississippi Valley: A Study of the Pammel Creek Oneota Site (47Lc61), La Crosse, Wisconsin. *Wisconsin Archeologist* 70: 1–281.

Asch, David L., and James A. Brown

1990   Stratigraphy and Site Chronology. In *At the Edge of Prehistory: Huber Phase Archaeology in the Chicago Area,* edited by James A. Brown and Patricia J. O'Brien, pp. 174–185. Illinois Department of Transportation, Springfield, and Center for American Archeology, Kampsville, IL.

Asch, David L., and Nancy Asch Sidell

1990   Archaeobotany. In *At the Edge of Prehistory: Huber Phase Archaeology in the Chicago Area,* edited by James A. Brown and Patricia J. O'Brien, pp. 241–265. Illinois Department of Transportation, Springfield, and Center for American Archeology, Kampsville, Illinois.

Asch, Nancy Buck, and David L. Asch

1975   Plant Remains from the Zimmerman Site—Grid A: A Quantitative Approach. In *The Zimmerman Site: Further Excavations at the Grand Village of Kaskaskia,* by Margaret Kimball Brown, pp. 116–120. Reports of Investigations no. 32. Illinois State Museum, Springfield.

Austin, Robert J., and Alfred J. Woods Jr.

1991   Archaeological Testing of a Proposed Road Alignment on Galt Island, Lee County, Florida. Report. Piper Archaeology/Janus Research, St. Petersburg, FL. Submitted to William Mills.

Babich, Jay, Natalie M. Kirshner, William C. Johnson, and Thomas S. Kirshner

1996   Archaeological Investigations at the Kirshner Site (36Wm213), a Middle Monongahela Period Village in the Youghiogheny River Valley: An Interim Report. Paper presented at the annual meeting of the Eastern States Archeological Federation, Huntington, WV.

Baby, Raymond S.

1971   Prehistoric Architecture: A Study of House Types in the Ohio Valley. *Ohio Journal of Science* 71 (4): 193–198.

Baerreis, David A., and Reid A. Bryson

1965   Climatic Episodes and the Dating of Mississippian Cultures. *Wisconsin Archeologist* 46 (4): 203–220.

Baerreis, David A., Reid A. Bryson, and J. E. Kutzbach

1976   Climate and Culture in the Western Great Lakes Region. *Midcontinental Journal of Archaeology* 1 (1): 39–58.

Bakeless, John

1950   *The Eyes of Discovery: America as Seen by the First Explorers.* J. B. Lippincott, New York.

Baker, S. W.

1988   Neale's Landing Site Ceramics: A Perspective on the Protohistoric Period from Blennerhasset Island. *West Virginia Archaeologist* 40 (2): 40–53.

Bamforth, Douglas B.

1990   An Empirical Perspective on Little Ice Age Climatic Change on the Great Plains. *Plains Anthropologist* 35: 359–366.

Banks, Philip O., and Rodney M. Feldmann

1970   *Guide to the Geology of Northeastern Ohio.* Northern Ohio Geological Society, Kent.

Barber, Michael

1991 The Preliminary Vertebrate Faunal Analysis of the Spessard Site (44FV134), Fluvanna County, Virginia. *Quarterly Bulletin of the Archaeological Society of Virginia* 46: 70–76.

1993 Native Americans on the Virginia Frontier in the Seventeenth Century: Recent Archaeological Excavations in the Southern Piedmont and Ridge and Valley Provinces of Virginia. Paper presented at the annual meeting of the Southeastern Archaeological Conference, Raleigh, NC.

Barber, Michael B., Michael F. Barber, and Christopher L. Bowen

1998 Phase III Excavations at the Hurt Power Plant Site, Pittsylvania County, Virginia: A Protohistoric Village on the Middle Roanoke (Staunton) River. Report. Preservation Technologies, Inc., Salem, Virginia. Manuscript on file, Virginia Department of Historic Resources, Richmond.

Barbour, Philip (editor)

1986 *The Complete Works of Captain John Smith (1580–1631).* 3 vols. University of North Carolina Press, Chapel Hill.

Battles, Mrs. Richard E.

1969 One Foot in a Grave. *Journal of Alabama Archaeology* 15 (1): 35–38.

1972 Copper and Lithic Artifacts. *Journal of Alabama Archaeology* 18: 32–35.

Bauxar, J. Joseph

1978 History of the Illinois Area. In *Handbook of North American Indians,* vol. 15, *Northeast,* edited by Bruce G. Trigger, pp. 594–601. Smithsonian Institution Press, Washington, DC.

Beauchamp, William M.

1900 *Aboriginal Occupation of New York.* Bulletin no. 32. New York State Museum, Albany, NY.

1907 *Aboriginal Place Names of New York.* Bulletin no. 108. New York State Museum, Albany.

1916 *Moravian Journals Relating to Central New York, 1745–66.* Onondaga Historical Asociation, Syracuse, NY.

Becker, Marshall Joseph

1972 An Analysis of Skeletal Remains from an Ossuary at the Harris Yard Site (33WO-1), Rossford, Ohio. *Michigan Archaeologist* 18 (1): 14–19.

1987 An Analysis of the Human Skeletal Remains from 46Hm73: A Susquehannock Population of the Mid-Sixteenth Century. *West Virginia Archaeologist* 39 (2): 37–53.

1991 The Stature of a Susquehannock Population of the Mid-Sixteenth Century Based on Skeletal Remains from 46Hm73. *Pennsylvania Archaeologist* 61 (2): 73–88.

Belovich, Stephanie J.

1985a *Archaeological Excavations at the Greenwood Village Site (33Cu92): Final Report.* Cleveland Archaeological Research Report no. 56. Cleveland Museum of Natural History.

1985b *Archaeological Testing, the Columbia Road Site (33Cu102), Cuyahoga Valley National Recreation Area.* Archaeological Research Report no. 49. Cleveland Museum of Natural History.

1991 The Staas Site, a Whittlesey Ceremonial/Mortuary Camp in Cuyahoga County, Ohio. Research manuscript on file, Cleveland Museum of Natural History.

Belovich, Stephanie J., and David S. Brose

1992 Late Woodland Fortifications of Northern Ohio. *Kirtlandia* 3: 3–23.

Benn, David W.

1989 Hawks, Serpents, and Bird-Men: Emergence of the Oneota Mode of Production. *Plains Anthropologist* 34: 233–260.

1998 Moon: A Fortified Mississippian-Period Village in Poinsett County, Arkansas. In *Changing Perspectives on the Archaeology of the Central Mississippi River Valley,* edited by M. J. O'Brien and R. C. Dunnell, pp. 225–257. University of Alabama Press, Tuscaloosa.

Benn, David W. (editor)

1992 Excavations at the Moon Site (3PO488), a Middle Mississippian Village in Northeastern Arkansas. Report. Center for Archaeological Research, Southwest Missouri State University, Springfield. Submitted to the Arkansas Highway and Transportation Department.

Beriault, John, Robert Carr, Jerry Stipp, Richard Johnson, and Jack Meeder

1981 The Archaeological Salvage of the Bay West Site, Collier County, Florida. *Florida Anthropologist* 34: 39–58.

Bernabo, J. C.

1981 Quantitative Estimates of Temperature Changes over the Last 2700 Years in Michigan Based on Pollen Data. *Quaternary Research* 15 (2): 143–159.

Bernhardt, Jack

1973 Excavation of a Late Woodland Occupation in Gillie's Cave, Twinsburg, Portage County, Ohio. Master's thesis, Department of Anthropology, Kent State University.

Bier, Donald Jr.

n.d. The Archaeology of the Eiden Site, Lorain County, Ohio, and the Late Prehistory of North-Central Ohio. Unpublished 1985–1990 research manuscript on file at the Cleveland Museum of Natural History and the Lorain County Metroparks.

Biggar, Henry P.

1922– *The Works of Samuel de Champlain.* 6 vols. The Cham-
1936 plain Society, Toronto.

Blaine, Martha Royce

1979 *The Ioway Indians.* University of Oklahoma Press, Norman.

Blair, Emma H. (editor)

1911 *The Indian Tribes of the Upper Mississippi Valley and Region of the Great Lakes as Described by Nicolas Perrot, French Commandant in the Northwest.* 2 vols. Arthur H. Clark, Cleveland, OH.

Blake, Leonard W., and Hugh C. Cutler

1975 Food Remains from the Zimmerman Site. In *The Zimmerman Site: Further Excavations at the Grand Village of the Kaskaskia,* by Margaret Kimball Brown, pp. 92–4. Reports of Investigations no. 32. Illinois State Museum, Springfield.

Blakely, Robert L., and B. Detweiler-Blakely

1989 The Impact of European Disease in the Sixteenth-Century Southeast: A Case Study. *Midcontinental Journal of Archaeology* 14 (1): 62–89.

Blakely, Robert, and David Mathews

1990   Bioarchaeological Evidence for a Spanish–Native American Conflict in the Sixteenth-Century Southeast. *American Antiquity* 55: 718–744.

Bland, Edward

1651   *The Discovery of New Brittaine.* Printed by Thomas Harper for John Stephenson, London.

Blassingham, Emily J.

1956   The Depopulation of the Illinois Indians. *Ethnohistory* 3: 193–224, 361–412.

Blau, Harold, Jack Campisi, and Elisabeth Tooker

1978   Onondaga. In *Handbook of North American Indians,* vol. 15, *Northeast,* edited by Bruce G. Trigger, pp. 491–499. Smithsonian Institution Press, Washington, DC.

Bluhm, Elaine A., and Gloria J. Fenner

1961   The Oak Forest Site. *Illinois Archaeological Survey Bulletin* 3: 138–161.

Bluhm, Elaine A., and Allen Liss

1961   The Anker Site. In *Chicago Area Archaeology,* edited by E. A. Bluhm, pp. 89–137. Bulletin no. 3. Illinois Archaeological Survey, Carbondale.

Bordewich, Fergus M.

1996   *Killing the White Man's Indian.* New York: Doubleday.

Boszhardt, Robert F.

1985   *Final Cultural Resources Investigations along CTH 'SN' in La Crosse County, Wisconsin,* with contributions by James Theler, Arthur Bettis, Dean Thompson, and Cynthia Stiles-Hanson. Reports of Investigations no. 33. Mississippi Valley Archaeology Center, University of Wisconsin–La Crosse.

1987   Midway Revisited: It's More and Less than What It Used to Be. Paper presented at the 32d annual Midwest Archaeological Conference, Milwaukee, WI.

1989   Ceramic Analysis and Site Chronology of the Pammel Creek Site. In *Human Adaptation in the Upper Mississippi Valley: A Study of the Pammel Creek Oneota Site (47Lc61), La Crosse, Wisconsin,* by Constance M. Arzigian, Robert F. Boszhardt, James L. Theler, Roland L. Rodell, and Michael J. Scott, pp. 41–94. *Wisconsin Archeologist* 70.

1991   Oneota South. Paper presented at the annual meeting of the Midwest Archaeological Conference, La Crosse, WI.

1992   *Phase III Archaeological Mitigation at the Trane Site (47LC447), La Crosse, Wisconsin,* with a contribution by Constance Arzigian. Reports of Investigations no. 138. Mississippi Valley Archaeology Center, University of Wisconsin–La Crosse.

1994   Oneota Group Continuity at La Crosse: The Brice Prairie, Pammel Creek, and Valley View Phases. *Wisconsin Archeologist* 75: 173–236.

1997   Ceramics from the Sand Lake Archaeological District, Wisconsin. *Journal of the Iowa Archeological Society* 44: 139–159.

Boszhardt, Robert F., James P. Gallagher, Thomas W. Bailey, Robert F. Sasso, and Katherine P. Stevenson

1984   *Archaeological Investigations at the Mouth of Sand Lake Coulee: The 1982 Season.* Reports of Investigations no. 8. Mississippi Valley Archaeology Center, University of Wisconsin–La Crosse.

Boszhardt, Robert F., James P. Gallagher, James L. Theler, Thomas W. Bailey, Arthur Bettis III, and Dean Thompson

1986   *Additional Cultural Resources Investigations at Selected Portions of the State Road Coulee-Pammel Creek Flood Control Project at La Crosse, Wisconsin.* Reports of Investigations no. 27. Mississippi Valley Archaeology Center, University of Wisconsin–La Crosse.

Boszhardt, Robert F., Wendy Holtz, and Jeremy Nienow

1995   A Compilation of Oneota Radiocarbon Dates as of 1995. In *Oneota Archaeology: Past, Present, and Future,* edited by William Green, pp. 203–227. Office of the State Archaeologist, University of Iowa, Iowa City.

Bourne, Edward G. (editor)

1904   *Narratives of the Career of Hernando de Soto in the Conquest of Florida as Told by a Knight of Elvas and in a Relation by Luys Hernandez de Biedma, Factor of the Expedition, Translated by Buckingham Smith, Together with an Account of de Soto's Expedition based on the Diary of Rodrigo Ranjel, His Probate Secretary, Translated from Oviedo's Historia General y Natural de las Indias.* 2 vols. A. S. Barnes, New York.

Bowen, Jonathan E.

1992   Archaeology of the Western Basin Area of Northwest and North-Central Ohio. Ph.D. dissertation, Department of Anthropology, Ohio State University, Columbus.

1994   *The Sandusky River Area of North-Central Ohio: 1300–1600.* Sandusky Valley Chapter, Archaeological Society of Ohio, Upper Sandusky, OH.

2000   The Ensign Locality: A Fifteenth-Century Settlement in Sandusky County, Ohio. Paper presented at the 19 May 2000 meeting of the Ohio Archaeological Council, Columbus.

Bowman, Irene

1979   The Draper Site: Historical Accounts of Vegetation in Pickering and Markham Townships with Special Reference to the Significance of a Large, Even-Aged Stand Adjacent to the Site. In *Settlement Patterns of the Draper and White Sites: 1973 Excavations,* edited by Brian Hayden, pp. 47–58. Department of Archaeology Publication 6. Simon Fraser University, Burnaby, BC, Canada.

Bowman, Robert

1904   Early History and Archaeology of Yazoo County. *Publications of the Mississippi Historical Society* 8: 427–441.

Boyce, Hettie L.

1985   The Novak Site: A Late Woodland Upland Monongahela Village. *Pennsylvania Archaeologist* 55 (3): 21–49.

Boyd, C. Clifford Jr.

1993   The Trigg Site (44MY3) and Other Late Woodland/Contact Period Sites along the New River Valley in Southwest Virginia. Paper presented at the annual meeting of the Southeastern Archaeological Conference, Raleigh, NC.

Boyd, Mark F.

1937   Expedition of Marcos Delgado, 1686. *Florida Historical Quarterly* 16: 2–32.

Boyer, William P.

1982   In Search of Jefferson's Mound. Manuscript on file, Virginia Department of Historic Landmarks, Richmond.

Boyle, David
1900 *Annual Archaeological Report for 1899.* Ontario Ministry of Education, Toronto.

Bradley, James W.
1979 The Onondaga Iroquois, 1500–1655: A Study in Cultural Change and Its Consequences. Ph.D. dissertation, Interdisciplinary Program in Social Sciences, Syracuse University, NY.

1987a *Evolution of the Onondaga Iroquois: Accommodating Change, 1500–1655.* Syracuse University Press, Syracuse, NY.

1987b Native Exchange and European Trade: Cross-Cultural Dynamics in the Sixteenth Century. *Man in the Northeast* 33: 31–46.

Bradley, James W., and S. Terry Childs
1991 Basque Earrings and Panther's Tails: The Form of Cross-Cultural Contact in Sixteenth-Century Iroquoia. In *Metals in Society, Theory beyond Analysis,* edited by Robert M. Ehrenreich, pp. 7–17. MASCA Research Papers in Science and Archaeology 8 (2). University Museum of Archaeology and Anthropology, University of Pennsylvania, Philadelphia.

n.d. Basque Earrings and Panther's Tails: The Form of Cross-Cultural Contact in Sixteenth-Century Iroquoia. Manuscript.

Brain, Jeffrey P.
1975 Artifacts of the Adelantado. *The Conference on Historic Site Archaeology* 8: 129–138.

1979 *Tunica Treasure.* Papers of the Peabody Museum of American Archaeology and Ethnology, vol. 71. Harvard University, Cambridge, MA, and Peabody Museum of Salem, Salem, MA.

1985 The Archaeology of the Hernando de Soto Expedition. In *Alabama and the Borderlands: From Prehistory to Statehood,* edited by R. Reid Badger and Lawrence A. Clayton, pp. 96–107. University of Alabama Press, Tuscaloosa.

1988 *Tunica Archaeology.* Papers of the Peabody Museum of American Archaeology and Ethnology, vol. 78. Harvard University, Cambridge, MA.

1989 *Winterville: Late Prehistoric Culture Contact in the Lower Mississippi Valley.* Archaeological Report no. 23. Mississippi Department of Archives and History, Jackson.

Brain, Jeffrey P., and P. Phillips
1996 *Shell Gorgets: Styles of the Late Prehistoric and Protohistoric Southeast.* Peabody Museum of American Archaeology and Ethnology, Harvard University, Cambridge, MA.

Brashler, Janet G.
1987 A Middle-Sixteenth-Century Susquehannock Village in Hampshire County, West Virginia. *West Virginia Archaeologist* 39 (2): 1–31.

Brashler, Janet G., and Ronald W. Moxley
1990 Late Prehistoric Engraved Shell Gorgets of West Virginia. *West Virginia Archaeologist* 42 (1): 1–10.

Braun, D. P.
1986 Midwestern Hopewellian Exchange and Supralocal Interaction. In *Peer Polity Interaction and Socio-Political Change,* edited by C. Renfrew and J. F. Cherry, pp. 117–126. Cambridge University Press, Cambridge.

Braun, Lucy
1950 *Deciduous Forests of Eastern North America.* Blakiston, Philadelphia.

Bray, Robert T.
1961 The Flynn Cemetery: An Orr Focus Oneota Burial Site in Allamakee County, Iowa. *Journal of the Iowa Archaeological Society* 10 (4): 15–25.

Breitburg, E.
1992 Vertebrate Faunal Remains. In *Fort Ancient Cultural Dynamics in the Middle Ohio Valley,* edited by A. G. Henderson, pp. 209–241. Monographs in World Archaeology no. 8. Prehistory Press, Madison, WI.

Brose, David S.
1971 The Southeast Ceremonial Complex in Northeast Ohio. *Ohio Archaeologist* 21 (4): 16–19.

1972 The Development of Archaeology in Northeastern America. In *The Development of North American Archaeology,* edited by J. Fitting, pp. 116–139. Natural History Press, New York.

1973 A Preliminary Analysis of Recent Excavations at the South Park Site, Cuyahoga County, Ohio. *Pennsylvania Archaeologist* 43: 25–52.

1974 American Indian History and Prehistory in Northern Ohio. *Aboriginal Research Bulletin* 3 (2): 57–104.

1975 *Preliminary Results of a Reconnaissance of the Area of Lower Tinkers Creek Valley.* Cuyahoga Valley National Park Board, Peninsula, OH.

1976a Introduction. In *The Late Prehistory of the Lake Erie Drainage Basin: A 1972 Symposium Revised,* edited by D. S. Brose, pp. 1–23. Scientific Papers of the Cleveland Museum of Natural History, Cleveland, OH.

1976b Locational Analysis in the Prehistory of Northeast Ohio. In *Cultural Change and Continuity: Essays in Honor of James B. Griffin,* edited by C. Cleland, pp. 3–18. Academic Press, New York.

1976c The Whittlesey Tradition of Northeastern Ohio. In *The Late Prehistory of the Lake Erie Drainage Basin: A 1972 Symposium Revised,* edited by D. S. Brose, pp. 25–47. Scientific Papers of the Cleveland Museum of Natural History, Cleveland, OH.

1977a *Archaeological Reconnaissance and Subsurface Investigations of the Proposed US Steel Company Greenfield Steel Plant, Ashtabula Co., Ohio, and Erie Co., Pennsylvania.* Archaeological Research Report no. 27. Cleveland Museum of Natural History.

1977b The Hillside Road Site: Fort Ancient Influence in a Whittlesey Occupation in Cuyahoga County, Ohio. *Ohio Archaeologist* 27 (1): 31–43.

1978a The Late Prehistory of the Upper Great Lakes. In *Handbook of North American Indians,* vol. 15, *Northeast,* edited by Bruce G. Trigger, pp. 569–582. Smithsonian Institution Press, Washington, DC.

1978b Lithic Technology and Cultural Ecology in Northeast Ohio. In *Lithic Technology and Prehistoric Subsistence,* edited by D. Davis, pp. 43–65. Publications in Anthropology no. 20. Vanderbilt University, Nashville, TN.

1983 Rethinking the French Presence in the Upper Great Lakes. In *Lulu Linear Punctated: Essays in Honor of George Irving Quimby,* edited by Robert C. Dunnell and Donald K. Grayson, pp. 209–252. Anthropological

Papers 72. Museum of Anthropology, University of Michigan, Ann Arbor.

1984   History as Handmaiden to Archaeology. *Ohio Archaeologist* 34 (1): 28–29.

1985a   A Study in Grey: Critical Evaluation of Some Recent Literature in Cultural Resource Management. *American Anthropologist* 87: 370–377.

1985b   RP3 Study Unit: The Late Woodland Period in Northeast Ohio, Study Unit B. Report. Ohio Historical Society and Cleveland Museum of Natural History. Submitted to the Ohio Historic Preservation Office, Columbus.

1985c   RP3 Study Unit: Late Prehistoric and Protohistoric Periods in Northeast Ohio, Study Unit B. Report. Ohio Historical Society and Cleveland Museum of Natural History. Submitted to the Ohio Historic Preservation Office, Columbus.

1987a   Early Explorations. In *The Encyclopedia of Cleveland History,* edited by D. VanTassel and J. Grabowski, pp. 384–385. Indiana University Press, Bloomington.

1987b   Material Culture, Radio-Carbon Chronology and Ceramic Type Sets Defining the Late Woodland Phases of the Whittlesey Tradition of Northeastern Ohio. Paper presented at the annual meeting of the Ohio Archaeological Council, Cleveland.

1988a   *Research Problems in Northeastern Ohio Archaeology.* Oberlin Research Seminars in Anthropology. Oberlin, OH.

1988b   Redaction of theses by Nick Toth and Kathy Shick, and reanalyses of lithics and grave lots at the Libben site (33OT6). Manuscripts on file at the Cleveland Museum of Natural History, Archaeology Department, Cleveland, OH.

1992   Late Whittlesey Social Organization as Reflected by the Ceramic Distributions of the South Park Site, Cuyahoga County, Ohio. Paper presented at the annual meeting of the Midwest Archaeological Conference, Grand Rapids, MI.

1993   Early Mississippian Earspools at the Late Woodland Mill Hollow Site, Erie County, Ohio. *Mid-Continental Journal of Archaeology* 18 (1): 97–130.

1994a   Trade and Exchange in the Midwestern United States. In *Prehistoric Exchange Systems in North America,* edited by J. Erikson and T. Baugh, pp. 215–240. Plenum Press, New York.

1994b   *The South Park Village Site and the Late Prehistoric Whittlesey Tradition of Northeast Ohio.* Monographs in World Archaeology no. 20. Prehistory Press, Madison, WI.

1997a   Cultural Relationships of the Late Prehistoric Whittlesey and Sandusky Traditions of Northern Ohio: A Response to Stothers, Murphy and Prufer. *North American Archaeologist* 18 (2): 177–204.

1997b   Reviews of "The Western Basin Tradition: Algonquin or Iroquois?" by D. Stothers, and "Cultural Change and Continuity: The Western Basin, Ontario Iroquois, and Sandusky Traditions—A 1982 Perspective" by D. Stothers and J. Graves. *North American Archaeologist* 18 (2): 151–164.

2000   Late Prehistoric Societies of Northeastern Ohio and Adjacent Portions of the South Shore of Lake Erie: A Review. In *Cultures before Contact: The Late Prehistory of Ohio and Surrounding Regions,* edited by R. A. Genheimer, pp. 96–123. Ohio Archaeological Council, Columbus.

Brose, David S., Michael Arsenijevic, Timothy Matson, and Michael Tevez

1988   Redaction of theses and notes by Mary L. Harrison with Orrin C. Shane III and reanalyses and reinterpretations of Late Woodland fauna, pipes, and shell artifacts from the Libben site (33OT6) in north-central Ohio. Manuscripts on file at the Cleveland Museum of Natural History, Archaeology Department, Cleveland, OH.

Brose, David S., Stephanie Belovich, Michael Brooslin, Robert Burns, John Hall, Harold Haller, Chris Pierce, and Carl Ubbeohde

1981   *Prehistoric and Historic Archaeological Investigations of the Cuyahoga Valley National Recreation Area, Ohio.* Archaeological Research Report no. 30. Cleveland Museum of Natural History.

Brose, David S., and Donald Bier Jr.

1978   *Investigations at the Prehistoric Archaeological Eiden Site, 33LO14, Lorain County Metropolitan Park District, Lorain County, Ohio: The 1977 Season.* Archaeological Research Report no. 29 (2). Cleveland Museum of Natural History, Cleveland, OH.

Brose, David S., and Patricia S. Essenpreis

1973   A Report of a Preliminary Archaeological Survey of Monroe County. *Michigan Archaeologist* 19 (1–2): 1–143.

Brose, David S., William C. Johnson, and Michael J. Hambacher

1979   Archaeological Investigations of the Eastwall Site, 33Ab41: Protohistoric Iroquoian Occupations of Northeast Ohio. Manuscripts and data analyses on file in the Cleveland Museum of Natural History Archaeological Laboratory Archives.

n.d.   Archaeological Investigations at the Eastwall Site, 33AB41: Protohistoric Iroquoian Occupations of Northeast Ohio. Research manuscript on file at the Cleveland Museum of Natural History, Archaeological Laboratory Archives.

Brose, David S., Alfred M. Lee, Steven McQuillin, John Hall, and Russell Weisman

1985a   *Archeological and Architectural Survey of Alternate Corridors, Eastern Extension, Lakeland Freeway, Lake and Ashtabula Counties, Ohio.* Archaeological Research Report no. 49. Cleveland Museum of Natural History.

1985b   *An Archaeological and Historical Architectural Survey of Ecological Transects: Upper Chagrin Drainage, Geauga County, Ohio.* Archaeological Research Report no. 54. Cleveland Museum of Natural History.

Brose, David S., Alfred M. Lee, and Renata Wolynec

1983   *Historic Resources Protection Plan for the Lake Erie Coastal Zone with a Predictive Model of Archaeological Site Location, Inventory of Known Properties, and Testing of the Elk Creek Site, Girard, Erie Co., Pennsylvania.* Northwest Institute of Research, Erie, PA.

Brose, David S., and Cheryl Munson

1986   Cultural Resource Management in the Midwest: Status and Directions. In *Society for American Archaeology: Regional Conferences Summary Report,* edited by C. Irwin-Williams and D. Fowler, pp. 68–77. Washington, DC.

Brose, David S., and G. Michael Pratt

1975 *Salvage Excavations at the Walnut Tree Site, 33Cu35: Archaeology of an Impacted Prehistoric Campsite.* Technical Report in Archaeology. Northeast Ohio Regional Sewer District, Cleveland.

Brose, David S., and John F. Scarry

1976 Boston Ledges: Spatial Analyses of an Early Late Woodland Rockshelter in Summit County, Ohio. *Mid-Continental Journal of Archaeology* 1 (2): 115–156.

Brose, David S., Russell Weisman, Elmer Bannon, and Richard Meindl

1988 Decorative and technological analyses, statistical inferences, and socioecological interpretations of Late Woodland ceramics at the Libben Site (33OT6) in North-Central Ohio. Research manuscripts and redactions of theses and notes by D. McKenzie and G. Harris. Manuscripts on file, Cleveland Museum of Natural History Archaeological Laboratory and Kent State University.

Brose, David S., Gregory Wentzel, Helga Bluestone, and Patricia Essenpreis

1976 Conneaut Fort: A Prehistoric Whittlesey Focus Village in Ashtabula County, Ohio. *Pennsylvania Archaeologist* 56 (4): 29–77.

Brose, David S., and N. M. White

1983 Recent Data on Fort Ancient Occupation in the Caesar Creek Valley, Southwestern Ohio. *West Virginia Archaeologist* 35 (2): 3–39.

Brown, D. M., G. A. McKay, and L. J. Chapman

1980 *The Climate of Southern Ontario.* Climatological Studies 5. Environment Canada, Atmospheric Environment Service, Toronto.

Brown, Ian W.

1981 A Study of Stone Box Graves in Eastern North America. *Tennessee Anthropologist* 6 (1): 1–26.

1989 The Calumet Ceremony in the Southeast and Its Archaeological Manifestations. *American Antiquity* 54: 311–331.

Brown, James A.

1975 The Impact of the European Presence on Indian Culture. In *Contest for Empire 1500–1755: Proceedings of an Indiana American Revolutionary Bicentennial Symposium,* edited by John B. Elliott, pp. 6–24. Indiana Historical Society, Indianapolis.

1982 What Kind of Economy Did the Oneota Have? In *Oneota Studies,* edited by Guy E. Gibbon, pp. 107–112. Publications in Anthropology no. 1. University of Minnesota, Minneapolis.

1989 On Style Divisions of the Southeastern Ceremonial Complex: A Revisionist Perspective. In *The Southeastern Ceremonial Complex: Artifacts and Analysis,* edited by Patricia Galloway, pp. 183–204. University of Nebraska Press, Lincoln.

1990 Ethnohistoric Connections. In *At the Edge of Prehistory: Huber Phase Archaeology in the Chicago Area,* edited by James A. Brown and Patricia J. O'Brien, pp. 155–160. Illinois Department of Transportation, Springfield, and Center for American Archaeology, Kampsville, IL.

1991 *Aboriginal Cultural Adaptations in the Midwestern Prairies.* Garland, New York.

Brown, James A. (editor)

1961 *The Zimmerman Site: A Report on Excavations at the Grand Village of Kaskaskia, La Salle County, Illinois.* Report of Investigations no. 9. Illinois State Museum, Springfield.

1990 The Oak Forest Site: Investigations into Oneota Subsistence-Settlement in the Cal-Sag Area of Cook County, Illinois. Part 2 of *At the Edge of Prehistory: Huber Phase Archaeology in the Chicago Area,* edited by J. A. Brown and P. J. O'Brien, pp. 121–308. Illinois Department of Transportation, Springfield, and Center for American Archeology, Kampsville, IL.

Brown, James A., Terrance J. Martin, J. C. Redmond, and Kathryn C. Egan

1995 Overview Report of Investigations at the Zimmerman Site West by Northwestern University. In *Northwestern Archaeological Field School Guide for 1995,* pp. 1–42. Department of Anthropology, Northwestern University, Evanston, IL.

Brown, James A., and J. Willis

1995 Reexamination of Danner Pottery from the Starved Rock Area. Paper presented at the Midwest Archaeological Conference, Beloit, WI.

Brown, James A., Roger W. Willis, Mary A. Barth, and George K. Neumann

1967 *The Gentleman Farm Site, La Salle County, Illinois.* Reports of Investigations no. 12. Illinois State Museum, Springfield.

Brown, Jeffrey D., and Shaune M. Skinner

1983 Monongahela on the Wrong Site of the River. Paper presented at the annual meeting of the Pennsylvania Archaeological Society.

Brown, Jennifer S. H., and Elizabeth Vibert (editors)

1996 *Reading Beyond Words: Contexts for Native History.* Broadview Press, Toronto.

Brown, Margaret Kimball

1972 Native-Made Glass Pendants from East of the Mississippi. *American Antiquity* 37: 432–439.

1973 Cultural Transformation among the Illinois: The Application of a Systems Model to Archaeological and Ethnohistorical Data. Ph.D. dissertation, Michigan State University, East Lansing.

1975 *The Zimmerman Site: Further Excavations at the Grand Village of the Kaskaskia.* Reports of Investigations no. 32. Illinois State Museum, Springfield.

Brown, Robin C.

1994 *Florida's First People.* Pineapple Press, Sarasota, FL.

Broyles, B. J.

1970 Burial of a Medicine Man. *Wonderful West Virginia* 34 (4): 12–13, 27.

Brumfiel, Elizabeth M.

1989 Factional Competition in Complex Society. In *Domination and Resistance,* edited by D. Miller, M. Rowlands, and C. Tilley, pp. 127–139. Unwin-Hyman, London.

Bryson, Reid A., D. A. Baerreis, and W. M. Wendland
  1970   The Character of Late-Glacial and Post-Glacial Cli-
          matic Changes. In *Pleistocene and Recent Environments
          of the Central Great Plains,* edited by W. Dort Jr. and
          J. K. Jones Jr., pp. 53–74. University Press of Kansas,
          Lawrence.

Bryson, Reid A., and Thomas J. Murray
  1977   *Climates of Hunger: Mankind and the World's Changing
          Weather.* University of Wisconsin Press, Madison.

Bryson, Reid A., and Wayne M. Wendland
  1967   Tentative Climatic Patterns for Some Late Glacial and
          Post-Glacial Episodes in Central North America. In
          Life, Land and Water, edited by William J. Mayer-
          Oakes, pp. 271–298. Occasional Papers no. 1. Depart-
          ment of Anthropology, University of Manitoba, Win-
          nipeg, Canada.

Buchanan, W. T. Jr.
  1984   *The Trigg Site, City of Radford, Virginia.* Archaeological
          Society of Virginia, Richmond.

Bugler, Caroline
  1979   *Dutch Painting in the Seventeenth Century.* Mayflower
          Books, New York.

Buikstra, Jane E.
  1976   *Hopewell in the Lower Illinois Valley.* Scientific Papers
          no. 2. Northwestern Archaeological Program,
          Evanston, IL.

Buikstra, Jane E., and George Milner
  1991   Isotopic and Archaeological Interpretations of Diet in
          the Central Mississippi Valley. *Journal of Archaeological
          Science* 18: 319–329.

Buker, William E.
  1968   The Archaeology of the McKees Rocks Late Prehis-
          toric Village Site. *Pennsylvania Archaeologist* 38 (1–4):
          3–49.
  1970   The Drew Site (36-AL-62). *Pennsylvania Archaeologist*
          40 (3–4): 21–68.
  1975   The Drew Phase of the Monongahela Complex.
          SPAAC Speaks 11 (1): 21–29.
  1993   The Portman Site (36AL40). *Pennsylvania Archaeologist*
          63 (2): 7–52.

Bullen, Ripley P.
  1964   *The Archaeology of Grenada, West Indies.* Contributions
          of the Florida State Museum, Social Sciences 11.
          Gainesville.

Bullen, Ripley P., and Adelaide K. Bullen
  1956   *Excavations on Cape Haze Peninsula, Florida.* Contribu-
          tions of the Florida State Museum, Social Sciences 1.
          Gainesville.
  1972   *Archaeological Investigations on St. Vincent and the
          Grenadines.* American Studies Report 8. Gainesville.
  1976   *The Palmer Site.* Publication 8. Florida Anthropological
          Society, Gainesville.

Bush, David R.
  1984   The Erie Indians and the Whittlesey Focus: Late Abo-
          riginal Life in Northeastern Ohio. *Lake County Histori-
          cal Quaterly* 26 (4): 1–25.
  1990   *Excavations at the Grantham Site in Lake County, Ohio.*
          Strata Data, newsletter of the Case Western Reserve
          University Laboratory of Archaeology, Cleveland, OH.

Bush, David R., and Charles Callender
  1984   Anybody but the Erie. *Ohio Archaeologist* 34 (1): 31–35.

Bushnell, Amy T.
  1986   Background and Beginnings of the Deerskin Trade:
          Spanish Documentary Evidence. Paper presented
          at the annual meeting of the American Society for
          Ethnohistory, Charleston, SC.

Bushnell, David I. Jr.
  1909   *The Choctaw of Bayou Lacomb, St. Tammany Parish,
          Louisiana.* Bulletin 48. Bureau of American Ethnol-
          ogy, Washington, DC.
  1914   The "Indian Grave": A Monacan Site in Albemarle
          County, Virginia. *William and Mary Quarterly* 23:
          106–112.
  1930   *The Five Monacan Towns of Virginia, 1607.* Smithsonian
          Miscellaneous Collections 82 (12).
  1935   *The Mannahoac Tribes in Virginia, 1608.* Smithsonian
          Miscellaneous Collections 94 (8).

Butler, Brian M.
  1991   Kincaid Revisited: The Mississippian Sequence in the
          Lower Ohio Valley. In *Cahokia and the Hinterlands:
          Middle Mississippian Cultures of the Midwest,* edited by
          Thomas E. Emerson and R. Barry Lewis, pp. 264–
          273. University of Illinois Press, Urbana.

Butler, Coleen
  1988   A Botanical Study of Feature 86–3 from the Spessard
          Site. Manuscript on file, Department of Anthropol-
          ogy, University of Virginia, Charlottesville.

Butler, Mary
  1939   *Three Archaeological Sites in Somerset County, Pennsylva-
          nia.* Bulletin 753. Pennsylvania Historical Commis-
          sion, Harrisburg.

Callender, Charles
  1962   *Social Organization of the Central Algonkian Indians.*
          Publications in Anthropology 7. Milwaukee Public
          Museum, Milwaukee, WI.
  1978a   Shawnee. In *Handbook of North American Indians,* vol.
          15, *Northeast,* edited by Bruce G. Trigger, pp. 622–
          635. Smithsonian Institution Press, Washington, DC.
  1978b   Illinois. In *Handbook of North American Indians,* vol. 15,
          Northeast, edited by Bruce G. Trigger, pp. 673–680.
          Smithsonian Institution Press, Washington, DC.

Cardinal, Elizabeth A.
  1975   Faunal Remains from the Zimmerman Site, 1970. In
          *The Zimmerman Site: Further Excavations at the Grand
          Village of Kaskaskia,* by Margaret Kimball Brown,
          pp. 73–79. Reports of Investigations 32. Illinois State
          Museum, Springfield.

Carpenter, E. S., K. R. Pfirman, and H. L. Schoff
  1949   The 28th Street Site. *Pennsylvania Archaeologist* 19 (1–
          2): 3–16.

Carr, Christopher, and Robert F. Maslowski
  1995   Cordage and Fabrics: Relating Form, Technology, and
          Social Process. In *Style, Society, and Person, Archaeologi-
          cal Perspectives,* edited by Christopher Carr and Jill E.
          Neitzel, pp. 297–343. Plenum Press, New York.

Carr, Lucian
  1877   *Report on the Exploration of a Mound in Lee County, Vir-
          ginia.* Tenth Annual Report of the Peabody Museum

of American Archaeology and Ethnology. Harvard University, Cambridge, MA.

Carr, Robert S.
1985   Prehistoric Circular Earthworks in South Florida. *Florida Anthropologist* 38: 288–301.

Carskadden, Jeff
1992   The Bosman Site, Muskingum County, Ohio. *Field Notes: The Newsletter of the West Virginia Archaeological Society* 34 (3): 3–4.
1994   Fort Ancient in the Central Muskingum Valley of Eastern Ohio: A View from the Philo II Site. Paper presented at "Cultures before Contact: A Conference on the Late Prehistory of the Ohio Region," Ohio Archaeological Council, Cincinnati.

Carskadden, Jeff, and J. Morton
1977   *The Richards Site and the Philo Phase of the Fort Ancient Tradition.* Occasional Papers in Muskingum Valley Archaeology, no. 1-9. Muskingum Archaeological Survey, Zanesville, OH.

Champlain, Samuel de
1907   *Voyages of Samuel de Champlain 1604–1618.* Original Narratives of Early American History. Charles Scribner's Sons, New York.

Chapman, Carl H., and Leo O. Anderson
1955   The Campbell Site: A Late Mississippi Town Site and Cemetery in Southeast Missouri. *Missouri Archaeologist* 17 (2–3): 10–119.

Chapman, Carl H., J. W. Cottier, D. Denman, D. R. Evans, D. E. Harvey, M. D. Reagan, B. L. Roper, M. D. Southard, and G. A. Waselkov
1977   Investigation and Comparison of Two Fortified Mississippi Tradition Archaeological Sites in Southeast Missouri: A Preliminary Compilation. *Missouri Archaeologist* 38.

Chapman, J., and B. Keel
1979   Candy Creek–Connestee Components in Eastern Tennessee and Western North Carolina and Their Relationship with Adena-Hopewell. In *Hopewell Archaeology,* edited by D. S. Brose and N. B. Greber, pp. 157–161. Kent State University Press, Kent, OH.

Childress, Mitchell R.
1992   Mortuary Vessels and Comparative Ceramic Analysis: An Example from the Chucalissa Site. *Southeastern Archaeology* 11 (1): 31–50.

Childs, S. Terry.
1994   Native Copper Technology and Society in Eastern North America. In *Precolumbian Technology and Archaeometry,* edited by David Scott. Getty Conservation Institute, Los Angeles.

Church, Florence
1987   An Inquiry into the Transition from Late Woodland to Late Prehistoric Cultures in the Central Scioto Valley, Ohio, circa A.D. 500 to A.D. 1250. Ph.D. dissertation, Department of Anthropology, Ohio State University.

Clark, Jerry
1971   Malone Terrace Oneota Site. In *Prehistoric Investigations,* edited by Marshall McKusick, pp. 80–85. Report 3. Office of the State Archaeologist, Iowa City.

Clark, Joshua V. H.
1849   *Onondaga: Or Reminiscences of Earlier and Later Times.* . . . 2 vols. Stoddard and Babcock, Syracuse, NY.

Clausen, Carl J., A. D. Cohen, Cesare Emiliani, J. A. Holman, and J. J. Stipp
1979   Little Salt Spring, Florida: A Unique Underwater Site. *Science* 203: 609–614.

Cleland, Charles E.
1966   *The Prehistoric Animal Ecology and Ethnozoology of the Upper Great Lakes Region.* Anthropological Papers of the Museum of Anthropology no. 29. University of Michigan, Ann Arbor.
1992   *Rites of Conquest: The History and Culture of Michigan's Native Americans.* University of Michigan Press, Ann Arbor.
1999   Cultural Transformations: The Archaeology of Historic Indian Sites in Michigan, 1670–1940. In *Retrieving Michigan's Buried Past: The Archaeology of the Great Lakes State,* edited by J. Halsey, pp. 279–290. Bulletin 64. Cranbrook Institute of Science, Bloomfield Hills, MI.

Cleland, Charles E. (editor)
1971   *The Lasanen Site: An Historic Burial Locality in Mackinac County, Michigan.* Publications of the Museum, Anthropological Series 1 (1). Michigan State University, East Lansing.

Coburn, Mona L.
1989   Mississippian Faunal Remains from the Lundy Site (11–Jd-140), Jo Daviess County, Illinois. *Illinois Archaeology* 1: 5–38.

Coe, Joffre L.
1952   The Cultural Sequence of the Carolina Piedmont. In *Archaeology of the Eastern United States,* edited by James B. Griffin, pp. 301–311. University of Chicago Press, Chicago.
1964   *The Formative Cultures of the Carolina Piedmont.* Transactions of the American Philosophical Society, n.s. 54 (5). American Philosophical Society, Philadelphia.

Coe, Joffre L., and Ernest Lewis
1952   Dan River Series Statement. In *Prehistoric Pottery of the Eastern United States,* edited by James B. Griffin, Museum of Anthropology, University of Michigan, Ann Arbor.

Cohen, Felix S.
1982   *Felix S. Cohen's Handbook of Federal Indian Law.* Revised edition, edited by Rennard Stickland. Bobbs-Merrill, Charlottesville, VA.

Collins, Henry B. Jr.
1929   The "Lost" Calusa Indians of Southwestern Florida. *Explorations and Field Work of the Smithsonian Institution in 1928,* pp. 151–156. Washington, DC.

Connolly, Bob, and Robin Anderson
1987   *First Contact: New Guinea's Highlanders Encounter the Outside World.* Viking, New York.

Connors, Dennis J., Laurence M. Hauptman, Ray Gonyea, and Fred R. Wolcott
1986   *Onondaga: Portrait of a Native People.* Syracuse University Press in association with the Everson Museum of Art, Syracuse, NY.

Conrad, Lawrence A.
1991   The Middle Mississippian Cultures of the Central Illinois River Valley. In *Cahokia and the Hinterlands: Middle Mississippian Cultures of the Midwest,* edited by Thomas E. Emerson and R. Barry Lewis, pp. 119–156. University of Illinois Press, Urbana.

Converse, Robert N.
1973   Fort Ancient Artifacts from the Hardin Village Site, Greenup County, Kentucky. *Ohio Archaeologist* 23 (1): 7–9.

Cordell, Ann S.
1992   Technological Investigation of Pottery Variability in Southwest Florida. In *Culture and Environment in the Domain of the Calusa,* edited by W. H. Marquardt, pp. 105–189. Monograph 1. Institute of Archaeology and Paleoenvironmental Studies, University of Florida, Gainesville.

1994   Pottery Variability and Chronology at Southwest Florida's Pineland Site Complex. Paper presented at the annual meeting of the Southeastern Archaeological Conference, Lexington, KY.

n.d.   Technological Investigation of Pottery Variability at the Pineland Site Complex. In *The Archaeology of Pineland: A Coastal Southwest Florida Site Complex, A.D. 50–1600,* edited by K. J. Walker and W. H. Marquardt. Monograph 4. Institute of Archaeology and Paleoenvironmental Studies, University of Florida, Gainesville. In preparation.

Cottrell, Ron
n.d.   Notes on fieldwork. Manuscript on file, Carnegie Museum of Natural History, Pittsburgh, PA.

Covington, James W.
1959   Trade Relations between Southwestern Florida and Cuba, 1600–1840. *Florida Historical Quarterly* 38: 114–128.

Cowan, C. Wesley
1986   Fort Ancient Chronology and Settlement Evaluation in the Great Miami Valley, vol. 2, Excavations and Chronology. Manuscript on file, Ohio Historic Preservation Office, Cincinnati.

1987   *First Farmers of the Middle Ohio Valley: Fort Ancient Societies, A.D. 1000–1670.* Cincinnati Museum of Natural History, Cincinnati, OH.

1988   From Pithouse to Longhouse, from Community to Chaos: Late Prehistoric and Protohistoric Developments in the Middle Ohio Valley. Paper presented at the Midwest Archaeological Conference, Champaign-Urbana, IL.

1992   The Dawn of History and the Demise of the Fort Ancient Cultures of the Central Ohio Valley. Publication version of paper presented at the annual meeting of the Society for American Archaeology, Pittsburgh, PA.

Cowan, C. W., S. Dunavan, J. P. Nass Jr., and S. Scott
1990   The Schomaker Site: A Middle Period Fort Ancient Town on the Great Miami River, Hamilton County, Ohio. *West Virginia Archaeologist* 42 (1): 11–35.

Cowan, C. Wesley, and Patty Jo Watson (editors)
1989   *The Origins of Agriculture: An International Perspective.* Smithsonian Institution Press, Washington, DC.

Crane, Verner
1981   *The Southern Frontier: 1670–1732.* W. W. Norton, New York.

Crawford, Gary W., David G. Smith, and Vandy E. Bowyer
1997   Dating the Entry of Corn (*Zea mays*) into the Lower Great Lakes. *American Antiquity* 62 (1): 112–120.

Cremin, William M.
1980   The Schwerdt Site: A Fifteenth-Century Fishing Station on the Lower Kalamazoo River, Southwest Michigan. *Wisconsin Archeologist* 61: 280–292.

1983   Late Prehistoric Adaptive Strategies on the Northern Periphery of the Carolinian Biotic Province: A Case Study from Southwest Michigan. *Midcontinental Journal of Archaeology* 8: 91–107.

1992   Researching the Void between History and Prehistory in Southwest Michigan. *Michigan Archaeologist* 38: 19–37.

1996   The Berrien Phase of Southwestern Michigan: Proto-Potawatomi? In *Investigating the Archaeological Record of the Great Lakes State: Essays in Honor of Elizabeth Baldwin Garland,* edited by Margaret B. Holman, Janet G. Brashler, and Kathryn E. Parker, pp. 383–413. New Issues Press, Kalamazoo, MI.

Cresson, Francis M. Jr.
n.d.   Hilltop and Valley Sites of Southwestern Pennsylvania. Manuscript on file, Pennsylvania Historical and Museum Commission, Harrisburg.

Cronon, William
1983   *Changes in the Land: Indians, Colonists, and the Ecology of New England.* Hill and Wang, New York.

Crosby, Alfred W.
1972   *The Columbian Exchange: Biological and Cultural Consequences of 1492.* Greenwood Press, Westport, CT.

Cumming, William P. (editor)
1958   *The Discoveries of John Lederer.* University of Virginia Press, Charlottesville.

Curren, Caleb
1984   *The Protohistoric Period in Central Alabama.* Alabama-Tombigbee Regional Commission, Camden, AL.

Curry, Dennis, and Maureen Kavanaugh
1991   The Middle to Late Woodland Transition in Maryland. *North American Archaeologist* 12: 3–28.

Curtis, S. A., and J. W. Hatch
1981   Cultural Resources in the Southern Lake Erie Basin: A Predictive Model. Report. Argonne National Laboratory, Chicago. Submitted to the United States Army, Corps of Engineers.

Cushing, Frank Hamilton
1897   Exploration of Ancient Key Dweller Remains on the Gulf Coast of Florida. *Proceedings of the American Philosophical Society* 35: 329–448. Philadelphia.

Davis, Christine E.
1993   A Unique Seventeenth-Century Settlement Pattern and Exchange Network in Western Pennsylvania: The Sony Site. Paper presented at the annual meeting of the Society for American Archaeology, St. Louis, MO.

Davis, R. P. Stephen Jr., and H. Trawick Ward
1987   A Comparison of Plowzone and *in Situ* Site Structure at the Fredricks Site, A Siouan Village in Piedmont

North Carolina. Paper presented at the annual meeting of the Southeastern Archaeological Conference, Charleston, SC.

1991a The Evolution of Siouan Communities in Piedmont North Carolina. *Southeastern Archaeology* 10 (1): 40–53.

1991b The Occaneechi and Their Role as Middlemen in the Seventeenth-Century Virginia–North Carolina Trade Network. Paper presented at the annual meeting of the Society for Historical Archaeology, Richmond, VA.

Davis, R. S., G. M. Pratt, and D. C. Wilkie

1976 A Prehistoric Village on Kelly's Island. *Explorer* 18 (3): 11–19.

DeBoer, Warren R.

1988 Subterranean Storage and the Organization of Surplus: The View from Eastern North America. *Southeastern Archaeology* 7: 1–20.

DeJarnette, David, and Asael T. Hansen

1960 *The Archaeology of the Childersburg Site, Alabama.* Notes in Anthropology no. 4. Florida State University, Tallahassee.

DeJarnette, David, Edward Kurjack, and Bennie Keel

1973 Archaeological Investigations in the Weiss Reservoir of the Coosa River in Alabama. *Journal of Alabama Archaeology* 19: 1–201.

Deloria, Vine Jr.

2000 Foreword. In *Skull Wars: Kennewick Man, Archaeology, and the Battle for Native American Identity,* by David Hurst Thomas. Basic Books, New York.

Denig, Edwin T.

1961 *Five Indian Tribes of the Upper Missouri.* University of Oklahoma Press, Norman.

DePratter, Chester B.

1983 Late Prehistoric and Early Historic Chiefdoms in the Southeastern United States. Ph.D. dissertation, Department of Anthropology, University of Georgia, Athens.

1989 Cofitachequi: Ethnohistorical and Archaeological Evidence. In *Studies in South Carolina Archaeology: Essays in Honor of Robert L. Stephenson,* edited by Albert C. Goodyear III and Glen T. Hanson, pp. 133–156. Anthropological Studies 9, Occasional Papers of the South Carolina Institute of Archaeology and Anthropology. University of South Carolina, Columbia.

1991 *Late Prehistoric and Early Historic Chiefdoms in the Southeastern United States.* Garland, New York.

DePratter, Chester B., Charles M. Hudson, and Marvin T. Smith

1985 The de Soto Expedition: From Chiaha to Mabila. In *Alabama and the Borderlands: From Prehistory to Statehood,* edited by Reid Badger and Lawrence Clayton, pp. 108–127. University of Alabama Press, Tuscaloosa.

Dice, Lee R.

1943 *The Biotic Provinces of North America.* University of Michigan Press, Ann Arbor.

Dickens, Roy S. Jr., H. Trawick Ward, and R. P. Stephen Davis Jr. (editors)

1987 *The Siouan Project: Seasons I and II.* Monograph Series 1. Research Laboratories of Anthropology, University of North Carolina, Chapel Hill.

Dickinson, Jonathan

1985 *Jonathan Dickinson's Journal, or God's Protecting Providence, Being the Narrative of a Journey from Port Royal in Jamaica to Philadelphia, August 23, 1696, to April 1st, 1697.* Florida Classics Library, Port Salerno, FL.

Dirst, Victoria, and Paul Kreisa

1982 Human Remains from the Cowling Portion of the Karow Cemetery Site (47/WN/198). *Wisconsin Archeologist* 63: 405–426.

Divale, William

1977 Living Floor Area and Marital Residence: A Replication. *Behavior Science Research* 12: 109–115.

Dobbs, Clark A.

1982 Oneota Origins and Development: The Radiocarbon Evidence. In *Oneota Studies,* edited by Guy E. Gibbon, pp. 91–105. Publications in Anthropology no. 1. University of Minnesota, Minneapolis.

Dobyns, Henry F.

1983 *Their Number Become Thinned: Native American Population Dynamics in Eastern North America.* University of Tennessee Press, Knoxville.

1989 More Methodological Perspectives on Historical Demography. *Ethnohistory* 36: 285–299.

1993 Disease Transfer at Contact. *Annual Review of Anthropology* 22: 273–391.

Dongoske, Kurt, Michael Yeatts, Roger Anyon, and T. J. Ferguson

1997 Archaeological Cultures and Cultural Affiliation: Hopi and Zuni Perspectives in the American Southwest. *American Antiquity* 62 (4): 600–608.

Doran, Glen H., and David N. Dickel

1988 Multidisciplinary Investigations at the Windover Site. In *Wet Site Archaeology,* edited by Barbara A. Purdy, pp. 263–289. Telford Press, Caldwell, NJ.

Dorwin, John

1971 The Bowen Site: An Archaeological Study of Cultural Processes in the Late Prehistory of Central Indiana. *Prehistory Research Series* 4 (4): 193–411. Indiana Historical Society, Indianapolis.

Douglas, John G.

1976 Collins: A Late Woodland Ceremonial Complex in the Woodfordian Northeast. Ph.D. dissertation, Department of Anthropology, University of Illinois at Champaign-Urbana.

Douglass, Andrew E.

1885 Ancient Canals on the Southwest Coast of Florida. *American Antiquarian and Oriental Journal* 7: 277–285.

Dragoo, Don W.

1955 Excavations at the Johnston Site, Indiana County, Pennsylvania. *Pennsylvania Archaeologist* 25 (2): 85–141.

1976 The Upper Allegheny Valley. In *The Late Prehistory of the Lake Erie Drainage Basin: A 1972 Symposium Revised,* edited by D. S. Brose, pp. 76–88. Scientific Papers of the Cleveland Museum of Natural History, Cleveland, OH.

Dragoo, Don W., Richard L. George, and Donald P. Tanner

1964 *Excavations at Selected Archeological Sites in the Chartiers Valley in Western Pennsylvania.* National Park Service Project no. 14-10-5-950-11. Chartiers Creek Flood Control Project, Carnegie Museum, Pittsburgh.

Drooker, Penelope B.

1994   Madisonville Focus Revisited: Reexcavating Fort Ancient from Museum Collections. Paper presented at "Cultures before Contact: A Conference on the Late Prehistory of the Ohio Region," Ohio Archaeological Council, Cincinnati.

1996   Madisonville Metal and Glass Artifacts: Implications for Western Fort Ancient Chronology and Interaction Networks. *Midcontinental Journal of Archaeology* 21 (2): 1–46.

1997a   *The View from Madisonville: Protohistoric Western Fort Ancient Interaction Patterns.* Memoir no. 31. Museum of Anthropology, University of Michigan, Ann Arbor.

1997b   Exotic Ceramics at Madisonville: Implications for Interaction. Paper presented at the joint symposium of the Ontario Archaeological Society and the Midwest Archaeological Conference, Toronto.

1998   *Zoom-In to Madisonville.* CD-ROM. University of Michigan Museum of Anthropology, Ann Arbor.

Dunavan, S. L.

1991   Fort Ancient Paleoethnobotany: New Data and Perspectives. Paper presented at the annual conference of the Society of Ethnobiology, St. Louis.

1993   Madisonville Paleoethnobotany: Crops and Other Plants. Paper presented at the annual meeting of the Society for American Archaeology, St. Louis.

Dunham, Gary

1994   Common Ground, Contesting Identities: The Emergence of Late Prehistoric Burial Ritual in Central Virginia. Ph.D. dissertation, Department of Anthropology, University of Virginia, Charlottesville.

Dunnell, Robert C.

1962   *The Hughes Farm Site (46-Oh-9), Ohio County, West Virginia.* Publication Series 7. West Virginia Archaeological Society, Moundsville, WV.

1980   A Monongahela Settlement in Central Ohio County, West Virginia. *West Virginia Archaeologist* 29: 1–37.

1998   The Langdon Site, Dunklin County, Missouri. In *Changing Perspectives on the Archaeology of the Central Mississippi River Valley,* edited by M. O'Brien and R. Dunnell, pp. 200–224. University of Alabama Press, Tuscaloosa.

Dye, David

1990   Warfare in the Sixteenth-Century Southeast: The de Soto Expedition in the Interior. In *Columbian Consequences,* vol. 2, *Archaeological and Historical Perspectives on the Spanish Borderlands East,* edited by David H. Thomas, pp. 211–222. Smithsonian Institution Press, Washington, DC.

Edging, Richard

1990   *The Turk Site: A Mississippi Period Town in Western Kentucky.* Kentucky Heritage Council, Frankfort.

Edic, Robert F.

1992   The Calusa Island Site (8LL45), Bokeelia (Lee County). Typescript report on file, Department of Anthropology, Florida Museum of Natural History, Gainesville, FL.

Egan, Kathryn C., and S. Loretta Brown

1995   Analysis of Floral Remains. In *The Tremaine Site Complex: Oneota Occupation in the La Crosse Locality, Wisconsin,* vol. 3, *The Tremaine Site (47Lc-95),* edited by Jodie O'Gorman, pp. 225–235. State Historical Society of Wisconsin, Madison.

Eggan, Fred R.

1952   The Ethnological Cultures and Their Archeological Backgrounds. In *Archeology of the Eastern United States,* edited by James B. Griffin, pp. 35–45. University of Chicago Press, Chicago.

Egloff, Keith

1992   The Late Woodland Period in Southwestern Virginia. In *The Middle and Late Woodland in Virginia: A Synthesis,* edited by T. R. Reinhart and M. E. Hodges, pp. 187–224. Special Publication of the Archaeological Society of Virginia no. 29. Dietz Press, Richmond.

Egloff, Keith, and Stephen R. Potter

1982   Indian Ceramics from Coastal Plain Virginia. *Archaeology of Eastern North America* 10: 95–117.

Egloff, Keith, and Deborah Woodward

1993   *First People: Native Inhabitants of Virginia.* Virginia Department of Historic Resources. University Press of Virginia, Charlottesville.

Eisert, Ronald W.

1981   The Wylie Site (36WH274). *Pennsylvania Archaeologist* 81 (1–2): 11–62.

1984   Structural Features of the Donley Site. *Pennsylvania Archaeologist* 51 (1–2): 32–39.

Ellis, Chris J., and Neal Ferris (editors)

1990   *The Archaeology of Southern Ontario to A.D. 1650.* Occasional Publication of the London Chapter no. 5. Ontario Archaeological Society, London, Ontario, Canada.

Ember, Melvin

1973   An Archaeological Indicator of Matrilocal versus Patrilocal Residence. *American Antiquity* 38: 177–182.

Emerson, Thomas E.

1989   Water, Serpents, and the Underworld: An Exploration into Cahokian Symbolism. In *The Southeastern Ceremonial Complex: Artifacts and Analysis,* edited by Patricia Galloway, pp. 45–92. University of Nebraska Press, Lincoln.

1991   Some Perspectives on Cahokia and the Northern Mississippian Expansion. In *Cahokia and the Hinterlands: Middle Mississippian Cultures of the Midwest,* edited by Thomas E. Emerson and R. Barry Lewis, pp. 221–238. University of Illinois Press, Urbana.

Emerson, Thomas E., and James A. Brown

1992   The Late Prehistory and Protohistory of Illinois. In *Calumet and Fleur-de-lys: Archaeology of Indian and French Contact in the Mid-Continent,* edited by John A. Walthall and Thomas E. Emerson, pp. 77–125. Smithsonian Institution Press, Washington, DC.

Emerson, Thomas E., and R. Barry Lewis (editors)

1991   *Cahokia and the Hinterlands: Middle Mississippian Cultures of the Midwest.* University of Illinois Press, Urbana.

Engberg, Robert M.

1930   Archaeological Report. *Western Pennsylvania Historical Magazine* 13 (2): 67–103.

Engelbrecht, William

1987   Factors Maintaining Low Population Density among

the Prehistoric New York Iroquois. *American Antiquity* 52 (1): 13–27.

Engelbrecht, William, Earl Sidler, and Michael Walko
1990　The Jefferson County Iroquoians. *Man in the Northeast* 39: 65–77.

Essenpreis, Patricia S.
1978　Fort Ancient Settlement: Differential Response at a Mississippian-Late Woodland Interface. In *Mississippian Settlement Patterns,* edited by Bruce D. Smith, pp. 141–167. Academic Press, New York.
1982　The Anderson Village Site: Redefining the Anderson Phase of the Fort Ancient Tradition of the Middle Ohio Valley. Ph.D. dissertation, Department of Anthropology, Harvard University.
1988　An Introduction to the Fort Ancient Cultural Complexes of the Middle Ohio Valley. In *A History of 17 Years of Excavation and Reconstruction: A Chronicle of Twelfth-Century Human Values and the Built Environment,* edited by J. M. Heilman, M. C. Lilias, and C. A. Turnbow, pp. 1–22. Dayton Museum of Natural History, Dayton, OH.

Evans, Clifford
1955　*A Ceramic Study of Virginia Archaeology.* Bulletin 160. Bureau of American Ethnology, Smithsonian Institution, Washington, DC.

Evans, S. J.
1994　Mortuary Data as Indicators of Social Organization at the Incinerator Site (33MY57). Paper presented at the Midwest Archaeological Conference, Lexington, KY.

Fagan, Brian
1991　*Ancient North America: The Archaeology of a Continent.* Thames and Hudson, London.

Farrow, Diana C.
1986　A Study of Monongahela Subsistence Patterns Based on Mass Spectrometric Analysis. *Midcontinental Journal of Archaeology* 11 (2): 153–179.

Faulkner, Charles H.
1964　The Rader Site. *Central States Archaeological Journal* 11: 90–96.
1972　*The Late Prehistoric Occupation of Northwestern Indiana: A Study of the Upper Mississippi Cultures of the Kankakee Valley.* Prehistoric Research Series 5, no. 1. Indiana Historical Society, Indianapolis.

Fausz, J. Frederick
1984　The Significance of the Beaver Trade on Anglo-Indian Relations in the Early Chesapeake. Paper presented at the Middle Atlantic Archaeological Conference, Rehoboth Beach, DE.
1985　Patterns of Anglo-Indian Aggression and Accommodation along the Mid-Atlantic Coast 1584–1634. In *Cultures in Contact: The Impact of European Contacts on Native American Cultural Institutions, A.D. 1000–1800,* edited and with commentary by William W. Fitzhugh, pp. 225–268. Smithsonian Institution Press, Washington, DC.

Fecteau, Rodolphe D.
1985　The Introduction and Diffusion of Cultivated Plants in Southern Ontario. Master's thesis, York University, Toronto.

Feinman, Gary, and Jill Neitzel
1984　Too Many Types: An Overview of Prestate Societies in the Americas. In *Advances in Archaeological Method and Theory,* vol. 7, edited by Michael B. Schiffer, pp. 39–102. Academic Press, New York.

Feldmann, Rodney, A. Coogan, and R. Heimlich
1977　*Southern Great Lakes: Geology Field Guide.* Kendal/Hunt, Dubuque, IA.

Fenneman, Nevin
1938　*Physiography of the Eastern United States.* McGraw-Hill, New York.

Fenton, William N.
1940　Problems Arising from the Historic Northeastern Position of the Iroquois. In *Essays in Historical Anthropology of North America,* pp. 159–251. Smithsonian Miscellaneous Collections 100. Smithsonian Institution Press, Washington, DC.
1951　Locality as a Basic Factor in the Development of Iroqois Social Structure. In *Symposium on Local Diversity in Iroquois Culture,* edited by William N. Fenton, pp. 39–54. Bulletin 149. Bureau of American Ethnology, Smithsonian Institution, Washington, DC.
1962　"This Island, the World on the Turtle's Back." *Journal of American Folklore* 75 (298): 283–300.
1987　*The False Faces of the Iroquois.* University of Oklahoma Press, Norman.

Fields, Peggy
1969　A Monongahela House Pattern. *SPAAC Speaks* 9 (1): 15–19.

Finlayson, William D.
1985　*The 1975 and 1978 Rescue Excavations at the Draper Site: Introduction and Settlement Patterns.* Mercury Series, Archaeological Survey of Canada, Paper 130. National Museum of Man, Ottawa.

Fischer, David Hackett
1970　*Historians' Fallacies: Toward a Logic of Historical Thought.* Harper and Row, New York.

Fisher, George S.
n.d.　Notes on fieldwork. Manuscript on file, Carnegie Museum of Natural History, Pittsburgh.

Fisher-Carroll, Rita L.
1997　Sociopolitical Organization at Upper Nodena (3MS4) from a Mortuary Perspective. Master's thesis, Department of Anthropology, University of Arkansas, Fayetteville.

Fisk, Harold N.
1944　*Geological Investigation of the Alluvial Valley of the Lower Mississippi River.* Mississippi River Commission Publication 52. War Department, US Army Corps of Engineers, Vicksburg.

Fitting, James E.
1964　Ceramic Relationships of Four Late Woodland Sites in Northern Ohio. *Wisconsin Archaeologist* 45 (4): 160–175.
1965　*Late Woodland Cultures of Southeastern Michigan.* Anthropology Papers no. 24. University of Michigan, Museum of Anthropology, Ann Arbor.
1970　*The Archaeology of Michigan.* Natural History Press, Bloomfield Hills and New York.

Fitting, James E., and Richard Zurrell
1976   The Detroit–St. Clair Region. In *The Late Prehistory of the Lake Erie Drainage Basin: A 1972 Symposium Revised,* edited by D. S. Brose, pp. 214–250. Scientific Papers of the Cleveland Museum of Natural History, Cleveland.

Fitzgerald, William R.
1982a   *Lest the Beaver Run Loose: The Early-Seventeenth-Century Christianson Site and Trends in Historic Neutral Archaeology.* Mercury Series, Archaeological Survey of Canada, Paper 111. National Museum of Man, Ottawa.
1982b   *In the Shadow of the Great Beaver: Alterations in Burial Offerings in the Spencer Creek Area of Historic Neutralia.* Report on file at the Ontario Heritage Foundation, Toronto.
1982c   A Refinement of Historic Neutral Chronologies: Evidence from Shaver Hill, Christianson and Dwyer. *Ontario Archaeology* 38: 31–46.
1983   Further Comments on Neutral Glass Bead Sequence. *Arch Notes* 83 (1): 17–25.
1990a   Chronology to Cultural Process: Lower Great Lakes Archaeology, 1500–1650. Ph.D. dissertation, Department of Anthropology, McGill University, Montreal, Canada.
1990b   Preliminary Observations on the Ivan Elliot (AiHa-16) Village and Raymond Reid (AiHa-4) Hamlet, Wellington County, Ontario. *Kewa* (Newsletter of the London Chapter, Ontario Archaeological Society) 90 (6): 2–16.
1991a   *The Archaeology of the Sixteenth-Century Neutral Iroquoian MacPherson (AhHa-21) Village.* Report on file at the Ministry of Culture and Communications, London.
1991b   More (or Less) on Iroquoian Semi-Subterranean "Sweat Lodges." *Arch Notes* (Newsletter of the Ontario Archaeological Society) 91 (2): 8–11.

Fitzgerald, William R., and James B. Jamieson
1985   An Alternate Interpretation of Late Iroquoian Development. Paper presented at a meeting of the Canadian Archaeological Association, Winnipeg.

Fitzgerald, William R., Dean H. Knight, and Allison Bain
1995   Untanglers of Matters Temporal and Cultural: Glass Beads and the Early Contact Period Huron Ball Site. *Canadian Journal of Archaeology* 19: 117–138.

Fitzgerald, William R., L. Turgeon, R. H. Whitehead, and J. W. Bradley
1993   Late Sixteenth-Century Basque Banded Copper Kettles. *Historical Archaeology* 27 (1): 44–57.

Fitzhugh, William
1984   *Cultures in Contact: The European Impact on Native Cultural Institutions in Eastern North America, A.D. 1000–1800.* Smithsonian Institution Press, Washington, DC.

Flinn, John J.
1893   *Official Guide to the World's Columbian Exposition in the City of Chicago, May 1 to October 26, 1893.* World's Columbian Exposition, Chicago.

Foley, P. M., and T. F. Lipscombe
1961   A Kentucky Fort Ancient Burial Site. *Ohio Archaeologist* 11 (4): 126–128.

Fontaneda, Do. d'Escalante
1944   *Memoir of Do. d'Escalante Fontaneda Respecting Florida, Written in Spain, about the Year 1575.* Translated by Buckingham Smith, with editorial comments by David O. True. Glades House, Coral Gables, FL.

Forbes, Jack D. (editor and contributor)
1964   *The Indian in America's Past.* Prentice Hall, Englewood Cliffs, NJ.

Ford, Michael J.
1982   *The Changing Climate: Responses of the Natural Flora and Fauna.* George Allen and Unwin, London.

Fowke, Gerard
1894   *Archeologic Investigations in James and Potomac Valleys.* Bulletin 23. Bureau of American Ethnology, Smithsonian Institution, Washington, DC.
1902   *Archaeological and Geological History of Ohio.* Ohio State Archaeological and Historical Society, Columbus.

Fowler, Melvin L., and Robert L. Hall
1978   Late Prehistory of the Illinois Area. In *Handbook of North American Indians,* vol. 15, *Northeast,* edited by Bruce G. Trigger, pp. 560–68. Smithsonian Institution Press, Washington, DC.

Fox, George R.
1916   Outagamie County Antiquities. *Wisconsin Archeologist* 15: 1–21.

Fox, William A.
1980   Of Projectile Points and Politics. *Arch Notes* (Newsletter of the Ontario Archaeological Society) 80 (2): 5–13.
1981   Nanticoke Triangular Points. *Kewa* (Newsletter of the London Chapter, Ontario Archaeological Society) 81 (4): 21.
1990   The Odawa. In *The Archaeology of Southern Ontario to A.D. 1650,* edited by Chris J. Ellis and Neal Ferris, pp. 457–473. Occasional Publication of the London Chapter no. 5. Ontario Archaeological Society, London, Ontario, Canada.

Fradkin, Arlene
1976   The Wrightman Site: A Study of Prehistoric Culture and Environment on Sanibel Island, Florida. Master's thesis, Department of Anthropology, University of Florida, Gainesville.

Frankfort, Henri
1956   *The Birth of Civilization in the Near East.* Doubleday Anchor Books, Garden City, NY.

Franquelin, Jean-Baptiste Louis
1684   "Carte de la Louisiane." Map Library, Lower Mississippi Survey, Peabody Museum of American Archaeology and Ethnology, Harvard University, Cambridge, MA.

Freidin, N.
1987   Report on the Investigations at Clover (46–Cb-40), West Virginia, by the Marshall University Archaeological Field School. Manuscript on file at the State Historic Preservation Office, Charleston.

Fried, Morton H.
1968   On the Concepts of "Tribe" and "Tribal Society." In *Essays on the Problem of Tribe,* edited by June Helm, pp. 3–20. Proceedings of the 1967 Annual Meeting of the American Ethnological Society. University of Washington Press, Seattle.

Fritts, H., G. R. Lofgren, and G. Gordon
1979   Variations in Climate since 1602 as Reconstructed from Tree Rings. *Quaternary Research* 12: 86–46.

Fuller, John William
1981 Developmental Change in Prehistoric Community Patterns: The Development of Nucleated Village Communities in Northern West Virginia. Ph.D. dissertation, University of Washington, Seattle.

Fuller, Richard S., and Diane E. Silvia
1984 Ceramic Rim Effigies in Southwest Alabama. *Journal of Alabama Archaeology* 30 (1): 1–48.

Fundaburk, Emma Lila
1958 *Southeastern Indians Life Portraits: A Catalogue of Portraits 1564–1860.* Published by the author, Luverne, AL.

Funkhouser, W. D., and W. S. Webb
1928 *Ancient Life in Kentucky.* Kentucky Geological Survey, Series 6, vol. 34. Kentucky Geological Survey, Frankfort.

Gailey, Christine Ward, and Thomas C. Patterson
1988 State Formation and Uneven Development. In *State and Society: The Emergence and Development of Social Hierarchy and Political Centralization,* edited by J. Gledhill, B. Bender, and M. T. Larsen, pp. 77–90. Unwin Hyman, London.

Gallagher, James P.
1990 *The Farley Village Site, 21Hu2, an Oneota/Ioway Site in Houston County, Minnesota.* Reports of Investigations no. 117. Mississippi Valley Archaeology Center, University of Wisconsin–La Crosse.
1992 Prehistoric Field Systems in the Upper Midwest. In *Late Prehistoric Agriculture: Observations from the Midwest,* edited by William I. Woods, pp. 95–135. Illinois Historic Preservation Agency, Springfield.

Gallagher, James P., Constance M. Arzigian, Robert F. Boszhardt, Charles R. Moffat, and James L. Theler
1992 *Phase III Excavations at the Tremaine Site, 47LC95: The Midvale Interceptor Project.* Reports of Investigations no. 133. Mississippi Valley Archaeology Center, University of Wisconsin–La Crosse.

Gallagher, James P., Robert F. Boszhardt, Robert F. Sasso, and Katherine P. Stevenson
1985 Oneota Ridged Field Agriculture in Southwestern Wisconsin. *American Antiquity* 50: 605–612.

Gallagher, James P., and Katherine P. Stevenson
1982 Oneota Subsistence and Settlement in Southwestern Wisconsin. In *Oneota Studies,* edited by Guy E. Gibbon, pp. 29–53. Publications in Anthropology no. 1. University of Minnesota, Minneapolis.

Gallagher, James P., Katherine Stevenson, Heidi Fassler, Christopher Hill, Margaret Mills, Toby Morrow, Karene Motivans, Sherry Neff, Teresa Weeth, and Randall Withrow
1981 The Overhead Site (47Lc20). Report. Submitted to the Historic Preservation Division, State Historical Society of Wisconsin. Copy on file, Mississippi Valley Archaeology Center, University of Wisconsin–La Crosse.

Gallivan, Martin
1995 The Wood Site (44NE143) in the James River Piedmont: Site Structure, Household, and Community at the Opening of the Late Woodland. Manuscript on file, Department of Anthropology, University of Virginia.
1997 The Leatherwood Creek Site: A Dan River Phase Site in the Southern Virginia Piedmont. *Quarterly Bulletin of the Archaeological Society of Virginia* 52: 150–171.
1999 The Late Prehistoric James River Village: Household, Community, and Regional Dynamics. Ph.D. dissertation, Department of Anthropology, University of Virginia, Charlottesville.

Galloway, Patricia K.
1993 Ethnohistory. In *The Development of Southeastern Archaeology,* edited by J. Johnson, pp. 78–108. University of Alabama Press, Tuscaloosa.

Gannett, Henry
1902 The Origin of Certain Place Names in the State of Mississippi. *Publications of the Mississippi Historical Society* 6: 339–349.

Gardner, William
1986 *Lost Arrowheads and Broken Pottery: Traces of Indians in the Shenandoah Valley.* Thunderbird, Manassas, VA.

Gaskell, Ivan
1990 *The Thyssen-Bornemisza Collection: Seventeenth-Century Dutch and Flemish Painting.* Philip Wilson, London.

Geier, Clarence R., and J. Craig Warren
1982 *The Huffman Site (44BA5): A Late Woodland Site on the Jackson River, Bath County, Virginia.* Occasional Paper 9. Archaeological Research Center, James Madison University, Harrisonburg, VA.

George, Richard L.
1974 Monongahela Settlement Patterns and the Ryan Site. *Pennsylvania Archaeologist* 44 (1–2): 1–22.
1975 Ceramics, Social Organization, and Monongahela. *SPAAC Speaks* 11 (1): 30–42.
1978 The McJunkin Site: A Preliminary Report. *Pennsylvania Archaeologist* 48 (4): 33–47.
1980 Notes on the Possible Cultural Affiliation of Monongahela. *Pennsylvania Archaeologist* 50 (1–2): 45–50.
1983 The Gnagey Site and the Monongahela Occupation of the Somerset Plateau. *Pennsylvania Archaeologist* 53 (4): 1–97.
1994 Revisiting the Monongahela Linguistic/Cultural Affiliation Mystery. *Pennsylvania Archaeologist* 64 (2): 54–59.
1996 What Ever Happened to the Drew Phase? Paper presented at the annual meeting of the Eastern States Archeological Federation, Huntington, WV.
1997 McFate Artifacts in a Monongahela Context: McJunkin, Johnson, and Squirrel Hill. *Pennsylvania Archaeologist* 67 (1): 35–44.
1998 Refining the Drew Phase. Paper presented at the annual meeting of the Society for Pennsylvania Archaeology, New Cumberland.

George, Richard L., Jay Babich, and Christine E. Davis
1990 The Household Site: Results of a Partial Excavation of a Late Monongahela Village in Westmoreland County, Pennsylvania. *Pennsylvania Archaeologist* 60 (2): 40–70.

George, Richard L., and Richard Scaglion
1992 Seriation Changes in Monongahela Triangular Lithic Projectiles. *Man in the Northeast* 44: 73–81.

Gersna, Charles
1966 Notes on a Series of Nine Burials from the Beazell Site, Washington Co., Pennsylvania 36WH34. *SPAAC Speaks* 6 (1): 7–18.

Gibbon, Edward
1777   *The History of the Decline and Fall of the Roman Empire.*
        3 vols. 1889 edition with critical notes by Oliphant
        Smeaton [1909], Everyman. Random House Modern
        Library reprint [1963], New York.

Gibbon, Guy
1970a   A Brief History of Oneota Research in Wisconsin.
        Wisconsin Magazine of History 53: 278–293.
1970b   The Midway Village Site: An Orr Phase Oneota Site in
        the Upper Mississippi River Valley. *Wisconsin Archeolo-
        gist* 51 (3): 79–162.
1972   Cultural Dynamics and the Development of the
        Oneota Life-way in Wisconsin. *American Antiquity* 37:
        166–185.

Gilliland, Marion S.
1975   *The Material Culture of Key Marco, Florida.* University
        Press of Florida, Gainesville.

Glass, S. A.
n.d.   Return to Fox Fields: The Mason County, Kentucky,
        Ft. Ancient Site. Manuscript in possession of the
        author.

Gleach, Frederic W.
1985   A Compilation of Radiocarbon Dates with Applicabil-
        ity to Central Virginia. *Quarterly Bulletin of the Archae-
        ological Society of Virginia* 40: 180–200.

Gleason, Patrick J., Arthur D. Cohen, William G. Smith,
H. Kelly Brooks, Peter A. Stone, Robert L. Goodrick, and
William Spackman Jr.
1984   The Environmental Significance of Holocene Sedi-
        ments from the Everglades and Saline Tidal Plain. In
        Environments of South Florida: Present and Past, edited
        by P. J. Gleason, pp. 297–351. Memoir 2. Revised edi-
        tion. Miami Geological Society, Coral Gables, FL.

Glowacki, D., C. Turnbow, and R. Fields
1993   New Perspectives on the Fort Ancient Ceramics of
        the Madisonville Site, Southwestern Ohio. Paper pre-
        sented at the annual meeting of the Society for Amer-
        ican Archaeology, St. Louis.

Goggin, John M., and William T. Sturtevant
1964   The Calusa: A Stratified Non-Agricultural Society
        (with Notes on Sibling Marriage). In *Explorations in
        Cultural Anthropology: Essays in Honor of George Peter
        Murdock,* edited by Ward Goodenough, pp. 179–219.
        McGraw-Hill, New York.

Gold, Debra L.
1988   Subsistence, Health, and Emergent Inequality in Late
        Prehistoric Interior Virginia. Ph.D. dissertation, De-
        partment of Anthropology, University of Michigan,
        Ann Arbor.

Goldstein, Lynne
1987   *The Southeastern Wisconsin Archaeology Project: 1986–87
        and Project Summary.* Report of Investigations no. 88.
        Archaeological Research Laboratory, University of
        Wisconsin–Milwaukee.
1991   The Implications of Aztalan's Location. In *New Per-
        spectives on Cahokia: Views from the Peripheries,* edited
        by James B. Stoltman, pp. 209–227. Prehistory Press,
        Madison, WI.

Goldstein, Lynne G., and John D. Richards
1991   Ancient Aztalan: The Cultural and Ecological Context

of a Late Prehistoric Site in the Midwest. In *Cahokia
        and the Hinterlands: Middle Mississippian Cultures of
        the Midwest,* edited by Thomas E. Emerson and
        R. Barry Lewis, pp. 193–206. University of Illinois
        Press, Urbana.

Goodman, Alan H., John Lallo, George J. Armelagos, and
Jerome C. Rose
1984   Health Changes at Dickson Mounds, Illinois (A.D.
        950–1300). In *Paleopathology at the Origins of Agricul-
        ture,* edited by Mark Nathan Cohen and George J.
        Armelagos, pp. 271–305. Academic Press, New York.

Gordon, Harry
1766   Journal of Captain Harry Gordon's Journey from
        Pittsburg down the Ohio and the Mississippi to New
        Orleans, Mobile, and Pensacola, 1766. In *Travels in the
        American Colonies,* edited by Newton D. Mereness,
        pp. 457–489. Macmillan, New York, 1916.

Gordon, Robert B.
1966   *Natural Vegetation of Ohio at the Time of Earliest Land
        Surveys.* Map. Ohio Biological Survey, Columbus.
1969   *The Natural Vegetation of Ohio in Pioneer Days.* Bulletin
        of the Ohio Biological Survey (n.s.) 3 (2). Ohio State
        University, Columbus.

Goss, A. F.
1988   Astronomical Alignments at the Incinerator Site. In *A
        History of 17 Years of Excavation and Research: A Chroni-
        cle of Twelfth-Century Human Values and the Built Envi-
        ronment,* edited by J. M. Heilman, M. C. Lilias, and
        C. A. Turnbow, pp. 314–334. Dayton Museum of
        Natural History, Dayton, OH.

Graham, J. Bennett
1966   An Archaeological Local Sequence Chronology in the
        Lock 3 Reservoir. Master's thesis, Department of So-
        ciology and Anthropology, University of Alabama.

Gramly, Richard Michael
1977   Deerskins and Hunting Territories: Competition for a
        Scarce Resource of the Northeastern Woodlands.
        American Antiquity 42: 601–605.

Granberry, Julian
1995   The Position of the Calusa Language in Florida Pre-
        history: A Working Hypothesis. *Florida Anthropologist*
        48: 156–173.

Grant, W. L., and H. P. Biggar
1907–   *The History of New France by Marc Lescarbot.* 8 vols.
1914   The Champlain Society, Toronto.

Grantham, Larry
1996   The Illini Village of the Marquette and Jolliet Voyage
        of 1673. *Missouri Archaeologist* 54: 1–20.

Grauer, Anne L.
1995   Tremaine Skeletal Data. In *The Tremaine Site Complex:
        Oneota Occupation in the La Crosse Locality, Wisconsin,*
        vol. 3, *The Tremaine Site (47Lc-95),* edited by Jodie
        O'Gorman, pp. 409–421. State Historical Society of
        Wisconsin, Madison.

Gravely, Richard P. Jr.
1969   The Madison Cemetery. *Eastern States Archaeological
        Federation Bulletin* 27: 11.
1983   Archaeological Sites in the Upper Dan River Drainage
        System. In *Piedmont Archaeology: Recent Research and
        Results,* edited by J. Mark Wittkofski and Lyle E.

Browning, pp. 118–124. Special Publication no. 10. Archaeological Society of Virginia, Richmond.

Graves, James

1984 Archaeological Investigations of the Indian Hills Site, Lucas County, Ohio. Master's thesis, Department of Anthropology, University of Toledo.

Gravier, Jacques

1900 Relation or Journal of the Voyage of Father Gravier, of the Society of Jesus, in 1700, from the Country of the Illinois to the Mouth of the Mississippi River. *The Jesuit Relations and Allied Documents* 65, edited by R. G. Thwaites, pp. 100–179. Cleveland, OH.

Graybill, Jeffrey R.

1980 Marietta Works, Ohio, and the Eastern Periphery of Fort Ancient. *Pennsylvania Archaeologist* 50 (1–2): 51–60.

1981 The Eastern Periphery of Fort Ancient (A.D. 1050–1650): A Diachronic Approach to Settlement Variability. Ph.D. dissertation, Department of Anthropology, University of Washington, Seattle.

1984 The Eastern Periphery of Fort Ancient. *Pennsylvania Archaeologist* 54 (1–2): 40–50.

1986 Fort Ancient–East: Origins, Change, and External Correlations. Paper presented at the Midwestern Archaeological Conference, Columbus, OH.

1987 Fort Ancient–Madisonville Horizon: Protohistoric Archaeology in the Middle Ohio Valley. Paper presented at the Upland Woodland Archaeology Conference, Morgantown, WV, and at the 3d annual Uplands Archaeology in the East Symposium, Harrisonburg, WV.

Graymont, Barbara

1972 *The Iroquois in the American Revolution.* Syracuse University Press, Syracuse, NY.

Green, Thomas J., and Cheryl A. Munson

1978 Mississippian Settlement Patterns in Southwestern Indiana. In *Mississippian Settlement Patterns,* edited by Bruce D. Smith, pp. 293–330. Academic Press, New York.

Green, William

1984 Protohistoric Depopulation in the Upper Midwest. Paper presented at the Midwest Archaeological Conference, Evanston, IL.

1993 Examining Protohistoric Depopulation in the Upper Midwest. *Wisconsin Archeologist* 74: 290–323.

1995 The 1837 Ioway Map. Paper presented at the annual meeting of the American Society for Ethnohistory, Kalamazoo, MI.

1998 The Erie/Westo Connection: Possible Evidence for Long-Distance Migration in the Eastern Woodlands during the Sixteenth and Seventeenth Centuries. Paper presented at the annual meeting of the Southeastern Archaeological Conference, Greenville, SC.

Greengo, Robert E.

1955 Unpublished field notes. Lower Mississippi Survey Archives, Peabody Museum of American Archaeology and Ethnology, Harvard University, Cambridge, MA.

Greenman, Emerson F.

1930 Field Notes of Survey and Excavation in Northern Ohio, 1929–1930. Division of Archaeology, Ohio Historical Society Archives, Columbus.

1935a Seven Prehistoric Sites in Northern Ohio. *Ohio Archaeological and Historical Quarterly* 44 (2): 220–237.

1935b Excavation of the Reeve Village Site, Lake County, Ohio. *Ohio Archaeological and Historical Quarterly* 44 (1): 2–64.

1937 Two Prehistoric Villages near Cleveland, Ohio. *Ohio Archaeological and Historical Quarterly* 46 (4): 305–366.

1957 Riviere au Vase Site. *Michigan Archaeologist* 3 (1): 9–11.

1958 Prehistoric Detroit. *Michigan Archaeologist* 4 (4): 81–98.

Greer, E. S.

1966 A Tukabahatchee Plate from the Coosa River. *Journal of Alabama Archaeology* 12: 156–58.

Gregg, Michael L.

1975 A Population Estimate for Cahokia. In *Perspectives in Cahokia Archaeology.* Bulletin 10. Illinois Archaeological Survey, Urbana.

Gremillion, Kristen J.

1987 Plant Remains from the Fredricks, Wall, and Mitchum Sites. In *The Siouan Project: Seasons I and II,* edited by Roy S. Dickens Jr., H. Trawick Ward and R. P. Stephen Davis Jr., pp. 259–277. Monograph Series 1. Research Laboratories of Anthropology, University of North Carolina, Chapel Hill.

1988 Plant Remains. In *Archaeology of the Historic Occaneechi Indians,* edited by H. Trawick Ward and R. P. Stephen Davis Jr. *Southern Indian Studies* 36–37: 95–117.

1989 Late Prehistoric and Historic Period Paleoethnobotany of the North Carolina Piedmont. Ph.D. dissertation, Department of Anthropology, University of North Carolina, Chapel Hill.

1993a Archaeobotany of the Graham-White Site. Report. Submitted to the Virginia Department of Historic Resources, Richmond.

1993b Appendix B: Paleoethnobotanical Evidence of Change and Continuity in Piedmont Subsistence. In *Indian Communities on the North Carolina Piedmont, A.D. 1000 to 1700,* by H. Trawick Ward and R. P. Stephen Davis Jr., pp. 457–468. Monograph 2. Research Laboratories of Anthropology, University of North Carolina, Chapel Hill.

Griffin, James B.

1943 *The Fort Ancient Aspect: Its Cultural and Chronological Position in Mississippi Valley Archaeology.* University of Michigan Press, Ann Arbor.

1944 The Iroquois in American Prehistory. *Papers of the Michigan Academy of Science, Arts, and Letters* 29: 357–374.

1945 An Interpretation of Siouan Archaeology in the Piedmont of North Carolina and Virginia. *American Antiquity* 10 (4): 321–330.

1946 Cultural Change and Continuity in Eastern United States Archaeology. In *Man in Northeastern North America,* edited by Frederick Johnson, pp. 37–95. Papers of the Robert S. Peabody Foundation for Archaeology no. 3. Andover, MA.

1960a A Hypothesis for the Prehistory of the Winnebago. In *Culture in History: Essays in Honor of Paul Radin,* edited by Stanley Diamond, pp. 809–865. Columbia University Press, New York.

1960b   Climatic Change: A Contributory Cause of the Growth and Decline of Northern Hopewell Culture. *Wisconsin Archeologist* 41: 21–33.

1961   Some Correlations of Climatic and Cultural Change in Eastern North American Prehistory. *Annals of the New York Academy of Sciences* 95: 710–717.

1978   Late Prehistory of the Ohio Valley. In *Handbook of North American Indians,* vol. 15, *Northeast,* edited by Bruce G. Trigger, pp. 547–59. Smithsonian Institution Press, Washington, DC.

1992   Fort Ancient Has No Class: The Absence of an Elite Group in Mississippian Societies in the Central Ohio Valley. In *Lords of the Southeast: Social Inequality and the Native Elites of Southeastern North America,* edited by A. W. Barker and T. R. Pauketat, pp. 53–59. Archaeological Papers no. 3. American Anthropological Association, Washington, DC.

Griffin, John
1988   *The Archaeology of Everglades National Park: A Synthesis.* National Park Service, Southeastern Archeological Center, Tallahassee, FL.

Griffin, John W., and Donald E. Wray
1945   Bison in Illinois Archaeology. *Transactions of the Illinois State Academy of Sciences* 38: 21–26.

Grimm, Eric C.
1983   Chronology and Dynamics of Vegetation Change in the Prairie-Woodland Region of Southern Minnesota, U.S.A. *New Phytologist* 93: 311–350.

Grove, Jean M.
1985   The Timing of the Little Ice Age in Scandinavia. In *The Climatic Scene,* edited by M. J. Tooley and G. M. Sheail, pp. 132–153. George Allen and Unwin, London.

1988   *The Little Ice Age.* Methuen, London.

Gruber, Jacob W.
1985   Archaeology, History, and Culture. In *American Archaeology, Past and Future: A Celebration of the SAA 1935–1985,* edited by D. Meltzer, D. Fowler, and J. Sabloff, pp. 163–186. Smithsonian Institution Press, Washington, DC.

Grumet, Robert
1990   *Historic Contact: Indians and Colonists in Northeastern North America, 1497–1783.* Mid-Atlantic Region, National Park Service, Cultural Resource Planning Branch.

Guldenzopf, D. B.
1986   The Colonial Transformation of Mohawk Iroquois Society. Ph.D. dissertation, State University of New York at Albany.

Halbert, Henry Sale
1899a   Choctaw Indian Names in Alabama and Mississippi. *Transactions of the Alabama Historical Society* 3: 64–77.

1899b   Nanih Waiya, the Sacred Mound of the Choctaws. *Publications of the Mississippi Historical Society* 2: 223–234.

1900   D'Anville's Map of East Mississippi. *Publications of the Mississippi Historical Society* 3: 367–371.

1901a   Last Indian Council on the Noxubee. *Publications of the Mississippi Historical Society* 4: 271–280.

1901b   District Divisions of the Choctaw Nation. *Publications of the Alabama Historical Society, Miscellaneous Collections* 1: 375–385.

1902a   Small Indian Tribes of Mississippi. *Publications of the Mississippi Historical Society* 5: 302–308.

1902b   Story of the Treaty of Dancing Rabbit Creek. *Publications of the Mississippi Historical Society* 6: 373–402.

1902c   Bernard Romans' Map of 1772. *Publications of the Mississippi Historical Society* 6: 415–439.

Hale, H. Stephen
1984   Prehistoric Environmental Exploitation around Lake Okeechobee. *Southeastern Archaeology* 3: 173–187.

Hall, Robert L.
1962   *The Archeology of Carcajou Point: With an Interpretation of the Development of Oneota Culture in Wisconsin.* 2 vols. University of Wisconsin Press, Madison.

1991   Cahokia Identity and Interaction Models of Cahokia Mississippian. In *Cahokia and the Hinterlands: Middle Mississippian Cultures of the Midwest,* edited by Thomas E. Emerson and R. Barry Lewis, pp. 3–34. University of Illinois Press, Urbana.

1993   Red Banks, Oneota, and the Winnebago: Views from a Distant Rock. *Wisconsin Archeologist* 74: 1–70.

1995   Relating the Big Fish and the Big Stone: The Archaeological Identity and Habitat of the Winnebago in 1634. In *Oneota Archaeology: Past, Present, and Future,* edited by William Green, pp. 19–30. Office of the State Archaeologist, University of Iowa, Iowa City.

1997   *An Archaeology of the Soul: North American Indian Belief and Ritual.* University of Illinois Press, Urbana.

Hally, David J.
1979   *Archaeological Investigations of the Little Egypt Site (9Mu102), Murray County, Ga., 1969 Season.* Laboratory of Archaeology Series, Report no. 18. University of Georgia.

1980   Archaeological Investigation of the Little Egypt Site (9Mu102), Murray County, Georgia, 1970–72 Seasons. Report. Department of Anthropology, University of Georgia. Submitted to the National Park Service.

1988   Archaeology and Settlement Plan of the King Site. In *The King Site: Continuity and Contact in Sixteenth-Century Georgia,* edited by Robert Blakely, pp. 3–16. University of Georgia Press, Athens.

1993   The 1992 and 1993 Excavations at the King Site (9FL5). *Early Georgia* 21 (2): 30–44.

Hally, David J., Patrick Garrow, and Wyman Trotti
1975   Preliminary Analysis of the King Site Settlement Plan. *Southeastern Archaeological Conference Bulletin* 18: 55–62.

Hally, David J., and James B. Langford Jr.
1988   *Mississippi Period Archaeology of the Georgia Valley and Ridge Province.* Laboratory of Archaeology Series, Report 25. Department of Anthropology, University of Georgia, Athens.

Hally, David J., Marvin T. Smith, and James B. Langford
1990   The Archaeological Reality of de Soto's Coosa. In *Columbian Consequences,* vol. 2, *Archaeological and Historical Perspectives on the Spanish Borderlands East,* edited by David H. Thomas, pp. 121–138. Smithsonian Institution Press, Washington, DC.

Halsey, John R. (editor)
1999   *Retrieving Michigan's Buried Past: The Archaeology of the*

Great Lakes State. Bulletin 64. Cranbrook Institute of
Science, Bloomfield Hills, MI.

Hamell, George R.
1987 Mythical Realities and European Contact in the
Northeast during the Sixteenth and Seventeenth
Centuries. *Man in the Northeast* 33: 63–87.
1992 The Iroquois and the World's Rim: Speculations on
Color, Culture, and Contact. *American Indian Quarterly* 16 (4): 451–469.

Hamell, George R., and Hazel Dean John
1987 Ethnology, Archaeology, History, and "Seneca Origins." Paper presented at the Annual Conference on
Iroquois Research, Rennselaerville, New York.

Hammer, C. U., H. B. Clausen, and W. Dansgaard
1980 Greenland Ice Sheet Evidence of Post-glacial Volcanism and Its Climatic Impact. *Nature* 288: 230–235.

Hammett, Julia E.
1987 Shell Artifacts from the Carolina Piedmont. In *The
Siouan Project: Seasons I and II,* edited by Roy S. Dickens Jr., H. Trawick Ward, and R. P. Stephen Davis Jr.,
pp. 167–183. Monograph Series 1. Research Laboratories of Anthropology, University of North Carolina,
Chapel Hill.

Hammond, E. A.
1973 The Spanish Fisheries of Charlotte Harbor. *Florida
Historical Quarterly* 51: 355–380.

Hamy, E.-T.
1968 *The Travels of the Naturalist Charles A. Lesueur in North
America, 1815–1837.* Edited by H. F. Raup; translated by
Milton Haber. Kent State University Press, Kent, OH.

Hann, John H.
1988 *Apalachee: The Land between the Rivers.* University Press
of Florida, Gainesville.
1991 *Missions to the Calusa.* Introduction by W. H. Marquardt; translations by John H. Hann. University of
Florida Press, Gainesville.
1996 Late Seventeenth-Century Forebears of the Lower
Creeks and Seminoles. *Southeastern Archaeology* 15:
66–80.

Hansinger, Michael J.
1992 Skeletal and Dental Analysis of Burials from the Collier Inn Site, Useppa Island. In *Culture and Environment
in the Domain of the Calusa,* edited by W. H. Marquardt, pp. 403–409. Monograph 1. Institute of Archaeology and Paleoenvironmental Studies, University of Florida, Gainesville.

Hanson, Lee H. Jr.
1966 *The Hardin Village Site.* Studies in Anthropology 4.
University of Kentucky Press, Lexington.
1975 *The Buffalo Site: A Late Seventeenth-Century Indian Village Site (46Pu31) in Putnam County, West Virginia.* Report of Archeological Investigations 5. West Virginia
Geological and Economic Survey, Morgantown, WV.

Hantman, Jeffrey L.
1985 *The Archaeology of Albemarle County.* University of Virginia Archaeological Survey, Monograph no. 2. Department of Anthropology, University of Virginia,
Charlottesville.
1990 Between Powhatan and Quirank: Reconstructing
Monacan Culture and History in the Context of

Jamestown. *American Anthropologist* 92 (3): 676–690.
1992 Monacan Archaeology and History. *Lynch's Ferry: A
Journal of Local History* 5: 6–12.
1993 Powhatan's Relations with the Piedmont Monacans.
In *Powhatan's Foreign Relations,* edited by H. Rountree,
pp. 94–111. University Press of Virginia, Charlottesville.
1998 "Ancestral Monacan Society"?: Cultural and Temporal
Boundedness in Indian History in Virginia. Paper presented at the annual meeting of the Society for American Archaeology, Seattle, WA.

Hantman, Jeffrey L., and Gary Dunham
1993 The Englightened Archaeologist. *Archaeology* 46:
44–49.

Hantman, Jeffrey L., Gary Dunham, and Sandra Olsen
1990 Ritual processes in prehistoric Virginia Mounds.
Paper presented at the annual meeting of the Society
for American Archaeology, Las Vegas, NV.

Hantman, Jeffrey L., Martin Gallivan, Mintcy Maxham, and
Daniel Hayes
1993 Late Woodland and Contact Era Village Excavations
in the Monacan Area of Virginia. Paper presented at
the annual meeting of the Southeastern Archaeological Conference, Raleigh, NC.

Hantman, Jeffrey L., and Michael J. Klein
1992 Middle and Late Woodland Archaeology in Piedmont
Virginia. In *Middle and Late Late Woodland Research in
Virginia,* edited by T. Reinhart, pp. 137–164. Special
Publication of the Archaeological Society of Virginia
no. 29. Dietz Press, Richmond.

Harding, Anthony F.
1982 Climatic Change and Archaeology. In *Climatic Change
in Later Prehistory,* edited by Anthony F. Harding,
pp. 1–10. Edinburgh University Press, Edinburgh.

Harn, Alan D.
1990 *The Prehistory of Dickson Mounds: The Dickson Excavation.* Reports of Investigations no. 35. Illinois State
Museum, Springfield.

Harper, B.
1994 Changing Settlement Patterns in the Anderson Phase
of Fort Ancient: New Evidence from South Fort Village. Paper presented at "Cultures before Contact: A
Conference on the Late Prehistory of the Ohio Region," Ohio Archaeological Council, Cincinnati.

Harrington, Mark
1922 *Cherokee and Earlier Remains on the Upper Tennessee
River.* Indian Notes and Monographs no. 24. Museum
of the American Indian, Heye Foundation, New York.

Hart, John P.
1990 Modeling Oneota Agricultural Production: A Cross-
Cultural Evaluation. *Current Anthropology* 31: 569–577.
1992 A Critique of the Adaptive Type Concept in Eastern
Woodlands Prehistory. Ph.D. dissertation, Northwestern University, Evanston, IL.
1994 Archaeological Investigations at the Mon City Site
(36WH737), Washington County, Pennsylvania. *Pennsylvania Archaeologist* 64 (2): 7–39.

Hart, John P., and Robert J. Jeske
1991 Models of Prehistoric Site Location for the Upper Illinois River Valley. *Illinois Archaeology* 3: 3–22.

Harvey, Amy E.
1979 *Oneota Culture in Northwestern Iowa.* Report 12. Office of the State Archaeologist, University of Iowa, Iowa City.

Hathcock, Roy
1988 *Ancient Indian Pottery of the Mississippi River Valley.* 2d ed. Walsworth, Marceline, MO.

Hauptman, Laurence M.
1981 *The Iroquois and the New Deal.* Syracuse University Press, Syracuse, NY.
1986 *The Iroquois Struggle for Survival: World War II to Red Power.* Syracuse University Press, Syracuse, NY.

Hauser, Raymond E.
1973 An Ethnohistory of the Illinois Indian Tribe, 1673–1832. Ph.D. dissertation, Northern Illinois University, Dekalb.

Hawkins, Rebecca A.
1994 Coming Full Circle: An Overview of the Fort Ancient Circular Village. Paper presented at "Cultures before Contact: A Conference on the Late Prehistory of the Ohio Region," Ohio Archaeological Council, Cincinnati.

Hayden, Brian
1978 Bigger Is Better? Factors Determining Ontario Iroquois Site Sizes. *Canadian Journal of Archaeology* 2: 107–116.

Hayes, Charles F. III
1989 An Introduction to the Shell and Shell Artifact Collection at the Rochester Museum and Science Center. In *Proceedings of the 1986 Shell Bead Conference: Selected Papers,* edited by Charles F. Hayes III, pp. 37–43. Research Records 20. Rochester Museum and Science Center, Rochester, NY.

Hayes, Daniel, and G. William Monaghan
1998 The Down and Dirty Approach to a Variable Archaeological Record: A Geomorphological Framework for Archaeological Site Formation, Preservation, and Discovery in the James and Potomac River Basins. Paper presented at the annual meeting of the Society for American Archaeology, Seattle, WA.

Hazel, Forest
1991 Occaneechi-Saponi Descendants in the North Carolina Piedmont: The Texas Community. *Southern Indian Studies* 40: 3–29.

Heidenreich, Conrad E.
1971 *Huronia: A History and Geography of the Huron Indians, 1600–1650.* McClelland and Stewart, Toronto.
1976 A Critical Study of the Maps of Samuel Champlain. *Cartographica* 17: 1–140.
1988 An Analysis of the Seventeenth-Century Map "Novvelle France." *Cartographica* 25 (3): 67–111.
1990 History of the St. Lawrence–Great Lakes Area to A.D. 1650. In *The Archaeology of Southern Ontario to A.D. 1650,* edited by Chris J. Ellis and Neal Ferris, pp. 475–492. Occasional Publication of the London Chapter no. 5. Ontario Archaeological Society, London, Ontario, Canada.

Heilman, J. M., and R. R. Hoefer
1981 Possible Astronomical Alignments in a Fort Ancient Settlement at the Incinerator Site in Dayton, Ohio. Paper presented at the annual meeting of the Society for American Archaeology, Philadelphia.

Heilman, J. M., M. C. Lilias, and C. A. Turnbow (editors)
1988 *A History of 17 Years of Excavation and Research: A Chronicle of Twelfth-Century Human Values and the Built Environment,* edited by J. M. Heilman, M. C. Lilias, and C. A. Turnbow. Dayton Museum of Natural History, Dayton, OH.

Hemmings, E. Thomas
1977 *Neale's Landing: An Archaeological Study of a Fort Ancient Settlement on Blennerhassett Island.* West Virginia Geological and Economic Survey, Morgantown.

Henderson, A. Gwynn
1992 Physical Setting. In *Fort Ancient Cultural Dynamics in the Middle Ohio Valley,* edited by A. G. Henderson, pp. 23–27. Monographs in World Archaeology no. 8. Prehistory Press, Madison, WI.

Henderson, A. Gwynn (editor)
1992 *Fort Ancient Cultural Dynamics in the Middle Ohio Valley,* Monographs in World Archaeology no. 8. Prehistory Press, Madison, WI.
1993 *Prehistoric Research at Petersburg, Boone County, Kentucky.* Archaeological Report 289. Program for Cultural Resource Assessment, University of Kentucky, Lexington.

Henderson, A. Gwynn, C. E. Jobe, and Christopher A. Turnbow
1986 Indian Occupation and Use in Northern and Eastern Kentucky during the Contact Period (1540–1795): An Initial Investigation. Manuscript on file, Kentucky Heritage Council, Frankfort.

Henderson, A. Gwynn, David Pollack, and Christopher A. Turnbow
1992 Chronology and Cultural Patterns. In *Fort Ancient Cultural Dynamics in the Middle Ohio Valley,* edited by A. G. Henderson, pp. 253–279. Monographs in World Archaeology no. 8. Prehistory Press, Madison, WI.

Henderson, A. Gwynn, and Christopher A. Turnbow
1987 Fort Ancient Developments in Northeastern Kentucky. In *Current Archaeological Research in Kentucky,* vol. 1, edited by D. Pollack, pp. 205–223. Kentucky Heritage Council, Frankfort.
1992 Previous Fort Ancient Chronologies. In *Fort Ancient Cultural Dynamics in the Middle Ohio Valley,* edited by A. G. Henderson, pp. 9–18. Monographs in World Archaeology no. 8. Prehistory Press, Madison, WI.

Henige, David
1989 On the Current Devaluation of the Notion of Evidence: A Rejoinder to Dobyns. *Ethnohistory* 36: 304–307.

Hennepin, R. P. Louis
1938 *Description of Louisiana, Newly Discovered to the Southwest of New France by Order of the King.* Translated by Marion E. Cross. University of Minnesota Press, Minneapolis.

Henning, Dale R.
1957 Malone II Rockshelter Revisited. *Iowa Archeological Society Newsletter* 23: 5–6.
1970 Development and Interrelationships of Oneota Culture in the Lower Missouri River Valley. *Missouri Archaeologist* 32: 1–180.

1995 Oneota Evolution and Interactions: A Perspective from Wever Terrace, Southeast Iowa. In *Oneota Archaeology: Past, Present, and Future,* edited by William Green, pp. 65–88. Office of the Iowa State Archaeologist, Ames, IA.

Herbstritt, James T.

1981 Bonnie Brook: A Multicomponent Aboriginal Locus in West-Central Pennsylvania. *Pennsylvania Archaeologist* 51 (3): 1–59.

1984 The Mystery of the Monongahela Culture: Archaeology at Foley Farm. *Pennsylvania Heritage* 10 (3): 26–31.

1988 Protohistoric Monongahela: The Beginning of an End. Paper presented at the annual meeting the West Virginia Archaeological Society, Parkersburg.

1993a Monongahela Culture at the Twilight of History. Paper presented at the 5th Monongahela Conference, California University of Pennsylvania, CA.

1993b Iroquoian Double Necked Pottery Jars: Age, Form, Context, and Distribution. Paper presented at the annual meeting of the Society for Pennsylvania Archaeology, Stroudsburg.

Herbstritt, James T., and Barry C. Kent

1990 Shenks Ferry Revisited: A New Look at an Old Culture. *Pennsylvania Heritage* 16 (1): 12–17.

Hodges, Mary Ellen N.

1993 The Archaeology of Native American Life in Virginia in the Context of European Contact: Review of Past Research. In *The Archaeology of Seventeenth-Century Virginia,* edited by T. R. Reinhart and D. Pogue, pp. 1–66. Special Publication of the Archaeological Society of Virginia no. 30. Dietz Press, Richmond, VA.

Hoffman, Bernard G.

1964 Observations on Certain Ancient Tribes of the Northern Appalachian Province. *Bulletin of the Bureau of American Ethnology* 191: 191–245. Smithsonian Institution, Washington, DC.

Hoffman, Michael P.

1977 The Kinkead-Mainard site, 3PU2: A Late Prehistoric Quapaw Phase Site near Little Rock, Arkansas. *Arkansas Archeologist* 16–18: 1–41.

1986 The Protohistoric Period in the Lower and Central Arkansas River Valley in Arkansas. In *The Protohistoric Period in the Mid-South: 1500–1700,* edited by David H. Dye and Ronald C. Brister, pp. 24–37. Mississippi Department of Archives and History, Jackson.

1993 The Depopulation and Abandonment of Northeastern Arkansas in the Protohistoric Period. In *Archaeology of Eastern North America: Papers in Honor of Stephen Williams,* edited by J. B. Stoltman, pp. 261–275. Archaeological Report no. 25. Mississippi Department of Archives and History, Jackson.

Hogue, Susan Homes

1988 A Bioarchaeological Study of Mortuary Practice and Change among the Piedmont Siouan Indians. Ph.D. dissertation, Department of Anthropology, University of North Carolina, Chapel Hill.

Holland, C. G.

1963 Excavations at the C. L. Davis Farm (BK-2). *Quarterly Bulletin of the Archaeological Society of Virginia* 17 (4): 3–12.

1978 Albemarle County Settlement: A Piedmont Model. *Quarterly Bulletin of the Society of Virginia* 33: 29–44.

1983 A Synthesis of Virginia Archaeology and Ethnology. Manuscript on file, Virginia Department of Historic Resources, Richmond.

Holland, C. G., D. van Roijen, and S. Spieden

1983 The Rapidan Mound Revisited. *Quarterly Bulletin of the Archaeological Society of Virginia* 38: 1–32.

Holland, Thomas D.

1991 An Archaeological and Biological Analysis of the Campbell Site. Ph.D. dissertation, University of Missouri.

Holley, George R.

1989 *The Archaeology of the Cahokia Mounds ICT-II: Ceramics.* Illinois Cultural Resources Study no. 11. Illinois Historic Preservation Agency, Springfield.

Hollinger, R. Eric

1995 Residence Patterns and Oneota Cultural Dynamics. In *Oneota Archaeology: Past, Present, and Future,* edited by William Green, pp. 141–174. Office of the State Archaeologist, University of Iowa, Iowa City.

Holm, Mary Ann

1987 Faunal Remains from the Wall and Fredricks Sites. In *The Siouan Project: Seasons I and II,* edited by Roy S. Dickens Jr., H. Trawick Ward, and R. P. Stephen Davis Jr., pp. 237–258. Monograph Series 1. Research Laboratories of Anthropology, University of North Carolina, Chapel Hill.

1993 Faunal Remains [The Holt Site]. In *Indian Communities on the North Carolina Piedmont, A.D. 1000 to 1700,* by H. Trawick Ward and R. P. Stephen Davis Jr., pp. 73–75. Monograph 2. Research Laboratories of Anthropology, University of North Carolina, Chapel Hill.

Holmes, W. F. S.

1994 Hardin Village: A Northern Kentucky Late Fort Ancient Site's Mortuary Patterns and Social Organization. Master's thesis, Department of Anthropology, University of Kentucky, Lexington.

Holmes, William H.

1886 Ancient Pottery of the Mississippi Valley. In *Fourth Annual Report for 1882–1883,* pp. 361–436. Bureau of American Ethnology, Smithsonian Institution, Washington, DC.

Holstein, Harry O., Curtis Hill, Keith Little, and Caleb Curren

1990 Ethnohistoric Archaeology and Hypothesis Testing: Archaeological Investigation of the Terrapin Creek Site. Draft report submitted to the Alabama de Soto Commission, Tuscaloosa, Alabama.

Holstein, Harry O., Keith Little, Curtis Hill, and Caleb Curren

1992 In Search of de Luna's Coosa. Paper presented at the annual meeting of the Society for American Archaeology, Pittsburgh.

Hooton, E. A., and C. C. Willoughby

1920 *Indian Village Site and Cemetery near Madisonville, Ohio.* Papers of the Peabody Museum of American Archaeology and Ethnology, vol. 8, no. 1. Harvard University, Cambridge, MA.

Houck, Peter, and Mintcy Maxham

1993 *Indian Island in Amherst County.* Warwick House, Lynchburg, VA.

House, John H.

1987 Kent Phase Investigations in Eastern Arkansas 1978–1984. *Mississippi Archaeology* 22: 46–60.

1991 Monitoring Mississippian Dynamics: Time, Settlement, and Ceramic Variation in the Kent Phase, Eastern Arkansas. Ph.D. dissertation, Southern Illinois University, Carbondale.

1993 Dating the Kent Phase. *Southeastern Archaeology* 12 (1): 21–32.

Howard, James H.

1965 *The Ponca Tribe.* Bulletin 195. Bureau of American Ethnology, Smithsonian Institution, Washington, DC.

Howe, Sally, and Thompson Webb

1983 Calibrating Pollen Data in Climatic Terms: Improving the Methods. *Quaternary Science Reviews* 2: 17–51.

Howells, William W.

1960 Estimating Population Numbers through Archaeological Skeletal Remains. In *The Application of Quantitative Methods in Archaeology,* edited by R. F. Heizer and S. F. Cook, pp. 158–185. Viking Fund Publications in Anthropology 28. Wenner-Gren Foundation, New York.

Huddleston, Lee E.

1967 *Origins of the American Indians: European Concepts 1492–1729.* University of Texas Press, Austin.

Hudson, C., and C. C. Tesser (editors)

1994 *The Forgotten Centuries: Indians and Europeans in the American South, 1521–1704.* University of Georgia Press, Athens.

Hudson, Charles M. Jr.

1970 *The Catawba Nation.* University of Georgia Press, Athens.

1990 *The Juan Pardo Expeditions.* Smithsonian Institution Press, Washington, DC.

1997 *Knights of Spain, Warriors of the Sun.* University of Georgia Press, Athens.

Hudson, Charles M. Jr., Marvin T. Smith, and Chester B. DePratter

1984 The Route of the de Soto Expedition from Apalachee to Chiaha. *Southeastern Archaeology* 3: 65–77.

1990 The Hernando de Soto Expedition: From Mabila to the Mississippi River. In *Towns and Temples along the Mississippi,* edited by David H. Dye and Cheryl Anne Cox, pp. 181–207. University of Alabama Press, Tuscaloosa.

Hudson, Charles M. Jr., Marvin T. Smith, Chester B. DePratter, and Emilia Kelley

1989 The Tristan de Luna Expedition, 1559–1561. *Southeastern Archaeology* 8: 31–45.

Hudson, Charles M. Jr., Marvin T. Smith, David J. Hally, Richard Polhemus, and Chester B. DePratter

1985 Coosa: A Chiefdom in the Sixteenth-Century Southeastern United States. *American Antiquity* 50: 723–737.

Hudson, Charles M. Jr., John E. Worth, and Chester B. DePratter

1990 Refinements in Hernando de Soto's Route through Georgia and South Carolina. In *Columbian Consequences,* vol. 2, *Archaeological and Historical Perspectives on the Spanish Borderlands East,* edited by David H. Thomas, pp. 107–119. Smithsonian Institution Press, Washington, DC.

Huey, Paul R.

1983 Glass Beads from Fort Orange (1624–1676), Albany, New York. In *Proceedings of the 1982 Glass Trade Bead Conference,* edited by Charles F. Hayes III, pp. 83–110. Research Records 16. Rochester Museum and Science Center, Rochester, NY.

Humpf, Dorothy A., and James W. Hatch

1994 Susquehannock Demography: A New Perspective on the Contact Period in Pennsylvania. In *Proceedings of the 1992 People to People Conference: Selected Papers,* edited by Charles F. Hayes, pp. 65–76. Research Records no. 23. Rochester Museum and Science Center, Rochester, NY.

Hunt, George T.

1940 *The Wars of the Iroquois: A Study in Intertribal Trade Relations.* University of Wisconsin Press, Madison.

Hunter, William A.

1959 The Historic Role of the Susquehannock. In *Susquehannock Miscellany,* edited by John Witthoft and W. Fred Kinsey, pp. 8–18. Pennsylvania Historical and Museum Commission, Harrisburg.

1978 History of the Ohio Valley. In *Handbook of North American Indians,* vol. 15, *Northeast,* edited by Bruce G. Trigger, pp. 588–593. Smithsonian Institution Press, Washington, DC.

Hutchinson, Dale L.

1992 Prehistoric Burials from Buck Key. In *Culture and Environment in the Domain of the Calusa,* edited by W. H. Marquardt, pp. 411–422. Monograph 1. Institute of Archaeology and Paleoenvironmental Studies, University of Florida, Gainesville.

1999 Precolumbian Human Skeletal Remains from Useppa Island. In *The Archaeology of Useppa Island,* edited by W. H. Marquardt. Monograph 3. Institute of Archaeology and Paleoenvironmental Studies, University of Florida, Gainesville.

Hyde, George E.

1962 *Indians of the Woodlands from Prehistoric Times to 1725.* University of Oklahoma Press, Norman.

Ingstad, Helge

1964 Vinland Ruins Prove Vikings Found the New World. *National Geographic* 126 (5): 708–734.

Jackson, Donald (editor)

1964 *Blackhawk: An Autobiography.* University of Illinois Press, Urbana.

James, James Alton

1928 *The Life of George Rogers Clark.* University of Chicago Press, Chicago.

Jamieson, James B.

1983 An Examination of Prisoner-Sacrifice and Cannibalism at the St. Lawrence Iroquoian Roebuck Site. *Canadian Journal of Archaeology* 7 (2): 159–176.

1990 The Archaeology of the St. Lawrence Iroquoians. In *The Archaeology of Southern Ontario to A.D. 1650,* edited by Chris J. Ellis and Neal Ferris, pp. 385–404. Occasional Publication of the London Chapter no. 5. Ontario Archaeological Society, London, Ontario, Canada.

Jefferson, Thomas

1982   *Notes on the State of Virginia.* W. W. Norton,
[1787] New York.

Jeffries, R.
1979 The Tunacunnhee Site: Hopewell in Northwest Georgia. In *Hopewell Archaeology*, edited by D. S. Brose and N. B. Greber, pp. 162–170. Kent State University Press, Kent, OH.

Jennings, Francis
1978 Susquehannock. In *Handbook of North American Indians*, vol. 15, *Northeast*, edited by Bruce G. Trigger, pp. 362–367. Smithsonian Institution Press, Washington, DC.
1984 *The Ambiguous Iroquois Empire: The Covenant Chain Confederation of Indian Tribes with English Colonies from Its Beginnings to the Lancaster Treaty of 1744.* W. W. Norton, New York.
1988 *Empire of Fortune: Crowns, Colonies, and Tribes in the Seven Years War in America.* W. W. Norton, New York.

Jennings, Jesse D.
1974 *Prehistory of North America.* McGraw-Hill, New York.

Jeske, Robert J.
1989 Horticultural Technology and Social Interaction at the Edge of the Prairie Peninsula. *Illinois Archaeology* 1: 103–120.
1990 Langford Tradition Subsistence, Settlement, and Technology. *Midcontinental Journal of Archaeology* 15: 221–249.

Jeter, Marvin D.
1989 Protohistoric and Historic Native Americans. In *Archeology and Bioarcheology of the Lower Mississippi Valley and Trans-Mississippi South in Arkansas and Louisiana*, edited by Marvin D. Jeter, Jerome C. Rose, G. Ishmael Williams Jr., and Anna M. Harmon, pp. 221–248. Research Series no. 37. Arkansas Archeological Survey, Fayetteville.

Johnson, Jay
1991a Aboriginal Settlement and First Contact in Northeast Mississippi. *National Geographic Research and Exploration* 7: 492–494.
1991b Settlement Patterns, GIS, Remote Sensing, and the Late Prehistory of the Black Prairie in East-Central Mississippi. In *Applications of Space-Age Technology in Anthropology*, organized by Clifford A. Behrens and Thomas L. Sever, pp. 111–119. Science and Technology Laboratory, John C. Stennis Space Center, Meriden, MS.

Johnson, William C.
1972 Late Prehistoric Monongahela Ceramics and Cultural Sequence in Southwestern Pennsylvania. Paper presented at the annual meeting of the Southeastern Archaeological Conference, Morgantown, WV.
1976 Late Prehistory of Northwestern Pennsylvania. In *The Late Prehistory of the Lake Erie Drainage Basin: A 1972 Symposium Revised*, edited by D. S. Brose, pp. 48–75. Scientific Papers of the Cleveland Museum of Natural History, Cleveland.
1979 *Archaeological Survey of the Erie National Wildlife Refuge, Erie and Crawford Counties, Pennsylvania.* University of Pittsburgh and Section of Man, Carnegie Museum.
1981 The Campbell Farm Site (36FA26) and Monongahela: A Preliminary Examination and Assessment. Paper presented at the 4th Monongahela Symposium, California, PA.

1990 The Protohistoric Monongahela and the Case for an Iroquoian Connection. Paper presented at the annual meeting of the Eastern States Archaeological Federation, Columbus, OH.
1992 The Protohistoric Monongahela and the Case for an Iroquoian Connection. Paper presented at the annual meeting of the Society for American Archaeology, Pittsburgh, PA.
1994a Tracing the Glaciated Allegheny Plateau Tradition: A Preliminary Culture History of the Late Woodland Period (ca. A.D. 1000–1600) on the Glaciated Allegheny Plateau Section of Northwestern Pennsylvania and Southwestern New York. Paper presented at the annual meeting of the Society for Pennsylvania Archaeology, Pittsburgh, PA.
1994b McFate Incised, Conemaugh Cord-Impressed, Chautauqua Simple-Stamped, and Chautauqua Cord-marked: Type Definitions, Refinements, and Preliminary Observations on Their Origins and Distributions. Paper presented at the annual meeting of the Society for Pennsylvania Archaeology, Pittsburgh, PA.

Johnson, William C., and William P. Athens
1998 Late Prehistoric Period Monongahela Culture Settlement Patterns in the Appalachian Plateau Section of the Upper Ohio River Valley: The Case for a Risk Reduction Subsistence Strategy. Paper presented at the annual meeting of the Society for Pennsylvania Archaeology, New Cumberland.

Johnson, William C., William P. Athens, Martin T. Fuess, Luis G. Jaramillo, Keith R. Bastianini, and Elizabeth Ramos
1989 Late Prehistoric Period Monongahela Culture Site and Cultural Resource Inventory. Report, Survey and Planning Grant. Cultural Resource Management Program, Department of Anthropology, University of Pittsburgh. Submitted to the Pennsylvania Historical and Museum Commission, Bureau for Historic Preservation, Harrisburg, PA.

Johnson, William C., and Jay Babich
1992 A New Monongahela Culture House Type. Paper presented at the annual meeting of the Eastern States Archaeological Federation, Pittsburgh, PA.

Johnson, William C., H. Dale Morgan, and Peter S. Cholock
1991 The Kiskiminetas Phase: A New Early Monongahela Period Complex. Paper presented at the annual meeting of the Society for Pennsylvania Archaeology, Brookville.

Johnson, William C., James B. Richardson III, and Allen S. Bohnert
1979 Archaeological Site Survey in Northwest Pennsylvania, Region IV. Report. Section of Man, Carnegie Museum of Natural History, Pittsburgh. Submitted to the Pennsylvania Historical and Museum Commission.

Johnson, William C., and D. Scott Speedy
1993 Cordage Twist Direction as a Tool in Delineating Territorial Boundaries and Demonstrating Population Continuity during the Late Woodland and Late Prehistoric Periods in the Upper Ohio River Valley. Paper presented at the 5th Monongahela Conference, California University of Pennsylvania, CA.

Jones, B. C.
  1981   Excavation of an Archaic Cemetery in Cocoa Beach,
          Florida. *Florida Anthropologist* 34: 81–89.
Joslyn Art Museum
  1984   *Karl Bodmer's America.* Joslyn Art Museum/University
          of Nebraska Press, Omaha.
Katz, S. H., M. L. Hediger, and L. A. Valleroy
  1974   Traditional Maize Processing Techniques in the New
          World. *Science* 184: 765–773.
Katzenberg, M. Anne, Shelley R. Saunders, and William R.
Fitzgerald
  1993   Age Differences in Stable Carbon and Nitrogen Iso-
          tope Ratios in a Population of Prehistoric Maize Hor-
          ticulturists. *American Journal of Physical Anthropology*
          90: 267–281.
Kavanaugh, Maureen
  1983   Prehistoric Occupation of the Monacacy River Re-
          gion, Maryland. In *Piedmont Archaeology: Recent Re-
          search and Results,* edited by J. Mark Wittkofski and
          Lyle E. Browning, pp. 40–54. Special Publication no.
          10. Archaeological Society of Virginia, Richmond.
Kay, Jeanne
  1979   Wisconsin Indian Hunting Patterns, 1634–1836.
          Annals of the Association of American Geographers 69:
          402–418.
Keel, Bennie C.
  1972   The Recovery of a Historic Indian Burial at Site Sk^{v}1a,
          Stokes County, North Carolina. Manuscript on file,
          Research Laboratories of Anthropology, University of
          North Carolina, Chapel Hill.
Keenleyside, David
  1977   *Late Prehistory of Point Pelee, Ontario, and Environs.* Ar-
          chaeological Survey of Canada, Paper 80. National
          Museum of Man, Ottawa.
Keigwin, Lloyd D.
  1996   The Little Ice Age and Medieval Warm Period in the
          Sargasso Sea. *Science* 274: 1504–1508.
Keller, Gordon N.
  1949   Fort Ancient Manifestations in the Starved Rock Area
          of Northern Illinois. Master's thesis, University of
          Chicago.
Kellogg, Louise P. (editor)
  1917   *Early Narratives of the Northwest, 1634–1699.* Charles
          Scribner's Sons, New York.
Kelly, A. R.
  1970   Explorations at Bell Field Mound and Village, Seasons
          1965, 1966, 1967, 1968. Report. University of Georgia,
          Athens. Submitted to the US National Park Service,
          Atlanta.
  1972   The 1970–1971 Field Seasons at Bell Field Mound,
          Carters Dam. Report. University of Georgia, Athens.
          Submitted to the US National Park Service, Atlanta.
Kelly, A. R., and Lewis H. Larson Jr.
  1956   Explorations at Etowah Indian Mounds near
          Cartersville, Georgia: Seasons 1954, 1955, 1956.
          Archaeology 10 (1): 39–48.
Kelly, A. R., Frank Schnell, Donald Smith, and Ann Schlosser
  1965   Explorations in Sixtoe Field, Carter's Dam, Murray
          County, Georgia: Seasons of 1962, 1963, 1964. Report.

University of Georgia, Athens. Submitted to the US
National Park Service, Atlanta.
Kennedy, William Jerald, Ryan Wheeler, Linda Spears Jester,
Jim Pepe, Nancy Sinks, and Clark Wernecke
  1993   *Archaeological Survey and Excavations at the Jupiter Inlet I
          Site (8PB34), DuBois Park, Palm Beach County, Florida.*
          Department of Anthropology, Florida Atlantic Uni-
          versity, Boca Raton, FL.
Kent, Barry C.
  1974   Locust Grove Pottery: A New Late Woodland Variety.
          Pennsylvania Archaeologist 44 (4): 1–5.
  1984   *Susquehanna's Indians.* Anthropological Series no. 6.
          Pennsylvania Historical and Museum Commission,
          Harrisburg, PA.
Kenworthy, Charles J.
  1875   [Written under pen name "Al Fresco"] Southwest
          Florida: Being Notes of a Tour of Exploration: By
          Our Own Commissioner [the eighth of twelve install-
          ments]. *Forest and Stream* 4 (14, May 13, 1875).
  1883   Ancient Canals in Florida. *Annual Report of the Smith-
          sonian Institution 1881,* pp. 631–635. Washington, DC.
Kenyon, Ian T.
  1972   The Neutral Sequence in the Hamilton Area. Paper
          presented at a meeting of the Canadian Archaeologi-
          cal Association, St. John's, Newfoundland.
Kenyon, Ian T., and William Fitzgerald
  1986   Dutch Glass Beads in the Northeast: An Ontario Per-
          spective. *Man in the Northeast* 32: 1–34.
Kenyon, Ian T., and Thomas Kenyon
  1983   Comments on Seventeenth-Century Glass Trade
          Beads from Ontario. In *Proceedings of the 1982 Glass
          Trade Bead Conference,* edited by C. F. Hayes III, pp. 59–
          74. Research Records no. 16. Rochester Museum and
          Science Center, Rochester, NY.
Kenyon, W. A.
  1982   *The Grimsby Site: A Historic Neutral Cemetery.* Royal On-
          tario Museum, Toronto, Canada.
Kidd, Kenneth E., and Martha Ann Kidd
  1970   A Classification System for Glass Beads for the Use of
          Field Archaeologists. In *Canadian Historic Sites: Occa-
          sional Papers in Archaeology and History 1,* pp. 45–89.
          National Historic Sites Service, Department of Indian
          Affairs and Northern Development, Ottawa, Canada.
  1983   A Classification System for Glass Beads for the Use of
          Field Archaeologists. In *Proceedings of the 1982 Glass
          Trade Bead Conference,* edited by C. F. Hayes III, N. Bol-
          ger, K. Karklins, and C. F. Wray, pp. 219–257. Re-
          search Records no. 16. Rochester Museum and Sci-
          ence Center, Rochester, NY.
Kidder, Tristam R.
  1992   Timing and Consequences of the Introduction of
          Maize Agriculture in the Lower Mississippi Valley.
          North American Archaeologist 13: 15–41.
King, Adam
  1997   A New Perspective on the Etowah Valley Mississip-
          pian Ceramic Sequence. *Early Georgia* 25 (2): 36–61.
King, Frances B.
  1993   Climate, Culture, and Oneota Subsistence in Central
          Illinois. In *Foraging and Farming in the Eastern Wood-*

lands, edited by C. Margaret Scarry, pp. 232–254. University Press of Florida, Gainesville.

King, James E.

1981   Late Quaternary Vegetational History of Illinois. *Ecological Monographs* 51: 43–62.

Kinietz, W. Vernon

1940   Memoir concerning the Different Indian Nations of North America, Antoine Denis Raudot. In *The Indians of the Western Great Lakes, 1615–1760,* pp. 339–410. Occasional Contributions no. 10. Museum of Anthropology, University of Michigan, Ann Arbor.

Kinnaird, Lawrence

1946   *Annual Report of the American Historical Association for the Year 1945,* vol. 4, *Spain in the Mississippi Valley, 1765–1794, Part 3: Problems of Frontier Defense, 1792–1794.* US Government Printing Office, Washington, DC.

Kinsey, W. Fred III

1959   Historic Susquehannock Pottery. In *Susquehannock Miscellany,* edited by John Witthoft and W. Fred Kinsey III, pp. 61–98. Pennsylvania Historical and Museum Commission, Harrisburg.

Klatka, Thomas S., and Michael J. Klein

1993   Preliminary Report on the Graham-White Site: A Late Prehistoric and Contact Period Site in Western Virginia. Paper presented at the annual meeting of the Southeastern Archaeological Conference, Raleigh, NC.

1998   Deciphering Site Occupational History at the Graham-White Site (44RN21). *Quarterly Bulletin of the Archaeological Society of Virginia* 53: 127–145.

Klein, Michael J.

1986   Settlement Patterns in Central Virginia Prehistory. Master's thesis, Department of Anthropology, University of Virginia, Charlottesville.

1994a   An Absolute Seriation Approach to Ceramic Chronology in the Potomac, James, and Roanoke River Drainages of Virginia and Maryland. Ph.D. dissertation, Department of Anthropology, University of Virginia, Charlottesville.

1994b   Results of a Recent Radiocarbon Dating Project in Virginia. *Quarterly Bulletin of the Archaeological Society of Virginia* 49: 17–24.

Knight, Vernon J.

1985   *East Alabama Archaeological Survey, 1985 Season.* Report of Investigations no. 47. Office of Archaeological Research, University of Alabama, Tuscaloosa.

1988   *A Summary of Alabama's de Soto Mapping Project and Project Bibliography.* De Soto Working Paper 9. State Museum of Natural History. University of Alabama, Tuscaloosa.

Kopas, Frank A.

1973   *Soil Survey of Fayette County, Pennsylvania.* USDA Soil Conservation Service, in cooperation with Pennsylvania State University and the Pennsylvania Department of Agriculture.

Krakker, James A.

1983   Changing Socio-Cultural Systems during the Late Prehistoric Period in Southeast Michigan. Ph.D. dissertation, Department of Anthropology, University of Michigan.

Kreisa, Paul P.

1986   The Furman Site (47Wn216), a Lake Winnebago Phase Burial Area near Oshkosh, Wisconsin. *Wisconsin Archeologist* 67: 71–96.

1993   Oneota Burial Patterns in Eastern Wisconsin. *Midcontinental Journal of Archaeology* 18: 35–60.

Kroeber, Alfred L.

1939   *Cultural and Natural Areas of Native North America.* Publications in American Archaeology and Ethnology, vol. 38. University of California, Berkeley.

Kuhn, R. D., R. E. Funk, and J. F. Pendergast

1993   Evidence for a Saint Lawrence Iroquoian Presence on Sixteenth-Century Mohawk Sites. *Man in the Northeast* 45: 77–86.

Kullen, Douglas

1994   The Comstock Trace: A Huber Phase Earthwork and Habitation Site near Joliet, Will County, Illinois. *Midcontinental Journal of Archaeology* 19: 3–38.

Lafferty, Robert H., and Michael C. Sierzchula

1989   *A Cultural Resources Survey of the Delta National Forest, Mississippi.* US Forest Service, Jackson, MS.

Langford, James B., and Marvin T. Smith

1990   Recent Investigations in the Core of the Coosa Province. In *Lamar Archaeology: Mississippian Chiefdoms in the Deep South,* edited by Mark Williams and Gary Shapiro, pp. 104–116. University of Alabama Press, Tuscaloosa.

Lapham, Heather A.

1995   The Analysis of European Glass Trade Beads Recovered from Monongahela Sites in Greene County, Pennsylvania. Report submitted to the Bead Society of Greater Washington, Washington, DC.

1997   Assessing the Impact of European Contact on Native American Economies in Southern Virginia, A.D. 1000–1700. Master's paper on file, Department of Anthropology, University of Virginia, Charlottesville.

1998   Some Thoughts on Glass Beads and Exchange Patterns in the Interior Chesapeake Bay Region. Paper presented at the annual meeting of the Society for American Archaeology, Seattle, WA.

Larsen, Clark Spencer

1994   In the Wake of Columbus: Native Population Biology in the Postcontact Americas. *Yearbook of Physical Anthropology* 37: 109–54.

2000   *Skeletons in Our Closet: Revealing Our Past through Bioarchaeology.* Princeton University Press, Princeton, NJ.

Larsen, Curtis E.

1985a   Geoarchaeological Interpretation of Great Lakes Coastal Environments. In *Archeological Sediments in Context,* edited by J. K. Stein and W. R. Farrand, pp. 91–110. Center for the Study of Early Man, Orono, ME.

1985b   *A Stratigraphic Study of Beach Features on the Southwestern Shore of Lake Michigan: New Evidence of Holocene Lake Level Fluctuations.* Environmental Geology Notes 112. Illinois State Geological Survey, Springfield.

Larson, Daniel O., and Joel Michaelsen

1990   Impacts of Climatic Variability and Population

Growth on Virgin Branch Anasazi Cultural Developments. *American Antiquity* 55 (2): 227–249.

Larson, Lewis H. Jr.

1971a   Settlement Distribution during the Mississippian Period. *Southeastern Archaeological Conference Bulletin* 13: 19–25.

1971b   Archaeological Implications of Social Stratification of the Etowah Site, Georgia. In *Approaches to the Social Dimensions of Mortuary Practices,* edited by James A. Brown, pp. 58–67. Memoir 25. Society for American Archaeology.

1972   Functional Considerations of Warfare in the Southeast during the Mississippian Period. *American Antiquity* 37: 383–392.

1989   The Etowah Site. In *The Southeastern Ceremonial Complex: Artifacts and Analysis,* edited by Patricia Galloway, pp. 133–141. University of Nebraska Press, Lincoln.

Latta, Martha A.

1987   Iroquoian Stemware. *American Antiquity* 52 (4): 717–724.

1990   The Stem of the Matter: Reply to Ramsden and Fitzgerald. *American Antiquity* 55 (1): 162–165.

Lawrence, William L., and Robert C. Mainfort Jr.

1993   Excavations at 40LK1, a Mississippian Substructural Mound in the Reelfoot Basin, Lake County, Tennessee. *Midcontinental Journal of Archaeology* 18 (1): 18–34.

1995   Otto Sharp: A Protohistoric Site in the Reelfoot Basin, Lake County, Tennessee. In *Current Archaeological Research in Kentucky,* vol. 3, edited by J. F. Doershuk, C. A. Bergman, and D. Pollack, pp. 265–277. Kentucky Heritage Commission, Frankfort, KY.

Lawson, John

1966   *A New Voyage to Carolina.* Readex Microprint. Originally published 1709, London.

Lawson, Sarah (translator)

1992   *A Foothold in Florida: The Eye-Witness Account of Four Voyages Made by the French to That Region and Their Attempt at Colonisation, 1562–1568.* Antique Atlas Publications, West Sussex, England.

Le Roy Ladurie, Emmanuel

1971   *Times of Feast, Times of Famine: A History of Climate since the Year 1000.* Doubleday, Garden City, NY.

Le Sueur, Pierre Charles

1700   *Journal du voyage de Lesueur sur le Mississippi.* Archives Nationales, Paris.

Leach, Edmund

1954   *Political Systems of Highland Burma.* Beacon Press, Boston.

Lee, Alfred M.

1981   *An Archaeological Reconnaissance of Selected Areas in Lake County, Ohio.* Archaeological Research Report no. 34 (3). Cleveland Museum of Natural History.

1986   Archaeological Recovery of Early, Middle and Early Late Woodland Remains from the Excavation of the Stanford Knoll Site in the Cuyahoga Valley National Recreation Area. Technical Report. Cleveland Museum of Natural History. Submitted to the National Park Service Midwestern Archaeological Center.

1988   *Archaeological Reconnaissance in Ashtabula County, Ohio.*

Archaeological Research Report no. 70. Cleveland Museum of Natural History.

Lee, Alfred M., and William Fienga

1982   The Bass Lake Site. Paper presented at the annual meeting of the Midwestern Archaeological Conference, Columbus.

Lee, Arthur R.

1993   Lab May Verify Heineken Dates. *Southwest Florida Archaeological Society Newsletter* 9 (2): 1–2. Naples, FL.

Lee, Thomas E.

1952   The Parker Earthwork, Corruna, Ontario. *Pennsylvania Archaeologist* 28 (1): 3–30.

1959   An Archaeological Survey of Southwestern Ontario and Manitoulin Island. *Pennsylvania Archaeologist* 29 (2): 80–92.

Lefler, Hugh T. (editor)

1967   *A New Voyage of Carolina, by John Lawson.* University of North Carolina Press, Chapel Hill.

Lehmer, Donald J.

1963   The Plains Bison Hunt: Prehistoric and Historic. *Plains Anthropologist* 8: 211–217.

Leland, Waldo G.

1924   The Lesueur Collection of American Sketches in the Museum of Natural History at Havre, Seine-Inferieure. *Mississippi Valley Historical Review* 10 (1):53–78.

Lenig, Donald

1977   *Of Dutchmen, Beaver Hats and Iroquoians.* New York State Archaeological Association Researches and Transactions, Rochester and Albany.

Lennox, Paul A.

1981   The Hamilton Site: A Late Historic Neutral Town. Mercury Series, Archaeological Survey of Canada, Paper 103, pp. 211–403. National Museum of Man, Ottawa.

1984a   The Bogle I and Bogle II Sites: Historic Neutral Hamlets of the Northern Tier. Mercury Series, Archaeological Survey of Canada, Paper 121, pp. 184–289. National Museum of Man, Ottawa.

1984b   The Hood Site: A Historic Neutral Town of A.D. 1640. Mercury Series, Archaeological Survey of Canada, Paper 121, pp. 1–183. National Museum of Man, Ottawa.

Lennox, Paul A., and William R. Fitzgerald

1990   The Culture History and Archaeology of the Neutral Iroquoians. In *The Archaeology of Southern Ontario to A.D. 1650,* edited by Chris J. Ellis and Neal Ferris, pp. 405–456. Occasional Publication of the London Chapter no. 5. Ontario Archaeological Society, London, Ontario, Canada.

Lewis, Clifford, and Albert J. Loomie

1953   *The Spanish Jesuit Mission in Virginia, 1570–1572.* University of North Carolina Press, Chapel Hill.

Lewis, Ernest

1951   The Sara Indians, 1540–1768: An Ethno-Archaeological Study. Master's thesis, Department of Sociology and Anthropology, University of North Carolina, Chapel Hill.

Lewis, R. Barry

1978   Land Leveling Salvage Investigations in South Mississippi County, Missouri: 1970. Report, Contract no. 14-10-2: 920–150. Submitted to the Midwest Region, US National Park Service.

1988 Old World Dice in the Protohistoric Southern United States. *Current Anthropology* 29: 759–768.

1990 The Late Prehistory of the Ohio-Mississippi Rivers Confluence Region, Kentucky and Missouri. In *Towns and Temples along the Mississippi,* edited by David H. Dye and Cheryl Anne Cox, pp. 38–58. University of Alabama Press, Tuscaloosa.

1991 The Early Mississippi Period in the Confluence Region and Its Northern Relationships. In *Cahokia and the Hinterlands: Middle Mississippian Cultures of the Midwest,* edited by Thomas E. Emerson and R. Barry Lewis, pp. 274–294. University of Illinois Press, Urbana.

Lewis, R. Barry (editor)
1986 *Mississippian Towns of the Western Kentucky Border: The Adams, Wickliffe, and Sassafras Ridge Sites.* Kentucky Heritage Council, Frankfort.

Lewis, Thomas M. N., and Madeline Kneberg
1941 *The Prehistory of the Chickamauga Basin in Tennessee: A Preview.* Tennessee Anthropology Papers no. 1. Division of Anthropology, University of Tennessee, Knoxville.

1946 *Hiwassee Island.* University of Tennessee Press, Knoxville.

1970 *Hiwassee Island: An Archaeological Account of Four Tennessee Indian Peoples.* University of Tennessee Press, Knoxville.

Lilias, M.
1988 History of the Dayton Museum of Natural History's Involvement with the Incinerator Site. In *A History of 17 Years of Excavation and Research: A Chronicle of Twelfth-Century Human Values and the Built Environment,* edited by J. M. Heilman, M. C. Lilias, and C. A. Turnbow, pp. 36–54. Dayton Museum of Natural History, Dayton, OH.

Lindsay, Mrs. E. M.
1964 Cooper Farm Salvage Project. *Journal of Alabama Archaeology* 10: 22–29.

Little, Keith
1985 A Sixteenth-Century European Sword from a Protohistoric Aboriginal Site in Northwest Georgia. *Early Georgia* 13: 1–14.

Little, Keith, and Caleb Curren
1981 Site 1Ce308: A Protohistoric Site on the Upper Coosa River in Alabama. *Journal of Alabama Archaeology* 27: 117–24.

1990 Conquest Archaeology of Alabama. In *Columbian Consequences,* vol. 2, *Archaeological and Historical Perspectives on the Spanish Borderlands East,* edited by David H. Thomas, pp. 169–195. Smithsonian Institution Press, Washington, DC.

Logan, Wilfred D.
1953 Archaeological Investigation of Spike Hollow Rockshelter, Allamakee County, Iowa. *Journal of the Iowa Archaeological Society* 2 (2–3): 4–30.

1976 *Woodland Complexes in Northeastern Iowa.* Publications in Archeology 15. US Department of the Interior, National Park Service, Washington, DC.

Luer, George M.
1989 Calusa Canals in Southwestern Florida: Routes of Tribute and Exchange. *Florida Anthropologist* 42 (2): 89–130.

1994 A Third Ceremonial Tablet from the Goodnow Mound, Highlands County, Florida, with Notes on Some Peninsular Tribes and Other Tablets. *Florida Anthropologist* 47: 180–188.

Luer, George, D. Allerton, D. Hazeltine, R. Hatfield, and D. Hood
1986 Whelk Shell Tool Blanks from Big Mound Key (8–10), Charlotte County, Florida: With Notes on Certain Whelk Shell Tools. In *Shells and Archaeology in Southern Florida,* edited by G. Luer, pp. 92–124. Publication 12. Florida Anthropological Society, Tallahassee.

Luer, George M., and Marion M. Almy
1987 The Laurel Mound (8SO98) and Radial Burials, with Comments on the Safety Harbor Period. *Florida Anthropologist* 40: 301–320.

Luer, George M., and Lauren C. Archibald
1988 *Archaeological Data Recovery at Mound A, Boggess Ridge (8–16), Charlotte Harbor State Reserve, Winter Field Season 1988.* Archaeological and Historical Conservancy, Miami.

Luer, George M., and Ryan J. Wheeler
1997 How the Pine Island Canal Worked: Topography, Hydraulics, and Engineering. *Florida Anthropologist* 50: 115–131.

Lumb, Lisa C., and Charles H. McNutt
1988 *Chucalissa: Excavations in Units 2 and 6, 1959–67.* Occasional Papers no. 15. Anthropological Research Center, Memphis State University, Memphis, TN.

Lurie, Nancy Oestreich
1960 Winnebago Protohistory. In *Culture in History,* edited by Stanley Diamond, pp. 790–808. Columbia University Press, New York.

Lurie, Rochelle
1994 New Insights on the Protohistoric Period in Northeastern Illinois: The New Lenox Site. Paper presented at the Midwest Archaeological Conference, Lexington, KY.

Lyon, Eugene
1983 *The Enterprise of Florida: Pedro Menéndez de Avilés and the Spanish Conquest of 1565–1568.* University Press of Florida, Gainesville.

MacCord, Howard A. Sr.
1952 The Susquehannock Indians in West Virginia, 1630–77. *West Virginia History* 13 (4): 239–246.

1974 The Wingina Site, Nelson County, Virginia. *Quarterly Bulletin of the Archaeological Society of Virginia* 28: 169–180.

1986 *The Lewis Creek Mound Culture in Virginia.* Privately printed, Richmond.

1989 The Intermontane Culture: A Middle Appalachian Late Woodland Manifestation. *Archaeology of Eastern North America* 17: 89–108.

1991 Linking Archaeological Cultures with Historic Indian Groups. *Quarterly Bulletin of the Archaeological Society of Virginia* 46 (3): 141–144.

MacDonald, Robert I.
    1986   The Coleman Site (AiHd-7): A Late Prehistoric Iroquoian Village in the Waterloo Region. Master's thesis, Trent University, Peterborough, Ontario.
    1988   Ontario Iroquoian Sweat Lodges. *Ontario Archaeology* 48: 17–26.

MacNeish, Richard S.
    1952   *Iroquois Pottery Types: A Technique for the Study of Iroquois Prehistory.* National Museum of Canada Bulletin 124. National Museum of Canada, Ottawa.

Mahon, John K.
    1985   *History of the Second Seminole War, 1835–1842.* Revised edition. University Press of Florida, Gainesville.
    1998   The First Seminole War, November 21, 1817–May 24, 1818. *Florida Historical Quarterly* 77: 62–67.

Mainfort, Robert C. Jr.
    1979   *Indian Social Dynamics in the Period of European Contact: Fletcher Site Cemetery, Bay County, Michigan.* Publications of the Museum, Anthropological Series 1 (4). Michigan State University, East Lansing.
    1985   Wealth, Space, and Status in an Historic Indian Cemetery. *American Antiquity* 50 (3): 555–579.
    1991   An Overview of Late Mississippian Sites in West Tennessee. Paper presented at the annual meeting of the Southeastern Archaeological Conference, Jackson, MS.
    1996a   Cultural History of the Reelfoot Lake Basin, Kentucky and Tennessee. In *Prehistory of the Central Mississippi Valley*, edited by C. H. McNutt, pp. 77–96. University of Alabama Press, Tuscaloosa.
    1996b   Late Period Chronology in the Central Mississippi Valley: A Western Tennessee Perspective. *Southeastern Archaeology* 15 (2): 172–181.
    1999   Late Period Phases in the Central Mississippi Valley: A Multivariate Approach. In *Arkansas Archeology: Papers in Honor of Dan and Phyllis Morse*, edited by R. C. Mainfort and M. D. Jeter, pp. 143–167. University of Arkansas Press, Fayetteville.

Mainfort, Robert C., and Michael C. Moore
    1998   Graves Lake: A Late Mississippian-Period Village in Lauderdale County, Tennessee. In *Changing Perspectives on the Archaeology of the Central Mississippi River Valley*, edited by M. O'Brien and R. Dunnell, pp. 99–123. University of Alabama Press, Tuscaloosa.

Manson, Carl P., and Howard A. MacCord
    1941   An Historic Iroquois Site near Romney, West Virginia. *West Virginia History* 2 (4): 290–293.
    1944   Additional Notes on the Herriott Farm Site. *West Virginia History* 5 (3): 201–211.

Manson, Carl P., Howard A. MacCord, and James B. Griffin
    1944   The Culture of the Keyser Farm Site. *Papers of the Michigan Academy of Science, Arts, and Letters* 29: 375–418.

Maples, William R.
    1987   *Analysis of Skeletal Remains Recovered at the Gauthier Site, Brevard County, Florida.* Miscellaneous Project Report Series 31. Florida Museum of Natural History, Department of Anthropology, Gainesville.

Markman, Charles W.
    1991   Above the American Bottom: The Late Woodland–Mississippian Transition in Northeast Illinois. In *New Perspectives on Cahokia: Views from the Periphery*, edited by James B. Stoltman, pp. 177–208. Prehistory Press, Madison, WI.

Marquardt, William H.
    1987a   The Calusa Social Formation in Protohistoric South Florida. In *Power Relations and State Formation*, edited by Thomas C. Patterson and Christine W. Gailey, pp. 98–116. Archaeology Section, American Anthropological Association, Washington, DC.
    1987b   South Floridian Contacts with the Bahamas: A Review and Some Speculations. Paper presented at the symposium, "Bahamas 1492: Its People and Environment," Freeport, Bahamas, November 1987.
    1988   Politics and Production among the Calusa of South Florida. In *Hunters and Gatherers*, vol. 1, *History, Evolution, and Social Change*, edited by Tim Ingold, David Riches, and James Woodburn, pp. 161–188. Berg, London.
    1991   Introduction. In *Missions to the Calusa*, by John H. Hann, pp. xv–xix. University Press of Florida, Gainesville.
    1992a   Calusa Culture and Environment: What Have We Learned? In *Culture and Environment in the Domain of the Calusa*, edited by W. H. Marquardt, pp. 423–436. Monograph 1. Institute of Archaeology and Paleoenvironmental Studies, University of Florida, Gainesville.
    1992b   Recent Archaeological and Paleoenvironmental Investigations in Southwest Florida. In *Culture and Environment in the Domain of the Calusa*, edited by W. H. Marquardt, pp. 9–57. Monograph 1. Institute of Archaeology and Paleoenvironmental Studies, University of Florida, Gainesville.
    1992c   Shell Artifacts from the Caloosahatchee Area. In *Culture and Environment in the Domain of the Calusa*, edited by W. H. Marquardt, pp. 191–227. Monograph 1. Institute of Archaeology and Paleoenvironmental Studies, University of Florida, Gainesville.
    1996   Four Discoveries: Environmental Archaeology in Southwest Florida. In *Case Studies in Environmental Archaeology*, edited by E. J. Reitz, L. A. Newsom, and S. J. Scudder, pp. 17–32. Plenum Press, New York.

Marquardt, William H. (editor)
    1992   *Culture and Environment in the Domain of the Calusa.* Monograph 1. Institute of Archaeology and Paleoenvironmental Studies, University of Florida, Gainesville.
    1999   *The Archaeology of Useppa Island.* Monograph 3. Institute of Archaeology and Paleoenvironmental Studies, University of Florida, Gainesville.

Marquardt, William H., Claudine Payne, and Karen Jo Walker
    1992   *Calusa News* no. 6. Institute of Archaeology and Paleoenvironmental Studies, Florida Museum of Natural History, Gainesville.

Marquardt, William H., and Jennifer Wallace
    1995   Salvage Excavation of a Human Burial on Useppa Island, 8LL51, Lee County, Florida. Report. Submitted to the Office of the State Archaeologist. Manuscript on file, Florida Museum of Natural History, Gainesville.

Martijn, Charles A.

1969 *Ile aux Basques and the Prehistoric Iroquois Occupation of Southern Quebec.* Cahiers d'Archéologie Québecoise, Trois-Rivières.

Martin, Patrick E., and Robert C. Mainfort Jr.

1985 The Battle Point Site: A Late Historic Cemetery in Ottawa County, Michigan. *Arctic Anthropology* 22 (2): 115–129.

Maslowski, Robert F.

1973 An Analysis of Cordmarked Watson Ware. *Pennsylvania Archaeologist* 43 (2): 1–12.

1984a The Significance of Cordage Attributes in the Analysis of Woodland Pottery. *Pennsylvania Archaeologist* 54 (1–2): 51–60.

1984b Protohistoric Villages in Southern West Virginia. In *Upland Archaeology in the East, Symposium 2,* edited by M. B. Barber, pp. 148–165. USDA Forest Service Southern Region, Atlanta, GA.

Mason, Carol I.

1976 Historic Identification and the Lake Winnebago Focus Oneota. In *Cultural Change and Continuity: Essays in Honor of James Bennett Griffin,* edited by Charles E. Cleland, pp. 335–348. Academic Press, New York.

1993 Historic Pottery and Tribal Identification in Wisconsin: A Review of the Evidence and the Problems. *Wisconsin Archeologist* 74: 258–271.

Mason, Ronald J.

1976 Ethnicity and Archaeology in the Upper Great Lakes. In *Cultural Change and Continuity: Essays in Honor of James Bennett Griffin,* edited by Charles E. Cleland, pp. 349–361. Academic Press, New York.

1981 *Great Lakes Archaeology.* Academic Press, Orlando, FL.

1983 The Archaeological Investigations of Rock Island III, Door County, Wisconsin. Special Paper. *Mid-Continental Journal of Archaeology* 5: 1–276.

1986 *Rock Island: Historical Indian Archaeology in the Northern Lake Michigan Basin.* MCJA Special Paper no. 6. Kent State University Press, Ohio.

1993 Oneota and Winnebago Ethnogenesis: An Overview. *Wisconsin Archeologist* 74: 400–421.

Mathews, Zena Pearlstone

1980 Of Man and Beast: The Chronology of Effigy Pipes among Ontario Iroquoians. *Ethnohistory* 27 (4): 295–307.

Matlack, Harry A.

1986 *Mystery of the Fort Field: The Bell Site Dig, C-36CD31.* Privately printed.

1987 *Pottery of the Bell Site.* Privately printed.

Mayer-Oakes, William J.

1954 The Scarem Site, Washington County, Pennsylvania. *Pennsylvania Archaeologist* 24 (2): 45–62.

1955 *Prehistory of the Upper Ohio Valley: An Introductory Archaeological Study.* Annals of the Carnegie Museum no. 34. Pittsburgh.

1993 Varner Site. Slide presentation at the Carnegie Museum of Natural History, Pittsburgh.

Maymon, Jeffrey H., and Thomas W. Davis

1998 A Contact Period Susquehannock Site in the Upper Potomac River Drainage: Data Recovery at Site 46HY89, Moorefield, West Virginia. Paper presented at the annual meeting of the Middle Atlantic Archaeological Conference, Cape May, NJ.

McAndrews, John H.

1988 Human Disturbance of North American Forests and Grasslands: The Fossil Pollen Record. In *Vegetation History,* edited by B. Huntley and T. Webb, pp. 673–697. Kluwer Academic, Dordrecht, Netherlands.

McCain, William D., and Charlotte Capers

1954 *Memoirs of Henry Tillinghast Ireys.* Papers of the Washington County Historical Society 1910–1915. Mississippi Department of Archives and History and Mississippi Historical Society, Jackson.

McGoun, William E.

1993 *Prehistoric Peoples of South Florida.* University of Alabama Press, Tuscaloosa.

McKenzie, Douglas H., and John Blank

1976 The Eiden Site: Late Woodland from the South-Central Lake Erie Region. In *The Late Prehistory of the Lake Erie Drainage Basin: A 1972 Symposium Revised,* edited by D. Brose, pp. 305–326. Scientific Papers of the Cleveland Museum of Natural History, Cleveland.

McKenzie, Douglas H., John E. Blank, James L. Murphy, Orin C. Shane III, and the Board of Park Commissioners, Lorain County Metropolitan Park District

1973 *The Eiden Site: Terminal Late Woodland on the South-Central Lake Erie Shore.* Lorain County Metropolitan Park District, Elyria, OH.

McKern, Will C.

1931 Archaeological Fieldwork in La Crosse, Vernon, and Crawford Counties. *Yearbook of the Public Museum of the City of Milwaukee, 1929* 9: 7–26.

1945 Preliminary Report on the Upper Mississippi Phase in Wisconsin. *Bulletin of the Public Museum of the City of Milwaukee* 16 (3): 109–285.

McKusick, Marshall B.

1973 *The Grant Oneota Village.* Report 4. Office of the State Archaeologist, Iowa City, IA.

McLaughlin, Robert H.

1998a The Antiquities Act of 1906: Politics and the Framing of an American Anthropology and Archaeology. *Oklahoma City University Law Review* 25 (1–2): 61–91.

1998b The American Archaeological Record: Authority to Dig, Power to Interpret. *International Journal of Cultural Property* 7 (2): 342–375.

McMichael, Edward V.

1968 *Introduction to West Virginia Archeology.* 2d ed., revised. West Virginia Geological and Economic Survey, Educational Series. Morgantown, WV.

Merrell, James H.

1982 Natives in a New World: The Catawba Indians of Carolina, 1650–1800. Ph.D. dissertation, Johns Hopkins University, Baltimore, MD.

1987 "This Western World": The Evolution of the Piedmont, 1525–1725. In *The Siouan Project: Seasons I and II,* edited by Roy S. Dickens Jr., H. Trawick Ward, and R. P. Stephen Davis Jr., pp. 19–27. Monograph Series 1. Research Laboratories of Anthropology, University of North Carolina, Chapel Hill.

1989 *The Indians of the New World: Catawbas and Their Neigh-*

bors from European Contact through the Era of Removal. University of North Carolina Press, Chapel Hill.

Michalik, Laura K.
1982   An Ecological Perspective on the Huber Phase Subsistence-Settlement System. In *Oneota Studies,* edited by Guy E. Gibbon, pp. 29–53. Publications in Anthropology no. 1. University of Minnesota, Minneapolis.

Michel, Louis
1916   Diary of a French Huegenot in Virginia. *Virginia Magazine of History and Biography* 24: 1–41.

Milanich, Jerald T.
1992   Native Societies and Spanish Empire in the Sixteenth-Century American Southeast. *Antiquity* 66: 140–152.
1995   *Florida Indians and the Invasion from Europe.* University Press of Florida, Gainesville.

Milanich, Jerald T., Jefferson Chapman, Ann S. Cordell, Stephen Hale, and Rochelle A. Marrinan
1984   Prehistoric Development of Calusa Society in Southwest Florida: Excavations on Useppa Island. In *Perspectives on Gulf Coast Prehistory,* edited by D. D. Davis, pp. 258–314. University Press of Florida, Gainesville.

Miller, Christopher L., and George R. Hamell
1986   A New Perspective on Indian-White Contact: Cultural Symbols and Colonial Trade. *Journal of American History* 73 (2): 311–328.

Miller, O., M. E. Becher, C. S. Weed, and M. Warner
1997   *Phase III Mitigation Investigations at the Turpin Archaeological District, for the Cinergy Corp.'s State Route 32 Pipeline Project, Hamilton County, Ohio.* Gray and Pape, Inc., Cincinnati, OH.

Mills, W. C.
1904   Explorations of the Gartner Mound and Village Site. In *Certain Mounds and Village Sites in Ohio,* vol. 1, part 2, pp. 1–65. Fred J. Heer, Columbus.
1906   Explorations of the Baum Village Site. In *Certain Mounds and Village Sites in Ohio,* vol. 1, part 3, pp. 1–96. Fred J. Heer, Columbus.
1917   Exploration of the Feurt Mounds and Village Site. *Ohio Archaeological and Historical Quarterly* 26 (3): 305–449.

Milner, George R.
1980   Epidemic Disease in the Postcontact Southeast: A Reappraisal. *Midcontinental Journal of Archaeology* 5: 39–56.
1990   The Late Prehistoric Cahokia Cultural System of the Mississippi River Valley: Foundations, Florescence, and Fragmentation. *Journal of World Prehistory* 4: 1–43.
1991   American Bottom Mississippian Cultures: Internal Developments and External Relations. In *New Perspectives from the Periphery,* edited by James B. Stoltman, pp. 29–48. Prehistory Press, Madison, WI.
1992   Tracking the Four Horsemen across the Post-Columbian Southeast. Keynote address presented at the annual meeting of the Southeastern Archaeological Conference, Little Rock, AR.

Milner, George R., Eve Anderson, and Virginia G. Smith
1991   Warfare in Late Prehistoric West-Central Illinois. *American Antiquity* 56: 581–603.

Milner, George, Clark Larsen, Dale Hutchinson, and Matt Williamson
1994   Conquistadors, Excavators, or Rodents? Paper presented at the annual meeting of the Southeastern Archaeological Conference, Lexington, KY.

Milner, George R., and Virginia G. Smith
1986   *New Deal Archaeology in Kentucky: Excavations, Collections, and Research.* Occasional Papers in Anthropology 5. Program for Cultural Resource Assessment, University of Kentucky, Lexington.
1990   Oneota Human Skeletal Remains. In *Archaeological Investigations at the Morton Village and Norris Farms 36 Cemetery,* edited by S. K. Santure, A. D. Harn, and D. Esarey, pp. 111–148. Reports of Investigations no. 45. Illinois State Museum, Springfield.

Milner, George R., Virginia G. Smith, and Eve Anderson
1991   Conflict, Mortality, and Community Health in an Illinois Oneota Population. In *Between Bands and States,* edited by Susan A. Gregg, pp. 245–264. Occasional Paper no. 9. Center for Archaeological Investigations, Southern Illinois University, Carbondale.

Mitchem, Jeffrey M.
1989   Redefining Safety Harbor: Late Prehistoric/Protohistoric Archaeology in West Peninsular Florida. Ph.D. dissertation, Department of Anthropology, University of Florida, Gainesville.
1996a   Mississippian Research at Parkin Archeological State Park. In *Proceedings of the 14th Mid-South Archaeological Conference,* edited by R. Walling, C. Wharey, and C. Stanley, pp. 25–39. Special Publications 1. Panamerican Consultants, Tuscaloosa, AL.
1996b   Investigations of the Possible Remains of de Soto's Cross at Parkin. *Arkansas Archeologist* 35: 87–95.

Moffat, Charles R.
1979   Some Observations on the Distribution and Significance of the Garden Beds in Wisconsin. *Wisconsin Archeologist* 60: 222–248.

Mooney, James P.
1894   *The Siouan Tribes of the East.* Bulletin 22. Bureau of American Ethnology, Smithsonian Institution, Washington, DC.

Moore, Alexander
1988   *Nairne's Muskhogean Journals.* University Presses of Mississippi, Jackson.

Moore, Clarence B.
1900   Certain Antiquities of the Florida West-Coast. *Journal of the Academy of Natural Sciences of Philadelphia* 11: 350–394.
1905   Miscellaneous Investigations in Florida. *Journal of the Academy of Natural Sciences of Philadelphia* 13: 296–325.

Moorehead, Warren K.
1932   *Etowah Papers.* Robert S. Peabody Foundation, Andover, MA.

Morgan, Lewis H.
1851   *League of the Ho-dé-no-sau-nee or Iroquois.* Sage and Brother, Rochester, NY.

Morgan, Richard C., and Holmes Ellis
1943   The Fairport Harbor Village Site, Lake County, Ohio. *Ohio State Archaeological and Historical Society Quarterly* 52 (1): 1–64.

Morgan, Richard G.
1952   Outline of Cultures in the Ohio Region. In *Archaeology of the Eastern United States,* edited by James B.

Griffin, pp. 83–98. University of Chicago Press, Chicago.

Morrell, L. Ross
1965   *The Woods Island Site in Southeastern Acculturation, 1625–1800.* Notes in Anthropology no. 11. Florida State University, Tallahassee.

Morse, Dan F.
1990   The Nodena Phase. In *Towns and Temples along the Mississippi,* edited by David H. Dye and Cheryl A. Cox, pp. 69–97. University of Alabama Press, Tuscaloosa.
1992   The Seventeenth-Century Michigamea Village Location in Arkansas. In *Calumet and Fleur-de-lys: Archaeology of Indian and French Contact in the Mid-Continent,* edited by John A. Walthall and Thomas E. Emerson, pp. 55–74. Smithsonian Institution Press, Washington, DC.
1993   Archaeology and the Population of Arkansas in 1541–1543. In *The Expedition of Hernando de Soto West of the Mississippi, 1541–1543,* edited by G. A. Young and M. P. Hoffman, pp. 29–35. University of Arkansas Press, Fayetteville.

Morse, Dan F. (editor)
1989   *Nodena.* Research Series no. 30. Arkansas Archeological Survey, Fayetteville.

Morse, Dan F., and Phyllis A. Morse
1983   *Archaeology of the Central Mississippi Valley.* Academic Press, New York.
1990   The Spanish Exploration of Arkansas. In *Columbian Consequences,* vol. 2, *Archaeological and Historical Perspectives on the Spanish Borderlands East,* edited by David H. Thomas, pp. 197–210. Smithsonian Institution Press, Washington, DC.

Morse, Phyllis A.
1981   *Parkin.* Research Series no. 13. Arkansas Archeological Survey, Fayetteville.
1990   The Parkin Site and the Parkin Phase. In *Towns and Temples along the Mississippi,* edited by D. H. Dye and C. A. Cox, pp. 118–134. University of Alabama Press, Tuscaloosa.

Morton, James
1992   Preliminary Observations on the Bosman Site Ceramic Assemblage and Speculations on Its Placement within Protohistory in the Upper Ohio Valley and Surrounding Areas. Paper distributed at the annual meeting of the Ohio Archaeological Council, Columbus.

Morton, James, and Brian DaRe
1996   Toward a Revised Taxonomy and Culture History Scheme for Eastern Ohio Late Prehistory. *Ohio Archaeologist* 46 (4): 32–39.

Mott, Mildred
1938   The Relation of Historic Indian Tribes to Archaeological Manifestations in Iowa. *Iowa Journal of History and Politics* 36: 227–314.

Mouer, L. Daniel
1981   Powhatan and Monacan Settlement Hierarchies. *Quarterly Bulletin of the Archaeological Society of Virginia* 36: 1–21.
1983   A Review of the Archaeology and Ethnohistory of the Monacan Indians. In *Piedmont Archaeology: Recent Research and Results,* edited by J. Mark Wittkofski and Lyle E. Browning, pp. 21–39. Special Publication no. 10. Archaeological Society of Virginia, Richmond.

Moxley, Ronald W.
1988a   The Orchard Site: A Proto-Historic Fort Ancient Village Site in Mason County, West Virginia. *West Virginia Archaeologist* 40 (1): 33–41.
1988b   The Orchard Site: A Proto-Historic Fort Ancient Village Site in Mason County, West Virginia. *Ohio Archaeologist* 38 (3): 4–11.

Muller, Jon D.
1986   *Archaeology of the Lower Ohio River Valley.* Academic Press, New York.
1989   The Southern Cult. In *The Southeastern Ceremonial Complex: Artifacts and Analysis,* edited by Patricia Galloway, pp. 11–26. University of Nebraska Press, Lincoln.
1997   *Mississippian Political Economy.* Plenum, New York.

Munson, Cheryl, David Pollack, and Mary Lucas Powell.
1988   Slack Farm Site. *Bulletin of the Society for American Archaeology* 6 (6): 122.

Murdock, George P.
1955   North American Social Organization. *Davidson Journal of Anthropology* 1: 85–97.

Murphy, Carl, and Neal Ferris
1990   The Late Woodland Western Basin Tradition in Southwestern Ontario. In *The Archaeology of Southern Ontario to* A.D. *1650,* edited by C. J. Ellis and N. Ferris, pp. 189–278. Occasional Publication of the London Chapter no. 5. Ontario Archaeological Society, London, Ontario, Canada.

Murphy, James L.
1971a   Whittlesey Pottery Types. *Ohio Archaeologist* 21 (1): 298–305.
1971b   The Lyman Site (33La2), Lake County, Ohio. *Pennsylvania Archaeologist* 41 (3): 12–25
1971c   The Fairport Harbor Site (33–La-5), Lake County, Ohio. *Pennsylvania Archaeologist* 41 (3): 26–43.
1972a   Notes on the South Park Ceramics. *Ohio Archaeologist* 22 (2).
1972b   Monongahela, Mayer-Oakes and Me. *Amwoki Chapter Newsletter, Society for Pennsylvania Archaeology* 3 (3): 1–11.

Nabokov, Peter, and Dean Snow
1992   Farmers of the Woodlands. In *America in 1492: The World of the Indian Peoples before the Arrival of Columbus,* edited by Alvin M. Josephy, pp. 119–145. Alfred Knopf, New York.

Nale, Robert F.
1963   The Salvage Excavation of the Boyle Site (36 Wh 19). *Pennsylvania Archaeologist* 38 (4): 164–194.

Nash, Charles H.
1972   *Chucalissa: Excavations and Burials through 1963.* Occasional Papers no. 6. Anthropological Research Center, Memphis State University, Memphis, TN.

Nass, J. P. Jr.
1987   Use-Wear Analysis and Household Archaeology: A Study of the Activity Structure of the Incinerator Site, an Anderson Phase Fort Ancient Community in Southwestern Ohio. Ph.D. dissertation, Ohio State University, Columbus.

Nass, J. P. Jr., and R. W. Yerkes
    1995   Social Differentiation in Mississippian and Fort An-
            cient Societies. In *Mississippian Communities and House-
            holds,* edited by J. D. Rogers and B. D. Smith, pp. 58–
            80. University of Alabama Press, Tuscaloosa.
National Geographic Society
    1988   *Historical Atlas of the United States.* National Geo-
            graphic Society, Washington, DC.
Navey, Liane
    1982   An Introduction to the Mortuary Practices of the His-
            toric Sara. Master's thesis, Department of Anthropol-
            ogy, University of North Carolina, Chapel Hill.
Neuman, Robert W.
    1984   *An Introduction to Louisiana Archaeology.* Louisiana
            State University Press, Baton Rouge.
Neumann, Thomas W., and Robert M. Sanford
    1986   Current Research. *American Antiquity* 51 (3): 645.
Neveret, Margo
    1992   Analyses of the Excavations of the Anderson Village
            Site on Old Woman Creek, Erie County, Ohio. Mas-
            ter's thesis, Department of Anthropology, Kent State
            University, Kent, OH.
Newsom, Lee A., and C. Margaret Scarry
    n.d.   Homegardens and Mangrove Swamps: Pineland
            Archaeobotanical Research. In *The Archaeology of
            Pineland: A Coastal Southwest Florida Site Complex,* A.D.
            50–1600, edited by K. J. Walker and W. H. Marquardt.
            Monograph 4. Institute of Archaeology and Paleo-
            environmental Studies, University of Florida,
            Gainesville. In preparation.
Noble, William C.
    1972   The Cleveland Neutral Village (AhHb-7): A Prelimi-
            nary Statement. Manuscript on file, Department
            of Anthropology, McMaster University, Hamilton,
            Ontario.
    1979   Ontario Iroquois Effigy Pipes. *Canadian Journal of
            Archaeology* 3: 69–90.
    1980   Thorold: An Early Historic Niagara Neutral Town. In
            Villages in the Niagara Peninsula, edited by John Burt-
            niak and Wesley B. Turner, pp. 43–55. Proceedings of
            the Niagara Peninsula History Conference, Brock
            University, St. Catharines, Ontario.
NPW Consultants
    1983   Excavation of Two Monongahela Sites: Late Wood-
            land Gensler (36GR63) and Historic Throckmorton
            (36GR160). Report. NPW Consultants, Inc., Union-
            town, PA. Submitted to Consolidation Coal Company,
            Pittsburgh, PA.
O'Brien, Michael J.
    1994   *Cat Monsters and Head Pots.* University of Missouri
            Press, Columbia.
    1995   Archaeological Research in the Central Mississippi
            Valley: Culture History Gone Awry. *Review of Archae-
            ology* 16 (1): 23–36.
O'Brien, Michael J., and Thomas D. Holland
    1994   Campbell. In *Cat Monsters and Head Pots,* by M. J.
            O'Brien, pp. 195–260. University of Missouri Press,
            Columbia.
O'Brien, Michael J., and J. Raymond Williams
    1994   Other Late Mississippian Period Sites. In *Cat Monsters

            and Head Pots,* by M. J. O'Brien, pp. 261–306. Univer-
            sity of Missouri Press, Columbia.
O'Callaghan, Edmund B., and Berthold Fernow (editors)
    1853–   *Documents Relative to the Colonial History of the State
    1887   of New York.* 15 vols. Weed Parsons, Albany, NY.
Oehler, C. M.
    1950   *Turpin Indians: A Report on the Findings of the Cincin-
            nati Museum of Natural History's Archaeological Explo-
            ration of the Turpin Site, Hamilton County, Ohio, 1946 to
            1949.* Popular Publication Series no. 1. Cincinnati Mu-
            seum of Natural History, Cincinnati.
    1973   Turpin Indians. *Journal of the Cincinnati Museum of
            Natural History* 23 (2).
O'Gorman, Jodie (editor)
    1995   *The Tremaine Site Complex: Oneota Occupation in the La
            Crosse Locality, Wisconsin,* vol. 3, *The Tremaine Site (47Lc-
            95).* State Historical Society of Wisconsin, Madison.
Ontario Corn Committee
    1992   *Ontario Hybrid Corn Performance Trials.* Ontario Min-
            istry of Agriculture and Food, Alliston.
Orr, Ellison
    1922   The New Albin Inscribed Tablet. *Proceedings of the
            Iowa Academy of Science* 29: 49–52.
Orr, Kenneth G.
    1949   *The Historic Upper Mississippi Phase in Northern Illinois:
            LaSalle County, Illinois.* Proceedings of the Fifth Plains
            Conference for Archaeology, pp. 100–105. Notebook
            1. Laboratory for Anthropology, University of Ne-
            braska, Lincoln.
Overstreet, David F.
    1978   Oneota Settlement Patterns in Eastern Wisconsin:
            Some Considerations of Time and Space. In *Mississip-
            pian Settlement Patterns,* edited by Bruce D. Smith,
            pp. 21–52. Academic Press, New York.
    1992   *Archaeology at Lac des Puans: The Lake Winnebago Phase,
            a Classic Horizon Expression of the Oneota Tradition in
            East-Central Wisconsin.* Reports of Investigations no.
            280. Great Lakes Archaeological Research Center,
            Milwaukee, WI.
    1993   McCauley, Astor, and Hanson: Candidates for the
            Provisional Dandy Phase. *Wisconsin Archeologist* 74:
            120–196.
    1995   The Eastern Wisconsin Oneota Regional Continuity.
            In *Oneota Archaeology: Past, Present, and Future,* edited
            by William Green, pp. 33–64. Office of the Iowa State
            Archaeologist, Ames, IA.
Parker, Arthur C.
    1907   *Excavations in an Erie Indian Village and Burial Site at
            Ripley, Chautauqua Co., New York.* Bulletin 117. New
            York State Museum, Albany.
Parker, Scott K.
    1989   Lithic Exchange in Prehistoric Virginia. Master's
            thesis, Department of Anthropology, University of
            Virginia, Charlottesville.
Parks, Arva Moore
    1985   *Where the River Found the Bay: Historical Study of the
            Granada Site. Archaeology and History of the Granada
            Site,* vol. 2. John W. Griffin, general editor. Florida
            Division of Archives, History, and Records Manage-
            ment, Tallahassee, FL.

Parry, M. L.
1981 Climatic Change and the Agricultural Frontier: A Research Strategy. In *Climate and History,* edited by T. M. L. Wigley, M. J. Ingram, and G. Farmer, pp. 319–336. Cambridge University Press, Cambridge.

Patterson, David K.
1984 *A Diachronic Study of Dental Paleopathology and Attritional Status of Prehistoric Ontario Pre-Iroquois and Iroquois Populations.* Mercury Series, Archaeological Survey of Canada, Paper 122. National Museum of Man, Ottawa.

Pauketat, Timothy R., and Thomas E. Emerson
1991 The Ideology of Authority and the Power of the Pot. *American Anthropologist* 93: 919–941.

Pease, Theodore C., and Raymond C. Werner (editors)
1934 De Gannes Memoir. In *The French Foundations, 1680–1693,* pp. 302–395. Illinois State Historical Library, Springfield.

Peckham, Howard H.
1947 *Pontiac and the Indian Uprising.* Princeton University Press, Princeton, NJ.

Peebles, Christopher S.
1986 Paradise Lost, Strayed, and Stolen: Prehistoric Social Devolution in the Southeast. In *The Burden of Being Civilized: An Anthropological Perspective on the Discontents of Civilization,* edited by Miles B. Richardson and Malcolm C. Webb, pp. 24–40. Southern Anthropological Society Proceedings. University of Georgia Press, Athens.
1987 The Rise and Fall of the Mississippian in Western Alabama: The Moundville and Summerville Phases, A.D. 1000 to 1600. *Mississippi Archaeology* 22 (1): 1–31.

Pendergast, James F.
1989 The Significance of Some Marine Shell Excavated on Iroquoian Archaeological Sites in Ontario. In *Proceedings of the 1986 Shell Bead Conference: Selected Papers,* edited by Charles F. Hayes III, pp. 97–112. Research Records 20. Rochester Museum and Science Center, Rochester, New York.
1991 *The Massawomeck: Raiders and Traders into the Chesapeake Bay in the Seventeenth Century.* Transactions of the American Philosophical Society 81, Part 2. Philadelphia.

Penman, John T.
1983 Archaeology and Choctaw Removal. In *Southeastern Natives and Their Pasts,* edited by D. G. Wyckoff and J. C. Hofman, pp. 283–299. Studies in Oklahoma's Past no. 11, Oklahoma Archaeological Survey, Norman, and Contribution no. 2, Cross Timbers Heritage Association, Norman, OK.
1988 Neo-Boreal Climatic Influences on the Late Prehistoric Agricultural Groups in the Upper Mississippi Valley. *Geoarchaeology* 3: 139–145.

Perry, Lynn
1948 Interpretation of Rainfall Records at Miami. *Quarterly Journal of the Florida Academy of Sciences* 10: 147–149.

Pertulla, Timothy K.
1998 Powers Fort: A Middle Mississippian-Period Fortified Community in the Western Lowlands of Missouri. In *Changing Perspectives on the Archaeology of the Central Mississippi River Valley,* edited by M. J. O'Brien and R. C. Dunnell, pp. 169–199. University of Alabama Press, Tuscaloosa.

Peterson, Randolph L.
1966 *The Mammals of Eastern Canada.* Oxford University Press, Toronto.

Petherick, Gary L.
1987 Architecture and Features at the Fredricks, Wall, and Mitchum Sites. In *The Siouan Project: Seasons I and II,* edited by Roy S. Dickens Jr., H. Trawick Ward, and R. P. Stephen Davis Jr., pp. 29–80. Monograph Series 1. Research Laboratories of Anthropology, University of North Carolina, Chapel Hill.

Pfeiffer, Susan, and Patricia King
1983 Cortical Bone Formation and Diet among Protohistoric Iroquoians. *American Journal of Physical Anthropology* 60: 23–28.

Pfister, Christian
1981 An Analysis of the Little Ice Age Climate in Switzerland and Its Consequences for Agricultural Production. In *Climate and History,* edited by T. M. L. Wigley, M. J. Ingram, and G. Farmer, pp. 214–248. Cambridge University Press, Cambridge.

Phillips, Philip
1970 *Archaeological Survey in the Lower Yazoo Basin, Mississippi, 1947–1955.* Papers of the Peabody Museum of American Archaeology and Ethnology 60, Parts 1 and 2. Harvard University, Cambridge, MA.

Phillips, Philip, James A. Ford, and James B. Griffin
1951 *Archaeological Survey in the Lower Mississippi Alluvial Valley, 1940–1947.* Papers of the Peabody Museum of American Archaeology and Ethnology, vol. 25. Harvard University, Cambridge.

Pollack, D., and A. G. Henderson
1984 A Mid-Eighteenth-Century Historic Indian Occupation in Greenup County, Kentucky. In *Late Prehistoric Research in Kentucky,* edited by D. Pollack, C. D. Hockensmith, and T. N. Sanders, pp. 1–24. Kentucky Heritage Council, Frankfort.

Pollack, D., M. L. Powell, and A. Adkins
1987 Preliminary Study of Mortuary Patterns at the Larkin Site, Bourbon County, Kentucky. In *Current Archaeological Research in Kentucky,* vol. 1, edited by D. Pollack, pp. 188–203. Kentucky Heritage Council, Frankfort.

Porter, Stephen C.
1981 Recent Glacier Variations and Volcanic Eruptions. *Nature* 291: 139–142.

Potter, Stephen
1989 Early English Effects on Virginia Algonquian Exchange and Tribute in the Tidewater Potomac. In *Powhatan's Mantle,* edited by P. Wood, G. Waselkov, and T. Hatley, pp. 151–172. University of Nebraska Press, Lincoln.
1993 *Commoners, Tribute, and Chiefs: The Development of Algonquian Culture in the Potomac Valley.* University Press of Virginia, Charlottesville.

Potter, William L.
1988 The Forts of Palos: Historiography and Comment on Fortified Sites near Chicago. *Rediscovery* 3: 1–14.

Powell, Mary L.

1989   The Nodena People. In *Nodena,* edited by Dan F. Morse, pp. 65–95. Research Series no. 30. Arkansas Archeological Survey, Fayetteville.

1990   Health and Disease at Nodena: A Late Mississippian Community in Northeastern Arkansas. In *Towns and Temples on the Mississippi River,* edited by D. H. Dye and C. A. Cox, pp. 98–117. University of Alabama Press, Tuscaloosa.

1992   In the Best of Health? In *Lords of the Southeast: Social Inequality and the Native Elites of the Southeastern United States,* edited by A. W. Barker and T. R. Pauketat, pp. 881–897. Archeological Papers of the American Anthropological Association no. 3. Washington, DC.

Prahl, Earl J., David S. Brose, and David M. Stothers

1976   A Preliminary Synthesis of Late Prehistoric Phenomena in the Western Basin of Lake Erie. In *The Late Prehistory of the Lake Erie Drainage Basin: A 1972 Symposium Revised,* edited by D. S. Brose, pp. 251–282. Scientific Papers of the Cleveland Museum of Natural History, Cleveland.

Pratt, G. Michael

1981   The Western Basin Tradition. Ph.D. dissertation, Department of Anthropology, Case Western Reserve University, Cleveland, OH.

Pratt, G. Michael, and D. S. Brose

1992   Cultural and Climatic Change along Lake Erie's South Shore. Paper presented at the annual meeting of the Society for American Archaeology, Pittsburgh.

Pratt, G. Michael, Pat Croninger, and Jan del Castillo

1983   Archaeology of the Harbor Site Area, Sandusky Co., Ohio. CRM Report, Heidleberg College, Tiffin, OH. Submitted to the Ohio Historic Preservation Office.

Pratt, Peter P.

1976   *Archaeology of the Oneida.* Occasional Publications in Northeast Archaeology no. 1. Man in the Northeast, George's Mills, New Hampshire.

n.d.   Onondaga Iroquois Acculturation at the Time of Frontenac's Invasion of 1696. Manuscript on file, Robert S. Peabody Museum, Andover, MA.

Prezzano, Susan C.

1988   Spatial Analysis of Post Mold Patterns at the Sackett Site, Ontario County, New York. *Man in the Northeast* 35: 27–45.

Price, James E.

1976   Prehistory of the Fourche Creek Watershed. In *An Assessment of the Cultural Resources of the Fourche Creek Watershed,* by James E. Price, Cynthia R. Price, and Suzanne E. Harris, pp. 35–51. Report, contract USDA-AG-29SCS-00527. American Archaeology Division, University of Missouri, Columbia. Submitted to USDA Soil Conservation Service, Springfield, MO.

Price, James E., and James B. Griffin

1979   *The Snodgrass Site of the Powers Phase of Southeast Missouri.* Anthropological Papers no. 66. University of Michigan, Ann Arbor.

Price, James E. and Cynthia R. Price

1990   Protohistoric/Early Historic Manifestations in Southeastern Missouri. In *Towns and Temples along the Mississippi,* edited by D. H. Dye and C. A. Cox, pp. 59–68. University of Alabama Press, Tuscaloosa.

Price, James E., Cynthia R. Price, and Suzanne E. Harris

1976   An Assessment of the Cultural Resources of the Fourche Creek Watershed. Report. American Archaeology Division, University of Missouri, Columbia. Submitted to the US Soil Conservation Service.

Prufer, Olaf H.

1967   Chesser Cave: A Late Woodland Phase in Southeastern Ohio. In *Studies in Ohio Archaeology,* edited by Olaf H. Prufer and Douglas H. McKenzie, pp. 1–62. The Press of Western Reserve University, Cleveland, OH.

Prufer, Olaf H., and E. Andors

1967   The Morrison Village Site (33Ro-3): A Terminal Prehistoric Site in Ross County, Ohio. In *Studies in Ohio Archaeology,* edited by Olaf H. Prufer and Douglas H. McKenzie, pp. 187–229. The Press of Western Reserve University, Cleveland.

Prufer, Olaf H., and D. H. McKenzie

1966   Peters Cave: Two Woodland Occupations in Ross County, Ohio. *Ohio Journal of Science* 66 (3): 233–253.

Prufer, Olaf H., Donald Metzger, and Dana Long

1989   *Krill Cave: A Stratified Rockshelter in Summit County, Ohio.* Research Papers in Archaeology no. 8. Kent State University.

Prufer, Olaf, and Orin C. Shane III

1970   *Blain Village and the Fort Ancient Tradition in Ohio.* Kent State University Press, Kent, OH.

1976   The Portage-Sandusky-Vermilion Region. In *The Late Prehistory of the Lake Erie Drainage Basin: A 1972 Symposium Revised,* edited by D. Brose, pp. 283–304. Scientific Papers of the Cleveland Museum of Natural History, Cleveland, OH.

Purdue, James R., and Bonnie W. Styles

1986   Dynamics of Mammalian Distribution in the Holocene of Illinois. *Illinois State Museum Reports of Investigations* 41: 1–63.

1987   Changes in the Mammalian Fauna of Illinois and Missouri during the Late Pleistocene and Holocene. In *Late Quaternary Mammalian Biogeography and Environments of the Great Plains and Prairies,* edited by R. W. Graham, H. A. Semken Jr., and M. A. Graham, pp. 144–174. Illinois State Museum Scientific Papers, vol. 22, Springfield.

Putnam, F. W.

1886   Report of the Curator. *Peabody Museum Annual Report* 18: 401–419, 477–502.

1973a   Archaeological Explorations at Madisonville and Other Sites in the Little Miami River Valley, Ohio. Sixteenth Annual Report, 1883. In *The Archeological Reports of Frederic Ward Putnam, Selected from the Annual Reports of the Peabody Museum of Archaeology and Ethnology, Harvard University, 1875–1903,* edited by P. Phillips, pp. 197–208. AMS Press, New York.

1973b   Archaeological Explorations at Madisonville, Ohio. Fifteenth Annual Report, 1882. In *The Archeological Reports of Frederic Ward Putnam, Selected from the Annual Reports of the Peabody Museum of Archaeology and Ethnology, Harvard University, 1875–1903,* edited by P. Phillips, pp. 185–190. AMS Press, New York.

Quimby, George Irving

1960   *Indians of the Upper Great Lakes.* University of Chicago Press, Chicago.

1966   *Indian Culture and European Trade Goods.* University of Wisconsin Press, Madison.

Quinn, David
1984   *Set Fair for Roanoke: Voyages and Colonies, 1584–1606.* University of North Carolina Press, Chapel Hill.

Quitmyer, Irvy R., and Melissa A. Massaro
1999   Seasonality and Subsistence in a Southwest Florida Estuary: A Faunal Analysis of Precolumbian Useppa Island. In *The Archaeology of Useppa Island,* edited by W. H. Marquardt. Monograph 3. Institute of Archaeology and Paleoenvironmental Studies, University of Florida, Gainesville.

Radin, Paul
1923   The Winnebago Tribe. *Annual Report of the Bureau of American Ethnology* 37: 35–560. Smithsonian Institution, Washington, DC.

Radisson, Pierre Esprit
1961   *The Explorations of Pierre Esprit Radisson: From the Original Manuscript in the Bodleian Library and the British Museum,* edited by Arthur T. Adams. Haines and Ross, Minneapolis.

Railey, J. A.
1992   Chipped Stone Artifacts. In *Fort Ancient Cultural Dynamics in the Middle Ohio Valley,* edited by A. G. Henderson, pp. 137–169. Monographs in World Archaeology no. 8. Prehistory Press, Madison, WI.

Ramenofsky, Ann F.
1987   *Vectors of Death: The Archaeology of European Contact.* University of New Mexico Press, Albuquerque.

Ramsden, Peter G.
1978   An Hypothesis concerning the Effects of Early European Trade among Some Ontario Iroquois. *Canadian Journal of Archaeology* 2: 101–106.
1989   Palisade Extension, Village Expansion and Immigration in Trent Valley Huron Prehistory. *Canadian Journal of Archaeology* 12: 177–183.
1990   The Hurons: Archaeology and Culture History. In *The Archaeology of Southern Ontario to A.D. 1650,* edited by Chris J. Ellis and Neal Ferris, pp. 361–384. Occasional Publication of the London Chapter no. 5. Ontario Archaeological Society, London, Ontario, Canada.

Ranjel, Rodrigo
1922   A Narrative of de Soto's Expedition Based on the Dairy of Rodrigo Ranjel. In *Narratives of the Career of Hernando de Soto,* edited by Edward G. Bourne, pp. 43–150. Allerton, New York.

Rapp, George, Eiler Henrickson, and James Allert
1990   Native Copper Sources of Artifact Copper in Pre-Columbian North America. In *Archaeological Geology of North America,* edited by Norman P. Lasca and Jack Donahue, pp. 479–498. Centennial Special Volume 4. Geological Society of America, Boulder, CO.

Redmond, Brian
1984   The Doctor's Site (33LU11): Younge Phase Cultural Dynamics in the Western Lake Erie Drainage Basin. Master's thesis, Department of Anthropology, University of Toledo.
1994   *The Archaeology of the Clampitt Site (12 Lr 329), an Oliver Phase Village in Lawrence County, Indiana.* Research Report no. 16. Glenn A. Black Laboratory of Archaeology, Indiana University, Bloomington.

1999   White Fort and the Middle Sandusky Tradition Occupation of the Black River Valley in Northern Ohio. *Archaeology of Eastern North America* 27: 109–156.
2000   Reviewing the Late Prehistory of Ohio. In *Cultures before Contact: The Late Prehistory of Ohio and Surrounding Regions,* edited by R. A. Genheimer, pp. 426–435. Ohio Archaeological Council, Columbus.

Richter, Daniel K.
1983   War and Culture: The Iroquois Experience. *William and Mary Quarterly* 40: 528–559.
1992   *The Ordeal of the Longhouse: The Peoples of the Iroquois League in the Era of European Colonization.* University of North Carolina Press, Chapel Hill.

Riggs, R. E.
1977   The Turpin Site Fort Ancient Burial Mound and Surrounding Burial Pattern (33 Ha 19): A Biological Comparison Using Non-Metric Traits of the Cranial and Post-Cranial Skeleton. Master's thesis, Department of Anthropology, University of Cincinnati, Cincinnati, OH.
1986   New Stratigraphic Sequences from the Lower Little Miami Valley. *West Virginia Archaeologist* 38 (2): 1–21.

Riley, Franklin L.
1915   *School History of Mississippi.* Revised edition. B. F. Johnson, Richmond, VA.

Riley, Thomas J.
1994   Ocmulgee and the Question of Mississippian Agronomic Practices. In *Ocmulgee Archaeology, 1936–1986,* edited by David J. Hally, pp. 96–104. University of Georgia Press, Athens.

Riley, Thomas J., and Glen Freimuth
1979   Field Systems and Frost Drainage in the Prehistoric Agriculture of the Upper Great Lakes. *American Antiquity* 44: 271–285.

Ritchie, William A.
1969   *The Archaeology of New York State.* Revised ed. Natural History Press, Garden City, NJ.

Ritchie, William A., and R. E. Funk
1973   *Aboriginal Settlement Patters in the Northeast.* New York State Museum and Science Service Memoir 20. New York State Museum and Science Service, Albany.

Ritchie, William A., and R. S. MacNeish
1949   The Pre-Iroquoian Pottery of New York State. *American Antiquity* 15: 97–124.

Roberts, William L.
1990   Frost Patterns and Their Implications for Aboriginal Settlement in Potter County, PA. Paper presented at the annual meeting of the Society for Pennsylvania Archaeology, Wilkes-Barre.

Robson, John
1958   A Comparison of Artifacts from the Indian Villages Quemahoning and Squirrel Hill. *Pennsylvania Archaeologist* 28 (3–4): 112–126.

Rodell, Roland L.
1989   The Pammel Creek Site Lithic Artifacts. *Wisconsin Archeologist* 70: 95–110.

Romain, William F.
1979   Archaeological Evaluation of Magico-Ritual Evidence through Analysis of Biocultural Variables: An Investigation of Mutilated Skeletal Elements from Libben.

Master's thesis, Department of Anthropology, Kent State University.

Roper, Donna C.

1991   John Dunbar's Journal of the 1834–35 Chawi Winter Hunt and Its Implications for Pawnee Archaeology. *Plains Anthropologist* 36: 193–214.

1992   Documentary Evidence for Changes in Protohistoric and Early Historic Pawnee Hunting Practices. *Plains Anthropologist* 37: 353–366.

Rossen, J.

1988   Botanical Remains. In *Muir: An Early Fort Ancient Site in the Inner Bluegrass,* edited by C. A. Turnbow and W. E. Sharp, pp. 243–264. Archaeological Report no. 165. Program for Cultural Resource Assessment, University of Kentucky, Lexington.

1992   Botanical Remains. In *Fort Ancient Cultural Dynamics in the Middle Ohio Valley,* edited by A. G. Henderson, pp. 189–208. Monographs in World Archaeology no. 8. Prehistory Press, Madison, WI.

Rossen, J., and R. B. Edging

1987   East Meets West: Patterns in Kentucky Late Prehistoric Subsistence. In *Current Archaeological Research in Kentucky,* vol. 1, edited by D. Pollack, pp. 225–234. Kentucky Heritage Council, Frankfort.

Rostlund, Erhard

1960   The Geographic Range of the Historic Bison in the Southeast. *Annals of the Association of American Geographers* 50: 395–407.

Rothschild, Nan A.

1979   Mortuary Behavior and Social Organization at Indian Knoll and Dickson Mounds. *American Antiquity* 44: 658–67.

Rountree, Helen

1989   *The Powhatan Indians of Virginia: Their Traditional Culture.* University of Oklahoma Press, Norman.

1991   *Pocahontas's People: The Powhatan Indians through Four Centuries.* University of Oklahoma Press, Norman.

Rountree, Helen (editor)

1993   *Powhatan Foreign Relations.* University Press of Virginia, Charlottesville.

Rumrill, Donald A.

1991   The Mohawk Glass Trade Bead Chronology: Ca. 1560–1785. *Beads (Journal of the Society of Bead Researchers)* 3: 5–45.

Rusch, Lynn A.

1985   The Springview Site: A Possible Late-Seventeenth-Century Mascouten Village. *Wisconsin Archeologist* 66: 157–175.

Russo, Michael

1991   Final Report on Horr's Island: The Archaeology of Archaic and Glades Settlement and Subsistence Patterns (with chapters by Ann Cordell, Lee Newsom, and Sylvia Scudder). Report. Florida Museum of Natural History, Gainesville, Florida. Submitted to Key Marco Developments. Copy on file, Florida Museum of Natural History, Gainesville.

1994   Why We Don't Believe in Archaic Ceremonial Mounds and Why We Should: The Case from Florida. *Southeastern Archaeology* 13: 93–109.

Rutter, William E.

1984   The Upper Mississippian Component at the Fort

Meigs Site, Northwest Ohio, with Special Emphasis on the Ceramic Assemblage. Master's thesis, Department of Anthropology, Western Michigan University, Kalamazoo.

Sagard, Gabriel

1635   *Le grand voyage du pays des Hurons situe en l'Amerique vers la mer douce . . . [The long voyage to the country of the Hurons . . .].* Translated by E. H. Langton and edited by G. M. Wrong. Publication no. 25. The Champlain Society [1939], Toronto.

Sampson, Kelvin W., and Duane Esarey

1993   A Survey of Elaborate Mississippian Copper Artifacts from Illinois. *Illinois Archaeology* 5: 452–480.

Sanford, Louis

1914   A Disk Pipe. *Wisconsin Archeologist,* o.s. 12 (1): 30–36.

Santure, Sharron, Alan Harn, and Duane Essary (editors)

1990   *Archaeological Investigations at the Morton Village and Norris Farms 36 Cemetery.* Reports of Investigations no. 45. Illinois State Museum, Springfield.

Sasso, Robert F.

1984   *Archaeological Data Recovery at the Overhead Site, 47Lc20, La Crosse County, Wisconsin.* Reports of Investigations no. 18. Mississippi Valley Archaeology Center, University of Wisconsin–La Crosse.

1987   The White Camp and Mounds Revisited. Paper presented at the Midwest Archaeological Conference, Milwaukee, WI.

1989   Oneota Settlement Practices in the LaCrosse Region: An Analysis of the Coon Creek Drainage in the Driftless Area of Western Wisconsin. Ph.D. dissertation, Northwestern University, Evanston, IL.

1992   Garden Beds and Corn Hills: Archaeological Manifestations of Aboriginal Midwestern Cultivation. Paper presented at the Midwest Archaeological Conference, Grand Rapids, MI.

1993   La Crosse Region Oneota Adaptations: Changing Late Prehistoric Subsistence and Settlement Patterns in the Upper Mississippi Valley. *Wisconsin Archeologist* 74: 316–361.

Sasso, Robert F., Robert F. Boszhardt, James C. Knox, James L. Theler, Katherine P. Stevenson, James P. Gallagher, and Cynthia Stiles-Hanson

1985   *Prehistoric Ridge Field Agriculture in the Upper Mississippi Valley.* Reports of Investigations no. 38. Mississippi Valley Archaeology Center, University of Wisconsin–LaCrosse.

Sasso, Robert F., and James A. Brown

1987   Land, Fields, and Maize: A Perspective on Oneota Agriculture. Paper presented at the annual meeting of the American Anthropological Association, Chicago, IL.

Sauer, Carl O.

1966   *The Early Spanish Main.* University of California Press, Berkeley.

1971   *Sixteenth-Century North America.* University of California Press, Berkeley.

Saunders, Shelley R.

1989   The MacPherson Site Burials. Manuscript on file, Department of Anthropology, McMaster University, Hamilton, Ontario.

Scarry, C. Margaret

1999   Precolumbian Use of Plants on Useppa Island. In *The*

Archaeology of Useppa Island, edited by W. H. Marquardt, pp. 129–137. Monograph 3. Institute of Archaeology and Paleoenvironmental Studies, University of Florida, Gainesville.

Scarry, C. Margaret, and Lee A. Newsom
1992   Archaeobotanical Research in the Calusa Heartland. In *Culture and Environment in the Domain of the Calusa,* edited by W. H. Marquardt, pp. 375–401. Monograph 1. Institute of Archaeology and Paleoenvironmental Studies, University of Florida, Gainesville.

Scarry, John
1973   The Eiden Site: A Late Woodland Site in the Black River Valley. *Toledo Area Aboriginal Research Club Bulletin* 2 (3): 42–57.

Schmitt, Karl
1952   Archaeological Chronology of the Middle Atlantic States. In *Archaeology of the Eastern United States,* edited by J. B. Griffin, pp. 59–70. University of Chicago Press, Chicago.

Schnell, Gail Schroeder
1974   *Hotel Plaza, An Early Historic Site with a Long Prehistory.* Reports of Investigations no. 29. Illinois State Museum, Springfield.

Schock, Jack
1976   Southwestern New York: The Chautauqua Phase and Other Late Woodland Occupation. In *The Late Prehistory of the Lake Erie Drainage Basin,* edited by David S. Brose, pp. 89–109. Cleveland Museum of Natural History Scientific Papers, Cleveland, OH.

Schoolcraft, Henry R.
1851–   *Historical and Statistical Information Respecting*
1887   *the History, Conditions, and Prospects of the Indian Tribes of the United States.* 6 vols. Lippincott, Grambo, Philadelphia.

Schurr, M. R., and M. J. Schoeninger
1995   Associations between Agricultural Intensification and Social Complexity: An Example from the Prehistoric Ohio Valley. *Journal of Anthropological Archaeology* 14: 315–339.

Schwarcz, H. P., F. J. Melbye, M. A. Katzenberg, and M. Knyf
1985   Stable Isotopes in Human Skeletons of Southern Ontario: Reconstructing Paleodiet. *Journal of Archaeological Science* 12: 187–206.

Sciulli, Paul W.
1995   Biological Indicators of Diet in Monongahela Populations. *Pennsylvania Archaeologist* 65 (2): 1–18.

Sciulli, Paul W., and Ronald C. Carlisle
1977   Analysis of the Dentition from Three Western Pennsylvania Late Woodland Sites, II: Wear and Pathology. *Pennsylvania Archaeologist* 47 (4): 53–59.

Sears, William H.
1982   *Fort Center: An Archaeological Site in the Lake Okeechobee Basin.* University Press of Florida, Gainesville.

Seckinger, Ernest W.
1977   Social Complexity during the Mississippian Period in Northwest Georgia. Master's thesis, University of Georgia.

Seminole Tribe of Florida
1998   *The Seminole Tribe of Florida: History.* Internet URL: http://www.seminoletribe.com/history/. September 20, 1998.

Sempowski, Martha J.
1989   Fluctuations through Time in the Use of Marine Shell at Seneca Iroquois Sites. In *Proceedings of the 1986 Shell Bead Conference: Selected Papers,* edited by Charles F. Hayes III, pp. 81–96. Research Records 20. Rochester Museum and Science Center, Rochester, New York.
1992   Preliminary Observations on Early Historic Period Exchange between the Seneca and the Susquehannock. Paper presented at the annual meeting of the Canadian Archaeological Association, London, Ontario.
1994   Early Historic Exchange between the Seneca and the Susquehannock. In *The Proceedings of the People to People Conference,* edited by C. F. Hayes III, C. C. Bodner, and L. P. Saunders, pp. 51–64. Research Records no. 23. Rochester Museum and Science Center, Rochester, NY.

Shane, Orin C. III
1967   The Mixter Site. In *Studies in Ohio Archaeology,* edited by O. Prufer and D. McKenzie, pp. 121–186. Western Reserve University Press, Cleveland, OH.
1974   Archaeological Survey along the Route of Ohio State Route 2, Lorain, Erie, Huron and Ottawa Counties, Ohio. Project Report. Kent State University. Submitted to the Bureau of Environmental Services, Ohio Department of Transportation, Kent, Ohio.

Sharp, W. E.
1990   Fort Ancient Period. In *The Archaeology of Kentucky: Past Accomplishments and Future Directions,* edited by D. Pollack, pp. 467–557. Kentucky Heritage Council, Frankfort.

Shay, C. Thomas
1978   Late Prehistoric Bison and Deer Use in the Eastern Prairie-Forest Border. In *Bison Procurement and Utilization: A Symposium,* edited by Leslie B. Davis and Michael Wilson, pp. 194–212. Plains Anthropologist Memoir 14.

Shea, John G. (editor)
1903   *Discovery and Exploration of the Mississippi Valley.* Joseph McDonough, Albany, NY.

Shelford, Victor E.
1963   *The Ecology of North America.* University of Illinois Press, Urbana.

Shetrone, H. C.
1926   The Campbell Island Village Site and the Hine Mound and Village Site. In *Certain Mounds and Village Sites in Ohio,* vol. 4, edited by W. C. Mills. F. J. Heer, Columbus.

Shott, Michael J.
1992   Radiocarbon Dating as a Probabilistic Technique: The Childers Site and Late Woodland Occupation in the Ohio Valley. *American Antiquity* 57: 202–230.

Simmons, William S.
1986   *Spirit of the New England Tribes.* University of New England Press, Hanover.

Sioui, Georges
1992   Les Nadoueks: Leur histoire des anneés 1000 a 1650 de notre ère. Paper presented at the "Transferts Culturels en Amérique et Ailleurs" conference, Québec.

Skinner, Alanson B.
1926   Ethnology of the Ioway Indians. *Bulletin of the Public Museum of the City of Milwaukee* 5: 181–354.

Smith, Bruce D.
1978   Variation in Mississippian Settlement Patterns. In *Mississippian Settlement Patterns,* edited by Bruce D. Smith, pp. 479–503. Academic Press, New York.
1984   Mississippian Expansion: Tracing the Historical Development of an Explanatory Model. *Southeastern Archaeology* 3 (1): 13–32.
1986   The Archaeology of the Southeastern United States: From Dalton to de Soto, 10,500–500 B.P. *Advances in World Archaeology* 5: 1–92.
1990   *The Mississippian Emergence.* Smithsonian Institution Press, Washington, DC.

Smith, Buckingham
1968   *Narratives of de Soto in the Conquest of Florida.* Palmetto Books, Gainesville, FL.

Smith, Gerald P.
1972   Explanatory Note. In *Chucalissa: Burials and Excavations through 1963,* by C. H. Nash, pp. ii–vi. Occasional Papers no. 6. Anthropological Research Center, Memphis State University, Memphis, TN.
1990   The Walls Phase and Its Neighbors. In *Towns and Temples along the Mississippi,* edited by D. H. Dye and C. A. Cox, pp. 135–169. University of Alabama Press, Tuscaloosa.

Smith, Gerald P., and Charles H. McNutt
1991   Recent and Reevaluated Dates from Chucalissa. Paper presented at the annual meeting of the Southeastern Archaeological Conference, Jackson, MS.

Smith, Hale G.
1951   *The Crable Site, Fulton County, Illinois: A Late Prehistoric Site in the Central Illinois Valley.* Anthropological Papers no. 7. Museum of Anthropology, University of Michigan, Ann Arbor.

Smith, H. I.
1910   *The Prehistoric Ethnology of a Kentucky Site.* Anthropological Papers of the American Museum of Natural History, vol. 6, part 2. New York.

Smith, Ira F. III
1984   *A Late Woodland Village Site in North-Central Pennsylvania: Its Role in Susquehannock Culture History.* Pennsylvania Historical and Museum Commission, William Penn Memorial Museum, Harrisburg.

Smith, Marvin T.
1977   The Early Historic Period (1540–1670) on the Upper Coosa River Drainage of Alabama and Georgia. *The Conference on Historic Site Archaeology Papers* 1976, 11: 151–67.
1987   *Archaeology of Aboriginal Culture Change in the Interior Southeast: Depopulation during the Early Historic Period.* Ripley P. Bullen Monographs in Anthropology and History no. 6. University Press of Florida and Florida State Museum, Gainesville.
1988   The Effect of European Contact on the Indians of the Southeast. Paper presented at the annual meeting of the West Virginia Archaeological Society, Parkersburg, WV.
1989a   Aboriginal Population Movements in the Early Historic Period Interior Southeast. In *Powhatan's Mantle: Indians in the Colonial Southeast,* edited by Peter H. Wood, Gregory A. Waselkov, and M. Thomas Hatley, pp. 21–34. University of Nebraska Press, Lincoln.
1989b   In the Wake of de Soto: Alabama's Seventeenth-Century Indians on the Coosa River. Report. Submitted to the Alabama de Soto Commission.
1994   Aboriginal Depopulation in the Postcontact Southeast. In *The Forgotten Centuries: Indians and Europeans in the American South, 1521–1704,* edited by Charles M. Hudson Jr. and Carmen Chaves Tesser, pp. 257–275. University of Georgia Press, Athens.
1995   Woods Island Revisited. *Journal of Alabama Archaeology* 41: 93–106.
2000   *Coosa: The Rise and Fall of a Southeastern Mississippian Chiefdom.* University Press of Florida, Gainesville.

Smith, Marvin T., Vernon J. Knight, Julie B. Smith, and Kenneth Turner
1993   The Milner Village (1Et1): A Mid-Seventeenth-Century Site near Gadsden, Alabama. In *Archaeological Survey and Excavations in the Coosa River Valley, Alabama,* edited by Vernon J. Knight Jr., pp. 49–61. Bulletin 15. Alabama Museum of Natural History, Tuscaloosa.

Smith, Marvin T., and Stephen A. Kowalewski
1980   Tentative Identification of a Prehistoric Province in Piedmont Georgia. *Early Georgia* 8: 1–13.

Smith, Marvin T., and Julie Barnes Smith
1989   Engraved Shell Masks in North America. *Southeastern Archaeology* 8 (1): 9–18.

Smith, Thomas
1977   *The Mapping of Ohio.* Kent State University Press, Kent, OH.

Snider, D.
1991   Eagle Creek Site, Brown County, Ohio: A Preliminary Assessment and Observation. *Ohio Archaeologist* 41 (1): 16–21.

Snow, Dean R.
1984   Iroquois Prehistory. In *Extending the Rafters: Interdisciplinary Approaches to Iroquoian Studies,* edited by M. K. Foster, J. Campisi, and M. Mithun. State University of New York Press, Albany.
1986   Historic Mohawk Settlement Patterns. Paper presented at a meeting of the Canadian Archaeological Association, Toronto.
1994a   *The Iroquois.* The Peoples of America. Blackwell, Cambridge, MA.
1994b   Iroquoians and Europeans: Disunited Nations in the Early Contact Period. In *Proceedings of the 1992 People to People Conference,* edited by Charles F. Hayes III, Connie C. Bodner, and Lorraine P. Saunders, pp. 1–5. Research Records no. 23. Rochester Museum and Science Center, Rochester, NY.
1995a   *Mohawk Valley Archaeology: The Sites.* Occasional Papers in Anthropology 23. Matson Museum of Anthropology, University Park, NY.
1995b   Migration in Prehistory: The Northern Iroquoian Case. *American Antiquity* 60 (1): 59–79.
1995c   Microchronology and Demographic Evidence Relating to the Size of Pre-Columbian North American Indian Populations. *Science* 268: 1601–1604.
1995d   *Mohawk Valley Archaeology: The Collections.* Occasional

Papers in Anthropology 22. Matson Museum of Anthropology, University Park, NY.

1996   More on Migration in Prehistory: Accommodating New Evidence in the Northern Iroquoian Case. *American Antiquity* 61: 791–796.

Snow, Dean R., and Kim M. Lanphear

1988   European Contact and Indian Depopulation in the Northeast: The Timing of the First Epidemics. *Ethnohistory* 35: 15–33.

1989   More Methodological Perspectives: A Rejoinder to Dobyns. *Ethnohistory* 36: 299–304.

Snow, Dean R., and William A. Starna

1989   Sixteenth-Century Depopulation: A View from the Mohawk Valley. *American Anthropologist* 91: 142–149.

Sohrweide, Anton G.

n.d.a   Report on the Indian Hill Site. Manuscript on file, Robert S. Peabody Museum, Andover, MA.

n.d.b   Report on the Weston Site. Manuscript on file, Robert S. Peabody Museum, Andover, MA.

Solís de Merás, Gonzalo

1964   *Pedro Menéndez de Avilés, Adelantado, Governor, and Captain-General of Florida: Memorial.* Facsimile reproduction of 1570 edition. University Press of Florida, Gainesville.

Spector, Janet D.

1975   Crabapple Point (Je 93): An Historic Winnebago Indian Site in Jefferson County, Wisconsin. *Wisconsin Archeologist* 56: 270–345.

Spence, Michael W.

1992   Three Burials from the Libby Site, Kent County, Ontario. Manuscript on file, Department of Anthropology, University of Western Ontario, London, Ontario.

Springer, James Warren, and Stanley R. Witkowski

1982   Siouan Historical Linguistics and Oneota Archaeology. In *Oneota Studies,* edited by Guy E. Gibbon, pp. 69–83. Publications in Anthropology no. 1. University of Minnesota, Minneapolis.

Squier, George Ephram, and Edwin H. Davis

1848   *Ancient Monuments of the Mississippi Valley.* Smithsonian Contributions to Knowledge, vol. 1. Washington, DC.

Staeck, John P.

1993   Chief's Daughters, Marriage Patterns, and the Construction of Past Identities: Some Suggestions on Alternative Methods for Modeling the Past. *Wisconsin Archeologist* 74: 370–399.

Stafford, Barbara D.

1989   *Central Illinois Expressway: Floodplain Archaic Occupations of the Illinois Valley Crossing.* Technical Report 4. Center for American Archeology, Kampsville, IL.

Stahle, D. W., M. K. Cleaveland, and J. G. Hehr

1985   A 450–Year Drought Reconstruction for Arkansas, United States. *Nature* 316 (6028): 530–532.

Stapor, Frank W. Jr., Thomas D. Mathews, and Fonda E. Lindfors-Kearns

1991   Barrier Island Progradation and Holocene Sea-Level History in Southwest Florida. *Journal of Coastal Research* 7: 815–838.

Stark, Kathryn J.

1995   European Glass Trade Beads and the Chronology of

Niagara Frontier Iroquois Sites. *Northeast Anthropology* 50: 61–89.

Starna, William A.

1988   Aboriginal Title and Traditional Iroquois Land Use: An Anthropological Perspective. In *Iroquois Land Claims,* edited by C. Vecsey and W. A. Starna, pp. 31–48. Syracuse University Press, Syracuse, NY.

Starr, Mary E.

1992   Preliminary Report on Ceramic Vessels from the 1991 Oliver Salvage. *Mississippi Archaeology* 27 (2): 40–55.

Steckley, John R.

1985   Finding a Home for Two Tribes. *Michigan Archaeologist* 31 (4): 123–129.

1990   The Early Map "Novvelle France": A Linguistic Analysis. *Ontario Archaeologist* 51: 17–29.

Steponaitis, Vincas P.

1983   *Ceramics, Chronology, and Community Patterns: An Archaeological Study of Moundville.* Academic Press, New York.

1991   Contrasting Patterns of Mississippian Settlement. In *Chiefdoms: Their Evolutionary Significance,* edited by Timothy Earle, pp. 193–228. Cambridge University Press, Cambridge.

Sternheimer, Patricia A.

1983   Classification and Analysis of the Grave Goods from the Trigg Site: A Late Woodland–Contact Period Burial Site from Southwestern Virginia. Master's thesis, Department of Anthropology, University of Virginia, Charlottesville.

Stevens, J. S.

1989   Environmental Site Predictors and Prehistoric Settlement Patterns in the Central Piedmont of Virginia. Paper presented at the Middle Atlantic Archaeological Conference.

Stevenson, Katherine

1984   *The Oneota Study Unit in Region 6, Western Wisconsin.* Reports of Investigations no. 20. Mississippi Valley Archaeology Center, University of Wisconsin–La Crosse.

1994   Chronological and Settlement Aspects of the Valley View Site (47 Lc 34). *Wisconsin Archeologist* 75: 237–284.

Stevenson, Katherine, and Robert F. Boszhardt

1993   *The Current Status of Oneota Sites and Research in Western Wisconsin: The Oneota Study Unit in Region 6, 1993 Update.* Reports of Investigations no. 163. Mississippi Valley Archaeology Center, University of Wisconsin–La Crosse.

Stewart, R. M.

1989   Trade and Exchange in Middle Atlantic Prehistory. *Archaeology of Eastern North America* 17: 47–78.

Stoltman, James B.

1973   The Overhead Site (47Lc20), an Orr Phase Site near LaCrosse, Wisconsin. *Wisconsin Archeologist* 54: 2–35.

1983   Ancient Peoples of the Upper Mississippi River Valley. In *Historic Lifestyles in the Upper Mississippi River Valley,* edited by John Wozniak, pp. 197–255. University Press of America, New York.

1986   The Appearance of the Mississippian Cultural Tradition in the Upper Mississippi Valley. In *Prehistoric*

Mound Builders of the Mississippi Valley, edited by James B. Stoltman, pp. 26–34. The Putnam Museum, Davenport, IA.

1991 Cahokia as Seen from the Peripheries. In *New Perspectives on Cahokia: Views from the Periphery*, edited by James B. Stoltman, pp. 349–354. Prehistory Press, Madison, WI.

Stoltman, James B., and David A. Baerreis

1983 The Evolution of Human Ecosystems in the Eastern United States. In *Late-Quaternary Environments of the United States*, vol. 2, *The Holocene*, edited by H. E. Wright Jr., pp. 252–268. University of Minnesota Press, Minneapolis.

Stothers, David M.

1978 The Western Basin Traditon: Algonquin or Iroquois? *Michigan Archaeologist* 24 (1): 11–36.

1981 Indian Hills (33WO4): A Protohistoric Assistaeronon Village in the Maumee River Valley of Northwestern Ohio. *Ontario Archaeology* 36: 47–56.

1983 The Lost Jesuit Map Found? *Ohio Archaeologist* 33 (4): 23–27.

1991 Lost in Time: The Forgotten Tribal Groups of Northern Ohio. *Ohio Archaeologist* 41 (3): 26–27

1994 The Protohistoric Time Period in the Southwestern Lake Erie Region: European-Derived Trade Material, Population Movement and Cultural Realignment. Paper presented at "Cultures before Contact: A Conference on the Late Prehistory of the Ohio Region," Ohio Archaeological Council, Cincinnati.

1995 The "Michigan Owasco" and the Iroquois Co-Tradition: Late Woodland Conflict, Conquest, and Cultural Realignment in the Western Lower Great Lakes. *Northeast Anthropology* 49: 5–41.

2000 The Protohistoric Time Period in the Southwestern Lake Erie Region: European-Derived Trade Material, Population Movement, and Cultural Realignment. In *Cultures before Contact: The Late Prehistory of Ohio and Surrounding Regions*, edited by R. A. Genheimer, pp. 52–95. Ohio Archaeological Council, Columbus.

Stothers, David M., and Timothy J. Abel

1989 The Position of the Pearson Complex in the Late Prehistory of Northern Ohio. *Archaeology of Eastern North America* 17: 109–142.

1991 Beads, Brass, and Beaver: Archaeological Reflections of Protohistoric "Fire Nation" Trade and Exchange. *Archaeology of Eastern North America* 19: 121–134.

Stothers, David M., and Susan K. Bechtel

1987 Stable Carbon Isotope Analysis: An Inter-Regional Perspective. *Archaeology of Eastern North America* 15: 137–154.

2000 The Land between the Lakes: New Perspectives on the Late Woodland (ca. A.D. 500–1300) Time Period in the Region of the St. Clair–Detroit River System. In *Cultures before Contact: The Late Prehistory of Ohio and Surrounding Regions*, edited by R. A. Genheimer, pp. 2–51. Ohio Archaeological Council, Columbus.

Stothers, David M., and James R. Graves

1978 The Western Basin Tradition: Algonquian or Iroquoian? *Michigan Archaeologist* 24 (1): 11–36.

1983 Cultural Continuity or Change: The Western Basin,

Ontario Iroquois and Sandusky Traditions—A 1982 Perspective. *Archaeology of Eastern North America* 11: 109–142.

Stothers, David M., James R. Graves, Susan K. Bechtel, and Timothy J. Abel

1994 Current Perspectives on the Late Prehistory of the Western Lake Erie Region: An Alternative to Murphy and Ferris. *Archaeology of Eastern North America* 22: 135–196.

Stothers, David M., and G. M. Pratt

1982 New Perspectives on the Late Woodland Cultures of the Western Lake Erie Region. *Mid-Continental Journal of Archaeology* 6 (2): 91–121.

Stothers, David M., Olaf H. Prufer, and James L. Murphy

1997 Review of "The South Park Village Site and the Late Prehistoric Whittlesey Tradition of Northeast Ohio" by David S. Brose. North American Archaeologist 18 (2): 165–176.

Stothers, David M., and William Rutter

1978 The LaSalle Site (33–WO-42): An Upper Mississippian Manifestation in the Western Lake Erie Basin. *Newsletter of the Toledo Area Aboriginal Research Club* 78 (5): 1–2.

Stout, Charles B.

1987 *Surface Distribution Patterns at the Adams Site, a Mississippian Town in Fulton County, Kentucky.* Western Kentucky Project Report no. 6. Department of Anthropology, University of Illinois, Urbana-Champaign.

Stout, David B., Erminie Wheeler-Voegelin, and Emily J. Blassingham

1974 *Indians of E. Missouri, W. Illinois, and S. Wisconsin from the Proto-historic Period to 1804.* Garland, New York.

Stowe, Noel R.

1989 The Pensacola Variant and the Southeastern Ceremonial Complex. In *The Southeastern Ceremonial Complex: Artifacts and Analysis*, edited by Patricia Galloway, pp. 125–132. University of Nebraska Press, Lincoln.

Strong, John A.

1989 The Mississippian Bird-Man Theme in Cross-Cultural Perspective. In *The Southeastern Ceremonial Complex: Artifacts and Analysis*, edited by Patricia Galloway, pp. 211–238. University of Nebraska Press, Lincoln.

Stuiver, Minze, and Paula J. Reimer

1993 Extended ^{14}C Data Base and Revised Calib 3.0 ^{14}C Age Calibration Program. *Radiocarbon* 35: 215–230.

Sturtevant, William C.

1953 Chakaika and the Spanish Indians: Documentary Sources Compared with Seminole Traditions. *Tequesta* 13: 35–73.

1983 Tribe and State in the Sixteenth and Twentieth Centuries. In *The Development of Political Organization in Native America*, edited by Elisabeth Tooker, pp. 3–16. American Ethnological Society, Washington, DC.

Styles, Bonnie W., and Karli White

1995 Analysis of Faunal Remains. In *The Tremaine Site Complex: Oneota Occupation in the La Crosse Locality, Wisconsin*, vol. 3, *The Tremaine Site (47Lc-95)*, edited by Jodie O'Gorman, pp. 197–223. State Historical Society of Wisconsin, Madison.

Sullivan, Lynne P., and Gwenyth A. D. Coffin

1995 Ripley Site Mortuary Customs. In *Reanalyzing the Rip-*

ley Site: Earthworks and Late Prehistory on the Lake Erie Plain, edited by Lynne P. Sullivan, pp. 157–186. New York State Museum Bulletin. State Education Department, Albany.

Sullivan, Lynne P., Sarah W. Neusius, and Phillip Neusius
  1995 Earthworks and Mortuary Sites on Lake Erie: Believe It or Not at the Ripley Site. *Mid-Continental Journal of Archaeology* 20 (2): 115–142.

Sullivan, Norman C.
  1990 Oneota Subsistence: Inferences from Dental and Skeletal Pathology. In *The Woodland Tradition in the Western Great Lakes: Papers in Honor of Elden Johnson,* edited by Guy E. Gibbon, pp. 11–17. Publications in Anthropology no. 4. University of Minnesota, Minneapolis.

Sulman, Felix G.
  1982 *Short- and Long-Term Changes in Climate.* CRC Press, Boca Raton, FL.

Swain, Albert M.
  1978 A History of Fire and Vegetation in Northeastern Minnesota as Recorded in Lake Sediments. *Quaternary Research* 3: 383–396.

Swanton, John R.
  1911 *Indian Tribes of the Lower Mississippi and Adjacent Coast of the Gulf of Mexico.* Bulletin 43. Bureau of American Ethnology, Smithsonian Institution, Washington, DC.
  1922 *Early History of the Creek Indians and Their Neighbors.* Bulletin 73. Bureau of American Ethnology, Smithsonian Institution, Washington, DC.
  1931 *Source Material for the Social and Ceremonial Life of the Choctaw Indians.* Bulletin 103. Bureau of American Ethnology, Smithsonian Institution, Washington, DC.
  1946 *The Indians of the Southeastern United States.* Bulletin 137. Bureau of American Ethnology, Smithsonian Institution, Washington, DC.
  1952 *Indian Tribes of North America.* Bulletin 145. Bureau of American Ethnology, Smithsonian Institution, Washington, DC.

Swauger, James L.
  1974 *Rock Art of the Upper Ohio Valley.* Academische Druck. U. Verlagsanstalt, Granz, Austria.

Tankersley, Kenneth B.
  1986a Bison Exploitation by Late Fort Ancient Peoples in the Central Ohio River Valley. *North American Archaeologist* 7 (4): 289–303.
  1986b The Geoarchaeology of the Madisonville Site. Paper presented at the Midwest Archaeological Conference, Columbus, Ohio.
  1992 Bison and Subsistence Change: The Protohistoric Ohio Valley and Illinois Valley Connection. In *Long-Term Subsistence Change in Prehistoric North America,* edited by Dale R. Croes, Rebecca A. Hawkins, and Barry L. Isaac, pp. 103–130. Research in Economic Anthropology, Supplement 6. JAI Press, Greenwich, CT.

Tankersley, K. B., and W. R. Adams
  1991 Holocene Bison Remains (*Bison bison*) from Greene County, Indiana. *Proceedings of the Indiana Academy of Science* 99 (2): 229–236.

Tanner, Helen Hornbeck
  1989 The Land and Water Communication Systems of the Southeastern Indians. In *Powhatan's Mantle,* edited by P. Wood, G. Waselkov, and T. Hatley, pp. 6–20. Lincoln, University of Nebraska Press.

Telster, Patrice A.
  1992 Settlement Context and Structure at County Line, Missouri. *Southeastern Archaeology* 11 (1): 14–30.

Temple, Wayne C.
  1958 *Indian Villages of the Illinois Country: Historic Tribes.* Scientific Papers 2, no. 2. Illinois State Museum, Springfield.

Temple, William
  1975 *Maps of the Illinois Country.* Part 2 (revision and addendum to Part 1, by S. Tucker.) Papers of Illinois State Museum, Springfield.

Thomas, Cyrus
  1894 *Report on the Mound Explorations of the Bureau of Ethnology.* Twelfth Annual Report of the Bureau of American Ethnology, Smithsonian Institution, Washington, DC.

Thomas, David H.
  1989 *Archaeology.* 2d ed. Holt, Rinehart, and Winston, New York.
  1990 Columbian Consequences: Probing the Spanish Borderlands East. In *Columbian Consequences,* vol. 2, *Archaeological and Historical Perspectives on the Spanish Borderlands East,* edited by David H. Thomas, pp. xiii–xv. Smithsonian Institution Press, Washington, DC.

Thomas, David H. (editor)
  1989 *Columbian Consequences,* vol. 1, *Archaeological and Historical Perspectives on the Spanish Borderlands West.* Smithsonian Institution Press, Washington, DC.
  1990 *Columbian Consequences,* vol. 2, *Archaeological and Historical Perspectives on the Spanish Borderlands East.* Smithsonian Institution Press, Washington, DC.

Thornton, Russell
  1987 *American Indian Holocaust and Survival: A Population History since 1492.* University of Oklahoma Press, Norman.
  1997 Aboriginal North American Population and Rates of Decline, ca. A.D. 1500–1900. *Current Anthropology* 38: 310–325.

Thwaites, Reuben G. (editor)
  1895 Narrative of Spoon Decorah. *Collections of the State Historical Society of Wisconsin* 13: 448–462.
  1896– *The Jesuit Relations and Allied Documents: Travel*
  1901 *and Explorations of the Jesuit Missionaries in New France, 1610–1791.* 73 vols. Burrows Brothers, Cleveland.
  1902 *The French Regime in Wisconsin.* Collections of the State Historical Society of Wisconsin, vol. 16. Madison, WI.

Todorov, Tzvetan
  1984 *The Conquest of America.* Harper and Row, New York.

Tooker, Elisabeth
  1963 The Iroquois Defeat of the Huron: A Review of Causes. *Pennsylvania Archaeologist* 33 (1–2): 115–123.
  1978a The League of the Iroquois: Its History, Politics, and Ritual. In *Handbook of North American Indians,* vol. 15, *Northeast,* edited by Bruce G. Trigger, pp. 418–441. Smithsonian Institution Press, Washington, DC.
  1978b Iroquois since 1820. In *Handbook of North American*

Indians, vol. 15, *Northeast,* edited by Bruce G. Trigger, pp. 449–465. Smithsonian Institution Press, Washington, DC.

Torrence, Corbett McP.
1999   The Archaic Period on Useppa Island: Excavations on Calusa Ridge. In *The Archaeology of Useppa Island,* edited by W. H. Marquardt. Monograph 3. Institute of Archaeology and Paleoenvironmental Studies, University of Florida, Gainesville.

Transeau, E. N.
1935   The Prairie Peninsula. *Ecology* 16: 423–437.

Trigger, Bruce G.
1969a   Criteria for Identifying the Locations of Historic Indian Sites: A Case Study from Montreal. *Ethnohistory* 16 (4): 303–316.
1969b   *The Huron: Farmers of the North.* Holt, Rinehart and Winston, New York.
1976   *The Children of Aataentsic: A History of the Huron People to 1660.* McGill-Queen's University Press, Montreal, Canada.
1978   Early Iroquoian Contacts with Europeans. In *Handbook of North American Indians,* vol. 15, *Northeast,* edited by Bruce G. Trigger, pp. 344–356. Smithsonian Institution Press, Washington, DC.
1981   Prehistoric Social and Political Organization: An Iroquoian Case Study. In *Foundations of Northeast Archeology,* edited by Dean R. Snow, pp. 1–50. Academic Press, New York.
1985   *Natives and Newcomers: Canada's "Historic Age" Reconsidered.* McGill-Queen's University Press, Montreal.
1991   Early Native North American Responses to European Contact: Romantic versus Rationalistic Interpretations. *Journal of American History* 77 (4): 1195–1215.

Trimble, Carmen Carreras
1996   Paleodiet in Virginia and North Carolina as Determined by Stable Isotope Analysis of Skeletal Remains. Master's thesis, Department of Environmental Sciences, University of Virginia, Charlottesville.

Trow, Thomas L.
1981   Surveying the Route of the Root: An Archaeological Reconnaissance in Southeastern Minnesota. In *Current Directions in Midwestern Archaeology,* edited by Scott F. Anderson, pp. 91–107. Occasional Publications in Minnesota Anthropology no. 9. Minnesota Anthropological Society, St. Paul.

Tuck, J. A.
1968   Iroquoian Cultural Development in Central New York. Ph.D. dissertation, Department of Anthropology, Syracuse University.
1971   *Onondaga Iroquois Prehistory: A Study in Settlement Pattern Archaeology.* Syracuse University Press, Syracuse, NY.
1978   Regional Cultural Development, 3000 to 300 B.C. In *Handbook of North American Indians,* vol. 15, *Northeast,* edited by Bruce G. Trigger, pp. 28–43. Smithsonian Institution Press, Washington, DC.

Turgeon, Laurier, and William Fitzgerald
1992   Les objets des échanges entre Français et Amérindiens au XVIe siècle. *Recherches amérindiennes au Québec* 22 (2–3): 152–167.

Turnbaugh, William A.
1979   Calumet Ceremonialism as a Nativistic Response. *American Antiquity* 44: 685–691.

Turnbow, C. A., and A. G. Henderson
1992   Ceramic Analysis. In *Fort Ancient Cultural Dynamics in the Middle Ohio Valley,* edited by A. G. Henderson, pp. 113–135. Monographs in World Archaeology no. 8. Prehistory Press, Madison, WI.

Turnbow, C. A., and W. E. Sharp
1988   *Muir: An Early Fort Ancient Site in the Inner Bluegrass.* Archaeological Report no. 165. Program for Cultural Resource Assessment, University of Kentucky, Lexington.

Turner, E. Randolph III
1978   An Intertribal Deer Exploitation Buffer Zone for the Virginia Coastal Plain–Piedmont Region. *Quarterly Bulletin of the Archaeologial Society of Virginia* 32: 42–48.
1985   Socio-political Organization within the Powhatan Chiefdom and the Effects of European Contact. In *Cultures in Contact: The Impact of European Contacts on Native American Cultural Institutions,* edited by W. W. Fitzhugh, pp. 193–224. Smithsonian Institution Press, Washington, DC.
1992   The Virginia Coastal Plain during the Late Woodland Period. In *Middle and Late Woodland Research in Virginia,* edited by T. R. Reinhart and M. E. Hodges, pp. 97–136. Special Publication of the Archaeological Society of Virginia no. 29. Dietz Press, Richmond.

Turner, E. Randolph III, and Robert S. Santley
1979   Deer Skins and Hunting Territories Reconsidered. *American Antiquity* 44: 810–816.

Ubelaker, Douglas H.
1988   North American Indian Population Size, A.D. 1500 to 1985. *American Journal of Physical Anthropology* 77: 289–294.

University of Alabama
1963   Archaeological Investigations of the Logan Martin Dam Reservoir in Talladega and St. Clair Counties, June 1, 1963–September 1, 1963. Progress report. Department of Sociology and Anthropology, University of Alabama. Submitted to the Alabama Power Company.
1964   Archaeological Investigations of the Lock Three Dam Reservoir in Etowah and St. Clair Counties, Alabama, January 1, 1964–December 31, 1964. Progress report. Department of Sociology and Anthropology, University of Alabama. Submitted to the Alabama Power Company.
1965   Archaeological Investigations in the Lock Three Dam Reservoir in Calhoun, Etowah, and St. Clair Counties, Alabama, January 1, 1965–December 31, 1965. Final progress report. Department of Sociology and Anthropology, University of Alabama. Submitted to the Alabama Power Company.

Upchurch, Sam B., Pliny Jewell IV, and Eric DeHaven
1992   Stratigraphy of Indian "Mounds" in the Charlotte Harbor Area, Florida: Sea-Level Rise and Paleoenvironments. In *Culture and Environment in the Domain of the Calusa,* edited by W. H. Marquardt, pp. 59–103.

Monograph 1. Institute of Archaeology and Paleoenvironmental Studies, University of Florida, Gainesville.

Valentine, Edward Pleasants
1892   *Report on the Excavation of the Hayes Creek Mound.* Valentine Museum, Richmond, VA.

Varner, John G., and Jeanette J. Varner
1951   *The Florida of the Inca by Garcilaso de la Vega.* University of Texas Press, Austin.

Vickery, K. D., and R. A. Genheimer
1994   Report of Excavations at the Fort Ancient State Line Site, 33Ha58, in the Central Ohio Valley. Paper presented at "Cultures before Contact: A Conference on the Late Prehistory of the Ohio Region," Ohio Archaeological Council, Cincinnati.

Vietzen, Raymond C.
1941   *Ancient Man in Northern Ohio.* McCahon, Lorain, OH.
1945   *The Immortal Eries.* Wilmot, Elyria, OH.
1965   *Indians of the Lake Erie Basin or Lost Nations.* Ludi, Wahoo, NE.
1972   *The Riker Site in Tuscarawas County.* Sugar Creek Chapter, Archaeological Society of Ohio, New Philadelphia, OH.
1974   *The Riker Site.* Archaeological Society of Ohio.
1989   *Prehistoric Americans.* White Horse, Elyria, OH.

Vradenburg, Joseph
1993   Analysis of Human Skeletal Remains. In *The Tremaine Site Complex: Oneota Occupation in the La Crosse Locality, Wisconsin,* vol. 1, *The OT Site,* edited by Jodie O'Gorman, pp. 141–155. State Historical Society of Wisconsin, Madison.
1998   A Bioarchaeological Investigation of the Characterization of the La Crosse Area Oneota Adaptation. Paper presented at the annual meeting of the Society for American Archaeology, Seattle, WA.

Waddell, Eugene
1980   *Indians of the South Carolina Lowcountry, 1521–1751.* The Reprint Company, Spartanburg, SC.

Wagers, C.
1993   The Atkinson Spider. *Central States Archaeological Journal* 40 (2): 55.

Wagner, G. E.
1987   Uses of Plants by the Fort Ancient Indians. Ph.D. dissertation, Department of Anthropology, Washington University, St. Louis.

Wagner, Norman E., Lawrence E. Toombs, and Eduard R. Riegert
1973   *The Moyer Site: A Prehistoric Village in Waterloo County.* Wilfrid Laurier University Publications, Waterloo, Ontario.

Walker, Joan, and Glenda Miller
1992   Life on the Levee: The Late Woodland Period in the Northern Great Valley of Virginia. In *Middle and Late Woodland Research in Virginia,* edited by T. R. Reinhart and M. E. Hodges, pp. 165–186. Special Publication of the Archaeological Society of Virginia no. 29. Dietz Press, Richmond.

Walker, Karen J.
1992   The Zooarchaeology of Charlotte Harbor's Prehistoric Maritime Adaptation: Spatial and Temporal Per-

spectives. In *Culture and Environment in the Domain of the Calusa,* edited by W. H. Marquardt, pp. 265–366. Monograph 1. Institute of Archaeology and Paleoenvironmental Studies, University of Florida, Gainesville.

Walker, Karen J., Frank W. Stapor Jr., and William H. Marquardt
1994   Episodic Sea Levels and Human Occupation at Southwest Florida's Wightman Site. *Florida Anthropologist* 47: 161–179.
1995   Archaeological Evidence for a 1750–1450 B.P. Higher-than-Present Sea Level along Florida's Gulf Coast. In *Holocene Cycles: Climate, Sea Levels, and Sedimentation,* edited by C. W. Finkl Jr., pp. 205–218. *Journal of Coastal Research,* Special Issue no. 17.

Wall, Robert D.
1983   The 1981 Survey of the Western Maryland Plateau Region. *Maryland Archeology* 19 (1): 18–34.
1984   Protohistoric Settlement of the Maryland Plateau Region: An Overview. In *Upland Archeology in the East: Symposium 2,* edited by Michael B. Barber, pp. 180–190. Cultural Resources Report 5. US Department of Agriculture, Forest Service, Southern Region.

Walthall, John A.
1992   Aboriginal Pottery and the Eighteenth-Century Illini. In *Calumet and Fleur-de-lys: Archaeology of Indian and French Contact in the Midcontinent,* edited by John A. Walthall and Thomas E. Emerson, pp. 155–174. Smithsonian Institution Press, Washington, DC.

Walthall, John A., and Thomas E. Emerson (editors)
1992   *Calumet and Fleur-de-lys: Archaeology of Indian and French Contact in the Midcontinent,* edited by John A. Walthall and Thomas E. Emerson. Smithsonian Institution Press, Washington, DC.

Walthall, John A., and G. R. Holley
1997   Mobility and Hunter-Gatherer Toolkit Design: Analysis of a Dalton Lithic Cache. *Southeastern Archaeology* 16 (2): 152–162.

Walthall, John A., F. Terry Norris, and Barbara D. Stafford
1992   Woman Chief's Village: An Illini Winter Camp. In *Calumet and Fleur-de-lys: Archaeology of Indian and French Contact in the Midcontinent,* edited by John A. Walthall and Thomas E. Emerson, pp. 129–153. Smithsonian Institution Press, Washington, DC.

Ward, H. Trawick
1980   The Spatial Analysis of the Plow Zone Artifact Distributions from Two Village Sites in North Carolina. Ph.D. dissertation, Department of Anthropology, University of North Carolina, Chapel Hill.
1985   Social Implications of Storage and Disposal Patterns. In *Structure and Process in Southeastern Archaeology,* edited by Roy S. Dickens Jr. and H. Trawick Ward, pp. 82–101. University of Alabama Press, Tuscaloosa.
1987   Mortuary Patterns at the Fredricks, Wall, and Mitchum Sites. In *The Siouan Project: Seasons I and II,* edited by Roy S. Dickens Jr., H. Trawick Ward, and R. P. Stephen Davis Jr., pp. 81–110. Monograph Series 1, Research Laboratories of Anthropology, University of North Carolina, Chapel Hill.

Ward, H. Trawick, and R. P. Stephen Davis Jr.
1991   The Impact of Old World Diseases on the Native In-

habitants of the North Carolina Piedmont. *Archaeology of Eastern North America* 19: 171–181.

1993   *Indian Communities on the North Carolina Piedmont A.D. 1000 to 1700.* Monograph 2. Research Laboratories of Anthropology, University of North Carolina, Chapel Hill.

1999   *Time before History: The Archaeology of North Carolina.* University of North Carolina Press, Chapel Hill.

Ward, H. Trawick, and R. P. Stephen Davis Jr. (editors)

1988   Archaeology of the Historic Occaneechi Indians. *Southern Indian Studies* 36–37.

Warrick, Gary A.

1984   Reconstructing Ontario Iroquoian Village Organization. Mercury Series, Archaeological Survey of Canada, Paper 124, pp. 1–180. National Museum of Man, Ottawa.

1990   A Population History of the Huron-Petun, A.D. 900–1650. Ph.D. dissertation, McGill University, Montreal, Quebec.

Waselkov, Gregory A.

1989   Seventeenth-Century Trade in the Colonial Southeast. *Southeastern Archaeology* 8 (2): 117–133.

Washburn, Wilcomb E. (editor)

1988   *Handbook of North American Indians,* vol. 4, *History of Indian-White Relations.* Smithsonian Institution Press, Washington, DC.

Watts, William A., and Barbara C. S. Hansen

1988   Environments of Florida in the Late Wisconsin and Holocene. In *Wet Site Archaeology,* edited by Barbara A. Purdy, pp. 307–323. Telford Press, Caldwell, NJ.

Wauchope, Robert

1966   *Archaeological Survey of Northern Georgia.* Memoir no. 21. Society for American Archaeology.

Webb, Thompson III

1981   The Reconstruction of Climatic Sequences from Botanical Data. In *Climate and History: Studies in Interdisciplinary History,* edited by R. I. Rothberg and T. K. Rabb, pp. 169–192. Princeton University Press, Princeton, NJ.

Webb, Thompson III, and Reid A. Bryson

1972   Late- and Postglacial Climatic Change in the Northern Midwest, U.S.A.: Quantitative Estimates Derived from Fossil Pollen Spectra by Multivariate Analysis. *Quaternary Research* 2: 70–115.

Webb, William S.

1938   *An Archaeological Survey of the Norris Basin in Eastern Tennessee.* Bulletin 118. Bureau of American Ethnology, Smithsonian Institution, Washington, DC.

Webb, William S., and W. D. Funkhouser

1933   *The McCleod Bluff Site.* Reports in Archaeology and Anthropology 3 (1). University of Kentucky, Lexington.

Webb, William S., and Charles Wilder

1951   *An Archaeological Survey of Guntersville Basin on the Tennessee River in Northern Alabama.* University of Kentucky Press, Lexington.

Weddle, R. S.

1985   *Spanish Sea: The Gulf of Mexico in North American Discovery.* Texas A&M University Press, College Station.

Wedel, Mildred M.

1959   Oneota Sites on the Upper Iowa River. *Missouri Archaeologist* 21 (2–4): 1–180.

1986   Peering at the Ioway Indians through the Mist of Time: 1650–circa 1700. *Journal of the Iowa Archaeological Society* 33: 1–74.

Weiskotten, Daniel H.

1988   Origins of the Oneida Iroquois, Fact and Fallacy, Past and Present. *Bulletin, Chenango Chapter, New York State Archaeological Association* 22 (4): 1–20.

Weisman, Brent R.

1989   *Like Beads on a String: A Culture History of the Seminole Indians in North Peninsular Florida.* University of Alabama Press, Tuscaloosa.

1991   *Archaeological Investigations at the "Backhoe Trench," Big Mound Key (8CH10).* Report on file, C.A.R.L. Archaeological Survey, Florida Bureau of Archaeological Research, Tallahassee. (Photocopy on file, Florida Museum of Natural History, Gainesville.)

Welch, Paul D.

1991   *Moundville's Economy.* University of Alabama Press, Tuscaloosa.

Weslager, C. A.

1948   Monongahela Woodland Culture and the Shawnee. *Pennsylvania Archaeologist* 18 (1–2): 19–22.

Wesler, Kit W.

1991a   *Archaeological Excavations at Wickliffe Mounds, 15BA4: North Village and Cemetery.* Report no. 4. Wickliffe Mounds Research Center, Wickliffe, KY.

1991b   Ceramics, Chronology, and Horizon Markers at Wickliffe Mounds. *American Antiquity* 56 (2): 278–290.

West, G. A.

1934   Tobacco, Pipes, and Smoking Customs of the American Indians. *Bulletin of the Public Museum of the City of Milwaukee* 17: 1–994.

Wharton, Barry R., George R. Ballo, and Mitchell E. Hope

1981   The Republic Groves Site, Hardee County, Florida. *Florida Anthropologist* 34: 59–80.

White, Hayden V.

1974   The Historical Text as Literary Artifact. *Clio* 3 (3): 81–101.

1985a   The Noble Savage Theme as Fetish. In *Tropics of Discourse: Essays in Cultural Criticism,* edited by H. V. White, pp. 183–197. Johns Hopkins University Press, Baltimore.

1985b   Introduction: Tropology, Discourse, and the Modes of Human Consciousness. In *Tropics of Discourse: Essays in Cultural Criticism,* edited by H. V. White, pp. 1–27. Johns Hopkins University Press, Baltimore.

White, Marian E.

1961   *Iroquois Culture History in the Niagara Frontier Area of New York State.* Anthropological Papers no. 16. University of Michigan Museum of Anthropology, Ann Arbor.

1967   *An Early Historic Niagara Frontier Iroquois Cemetery in Erie County, New York.* Researches and Transactions of the New York State Archeological Association 16 (1). Rochester.

1976   Late Woodland Archaeology in the Niagara Frontier

of New York and Ontario. In *The Late Prehistory of the Lake Erie Drainage Basin: A Symposium Revised,* edited by David S. Brose, pp. 110–136. Cleveland Museum of Natural History Scientific Papers, Cleveland.

1978   Neutral and Wenro Erie. In *Handbook of North American Indians,* vol. 15, *Northeast,* edited by Bruce Trigger, pp. 407–418. Smithsonian Institution Press, Washington, DC.

White, Richard

1983   *The Roots of Dependency: Subsistence, Environment, and Social Change among the Choctaws, Pawnees, and Navajos.* University of Nebraska Press, Lincoln.

1991   *The Middle Ground: Indians, Empires, and Republics in the Great Lakes Region, 1650–1815.* Cambridge University Press, Cambridge.

Whitman, Janice R.

1975a   An Analysis of the Ceramics from the Riker Site, Tuscrawas County, Ohio. Master's thesis, Department of Anthropology, Sociology and Criminal Justice, Kent State University, Kent, OH.

1975b   A Cursory Analysis of Monongahela Traits Appearing in Four Sites in Southeastern Ohio. *SPAAC Speaks* 11 (1): 6–20.

Whitman, William

1937   *The Oto.* Contributions to Anthropology 28. Columbia University, New York.

Whitney, Theodore

1974   Aboriginal Art and Ritual Objects. *Chenango Chapter NYSAA* 14 (1).

Whittlesey, Charles

1851   *Ancient Earthworks of the Cuyahoga River Valley.* Contributions to Knowledge 3. Smithsonian Institution, Washington, DC.

1871   *Ancient Earth Forts of the Cuyahoga Valley, Ohio.* Tract no. 5. Western Reserve and Northern Ohio Historical Society, Cleveland.

Whyte, Thomas, and Clarence Geier

1982   *The Perkins Point Site (44BA3): A Protohistoric Stockaded Village on the Jackson River, Bath County, Virginia.* Occasional Papers in Anthropology 11. Archaeological Research Center, James Madison University, Harrisonburg, VA.

Widmer, Randolph J.

1988   *The Evolution of the Calusa: A Non-Agricultural Chiefdom on the Southwest Florida Coast.* University of Alabama Press, Tuscaloosa.

Wiegers, Robert P.

1988   A Proposal for Indian Slave Trading in the Mississippi Valley and Its Impact on the Osage. *Plains Anthropologist* 33: 187–202.

Wilford, Lloyd A., and John Brink

1974   The Hogback Site. *Minnesota Archaeologist* 33: 1–79.

Willey, Gordon R.

1949   *Archeology of the Florida Gulf Coast.* Smithsonian Miscellaneous Collections 113. Smithsonian Institution, Washington, DC.

Willey, Gordon, and Jeremy A. Sabloff

1974   *A History of American Archaeology.* W. H. Freeman, San Francisco.

Williams, J. Mark, and Gary Shapiro

1987   The Changing Contexts of Oconee Valley Political Power. Paper presented at the annual meeting of the Southeastern Archaeological Conference, Charleston, SC.

Williams, Ray

1968   Southeast Missouri Land Leveling Salvage Archaeology: 1967. Report. Submitted to the Midwest Region, US National Park Service.

1972   Land Leveling Salvage Archaeology in Missouri: 1968. Report. Submitted to the Midwest Region, US National Park Service.

Williams, Stephen

1954   An Archaeological Study of the Mississippian Culture in Southeast Missouri. Ph.D. dissertation, Yale University.

1956   Settlement Patterns in the Lower Mississippi Valley. In *Prehistoric Settlement Patterns in the New World,* edited by Gordon R. Willey, pp. 52–62. Wenner-Gren Publications in Archaeology no. 23. New York.

1962   Historic Archaeology in the Lower Mississippi Valley. *Southeastern Archaeological Conference Newsletter* 9 (1): 53–63.

1966   *Historic Archaeology, Past and Present: Annual Report for 1966,* pp. 23–29. School of American Research, Sante Fe.

1967   On the Location of the Historic Taensa Villages. *The Conference on Historic Site Archaeology Papers 1965–1966* 1: 3–13.

1980   Armorel: A Very Late Phase in the Lower Mississippi Valley. *Southeastern Archaeological Conference Bulletin* 22: 105–110.

1981a   Some Reflections on the Long, Happy, and Productive Life of Robert Stuart Neitzel. *Southeastern Archaeological Conference Bulletin* 24: 7–9.

1981b   Some Historic Perspectives on Southeastern Ceramic Traditions. *Geoscience and Man* 22: 115–122.

1983   Some Ruminations on the Current Strategy of Archaeology in the Southeast. *Southeastern Archaeological Conference Bulletin* 21: 72–81.

1988   Foreword. In *Tunica Archaeology,* by Jeffrey P. Brain, p. xv. Papers of the Peabody Museum of American Archaeology and Ethnology, vol. 78. Harvard University, Cambridge, MA.

1990   The Vacant Quarter and Other Late Events in the Lower Valley. In *Towns and Temples along the Mississippi,* edited by David H. Dye and Cheryl A. Cox, pp. 170–180. University of Alabama Press, Tuscaloosa.

Williams, Stephen, and Jeffrey P. Brain

1983   *Excavations at the Lake George Site, Yazoo County, Mississippi, 1958–1960.* Papers of the Peabody Museum of American Archaeology and Ethnology, vol. 74. Harvard University, Cambridge, MA.

Willis, Raymond F., and Robert E. Johnson

1980   AMAX Pine Level Survey: An Archaeological and Historical Survey of Properties in Manatee and DeSoto Counties, Florida. Report. Submitted to Environmental Science and Engineering, Inc., Gainesville.

Wilson, Charles J.
1982 *The Indian Presence: Archaeology of Sanibel, Capitiva, and Adjacent Islands in Pine Island Sound.* Sanibel-Captiva Conservation Foundation, Sanibel, Florida.

Wilson, H. Clyde
1956 A New Interpretation of the Wild Rice District of Wisconsin. *American Anthropologist* 58: 1059–1064.

Wilson, Jack H. Jr.
1977 Feature Fill, Plant Utilization, and Disposal among the Historic Sara Indians. Master's thesis, Department of Anthropology, University of North Carolina, Chapel Hill.
1983 A Study of Late Prehistoric, Protohistoric, and Historic Indians of the Carolina and Virginia Piedmont: Structure, Process, and Ecology. Ph.D. dissertation, Department of Anthropology, University of North Carolina, Chapel Hill.

Windsor, Justin
1894 *Narrative and Critical History of America,* vol. 2. Little Brown, Boston.

Withrow, Randall
1988 Archaeological Manifestations of the Seventeenth-Century Ioway in the Upper Mississippi River Valley. Paper presented at the 46th annual Plains Anthropological Conference, Wichita, KS.
n.d. Miscellaneous Survey and Excavation Records, Site Inventories, and Notes Related to Archaeological Research in the Root River Valley of Southeastern Minnesota. Copy in the author's possession.

Withrow, Randall, and Roland L. Rodell
1984 *Archaeological Investigations in Southeastern Minnesota: The 1984 Root River Survey.* Reports of Investigations no. 29. Mississippi Valley Archaeology Center, University of Wisconsin–La Crosse.

Witthoft, John
1952 Comments on the Cultural Position of the Herriot Farm Site. *West Virginia History* 13 (4): 249–253.
1959 Ancestry of the Susquehannocks. In *Susquehannock Miscellany,* edited by John Witthoft and W. Fred Kinsey, pp. 19–60. Pennsylvania Historical and Museum Commission, Harrisburg.

Wittry, Warren L.
1963 The Bell Site, Wn9, an Early Historic Fox Village. *Wisconsin Archeologist* 44: 1–57.

Wolf, Eric R.
1982 *Europe and the People without History.* University of California Press, Berkeley.

Wood, Peter
1987 The Impact of Smallpox on the Native Populations of the Eighteenth-Century South. *New York State Journal of Medicine* 87: 30–36.

Woodley, Philip, Rebecca Southern, and William Fitzgerald
1992 The Archaeological Assessment and Partial Mitigation of the Zamboni Cemetery (AgHb-144), Brantford. Manuscript on file, Ministry of Culture and Communications, Toronto.

Worth, John E.
1995 Fontaneda Revisited: Five Descriptions of Sixteenth-Century Florida. *Florida Historical Quarterly* 73: 339–352.

Wray, Charles F.
1983 Seneca Glass Trade Beads c. A.D. 1550–1820. In *Proceedings of the 1982 Glass Trade Bead Conference.* Research Records 16, pp. 41–49. Rochester Museum and Science Center, Rochester, NY.

Wray, Charles F., Martha L. Sempowski, and Lorraine P. Saunders
1991 *Tram and Cameron Sites: Two Early Contact Era Seneca Sites.* The Charles F. Wray Series in Seneca Archaeology, vol. 2, edited by Charles F. Hayes III. Research Records 19. Rochester Museum and Science Center, Rochester, NY.

Wray, Donald E., and Hale G. Smith
1944 An Hypothesis for the Identification of the Illinois Confederacy with the Middle Mississippi Culture in Illinois. *American Antiquity* 10: 23–27.

Wright, Gary A.
1967 Some Aspects of Early and Mid-Seventeenth-Century Exchange Networks in the Western Great Lakes. *Michigan Archaeologist* 13 (4): 181–197.

Wright, James V.
1966 *The Ontario Iroquois Tradition.* Bulletin 210. National Museum of Canada, Ottawa.
1972 *Ontario Prehistory.* National Museum of Canada, National Museum of Man, Ottawa.

Wright, Milton J.
1981 *The Walker Site.* Mercury Series, Archaeological Survey of Canada, Paper 103. National Museum of Man, Ottawa.

Young, Gloria A., and Michael P. Hoffman (editors)
1993 *The Expedition of Hernando de Soto West of the Mississippi, 1541–1543.* University of Arkansas Press, Fayetteville.

Zitomersky, J.
1994 *French Americans—Native Americans in Eighteenth-Century French Colonial Louisiana: The Population Geography of the Illinois Indians, 1670s–1760s.* Lund University Press, Lund, Sweden.

Zubrow, Ezra
1990 The Depopulation of Native America. *Antiquity* 64: 754–765.